SELECT ORATIONS

OF

CICERO.

THE

FOUR ORATIONS AGAINST CATILINE

with an

Interlinear Translation on the Hamiltonian System.

BY

WILLIAM UNDERWOOD,

Son-in-law and partner of the late Hamilton.

THE

SEVEN REMAINING ORATIONS

with an

Interlinear Translation on the System of Locke

BY

THOMAS CLARK,

PHILADELPHIA:
DAVID McKAY COMPANY
WASHINGTON SQUARE.

Printed in the United States of America

PREFACE.

In this interlinear translation of Cicero, the four orations against Catiline are translated, according to the Hamiltonian system, by Underwood, the son-in-law and partner of Hamilton. The London edition of these four orations has been carefully revised, and the errors and omissions corrected and supplied; for without the greatest care on the part of the editor, errors and omissions are very apt to occur in interlinear translations.

As these four orations against Catiline constitute so small a portion of the present publication, it may be considered as almost altogether an original interlinear translation of the select orations of Cicero; and that nearly on the plan suggested by the great poet and distinguished Latin scholar, Milton, and the celebrated metaphysician and writer on education, Locke.

The orations expressly translated by the American editor of this Philadelphia edition are: the ORATIO PRO ARCHIA POETA — PRO MARCELLO — PRO LEGE MANILIA — PRO L. MURENA — PRO Q. LIGARIO — PRO REGE DEIOTARIO — PRO T. ANNIO MILONE. Thus making a more complete collection of select orations of Cicero than any published in the United States; containing all the orations that are read in any of the schools and colleges of this country, and comprising all those in the editions of Anthon, Bullions, Johnson, and others.

As a mere verbal translation would be inadequate to convey the meaning of Cicero in his orations, it has become necessary to add thereto. When such additions only express the thought of the author more intelligibly in English, they are denoted by being placed between parentheses ( ), and constitute a part of the sentence; but when such additions are, as it were, explanations, and do not properly constitute a part of the sentence, they are placed between brackets [ ], and may be considered as short explanatory notes. This applies only to those orations translated by the American editor.

When several words in English are necessary to express a Latin word, such words are united together by hyphens, as:

Quod nuntiaret
What might-he-announce

but when, in forming an English sentence, a word intervenes between such two or more words that denote a Latin one, the figure ¹ is placed before the words thus separated, as:

Palam fecerat testamentum.
¹He-had openly ¹made (his) will.

This also only applies to the orations translated by the American editor.

THOMAS CLARK.

TESTIMONIALS

AS TO

THE MERITS OF

The Interlinear Translation of the Classics.

Testimony of celebrated men in favour of the interlineary system of translations, as being best adapted for learning a language.

MILTON.—We do amiss to spend seven or eight years merely in scraping together as much Latin and Greek as might be learned easily and delightfully in one year.

If, after some preparatory grounds of speech by their certain forms got into memory, they were led to the *praxis* thereof in some chosen short book *lessoned thoroughly to them*, [that is, read and translated to them], which would bring the whole language quickly into their power. This I take to be the most natural and most profitable way of learning languages.

[Children] should begin with the chief and necessary rules of some good grammar, either that now used, or any better; and while this is doing, their speech is to be fashioned to a distinct and clear pronunciation, as near as may be to the Italian, especially in the vowels. Next, to make them expert in the usefullest points of grammar, some easy and delightful book should be read to them.

[By this, Milton means that the teacher should read some easy Latin book to his pupils, and translate and explain it repeatedly, until they understand such Latin book, and can themselves translate it.]

(v)

JOHN LOCKE, author of the "Essay on the Human Under-standing."—When I consider what ado is made about a little Latin and Greek, how many years are spent in it, and what a noise and business it makes to no purpose, I can hardly forbear thinking that the parents of children still live in fear of the schoolmaster's rod, which they look on as the only instrument of education; as a language or two to be his whole business. How else is it possible that a child should be chained to the oar, seven, eight, or ten of the best years of his life, to get a language or two, which, I think, might be had at a great deal cheaper rate of pains and time, and be learned almost in playing.

[The first project of Locke] is to trouble the child with no grammar at all, but to have Latin as English has been, without the perplexity of rules, talked into him, for, if you will consider it, Latin is no more unknown to a child, when he comes into the world, than English; and yet he learns English without a master, rule, or grammar; and so might he Latin, too, as Tully did, if he had somebody always to talk to him in this language. And when we so often see a French woman teach an English girl to speak and read French perfectly in a year or two, without any rule of grammar, or anything else but prattling to her, I cannot but wonder how gentlemen have overseen this way for their sons. If, therefore, a man could be got, who, himself speaking good Latin, would always be about your son, talk constantly to him, and suffer him to speak and read nothing else, this would be the true and genuine way, and that which I would propose, not only as the easiest and best, wherein a child might, without pains or chiding, get a language which others are wont to be whipt for at school six or seven years together; but also as that wherein, at the same time, he might have his mind and manners formed, and be instructed in all other parts of knowledge of things that fall under the senses, and require little more than memory. But if such a man cannot be got who speaks good Latin, the next best thing is to have him taught as near this way as may be, which is by taking some easy and pleasant book, such as Æsop's Fables, and writing the English translation (made as literal as can be) in one line, and the Latin words which answer each of them, just over it in another. These let him read every day, over and over again, till he perfectly understands the Latin; and then go on to another Fable till he is also perfect in that, not omitting what he is already perfect in, but sometimes reviewing that to keep it in his memory.

The formation of the verb first, and afterwards the declensions of the nouns and pronouns, perfectly learned by heart, facilitate his acquaintance with the genius and manner of the Latin tongue, which varies the signification of verbs and nouns, not as the modern languages do, by particles prefixed, but by changing the last syllable. More than this of grammar, I think, he need not have, till he can read himself Sanctii Minerva.

As he advances in acquiring a knowledge of words, he must advance, *pari pasu*, in obtaining a thorough and critical knowledge of grammar. When by this way of interlining Latin and English one with another, he has got a moderate knowledge of the Latin tongue, he may then be advanced a little farther, to the reading of some other easy Latin book, such as Justin, or Eutropius; and, to make the reading and understanding of it the less tedious and difficult to him, let him help himself with the English translation. Nor let the objection, that he will then know it only by rote, fright any one. This, when well considered, is not of any moment against, but plainly for, this way of learning a language. For languages are only to be learned by rote; and a man who does not speak English and Latin perfectly by rote, so that having thought of the thing he would speak of, his tongue, of course without thought of rule or grammar, falls into the proper expression and idiom of that language, does not speak it well, nor is master of it. Languages were made, not by rules of art, but by accident, and the common use of the people; and he that speaks them well has no other rule but that, nor anything to trust to but his memory, and the habit of speaking, after the fashion learned from those that are allowed to speak properly, which, in other words, is only to speak by rote.

SYDNEY SMITH.—The Hamiltonian system, on the other hand: 1st. Teaches an unknown tongue by the closest interlinear translations, instead of leaving a boy to explore his way by the lexicon or dictionary. 2d. It postpones the study of grammar till a considerable progress has been made in the language, and a great degree of practical grammar has been acquired. 3d. It substitutes the cheerfulness and competition of the Lancasterian system for the dull solitude of the dictionary. By these means a boy finds he is making a progress, and learning something from the very beginning. He is not overwhelmed with the first appearance of insuperable difficulties; he receives some little pay from the first moment of his apprenticeship, and is not compelled to wait for remuneration till he is out of his time. The student, having acquired the great art of understanding the sense of what is written in another tongue, may go into the study of the language as deeply and as extensively as he pleases. The old system aims at beginning with a depth and accuracy which many men never will want, which disgusts many from arriving even at moderate attainments, and is a less easy, and not more certain road to a profound skill in a language, than if attention to grammar had been deferred to a later period.

In fine, we are strongly persuaded that, the time being given, this system will make better scholars; and, the degree of scholarship being given, a much shorter time will be needed. If there is any truth in this, it will make Mr. Hamilton one of the most useful men of his age; for, if there is anything which fills reflecting men with melancholy and regret, it is the waste of mortal time, parental money, and puerile happiness, in the present method of pursuing Latin and Greek.

PRIMA ORATIO
THE FIRST ORATION

MARCI TULLII CICERONIS IN LUCIUM CATILINAM,

OF MARCUS TULLIUS CICERO AGAINST LUCIUS CATILINE,

HABITA IN SENATU.
HELD (DELIVERED) *IN THE SENATE.*

~~~~~~~~

1. Quousque   tandem   abutêre   nostrâ
How far   at length   wilt thou abuse   with our

patientiâ, Catilina?   Quamdiu etiam iste tuus
patience,   O Catiline?   How long also that thy

furor   eludet   nos? ad quem finem   effrenata
fury will (it) elude us? to what end (thy) unbridled

audacia   jactabit   sese?   ne   nocturnum
audacity will (it) boast itself? whether the nightly

præsidium   Palatii   (movit)   te
guard   of the Palatium (has (that) moved) thee

nihil   vigiliæ urbis
nothing (has that in no respect affected thee), the watches of the city

(moverunt)   nihil,   timor   populi
have (they) moved (thee; nothing, the fear of the people

nihil, concursus omnium bonorum
(has that moved thee) nothing, the assemblage of all the good

nihil,   hic munitissimus locus
(has that moved thee) nothing, this most fortified place

senatûs   habendi
of a senate to be held   (of holding a senate) (has that moved thee)

nihil,   ora   que vultus horum   move
nothing, the faces and looks of these (senators) have (these

runt nihil? Sentis **non** tua **consilia**
moved (thee) nothing? Perceivest thou not thy counsels

patere? Vides non tuam conjurationem
to be open (to be exposed)? Seest thou not thy conspiracy

jam teneri constrictam conscientiâ omnium
already to be held bound by the consciousness of all

horum? Quem nostrûm arbitraris
these (senators)? Whom of us supposest thou

ignorare quid egeris proximâ,
to be ignorant what thou mayest have acted on the nearest

quid superiore necte, ubi fueris,
(last night), what on the former night, where thou mayest have been,

quos convocaveris, quid consilii
whom thou mayest have called together, what of counsel

ceperis? O tempora! O mores. Senatus
thou mayest have taken? O the times! O the manners. The senate

intelligit hæc, consul videt, tamen hic vivit.
understands this, the consul sees (it), yet this (Catiline) lives.

Vivit? imo, verò; etiam venit in senatum. Fit
Lives? yes, truly; even comes into the senate. He becomes

particeps publici consilii: notat et **designat**
a partaker of the public counsel: he notes and marks out

oculis unumquemque nostrûm ad cædem.
with (his) eyes each of us to (for) slaughter

Autem nos fortes viri videmur satisfacere reipublicæ,
But we brave men seem to do enough for the republic,

si vitemus furorem, ac tela istius.
if we may avoid the fury, and the weapons of that (Catiline).

Oportebat te, Catilina, jampridem duci ad
It did behove thee, O Catiline, long since to be led to

mortem jussu consulis: istam pestem,
death by order of the consul: (it behoved) that pest (destruction),

quam tu machinaris jam diu in nos omnes,
which thou contrivest already a long time against us all,

conferri in te. Verò an amplissimus
to be brought upon thee. But whether the most ample (most hon-

vir, P. Scipio, maximus pontifex, privatus
ourable) man, P Scipio, the greatest priest, (as) a private (person)

interfecit Tiberium Gracchum, mediocriter labe-
slew   Tiberius Gracchus,   moderately   making

factantem statum reipublicæ : verò nos consules
to totter   the state   of the republic :   but we consuls,

perferemus Catilinam cupientem vastare orbem
shall we endure   Catiline   desiring   to lay waste the globe

terræ cæde, atque incendiis ? Nam
of the earth with slaughter, and with conflagrations ?   For

prætereo illa nimis antiqua, quòd Q. Servilius
I pass over those too ancient (examples) that   Q. Servilius

Ahala occidit suâ manu Spurium Melium,
Ahala killed with his own hand Spurius   Melius,

studentem novis rebus. Ista
studying for new things (having revolutionary designs). That

virtus fuit, fuit quondam in hâc republicâ, ut
virtue has been, has been once in this republic, that

fortes viri coërcerent perniciosum civem acrioribus
brave men would check a pernicious citizen with sharper

suppliciis quàm acerbissimum hostem. Enim
(more severe) punishments than the most bitter enemy.   For

habemus vehemens et grave senatusconsultum
we have a vehement and heavy (severe) decree of the senate

in te, Catilina : non consilium neque auctoritas
against thee, O Catiline : not the counsel nor the authority

hujus ordinis deest reipublicæ; nos dico
of this order (of the senate) is wanting to the republic; we I say

apertè, nos consules desumus.
openly we consuls are wanting (to it).

2. Senatus quondam decrevit, ut L. Opimius
The senate once decreed, that L. Opimius

consul videret, ne respublica caperet quid
the consul should see, lest the republic might take any (thing)

detrimenti : nulla nox intercessit ; C. Gracchus,
of detriment : no night intervened ;   C. Gracchus,

clarissimo patre, avo, majoribus,
born from a most famous father, grandfather, (and) ancestors,

interfectus est propter quasdam suspiciones seditionum :
was slain because of some suspicions of seditions

M. Fulvius, consularis,   occisus est, cum   liberis.
M. Fulvius,   a consular (man),   was killed,   with (his) children.

Simili   senatusconsulto   respublica   permissa est
By a like   decree of the senate   the republic   was permitted

C. Mario et   L. Valerio consulibus; num
(confided) to C. Marius   and to L. Valerius   the consuls; whether

mors ac pœna   reipublicæ remorata est
death and the punishment of the republic   retarded (fail to overtake)

L. Saturninum,   tribunum   plebis,   et
L. Saturninus,   tribune   of the common people,   and

C. Servilium, prætorem, unum diem postea? At non
C. Servilius,   the prætor,   one   day afterwards? But   we

patimur   aciem   auctoritatis   horum
suffer   the edge   of the authority   of these (the senators)

hebescere   jam   vicesimum diem. Enim habemus
to become blunt already   the twentieth   day.   For   we have

senatusconsultum   hujusmodi, verumtamen inclusum
a decree of the senate   of this sort,   nevertheless   inclosed

in tabulis, tanquam gladium reconditum in   vagina :
in the tablets,   as if   a sword   hidden   in   the scabbard:

ex quo   senatusconsulto   convenit   te,   Catilina,
from which decree of the senate   it was fit   thee,   O Catiline,

interfectum esse   confestim. Vivis;   et   vivis
to have been slain   immediately. Thou livest; and   thou livest

non ad   audaciam deponendam, sed ad
not   to (for) audacity   to be placed down,   but   to (for thy audacity)

confirmandam.   Conscripti   Patres,   cupio   me
to be confirmed.   Conscript   Fathers,   I desire myself

esse clementem ;   cupio   me   non   videri dissolutum
to be mild;   I desire myself   not   to seem   dissolute

in   tantis   periculis reipublicæ: sed jam
(negligent) in   so great   dangers   of the republic: but   now

condemno   me ipsum   inertiæ   que   nequitiæ.
I condemn   myself   of inactivity   and   of negligence.

Castra collocata sunt in Italiâ contra rempublicam,
Camps have been placed   in   Italy   against   the republic,

in faucibus   Etruriæ: numerus   hostium
in   the jaws (passage) of Tuscany: the number   of the enemies

crescit in singulos dies: autem videmus
increases into single days (daily): but we see

imperatorem eorum castrorum, que ducem hostium,
the commander of those camps, and leader of the enemies,

intra mœnia, atque adeo in senatu, molientem
within the walls, and even in the senate, attempting

quotidie aliquam intestinam perniciem reipublicæ. S,
daily some intestine destruction to the republic. If

jussero te, Catilina, jam comprehendi; si
I shall have ordered thee, O Catiline, now to be seized; if

interfici, credo, erit verendum
(I shall have ordered thee) to be slain, I believe, it will be to be feared

mihi, ne omnes boni hoc factum esse
to me (by me), lest all the good (may say) this to have been done

non serius à me, potius quam quisquam dicat
not too late by me, rather than any (person) may say

crudelius. Verum ego nondum
(it to have been done) too cruelly. But I not yet

adducor ut faciam hoc, quod oportuit factum esse
am led that I may do this, which it has behoved to have been done

jampridem, de certâ causâ. Tum denique
long since, from a certain cause. Then at last

interficiam te, cum jam nemo poterit inveniri
I will slay thee, when now nobody will be able to be found

tam improbus, tam perditus, tam similis tui,
so wicked, so lost (abandoned), so like of thyself,

qui fateatur non id factum esse jure.
who may confess not that to have been done by right.

Quamdiu quisquam erit, qui audeat defendere te,
As long as any (person) shall be, who may dare to defend thee,

vives; et vives ita ut vivis nunc,
thou shalt live; and thou shalt live so as thou livest now,

obsessus meis multis et firmis præsidiis, ne
beset by my many and firm guards, lest

possis commovere te contra rempublicam.
thou mayest be able to move thyself against the republic.

Etiam oculi et aures multorum speculabuntur atque
Also the eyes and ears of many shall spy and

custodient te non sentientem, sicut fecerunt
shall watch thee not perceiving, so as they have done

adhuc.
hitherto.

3. Etenim quid est quod expectes jam
For what is it which thou mayest expect now

amplius, Catilina, si neque nox potest obscurare
more, Catiline, if neither night is able to conceal

tenebris nefarios cœtus nec privata domus
with darknesses (thy) impious assemblies, nor a private house

continere vocem tuæ conjurationis parietibus? si
to contain the voice of thy conspiracy with (its) walls? if

omnia illustrantur, si erumpunt? Muta
all (things) are brought to light, if they burst forth? Change

jam istam mentem: crede mihi: obliviscere cædis
now that mind: believe to me: forget of slaughter

atque incendiorum: teneris undique: omnia
and of conflagrations: thou art held on all sides: all

tua consilia sunt clariora nobis luce: quæ
thy counsels are clearer to us than light: which (things)

licet etiam recognoscas mecum. Ne
it is allowed even thou mayest recognise with me. Whether

meministi me dicere in senatu ante
hast thou remembered me to say in the senate before

duodecimum diem kalendarum Novembris, C. Manlium,
the twelfth day of the calends of November, C. Manlius,

satellitem atque administrum tuæ audaciæ, fore
the attendant and assistant of thy audacity, to be about to be

in armis certo die, qui dies esset futurus ante
in arms on a certain day, which day might be about to be before

sextum diem kalendarum Novembris? Num
the sixth day of the calends of November? Whether

Catilina non modo tanta, tam atrox, tam
Catiline not only so great, so atrocious, so

incredibilis res fefellit me, verum, id quod est
incredible a thing deceived me, but, that which is

multo magis admirandum, dies? Ego idem
by much more to be wondered at, the day? I the same (person)

dixi in senatu, te contulisse cædem
said in senate, thee to have appointed the slaughter

optimatum in ante quintum diem kalendarum
of the aristocracy unto (the day) before the fifth day of the calends

Novembris, tum cum multi principes civitatis
of November, then when many chief (persons) of the state

profugerunt Româ, non tam causâ sui
fled from Rome, not so (much) for the sake of themselves

conservandi, quam tuorum consiliorum reprimendorum.
to be preserved, as of thy counsels to be repressed

Num potes
(as for the sake of repressing thy designs). Whether art thou able

infitiari, te circumclusum meis præsidiis, meâ
to deny thyself being closed around by my guards, by my

diligentiâ illo die ipso, potuisse non commovere
diligence on that day itself, to have been able not to move

te contra rempublicam? cum tu, discessu
thyself against the republic? when thou, at the departure

cæterorum, dicebas te esse contentum tamen nostrâ
of the rest, didst say thyself to be content yet with our

cæde qui remansissemus. Quid!
slaughter (with the slaughter of us) who might have remained. What!

cum tu confideres te esse occupaturum Præneste
when thou mightest trust thyself to be about to occupy Præneste

nocturno impetu kalendis ipsis Novembris:
by a nocturnal attack on the calends themselves of November:

ne sensisti illam coloniam munitam esse
whether hast thou perceived that colony to have been fortified

meo jussu, meis præsidiis, custodiis, que vigiliis?
by my order, by my garrisons, guards, and watches?

Agis nihil, moliris nihil, cogitas
Thou actest nothing, thou attemptest nothing, thou thinkest (devisest)

nihil, quod ego non modo audiam non, sed etiam
nothing, which I not only may hear not, but even

videam non, que planè sentiam.
may see not, and plainly may perceive.

4. Recognosce tandem mecum illam superiorem
Recognise (call to mind) at length with me that former

noctem: jam intelliges me vigilare multo
night: now thou wilt understand me to watch by much

acrius ad salutem reipublicæ quam te ad
more sharply to (for) the safety of the republic than thyself to (for)

perniciem. Dico te venisse priori nocte
the destruction (of it). I say thee to have come on the former night

inter falcarios (agam
mong scythe-makers (into the scythe-maker's street) (I will act (speak)

non obscure), in domum M. Leccæ: complures
not obscurely), into the house of M. Lecca: (I say) many

socios ejusdem amentiæ que sceleris convenisse
partners of the same madness and crime to have come together

eodem. Num audes negare? Quid!
to the same place. Whether darest thou to deny (it)? What!

taces? Convincam, si negas. Enim
art thou silent? I will convict (thee), if thou deniest. For

video quosdam esse hic in senatu qui fuere
I see some (persons) to be here in the senate who were

unà cum te. O immortales dii! ubinam gentium
together with thee. O immortal gods! where of nations

sumus? in qua urbe vivimus? quam
(where in the world) are we? in what city do we live? what

rempublicam habemus? Sunt hic, hic in
republic have we? There are (persons) here, here in

nostro numero, conscripti patres, in hoc sanctissimo
our number, conscript fathers, in this most sacred

que gravissimo consilio orbis terræ, qui
and most weighty (dignified) council of the globe of the earth, who

cogitent de meo interitu, que
may devise concerning my destruction, and (the destruction)

nostrûm omnium, qui de exitio hujus
of us all, who (devise) concerning the destruction of this

urbis, atque adeo orbis terrarum. Ego consul
city, and even of the globe of the earths. I the consul

video hosce, et rogo sententiam de republica:
see these (persons), and I ask opinion concerning the republic:

et vulnero eos nondum voce, quos oportebat
and I wound those not yet with (my) voice, whom it did behove

trucidari **ferro.** **Igitur,** **Catilina,**
to be slaughtered with the iron (sword). Therefore, Catiline,

fuisti **apud** **Leccam** **illâ** **nocte :**
thou wast at Lecca (at Lecca's house) on that night.

distribuisti **partes** **Italiæ ;** **statuisti** **quo**
thou distributedst the parts of Italy ; thou appointedst whither

placeret **quemque** **proficisci ;** **delegisti**
it might please (thee) each to depart ; thou selected it

quos **relinqueres** **Romæ,** **quos** **educeres**
whom thou mightest leave of (at) Rome, whom thou mightest lead out

cum **te ;** **descripsisti** **partes** **urbis** **ad**
with thee ; thou describedst parts of the city to (for)

incendia ; **confirmasti** **te ipsum jam**
conflagrations ; thou confirmedst (affirmedst) thyself now (soon)

esse **exiturum ;** **dixisti** **esse** **etiam tum**
to be about to go out ; thou saidst to be (that there was) even then

paullulum **moræ** **tibi,** **quod** **ego** **viverem.** **Duo**
a very little of delay to thee, because I might live. Two

Romani equites **reperti sunt** **qui** **liberarent te** **istâ**
Roman knights were found who might free thee from that

curâ, **et** **pollicerentur** **sese** **interfecturos**
care, and might promise themselves (to be) about to slay

me in meo lectulo illâ nocte ipsâ, paullo ante
me in my little bed on that night itself, a little before

lucem. **Ego comperi** **omnia hæc,** **etiam vestro**
light. I discovered all these (things), even your

cœtu **vix dum** **dimisso :** **munivi** **atque**
assembly scarcely yet being dismissed : I fortified and

firmavi **meam domum majoribus** **præsidiis ;**
I strengthened my house with greater (stronger) guards ;

exclusi eos quos tu miseras ad me **mane**
I excluded those whom thou hadst sent to me in the morning

salutatum, cum illi **ipsi** **venissent, quos**
to salute (me), when those (persons) themselves might have come, whom

ego jam prædixeram multis ac summis viris
I already had foretold to many and to the highest men

esse venturos ad me id temporis.
to be about to come to me (at) that of time.

5. Cum quæ sint ita, Catilina,
When (since) which (things) may be thus, Catiline,

perge quò cœpisti; egredere aliquando
proceed whither thou hast begun; go out sometimes

ex urbe; portæ patent, proficiscere: illa
(at length) out of the city; the gates are open, depart: those

tua Manliana castra desiderant nimium diu te
thy Manlian camps want too long thee (their)

imperatorem. Educ cum te etiam omnes tuos;
commander. Lead out with thee also all thy

si minus, quam plurimos: purga
(associates); if less (if not all), as many as possible: cleanse

urbem: liberabis me magno metu, dummodo
the city: thou wilt free me from great fear, provided that

murus intersit inter me atque te:
the wall (the city wall) may be between between me and thee:

potes non versari jam diutius cum nobis:
thou art able not to be engaged now longer with us:

feram non, patiar non, sinam non.
I will bear (it) not, I will suffer (it) not, I will permit (it) not.

Magna gratia est habenda
Great favour is to be had (great thanks must be given)

immortalibus diis, atque huic Jovi Statori ipsi,
to the immortal gods, and to this Jupiter Stator himself,

antiquissimo custodi hujus urbis, quòd effugimus
the most ancient guardian of this city, that we have escaped

jam toties hanc tam tætram, tam horribilem
now so many times this so foul, so horrible

pestem que tam infestam reipublicæ. Summa salus
plague and so hostile to the republic. The highest safety

reipublicæ est non periclitanda sæpius in uno
of the republic is not to be endangered too often in one

homine. Quamdiu insidiatus es mihi, consuli
man. As long as thou plottedst against to me, the consul

designato, Catilina defendi me non publico
elect, Catiline I defended myself not by a public

præsidio, sed privatâ diligentiâ: cum proximis
guard but by private diligence: when at the nearest (last

consularibus comitiis voluisti interficere me, consulem,
consular   elections thou wishedst   to slay   me,   the consul,

et competitores in campo,
and (thy)   competitors   in   the plain, (the Campus Martius),

compressi tuos nefarios conatus præsidio et copiis
I repressed thy impious attempts with a guard and forces

amicorum, nullo tumultu concitato publice: denique,
of friends,   no   tumult being excited publicly: lastly,

quotiescunque petisti me, obstiti tibi
as often as   thou hast sought (aimed at) me, I have opposed to thee

per me, quamquam videbam meam perniciem esse
(by) myself, although I did see my destruction to be

conjunctam cum magnâ calamitate reipublicæ.
conjoined with a great calamity of the republic.

Nunc jam petis universam rempublicam
Even now thou seekest (aimest at) the whole   republic

aperte. Vocas templa immortalium deorum,
openly. **Thou callest** the temples of the immortal   gods,

tecta urbis, vitam omnium civium,
the roofs (houses) of the city, the life of all the citizens,

denique, totam Italiam, ad exitium et vastitatem.
lastly (in fine), the whole Italy, to destruction and devastation.

Quare quoniam audeo nondum facere id, quod est
Wherefore because I dare not yet to do that, which is

primum atque proprium hujus imperii
the first and proper (peculiar duty) of this command (of the

que disciplinæ majorum:
consular power) and of the discipline (custom) of (our) ancestors:

faciam id quod est lenius ad severitatem,
I will do that which is milder to (as to)   severity,

et utilius ad communem salutem; nam si
and more useful to (as to) the common safety; for if

jussero te interfici, reliqua manus
I shall have ordered thee to be slain, the remaining hand (band

conjuratorum residebit in republica: sin tu
of the conspirators will settle in the republic: but if thou

exieris, (quod hortor te jamdudum), magna
shalt have gone out (which I exhort thee long since), the great

et perniciosa sentina [reipublicæ], tuorum comitum,
and pernicious sink [to the republic], of thy companions,

exhaurietur ex urbe. Quid est, Catilina?
will be drawn off out of the city. What is it, Catiline?

Num dubitas facere id, me
Whether doubtest thou (dost thou hesitate) to do that, me

imperante, quod jam faciebas
commanding, which now (just now) thou didst do (wast about to do)

tuâ sponte? Consul jubet hostem exire
by thy own accord? The consul orders (thee) an enemy to go out

ex urbe: interrogas me, num in exilium? Jubeo
out of the city: dost thou ask me, whether into exile? I order

non; sed si consulis me, suadeo.
(thee) not; but if thou consultest me, I persuade (thee to do so).

6. Enim quid, Catilina, est, quod jam possit
For what, Catiline, is there, which now may be able

delectare te in hâc urbe? In quâ est nemo,
to delight thee in this city? In which there is no one,

extra istam conjurationem perditorum
without (unconnected with) that conspiracy of lost (aban-

hominum, qui metuit non te; nemo qui
doned) men, who fears not thee; no one who

oderit non. Quæ nota domesticæ turpitudinis
may have hated not (thee). What mark of domestic turpitude

est non inusta tuæ vitæ? Quod dedecus privatarum
is not branded to thy life? What disgrace of private

rerum hæret non infamiæ? Quæ libido abfuit
things adheres not to (thy) infamy? What lust has been absent

ab oculis, quod facinus umquam à
from (thy) eyes, what bad deed (has been absent) ever from

tuis manibus, quod flagitium a toto corpore?
thy hands, what villany from (thy) whole body?

Cui adolescentulo, quem irretisses
To what youth, whom thou mightest have ensnared

illecebris corruptelarum, tu prætulisti non
by the allurements of debaucheries, thou hast borne before not

aut ferrum ad audaciam, aut facem ad libidinem?
either a sword to (for) audacity, or a torch to (for) lust?

Vero quid! nuper cum morte
But what (why shall I mention)! lately when at the death

superioris uxoris vacuefecisses domum
of (thy) former wife thou mightest have made vacant (thy) house

novis nuptiis, ne cumulasti non hoc
for new nuptials, whether hast thou heaped up (augmented) not this

scelus etiam alio incredibili scelere? Quod ego
crime also by another incredible crime? Which I

prætermitto, et facile patior sileri, ne
pass by (omit), and easily suffer to be kept silent, lest

immanitas tanti facinoris videatur aut
the monstrousness of so great a wicked deed may seem either

extitisse in hâc civitate, aut non vindicata esse.
to have existed in this state, or not to have been punished.

Prætermitto ruinas tuarum fortunarum, omnes quas
I pass by the ruins of thy fortunes, all which

senties impendere tibi proximis Idibus:
thou wilt perceive to hang over to thee at the nearest (next) Ides:

venio ad illa quæ pertinent non ad privatam
I come to those (things) which pertain not to the private

ignominiam tuorum vitiorum, non ad tuam domesticam
disgrace of thy vices, not to thy domestic

difficultatem ac turpitudinem, sed ad summam
difficulty and turpitude, but to the sum (the whole)

reipublicæ, atque ad vitam que salutem nostrûm
of the republic, and to the life and the safety of us

omnium. Ne lux hujus vitæ, aut spiritus hujus
all. Whether the light of this life, or the breadth of this

cœli potest esse jucundus tibi, Catilina,
heaven (atmosphere) is able to be pleasant to thee, Catiline,

cum scias, esse neminem horum
when thou mayest know, to be (that there is) no one of these (sena-

qui nesciat te stetisse cum
tors) who may not know thee to have stood (that you stood) with

telo in comitio pridie kalendas
a weapon in the assembly house the day before the calends

Januarias, Lepido et Tullo consulibus?
belonging to January, Lepidus and Tullus (being) consuls?

Paravisse manum causâ consulum et
To have prepared a hand (band) for the sake of the consuls and

principum civitatis interficiendorum? Non
of the chief (persons) of the state to be slain? Not

aliquam mentem, aut tuum timorem, sed
any mind, or thy fear (fear of thine) but

fortunam reipublicæ obstitisse tuo scelere
the (good) fortune of the republic to have opposed to thy wickedness

ac furori? Ac jam omitto illa: enim neque
and fury? And now I omit those (things): for neither

sunt commissa post obscura, aut non
are (the crimes) committed (by thee) afterwards obscure, or not

multa. Quoties tu conatus es interficere me
many. How often thou hast endeavoured to slay me

designatum; quoties consulem?
(being consul) elect; how often (being) consul?

Quot tuas petitiones ita conjectas,
How many thy aims (how many thrusts of thine) so cast (directed),

ut viderentur non posse vitari, ego effugi
that they might seem not to be able to be avoided, I have escaped

quadam parvâ declinatione, et, ut aiunt, corpore?
by a certain small bending, and, as they say, with the body?

Agis nihil, assequeris nihil, moliris nihil,
Thou actest nothing, thou attainest nothing, thou attemptest nothing,

quod valeat latere mihi, in tempore: neque
which may be able to lie hid from me, in the time: nor

tamen desistis conari ac velle. Quoties
yet dost thou desist to endeavour and to wish. How often

jam ista sica extorta est tibi de
now (already) that poniard has been wrested from thee from

manibus? Vero quoties excidit et elapsa est
the hands? But how often it has fallen out and has slipped out

aliquo casu? Tamen potes non carere eâ
by some accident? Yet thou art able not to be without it

diutius: quæ quidem quibus sacris
longer: which (poniard) indeed to what sacred rites

initiata sit ac devota abs te nescio, quod
it may have been initiated and devoted by thee I know not that

putas   necesse   defigere   eam   in   corpore
thou thinkest (it)   necessary   to fix   it   in   the body

consulis.
of the consul.

7. Vero nunc, quæ est ista tua vita? Enim jam
   But   now,   what is that thy life?   For now

loquar   cum te sic, ut videar non esse permotus
I will speak with thee so, that I may seem not to be   moved

odio   quo   debeo, sed ut
with the hatred with which I ought, but that (I may seem to be moved)

misericordiâ, quæ nulla   debetur tibi,
with pity,   which none (none of which)   is due to thee.

Venisti   paullo ante in senatum: quis ex hâc
Thou camest a little before into the senate: who out of this

tantâ   frequentiâ,   ex   tot   tuis amicis   ac
so great assemblage,   out of so many   thy friends   and

necessariis, salutavit te? Si hoc contigit nemini
acquaintances, saluted   thee? If this has befallen to no one

post   memoriam hominum, expectas contumeliam
after (since) the memory   of men, dost thou wait for   reproach

vocis cum   sis   oppressus   gravissimo
of voice when thou mayst be (thou art) oppressed by the most heavy

judicio taciturnitatis? Quid,   quod tuo
judgment of silence?   Why (why should I mention), that at thy

adventu ista subsellia vacuefacta sunt? Quod omnes
arrival   those seats   were made vacant?   That   all

consulares,   qui persæpe fuerunt constituti
the consular (persons), who very often have been   appointed

tibi   ad   cædem, reliquerunt istam partem
to (by) thee to (for) slaughter,   left   that   part

subselliorum nudam atque inanem simul atque
of the seats   naked   and   empty   as soon as

assedisti? Quo animo tandem putas hoc
thou satest near? With what mind at length dost thou think this

ferendum tibi? Mehercle, si mei servi metuerent
be borne to (by) thee? By Hercules, if my slaves   might fear

me isto   pacto,   ut omnes tui cives
me by that agreement (in that manner), as all   thy citizens

metuunt   te,   putarem   meam   domum
fear   thee,   I should think   my   house   (ought)

relinquendam: arbitraris tu non   urbem
to be left: thinkest thou not (that) the city (ought to be

tibi?   Et, si   viderem   me tam graviter
left) to (by) thee? And, if I might see myself so   heavily

suspectum atque offensum meis civibus   injuriâ,
suspected   and   offensive to my citizens (even) with injustice,

mallem   me   carere   aspectu   civium   quam
I would rather myself to be-without the sight of (my citizens),   than

conspici   infestis   oculis   omnium: cum   tu
to be-viewed with the hostile   eyes   of all: when thou

agnoscas   conscientiâ   tuorum scelerum justum
mayst-recognise by a consciousness of thy   crimes   the just

odium omnium, et jam   diu debitum tibi,   dubitas
hatred   of all,   and now a-long-time due to thee, doubtest thou

vitare aspectum que præsentiam eorum,
(dost thou hesitate) to avoid the sight and the presence of those,

mentes   que sensus   quorum   vulneras?   Si tui
the minds and feelings of whom   thou woundest?   If thy

parentes   timerent   atque   odissent   te,   neque
parents   might-fear   and might-have-hated thee,   neither

posses   placare   eos ullâ ratione,
thou mightest-be-able to appease them by any   reason (means),

concederes,   ut opinor, aliquo   ab oculis eorum:
thou shouldst-retire, as I think, some-whither from the eyes of them:

nunc patria,   quæ est communis parens nostrûm
now the country, which is the common   parent   of us

omnium, odit   ac metuit te; et jam   diu
all,   has-hated (hates) and fears thee; and already a long-time

judicat nihil   de   te, nisi cogitare
judges nothing concerning thee, unless to devise (that you devise)

te   suo parricidio.   Tu verebere   neque
concerning her parricide (destruction). Wilt-thou-reverence   neither

auctoritatem hujus,   neque   sequere
the authority of this (of her),   nor   wilt-thou-follow (her)

judicium, neque   pertimesces   vim?   Quæ
judgment,   nor   wilt-thou-fear (her) force?   Which

sic agit cum te, Catilina, et
(the country) thus acts (pleads) with thee, Catiline, and

quodammodo tacita loquitur. Nullum facinus
in some-manner silent speaks. No wicked-deed

exstitit jam aliquot annis, nisi per te; nullum
has-existed now (for) some years, unless through thee; no

flagitium sine te: tibi uni neces multorum
villany without thee: to thee one (alone) the deaths of many

civium, tibi vexatio que direptio sociorum
citizens, to thee (alone) the harassing and plundering of allies

fuit impunita ac libera: tu valuisti non solum
has been unpunished and free: thou hast-been-able not only

ad leges ac quæstiones negligendas, verum
to (for) laws and (judicial) inquiries to be neglected, but

etiam ad evertendas que perfringendas.
even to (for them) to-be-overturned and to-be-broken-through.

Quamquam illa superiora fuerunt non ferenda,
Although those former (villanies) have-been not to be borne

tamen tuli ut
(ought not to have been borne), yet I have borne (them), as

potui: vero nunc totam me esse in
I was-able: but now the whole myself (for my whole self) to be in

metu propter te unum; quidquid increpuerit,
fear because-of thee one (alone); whatever may-have-made-a-noise,

Catilinam timeri;
Catiline is to be-feared; (that Catiline should be the sole cause of

nullum consilium videri posse
fear in every disturbance); (for) no design to seem to be-able

iniri contra me, quod abhorreat
to be-entered-on against me, which may-abhor (be inconsistent with)

a tuo scelere; est non ferendum. Quamobrem
from thy crime; (this) is not to be-borne. Wherefore

discede, atque eripe hunc timorem mihi, ne
depart, and take away this fear from me, lest

opprimar, si est verus;
I may-be-oppressed (that I may not be oppressed), if it is a true (fear),

sin falsus, ut tandem aliquando desinam timere.
but-if false, that at-length sometimes I may-cease to fear.

8. Si   patria loquatur hæc   cum te, ut
If (thy) country may-speak these (things) with thee, as

dixi,   ne   debeat non   impetrare,
I have-said, whether may-she-owe not (ought she not)   to obtain

etiam si   possit   non adhibere vim?
(her request), even   if she may-be-able not to apply   force?

Quid?   quod tu ipse dedisti   te
What (why should I mention)? that thou-thyself hast-given thyself

in custodiam? Quid?   quod causâ suspicionis
into custody?   What (why)? that for-the-sake of suspicion

vitandæ, dixisti te velle   habitare
to be-avoided, thou saidst thyself to wish (that thou wishedst) to reside

apud M. Lepidum? A quo receptus non,   ausus es
at   M. Lepidus? By whom being-received not, thou hast-dared

etiam venire ad me; atque   rogasti ut
even   to come to me; and   thou askedst (me) that

asservarem te meæ   domi: cum   tulisses
I-would-guard you in my house: when   thou mightest-have-borne

id responsum quoque a me,   me
(thou hadst received) that answer also   from me, myself

posse esse   tuto nullo modo cum te
to be-able to be (that I could be) safely in no manner with thee

iisdem parietibus,   qui essem in magno periculo,
in the same walls (of a house), who might-be in great   danger,

quod   contineremur   iisdem mœnibus; venisti
because we might-be-contained in the same city-walls; thou camest

ad Q. Metellum, prætorem: a quo repudiatus,
to Q. Metellus,   the prætor: by whom being-rejected,

demigrasti ad tuum sodalem, optimum virum,
thou wentest-over to thy companion, the best   man

M. Marcellum, quem tu videlicet
(that very good man), M. Marcellus, whom thou forsooth

putasti   fore   et diligentissimum
thoughtest to be-about-to-be (would be) both   most-diligent

ad te custodiendum   et sagacissimum ad
to (for) thee to be-guarded (to guard thee), and most-sagacious te

suspicandum   et fortissimum ad
(for) suspecting (thee) and most-brave to (for thee)

vindicandum.   **Sed quam longe   videtur**
to be-punished (for punishing thee). But how far does-he-seem

debere abesse   a carcere atque a vinculis, qui
to-ought to be-absent from prison and from bonds, who

ipse jam   judicaverit se dignum custodiâ?
himself now (already) may have-judged himself worthy with custody

          Cum   quæ   sint ita, Catilina,
(of custody)? When (since' which (things) may-be thus, Catiline,

dubitas,   si potes   non morari hic
doubtest thou (dost thou hesitate), if thou-art-able not to delay nere

æquo animo, abire   in   aliquas terras, et
with an equal mind, to go-away into some lands, and

mandare istam vitam,   ereptam multis justis
to commit that life (of thine), rescued from many just

que debitis suppliciis, fugæ que solitudini? Refer,
and due punishments, to flight and to solitude? Refer,

inquis, ad senatum (enim postulas id), et, si hic
thou sayest, to the senate (for thou demandest that), and, if this

ordo   decreverit placere sibi,
order (the senate) shall-have-decreed to please to itself, (that it pleases

         te ire in exsilium, dicis   te   esse
them), thee to go into exile, thou sayest thyself to be

obtemperaturum. Referam non id, quod abhorret à
about-to-comply. I will-refer not that, which abhors from

       meis moribus: et tamen   faciam
(is inconsistent with) my manners: and yet I will-make

ut intelligas,   quid hi   sentiant
that thou mayest-understand, what these (the senators) may perceive

       de   te. Egredere ex urbe, Catilina:
(think) concerning thee. Go-out out-of the city, Catiline:

libera rempublicam metu: proficiscere in exsilium,
free the republic from fear: depart into exile,

si expectas hanc vocem.   Quid est, Catilina?
if thou waitest-for this voice (word). What is-it, Catiline?

ecquid attendis, ecquid animadvertis silentium
whether dost-thou-observe, whether dost-thou-perceive the silence

horum?   patiuntur, tacent.   Quid
of these (senators)? they suffer (it), they are-silent. What (why

expectas   auctoritatem   loquentium,   voluntatem
dost-thou-wait-for   the authority   of (them) speaking,   the will

quorum   tacitorum perspicis?   At si   dixissem
of whom (being)   silent   thou-plainly-seest?   But if   I might-have-said

hoc idem   huic   optimo   adolescenti,
this   same (thing)   to this   best (excellent)   young-man,

P. Sextio,   si   fortissimo   viro, M. Marcello;   jam
P. Sextius,   if   to the most-brave   man,   M. Marcellus;   now

      senatus   intulisset   vim et
immediately)   the senate   would-have-brought-on (inflicted)   force and

manus optimo   jure   mihi   consuli in hoc templo
hands   with the best   right   to me   the consul   in   this   temple

ipso; autem cum   quiescunt   de   te, Catilina,
itself;   but   when   they are-quiet   concerning thee,   Catiline,

probant; cum patiuntur,   decernunt; cum   tacent,
they approve; when   they suffer (it),   they decree;   when they are-silent,

clamant. Neque hi   solum, auctoritas quorum
they exclaim. Neither these (senators) alone,   the authority   of whom

videlicet est cara tibi,   vita   vilissima;   sed
forsooth   is   dear   to thee, (their)   life (is)   most cheap;   but

etiam illi Romani equites, honestissimi atque optimi
also   those   Roman   knights,   most-honourable   and   best

viri, que ceteri fortissimi cives, qui circumstant
men,   and   the other   most-brave   citizens,   who   stand-around

senatum, et frequentiam quorum tu   potuisti videre,
the senate,   and the assemblage   of whom thou hast-been-able   to see,

et perspicere   studia, et paulo ante
and to see-plainly (their)   desires,   and   a little   before (a little while

     exaudire   voces: manus   ac   tela
ago)   to hear   their voices (shouts):   the hands   and   weapons

quorum   jam   diu   ego   vix contineo abs te,
of whom   already   a long-time   I   scarcely restrain   from thee,

adducam eosdem facile,   ut
I may-lead   the same   easily   (I could easily induce the same),   that

prosequantur usque ad   portas, te relinquentem
they may-follow   until   to   the gates, thee   leaving

hæc,   quæ   studes jampridem vastare.
these (things), which   thou studiest   long-since   to lay-waste.

9. Quamquam quid loquor? ut ulla res
Although what (why) do I speak? that any thing

frangat te? ut tu umquam corrigas te? ut
may-break thee? that thou ever mayst-correct thee? that

tu meditere ullam fugam? ut tu cogites ullum
thou mayst-meditate any flight? that thou mayst-devise any

exsilium? Utinam immortales Dii duint istam
exile? O that the immortal Gods may-give that

mentem tibi! Tametsi video, si perterritus meâ
mind to thee! Although I see, if being-alarmed by my

voce induxeris animum ire in exsilium,
voice thou shalt-have-induced (thy) mind to go into exile,

quanta tempestas invidiæ impendeat nobis,
how-great a tempest of envy (unpopularity) may impend to us

si minus in præsens tempus, recenti
me), if-not unto (for) the present time, by the recent

memoriâ tuorum scelerum, at in posteritatem.
memory of thy crimes, but unto posterity (at a future

Sed est tanti mihi;
time). But it-is of so-much (consequence) to me (it is worth the

dummodo ista sit privata calamitas, et
sacrifice); provided-that that may-be a private calamity, and

sejungatur a periculis reipublicæ. Sed est
may-be-separated from the dangers of the republic. But it-is

non postulandum, ut tu commoveare tuis vitiis,
not to be-demanded, that thou mayst-be-moved from thy vices,

ut pertimescas pœnas legum, ut
that thou mayst-fear the penalties of the laws, that

concedas temporibus reipublicæ; enim
thou mayst-concede to the times (circumstances) of the republic; for

neque es is, Catilina, ut aut pudor
either art-thou that (person), Catiline, that either shame

revocarit te a turpitudine, aut metus a
may have-recalled thee from turpitude, or fear from

periculo, aut ratio a furore. Quamobrem proficiscere,
danger, or reason from fury. Wherefore depart,

ut dixi jam sæpe: ac, si vis conflare
as I have-said already often: and, if thou wishest to blow-together

invidıam   mihi   tuo   inimico,   ut
(produce)   envy (unpopularity) to me   thy   enemy,   as

prædicas;   perge   recta   in   exsilium :   vix
thou declarest;   proceed   straightway   into   exile :   searcely

feram   sermones   hominum,   si   feceris   id :
shall-I-bear   the speeches   of men,   if   thou-shalt-have-done   that :

vix   sustınebo   molem   istius   invidiæ,   si
scarcely   shall-I-support   the mass   of that   envy,   if

ieris   in   exsilium   jussu   consulis :
thou shalt-have-gone in   exile   by the order   of the consul :

sin autem   mavis   servire meæ laudi et gloriæ,
but-if   thou wishest-rather to serve   to my   praise and   glory

egredere cum   importunâ manu   sceleratorum ;
go-out   with (thy)   troublesome   hand (band)   of wicked

confer   te   ad Manlium : concita perditos
(associates) ;   betake thyself to   Manlius :   excite   lost

cives :   secerne   te   a bonis :   infer
(abandoned) citizens :   separate thyself from the good :   bring-on

bellum   patriæ :   exsulta impio latrocinio,
war   to (thy) country :   exult   in impious   robbery (warfare),

ut   videaris   non   isse   ejectus a me ad alienos,
that thou-mayst-seem not to-have-gone cast-out by me   to   aliens,

sed invitatus ad   tuos.   Quamquam quid
but   being-invited   to   thy-own (friends).   Although   what

ego invitem   te, a   quo   sciam   jam
(why)   may-I-invite   thee, by whom I may-know (persons)   now

præmissos esse   qui præstolarentur   tibi
(already) to have-been-sent-before who   should-wait   for thee

armati   ad   Aurelium   forum ?   Sciam   diem
armed   to (at)   the Aurelian   forum ?   I may know the day

pactam esse   et constitutam cum Manlio ? A quo
to-have-been-agreed-on and   appointed   with Manlius ? By whom

sciam   etiam   illam   argenteam aquilam,   quam
I may-know   even   that   silver   eagle,   which

confido futuram esse perniciosam et funestam tibi,
I trust   to be-about-to-be   destructive   and   fatal   to thee,

ac omnibus tuis,   cui   sacrarium tuorum
and   to all   thy (friends), to which   a shrine   of thy

scelerum fuit constitutum tuæ domi,
crimes was appointed of thy (at thy) house,

præmissam esse? Ut tu possis carere illâ
to have-been-sent-before? How mayst-thou-be-able to be-without that

diutius, quam solebas venerari,
(eagle) any longer, which thou-wast-accustomed to worship,

proficiscens ad cædem? A altaribus cujus
departing to slaughter? From the altars of which

transtulisti sæpe istam impiam dexteram ad
thou-hast-transferred often that impious right-hand to

necem civium?
the death (slaughter) of citizens?

10. Ibis aliquando tandem, quo ista tua
Thou-wilt-go at length, whither that thy

effrenata ac furiosa cupiditas jampridem rapiebat
unbridled and furious desire long-since did-seize

te. Enim neque hæc res affert dolorem
(hurry) thee. For neither this thing brings pain

tibi, sed quandam incredibilem voluptatem:
to thee, but some (a certain) incredible pleasure;

natura peperit te ad hanc amentiam, voluntas
nature has-produced thee to this madness, (thy) will

exercuit, fortuna servavit: tu
has exercised (thee in it), fortune has-preserved (thee for it): thou

nunquam concupisti non modo otium, sed ne quidem
never hast-coveted not only ease, but not-even

bellum, nisi nefarium: nactus es manum
war, unless a nefarious (war): thou hast-obtained a band

improborum conflatam ex perditis,
of dishonest (men) blown-together (formed) out of lost

atque derelictis non modo ab omni
(abandoned men), and forsaken not only by every

fortunâ, verum etiam spe. Quâ lætitiâ
fortune, but even hope. With what gladness

tu perfruere hic? quibus gaudiis exsultabis? in
wilt-thou-enjoy here? in what joys wilt-thou-exult? in

quantâ voluptate bacchabere, cum in tanto numero
how-great pleasure wilt-thou-revel, when in so-great a number

tuorum   nəque   audies   neque   videbis
of thy (associates)   neither   wilt-thou-hear   nor   wilt-see

quemquam bonum virum?   Illi   tui labores,   qui
any   good   man?   Those   thy labours,   which

feruntur,   meditati sunt
are-borne (are commonly reported),   have-been-meditated (practised)

ad studium   hujus   vitæ: jacere
to (for) the study (purpose) of this (kind of) life: to lie

humi,   non modo ad   stuprum   obsidendum,
on-the-ground, not only to (for) adultery   to-be-lain-in-wait-for,

verum etiam ad   facinus   obeundum; vigilare,
but   even   to (for) a daring-deed to be-gone-through; to watch,

non solum insidiantem   somno   maritorum, verum
not   only   lying-in-wait for the sleep of husbands,   but

etiam bonis   occisorum. Habes ubi   ostentes
even for the goods of (them) slain. Thou hast where thou mayst display

illam tuam præclaram patientiam famis, frigoris,
that   thy   famous   patience   of hunger,   of cold,

inopiæ omnium rerum;   quibus   senties   te
of want of all   things; with which thou wilt-perceive thyself

esse confectum brevi tempore. Profeci tantum tum,
to be   wasted   in a short   time. I profited so-much then,

cum repuli te   a   consulatu, ut   posses
when I repelled thee from the consulship, that thou mightest-be-able

potius tentare   rempublicam   *exul,*   quam
rather to try (attack) the republic (as) an exile,   than

vexare   *consul:*   atque ut   id,   quod
to harass (it) (as) a consul: and that that,   which

susceptum esset scelerate a   te   nominaretur
might have-been-undertaken wickedly by thee should-be-named

latrocinium potius quam *bellum.*
a robbery   rather than   a war.

11. Nunc, conscripti patres, ut detester   ac
Now,   conscript fathers, that I may detest (avoid) and

deprecer   a   me, quandam   prope
may-deprecate from myself, some (a certain) nearly (almost

justam quærimoniam patriæ: percipite diligenter
last   complaint of (my) country: attend-to   diligently

quæso,   quæ   dicam,   et   mandate   ea
I pray, (twe things) which   I may-say,   and   commit   th m

penitus vestris animis que mentibus.   Etenim, si
inwardly to your   minds   and understandings.   For,   if

     patria, quæ est multo carior mihi meâ vitâ, si
(my) country, which is by-much dearer to me tnan my life, if

cuncta Italia, si omnis respublica loquatur cum me:
the whole Italy, if   all   the republic may-speak with   me:

M. Tulli,   quid   agis?   ne   tu patieris   eum
M. Tullius,   what actest-thou? whether wilt-thou-suffer   him

exire,   quem   comperisti   esse hostem: quem
to go-out   whom thou hast-discovered to be   an enemy: whom

vides futurum   ducem   belli: quem   sentis
thou seest about-to-be a leader of the war: whom thou perceivest

exspectari   imperatorem in castris   hostium,
to be-waited-for (as)   commander   in the camps of the enemies,

auctorem   sceleris,   principem   conjurationis,
the author   of the wickedness,   the chief   of the conspiracy,

evocatorem   servorum et perditorum   civium,
the summoner (to war) of slaves and of lost (abandoned) citizens,

ut videatur non esse emissus ex urbe abs te,
that he may-seem   not to be sent-out out-of the city by thee,

sed immissus in urbem?   Nonne imperabis hunc
but   sent-in into the city?   Wilt-thou-not-command   this

      duci in vincula, non   rapi   ad
(Catiline) to-be-led into bonds, not to be-seized (hurried) to

mortem, non mactari summo   supplicio? Quid
death,   not to be-slain with the highest punishment?   What

tandem impedit te? ne   mos   majorum?
at-length hinders you? whether the custom of (our) ancestors?

At persæpe etiam privati   multarunt
But very-often even   private (persons)   have fined (punished)

perniciosos cives morte in hac republicâ.   An
destructive   citizens with death in this   republic.   Whether

leges quæ rogatæ sunt   de   supplicio
the laws which have-been-begged (passed) concerning the punishment

Romanorum civium?   At nunquam in
of Roman   citizens (do these prevent thee)? But   never   is

hâc urbe ii tenuerunt jura civium, qui
this city those have-held (retained) the rights of citizens, who

defecerunt a republicâ. An times invidiam
have-revolted from the republic. Whether fearest-thou the envy

posteritatis? Vero refers præclaram
(displeasure) of posterity? But thou returnest a famous

gratiam Romano populo, qui extulit te,
acknowledgment to the Roman people, which has-raised thee,

hominem cognitum per te, nullâ
a man known through thyself (alone), with no

commendatione majorum, per omnes gradus
recommendation of ancestors, through all steps

honorum tam mature ad summum imperium,
(degrees) of honours so early to the highest command,

si propter invidiam, aut metum alicujus periculi,
if because-of envy, or fear of some danger,

negligis salutem tuorum civium. Sed si est
thou neglectest the safety of thy citizens. But if there-is

quis metus invidiæ, num est invidia severitatis
any fear of envy (displeasure), whether is the envy of severity

ac fortitudinis pertimescenda vehementius, quam
and of fortitude to-be-feared more-violently, than (that)

inertiæ ac nequitiæ? An, cum Italia
of inactivity and of negligence? Whether, when Italy

vastabitur bello, urbes vexabuntur, tecta
shall-be-devastated with war, cities shall-be-harassed, roofs

ardebunt: existimas te non
(houses) shall-be-on-fire: dost-thou-think thyself not (to be)

conflagraturum tum incendio invidiæ?
about-to-burn then with a conflagration of envy (unpopularity)?

12. Ego respondebo pauca his sanctissimis
I will-answer a few (words) to these most-sacred

vocibus reipublicæ, et mentibus hominum, qui
voices (words) of the republic, and to the minds of men, who

sentiunt idem. Si ego judicarem
feel the same (have similar sentiments). If I might-judge

hoc optimum factu, conscripti patres, Catilinam
this best to be-done, conscript fathers, Catiline

multari   **morte;**   **dedissem**   **non**
to be-fined (punished)   with death;   I would-have-given   not

usuram unius horæ ad vivendum   **isti**
the use   of one   hour   to   to be-lived (for living)   to that

gladiatori. Etenim, si summi viri, et clarissimi
gladiator.   For,   if the highest men, and the most-famous

cives non modo contaminarunt non, sed etiam
citizens not only   have contaminated   not,   but   even

honestarunt se, sanguine Saturnini, et
have-ennobled themselves, by the blood   of Saturninus,   and

Gracchorum, et Flacci, et complurium superiorum;
of the Gracchi, and of Flaccus, and   of many   superiors;

certe erat non verendum mihi, ne quid
certainly it was not to-be-feared to (by) me, lest any (thing)

invidiæ redundaret mihi in posteritatem, hoc
of unpopularity might-redound to me unto   posterity,   this

parricidâ civium interfecto. Quod si ea impenderet
parricide of citizens being-slain.   But-if it   might-impend

mihi maxime, tamen fui semper
(threaten) to me mostly (very much), yet I have-been always

hoc animo, ut putarem invidiam partam virtute,
with this mind, that I might-think envy   produced by virtue,

gloriam, non invidiam. Quamquam sunt nonnulli in
glory,   not envy.   Although there-are some   in

hoc ordine, qui aut videant non ea
this order (assembly), who either may-see not those (things)

quæ imminent, aut dissimulent ea, quæ
which impend,   or may-dissemble those (things), which

vident: qui aluerunt spem Catilinæ mollibus
they-see: who have-nourished the hope of Catiline by soft (mild)

sententiis, que corroboraverunt nascentem
opinions,   and   have-strengthened   the growing

conjurationem credendo non. Auctoritatem
conspiracy by believing (it)   not.   The authority

quorum multi secuti, non solum improbi,
of whom many having-followed, not only the dishonest,

verum etiam imperiti, si animadvertissem in
but   also the unskilful, if I might-have-animadverted upon

hunc, **dicerent** **factum esse crudeliter**
him (if I had punished him), would-say (it) to have-been-done cruelly

et regie. **Nunc intelligo, si iste**
and royally (tyrannically). Now I understand, if that (Catiline)

pervenerit quo intendit, **in Manliana**
shall-have-arrived whither he stretches (purposes), into the Manlian

castra, neminem fore tam stultum, qui videat
camps, no-one to be-about-to-be so foolish, who may-see

non conjurationem factam esse; neminem tam
not a conspiracy to have-been-made; no-one so

improbum, qui fateatur non. Autem hoc uno
dishonest, who may-confess (it) not. But this one

interfecto, intelligo, hanc pestem
(Catiline alone) being-slain, I understand, this pest

reipublicæ reprimi paullisper, non posse
of the republic to be-repressed for-a-little-while, not to be-able

comprimi in perpetuum. **Quod si**
to be-compressed unto perpetual (for ever). But-if

ejecerit se, que eduxerit suos
he shall-have-cast-out himself, and shall-have-led-out his-own

cum se, et aggregaverit ceteros
(associates) with himself, and shall-have-gathered-together the other

naufragos collectos undique eodem;
shipwrecked (ruined persons) collected from-all-sides to-the-same-place;

non modo hæc tam adulta pestis reipublicæ, verum
not only this so adult pest of the republic, but

etiam stirps ac semen omnium malorum
also the roots and seed of all evils

exstinguetur, atque delebitur.
will-be-extinguished, and will-be-blotted-out (destroyed).

13. Etenim jam diu, conscripti patres
For already a long-time, conscript fathers

versamur in his periculis conjurationis que insidiis:
we-are-engaged in these dangers of conspiracy and in snares

sed nescio quo pacto, maturitas
but I know-not by what agreement (by what means), the maturity

omnium scelerum, ac veteris furoris et audaciæ
of all crimes, and of old fury and audacity

erupit in tempus nostri consulatûs. Quod si
has-broken-out into the time of our (of my) consulship. But-if

ex tanto latrocinio iste unus
out-of so-great robbery (conspiracy) that one (Catiline alone)

tolletur; videbimur fortasse esse relevati
shall-be-taken-away; we-shall-seem perhaps to be relieved

curâ et metu ad quoddam breve tempus: autem
from care and fear to (for) some short time: but

periculum residebit, et erit inclusum penitus in
the danger will-settle, and will-be inclosed inwardly in

venis atque in visceribus reipublicæ. Ut sæpe homines
the veins and in the viscera of the republic. As often men

ægri gravi morbo, cum jactantur æstu que
sick with a heavy disease, when they are-tossed with heat and

febri, si biberint gelidam aquam, videntur
with fever, if they may-have-drunk cold water, seem

primo relevari, deinde afflictantur multo gravius
at-first to be-relieved, afterwards are-afflicted by much more-heavily

que vehementius; sic hic morbus, qui est in republicâ,
and more-violently; so this disease, which is in the republic,

relevatus pœnâ istius ingravescet
being-relieved by the punishment of that (Catiline) will grow-grievous

reliquis civibus. Quare, conscripti patres,
to the remaining citizens. Wherefore, conscript fathers,

improbi secedant, secernant se
the dishonest may retire (let them retire), let-them-separate themselves

a bonis, congregentur in unum locum; denique,
from the good, let-them-be-assembled into one place; finally,

id quod jam dixi sæpe, secernantur a
that which already I have-said often, let-them-be-separated from

nobis muro, desinant insidiari
us by the wall (of the city), let-them-cease to lie-in-wait

consuli suæ domi, circumstare
for the consul of his-own house (at his own house), to stand-around

tribunal urbani prætoris, obsidere curiam
the tribunal of the civic prætor, to beset the council-house

cum gladiis, comparare malleolos et faces ad
with swords, to prepare combustibles and torches to (for)

urbem inflammandam. Denique, sit inscriptum
the city to be-set-on-fire. Finally, let-it-be inscribed

in fronte uniuscujusque civis, quid sentiat
in (on) the forehead of each citizen, what ne may-feel

de republicâ. Polliceor hoc
(wnat are his sentiments) concerning the republic. I promise this

vobis, conscripti patres, tantam diligentiam fore
to you, conscript fathers, so-great diligence to-be-about-to-be

in nobis consulibus, tantam auctoritatem in
(will be) in us consuls, so-great authority in

vobis, tantam virtutem in Romanis equitibus,
you, so-great virtue (valour) in the Roman knights,

tantam consensionem in omnibus bonis, ut
so-great agreement in all the-good, that

profectione Catilinæ videatis omnia esse
by the departure of Catiline you-may-see all (things) to be

patefacta, illustrata, oppressa, vindicata. Hisce
exposed, brought-to-light, oppressed, punished. With these

ominibus, Catilina, cum summâ salute reipublicæ,
omens, Catiline, with the highest safety of the republic,

et cum tuâ peste ac pernicie, que cum exitio
and with thy-own pest and destruction, and with the destruction

eorum qui junxerunt se cum te omni scelere
of those who have-joined themselves with thee in every crime

que parricidio, proficiscere ad impium ac nefarium
and parricide, depart to an impious and nefarious

bellum. Tum tu, Jupiter, qui constitutus es a
war. Then thou, Jupiter, who has-been-established by

Romulo iisdem auspiciis quibus hæc urbs;
Romulus with the same auspices with which this city (wa.

quem nominamus vere Statorem hujus
established); whom we name truly the Stator of this

urbis atque imperii, arcebis hunc et socios
city and empire, wilt-ward-off this (Catiline) and the companions

hujus a tuis aris que ceteris templis, a tectis
of this from thy altars and from the other temples, from the roofs

ac mœnibus urbis, a vitâ que fortunis
(houses) and the walls of the city, from the life and the fortunes

omnium civium; et mactabis omnes
of all the citizens; and thou wilt-sacrifice (destroy) all

inimicos bonorum, hostes patriæ, latrones Italiæ,
enemies of the good, enemies of the country, the robbers of Italy,

conjunctos inter se fœdere scelerum ac
united among themselves by a covenant of crimes and

nefariâ societate, vivos que mortuos, æternis
by nefarious society, alive and dead, with eternal

suppliciis.
punishments

SECUNDA ORATIO
THE SECOND ORATION

AD QUIRITES.
TO THE ROMANS.

~~~~~~~~~~

1. **Tandem aliquando,** Quirites, vel ejecimus
At-length, Romans, either we-have-cast-out

ex urbe, L. Catilinam, furentem audaciâ, anhelantem
out-of the city, L. Catiline, raging with audacity, panting-after

scelus, molientem nefarie pestem patriæ,
crime, attempting nefariously the pest (destruction) of the country,

minitantem ferrum que flammam vobis atque huic urbi,
threatening sword and flame to you and to this city,

vel emisimus vel prosecuti sumus verbis
or we-have-sent (him) out, or we-have-followed with words

ipsum egredientem. Abiit, excessit, evasit,
himself going-out. He has-departed, he has-gone-out, he has-escaped,

erupit. Jam nulla pernicies comparabitur intra
he has-burst-out. Now no destruction will be-prepared within

mœnia mœnibus ipsis a illo monstro atque
the walls for the walls themselves by that monster and

prodigio. Atque sine controversiâ vicimus
prodigy (of wickedness). And without controversy we-have-conquered

quidem hunc unum ducem domestici belli. Enim jam
indeed this one leader of domestic war. For now

illa sica versabitur non inter nostra latera :
that poniard will be-engaged not among our sides

pertimescemus non in campo,
(will not be aimed at our sides): we shall-fear (it) not in the plain

non in foro, non in curiâ,
(the Campus Martius), not in the forum, not in the council-house.

deniqe, non intra   domesticos parietes. Ille motus est
finally,   not within (our) domestic   walls.   He was-moved

loco,   cum   depulsus est   ex   urbe.   Jam
from (his) place,   when   he was-driven   out-of   the city.   Now

geremus   palam justum bellum cum hoste,   nullo
we shall-carry on openly   a just   war   with an enemy, no-one

impediente.   Sine   dubio perdidimus, que magnifice
hindering.   Without   doubt   we destroyed,   and magnificently

vicimus hominem, cum conjecimus illum ex occultis
conquered   the man,   when   we cast   him out-of   hidden

insidiis   in   apertum latrocinium.   Vero   quanto
snares   into   open   robbery (war).   But with how-great

mœrore tandem   putatis   illum   esse   afflictum et
sorrow   at-length do you-think   him   to be   afflicted   and

profligatum,   quod   extulit   non   mucronem
cast-down,   because he has-carried-out   not   the sword-blade

cruentum, ut voluit, quod egressus est, nobis vivis,
bloody,   as he wished, because   he went-out,   ourselves   alive

         quod   extorsimus   ferrum   ei   de
(I being alive), because   we have-wrested   the sword from him   from

manibus,   quod reliquit   cives   incolumes,   quod
the hands,   because he has-left the citizens   safe,   because

      urbem stantem?   Ille nunc jacet prostratus,
(he has left) the city   standing?   He   now   lies   overthrown,

Quirites, et sentit   se esse perculsum atque abjectum,
Romans,   and perceives himself to be   struck   and   cast-down,

et profecto retorquet sæpe   oculos ad hanc urbem
and   indeed   turns-back   often (his)   eyes   to   this   city

quam luget   ereptam esse   ex   suis faucibus,
which   he mourns to have-been-snatched   out-of   his   jaws

quæ   videtur   mihi   quidem   lætari,   quod
which (city)   seems   to me   indeed   to rejoice,   because

evomuerit   tantam pestem, que   projecerit
it may have-vomited-out   so-great   a pest   and may-have-cast (it)

foras.
without.

   2. At si quis   est talis, quales oportebat omnes
    But if any (person) is   such   like-as   it did-behove   all

esse, qui accuset me vehementer in hoc   ipso,
to be, who may accuse me   violently   in this (thing' itself.

in quo mea oratio exsultat et triumphat, quod
in which my speech exults and triumphs, because

comprehenderim non tam capitalem hostem, potius
I may have-seized not so capital an enemy, rather

quam   emiserim: ista est non mea culpa,
than I may have-sent (him)-out: that is not my fault,

Quirites, sed   temporum. Oportebat jampridem
Romans, but (the fault) of the times. It-did-behove long-since

L. Catilinam interemtum esse, et affectum gravissimo
L. Catiline   to have-been-slain, and affected with the heaviest

supplicio; que et mos majorum, et severitas
punishment; and both the custom of (our) ancestors, and the severity

hujus imperii,   et respublica postulabat
of this command (of the consular power), and the republic did demand

id a me. Sed quam multos putatis fuisse, qui
that from me. But how many do you-think to have-been who

crederent non   quæ ego deferrem? quam
would believe not (the things) which I might-allege? how

multos, qui putarent   non   propter
many, who would-think (them) not (to exist) because-of

stultitiam? quam multos, qui etiam defenderent?
folly?   how many, who even would-defend (them)?

quam multos, qui faverent   propter improbitatem?
how many, who would-favour (them) because-of dishonesty?

Ac si, illo   sublato, judicarem omne
And if, he (Catiline) being-removed, I might-judge every

periculum depelli a vobis; jampridem ego
danger to be-repelled from you; long-since I

sustulissem L. Catilinam, non modo periculo
would-have-removed L. Catiline, not only with danger

    meæ invidiæ,   verum etiam vitæ.
(at the peril) of my envy (unpopularity), but even of life.

Sed cum viderem, re etiam tum probatâ
But when I might-see, the thing even then being-approved

ne quidem vobis omnibus si   multassem
not-even to (by) you all (the senators), if I might-have-punished

illum morte, ut meritus erat, fore
him with death, as he had-deserved, to be-about-to-be (it might be)

ut oppressus invidiâ, possem non persequi
that being-oppressed with unpopularity, I should-be-able not to pursue

socios ejus: deduxi rem huc,
the companions of him: I have-brought-down the thing hither (to this),

ut possetis pugnare palam tum, cum videretis
that you might-be-able to fight openly then, when you might-see

hostem aperte. Quem hostem, quidem, Quirites,
the enemy openly. Which enemy, indeed, Romans,

quam vehementer ego putem esse timendum foris,
how violently I may think to be to-be-feared without

licet intelligatis
being out of the city), it may-be-allowed (that) you may-understand

hinc, quod fero etiam illud moleste,
hence (you may learn from this), that I bear even this grievously,

quod exierit ex urbe parum comitatus.
that he may-have-gone-out out-of the city little accompanied.

Utinam ille eduxisset omnes suas copias cum
O that he might-have-led-out all his forces with

se! Eduxit mihi Tongillum, quem cœperat
himself! He has-led-out for me Tongillus, whom he had-begun

amare calumniâ in prætextâ:
to love with calumny (feigned love) in the prætexta (in youth): (he has

Publicium et Munacium, alienum æs quorum
led out) Publicius and Munacius, the debt of whom

contractum in popinâ poterat afferre nullum motum
contracted in the tavern was-able to bring no movement

reipublicæ: quos viros reliquit? quanto
(commotion) to the republic: what men has-he-left? with how-great

ære alieno, quam valentes, quam nobiles?
debt, how powerful, how noble?

8. Itaque ego contemno magnopere illum exercitum,
Therefore I despise greatly that army

et Gallicanis legionibus, et hoc delectu,
(of Catiline), both with the Gallic legions, and with this choice

quem Q. Metellus habuit in Piceno et Gallico
(levy), which Q. Metellus has had in the Picenian and Gallic

agro,   et   his   copiis,   quæ   comparantur   **a**
field (territory),   and with these   forces,   which   are-prepared   by

nobis quotidie;   collectum   ex   desperatis
us   daily (I despise that army);   collected   out-of   hopeless

senibus,   ex   agresti luxuriâ,   ex   rusticis decoctoribus,
old-men,   out-of   rural   luxury,   out-of   rustic   spendthrifts,

ex   iis   qui   maluerunt   deserere   vadimonia
out-of those   who   have-wished-rather   to desert (their)   recognisances

quam illum exercitum: quibus si ego   ostendero   non
than   that   army: to whom if   I   shall-have-shown   not

modo aciem nostri exercitus, verum etiam si
only   the array of our   army,   but   even   if (I shall have

          edictum prætoris, concident.   Mallem
shown)   the edict   of the prætor,   they will-fall (faint).   I would-rather

eduxisset   cum   se   suos   milites hos, quos
he might-have-led-out   with   himself (as)   his   soldiers   these, whom

video   volitare   in   foro,   quos   stare ad
I see   to flutter-about   in   the forum,   whom (I see) to stand   to (at)

curiam,   quos   venire etiam in senatum: qui
the council-house,   whom (I see)   to come   even   into the senate: who

nitent   unguentis,   qui   fulgent   purpurâ: qui   si
shine   with perfumes,   who   glitter   in purple: who   if

permanent hic, mementote illum exercitum non tam
they remain   here,   remember   that   army   not   so

          quam hos,   qui   deseruerunt   exercitum   esse
(much)   as   these,   who   have-deserted   the army   to be

pertimescendos nobis.   Atque sunt etiam   timendi
to-be-feared   to (by) us.   And   they-are   even   to be-feared

hoc   magis,   quod   sentiunt   me   scire   quid
by this   more,   because   they perceive   me   to know   what

cogitent,   neque tamen permoventur.   Video   cui
they may-devise,   nor   yet   are-moved.   I see   to whom

Apulia   attributa sit,   qui habeat Etruriam, qui
Apulia   may have-been-assigned,   who may-have   Etruria.   who

Picenum agrum,   qui Gallicum, qui   depoposcerit
the Picenian   field (territory),   who   the Gallic,   who may have-demanded

sibi   has urbanas insidias cædis atque incendiorum.
to himself these   civic   snares   of slaughter   and   of conflagrations

Sentiunt omnia consilia superioris noctis
They perceive all the counsels of the former night

delata esse ad me: patefeci in
to-have-been-brought (reported) to me: I exposed (them) in

senatu hesterno die: Catilina ipse pertimuit, profugit:
the senate yesterday: Catiline himself feared, fled:

quid hi exspectant? Næ illi errant vehementer,
what (why) these wait? Truly they err violently

si sperant illam meam pristinam
(very much), if they hope (expect) that my former

lenitatem futuram perpetuam.
mildness about-to-be perpetual.

4. Jam assecutus sum quod exspectavi, ut vos
Already I have-attained what I waited-for, that you

omnes videretis conjurationem factam esse aperte
all might-see a conspiracy to have-been-made openly

contra rempublicam. Nisi, vero, si est quis
against the republic. Unless, indeed, if there-is any (person)

qui putet similes Catilinæ non sentire
who may-think the like of Catiline (think like Catiline) not to feel

cum Catilinâ. Jam est non locus lenitati; res
with Catiline. Now there-is not place for mildness; the thing

ipsa flagitat severitatem. Etiam nunc concedam
itself demands severity. Even now I will-concede

unum: exeant; proficiscantur; patiantur ne
one (thing): let-them-go-out; let-them-depart; let-them-suffer not

miserum Catilinam tabescere desiderio sui;
the wretched Catiline to pine-away with the want of them

demonstrabo iter. Profectus est Aureliâ viâ:
I will-point-out the journey. He departed by the Aurelian way:

si volent accelerare, consequentur ad vesperam.
if they-shall-wish to hasten, they will-overtake (him) to (at) evening.

O fortunatam rempublicam, si quidem, ejecerit
O fortunate republic, if indeed, she may-have-cast-out

hanc sentinam hujus urbis! Mehercule, Catilinâ uno
this sink of this city! By-Hercules, Catiline one

exhausto, respublica videtur mihi relevata
alone, being-drawn-off, the republic seems to me relieved

et recreata. Enim quid mali aut sceleris potest
and refreshed. For what of evil or of crime is-able

fingi aut excogitari, quod ille conceperit
to be-fashioned or to be-devised, which he may have-conceived

non? Quis veneficus totâ Italiâ, quis gladiator,
not? What poisoner in whole (all) Italy, what gladiator

quis latro, quis sicarius, quis parricida, quis subjector
what robber, what assassin, what parricide, what substitutor

testamentorum, quis circumscriptor, quis ganeo,
of wills, what over-reacher, what debauchee,

quis nepos, quis adulter, quæ infamis mulier,
what spendthrift, what adulterer, what infamous woman,

quis corruptor juventutis, quis corruptus quis
what corruptor of youth, what corrupted (person), what

perditus potest inveniri, qui fateatur
lost (abandoned person) is-able to be-found, who may-confess

non se vixisse familiarissime cum Catilinâ?
not himself to have-lived most-familiarly with Catiline?

Quæ cædes facta est per hosce annos
What slaughter (murder) has-been-done through these-here years

sine illo? Quod nefarium stuprum
(of late years) without him? What nefarious debauchery

non per illum? Vero jam, quæ tanta illecebra
not through him? But now, what so-great allurement

juventutis fuit umquam in ullo homine, quanta in
of youth has been ever in any man, as-great-as in

illo? qui ipse amabat alios turpissime, serviebat
him? who himself did-love others most-basely, did serve

flagitiosissime amori aliorum:
(was subservient) most-villanously to the love of others

pollicebatur aliis fructum libidinum,
he did promise to others (to some) the fruit (enjoyment) of desires,

aliis mortem parentum, non modo impellendo, verum
to others the death of parents, not only by impelling, but

etiam adjuvando. Vero nunc quam subito collegerat
even by assisting. But now how-suddenly he had-collected

ingentem numerum perditorum hominum, non
a large number of lost (abandoned) men, not

solum ex urbe, verum etiam ex agris? Nemo,
only out-of the city, but even out of the fields? No-one,

nor modo Romæ, sed nec in ullo angulo
not only of Rome (at Rome), but neither in any corner

totius Italiæ, fuit oppressus alieno ære, quem
of the whole Italy, was oppressed with-debt, whom

adsciverit non ad hoc incredibile fœdus
he may-have-attached not to this incredible covenant

sceleris.
of crime.

5. Atque ut possitis perspicere diversa studia
And that you-may-be-able to see-plainly the different studies

ejus in dissimili ratione, est nemo in
of him in a dissimilar reason (manner), there-is no-one in

gladiatorio ludo paullo audacior ad facinus, qui
the gladiatory play (school) a little more-bold to daring-deed, who

fateatur non se esse intimum Catilinæ:
may-confess not himself to be the intimate (friend) of Catiline

nemo levior et nequior in
no-one lighter (more unsteady) and more profligate in (on)

scenâ, qui commemoret non se fuisse prope
the stage, who may-mention not himself to have-been nearly

sodalem ejusdem. Atque tamen idem,
the companion of the same. And yet the same (Catiline),

assuefactus exercitatione stuprorum et scelerum,
accustomed by the exercise of debaucheries and of crimes,

frigore, et fame, et siti, ac vigiliis perferendis,
in cold, and in hunger, and in thirst, and in watchings to be-borne,

prædicabatur fortis ab istis; cum subsidia
was-declared brave by those (persons); when the aids

industriæ atque instrumenta virtutis consumerentur
of industry and the instruments of virtue might-be-consumed

in libidine que audaciâ. Vero si sui comites
in desire and audacity. But if his companions

secuti fuerint hunc; si flagitiosi greges
may-have-followed this (Catiline); if the villanous flocks

desperatorum hominum exierint ex urbe; O
of hopeless men may-have-gone-out out-of the city; O

beatos nos, O fortunatam rempublicam, O præc.aram
happy   us, O fortunate   republic,   O   famous

laudem mei consulatûs! Enim jam libidines hominum
praise of my consulship! For now the desires of the men

sunt non mediocres,   audaciæ non humanæ ac
are   not moderate, (their) audacities not   human   and

tolerandæ: cogitant nihil, nisi   cædes,   nisi
to be-supported: they devise nothing, unless slaughters, unless

incendia, nisi rapinas;   profuderunt
conflagrations, unless rapines; they have-poured-forth (squandered)

sua   patrimonia;   abligurierunt   suas fortunas;
their-own patrimonies; they have-spent-in-feasting their   fortunes;

res   eos jampridem; fides   nuper
thing (property has failed) them long-since; faith (credit) lately

cœpit deficere;   tamen illa eadem libido, quæ
has-begun to fail (them); yet that same desire, which

erat in   abundantiâ, permanet. Quod si in vino
was   in (their) abundance, remains.   But-if in wine

et aleâ quærerent solum comissationes et   scorta,
and dice they-might-seek only revellings and prostitutes,

illi essent   desperandi   quidem; sed tamen
they would-be to be-despaired-of indeed;   but   yet

essent   ferendi. Vero quis possit ferre hoc,
they would-be to be-borne. But who may-be-able to bear this, (for)

inertes homines   insidiari   fortissimis   viris,
inactive   men   to lie-in-wait for the bravest   men,

stultissimos   prudentissimis,   ebriosos   sobriis,
the most-foolish for the most-prudent, the drunken for the sober

dormientes vigilantibus?   Qui mihi,   accubantes
the sleeping for the watching? Who (for me),   reclining

in conviviis, complexi impudicas mulieres, languidi
in banquets, having-embraced unchaste women,   languid

vino, conferti cibo, redimiti sertis, obliti
with wine, filled with food, crowned with garlands, besmeared

unguentis,   debilitati   stupris,   eructant   suis
with perfumes, weakened with debaucheries, belch-out in their

sermonibus cædem bonorum, atque   incendia
discourses   the slaughter of the good, and   the

urbis. Quibus, ego confido, aliquod fatum impendere:
of the city. To whom, I trust, some fate to impend:

et pœnas jam diu debitas improbitati,
and the penalties already a long-time due to dishonesty,

nequitiæ, sceleri, libidini, aut jam plane
to licentiousness, to crime, to desire, either already plainly

instare, aut certe jam appropinquare. Quos si
to be-at-hand, or certainly already to approach. Whom if

meus consulatus, quoniam potest non sanare,
my consulship, since it is-able not to cure,

sustulerit; propagarit
may have-removed; it will have propagated (it will have added a duration)

non nescio quod breve tempus, sed multa sæcula
not I know-not what short time, but many ages

reipublicæ. Enim est nulla natio quam
to the republic. For there-is no nation which

pertimescamus; nullus rex qui possit facere bellum
we may-fear; no king who may be-able to make war

Romano populo. Omnia externa, terrâ que
to the Roman people. All external (things), by land and

mari pacata sunt virtute unius:
by sea have-been-appeased by the valour of one (Pompey alone):

domesticum bellum manet; insidiæ sunt intus;
a domestic war remains; the snares are within;

periculum est inclusum intus; hostis est intus;
the danger is inclosed within; the enemy is within;

est certandum nobis cum luxuriâ, cum amentiâ,
it-is to be-contended to (by) us with luxury, with madness,

cum scelere. Quirites, ego profiteor me ducem
with crime. Romans, I profess (declare) myself the leader

huic bello; suscipio inimicitias
to this war; I take-up (I take upon myself) the enmities

perditorum hominum. Quæ poterunt
of the lost (abandoned) men. What (things) shall-be-able

sanari, sanabo quâcunque ratione; quæ
to be-cured, I will-cure by whatsoever reason (means); what

erunt resecanda, patiar non manere ad
things) shall-be to be-cut-off. I will-suffer not to remain to

perniciem civitatis. Proinde, aut   exeant,   aut
the destruction of the state.   Therefore, either   let-them-go-out,   or

quiescant;   aut, si et permanent in urbe, et
let-them-remain-quiet; or,   if both they remain in the city, and

in eâdem mente,   exspectent   ea   quæ
in the same mind,   let-them-expect   those (things) which

merentur.
they deserve.

6. At etiam sunt,   Quirites, qui dican
     But even there-are (persons),   Romans,   who may-say

Catilinam ejectum esse   a me in exsilium. Quod
Catiline   to-have-been-cast-out by me into   exile.   Which

si ego possem assequi verbo, ejicerem istos
if I   might-be-able to attain by word, I would-cast-out those

     ipsos, qui loquuntur hæc.   Videlicet
(persons) themselves, who   speak   these (things). That-is-to-say

     timidus, et permodestus homo potuit non
(forsooth) the timid, and   very-modest   man   was-able   not

ferre vocem consulis: simul atque jussus est ire
to bear the voice of the consul: as-soon-as he was-ordered to go

in exsilium, paruit ivit. Hesterno die, cum
into exile,   he obeyed, he went. On-yesterday, when

interfectus essem pæne meæ domi,
I might-have-been-slain almost of my house (at my own house),

vocavi senatum in ædem Jovis Statoris:
I called the senate into the temple of Jupiter Stator:

detuli omnem rem   ad conscriptos patres.
I referred all   the thing (affair) to the conscript fathers.

Quo, cum Catilina venisset, quis senator appellavit
Whither, when Catiline might-have-come, what senator addressed

eum? quis salutavit? denique, quis ita aspexit
him? who saluted (him)? finally, who so looked-on (him)

ut perditum civem, ac non potius ut
as a lost (abandoned) citizen, and not rather as

importunissimum hostem? Quin etiam principes ejus
a most-troublesome enemy? But even the chiefs of that

ordinis,   reliquerunt illam partem subselliorum
order (the senatorial),   left   that part   of the seats

ad quam ille accesserat nudam atque inanem. **Hic**
to   which   he   had approached   naked   and   empty.   Here

ego, ille vehemens consul, qui ejicio cives in
I,   that   violent   consul,   who   cast-out   citizens   into

exsilium verbo, quæsivi a Catilinâ, an fuisset
exile   by a word, asked   from Catiline, whether he might-have-been

nocturno conventu apud   M. Leccam, necne.
in the nocturnal   assembly   with (at the house of) M. Lecca,   or-not.

Cum ille audacissimus homo, convictus conscientiâ,
When that   most-audacious   man,   convicted   by consciousness,

primo reticuisset: patefeci cetera.
at-first   might-have-kept-silent: I exposed   the other (things).

Edocui quid egisset eâ nocte [ubi
I informed   what he might-have-acted   on that   night   [where

fuisset], quid constituisset in proximam,
he might-have-been], what he might-have-appointed   upon   the next

quemadmodum ratio totius belli
(night),   in what-manner   the reason (plan) of the whole   war

descripta esse ei. Cum hæsitaret,
might-have-been-described   to (by) him.   When he might-hesitate,

cum teneretur; quæsivi, quid
when he might-be-held (when he was convicted); I asked,   what (why)

dubitaret proficisci eò, quo pararat
he might-doubt (hesitate)   to depart thither, whither he had-prepared

jampridem: cum scirem arma, cum secures,
(to go)   long-since: when I might-know arms,   when   axes,

cum fasces, cum tubas, cum militaria signa,
when   fasces,   when trumpets,   when   military   signs (ensigns),

cum illam argenteam aquilam, cui ille etiam
when   that   silver   eagle,   to which he   even

fecerat sacrarium scelerum suæ domi,
had-made   a shrine   of crimes of his-own house (at his own house),

præmissam esse. Ejiciebam in exsilium,
to have-been-sent-before.   Did-I-cast-out   into   exile (him),

quem videbam jam ingressum esse in bellum?
whom   I did-see   already   to have-entered   into   war?

Etenim, credo iste Manlius centurio, qui
For,   I believe (forsooth)   that Manlius   the centurion,   who

posuit **castra** in Fesulano agro, indixit
has-placed camps in the Fesulanian field (territory), ha s-declared

bellum Romano populo suo nomine: et illa
war to (on) the Roman people in his-own name: and those

cast*a nunc exspectant non Catilinam ducem: et
camp now await not Catiline (as) leader: and

ille, ejectus in exsilium, conferet se
he, being-cast-out into exile, will-betake himself (to

Massiliam, ut aiunt, non in hæc castra.
Marseilles, as they say, not into these camps.

7. O miseram conditionem, non modo reipublicæ
O wretched condition, not only of the republic

administrandæ, verum etiam conservandæ? Nunc, si
to be-managed, but even to-be-preserved? Now, if

L. Catilina, circumclusus ac debilitatus meis consiliis,
L. Catiline, closed-around and weakened by my counsels,

laboribus, periculis, pertimuerit subito,
labours, (and) dangers, may have-feared suddenly,

mutaverit sententiam, deseruerit suos,
may have-changed (his) opinion, may have-deserted his-own

abjecerit consilium belli faciundi,
(associates), may have-cast-off the counsel of war to be-made

converterit iter ex hoc
the design of making war), may have-turned (his) journey out-of this

cursu sceleris et belli ad fugam atque in exsilium;
course of crime and of war to flight and into exile;

ille dicetur non spoliatus esse a me armis
he will-be-said not to-have-been-despoiled by me from the arms

audaciæ, non obstupefactus ac perterritus meâ
of audacity, not astonished and frightened by my

diligentiâ, non depulsus de spe que conatu, sed
diligence, not driven-off from (his) hope and attempt, but

indemnatus, innocens ejectus in exsilium a
uncondemned, innocent (to have been) cast-out into exile by

consule vi et minis: et erunt qui
the consul by force and by threats: and there-will-be (persons) who

velint illum, si fecerit hoc, existimari non
may-wish him, if he shall-have-done this, to be-thought not

improbum, sed miserum: me non diligentissimum
dishonest, but wretched: me not a most-diligent

consulem, sed crudelissimum tyrannum. Est tanti
consul, but a most-cruel tyrant. It-is-of so-much

mihi, Quirites, subire tempestatem
to me (I think it worth the while), Romans, to undergo the tempest

hujus falsæ atque iniquæ invidiæ, dummodo
of this false and unjust envy (unpopularity), provided-that

periculum hujus horribilis ac nefarii belli
the danger of this horrible and nefarious war

depellatur a vobis. Sane dicatur
may-be-driven-off from you. Truly he may-be-said

ejectus esse a me, dummodo eat in exsilium.
to have-been-cast-out by me, provided-that he may-go into exile.

Sed credite mihi, est non iturus. Ego numquam
But believe to me, he-is not about-to-go. I never

optabo a immortalibus diis, Quirites, causâ meæ
shall-wish from the immortal gods, Romans, for-the-sake of my

invidiæ levandæ, ut audiatis L. Catilinam
unpopularity to be-relieved, that you may-hear L. Catiline

ducere exercitum hostium, atque volitare in
to lead an army of the enemies, and to flutter-about in

armis: sed tamen audietis triduo: que
arms: but yet you will-hear (it) in the-space-of-three-days: and

timeo illud multo magis, ne aliquando sit invidiosum
I fear this by much more, lest at-length it may-be envious

mihi, quod emiserim potius
(producing unpopularity) to me, that I may-have-sent-out rather

quam quod ejecerim illum. Sed cum
than that I may have-cast-out him. But when (since)

sint homines, qui dicant illum ejectum esse
there-may-be men, who may-say him to have-been-cast-out

cum profectus sit, iidem quid dicerent,
when he may-have-departed, the same (persons) what would (they) say,

si interfectus esset? Quamquam isti, qui dictitant
if he might-have-been-slain? Although those, who say-often

Catilinam ire Massiliam, queruntur non
Catiline to go (is going to) Marseilles, complain-of not

5 *

tam,   quam verentur hoc.   Est   nemo istorum
so (so much),   as   they fear   this.   There-is no-one   of those

tam misericors, qui   malit   non
so   merciful,   who may wish-rather not (who would not prefer)

illum ire ad Manlium quam ad   Massilienses.
him   to go to   Manlius   than   to   the people-of-Marseilles.

Autem Mehercule, si ille numquam ante   cogitasset
But   by-Hercules, if he   never   before might-have-devised

hoc, quod agit,   tamen   mallet   se
this, which he acts (he is doing), yet   he would-wish-rather himself

interfici latrocinantem   quam vivere
to be-slain   robbing (warring against his country) than   to live

exsulem. Vero nunc, cum nihil adhuc   acciderit
an exile.   But now, when nothing as-yet may-have-happened

ei   præter   voluntatem que cogitationem
to him beside (contrary to)   the wish   and   the thought

ipsius, nisi quod profectus est Româ nobis
of himself, unless that he has-departed from Rome us (being)

vivis, optemus   potius ut   eat   in
alive, we may-wish (let us wish) rather that he may-go into

exsilium quam   queramur.
exile   than (that) we may-complain (of it).

8. Sed cur loquimur tam diu   de   uno
    But why do we-speak so long-time concerning one

hoste, et   de   eo hoste qui   jam fatetur
enemy, and concerning that enemy who already confesses

se   esse hostem, et quem timeo non, quia murus
himself to be an enemy, and whom I fear not, because the wall

     interest, quod volui semper? dicimus
(of the city) is-between, which I have-wished always? do we-say

nihil   de   his qui dissimulant, qui remanent
nothing concerning those who dissemble, who remain

Romæ,   qui sunt cum nobis? Quos ego quidem
of Rome (at Rome), who are with us? Whom I indeed

studeo   non tam   ulcisci, quam
study (greatly desire) not so (so much) to take-revenge-on, as

sanare, et placare   eos reipublicæ, si
to cure, to to appease (to reconcile) them to the republic, if

possit fieri ullo modo; neque intelligo
it-may-be-able to be-done in any manner; nor do I understand

quare id possit non fieri, si volent
wherefore that may be-able not to be-done, if they shall-wish

audire me. Enim exponam vobis, Quirites, ex
to hear me. For I will explain to you, Romans, out-of

quibus generibus hominum istæ copiæ comparentur:
what kinds of men those forces may be-prepared

deinde afferam singulis (plur.) medicinam
(raised): afterwards I will-bring to each the medicine

consilii atque meæ orationis, si potero
of (my) counsel and of my speech, if I shall-be-able (to offer)

quam. Est unum genus eorum, qui in magno
any. There-is one kind of those, who (being) in great

ære alieno, etiam habent majores possessiones:
debt, also have greater possessions:

adducti amore quarum, possunt dissolvi
led by the love of which, they are-able to be-dissolved

nullo modo. Species horum
(to be detached from them) in no manner. The appearance of these

hominum est honestissima (enim sunt locupletes);
men is the most-honourable (for they-are wealthy):

vero voluntas et causa impudentissima. Tu
but (their) wish and cause (is) most-shameless. Thou

sis ornatus et copiosus agris, tu
mayest-be adorned (furnished) and abundant in fields, thou (mayest

ædificiis, tu argento, tu familiâ,
be well furnished) with edifices, thou with silver, thou with household,

tu omnibus rebus; et dubites
thou with all things; and mayest-thou-doubt (dost thou hesitate)

detrahere de possessione, acquirere ad
to withdraw from (to diminish) thy possession, to acquire to

fidem? Enim quid exspectas bellum?
faith (to gain in credit)? For what dost-thou-expect war?

quid! ergo in vastatione omnium putas
what! therefore in the laying-waste of all (things) dost-thou-think

tuas possessiones futuras sacrosanctas?
thy possessions about-to-be sacred (inviolable)?

an   novas tabulas ?   **errant,**
whether (dost thou expect) new   tablets (an abolition of debts) ?   they err,

qui   exspectant   istas   a   Catilinâ.   [Novæ]   tabulæ
who   expect   those   from   Catiline.   [New]   tablets

proferentur   meo beneficio, verum auctionariæ.
shall be-brought-forward by my kindness,   but   auctionary

               Enim neque isti qui habent
(tablets — catalogues of sale).   For   neither those who   have

possessiones possunt esse salvi ullâ aliâ ratione.
possessions   are-able   to be   safe   in any   other   manner.

Quod si   voluissent   facere maturius,   neque
But-if   they might-have-wished   to do (it)   earlier,   nor

(id   quod   est   stultissimum)   certare   cum   usuris
(that   which   is   most-foolish)   to contend   with   usuries

fractibus   prædiorum ;   uteremur   his
with the fruits   of (their) farms ;   we should-use (experience) with these

          locupletioribus et melioribus civibus. Sed
(would have them)   wealthier   and   better   citizens.   But

puto   hosce   homines   minime   pertimescendos,
I think   these   men   least (very little)   to be-feared,

quod   aut   possunt   deduci   de   sententiâ ,
because   either   they are-able   to be-led-away   from (their) opinion ,

aut,   si   permanebunt,   videntur   mihi   magis
or,   if   they shall-remain,   they seem   to me   more (rather)

facturi   vota   contra   rempublicam   quam
about-to-make   vows (wishes) against   the republic   than

laturi   arma.
about-to-bear   arms.

   9.   Est   alterum genus eorum, qui quamquam
     There-is   another   kind   of those,   who   although

premuntur   ære alieno,   tamen   exspectant
they are-pressed   with debt,   yet   expect

dominiationem :   volunt   potiri   rerum :
dominion (authority) :   they wish   to possess   of things (power) :

arbitrantur   se   posse consequi honores, republicâ
they think   themselves to be-able to attain   honours,   the republic

perturbatâ,   quos   desperant   quietâ.
being-disturbed,   which   they despair (the republic being)   quiet.

Quibus hoc videtur præcipiendum, scilicet unum
To whom this   seems (fit)   to be-advised, that-is-to-say   one

et idem   quod omnibus ceteris, ut   desperent
and the same (thing) which   to all   the rest, that they may-despair

se   posse consequi id, quod conantur: primum
themselves to be-able to attain that, which they attempt: first

omnium me ipsum vigilare, adesse, providere
of all   myself   to watch, to be-present, to foresee (provide)

reipublicæ: deinde   magnos animos
for the republic: afterwards (secondly)   great   minds (spirit)

esse in bonis viris, magnam concordiam,
to be in good   men,   great   agreement (unanimity)

maximam multitudinem,   præterea magnas copias
a very-great   multitude (of them),   besides   great   forces

militum: denique, immortales deos præsentes,
of soldiers: finally,   the immortal gods being-present (propitious),

esse laturos   auxilium huic invicto   populo,
to-be about-to-bear   aid   to this unconquered people,

clarissimo imperio,   pulcherrimæ urbi,
(to this) most-famous   empire,   (to this) most-beautiful   city,

contra tantam vim sceleris. Quod si   jam
against so-great violence of crime. But-if   already

adepti sint   id, quod cupiunt cum summo
they may have-obtained that, which they desire with the highest

furore: num sperant illi   se   futuros consules,
fury: whether hope   they themselves about-to-be consuls,

ac dictatores, aut etiam reges in cinere (sing.) urbis,
and dictators,   or even kings in the ashes   of the city,

et sanguine civium, quæ   concupierunt
and in the blood of the citizens, which (things) they have-coveted

conscelerata ac nefaria mente? Vident non
with criminal   and nefarious   mind?   Do they-see   not

se   cupere   id,   quod si
themselves to desire (that they desire)   that,   which if

adepti fuerint,   sit necesse concedi alicui
they shall-have-obtained, may-be necessary to be-conceded to some

fugitivo aut gladiatori? Tertium genus est jam
fugitive   or   gladiator?   The third kind is   already

affectum ætate, sed tamen robustum
affected by age (is old) but yet robust

exercitatione: ex quo genere est Manlius ipse,
by exercise: out-of which kind is Manlius himself,

cui Catilina nunc succedit. Hi sunt homines ex
to whom Catiline now succeeds. These are men out-of

iis coloniis quas Sulla constituit Fesulis, universas
those colonies which Sulla established at Fesulæ, the whole

quas ego sentio esse optimorum civium, et
which I perceive to be of the best citizens, and

fortissimorum virorum: sed tamen hi sunt coloni,
of the bravest men: but yet these are colonists,

qui jactarunt se sumtuosius que insolentius
who have-boasted themselves too-expencively and too-insolently

in insperatis que repentinis pecuniis. Dum hi
in (their) unhoped-for and sudden monies. While these

ædificant, tamquam beati: dum delectantur
build as-if happy (wealthy): while they are-delighted

prædiis, lecticis, magnis familiis,
with (their) farms, with couches, with great households.

apparatis conviviis, inciderunt in
with prepared (magnificent) banquets, they have-fallen-in into

tantum æs alienum, ut si velint esse salvi,
so-great debt, that if they may-wish to-be safe,

Sulla sit excitandus iis ab
Sulla may to be-roused to them (Sulla must be raised by them) from

inferis: qui etiam impulerunt nonullos agrestes,
the shades-below: who also have-impelled some rustics,

tenues atque egentes homines, in illam eandem
slender (poor) and needy men, into that same

spem veterum rapinarum. Utrosque quos ego,
hope of old rapines. Both whom I,

Quirites, pono in eodem genere prædatorum que
Romans, place in the same kind of plunderers and

direptorum. Sed moneo eos hoc: desinant furere,
of pillagers. But I advise them this: let them-cease to rage,

ac cogitare proscriptiones et dictaturas. Enim
and to devise proscriptions and dictatorships. For

tantus   dolor illorum temporum est inustus   civitati,
so-great grief of those   times   is branded ts the state,

ut jam non modo homines, sed ne quidem pecudes
hat now not only   men,   but   not-even   cattle

videantur mihi esse passuræ   ista.
may-seem   to me to be about-to-suffer those (things).

  10. Quartum genus est sane varium, et mistum,
    The fourth   kind   is truly various, and   mixed,

et turbulentum: qui jampridem premuntur;
and   turbulent: who long-since are-pressed (with debt);

qui nunquam emergent: qui vacillant in
who   never   will emerge (therefrom): who   totter   in

vetere ære alieno, partim inertiâ, partim   negotio
old   debt,   partly by sloth, partly by business

gerendo   male,   partim
to be-carried-on badly (by conducting their business badly),   partly

etiam sumtibus;   qui   defatigati   vadimoniis,
also   by expenses; who being-harassed by recognisances,

judiciis,   proscriptionibus   bonorum,
by judgments,   by proscriptions (sequestrations)   of goods,

permulti dicuntur conferre   se   et   ex   urbe
very-many are-said to betake themselves both out-of the city

et   ex   agris   in illa castra. Ego arbitror
and out-of the fields into those camps.   I   think

hosce   esse non tam   acres milites quam
these (latter) to be not so (so much) active soldiers   as

lentos infitiatores. Primum qui homines si possunt
slow   cheats.   First which men if they are-able

non stare,   corruant; sed ita, ut non modo
not to stand, let-them-fall; but so, that not only

civitas, sed ne quidem proximi vicini sentiant.
the state, but not-even the nearest neighbours may perceive.

Nam intelligo non illud, quamobrem, si possunt
For   I understand not this, wherefore, if they are-able

non vivere honeste,   velint   perire turpiter;
not to live honourably, they may-wish to perish basely;

aut cur arbitrentur   se   perituros minore
or   why they may-think themselves about-to perish with les

dolore **cum** multis quam si pereant soli. **Quintum**
pain   with   many   than   if they may-perish alone.   The fifth

genus est parricidarum, sicariorum, denique, omnium
genus   is   of parricides,   of assassins,   finally,   of all

facinorosorum, quos ego revoco non a Catilinâ.
the villanous,   whom   I   call-back   not from   Catiline

Nam neque possunt divelli ab eo; et **sane**
For   neither are-they-able to-be-torn-away from him; and truly

pereant in latrocinio, quoniam sunt ita multi
let-them-perish in   robbery (war),   since   they-are so many

ut carcer possit non capere eos. **Autem**
that the prison may-be-able not to take (to hold) them.   But

postremum genus non solum numero, verum etiam
the last   kind   not only   in number,   but   also

genere ipso atque vitâ est: quod est proprium
in kind   itself   and in life is (this): which is   proper

Catilinæ, de delectu ejus, immo vero
to Catiline (peculiarly his own), from the choice of him,   yea-even

de complexu ac sinu ejus: **quos**
from the embrace and bosom of (his bosom friends): whom

videtis pexo capillo, nitidos, **aut**
you see with combed (curled) hair,   neat (elegant), either

imberbes, aut barbatos bene; **tunicis**
beardless,   or   bearded well (exquisitely); with tunics

municatis et talaribus; amictos velis,
having-sleeves and reaching-to-the-ancles; clothed with veils,

non togis: omnis industria vitæ quorum et
not with togas: all   the industry of the life of whom and

labor vigilandi expromitur in **cœnis**
labour of watching is-brought-out (exhibited) in   suppers

antelucanis. Omnes aleatores, omnes adulteri, omnes
before-day-break.   All   gamesters,   all   adulterers,   all

impuri que impudici versantur in his
impure and unchaste (persons) are-engaged (associate) in these

gregibus: hi tam lepidi ac delicati pueri didicerunt
flocks: these so pretty and delicate boys   have-learnt

non solum amare et amari, neque cantare **et**
not   only to love, and to be loved,   nor to sing   and

saltare, sed etiam vibrare sicas, et **spargere**
to dance, but also to brandish poniards, and to scatter

venena : qui nisi exeunt, nisi pereunt, etiamsi
poisons : who unless they go-out, unless they-perish, even-if

Catilina perierit, scitote hoc futurum
Catiline may have-perished, know-ye this about-to-be (that this will be)

Catilinarium seminarium in republicâ. Verumtamen
a Catilinarian seminary (nursery) in the republic. Nevertheless

quid isti miseri volunt sibi ? Num
what (do) those wretched (persons) wish for themselves ? Whether

sunt ducturi suas mulierculas cum
are-they about-to-lead their little-women (their women) with

se in castra ? Autem quemadmodum poterunt
themselves into the camps ? But how will they-be-able

carere illis, præsertim jam his noctibus ?
to be-without them, especially now in these nights (of November) ?

Autem quo pacto illi perferent
But by-what agreement (in what manner) will-they-bear

Apenninum, atque illas pruinas ac nives ? Nisi
the Apennine, and those frosts and snows ? Unless

putant se toleraturos hiemem facilius
they think themselves about-to-support winter more-easily

idcirco, quod didicerunt saltare nudi in
on-this-account, because they-have-learnt to dance naked in

conviviis.
banquets.

11. O bellum magnopere pertimescendum, cum
O war greatly to be-feared, when

Catilina sit habiturus hanc prætoriam cohortem
Catiline may-be about-to-have this prætorian cohort

scortorum. Instruite nunc, Quirites, vestra
(body guard) of debauchees. Array now, Romans, your

præsidia, que vestros exercitus contra has tam
guards, and your armies against these so

præclaras copias Catilinæ : et primum opponite
famous forces of Catiline : and first oppose

vestros consules que imperatores illi confecto et
your consuls and commanders to that exhausted and

saucio   gladiatori :   deinde   educite   florem   a.
wounded   gladiator :   afterwards   lead-out   the flower   and

robur   totius   Italiæ   contra   illam   ejectam   ac
strength   of the whole   of Italy   against   that   out-cast   and

debilitatam manum   naufragorum.   Vero
debilitated   hand (band) of shipwrecked (of ruined men).   But

jam urbes   coloniarum   ac   municipiorum
now   the cities   of (your) colonies   and   of (your) municipal-towns

respondebunt   silvestribus   tumulis
will-answer   (will oppose)   to the woody   (rustic)   hillocks

Catilinæ.   Neque vero   debeo   conferre   cæteras
of Catiline.   Nor   truly   ought-I   to compare (your)   other

copias, vestra ornamenta, præsidia, cum inopiâ atque
forces,   your   equipments,   guards,   with the need   and

egestate illius latronis.   Sed si,   omnibus his rebus
want   of that   robber.   But if,   all   these things

omissis,   quibus nos   suppeditamur,   ille   eget,
being-omitted,   in which   we   are-supplied,   he   is without,

senatu, Romanis equitibus, populo, urbe, ærario,
a senate,   Roman   knights,   a people, the city,   ι treasury,

vectigalibus,   cunctâ Italiâ, omnibus provinciis,
revenues,   the whole   Italy,   all   the provinces,

exteris nationibus : si, his rebus omissis,   velimus
foreign   nations :   if, these things being-omitted, we may-wish

contendere   causas   ipsas,   quæ confligunt
to contend   (to compare)   the causes   themselves,   which   conflict

ınter   se,   possumus   intelligere   ex   eo
between   themselves,   we are-able   to understand   out-of   that

ipso quam   valde   illi jaceant.   Enim
(thing) itself   how   very-much   they   may-lie (are fallen).   For

ex   hâc parte   pudor pugnat,   illinc
out-of   this   part (on this side)   modesty   fights,   thence (on the

petulantia ;   hinc   pudicitia, illinc
other side)   insolence ;   henc∘ (on this side)   chastity,   thence

stuprum ;   hinc fides,   illinc fraudatio ;   hinc pietas,
adultery ;   hence   faith,   thence   cheating ;   hence   piety,

illınc scelus ;   hinc constantia, illinc furor ι hinc
thence   crime ;   hence   constancy,   thence   madness ;   hence

nonestas, illinc turpitudo; hinc continentia, illinc
honesty, thence baseness; hence continence, thence

'ubido; denique, æquitas, temperantia, fortitudɔ,
lust; finally, equity, temperance, fortitude,

prudentia, omnes virtutes certant cum iniquitate, cum
prudence, all virtues contend with iniquity, with

luxuriâ, cum ignaviâ, cum temeritate, cum omnibus
luxury, with idleness, with rashness, with all

vitiis; postremo, copiæ cum egestate, bona
vices; lastly, forces (supplies) with want, good

ratio cum perdita, sana mens cum
reason with lost (reason), a healthy (sound) mind with

amentiâ; denique, bona spes confligit cum desperatione
madness; finally, good hope conflicts with despair

omnium rerum. In certamine ac prælio hujusmodi,
of all things. In a contest and battle of this sort,

nonne, etiamsi studia hominum
whether-or-not, even-if the desires (support) of men

deficiant, immortales dii ipsi cogent tot
may-fail, the immortal gods themselves will force so-many

et tanta vitia superari ab his præclarissimis
and so-great vices to be-overcome by these most-famous

virtutibus?
virtues?

12. Cum quæ sint ita, Quirites, vos defendite
Since which (things) may-be thus, Romans, do you-defend

vestra tecta quemadmodum jam antea custodiis que
your roofs as already before with guards and

vigiliis: consultum est ac
with watches: it has-been-consulted (it has been cared for) and

provisum mihi, ut esset satis præsidii
provided to be (by me), that there-should-be enough of guard

urbi sine vestro motu, ac sine
to the city without your motion (without disturbing you), and without

ullo tumultu. Omnes vestri coloni que municipes
any tumult. All your colonists and municipal

facti certiores a me de
(citizens) being-made more-certain (being informed) by me concerning

hâc nocturnâ excursione Catilinæ, defendent facile
this   nocturnal   excursion   of Catiline,   will defend   easily

suas urbes que fines: gladiatores, quam ille
their   cities   and   territories: the gladiators,   which   he (Catiline)

putavit fore maximam et certissimam
thought   to be-about-to-be   a very-great   and   a very-certain

manum sibi, quamquam sunt meliore animo
hand (band)   to himself,   although   they-are   with better   mind

quam pars patriciorum, tamen continebuntur
than   a part   of the patricians,   yet   shall-be-retained

nostrâ potestate. Q. Metellus, quem ego,
(held in check) by our   power.   Q. Metellus,   whom   I,

prospiciens hoc, præmisi in Gallicanum que
foreseeing   this,   sent-before   into   the Gallic   and

Picenum agrum, aut opprimet hominem, aut
the Picenian   land,   either   will-oppress   the man,   or

prohibebit omnes motus que conatus ejus. Autem
will hinder   all   the movements and attempts   of him.   But

de reliquis rebus constituendis, maturandis,
concerning   the remaining   things   to-be-appointed,   to-be-hastened,

agendis, referemus jam ad senatum, quem videtis
to be-acted,   we will-refer   now   to   the senate,   which   you see

vocari. Nunc etiam atque etiam volo
to be-called.   Now   also   and   also (again and again)   I wish

illos monitos qui remanserunt in urbe, atque adeo,
those (to be) advised   who   have-remained   in the city,   and-moreover,

qui relicti sunt a Catilinâ contra salutem urbis,
who   have-been-left   by   Catiline   against   the safety   of the city,

que omnium vestrûm, quamquam sunt hostes, tamen
and   of all   you,   although   they-are   enemies,   yet

quia nati sunt cives. Si mea lenitas adhuc
because   they have-been-born   citizens.   If   my   mildness   hitherto

visa est cui solutior, exspectavit
has-seemed   to any (person)   too-loose   (too lax),   it has-waited-for

hoc, ut id erumperet quod latebat. Quod
this,   that   that   might-burst-forth   which   did lie-concealed.   What

est reliquum, possum non jam
*   remaining (as far as regards the future).   I am-able   not   now

oblivisci hanc esse meam patriam, me esse consulem
to forget this to be my country, myself to be the consul

horum ; aut esse vivendum mihi
of these; either to be to be-lived to (by) me (that I must either live)

cum his, aut moriendum pro his
with this, or to be-died for these (or die in defence of these).

Est nullus custos portæ, nullus insidiator
There-is no keeper of the gate (of the city), no plotter

viæ ; si qui volunt exire, possunt
of the way (way-layer); if any wish to go-out, they are-able

consulere sibi. Vero qui commoverit se
to consult for themselves. But (he) who shall-have-moved himself

in urbe, cujus ego deprehendero non modo
in the city, of whom I shall-have-detected not only

ullum factum, sed inceptum ve conatum; sentiet
any deed, but undertaking or attempt; shall-perceive

esse in hâc urbe vigilantes consules, esse
to be (that there are) in this city vigilant consuls, to be

egregios magistratus, esse fortem senatum, esse arma,
excellent magistrates, to be a bold senate, to be arms,

esse carcerem, quem nostri majores voluerunt esse
to be a prison, which our ancestors have-wished to be

vindicem nefariorum ac manifestorum scelerum.
the avenger of nefarious and of manifest crimes.

13. Atque omnia hæc agentur si
And all these (things) shall-be-acted (done) a,

Quirites, ut maximæ res minimo motu, summa
Romans, that the greatest things with the least commotion, the highest

pericula nullo tumultu, intestinum ac domesticum
dangers with no tumult, an intestine and domestic

bellum, crudelissimum ac maximum post memoriam
war, the most-cruel and the greatest after (since) the memory

hominum, sedetur, me uno
of men, may-be-allayed, myself one (an individual)

togato duce et imperatore. Quod ego
wearing-the-toga (being) the leader and commander. Which I

administrabo sic, Quirites, ut si poterit fieri
will administer so, Romans, that if it shall-be-able to be-done

ullo   modo,   ne quidem   quisquam   improbus
in any   manner,   not-even   any   dishonest (person)

sufferat   pœnam   sui   sceleris in hâc urbe.   Sed
may undergo   the penalty   of his   crime   in this   city.   But

si   vis   manifestæ audaciæ, si periculum impendens
if the violence of manifest   audacity,   if   the danger   hanging-over

patriæ   deduxerint   me   necessario   de   hâc
to (my) country shall have-led-away   me   necessarily   from   this

lenitate animi;   perficiam profecto illud quod videtur
lenity   of mind;   I will-perform   indeed   that which   seems

vix   optandum   in   tanto   et   tam
scarcely   to be-wished-for (expected)   in   so-great   and   so

insidioso bello, ut ne quis bonus   intereat, que
deceitful   war,   that not any   good (person) may-perish,   and

vos omnes jam   possitis   esse   salvi   pœnâ
you   all   now   may-be-able   to be   safe   by the penalty

paucorum.   Quæ   quidem ego polliceor
(punishment) of a few.   Which (things) indeed   I   promise

vobis, Quirites, fretus neque   meâ   prudentiâ, neque
to you,   Romans,   relying   neither on my-own prudence,   nor

humanis   consiliis;   sed   multis   et   non   dubiis
on human   counsels;   but   on many   and   not   doubtful

significationibus   immortalium   deorum,   quibus
significations (omens)   of the immortal   gods,   who

ducibus ego ingressus sum in hanc spem que
(being) leaders   I   have-entered   into this   hope   and

sententiam; qui jam defendunt non   sua   templa
opinion;   who now   defend   not their-own temples

atque   tecta   urbis   procul, ut quondam
and   the roofs (houses) of the city   afar-off,   as   once

solebant,   ab externo atque longinquo hoste,
they were-accustomed, from an external   and   distant   enemy

sed hic præsentes   suo   numine atque auxilio :
but here   present with their-own influence   and   aid:

quos vos, Quirites, debetis precari, venerari, atque
whom you,   Romans,   ought   to pray-to,   to adore,   and

implorare,   ut   defendant   a   nefario   scelere
to implore,   that   they may-defend   from   the nefarious   crime

perditissimorum civium, hanc urbem, quam
of most-lost (abandoned) citizens. this city, which

voluerunt esse pulcherrimam, florentissimam,
they have-wished to be the most-beautiful, the most flourishing,

que potentissimam, omnibus **copiis hostium**
and the most-powerful, all the forces of enemies

superatis terrâ que mari.
being-overcome by land and by sea.

TERTIA ORATIO
THE THIRD ORATION

AD QUIRITES.
TO THE ROMANS.

~~~~~~~~~~

1. QUIRITES, videtis rempublicam, que vitam
Romans, you see the republic, and the life

vestrûm omnium, bona, fortunas, conjuges, que vestros
or you all, goods, fortunes, wives, and your

liberos, atque hoc domicilium clarissimi imperii,
children, and this abode of a most-famous empire,

fortunatissimam que pulcherrimam urbem, ereptam
a most-fortunate and most-beautiful city, snatched

ex flammâ atque ferro, ac pæne ex faucibus
out-of flame and sword, and almost out-of the jaws

fati, et conservatam ac restitutam vobis, hodierno die,
of fate, and preserved and restored to you, on-this-day,

summo amore immortalium deorum
by the highest (very great) love of the immortal gods

erga vos, meis laboribus, consiliis que periculis
towards you, by my labours, counsels and dangers.

Et si ii dies quibus conservamur sunt non minus
And if those days in which we are-preserved are not less

jucundi atque illustres nobis quam illi quibus
pleasant and illustrious to us than those in which

nascimur; quod lætitia salutis est certa, conditio
we are-born; because the joy of safety is certain, the condition

nascendi incerta; et quod nascimur sine
of being-born (is) uncertain; and because we are-born without

sensu, servamur cum voluptate: profecto quoniam
feeling, we are-preserved with pleasure: indeed because

(68)

sustulimus illum Romulum, qui condidit hanc urbem,
we have-raised that Romulus, who founded this city,

ad immortales deos benevolentiâ que famâ:
to the immortal gods with benevolence and with fame:

is debebit esse in honore apud vos que vestros
he will-ought to be in honour with (among) you and your

posteros, qui servavit hanc eandem urbem conditam
descendants, who has-preserved this same city being-founded

que amplificatam. Nam restinximus ignes jam
and enlarged. For we-have-extinguished the fires already

prope subjectos que circumdatos toti urbi, templis,
nearly cast-under and placed-around to the whole city, to the temples,

delubris, tectis, ac mœnibus; que
to the shrines, to the roofs (houses), and to the walls; and (we)

iidem retudimus gladios destrictos in rempublicam,
the same have-blunted the swords drawn against the republic,

que dejecimus mucrones eorum ab
and we-have-cast-down the points of them (of the swords) from

vestris jugulis. Quæ quoniam
your throats. Which (things) because

illustrata sunt, patefacta, comperta in
they have-been-brought-to-light, made-open, discovered in

senatu per me, exponam jam breviter vobis,
the senate through me, I will-explain now briefly to you,

Quirites, ut vos, qui ignoratis, possitis
Romans, that you, who are-ignorant-of (them), may be-able

scire ex actis, et quanta et quam manifesta,
to know out-of (from) acts, both how-great and how manifest

et quâ ratione investigata sint
(they are), and by what reason (manner) they may have-been-traced

et comprehensa. Principio, ut Catilina erupit
and detected. In the beginning, when Catiline burst-out

ex urbe paucis diebus ante, cum reliquisset
out-of the city by a few days before, when he might-have-left

Romæ socios sui sceleris, acerrimos
of Rome (at Rome) the partners of his crime, the most-active

duces hujusce nefarii belli: vigilavi semper, et
leaders of this nefarious war: I have-watched always, and

providi,   Quirites,   quemadmodum   possemus   esse
have-foreseen,   Romans,   in-what-manner   we might-be-able to be

salvi in   tantis   et   tam absconditis insidiis.
safe   in   so-great and   so   hidden   snares.

2. Nam tum, cum   ejiciebam   Catilinam   ex   urbe
For   then, when   I did-cast-out   Catiline   out-of the city

(enim vereor non jam invidiam   hujus verbi,
(for   I fear   not   now   the envy (unpopularity) of this   word,

cum illa   sit   magis   timenda,   quod   exierit
since that may-be more   to-be-feared, because he may have-gone-out

vivus),   sed tum cum   volebam   illum   exterminari,
alive),   but then when   I did-wish   him   to be-banished

putabam   aut   reliquam   manum   conjuratorum
I did-think   either   the remaining   band   of conspirators

exituram   simul,   aut   eos   qui   restitissent
about-to-go-out together,   or   those   who might-have-remained

fore   infirmos ac debiles   sine   illo.   Atque
to be-about-to-be infirm   and   weak   without him.   And

ego, ut   vidi eos, quos   sciebam   esse inflammatos
I,   when I saw those, whom   I did-know   to be   inflamed

maximo   furore et scelere, esse cum nobis,   et
with the greatest fury   and   crime,   to be with   us,   and

remansisse   Romæ, consumsi omnes   dies   que
to have-remained at Rome, consumed   all (my) days   and

noctes in eo,   ut   sentirem   ac   viderem   quid
nights   in this,   that   I might-perceive and   I might-see   what

agerent,   quid   molirentur :   ut,   quoniam mea
they might-act,   what they might-attempt : that,   because   my

oratio   faceret   minorem   fidem   vestris   auribus,
oration   might-make   less   faith   to your   ears,

           propter incredibilem magnitudinem
(would gain little credit), because of   the incredible   greatness

sceleris, comprehenderem rem ita,   ut tum demum
of the crime,   I might-detect   the thing so,   that then at-length

provideretis   vestræ saluti   animis,   cum
you might-foresee (provide) for your safety with (your) minds, when

videretis maleficium ipsum   oculis.   Itaque
you might-see the mischief   itself   with (your) eyes.   Therefore

ut   **comperi**   legatos   **Allobrogum**
when   I discovered   the ambassadors   of the Allobroges

sollicitatos esse a P. Lentulo, **causâ** Transalpini
to have-been-solicited by   P. Lentulus,   for-the-sake of a Transalpine

belli, et Gallici tumultûs excitandi, que ecs
war,   and   of a Gallic   tumult   to be-excited,   and   those

missos esse in Galliam ad suos cives, que eodem
to have-been-sent into   Gaul   to their citizens, and by the same

itinere, cum litteris que mandatis ad Catilinam, que
journey,   with   letters   and commands   to   Catiline,   and

Vulturcium adjunctum comitem iis, atque literas
Vulturcius   joined (as) a companion to them, and   le ters

datas esse huic ad Catilinam, putavi facultatem
to have-been-given to him to   Catiline,   I thought   the means

oblatam mihi, ut quod erat difficillimum, que
offered   to me, that (a thing) which was   most-difficult,   and

quod ego semper optabam a immortalibus diis,
which   I   always   did-wish-for   from   the immortal   gods,

    tota res deprehenderetur manifesto non solum
that the whole thing   might-be-detected   manifestly   not   only

a me sed etiam a senatu, et a vobis. Itâque
by me but   also   by the senate, and by   you.   Therefore

hesterno die vocavi ad me L. Flaccum et C. Pomtinum,
on-yesterday   I called to me   L. Flaccus and   C. Pomtinus,

fortissimos prætores, atque viros amantissimos
the most-bold   prætors,   and   men   most-loving

reipublicæ: exposui omnem rem; ostendi quid
of the republic: I explained   all   the things;   I showed   what

placeret fieri. Autem illi, qui
it might-please (what I thought proper) to be-done.   But   they, who

sentirent omnia præclara atque egregia
might-feel   all   illustrious   and   excellent (sentiments)

de republicâ, susceperunt negotium sine
concerning   the republic,   took-up   the business   without

recusatione, ac sine ullâ morâ, et cum
refusal,   and   without   any   delay,   and   when

advesperasceret, pervenerunt occulte ad Mu.vium
it might-become-evening,   they-arrived   secretly to (at) the Mulvian

pontem, atque fuerunt ibi in proximis villis,
bridge, and were there in the nearest country-houses,

ita bipartito, ut Tiberis et pons interesset
so in-two-parties, that the Tiber and the bridge might-be-between

inter eos. Autem et ipsi eduxerunt multos fortes
between them. But both they led-out many bold

viros eodem sine suspicione cujusquam, et
men to-the-same-place without the suspicion of-any-one, and

ego miseram ex Reatinâ præfecturâ complures
I had-sent out-of the Reatinian prefecture many

delectos adolescentes, operâ quorum utor
chosen young-men, with the assistance of whom I use

assidue in republicâ, præsidio cum gladiis.
constantly in the republic, to a guard (as a guard) with swords.

Interim tertiâ vigiliâ fere exactâ, cum
In-the-mean-time the third watch almost being-completed, when

legati Allobrogum inciperent jam ingredi
the ambassadors of the Allobroges might-begin already to enter-upon

Mulvium pontem cum magno comitatu, que
the Mulvian bridge with a great attendance, and

Vulturcius unà, impetus fit in eos:
Vulturcius together (with them), an attack is-made upon them:

gladii educuntur et ab illis, et a nostris; res
swords are-drawn-out both by them, and by our (men); the thing

erat nota prætoribus solis; ignorabatur a
was known to the prætors alone; it-was-unknown by

ceteris.
the rest.

3. Tum interventu Pomtini
Then at-the-coming-between (on the intervention) of Pomtinus

atque Flacci, pugna, quæ commissa erat, sedatur
and of Flaccus, the fight, which had-been-engaged, is-appeased.

Quæcunque litteræ erant in eo comitatu
Whatever letters were in that attendance (company)

traduntur prætoribus, signis integris;
are-delivered-up to the prætors, with the signs (seals) entire

ipsi comprehensi deducuntur ad me, cum
themselves being-seized are-led-down to me, when

dilucesceret jam. Atque vocavi statim ad
it might-become-daybreak already. And I called immediately to

me Cimbrum Gabinium, improbissimum machinatorem
me Cimbrus Gabinius, the most-wicked contriver

omnium horum scelerum, suspicantem nihildum.
of all these crimes, (he) suspecting nothing-as-yet

Deinde item L. Statilius arcessitur, et post eum
Then also L. Statilius is-sent-for, and after him

C. Cethegus; autem Lentulus venit tardissime, credo
C. Cethegus; but Lentulus came most-slowly, I believe

quod vigilarat proximâ nocte præter
because he-had-watched on the-nearest (last) night beyond

consuetudinem litteris dandis.
(his) custom in letters to-be-given (in giving the letters).

Vero cum placeret summis ac clarissimis
But when it might-please (seem fit) to the-highest and most-famous

viris hujus civitatis, qui, re auditâ, convenerant
men of this state, who, the thing being-heard, had-come-together

frequentes ad me mane, litteras aperiri
frequent (in numbers) to me in-the-morning, the letters to-be-opened

a me prius quam deferri ad senatum; ne, si nihil
by me before than to-be-referred to the senate; lest, if nothing

inventum esset, tantus tumultus videretur
might-have-been-found, so-great disturbance might-seem (to be)

injectus civitati a me temere; negavi me esse
cast-in to the state by me rashly; I denied myself to be

facturum, ut deferrem non integram rem
about-to-make, that I should-refer not the entire thing

de publico periculo ad publicum consilium.
concerning the public danger to the public council.

Etenim, Quirites, si ea, quæ delata erant
For, Romans, if those (things), which had-been-referred

ad me, reperta essent non; tamen ego
(reported) to me, might-have-been-found not; yet I

arbitrabar non nimiam diligentiam esse pertimescendam
did-think not too-great diligence to be to-be-feared

mihi in tantis periculis reipublicæ. Coëgi
to me (by me) in so-great dangers of the republic. I collected

celeriter frequentem   senatum, ut   vidistis
quickly   a frequent (numerous)   senate,   as you have-seen.

Atque   interea,   admonitu   Allobrogum, misi
And   in-the-mean-time, by the advice of the Allobroges, I sent

statim C. Sulpicium, prætorem, fortem virum, qui,
immediately C. Sulpicius, the prætor, a bold man, who,

si   esset   quid   telorum,   efferret
if there-might-be any (thing) of weapons, might-bring-(them)-out

ex ædibus (*plur.*) Cethegi; ex quibus ille
out-of the house of Cethegus; out-of which he

extulit maximum   numerum   sicarum et
brought-out a very-great number of poniards and

gladiorum.
of swords.

4. Introduxi Vulturcium sine Gallis; dedi
I led-in Vulturcius without the Gauls; I gave

ei publicam fidem, jussu senatus; hortatus sum
to him the public faith, by order of the senate; I exhorted

ut   indicaret ea,   quæ   sciret   sine
that he should-indicate those (things), which he might-know without

timore. Tum ille, cum recreasset se vix
fear. Then he, when he might-have-recovered himself scarcely

ex magno timore, dixit, se habere mandata et
out-of the great fear, said, himself to have commands and

litteras a P. Lentulo ad Catilinam, ut uteretur
letters from P. Lentulus to **Catiline,** that he-should-use

præsidio   servorum, et accederet cum
with guard (the help) of slaves, and should-approach with

exercitu ad urbem quam primum; autem id eo
the army to the city as-soon-as-possible; but that with this

consilio, ut cum incendissent urbem ex
design, that when they might-have-set-fire-to the city out-of

omnibus partibus, quemadmodum descriptum erat
all parts, as it-had-been-described

que distributum, que fecissent infinitam cædem
and distributed, and might-have-made an infinite slaughter

civium, ille esset præsto qui et exciperet
of citizens, he might-be at-hand who both might catch (those)

fugientes, et conjungeret se cum his ducibus
fleeing, and might-unite himself with these leaders

urbanis. Autem Galli introducti dixerunt
belonging-to-the-city. But the Gauls being-led-in said

jusjurandum et litteras datas esse sibi a
an oath and letters to-have-given to-themselves by

P Lentulo, Cethego, Statilio ad suam gentem;
P. Lentulus, Cethegus, (and) Statilius to their nation;

atque ita praescriptum esse sibi ab his et a
and thus to-have-been-prescribed to-themselves by these and by

L. Cassio, ut mitterent equitatum in Italiam
L. Cassius, that they-should-send cavalry into Italy

quam primum, pedestres copias non defuturas
as-soon-as-possible, foot-forces not about-to-be-wanting

sibi; autem Lentulum confirmasse sibi ex
to-them; but Lentulus to-have-confirmed to-them out-of

Sibyllinis fatis que responsis haruspicum, se esse
the Sybilline fates and the-answers of-diviners, himself to-be

illum tertium Cornelium, ad quem esset necesse
that third Cornelius, to whom it-might-be necessary

regnum hujus urbis atque imperium pervenire:
the-kingdom (rule) of-this city and the-command to-arrive:

Cinnam et Sullam fuisse ante se; que eundem
Cinna and Sulla to-have-been before himself; and the-same

dixisse hunc esse annum fatalem ad
(person) to-have-said this to-be the-year ordained-by-fate to (for)

interitum hujus urbis atque imperii, qui esset
the destruction of-this city and empire, which might-be

decimus annus post absolutionem virginum, autem
the tenth year after the-acquitting of-the-virgins, but

vicesimus post incensionem Capitolii. Autem
the-twentieth after the-setting-on-fire of-the-Capitol. But

dixerunt hanc controversiam fuisse Cethego cum
they said this dispute to-have-been to Cethegus with

caeteris, quod, placeret Lentulo et ceteris
the-rest, because, it-might-please to-Lentulus and to-the-rest

caedem fieri, atque urbem incendi
the-slaughter to-be-made, and the-city to-be set-on-fire

Saturnalibus,   id   videri   nimium longum
on the Saturnalia,   that   to-seem   too-long

Cethego.
to Cethegus.

5. Ac, ne   sit   longum,   Quirites,   jussimus
And, lest it may-be long (tedious), Romans,   we-ordered

tabellas   proferri,   quæ   dicebantur
the tablets (letters) to be-brought-forward, which   were said

datæ (esse)   a quoque : primum ostendimus signum
to have been-given by each :   first   we showed   the sign (seal)

Cethego ;   cognovit :   nos incidimus   linum ;
to Cethegus ; he acknowledged (it) : we   cut   the thread

legimus ;   erat scriptum manu   ipsius   senatui
we read ;   it was written with the hand of himself to the senate

et   populo   Allobrogum,   sese   esse   facturum
and   to the people of the Allobroges,   himself to be about-to-do

        quæ   confirmasset   legatis
(the things) which he might-have-confirmed (affirmed) to the ambassadors

eorum :   orare   ut   item   illi   facerent   quæ
of them : to beg that also   they   would-do (the things) which

legati   eorum recipissent sibi.
the ambassadors of them   received   to them (might have taken on

                Tum Cethegus, qui paulo ante
themselves to promise). Then   Cethegus, who a little before

respondisset   aliquid   de   gladiis ac   sicis
might-have-answered some (thing) concerning the swords and poniards,

quæ   deprehensæ erant   apud   ipsum,   quæ
which   had been-discovered   with   him (at his house),   and

dixisset   se   semper fuisse studiosum
might-have-said himself always to have-been studious (an admirer)

bonorum ferramentorum, debilitatus atque abjectus,
of good   weapons,   weakened   and   cast-down,

litteris   recitatis, convictus conscientiâ, repente
the letters being-read-aloud, convicted   by consciousness,   suddenly

conticuit. Statilius introductus cognovit   manum
became-silent. Statilius being-led-in acknowledged (his) hand

et suum signum ; tabellæ   recitatæ sunt in fere
and his   seal ; tablets (letters) were-read-aloud unto nearly

ᴜandem sententiam; confessus est. Tum ostendi
the same   purpose;   he confessed.   Then   I showed

tabellas   Lentulo,   et   quæsivi   ne
the tablets (letters)   to Lentulus,   and   I sought (asked) whether

cognosceret   signum;   annuit;   vero   signum
he would-acknowledge the seal; he nodded-assent; but   the seal

quidem est notum, inquam, imago   clarissimi
indeed   is known,   I said, the image of the most-famous

viri tui avi, qui amavit patriam et suos cives
man thy grandfather, who loved (his) country and his citizens

unice, quæ   quidem etiam   muta debuit
singularly, which (image) indeed even (although) dumb ought

revocare te a tanto scelere. Litteræ ad senatum
to recall thee from so-great crime. The letters to the senate

que populum Allobrogum leguntur eâdem ratione:
and people of the Allobroges are-read in the same reason

si vellet dicere quid   de   his
manner): if he might-wish to say any (thing) concerning these

rebus, feci   potestatem. Atque ille quidem primo
things, I made (gave) power.   And he indeed at-first

negavit; autem aliquanto post, toto indicio
denied;   but   somewhat after, the whole discovery

exposito atque edito, surrexit: quæsivit   a
being-explained and being-published, he rose: he sought (asked) from

Gallis, quid esset sibi cum iis,
the Gauls, what might-be to himself with them (what he had to do

quamobrem venissent suam domum;
with them),   wherefore they should-have-come (to) his house;

que iteᴍ a Vulturcio. Qui cum respondissent
and also from Vulturcius. Who when they-might-have-answered

illi breviter que constanter, per quem que quoties
to him briefly and constantly, through whom and how-often

venissent ad eum; que quæsissent
they might-have-come to him; and they might-have-sought (asked)

ab eo ne   locutus esset nihil secum
from him whether he might-have-spoken nothing with-them

de   Sibyllinis fatis: tum ille, subito demens
concerning the Sibylline fates: then he, suddenly mad

scelere,   ostendit   quanta   vis   conscientiæ
with crime,   showed   how-great   the force   of consciousness

esset;   nam cum   posset   inficiari   id,   repente
might-be;   for   when he might-be-able   to deny   that,   suddenly

præter   opinionem omnium, confessus est: ita
beyond (contrary to)   the opinion   of all,   he confessed: thus

non modo illud ingenium et exercitatio dicendi,
not   only   that   ability   and   exercise   of speaking,

quâ   valuit   semper, sed etiam, propter   vim
in which he prevailed   always,   but   also,   because-of the force

manifesti atque deprehensi sceleris,   impudentia,
of manifest   and   of detected   crime,   (his)   impudence,

quâ   superabat   omnes, que improbitas defecit.
in which he did-surpass   all,   and   dishonesty   failed (him).

Vero Vulturcius subito jussit litteras   proferri
But   Vulturcius   suddenly ordered the letters to be-brought-forward

atque aperiri, quas dicebat   datas esse   sibi
and   to-be-opened, which he did-say to have-been-given to him

a Lentulo ad   Catilinam. Atque ibi   Lentulus
by Lentulus to (for) Catiline.   And   there (then)   Lentulus

perturbatus vehementissime, tamen cognovit   et
being-disturbed   most-violently,   yet   acknowledged both

suum signum et manum; autem   erant   scriptæ
his   the seal and   hand;   but   they were   written

sine nomine, sed ita: "Cognosces qui sim   ex
without a name,   but thus: "Thou wilt-know who I may-be out-of

eo quem misi ad te.   Cura ut   sis
(from) him whom I have-sent to thee. Take-care that thou mayst-be

vir, et cogita   in quem locum   progressus sis,
a man, and think (consider) into what a place thou mayst-have-advanced,

et vide quid jam   sit   necesse tibi.   Cura   ut
and   see   what   now   may-be necessary for you. Take-care that

adjungas   tibi   auxilia omnium, etiam infimorum."
thou mayst-join to thee the aids   of all,   even   of the lowest."

Deinde Gabinius introductus cum primo   cœpisset
Then   Gabinius   being-led-in when at-first he might-have-begun

respondere impudenter, ad extremum negavit nihil
to answer   impudently, to (at) the last he denied nothing

ex   iis   quæ Galli insimulabant
out-of those (things) which the Gauls   did accuse (lay to his charge)

Ac cum illa   visa sunt mihi quidem, Quirites,
And when those (things) seemed to me indeed, Romans,

certissima argumenta atque indicia sceleris, tabellæ,
most-certain arguments and discoveries of crime, the letters,

signa, manus, denique,   confessio uniuscujusque:
seals, the hands, lastly, the confession of each:

tum   illa   multo certiora,   color,
then (so) these (seemed to me) by much more-certain, the colour,

oculi, vultus, taciturnitas. Enim   obstupuerant
the eyes, the look, the silence. For they had-become-astonished

sic,   intuebantur   terram sic, nonnumquam
so, they did-look-upon the earth so, sometimes

adspiciebant inter   se   sic furtim,
they did-look among themselves (one upon the other) so by-stealth,

ut   viderentur non jam indicari ab aliis, sed
that they might-seem not now to be-denounced by others, but

ipsi   indicare   se.
themselves to denounce themselves.

6. **Indiciis   expositis atque   editis,**
The discoveries being-explained and being-published,

Quirites, consului senatum, quid placeret
Romans, I consulted the senate, what it might-please (them)

fieri   de   summâ republicâ. Acerrimæ ac
to be-done concerning the chief republic. Most-severe and

fortissimæ sententiæ dictæ sunt a principibus,
most-bold opinions were-said by the chief (senators),

quas senatus consecutus est sine ullâ varietate. Et
which the senate followed without any variety. And

quoniam consultum senatus nondum perscriptum est,
since the decree of the senate not-yet has-been-transcribed,

exponam ex memoriâ vobis, Quirites, quid
I will-explain out-of memory to-you, Romans, what

senatus censuerit.   Primum gratiæ aguntur
the senate may-have-voted. First thanks are-acted (given)

mihi amplissimis verbis, quod respublica
to me in most-ample words. because the republic

liberata sit maximis periculis virtute,
may have-been-liberated from the greatest dangers by (my) valour,

consilio, meâ providentiâ : deinde L. Flaccus et
by (my) counsel, by my foresight : then L. Flaccus and

C. Pomtinus, prætores, laudantur merito ac jure,
C. Pomtinus, the prætors, are-praised deservedly and with right,

quod usus essem forti que fideli
because I might-have-used (experienced) with the bold and faithful

operâ eorum ; atque etiam laus impertitur forti
assistance of them ; and also praise is-imparted to the bold

viro, meo collegæ, quod removisset a suis
man, to my colleague, because he might-have-removed from his-own

consiliis et   reipublicæ eos qui fuissent
counsels and (from those) of the republic those who might-have-been

participes hujus conjurationis. Atque censuerunt ita,
partakers of this conspiracy. And they voted thus,

ut P. Lentulus, cum abdicasset se
that P. Lentulus, when he-might-have-abdicated himself

præturâ, tum traderetur in custodiam ;
from the prætorship, then should-be-delivered-up into custody ;

que item uti C. Cethegus, L. Statilius, P. Gabinius,
and also that C. Cethegus, L. Statilius, P. Gabinius,

qui omnes erant præsentes, traderentur in
who all were present, should-be-delivered-up into

custodiam ; atque hoc idem decretum est in
custody ; and this same (thing) was-decreed against

L. Cassium, qui depoposcerat sibi procurationem
L. Cassius, who had-required for himself the management

urbis incendendæ : in M. Cæparium, cui
of the city to be-set-on-fire : against M. Cæparius, to whom

indicatum erat   Apuliam attributam esse
it had-been-indicated (it appeared) Apulia to have-been-assigned

ad pastores sollicitandos : in P. Furium, qui
to (for) the shepherds to be-solicited : against P. Furius, who

est ex his colonis, quos L. Sulla deduxit
is out-of (from) those colonists, whom L. Sulla led-down (to)

Fæsulas ; in Q. Manlium Chilonem, qui semper
Fæsulæ · against Q. Manlius Chilo, who always

versatus erat una cum hoc Furio in hâc
had-been-engaged together with this Furius in this

sollicitatione Allobrogum; in P. Umbrenum,
solicitation of the Allobroges; against P. Umbrenus,

libertinum hominem, a quo constabat Gallos
a freed-man, by whom it was-evident the Gauls

primum perductos esse ad Gabinium. Atque senatus
first to have-been-led to Gabinius. And the senate

usus est eâ lenitate, Quirites, ut ex tantâ
used with that mildness, Romans, that out-of so-great

conjuratione, que tantâ vi ac multitudine
a conspiracy, and so-great force and multitude

domesticorum hostium, republicâ conservatâ,
of domestic enemies, the republic being-preserved,

arbitraretur mentes reliquorum posse sanari
it might-think the minds of the rest to be-able to be-cured

pœnâ novem perditissimorum hominum.
by the punishment of nine most-lost (most abandoned) men.

Atque etiam, Quirites, supplicatio decreta est meo
And also, Romans, a thanksgiving was-decreed in my

nomine immortalibus diis, pro singulari merito
name to the immortal gods, for the singular merit

eorum; quod contigit primum mihi
of these (things); which (thing) has happened first to me

togato post hanc urbem conditam;
wearing-the-toga (a civilian) after (since) this city being-built;

et decreta est his verbis, "Quod liberassem
and it was-decreed in these words, "Because I might-have-freed

urbem incendiis, cives cæde, Italiam
the city from conflagrations, the citizens from slaughter, Italy

bello." Si quæ supplicatio conferatur cum ceteris,
from war." If which thanksgiving may be-compared with others,

Quirites, hoc intersit, quod ceteræ,
Romans, this may be-the-difference, that others (have been appointed),

republicâ gestâ bene, hæc una constituta est,
the republic being-carried-on well, this alone has been-appointed

conservatâ. Atque illud, quod fuit faciendum
(the state) being-preserved. And this, which was to-be-done

primum, factum est atque transactum. Nam quamquam
first,   was-done and   dispatched.   For   although

P. Lentulus,   patefactus   indiciis   et   suis
P. Lentulus,   being-exposed by discoveries and by his-own

confessionibus,   judicio   senatûs,   amiserat   non
confessions,   by the judgment of the senate,   had-lost   not

modo   jus   prætoris,   verum etiam   civis;   tamen
only   the right of prætor,   but   also   of citizen;   yet

abdicavit   se   magistratu;   ut quæ religio
he abdicated   himself from the magistracy;   that what scruple

fuerat   non C. Mario   clarissimo viro,   quo   minus
had-been not to C. Marius a most-famous man, by which less

occideret C. Glauciam, prætorem,   de   quo   nihil
he should kill C. Glaucias,   a prætor, concerning whom nothing

decretum erat nominatim, nos   liberaremur   eâ
had-been-decreed by-name,   we   should-be-freed from that

religione in P. Lentulo privato   puniendo.
scruple   in P. Lentulus a private (person) to be-punished.

7. Nunc quoniam, Quirites, tenetis   nefarios
   Now   since,   Romans,   you-hold   the nefarious

duces   sceleratissimi   que periculosissimi belli
leaders of (this) most-wicked and most-dangerous   war

jam captos et comprehensos, debetis existimare
already taken and detected,   you ought to think

omnes copias Catilinæ, omnes   spes atque   opes,
all   the forces of Catiline, all (his) hopes and resources,

concidisse, his periculis urbis depulsis.   Quem
to have-fallen, this dangers of the city being-driven-off. Whom

quidem ego,   cum ego pellebam   ex   urbe,
indeed   I,   when   I   did-drive out-of the city,

providebam hoc animo, Quirites, Catilinâ remoto,
did-foresee this in (my) mind, Romans, Catiline being-removed,

nec somnum P. Lentuli, nec adipem L. Cassii,
neither the sleep of P. Lentulus, nor the fat of L. Cassius,

nor furiosam temeritatem Cethegi esse pertimescendam
nor the furious rashness of Cethegus to be to be-feared

mihi. Ille unus   ex   omnibus his erat
to (by) me. He one (alone) (Catiline) out-of all these was

timendus, sed tamdiu dum continebatur mœnibus
to be-feared, but (only) so-long while he was-contained by the walls

urbis. Norat omnia, tenebat
of the city. He had-known (he knew) all (things), he did-hold

aditus omnium; poterat audebat
(understand) the accesses of all; he was-able (and) did-dare

appellare, tentare, sollicitare: erat ei
to call (salute), to try, to solicit: there-was to him (he had

consilium aptum ad facinus; autem neque lingua
counsel fit to (for) daring-deed; but neither (his) tongue

neque manus deerat consilio. Jam habebat
nor hand was-wanting to (that) counsel. Already he did-have

certos homines delectos ac descriptos ad
certain men chosen and described (appointed) to (for)

certas res conficiendas. Vero neque, cum
certain things to be-completed. But neither, when

mandaverat aliquid, putabat confectum.
he had-commanded some (thing), did he think (it) completed.

Erat nihil quod ipse obiret non, occurreret,
There-was nothing which himself would-undergo not, would-oppose

vigilaret, laboraret: poterat
(would lend aid to), would-watch, would-labour (not): he was-able

ferre frigus, sitim, famem Nisi ego compulissem
to bear cold, thirst, hunger. Unless I might-have-driven

hunc hominem tam acrem, tam paratum, tam audacem,
this man so active, so prepared, so bold,

tam callidum, tam vigilantem in scelere, tam diligentem
so cunning, so vigilant in crime, so diligent

in perditis rebus, ex domesticis insidiis in
in lost (abandoned) things, out-of domestic snares into

latrocinium castrense (dicam id,
robbery belonging-to-the-camp (war) (I will-say that,

quod sentio, Quirites), depulissem non facile
which I think, Romans), I should-have-driven-off not easily

hanc tantam molem mali a vestris cervicibus. Ille
this so-great mass of evil from your necks. He

constituisset non Saturnalia nobis, neque
would-have-appointed not the Saturnalia for us, nor

denuntiasset   tanto   ante   diem   exitii   **et**
would-have-denounced by so-much before the day of destruction **and**

fati reipublicæ,   neque   commisisset,   ut
of fate to the republic,   nor would he-have-committed, that (his)

signum, ut denique suæ litteræ deprehenderentur
seal,   that   in-fine his-own letters   should-be-discovered

testes manifesti sceleris.   Quæ   nunc
witnesses of manifest   crime.   Which (things) now

gesta sunt,   illc   absente   sic, ut nullum furtum
have-been-carried-on, he being-absent so, that   no   theft

in privatâ domo umquam   inventum sit   tam
in a private house   ever may-have-been-found-out   so

palam, quam hæc tanta conjuratio in republica
openly,   as   this so-great conspiracy in the republic

inventa est atque deprehensa manifesto.   Quod si
has-been-found-out and   discovered   manifestly.   But-if

Catilina remansisset in urbe   ad hanc diem,
Catiline might-have-remained in the city to this   day,

quamquam quoad fuit   occurri atque obstiti
although as-long-as he was (here) I met   and I opposed

omnibus consiliis   ejus, tamen, ut   dicam
to all the counsels (designs) of him, yet, that I may-say

levissime,   fuisset   dimicandum
most-lightly (to say the least), it would-have-been to be-fought

nobis cum illo, neque nos umquam, dum ille hostis
to (by) us with him,   nor   we   ever,   while that enemy

  fuisset in urbe, liberassemus rempublicam
might-have-been in the city, should-have-freed   the republic

tantis periculis, tantâ pace, tanto otio,
from so-great dangers, with so-great peace, with so-great ease,

  tanto silentio.
with so-great silence.

   8. Quamquam   omnia   hæc,   **Quirites,**
     Although   all   these (things)   Romans,

administrata sunt a me ita, ut videantur et
have-been-managed by me so, that they may-seem both

  gesta esse et provisa   nutu
to have-been-carried-on and foreseen (provided for) at the nod (will)

atque   consilio   immortalium   deorum.   Que   cum
and   counsel   of the immortal   gods.   And   when

possumus consequi id conjecturâ, quod gubernatio
we are-able to arrive-at that by-conjecture, because the governance

tantarum rerum videtur vix   potuisse   esse
of so-great things seems scarcely to-have-been-able to be (the work)

humani consilii : vero tum ita præsentes   tulerunt
of human counsel : but then so present they brought

opem   et   auxilium nobis his temporibus, ut
assistance and   aid   to us in these   times,   that

possemus   pæne videre eos oculis.   Nam, ut
we might-be-able almost to see them with the eyes. For, that

omittam illa,   faces que ardorem   cœli
I may-omit these (things), the torches and the burning of the heaven

visas ab occidente nocturno tempore, ut
seen from the west in the nocturnal time, that (I may omit)

jactus   fulminum, ut motus terræ, ut
the castings of lightnings, that the motions of the earth, that (I may omit)

cetera,   quæ   tam multa facta sunt,
other (things), which (being) so many were-done (happened),

nobis   consulibus, ut immortales dii viderentur
us (being) consuls, so-that the immortal gods might-seem

canere   hæc   quæ nunc   fiunt :
to sing (foretel) these (things) which now are-done (happen) :

certe, Quirites, hoc quod sum dicturus est neque
certainly, Romans, this which I am about-to-say is neither

prætermittendum neque relinquendum. Nam profecto
to be-passed-over nor to be-left. For indeed

tenetis memoriâ, Cottâ et Torquato   consulibus,
you hold in memory, Cotta and Torquatus (being) consuls,

complures res in Capitolio percussas esse de cœlo,
many things in the Capitol to-have-been-struck from heaven,

cum et simulacra immortalium deorum depulsa sunt,
when both the images of the immortal gods were-thrust-down,

et statuæ veterum hominum dejectæ, et æra (plur.)
and the statues of ancient men cast-down, and the brass

legum   liquefacta. Etiam ille Romulus,
(brazen tablets) of the laws melted. Also that Romulus

qui condidit hanc urbem, tactus est: quem
who founded this city, was-touched (scathed): whom

meministis fuisse in Capitolio inauratum
you-remembered to have-been in the Capitol overlaid-with-gold

parvum atque lactentem, inhiantem uberibus
little and sucking, gaping-after to the teats

lupinis. Quo tempore quidem, cum
belonging-to-the-wolf. At which time indeed, when

aruspices convenissent ex totâ Etruriâ,
diviners might-have-come-together out of the whole Tuscany,

dixerunt cædes atque incendia, et interitum
they said slaughters and conflagrations, and the destruction

egum, et civile ac domesticum bellum, et occasum
of the laws, and civil and domestic war, and the fall

totius urbis atque imperii appropinquare, nisi
of the whole city and empire to approach, unless

mmortales dii placati omni ratione,
the immortal gods being-appeased in every reason (manner),

flexissent prope fata ipsa suo
might-have-bent (diverted) almost the fates themselves by their

numine. Itaque responsis illorum tunc
divinity (influence). Therefore at the answers of them then

et ludi facti sunt per decem dies, neque ulla
both games were-made through ten days, neither any

res prætermissa est quæ pertineret ad
thing was-omitted which might-pertain (tend) to

placandum deos; que iidem jusserunt facere
appeasing the gods; and the same (diviners) ordered to make

simulacrum Jovis majus, et collocare in excelso,
the image of Jupiter greater, and to place (it) in a lofty

et contra atque fuerat ante,
(situation), and on-the-contrary and (than) it had-been before,

convertere ad orientem; ac dixerunt se sperare,
to turn (it) to the east; and they said themselves to hope,

si illud signum, quod videtis, conspiceret
if that sign (statue), which you see, should-view (should look

ortum solis, et forum, que curiam,
towards) the rising of the sun, and the forum, and the council-house.

fore,   ut   ea   consilia,   quæ
to be-about-to-be (that it would be)   that those counsels,   which

inita essent   clam   contra salutem   urbis
might-have-been-entered-into secretly against the safety of tne city

atque   imperii,   illustrarentur,   ut
and   of the empire,   would-be-brought-so-clearly-to-light, that

possent   perspici   a   senatu que Romano
they might-be-able to be seen-through by the senate and   Roman

populo. Atque illi consules locaverunt
people. And those consuls   placed-out (made arrangements for)

illud collocandum ita; sed   tanta   fuit   tarditas
that   to be-placed thus; but so-great was the slowness

operis,   ut   collocaretur   neque a   superioribus
of the work, that it might-be-placed neither by the former

consulibus, neque a nobis ante hodiernum diem.
consuls,   nor by us before   this-day.

9. Hic quis potest, Quirites, esse tam aversus
   Here who is-able, Romans, to be so   averse

a   vero, tam præceps, tam captus mente,
from the truth, so headlong, so taken in mind (deprived

qui   neget omnia hæc   quæ
of understanding), who may deny all   these (things) which

videmus, que præcipue hanc urbem, administrari
we see,   and especially this city,   to be-managed

nutu   atque   potestate immortalium Deorum?
by the nod and   by the power of the immortal Gods?

Etenim cum   responsum esset   ita,   cædes,
For   when   it might-have-been-answered thus, slaughters,

incendia, que interitum reipublicæ comparari,
conflagrations, and the destruction of the republic to be-prepared

et   ea   a perditis   civibus; quæ
and these (things) by lost (abandoned) citizens; which (things)

tum   videbantur nonnullis incredibilia propter
then   did-seem   to some   incredible   because of

magnitudinem scelerum: sensistis   ea
the greatness of the crimes: you have-perceived these (things)

non modo cogitata esse, verum etiam suscepta a
not only to have-been-devised, but even   undertaken by

nefariis civibus.   Vero nonne est illud ita præsens,
nefarious citizens.   But   is-not this so   present,

ut videatur   factum esse   nutu   optimi.
that it may-seem to have-been-done by the nod of the best,

maximi Jovis, ut, cum hodierno die mane   et
the greatest Jupiter, that, when on this-day in the morning both

conjurati   et indices   eorum
the conspired (the conspirators) and the discoverers (accusers) of them

ducerentur meo jussu per forum in ædem
might-be-led by my order through the forum into the temple

Concordiæ,   eo   tempore ipso   signum
of Concord,   in that   time   itself   the sign (statue)

statueretur?   Quo collocato atque converso ad
might-be-erected? Which being-placed and being-turned to

vos que senatum, et senatus et vos vidistis omnia
you and the senate, both the senate and you saw   all

quæ cogitata erant contra salutem omnium,
'(things) which had-been-devised against the safety of all,

illustrata   et patefacta.   Quo   isti
brought-to-light and   exposed. By which (for which reason) those

sunt digni etiam majore odio que supplicio,
(persons) are worthy even with greater hatred and punishment,

qui   conati sunt   inferre funestos ac nefarios
who have-endeavoured to bring-on fatal   and nefarious

ignes non solum vestris domiciliis atque tectis, sed
fires not only to your   abodes   and to your roofs, but

etiam templis atque   delubris Deorum. Quibus
also to the temples and to the shrines of the Gods. To whom

si ego dicam me   restitisse,   sumam nimium
if I may-say myself to have-resisted, I shall-take too-much

mihi, et sim non ferendus. Ille, ille Jupiter
to myself, and may-be not to be borne. That, that Jupiter

restitit : ille voluit Capitolium, ille hæc templa, ille
resisted : he wished the Capitol, he these temples, he

hanc urbem, ille   vos omnes esse salvos. Ego
this   city, he (wished) you all to be safe.   I

suscepi   hanc mentem que voluntatem, Quirites,
nave-taken-up this   mind and   wish,   Romans.

immortalibus Diis ducibus, atque perveni ad
the immortal   Gods (being)   leaders,   and   I have arrived   to

hæc tanta indicia. Vero jam illa sollicitatio
these   so-great   discoveries.   But   now   that   solicitation

Allobrogum, tanta res, numquam credita (esset)
of the Allobroges, so-great a thing,   never   would-have-been-trusted

sic a Lentulo que ceteris domesticis hostibus, tam
thus by Lentulus and by the other domestic   enemies,   so

dementer et ignotis et barbaris,
madly   both to unknown and to barbarous (foreign persons)

que litteræ profecto numquam commissæ essent,
and the letters indeed   never   would-have-been-entrusted,

nisi consilium ereptum esset huic
unless counsel (discretion) might-have-been-snatched-away from this

tantæ audaciæ a immortalibus Diis. Vero quid?
so-great audacity by the immortal Gods.   But   what

ut homines Galli, ex civitate
(why shall I mention)? that   men   Gauls,   out-of   a state

male pacatâ, quæ una gens restat, quæ videatur
ill   appeased, which one (only) nation remains, which may-seem

et posse et non nolle facere bellum Romano
both to be-able and not to be-unwilling to make   war to the Roman

populo, negligerent spem imperii et amplissimarum
people,   should-neglect the hope of empire and of the most-ample

rerum ultro oblatam sibi a patriciis hominibus,
things willingly offered to themselves by patrician   men,

que anteponerent vestram salutem suis opibus:
and should-prefer   your   safety to their-own powers:

putatis id non factum esse divinitus? præsertim
do you-think that not to-have-been-done divinely?   especially

qui superarent nos non pugnando, sed tacendo.
who might-overcome us not by fighting, but by keeping-silence.

10. Quamobrem, Quirites, quoniam supplicatio
Wherefore,   Romans,   since   a thanksgiving

decreta est ad omnia pulvinaria, celebratote
has been-decreed to (at) all the cushions (temples),   celebrate

illos dies cum vestris conjugibus ac liberis. Nam
those days with your   wives   and children.   For

sæpe   multi   justi   honores   habiti sunt   ac   debita
often   many   just   honours   have-been-held   and   due

immortalibus Diis,   sed   profecto   numquam   justiores.
to the immortal Gods,   but   indeed   never   more-just

                Enim   erepti   ex   crudelissimo   ac
(than these).   For   being-snatched   out-of   the most-cruel   and

miserrimo   interitu,   et   erepti   sine   cæde,
most-wretched   destruction,   and   being-snatched   without   slaughter,

sine   sanguine,   sine   exercitu,   sine   dimicatione,
without   blood,   without   an army,   without   fighting,

        togati   vicistis,   me   uno
(you) wearing-the-toga   have-conquered,   me   one (person)

        togato   duce   et   imperatore.   Etenim
wearing-the-toga (being) leader   and   commander.   For

recordamini,   Quirites,   omnes   civiles   dissensiones,
you-recollect,   Romans,   all   the civil   disagreements,

neque   solum   eas,   quas   audistis,   sed et
nor (and not)   only   those,   which you have-heard,   but and (also)

has,   quas   vosmetipsi   meministis   et   vidistis.
these,   which   you-yourselves   have-remembered   and   have-seen.

L. Sulla oppressit   P. Sulpicium: ejecit   ex
L. Sulla   oppressed (destroyed)   P. Sulpicius: he cast-out   out-of

urbe   C. Marium,   custodem hujus urbis,   que partim
the city   C. Marius,   the keeper   of this   city,   and   partly

ejecit   ex   civitate,   partim   interemit multos fortes
cast-out   out-of   the state,   partly   slew   many   bold

viros.   Cn. Octavius,   consul,   expulit suum collegam
men.   Cn. Octavius,   the consul,   expelled   his   colleague

ex   urbe   armis: omnis   hic   locus   redundavit
out-of the city   by arms: all   this   place   has-overflowed

            acervis   corporum   et   sanguine   civium.
(abounded)   with heaps   of bodies   and   with the blood   of citizens.

Postea   Cinna cum Mario superavit:
Afterwards   Cinna   with   Marius   overcame (got the upper hand):

vero   tum,   clarissimis   viris   interfectis,   lumina
but   then,   the most-famous   men   being-slain,   the lights

civitatis   exstincta sunt.   Postea   Sulla   ultus est
of the state   were-extinguished.   Afterwards   Sulla   revenged

crudelitatem hujus victoriæ : neque est quidem
the cruelty   of this   victory :   nor   is-it   indeed

opus dici, quantâ diminutione civium,
necessary to be-said,   with how-great   diminution   of citizens,

et quantâ calamitate reipublicæ. M. Lepidus
and with how-great   calamity   of the republic.   M. Lepidus

dissensit a clarissimo et fortissimo viro,
dissented   from   the most-famous   and   most-brave   man,

Q. Catulo : interitus ipsius attulit non luctum
Q. Catulus :   the destruction   of himself   brought   not   grief

reipublicæ tam, quam ceterorum.
to the republic   so (so much),   as (did the destruction) of the rest.

Atque tamen omnes illæ dissensiones erant
And   however   all   those   disagreements   were

hujusmodi, Quirites, quæ pertinerent non ad
of this-sort,   Romans,   which   might-pertain   not   to

rempublicam delendam, sed ad
the republic   to be-destroyed,   but   to (the republic)

commutandam : illi voluerunt non nullam rempublicam
to be-changed :   they   wished   not   no   republic

esse, sed se esse principes in eâ quæ
to be, but (they wished) themselves to be   chiefs   in   that which

esset : neque hanc urbem conflagrare, sed
might-be :   nor (did they wish)   this   city   to be-on-fire,   but

se florere in hac urbe. Atque tamen omnes
themselves to flourish   in   this   city.   And   yet   all

illæ dissensiones, nulla quarum quæsivit exitium
those   disagreements,   no-one   of which   sought   the destruction

reipublicæ, fuerunt ejusmodi, ut dijudicatæ sint
of the republic,   were   of that-sort,   that they may have-been-settled

non reconciliatione concordiæ, sed internecione
not   by a reconciliation   of concord,   but   by the slaughter

civium. Autem in hoc maximo que crudelissimo
of citizens.   But   in   this   greatest   and   most-cruel

bello uno post memoriam hominum, bellum quale
war   alone after (since) the memory   of men,   a war   like-as

nulla barbaria umquam gessit cum suâ gente,
no   barbarous-country   ever   carried-on with   its   nation,

in quo bello hæc lex fuit constituta a Lentulo,
In which war this law was appointed by Lentulus,

Catilinâ, Cassio, Cethego, ut omnes, qui possent
Catiline, Cassius, Cethegus, that all, who might be-able

esse salvi, urbe salvâ, hi ducerentur
to be safe, the city (being) safe, these should-be-led (deemed)

in numero hostium; gessi me ita,
in the number of the enemies; I have-borne (conducted) myself so,

Quirites, ut conservaremini omnes salvi; et
Romans, that you might-be-preserved all safe; and

cum vestri hostes putassent tantum civium
when your enemies might-have-thought so-much of citizens

superfuturum, quantum restitisset infinitæ
about-to-survive, as might-have-remained from infinite

cædi, autem tantum urbis, quantum flamma
slaughter, (and) but so-much of the city, as the flame

potuisset non obire: servavi et urbem
might-have-been-able not to-go-over: I have-kept both the city

et cives integros que incolumes.
and the citizens entire and safe.

11. Pro quibus tantis rebus, Quirites, ego postulo
For which so-great things, Romans, I require

nullum præmium virtutis a vobis, nullum insigne
no reward of virtue from you, no mark

honoris, nullum monumentum laudis, præterquam
of honour, no monument of praise, except

sempiternam memoriam hujus diei. Ego volo omnes
the eternal memory of this day. I wish all

meos triumphos, omnia ornamenta honoris, monumenta
my triumphs, all ornaments of honour, monuments

gloriæ, insignia laudis condi et collocari
of glory, marks of praise to be-hid (treasured) and to be-placed

in vestris animis. Nihil mutum potest delectare
in your minds. Nothing dumb is-able to delight

me, nihil tacitum, denique, nihil hujusmodi, quod
me, nothing silent, finally, nothing of this-sort, which

etiam minus digni possint assequi.
even less worthy (persons) may be-able to attain

Nostræ res, Quirites, alentur vestrâ
Our things (affairs), Romans, shall-be-cherished in your

memoriâ, crescent sermonibus, inveterascent et
memory, shall-increase in discourses, shall grow-old and

corroborabuntur monumentis literarum; que
shall be-strengthened in the monuments of letters; and

intelligo eandem diem, quam spero
I understand (feel convinced) this same day, which I hope

fore æternam, propagatam et ad salutem
to be-about-to-be eternal, propagated both to the safety

urbis, et ad memoriam mei consulatus; que
of the city, and to the memory of my consulship; and

uno tempore duos cives extitisse in hâc
at one time two citizens to have-existed in this

republicâ, alter quorum terminaret fines
republic, the other (one) of whom should bound the limits

vestri imperii non regionibus terræ, sed
of your empire not by the regions of the earth, but

cœli; alter servaret domicilium que sedem
of heaven; the other should-preserve the-abode and seat

ejusdem imperii.
of the same empire.

12. Sed, quoniam fortuna atque conditio earum
But, since the fortune and condition of those

rerum quas ego gessi, est non eadem, quæ
things which I have-carried-on is not the same, which

illorum qui gesserunt externa bella; quod
(that is) of those who have-carried-on foreign wars; because

sit vivendum mihi cum his quos
it may-be to be-lived to me (I must live) with those whom

vici ac subegi; isti reliquerunt
have-conquered and have subdued; those have-left (their)

hostes aut interfectos aut oppressos: est vestrum,
enemies either slain or oppressed: it-is your

Quirites, providere, si sua facta prosunt
(duty), Romans, to provide, if their deeds profit

ceteris, ne mea quando obsint mihi. Enim
to others, lest mine at-any-time may-injure to me. For

ego   providi   ne   sceleratæ   ac   nefariæ
I   have-provided   lest   the wicked   and   nefarious

mentes   audacissimorum   hominum   possent
minds (intentions)   of the most-daring   men   might be-able

nocere vobis;   est vestrum   providere ne   noceant
to hurt to you;   it-is your (duty)   to provide lest   they may-hurt

mihi.   Quamquam,   Quirites,   potest   noceri
to me.   Although,   Romans,   it is-able   to be-hurt

mihi ipsi   nihil   quidem   jam   ab   istis.
to myself   nothing (not at all)   indeed   now   by   those.

                Enim   est   magnum
(These persons can do me no injury.)   For   there-is   a great

præsidium   in bonis,   quod   est   comparatum
guard (protection)   in good (men), which   is   provided

mihi   in   perpetuum: magna   dignitas   in
to me   unto   perpetual (time):   great   dignity   in

republicâ,   quæ   tacita   semper   defendet   me:
the republic,   which   silent   always   will defend   me:

magna   est   vis   conscientiæ,   quam   qui
great   is   the force   of consciousness,   which (those)   who

negligent,   cum   volent   violare   me,   ipsi
shall-neglect,   when they shall-wish to do-violence-to   me,   themselves

indicabunt   se.   Etiam   is
will-discover   themselves (will expose themselves).   Also   that

animus   est   in   nobis,   Quirites,   ut   non   modo
mind   is   in   us (me),   Romans,   that   not   only

cedamus   audaciæ   nullius,   sed   etiam
we may-yield   to the audacity   of no (person),   but   also

lacessamus   semper   ultro   omnes   improbos.
we may-assail   always   willingly   all   the dishonest.

Quod si   omnis   impetus   domesticorum   hostium
But-if   every   attack   of domestic   enemies

depulsus   a   vobis, convertit   se   in   me unum:
driven-off   from   you,   turns   itself   upon   me   one

       erit   providendum   vobis,   Quirites,
(alone):   it will-be   to be-provided   to you (by you),   Romans,

quâ   conditione   posthac   velitis   eos   esse   qu:
in what   condition   hereafter   you may wish those   to be   who

obtulerint　　　se　　　invidiæ que omnibus periculis
may-have-offered　themselves　to envy　and　　to all　　dangers

pro vestrâ salute.　Quid quidem est quod　　possit
for　your　safety.　What　indeed　is-there which may-be-able

jam　acquiri　mihi ipsi　ad　　　fructum
now　to be-acquired　for myself　to (for)　the fruit (enjoyment)

vitæ, præsertim cum videam neque　quidquam
of life,　especially　when I may-see　neither　any　(thing)

altius in vestro honore, neque in gloriâ virtutis,
higher in　your　honour,　nor　in the glory　of virtue,

quo　quidem　　　libeat　　　mihi adscendere?
whither　indeed　it may-be-pleasing　to me　to ascend?

Perficiam　illud　profecto,　Quirites,　ut
I will-complete　this　indeed,　Romans,　that (being)

privatus　　　tuear　atque　ornem　ea
a private (person) I may-defend　and　I may-adorn　those

　　quæ　gessi　in　consulatu: ut, si qua
(things) which I carried-on in (my) consulship:　that, if any

invidia　suscepta est　in　republicâ　conservandâ,
envy　has-been-taken-up　in　the republic　to be-preserved

　　　　lædat　　　invidos,　valeat
(in preserving the republic), it may-hurt　the envious,　it may-avail

mihi　ad　gloriam.　Denique,　tractabo
to me　to　glory.　Finally,　I will-handle (conduct)

me　ita　in　republicâ,　ut　meminerim
myself　so　in　the republic,　that　I may-have-remembered

　　　semper quæ　　gesserim,　que
(may remember) always　what (things) I may-have-carried-on,　and

curem　ut　ea　videantur　gesta esse
I may take-care that　these (things) may-seem to have-been-carried-on

virtute non　casu.　Vos, Quirites, quoniam est
by virtue　not by accident.　You, Romans,　since　it-is

jam nox, veneramini illum Jovem, custodem hujus
now night,　worship　that　Jupiter,　the keeper　of this

urbis ac vestrûm, atque discedite in vestra tecta:
city　and　of you,　and　depart　into　your　roofs

　　et, quamquam periculum est jam depulsum,
(houses): and,　although　danger　is　now　driven-away,

tamen defendite ea, æque ac priori
yeu defend them, equally and (as) on the former

nocte, custodiis que vigiliis. Providebo,
night, with guards and with watches. I will-provide,

Quirites, ne id sit faciendum
Romans, lest that may-be (that that may not be) to be-done

diutius vobis, atque ut possitis esse in
longer to you (by you), and that you may-be-able to be in

perpetuâ pace.
perpetual peace.

QUARTA ORATIO
THE FOURTH ORATION

HABITA IN SENATU.
HELD IN THE SENATE.

~~~~~~~~

1. CONSCRIPTI patres, video ora atque
Conscript fathers, I see the countenances and

oculos vestrûm omnium esse conversos in me:
the eyes of you all to be turned unto me:

video vos esse sollicitos non solum de vestro
I see you to be solicitous not only concerning your

periculo ac reipublicæ, verum etiam, si id
danger and (that) of the republic, but also, if that

depulsum sit, de meo periculo. Vestra
may-have-been-driven-off, concerning my danger. Your

voluntas erga me est jucunda mihi in malis,
good-will towards me is pleasant to me in evils (dangers),

et grata in dolore: sed, quæso per immortales
and grateful in grief: but, I pray by the immortal

deos, deponite eam, atque obliti meæ
gods, put-down (lay aside) it, and having-forgotten of my

salutis, cogitate de vobis ac de vestris
safety, think concerning yourselves and concerning your

liberis. Si hæc conditio quidem consulatus
children. If this condition indeed of the consulship

data est mihi, ut perferrem omnes acerbitates,
has-been-given to me, that I should-bear all bitternesses,

omnes dolores que cruciatus, feram non
all griefs and torments, I will-bear (them) not

solum fortiter, sed etiam libenter, dummodo dignitas
only boldly, but even willingly, provided-that dignity

(97)

que   salus   pariatur   meis laboribus vobis que
and   safety may-be-produced by my   labours to you and

Romano   populo. Ego sum ille consul, conscripti
to the Roman people.   I   am that consul,   conscript

patres, cui non forum, in quo omnis æquitas
fathers, to whom not the forum, in which all   equity

continetur; non campus,   consecratus
is-contained;   not the plain (Campus Martius), consecrated

consularibus auspiciis;   non curia, summum
to consular   auspices; not the council-house, the highest

auxilium omnium gentium; non domus, commune
aid   of all nations; not (my) house, the common

perfugium; non lectus, datus ad quietem;
refuge;   not (my) bed, given to (for) rest;

denique, non hæc sedes honoris fuit umquam vacua
finally,   not this seat of honour has-been ever   free

periculo mortis atque insidiis. Ego tacui
from danger of death and from snares. I have-kept-silent

multa,   pertuli multa,   concessi multa,
many (things), I have-borne many (things), I have-yielded many

sanavi multa   quodam meo dolore,
(things), I have-cured many (things) with some my-own grief

in   vestro timore. Nunc, si
(with some pain to myself), in (amid) your fear. Now, if

immortales dii voluerunt hunc esse exitum mei
the immortal gods have-wished this to be the issue of my

consulatus, ut eriperem   vos, conscripti
consulship, that I might-snatch-out (rescue) you, conscript

patres, que Romanum populum ex miserâ cæde,
fathers, and the Roman people out-of wretched slaughter,

conjuges, que vestros liberos, que vestales
(your) wives, and your children, and the vestal

virgines ex acerbissimâ vexatione; templa atque
virgins out-of the most-bitter vexation; the temples and

delubra, hanc pulcherrimam patriam nostrûm omnium
shrines, this most-beautiful country of us all

ex foedissimâ flammâ; totam Italiam ex bello
out-of the foulest flame; the whole Italy out-of war

at vastitate: quæcunque fortuna proponetur mihi
and devastation: whatever fortune shall be-proposed to me

uni, subeatur. Etenim si P. Lentulus, inductus
alone, may be-undergone. For if P. Lentulus, induced

a vatibus, putavit suum nomen fore fatale
by prophets, thought his name to be-about-to-be ordained-by-fate

ad perniciem reipublicæ, cur ego læter non
to the destruction of the republic, why may-I-rejoice not

meum consulatum extitisse prope fatalem ad
my consulship to have-existed almost ordained-by-fate to

salutem reipublicæ?
the safety of the republic?

2. Quare, conscripti patres, consulite vobis
Wherefore, conscript fathers, consult for yourselves

prospicite patriæ, conservate vos, conjuges,
look to your country, preserve yourselves, wives,

liberos, que vestras fortunas, defendite nomen que
children, and your fortunes, defend the name and

salutem Romani populi: desinite parcere mihi, ac
safety of the Roman people: cease to spare to me, and

cogitare de me. Nam primum debeo sperare
to think concerning me. For first I ought to hope

omnes deos, qui præsident huic urbi, esse
all the gods, who preside-over to this city, to be

relaturos gratiam mihi pro eo ac mereor:
about-to-return the favour to me according-to that as I deserve.

deinde si quid obtigerit, moriar
then (in the next place) if any (thing) shall-have-befallen, I shall-die

æquo que parato animo. Enim neque turpis mors
with an equal and prepared mind. For neither a base death

potest accidere forti viro, neque immatura
is-able to happen to a brave man, nor an immature (death)

consulari, nec misera sapienti. Nec
to a consular (man), nor a wretched (death) to a wise (man). Nor

tamen sum ego ille ferreus, qui movear non
yet am I that iron (person), who may-be-moved not

mœrore carissimi atque amantissimi fratris
by the sorrow of (my) dearest and most-loving brother

præsentis, que lacrymis omnium horum, a quibus
being-present, and by the tears of all these, by whom

videtis me circumsessum. Neque exanimata uxor
you see me surrounded. Neither (my) fainting wife

revocat non sæpe meam mentem domum, filia
calls-back not often my mind home, (and) daughter

abjecta metu, et parvulus filius, quem respublica
cast-down with fear, and (my) very-little son, whom the republi

videtur mihi amplecti tamquam obsidem mei
seems to me to embrace as-if a hostage (pledge) of my

consulatus: neque ille gener, qui exspectans
consulship: nor that son-in-law, who awaiting

exitum hujus diei, adstat in meo conspectu.
the issue of this day, stands-near in my sight.

Moveor omnibus his rebus, sed in eam partem,
I am-moved by all these things, but unto that part,

ut sint omnes salvi vobiscum, etiamsi aliqua
that they may-be all safe with you, even-if some

vis oppresserit me, potius quam et illi
violence may-have-oppressed me, rather than both they

et nos pereamus una cum republicâ. Quare,
and we may-perish together with the republic. Wherefore,

conscripti patres, incumbite ad salutem reipublicæ:
conscript fathers, apply to the safety of the republic:

circumspicite omnes procellas, quæ impendent,
look-around-upon all the storms, which hang-over (threaten),

nisi providetis. Non Tib. Gracchus, qui voluit
unless you provide. Not Tib. Gracchus, who wished

fieri iterum tribunus plebis: non C. Gracchus,
to be-made again tribune of the people: not C. Gracchus,

qui conatus est concitare agrarios: non L. Saturninus,
who endeavoured to excite the agrarians: not L. Saturninus,

qui occidit C. Memmium, adducitur in aliquod
who slew C. Memmius, is-brought into some

discrimen, atque in judicium vestræ
distinction (controversy), and into the judgment of your

severitatis. Ii tenentur, qui restiterunt Romæ,
severity Those are-held, who have-remained at Rome,

ad   **incendium**   **urbis,**   **ad vestram**   **cædem**
to (for)   the conflagration   of the city,   to   your   slaughter

omnium,   **ad Catilinam accipiendum :**
of all (for the slaughter of you all), to (for) Catiline   to be-received :

litteræ,   **signa,**   **manus,**   **denique**   **confessio**
the letters,   seals,   hand,   finally   the confession

uniuscujusque   **tenentur;**   **Allobroges**   **sollicitantur;**
of each   are-held;   the Allobroges   are-solicited;

servitia excitantur; Catilina arcessitur; id consilium
the slaves   are-excited;   Catiline   is-sent-for;   that   counsel

initum est,   **ut,**   **omnibus**   **interfectis,**   **nemo**
has-been-entered-into,   that,   all   being-slain,   no-one

relinquatur   **ne quidem**   **ad**   **nomen**   **reipublicæ**
may-be-left   not-even   to (for) the name   of the republic

deplorandum,   **atque**   **ad**   **calamitatem**   **tanti**
to be-deplored,   and   to (for) the calamity   of so-great

imperii lamentandam.
an empire   to be-lamented.

8. Indices   **detulerunt**   **omnia hæc,**
The informers   have-brought (reported)   all   these (things),

rei   **confessi sunt;**   **vos**   **jam**   **judicastis**
the accused   have-confessed (them);   you   already   have-judged

multis   **judiciis:**   **primum,**   **quod**   **egistis**
(them) by many   judgments: first,   because   you acted

gratias mihi singularibus verbis :
(have given) thanks to me   in singular   words (in extraordinary

et decrevistis   **conjurationem perditorum**
terms): and   you decreed (decided)   a conspiracy   of

hominum patefactam esse meâ virtute atque
(abandoned)   men   to have-been-exposed by my   virtue   and

diligentiâ: deinde quod coëgistis P. Lentulum, ut
diligence: then   because   you-forced   P. Lentulus   that

abdicaret   **se**   **præturâ:**   **tum quod**
he should-abdicate   himself   from the prætorship: then because

censuistis eum, et ceteros, de quibus judicastis,
you voted   him,   and the others, concerning   whom   you judged,

dandos   **in**   **custodiam: que maxime**   **quod**
to be-given into   custody: and   mostly (especially)   because

decrevistis supplicationem meo nomine, qui honos
you decreed   a thanksgiving in my name, which honour

habitus est nemini togato ante me: postremo
has-been-held to no-one wearing-the-toga before me: lastly,

hesterno die dedistis amplissima præmia legatis
on yesterday you gave most ample rewards to the ambassadors

Allobrogum, que Tito Vulturcio. Omnia quæ
of the Allobroges, and to Titus Vulturcius. All which

sunt ejusmodi, ut ii, qui dati sunt
(things) are of this-sort, that those, who have-been-given

nominatim in custodiam, videantur sine ullâ
by-name into custody, may-seem without any

dubitatione damnati esse a vobis. Sed ego
doubt   to have-been-condemned by you. But I

institui referre ad vos, conscripti patres,
have-determined to refer to you, conscript fathers,

tamquam integrum, et quid judicetis
as-if an entire (a new matter), both what you may-judge

de facto, et quid censeatis de
concerning the deed, and what you may-vote concerning

pœnâ; prædicam illa, quæ sunt
the punishment; I will-previously-say those (things), which are

consulis. Ego videbam jampridem magnum
(the business) of a consul. I did see long-since great

furorem versari in republicâ, et
madness to be-engaged (to be prevalent) in the republic, and

quædam nova mala misceri et concitari: sed
some new evils to be-mingled and to be-excited: but

nunquam putavi hanc tantam, tam exitiosam
never I thought this so-great, so destructive

conjurationem haberi a civibus. Nunc, quidquid
conspiracy to be-held by citizens. Now, whatever

est, quocunque vestræ mentes atque sententiæ
it-is, whither-soever your minds and opinions

inclinant, est statuendum vobis ante noctem.
incline, it-is to be-determined to you (by you) before night.

Videtis quantum facinus delatum sit
you see how-great a daring-deed may have-been-brought (reported)

ad vos: si putatis paucos esse affines huic,
to you: if you think few to be bordering (accessary) to this,

erratis vehementer. Hoc malum disseminatum est
you err violently. This evil has-been disseminated

latius opinione: manavit nor
more-widely than opinion (than is supposed): it has-flowed not

solum per Italiam, verum etiam transcendit Alpes,
only through Italy, but even has-passed-over the Alps,

et serpens obscure, jam occupavit multas
and creeping obscurely, already has-occupied many

provincias. Id nullo pacto potest opprimi
provinces. That by no agreement (means) is-able to be-oppressed

sustentando ac prolatando. Quâcunque ratione
by supporting and by deferring. In whatever reason

placet, est vindicandum vobis celeritir.
(manner) it pleases, it-is to be-punished to you (by you) quickly.

4. Video duas sententias esse adhuc;
I see two opinions to be hitherto (that there are

unam D. Silani, qui censet, eos
hitherto two opinions); one of D. Silanus, who votes, those

qui conati sunt delere hæc esse multandos
who have-endeavoured to destroy these (things) to be to be-fined

morte: alteram C. Cæsaris, qui removet
(punished) with death: the other of C. Cæsar, who removes

pœnam mortis, amplecitur omnes acerbitates
the penalty of death, embraces all the bitterness

ceterorum suppliciorum. Uterque versatur in summâ
of other punishments. Each is-engaged in the highest

severitate et pro suâ dignitate, et pro
severity both for (according to) his-own dignity, and for

magnitudine rerum. Alter putat oportere
the greatness of things. The other (the one) thinks (it) to behove

non eos qui conati sunt privare nos omnes,
not those who have-endeavoured to deprive us all,

qui Romanum populum vitâ
who (have endeavoured to deprive) the Roman people with life

qui delere imperium, qui
(of life). who (have attempted) to destroy the empire, who

exstinguere nomen Romani populi, frui vitâ,
to extinguish the name of the Roman people, to enjoy with life,

et hoc communi spiritu
and with this common breath (the air breathed by us all)

punctum temporis: atque recordatur hoc genus
a point of time (a moment): and calls-to-mind this kind

poenæ usurpatum esse sæpe in hâc republicâ
of punishment to have-been-used often in this republic

in improbos cives. Alter intelligit mortem non
against dishonest citizens. The other understands death not

constitutam esse a immortalibus dus causâ
to have-been-appointed by the immortal gods for-the-sake

supplicii, sed esse aut necessitatem naturæ, aut
of punishment, but to be either a necessity of nature, or

quietem laborum ac miseriarum. Itaque sapientes
a rest of labours and of miseries. Therefore wise (men)

numquam inviti, fortes etiam sæpe libenter
never unwillingly, the bold even often willingly

oppetiverunt eam. Vero vincula, et ea sempiterna,
have-undergone it. But bonds, and those eternal

certe inventa sunt ad singularem
(for life), certainly have-been-invented to (for) the singular

poenam nefarii sceleris. Jubet dispertiri
punishment of nefarious crime. He orders (them) to be-distributed

municipiis. Ista res videtur habere
to the municipal-towns. That thing seems to have

iniquitatem, si velis imperare; difficultatem,
injustice, if thou-mayest-wish to command (it); difficulty,

si rogare: tamen decernatur, si placet.
if to ask (it): yet let-it-be-decreed, if it pleases (you).

Enim ego suscipiam, et, ut spero,
For I will-take-up (will take upon myself), and, as I hope,

reperiam, qui putent esse non suæ
will-find (those), who may think (it) to be not (the part) of their

dignitatis recusare id, quod statueritis
dignity to refuse that, which you shall-have-appointed

causâ salutis omnium. Adjungit gravem
for-the-sake of the safety of all. He adjoins a heavy

poenam　　　　municipibus,　　　si　quis
punishment　to the inhabitants of the municipal towns,　if　any-one

eorum　　　　　ruperit　vincula:
of them (the conspirators) shall-have-broken　the bonds (escaped):

circumdat　horribiles custodias,　et sancit
he places-around　dreadful　guards,　and sanctions (things)

digna scelere perditorum　hominum, ne quis
worthy with the crime of lost (abandoned) men,　lest any-one

possit levare poenam eorum, quos condemnat,
may-be-able to lighten the punishment of those, whom he condemns,

aut　per senatum, aut per populum. Etiam
either through the senate, or through the people. Also (even)

eripit　spem,　quæ sola solet consolari
he snatches-away hope,　which alone is-accustomed to console

hominem in miseriis. Præterea,　jubet　bona
a man　in miseries.　Besides,　he orders (their) goods

publicari:　relinquit vitam solam nefariis
to be-confiscated:　he leaves　life　alone to the nefarious

hominibus:　quam si　eripuisset,
men:　which if　he might-have-snatched-away,

ademisset　multas poenas animi atque
he would-have taken-away many punishments of mind and

corporis, et omnes　scelerum, uno dolore.
of body,　and all (the punishments) of crimes, by one pain.

Itaque, ut aliqua formido esset posita improbis
Therefore, that some dread might-be placed to the dishonest

in vitâ, illi antiqui voluerunt quædam supplicia
in life, those ancients wished some punishments

ejusmodi esse constituta impiis apud
of that-sort to be appointed to the impious with (among)

inferos:　videlicet,　quod　intelligebant,
the shades-below:　that-is-to-say,　because they did-understand,

his remotis, mortem ipsam non esse pertimescendam.
these being-removed, death itself not to be to be-feared.

5. Nunc, conscripti patres, ego video quid intersit
Now, conscript fathers, I see what it may-interest

meâ.　　　　　　Si　secuti eritis
with mine (how much it may be to my interest). If you shall have-followed

sententiam C. Cæsaris, quoniam is secutus est hanc
the opinion of C. Cæsar, since he has-followed this

viam in republicâ, quæ habetur popularis,
way in the republic, which is-held (is accounted) the popular

fortasse populares impetus erunt minus
(way), perhaps popular attacks will-be less

pertimescendi mihi, hoc auctore et
to be-feared to me (by me), this (person being) the author and

cognitore hujusce sententiæ. Sin illam
acknowledger of this opinion. But-if (you follow) that

alteram, nescio an amplius negotii
other, I know-not whether more of business (trouble)

contrahatur mihi. Sed tamen utilitas reipublicæ
may be-contracted for me. But yet the advantage of the republic

vincat rationes meorum periculorum.
et (it) conquer the reasons (calculations) of my dangers.

Enim habemus a C. Cæsare, sicut dignitas ipsius
For we have from C. Cæsar, as the dignity of himself

et amplitudo majorum ejus postulabat,
and the greatness (nobility) of the ancestors of him did-require,

sententiam, tanquam obsidem perpetuæ
an opinion, as-if an hostage (pledge) of (his) perpetual

voluntatis in rempublicam. Intellectum est, quid
good-will unto the republic. It has-been-understood, what

intersit inter levitatem concionatorum et
may be-the-difference between the levity of public-speakers and

animum vere popularem, consulentem saluti
a mind truly popular, consulting for the safety

populi. Video non neminem de istis qui
of the people. I see not no-one (some one) from those who

volunt se haberi populares, abesse,
wish themselves to be-held (to be accounted) popular, to be-absent,

videlicet, ne ferat sententiam de capite
that-is-to-say, lest he may-bear an opinion concerning the head (life)

Romanorum civium. Is, nudiustertius, et
of Roman citizens. He, the-day-before-yesterday, both

dedit Romanos cives in custodiam, et decrevit
gave Roman citizens into custody, and decreed

mihi supplicationem, et hesterno die affecit indices
to me   a thanksgiving,   and on-yesterday   affected the informers

maximis præmiis. Jam hoc est dubium nemini,
with the greatest rewards.   Now this is doubtful to no-one,

quid judicarit de totâ re et causâ,
what he may-have-judged concerning the whole thing and cause,

qui decrevit custodiam reo, gratulationem
who has-decreed   custody to the accused,   congratulation

quæsitori, præmium indici. At, vero, C. Cæsar
to the inquirer, reward to the informer. But, truly, C. Cæsar

intelligit Semproniam legem constitutam esse
understands the Sempronian law   to have-been-appointed

de Romanis civibus; autem qui sit hostis
concerning Roman citizens; but who may-be an enemy

reipublicæ, eum posse nullo modo esse civem:
of the republic, him to be-able in no manner to be a citizen:

denique, latorem ipsum Semproniæ legis,
finally, the bearer (maker) himself of the Sempronian law,

dependisse pœnas reipublicæ jussu populi.
to have-paid penalties to the republic by-the-order of the people.

Idem putat largitorem et prodigum Lentulum
The same (person) thinks the briber and prodigal Lentulus

non posse appellari popularem, cum
not to be-able to be-called belonging-to-the-people, since

cogitarit tam acerbe que tam crudeliter
he may-have-devised so bitterly and so   cruelly

de pernicie Romani populi, exitio
concerning the destruction of the Roman people, the ruin

hujus urbis. Itaque, mitissimus atque lenissimus
of this city. Therefore, the most-mild and most-gentle

homo dubitat non mandare P. Lentulum
man (Cæsar) doubts (hesitates) not to commit P. Lentulus

æternis tenebris que vinculis; et sancit in posterum,
te eternal darkness and to bonds; and sanctions unto after (time),

ne quis possit jactare se
est any (person) may-be-able to toss himself (to be officious)

supplicio hujus levando,
in the punishment of him to be lightened (in lightening his punishment),

et posthac esse popularis in pernicie Romam
and hereafter to be popular in the destruction of the Roman

populi. Etiam adjungit publicationem bonorum, ut
people. Also he adjoins confiscation of goods, that

etiam egestas ac mendicitas consequator omnes
even want and beggary may-follow all

cruciatus animi et corporis.
torments of mind and of body.

6. Quamobrem, sive statueritis hoc,
Wherefore, whether you shall-have-appointed this,

dederitis mihi comitem ad concionem
you will-have-given to me a companion (Cæsar) to the public-assembly

carum atque jucundum populo; sive
dear and acceptable to-the-people; or-if

malueritis sequi sententiam Silani,
you shall-have-wished-rather to follow the opinion of Silanus,

defendetis facile me atque vos a vituperatione
you will-defend easily me and yourselves from the blame

crudelitatis, atque obtinebo eam fuisse
of cruelty, and I shall-obtain (maintain) it to-have-been

multo leviorem. Quamquam, conscripti patres, quæ
by much lighter. Although, conscript fathers, what

crudelitas potest esse in immanitate tanti
cruelty is-able to be in the outrageousness of so-great

sceleris puniendâ? Enim ego judico de meo
a crime to be-punished? For I judge from my-own

sensu. Nam ita liceat mihi perfrui vobiscum
feeling. Nor thus it may-be-allowed to me to enjoy with you

salvâ republicâ, ut ego, quod sum vehementior in
a safe republic, that I, because I am more-vehement in

hâc causâ, moveor non atrocitate animi, (enim quis
this cause, am-moved not by cruelty of mind, (for who

est mitior me?) sed quâdam singulari humanitate
is milder than I?) but by some singular humanity

et misericordiâ. Enim videor mihi videre hanc
and mercy. For I seem to myself to see this

urbem, lucem orbis terrarum, atque arcem
city, the light of the globe of the earths, and the citadel

omnium gentium, subito concidentem uno incendio;
of all   nations,   suddenly   falling   by one conflagration;

cerno   animo   miseros atque insepultos **acervos**
I discern   in (my) mind wretched   and   unburied   heaps

civium in   sepultâ patriâ; aspectus   et **furor**
of citizens in (my) buried   country; the appearance and   fury

Cethegi bacchantis in vestrâ cæde versatur
of Cethegus revelling   in   your   slaughter is-engaged (revolved)

ante oculos mihi. Vero cum proposui
before the eyes to me. But when I have-proposed (represented)

mihi Lentulum regnantem, sicut ipse confessus est
to myself Lentulus   ruling,   as   himself   confessed

se   sperasse ex   fatis, hunc Gabinium
himself to have-hoped out-of (according-to) the fates, this   Gabinius

esse purpuratum, Catilinam venisse cum exercitu,
to be clothed-in-purple,   Catiline   to have-come with (his) army,

tum perhorresco lamentationem matrumfamilias; **tum**
then   I dread   the lamentation of mothers-of-families; then

fugam virginum atque puerorum, ac vexationem
the flight of virgins   and   of boys,   and   the harassing

vestalium virginum; et quia hæc   videntur
of vestal   virgins; and because these (things)   seem

mihi vehementer misera atque miseranda, idcirco
to me   violently   wretched and   to be-pitied, on-that-account

præbeo   me   severum que vehementem   in
I afford (I show) myself severe   and   violent   against

eos qui voluerunt perficere ea. Etenim quæro
those who have-wished to perform them. For   I seek (ask)

si quis paterfamilias, suis liberis interfectis a servo,
if   any father-of-a-family, his children being-slain by a slave,

uxore occisâ,   domo incensâ,   sumserit
(his) wife being-killed, (his) house being-set-on-fire, shall-have-taken

non quam acerbissimum supplicium de   servis;
not   as-bitter-as-possible   punishment of (his) slaves;

utrum is videatur esse clemens ac misericors, an
whether he may-seem to be clement and   merciful,   or

inhumanissimus et crudelissimus? Vero   mihi
most-inhuman and   most-cruel?   But (he would seem) to me

importunus   ac   ferreus   qui   lenierit   non
importunate (cruel) and made-of-iron who shall-have-soothed not

suum dolorem que cruciatum   dolore   ac   cruciatu
his-own grief   and   torment   by the grief and   torment

            nocentis.   Sic nos in his hominibus, qui
of (the person) injuring. Thus we in these men,   who

voluerunt   trucidare   nos,   qui
have-wished   to slaughter   us,   who (have wished to slaughter

        conjuges, qui nostros liberos ; qui   conati sunt
(our)   wives,   who   our   children ; who   have-endeavoured

delere   singulas   domos uniuscujusque nostrum, et
to destroy the several houses   of each-one   of us,   and

hoc universum domicilium reipublicæ ;   qui egerunt
this   whole   abode   of the republic ; who have-acted

            id,   ut collocarent   gentem   Allobrogum
(attempted) this, that they might-place the nation of the Allobroges

in vestigiis hujus urbis, atque in   cinere (*sing.*)
in   the traces of this city,   and   in   the ashes

deflagrati   imperii : si fuerimus   vehementissimi
of the consumed empire : if we-shall-have-been very-vehement

habebimur   misericordes ; sin   voluerimus
we shall-be-held (accounted) merciful ;   but-if we-shall-have-wished

esse remissiores,   fama   summæ   crudelitatis, in
to be more-remiss, the report of the highest cruelty,   in

pernicie   patriæ   que   civium,   est   subeunda
the destruction of country and of citizens,   is   to be-undergone

nobis.   Nisi, vero, L. Cæsar, fortissimus vir, et
to us (by us). Unless, truly, L. Cæsar, a most-bold man, and

amantissimus reipublicæ, visus est cuipiam crudelior,
most-loving   of the republic, seemed to any-one more-cruel,

cum dixit virum   suæ sororis, electissimæ
when he said the man (husband) of his-own sister,   a most-select

feminæ, præsentem et audientem, esse   privandum
woman,   being-present and hearing,   to be to be-deprived

vitâ ;   cum dixit   avum   interfectum esse,
from life (of life); when he said (his) grand-father to have-been-slain,

jussu   consulis,   que   filium ejus   impuberem,
by order of-the-consul, and the son of him not-being-of-age,

missum legatum a patre, necatum esse in
being-sent ambassador by the father, to have-been-killed in

carcere. Quorum quod simile factum (est)? Quod
prison. Of whom what like (thing) was-done? What

consilium reipublicæ delendæ initum (est)?
design of the republic to be-destroyed was-entered-into?

Voluntas largitionis versata est
A wish of giving-liberally (to-the-people) was-engaged (existed)

tum in republicâ, et quædam contentio partium.
then in the republic, and some contention of parts

Atque illo tempore avus hujus
(of parties). And at that time the grandfather of this

Lentuli, clarissimus vir, armatus persecutus est
Lentulus, a most-famous man, being-armed pursued

Gracchum: ille etiam tum accepit grave vulnus, ne
Gracchus: he also then received a heavy wound, lest

quid minueretur de summâ republicâ:
any (thing) might-be-diminished from the highest republic:

hic arcessit Gallos ad fundamenta
this (Lentulus) sends-for the Gauls to (for) the foundations

reipublicæ evertenda, concitat servitia, vocat
of the republic to be-overturned, excites the slaves, calls

Catilinam, attribuit nos Cethego trucidandos,
Catiline, assigns us to Cethegus to be-slaughtered,

ceteros cives Gabinio interficiendos, urbem Cassio
the other citizens to Gabinius to be-slain, the city to Cassius

inflammandam, totam Italiam Catilinæ vastandam
to be-set-on-fire, the whole Italy to Catiline to be-laid-waste

que diripiendam. Vereamini, censeo, ne in hoc
and to be-plundered. You should-fear, I judge, lest in this

tam immani ac nefando scelere, videamini
so outrageous and impious crime, you may-seem

statuisse aliquid nimis severe; cum sit
to have-determined something too severely; when it-may-be

verendum multo magis, ne remissione pœnæ
to be-feared by much more, less by permission of punishment

videamur fuisse crudeles in patriam, quam
we may-seem to have-been cruel unto the country than

ne   ssveritate   animadversionis   nimis   vehementes
lest by the severity   of punishment   too   violent

in   acerbissimos hostes.
against the most-bitter enemies.

7. Sed, conscripti pa:res, possum non dissimulare
But,   conscript   fathers, I am-able not to dissemble

ea   quæ exaudio. Enim voces   jaciuntur,
those (things) which I hear. For   voices (speeches) are-cast

quæ perveniunt ad meas aures, eorum qui
(uttered), which   arrive   to my   ears, of those who

videntur vereri, ut habeam satis præsidii ad
seem   to fear, that I may-have enough of guard to (for)

ea   transigunda   quæ vos
these (things) to be-performed (for performing those things) which you

statueritis   hodierno-die. Omnia   et
shall have-determined   on-this-day.   All (things) both

provisa sunt,   et parata, et constituta, conscripti
have-been-foreseen, and prepared, and appointed,   conscript

patres, cum   meâ summâ curâ atque diligentiâ,
fathers, when (as well) by my highest care and   diligence,

tum   etiam multo majore voluntate   Romani
then (as) also by a much greater   wish   of the Roman

populi ad   summum imperium   retinendum, et
people to (for) the highest empire (rule) to-be-retained, and

ad   communes fortunas   conservandas. Omnes
to (for) the common   fortunes   to-be-preserved.   All

homines omnium ordinum, denique omnium ætatum
men   of all   orders,   finally of all   ages

adsunt: forum est plenum, templa circa forum
are-present: the forum is   full, the temples about the forum

plena, omnes   aditus   hujus loci ac templi pleni.
full,   all the approaches of this place and temple full.

Enim hæc causa sola inventa est post   urbem
For this cause alone has-been-found after (since) the city

conditam, in quâ omnes sentirent unum atque
being-founded, in which all might-think one   and

idem,   præter eos, qui cum viderent   esse
the same (thing), except those, who when they might-see (it) to be

pereundum **sibi,** **voluerunt**
to be-perished to (by) themselves (that they must perish), wished

potius perire cum omnibus, quam soli. Ego excipio
rather to perish with all, than alone. I except

et libenter secerno hosce homines: enim neque
and willingly separate these men: for neither

puto habendos in numero improborum
do-I-think (them) to be-held (accounted) in the number of dishonest

civium, sed in acerbissimorum hostium. Vero
citizens, but the (number) of most-bitter enemies. But

ceteri, immortales dii! quâ frequentiâ, quo
the rest, immortal gods! with what attendance (number), with what

studio, quâ virtute consentiunt ad communem
ardour, with what virtue (boldness) they-agree to the common

dignitatem que salutem? Quid ego commemorem hic
dignity and safety? Why may-I-mention here

Romanos equites? Qui ita concedunt vobis summam
the Roman knights? Who so concede to you the sum

ordinis que consilii, ut certent
(the chief place) of rank and of counsel, that they may-contend

vobiscum de amore reipublicæ: quos revocatos
with-you concerning love of the republic: whom being-recalled

ex dissensione multorum annorum ad societatem
out-of a disagreement of many years to the society

que concordiam hujus ordinis, hodiernus dies
and concord of this order (the senators), this-day

atque hæc causa conjungit vobiscum: quam
and this cause unites with you: which

conjunctionem confirmatam in meo consulatu, si
union confirmed in my consulship, if

tenuerimus perpetuam in republicâ, confirmo
we shall-have-held (it) perpetual in the republic, I confirm

vobis, nullum civile ac domesticum malum esse
to you, no civil and domestic evil to be

venturum posthac ad ullam partem reipublicæ.
about-to-come hereafter to any part of the republic,

Video tribunos ærarios,
I see the tribunes belonging-to-the-treasury (the receivers general)

fortissimos   viros   convenisse   pari   studio
most-bold   men   to have-come-together   with like   ardour

reipublicæ   defendendæ;   item universos   scribas:
of the republic   to be-defended;   also   all   the clerks:

quos cum   hæc dies   casu   frequentasset   ad
whom since   this   day   by accident   might-have-collected   to

ærarium,   video   esse   conversos   ab   exspectatione
the treasury,   I see   to be   turned   from   the expectation

    sortis   ad communem salutem.   Omnis   multitudo
of (their) lot   to   the common   safety.   All   the multitude

ingenuorum,   etiam   tenuissimorum,
of freeborn (citizens),   even   of the-most-slender (poorest),

adest.   Enim quis est,   cui   hæc templa, aspectus
is-present.   For   who is there, to whom   these temples,   the sight

urbis,   possessio libertatis, denique hæc lux ipsa,
of the city,   the possession   of liberty,   finally   this   light itself,

et hoc commune solum patriæ,   sit   non cum
and this   common   soil   of country,   may-be   not   when

     carum, tum   vero dulce atque jucundum?
(as well) dear,   then (as) truly   sweet   and   pleasant?

   8. Est pretium operæ,   conscripti patres,
    It-is the price of labour (it is worth while), conscript   fathers,

cognoscere   studia
to know   (to acquaint yourselves with)   the studies (ardour)

libertinorum hominum, qui suâ virtute   consecuti
of the freed-men,   who by their   virtue   having-attained

fortunam civitatis, judicant hanc esse vere   suam
the fortune   of the state,   judge   this   to-be   truly   their-own

patriam: quam quidam   nati hinc,   et   nati
country: which   some (persons) born hence,   and   born

  summo   loco,   judicaverunt non esse   suam
in the highest place (condition),   have-judged   not to be their-own

patriam, sed urbem hostium. Sed quid ego commemorem
country,   but a city of enemies. But why   may I-mention

homines hujusce ordinis, quos privatæ fortunæ, quos
the men   of this   order,   whom   private   fortunes,   whom

communis respublica, quos denique ea libertas, quæ
the common   republic,   whom   finally   that   liberty,   which

est dulcissima, excitavit ad salutem patriæ
is most-sweet, has-excited to the safety of (their) country

defendendam? Est nemo servus, qui sit modo
to be-defended? There-is no-one a slave, who may-be only

tolerabili conditione servitutis, qui perhorrescat non
in a tolerable condition of slavery, who may-dread not

audaciam perditorum civium, qui cupiat non
the audacity of lost (abandoned) citizens, who may-desire not

hæc stare, qui conferat non tantum voluntatis
these (things) to-stand, who may-confer not so-much of good-will

quantum audet, et quantum potest ad communem
as he dares, and as he-is-able to the common

salutem. Quare si forte hoc quod auditum est
safety. Wherefore if by-chance this which has-been-heard

commovet quem vestrûm, quendam lenonem Lentuli
moves any-one of you, a certain pimp of Lentulus

concursare circum tabernas, sperantem animos
to run-about around the shops, hoping the minds

egentium atque imperitorum posse sollicitari
of the needy and of the unskilful to be-able to be-solicited

pretio; id quidem cœptum (est) atque
by a price (reward); that indeed has been-begun and

tentatum: sed nulli inventi sunt aut tam miseri
tried: but none have-been-found either so wretched

fortunâ, aut tam perditi voluntate, qui velint
in fortune, or so lost (abandoned) in will, who may-wish

non illum locum ipsum sellæ atque operis, et
not that place itself of (their) seat (stall) and of work, and

quotidiani quæstus, qui non suum cubile ac
of daily gain, who (may wish) not his couch and

lectulum, denique qui non hunc otiosum
little-bed, finally who (may wish) not this idle (peaceable)

cursum suæ vitæ esse salvum. Vero multo maxima
course of their life to be safe. But by much the greatest

pars eorum, qui sunt in tabernis, immo vero (enim
part of those, who are in the shops, yes truly (for

id est potius dicendum) universum hoc genus,
that is rather to be-said) the whole this kind (class)

est amantissimum otii.   Etenim omne instrumentum,
is   most-loving   of ease.   For   all   the apparatus,

omnis   opera,   ac   quæstus   eorum   sustinetur
all   the labour,   and   gain   of them   is-supported

frequentiâ   civium,   alitur   otio: si   quæstus
by-assemblage   of citizens,   is-cherished by ease: if   the gain

quorum   solet   minui,   tabernis occlusis,   quid
of whom   is-accustomed   to be-diminished,   the shops being-shut,   what

tandem   est   futurum,   incensis.   Cum
at-length   is   about-to-be, (the shops) being-set-on-fire.   Since

quæ   sint ita, conscripti patres, præsidia
which (things) may-be thus,   conscript   fathers,   the guards (protection)

Romani   populi   desunt   non vobis: providete ne
of the Roman   people   are-wanting   not   to you: foresee   lest

vos videamini   deesse   Romano   populo.
you   may-seem   to-be-wanting   to the Roman   people.

9. Habetis   consulem reservatum   ex   plurimis
   You have   a consul   reserved   out-of   very-many

periculis et   insidiis, atque   ex   mediâ morte, non
dangers   and   snares,   and   out-of   middle death,   not

ad   suam   vitam, sed ad   vestram   salutem:
to (for)   his-own   life,   but   to (for)   your   safety:

omnes ordines   consentiunt   mente,   voluntate,
all   orders (ranks)   agree   in mind,   in will,

studio,   virtute,   voce   ad   rempublicam
In ardour,   in valour,   in voice   to (for)   the republic

conservandam: communis patria obsessa   facibus
to be-preserved: (your)   common   country   beset   with the torches

et   telis   impiæ conjurationis, supplex tendit
and weapons   of an impious   conspiracy,   suppliant stretches (her)

manus vobis: commendat   vobis   se,   vobis vitam
hands   to you: she commends   to you   herself,   to you   the life

omnium   civium,   vobis   arcem   et   Capitolium
of all   the citizens,   to you   the citadel   and   the Capitol

vobis   aras   Penatium,   vobis illum perpetuum ac
to you   the altars   of the Penates,   to you   that   perpetual   and

sempiternum   ignem Vestæ,   vobis   omnia   templa
eternal   fire   of Vesta,   to you   all   the temples

atque delubra deorum, vobis muros atque tecta
and   shrines   of the gods,   to you the walls   and   roofs (houses

urbis.   Præterea   est   judicandum   vobis
of the city.   Besides   it is   to be-judged   to you   (by you)

hodierno die   de   vestrâ vitâ,   de   animâ
on-this-day   concerning   your   life,   concerning   the life

vestrarum conjugum ac liberorum,   de   fortunis
of your   wives   and   children,   concerning the fortunes

omnium,   de   sedibus,   de   vestris
of all,   concerning (your)   seats (abodes),   concerning   your

focis.   Habetis   ducem   memorem   vestri,   oblitum
hearths.   You have   a leader   mindful   of you,   forgetful

sui,   quæ facultas   datur   non semper: habetis
of himself, which   means   is-given   not   always: you have

omnes ordines, omnes homines, universum Romanum
all   ranks,   all   men,   the whole   Roman

populum,   id   quod   videmus   primum   in
people,   that   which   we-see   first (for the first time) in

civili   causâ hodierno die, sentientem unum atque
a civil   cause   on-this-day,   thinking   one   and

idem.   Cogitate una nox pæne   delerit
the same (thing). Think   one   night   almost   may have-destroyed

imperium fundatum quantis laboribus, libertatem
an empire   founded   with how-great   labours,   liberty

stabilitam   quantâ   virtute,   fortunas   auctas   que
established   by how-great   valour,   fortunes   increased   and

exaggeratas   quantâ   benignitate   deorum.   Est
heaped-up   by how-great   kindness   of the gods.   It-is

providendum hodierno die, non modo ne id   possit
to be-foreseen   on this-day,   not only   lest that may be-able

umquam   posthac   confici,   sed   ne quidem
ever   hereafter   to be-performed,   but   not-even

cogitari   a civibus. Atque locutus sum hæc,
to be-thought (devised) by   citizens.   And   I have-spoken   these

non ut excitarem vos, qui pæne præcurritis
(things), not   that I might-excite   you,   who almost   run-before

mihi   studio; sed ut mea vox, quæ debet
to me (outstrip me) in ardour;   but   that   my   voice, which   ought

esse princeps   in republicâ,   videretur   functa (esse,
to be   chief (first)   in the republic,   might-seem to have-discharged

consulari   officio.
with the consular   duty (to have-discharged the consular duty).

10. Nunc, conscripti patres, antequam   redeo ad
Now,   conscript   fathers,   before-that   I return   to

sententiam,   dicam   pauca   de   me.
the opinion,   I will-say   a few (things) concerning   myself.

Ego video me   suscepisse   tantam multitudinem
I   see   myself to have-taken-up so-great   a multitude

inimicorum,   quanta   manus   conjuratorum   est,
of enemies,   as-great-as   the band   of the conspirators   is,

quam videtis esse permagnam: sed judico eam esse
which   you see to be   very-great: but I judge it   to be

turpem   et   infirmam,   contemtam   et   abjectam.
base   and   weak,   despised   and   abject.

Quod si aliquando, ista manus concitata   furore
But-if   at-sometime, that band being-excited by the fury

et   scelere alicujus,   valuerit   plus quam
and by the crime of some-one, shall-have-prevailed more   than

vestra dignitas ac   reipublicæ; tamen, conscripti
your   dignity and (that) of the republic;   yet,   conscript

patres,   pœnitebit me numquam meorum factorum
fathers,   it will-repent me   never   of my   deeds

atque consiliorum. Etenim mors, quam illi fortasse
and   counsels.   For   death, which they   perhaps

minitantur mihi, est   parata   omnibus: nemo
threaten   to me,   is   prepared   for all: no-one

assecutus est tantam laudem vitæ,   quantâ   vos
has-attained   so-great   praise of life, with as-great-as you

honestastis me vestris decretis. Enim   decrevistis
have-ennobled me by your   decrees.   For   you have-decreed

semper ceteris gratulationem reipublicæ   gestæ
always   to others   thanksgiving   of the republic being-carried-on

bene, mihi uni   reipublicæ   conservatæ.   Ille
well   to me one (alone) of the republic being-preserved.   That

Scipio sit clarus, consilio que virtute   cujus
Scipio may-be famous, by the counsel and by the valour of whom

Hannibal coactus est redire in Africam, atque
Hannibal was-forced to return into Africa, and

decedere ex Italiâ: alter Africanus
to depart out-of Italy: the other (Scipio) Africanus

ornetur eximiâ laude, qui delevit duas
may-be-adorned with excellent praise, who destroyed the two

urbes infestissimas huic imperio, Carthaginem que
cities most-hostile to this empire, Carthage and

Numantiam: ille L. Paullus habeatur egregius
Numantia: that L. Paullus may-be-held (accounted) an excellent

vir, currum cujus Perses, rex quondam
man, the chariot of whom Perses, a king once

potentissimus et nobilissimus, honestavit: Marius
most-powerful and most-noble, ennobled: Marius

sit in æternâ gloriâ, qui bis liberavit Italiam
may-be in eternal glory, who twice freed Italy

obsidione et metu servitutis: Pompeius
from siege and from fear of slavery: Pompey

anteponatur omnibus, res gestæ
may-be-placed-before (preferred) to all, the things carried-on

atque virtutes cujus continentur iisdem
(the exploits) and virtues of whom are-bounded by the same

regionibus ac terminis quibus cursus solis.
regions and limits by which the course of the sun

Erit profecto inter laudes horum
(is bounded). There-will-be indeed among the praises of these

aliquid loci nostræ gloriæ: nisi forte
something of place to our (for my) glory: unless by chance

est majus patefacere provincias nobis, quo
it-is a greater (thing) to open provinces to us, whither

possimus exire, quam curare ut etiam illi
we may-be-able to go-out, than to take-care that even those

qui absunt habeant quo victores
who are-absent may have (a place) whither (being) conquerors

revertantur. Quamquam uno loco conditio
they may-return. Although in one place (respect) the condition

externæ victoriæ est melior quam domesticæ;
of external victory is better than (that) of domestic (victory)

quod hostes, alienigenæ, aut oppressi serviunt
because enemies, foreigners, either being-oppressed serve

aut, recepti, putant
(become subservient), or, being-received (into friendship), think

se obligatos beneficio: autem, ex numero
themselves obliged by the favour: but, out-of the number

civium, qui depravati aliqua dementiâ,
of citizens, (those) who being-depraved by some madness,

cœperunt semel esse hostes patriæ, cum
have-begun once to be enemies of the country, when

repuleris a pernicie reipublicæ,
thou mayst-have-repulsed (them) from the destruction of the republic,

possis nec coërcere eos vi nec placare
thou mayst-be-able neither to restrain them by force nor to appease

beneficio. Quare video æternum bellum
by kindness. Wherefore I see an eternal war

susceptum esse mihi cum perditis
to have-been-undertaken to me (by me) with lost (abandoned)

civibus: quod, vestro auxilio, que omnium
citizens: which, by your aid, and (by that) of all

bonorum, que memoriâ tantorum periculorum,
the good, and by the memory of so-great dangers,

quæ semper hærebit, non modo in hoc populo qui
which always will adhere, not only in this people which

servatus est, sed etiam in sermonibus ac mentibus
has-been-preserved, but also in the discourses and the mind

omnium gentium, ego confido posse facile propulsari
of all nations, I trust to be-able easily to be-repulsed

a me atque a meis. Neque profecto ulla tanta
from me and from mine. Nor indeed any so-great

vis reperietur, quæ possit perfringere et
violence will be-found, which may-be-able to break-through and

labefactare vestram conjunctionem que Romanorum
to overthrow your union and (that) of the Roman

equitum, et tantam conspirationem omnium bonorum.
knights, and so-great agreement of all the good.

11. Cum quæ sint ita, conscripti patres,
Since which (things) may-be so, conscript fathers,

pro imperio, pro exercitu, pro provinciâ, quam
for the command, for the army, for the province, which

neglexi, pro triumpho, que ceteris insignibus
I have-neglected, for the triumph, and the other marks

laudis, quæ repudiata sunt a me, propter
of praise, which have-been-rejected by me, because-of

custodiam urbis que vestræ salutis, pro
the guardianship of the city and of your safety, for

clientelis que hospitiis provincialibus,
the clientships and friendships belonging-to-the-provinces (for my

quæ tamen tueor
clients and friends in the provinces), which yet I defend

opibus urbanis non minore labore
by the resources belonging-to-the-city not with less labour

quam comparo: igitur pro omnibus his
than I procure (them): therefore for all these

rebus, pro meis singularibus studiis in vos,
things, for my singular studies (ardour) unto you,

que pro hâc diligentiâ, quam conspicitis, ad
and for this (my) diligence, which you perceive, to (for)

rempublicam conservandam, postulo nihil aliud
the republic to be-preserved, I require nothing other (else)

a vobis, nisi memoriam hujus temporis,
from you, unless the memory (remembrance) of this time,

que totius mei consulatus: dum quæ erit
and of the whole of my consulship: while which shall-be

infixa vestris mentibus arbitrator me esse septum
infixed to your minds I shall-think myself to be inclosed

firmissimo muro. Quod si vis improborum
by a most-strong wall. But-if the violence of the dishonest

fefellerit atque superaverit meam spem,
shall-have-deceived and shall-have-overcome my hope,

commendo vobis meum parvum filium; cui profecto
I commend to you my little son; to whom indeed

erit satis præsidii, non solum ad
there will-be enough of guard (protection), not only to (for)

salutem, verum etiam ad dignitatem, si
safety, but even to (for) dignity, if

memineritis illum esse filium ejus
you shall-have-remembered him to be the son of that person

qui solus conservaverit omnia hæc suo
who alone may-have-preserved all these (things) at his-own

periculo. Quapropter, conscripti patres, decernite
danger. On-which-account, conscript fathers, decree

diligenter, ut instituistis, ac fortiter, de
diligently, as you have-begun, and boldly, concerning

vestrâ summâ salute, que Romani populi,
your highest safety, and (that) of the Roman people,

de vestris conjugibus ac liberis, de
concerning your wives and children, concerning

aris ac focis, de fanis ac templis,
(your) altars and hearths, concerning (your) fanes and temples.

de tectis ac sedibus totius urbis,
concerning the roofs and seats (abodes) of the whole city,

de imperio, de libertate, de salute
concerning the empire, concerning liberty, concerning the safety

Italiæ, que de universâ republicâ. Enim
of Italy, and concerning the whole republic. For

habetis eum consulem qui dubitet non et
you have that consul who may-doubt (hesitate) not both

parere vestris decretis, et defendere ea
to obey to your decrees, and to defend those (things)

quæ statueritis quoad vivet, et
which you shall-have-determined as-long-as he shall-live, and

præstare per se ipsum, possit.
to perform (them) by himself, (as-long-as) he may-be-able.

ORATIO
THE ORATION

MARCI TULLII CICERONIS,
OF MARCUS TULLIUS CICERO

PRO
FOR

A. LICINIO ARCHIA POËTA.
A. LICINUS ARCHIAS THE POET.

1. Si quid ingenii est in me judices, quod
If aught of talent is in me O judges, (and) which

quam exiguum sit sentio; aut si qua exercitatio
how slight it-is I-feel; or if any practice

dicendi, in quâ non infitior me esse
in (public) speaking, in which I do not deny (that) I am

mediocriter versatum; aut si aliqua ratio
moderately experienced; or if any method [systematic

hujusce rei
knowledge] of-this-same thing [of this same art of public speaking]

profecta ab studiis optimarum artium
arising from the-study of-the-best arts [liberal sciences]

ac disciplinâ, a quâ ego confiteor nullum
and from-instruction, from which I confess no

tempus meæ ætatis abhoruisse.
time [part] of-my life to-have-been-averse [to have been

Hic A. Licinus debet vel in
estranged] This A. Licinus ought [is entitled] even in [among]

primis repetere a me fructum omnium
the-first to-claim-in-return from me the fruit [benefit] of all

(123)

earum **rerum** **prope** **sue**
these things [of all these mental endowments] nearly-(as) his

jure. **Nam** **quoad** **longissimè** **mea** **mens**
(own peculiar) right. For as far (as) my mind

potest **respicere** **spatium** **præteriti** **temporis,** **et**
can look-back (on) the space of past time, and

recordari **ultimam** **memoriam** **pueritiæ,**
(can) recall the-most-remote remembrance (of early) youth,

repetens **inde** **usque,** **video**
repeating [tracing] (my life) thence even-to (the present time), I-see

hunc **exstitisse** **mihi** **principem,**
this (man) to-have-been to-me (my) principal (leader);

et ad suscipiendam, **et ad ingrediendam**
both in undertaking, and in entering-on (progressing in)

rationem **horum** **studiorum.** **Quod** **si**
the-method [principles] of these studies. Because [and] if

hæc vox **conformata** **hortatu** **que**
this voice (of mine) formed by-the-encouragement and

præceptis hujus, **fuit aliquando** **saluti**
precepts of this (man), was at-any-time a means (of) safety

nonnullis, debemus profectò quantum **est situm in**
to some, we ought certainly as much (as) is placed in

nobis **fere** **et** **opem** **et** **salutem**
us [as far as lies in our power] to bring both aid and safety

huic **ipsi,** **a** **quo** **accepimus** **id,** **quo**
to this (man) himself, from whom we-have-received that, by which

possemus **opitulari** **et** **servare** **alios.** **Ac ne**
we-might (be able) to aid and to-save others. And lest

quis **a** **nobis** **forte** **miretur** **hoc ita**
any-one from (among) us by-chance might-wonder (at) this so

dici, **quod** **sit** **in** **hoc** **quædam** **alia**
said (by me), because there-is in this (Archias) some other

facultas ingenii **que** **ne** **hæc**
faculty of-genius (a somewhat different talent) and not this

ratio **aut disciplina** **dicendi,**
science, or discipline (of public) speaking (which we may possess),

ne quidem fuimus nos **unquam penitùs dediti**
nor indeed were we (ourselves) ever entirely given

huic uni studio. Etenim omnes artes, quæ
to-this one study (of oratory). For all the arts, which

pertinent ad humanitatem habent
may-relate to humanity [to liberal and polite studies] have

quoddam commune vinculum, et continentur
some common bond (of union) and are contained

quasi quâdam cognatione inte
[are connected together] as-if by some relationship amon

se.
themselves.

2. Sed ne videatur esse mirum cui
But (that) it' may not 'appear to be wonderful to-any (one)

vestrum, me in legitimâ questione, et in publico
of you, (that) I in a legal question, and in a public

judicio, cum res agatur apud
court (of justice) when the thing (the action) is tried before

prætorem Romani populi lectissimum virum,
a prætor of-the-Roman people the-most-select of men

et apud severissimos judices,
[a most meritorious man], and before most-grave [strict] judges,

tanto conventu ac frequentiâ hominum uti
(and) in such an assembly and multitude of men should use

hoc genere dicendi, quod abhorreat non modò
this kind (of public) speaking, which is at variance not only

a consuetudine judiciorum verum etiam a
with the custom of courts (of justice) but also with

forensi sermone : quæso a vobis, ut
forensic speech [pleading at the bar]: I request of you, that

detis mihi, in hac causâ, hanc veniam,
you-may-grant me, in this case, that indulgence,

accommodatam huic reo, quemadmodum spero
suitable to this defendant, (and) as I-hop

non molestam vobis, ut patiamini me dicentem pro
not disagreeable to-you, that you may allow me pleading for

summo poëtâ atque eruditissimo homine, hoc
a distinguished poet and for-a-most-learned man, in this

concursu literatissimorum hominum, hac vestrâ
concourse of-most-instructed men, before-this your

humanitate,
humanity [before a court constituted of men distinguished for such liberal

denique, hoc prætore exercente judicium,
knowledge], in-fine, such-a prætor exercising judicature

loqui paullò liberiùs de studiis
[presiding at the trial], to speak a little more-freely of the studies

humanitatis ac literarum, et in personâ ejusmodi,
of-the-liberal-arts and literature, and in a character such-as-this,

quæ, propter otium ac studium, est minimè
who, on account (of his) quiet-life and studies, 'is very little

tractata in judiciis que periculis, uti propè
conversant in public trials and (their) risks, to use nearly

quodam novo et inusitato genere dicendi.
a certain new and unusual mode of-speaking.

Quod si sentiam tribui que
Which (indulgence) if (as) I feel is to be granted and

concedi mihi a vobis, profectò perficiam, ut
allowed to me by you, assuredly I-will-effect, that

putetis, hunc A. Licinium non modo non
you-may-think, (that) this A. Licinium 'is not only not

segregandum a numero civium
to be separated from the number of citizens [to be deprived of the

cum sit civis, verùm etiam, si
rights of citizenship] when he is a-citizen, but (that) also, if

esset non, fuisse adsciscendum.
ne were not (a citizen), he-ought-to-have-been admitted (among them).

3. Nam ut Archias primum excessit ex pueris,
For as Archias first grew-out of boyhood,

atque ab iis artibus, quibus puerilis ætas
and from (the study of) those arts, by-which puerile age

solet informari ad humanitatem contulit se ad
is-wont to be trained to liberal knowledge he devoted himself to

studium scribendi : primùm Antiochiæ
to-the-study of writing [poetic composition] : at first at Antioch

nam natus est ibi nobili loco)
for he-was-born there in-an-illustrious rank) [of a noble family]

quondam celebri et copiosâ urbe, atque affluenti,
formerly a celebrated and rich city, and abounding,

eruditissimis hominibus, que   liberalissimis
with-the-most-learned   men,   and (celebrated for)   liberal

studiis, contigit   celeriter antecellere omnibus
studies,   it-happened (to him) speedily   to excel   all

glorià   ingenii. Pòst in ceteris partibus
in the renown (of his) talents. Afterwards in   other   parts

Asiæ que cunctæ Græciæ, ejus adventus celebrabantur
of-Asia and of all Greece,   his   arrivals   were celebrated

sic,   ut exspectatio   hominis
so [were so much talked of], that the expectation of-the-man [desire

superaret   famam   ingenii,
of seeing the man] might exceed (even) the fame of (his) talents (but),

adventus ipsius que admiratio
the arrival of himself and the admiration (it caused even surpassed)

exspectationem. Italia erat tunc plena Græcarum
the expectation.   Italy was then full   of-Greek

artium ac disciplinarum, que hæc studia colebantur
arts   and   culture,   and these studies were cultivated

et tum in Latio vehementiùs, quam   nunc in
both then in Latium more ardently, than (they are) now in

iisdem   oppidis, et hìc Romæ   propter
the-same   towns,   and here at-Rome (for) on-account-of

tranquillitatem reipublicæ   non negligebantur
the tranquillity of the republic 'they were not 'neglected (but

Itaque et Tarentini et Rhegini
flourished greatly). Therefore both the Tarentinians and the Rhegians

et Neapolitani donarunt hunc civitate
and the Neapolitans rewarded   him with-the-city [granted him

que ceteris præmiis; et omnes
the rights of citizenship] and with-other gifts; and all (men)

qui poterant judicare aliquid de ingeniis
who could   judge   any-thing of talents [who had discern

existimarunt dignum
ment enough to distinguish merit] thought (him) worthy (of their)

cognitione atque hospitio. Cum esset jam notus
acquaintance and hospitality. When he-was already known

hac tantâ celebritate famæ absentibus, venit
by-this so-great celebrity of reputation to-those-absent, he came

Romam, Mario   consule,   et Catulo.   Nactus est,
to-Rome,   Marius   being-consul, and   Catulus.   He-found,

primùm, eos consules, quorum alter posset adhibere
at first,   those consuls, of whom the one could   furnish (him)

maximas   res   ad   scribendum,   cum   alter
the greatest subjects to be-written-on, when the other (could not

        res   gestas,   tum etiam
only furnish him) things performed [military achievements], but   also

            studium atque   aures.   Statim
(an attachment to liberal) studies and (correct) ears. Immediately

Luculli, cum Aarchias esset etiam tum prætextatus,
the Luculli, though Aarchias was   even   then   a young-man,

receperunt   eum   suam   domum.   Sed hoc
received   him 'into   their   'house.   But this (was)

non solum   ingenii ac   literarum,
not   only (on account 'of his) 'talents and 'of (his) 'learning,

verùm etiam   naturæ   atque
but   also 'of (his) 'nature [good natural disposition]   and

  virtutis,   ut domus, quæ fuerit prima
'of (his) 'virtue, that the house, which had been the first (residence)

hujus adolescentiæ, eadem esset familiarissima
of his   youth,   the same   was   most-familiar

  senectuti.   Erat illis temporibus jucundus
'to (his) 'old age. He was at-that   time   agreeable

              Q. Metello illi   Numidico,
[held in affectionate esteem] to Q. Metellus that (celebrated) Numidicus,

et ejus filio Pio.   Audiebatur a M. Æmilio;
and his son Pius. He-was-listened-to by   M. Æmilius;

vivebat   cum Q. Catulo, et patre et
he lived (on terms of intimacy) with Q. Catulus, both father and

filio ;   colebatur   a L. Crasso. Cum   teneret
son ; he-was-greatly-esteemed by L. Crassus. When (as also) he held

devinctam   consuetudine   Lucullos vero,
attached (to himself) by habits (of intimacy) the-Luculli indeed,

et Drusum, et Octavios, et Catonem, et   totam
also Drusus, and the-Octavii, and   Cato,   and the-whole

domum Hortensiorum,   afficiebatur   summo
family   of the Hortensii, he-was-rewarded with-the-greatest

honore;   quod
honour [he was held by them in the greatest honour and esteem];   for

non solum   colebant eum,   qui
not   only (those) cultivated him [courted his acquaintance], who

studebant percipere atque audire aliquid, verùm
studied   to learn   and   to hear something,   but

etiam, si qui   forte simulabant.
also,   if any one by chance affected (this).

4.   Interim,   satis   longo   intervallo,
In-the-meanwhile, a sufficiently long   interval (of time

           cum esset profectus cum L. Lucullo in
having elapsed), when he had   gone   with L. Lucullo into

Siciliam, et cum decederet ex eâ provinciâ cum
Sicily,   and when he departed from that province with

eodem Lucullo, venit Heracleam. Quæ cum esset
the-same Lucullus, he came to Heraclea. Which as it-was

civitas   æquissimo   jure   ac
a-city (enjoying) the-very-same rights (and privileges with Rome) and

        fœdere   voluit   adscribi   se   in
'in (strict) 'alliance (therewith) he desired to-be-enrolled himself in

eam civitatem;   que cum ipse putaretur dignus
that   city (as a citizen); and as he was thought worthy

        per se,   tum auctoritate et graciâ Luculli
(of it) by himself, as-well-as by-the-authority and favour of Lucullus

impetravit id ab Heracleensibus.   Civitas
he obtained this from the Heracleans. The-rights-of-Roman-citizenship

est data   lege   Silvani et Carbonis. "Si
was granted (to him) by-the-law of-Silvanus and of Carbo. "If

qui   fuissent adscripti fœderatis   civitatibus;
any-persons had-been enrolled among-the-confederated cities;

si cum lex   ferebatur habuissent domicilium in
if when the-law was-passed they had   a-residence in

Italiâ; et si sexaginta diebus essent professi apud
Italy;   and if in sixty days they had declared before

prætorem."   Cum hic haberet
the prætor (their wish to be enrolled as citizens)." As he   had

jam domicilium multos annos, professus est
already a residence (of) many years, he-declared (his intention)

apud Q. Metellum, prætorem, suum familiarissimum.
before   Q. Metellus,   the prætor,   his   most-intimate-friend.

Si dicimus nihil aliud nise de   civitate ac lege,
If   we-say nothing else except about (his) citizenship and the law

dico   nihil   ampliùs;   causa
(as relates to it), 'I (need) 'say nothing more;   the cause

dicta est.   Enim quid horum   Grati
is-pleaded (and is gained). For which of these (statements) O Gratius

potest infirmari?   ne negabis   esse
can   be-invalidated? 'you 'will not 'deny (that) he-was

adscriptum tum   Heracleæ?   Adest
enrolled   then (among the citizens) at Heraclea? There is present

vir   summâ auctoritate, et religione
a man (having) the highest   authority,   and   religion [scrupulous

et fide, L. Lucullus, qui dicit   se
regard for truth] and integrity, L. Lucullus, who says (that) he

non opinari, sed   scire,   non
does not think, but (that) he knows (it to be so), (that) 'he 'did not

audivise, sed vidisse   non interfuisse,
'hear, but saw (it) (that) 'he 'was not only 'present,

sed egisse.   Heracleenses legati adsunt,
but acted (in the affair). Heraclean delegates are present,

nobilissimi homines;   venerunt causâ
most-celebrated men (of the highest rank); they-have-come on account

hujus judicii, cum mandatis   et cum publico
of this trial, with instructions (from their city) and with public

testimonio; qui dicunt hunc   adscriptum
testimony; who say (that) he (was) a naturalized

Heracleensem. Hìc tu desideras publicas tabulas
Heraclean. Here you desire the public registers

Heracleensium, quas omnes scimus interisse
of the Heracleans, which 'we all 'know to-have-perished

Italico   bello, tabulario incenso. Est ridiculum,
in the-Italian war, the registry being burned. It is ridiculous,

dicere nihil ad ea   quæ habemus; quærere
to say nothing to those (proofs) which we have; (but) to ask-for

quæ possumus non habere; et tacere
(those) which we can not have; and to be silent

de **memoriâ** **hominum,** **flagitare**
concerning the recollection [testimony] of men, (and) to-insist-on

memoriam **literarum;** **et** **cum** **habeas**
the testimony of records; and when you-may-have

religionem **amplissimi** **viri,**
the conscientious-testimony of a most-honourable man, (and)

jusjurandum **que** **fidem** **integerrimi** **municipii,**
the oath and faith of a most-respectable municipality,

epudiare **ea,** **quæ** **possunt** **nullo** **modo**
to reject these (things), which can in no manner

depravari **desiderare** **tabulas,** **quas** **idem** **dicis**
be falsified (and) to require registers, which even you-say

solere **corrumpi.** **At habuit non domicilium in**
are accustomed to be altered. But he-had not a domicile in

Italiâ: **is qui** **tot** **annis ante civitatem datam,**
Italy: (not) he who for-so-many years before citizenship was granted

collocavit sedem **omnium** **suarum** **rerum** **ac**
(him), had placed the seat of all his effects and

fortunarum **Romæ?** **At** **non est professus?**
of all his fortunes at Rome? But 'he 'did not declare (his

Immo vero **iis**
intention of becoming a citizen)? Yes indeed (he did, and) in-those

tabulis **professus** **quæ** **solæ** **ex** **illâ**
registers did he declare (his intention) which alone out-of that

professione, **que** **collegio** **prætorum** **obtinent**
declaration, and college of prætors obtains

autoritatem publicarum tabularum.
the authority of public registers.

5. Nam cum tabulæ **Appii dicerentur** **asservatæ**
For as the registers of Appius were-said (to) have-been-kept

negligentius, **levitas** **Gabinii**
very carelessly, the trifling (and inconsistent conduct) of Gabinus

quamdiu **fuit** **incolumis,** **calamitas** **post**
as-long-as he-was safe (and), the misfortune after (his)

damnationem, **resignasset** **omnem fidem tabularum;**
condemnation, had-taken-away all the faith of the registers

Metellus, **homo**
[had deprived his registers of all credit]; Metellus, a man

sanctissimus que modestissimus omnium,   fuit tanta
the most pure   and   scrupulous   of all (men), was   so

    diligentia,   ut   venerit   ad   L. Lentulum
(full of)   care,   that   he came   to   L. Lentulus

prætorem,   et   ad judices,   et   dixerit,   se esse
the prætor,   and   to the judges,   and   said (that),   he was

commotum   liturâ   unius nominis. Igitur   his
disturbed   by-the-erasure of-a-single   name.   Therefore in these

tabulis videtis nullam lituram in nomen A. Licinii.
registers you-see   no   erasure   in the name of A. Licinius.

Quæ   cum sint ita, quid est quod   dubitetis
Which (things) when they are so, what is there that you-may-doubt

de ejus civitate, præsertim cum fuerit adscriptus
about his citizenship,   especially   as   he was   enrolled

quoque in aliis civitatibus?   Etenim cum
also   in other   cities (as a citizen)?   For   when

homines in Græciâ   impertiebantur
the men   in   Greece [Magna Græcia, or Southern Italy]   granted

    civitatem   multis mediocribus, et præditis
the-rights-of-citizenship   to many   ordinary-men,   and   endowed

aut nullâ arte aut aliquâ humili,   gratuitò,
either with no profession or   some low-one, (and this) gratuitously

    credo   Rheginos   aut   Locrenses,   aut
(can) I believe, (that) the Rhegians   or   the Locrians,   or

Neapolitanos, aut Tarentinos noluisse   id huic
the Neapolitans,   or   Tarentines would not (give) that to him

prædito summâ gloriâ ingenii, quod   solebant
endowed-with the greatest renown of talent, which they-were-accustomed

largiri scenicis artificibus. Quid? cum ceteri, non
to grant to theatrical   artists.   What? when others,   not

modo post civitatem   datam,   sed etiam
only   after   citizenship had-been-granted (to them), but   also

post Papiam legem, irrepserint aliquo modo in
after   the Papian law,   had crept   by some means into

tabulas eorum municiporum; hic rejicietur, qui
the registers of these   municipalities; [1]will-he-be [1]rejected,   who

ne utitur   quidem illis in quibus est
does not [1]avail (himself) indeed of those in   which   he is

scriptus, quòd semper voluit se esse
enrolled, because ¹he always ¹wished himself to be (considered)

Heracleensem. Requiris nostros census
a Heraclean. You demand our census [the censor's lists]

scilicet. Est enim obscurum, proximis censoribus
indeed. It is then unknown (that), under-the-last censors

hunc fuisse cum
[at the time of taking the last census] he was with

clarissimo imperatore L. Lucullo apud exercitum;
the-most-illustrious commander L. Lucullus with the army;

superioribus fuisse cum
(that at the time of) the-preceding (census to this last) he-was with

eodem quæstore in Asiâ;
the same (person when he was) quæstor in Asia; (that)

primis Julio et Crasso
in-the-first (census, after he became a citizen) Julius and Crassus

nullam partem populi esse censam.
(being censors) no part of-the-people was rated

Sed quoniam census non
[no census was taken]. But as the census ¹does not

confirmat jus civitatis, ac tantummodò indicat
¹confirm the-right of-citizenship, and only indicates

eum, qui sit census se
(that) he, who may-be rated [returned in the census] (that) he

jam tum gessisse ita, pro cive;
already then had-conducted (himself) so, as a citizen (as to claim

iis temporibus, quæ tu criminaris
enrollment); at-the-same time, that you charge (that)

ne quidem ipsius judicio eum versatum esse
not even ¹in his-own ¹opinion ¹did he ¹exercise

jure Romanorum civium, et sæpe fecit
the right of Roman citizens, ¹he both often ¹made

testamentum nostris legibus, et adiit
a will (according) to our laws. and he entered on

hæreditas Romanorum civium, et
inheritances (left to him by) Roman citizens, and (his name)

delatus est ad ærarium in beneficiis,
was-carried to the-public-treasury among the-beneficiaries [and the

a L.
honourable mention of his name was enrolled in the public treastry], by L.

Lucullo proconsule.
Lucullus the proconsul.

6. Quære argumenta, si potes quæ
Seek (for other) proofs, if you can (find) any

Enim hic nunquam revincetur neque suo
For this (Archias) never will-be-refuted either by-his-own

judicio, neque amicorum.
opinion, or (that of his) friends.

Quæres a nobis, Grati, cur tantopere
You ask of us, O Gratius, why ¹we ¹are so greatly

delectemur hoc homine. Quia suppeditat nobis
¹taken-up with-this man. Because he supplies us

ubi et animus reficiatur ex hoc forensi
(with that) whereby both the mind may-be-refreshed after this forensic

strepitu et aures defessæ convicio
noise [after the noise of the forum] and the ears fatigued with wrangling

conquiescant. An tu existimas, aut posse
may-find-repose. Or do you suppose, either (that it) would-be-possible

nobis suppetere, quod
for us to-have-a sufficient supply (of subjects), which

dicamus quotidie, in tantâ varietate rerum,
we-might-discourse-on daily, in such a-variety of things

nisi excolamus nostros animos
[pleadings], unless we-cultivated our minds

doctrinâ, aut animos posse ferre
by the study of literature, or (that) (our) minds could bear

tantam contentionem, nisi relaxemus eos eâdem
such (great) efforts, unless we relaxed them by-the-same

doctrinâ? Ego vero fateor, me esse deditum
tudies? I indeed confess (that), I am given

his studiis; pudeat ceteros si qui ita
to-these studies; ¹let others ¹be ashamed, if they ¹have so

abdiderunt se literis, ut possint
¹buried themselves in literature [in the study of], that they can

affere   nihil   ex   his,   neque   ad   communem
bring   nothing   from   these (studies), either   for   the common

fructum, neque   profere   in   adspectum
advantage,   or   to-bring-forth (any thing) to   the view (of men)

que   lucem.
and   the-light [or to publish any thing that may bear inspection].

Autem   quid   me   pudeat,   judices,   qui   tot
But   why (need)   I   be ashamed,   O judges,   who   so-many

annos   vivo   ita,   ut   unquam   aut   meum
years   live [have lived] so,   that   ever   either   my

otium   abstraxerit   me,   aut   voluptas
leisure [love of tranquillity] may-have-drawn   me from,   or   pleasure

avocarit,   aut   denique   somnus
may-have-called (me) from,   or   in fine   sleep

retardarit   tempore   aut   commodo
may-have-retarded (me) from   the dangers   or   advantage

nullius ?
of any one [from defending those in danger, or forwarding the advan-

Quare quis tandem reprehendat
tageous claims of others]? Wherefore who   in fine   may-reproach

me, aut quis jure   succenseat   mihi,   si   quantum
me,   or   who by right   may-be-angry   with me,   if   as-much

temporum conceditur ceteris, ad obeundas suas   res,
time (as)   is conceded   to others,   for   transacting their   affairs,

quantum   ad celebrandos festos dies ludorum,
as-much (as is given) for   celebrating   festival days   of games,

quantum   ad alias voluptates, et ad requiem
as-much (as is given) to   other   pleasures,   and to   the rest

ipsam   animi   et   corporis;   quantum   alii
itself   of the mind and   of the body;   as-much (time as) others

tribuunt   tempestivis   conviviis,
devote   to early   banquets [to the pleasures of the table

quantum denique   aleæ,   quantum
as-much   in-fine (as is devoted) to dice [games of hazard],   as-much

pilæ;   tantum   egomet sumpsero
(as is devoted to) ball-playing; so-much   (time)   I shall-have-taken

mihi   ad   recolenda   hæc
to myself [may I not take the same time] for   again-cultivating   these

studia? Atque hoc est adeo magis concedendum
studies? And this is so-much the more to-be-allowed

mihi, quòd ex his studiis quoque hæc facultas et
to me, because from these studies also this faculty and

oratio crescit, quæ,
speaking [this faculty of public speaking] improves (in me), which,

quantacunque est in me, nunquam defuit
in-whatever-degree it exists in me, never was-wanting

periculis amicorum.
to-the-dangers 'of (my) 'friends [never was refused to defend my friends

Quæ si videtur levior cui, certe
a danger]. Which if it-may-seem trifling to-any-one, certainly

quidem sentio, ex quo fonte hauriam, illa
indeed I-know, from what source I-may-draw, those (subjects

quæ sunt summa. Nam, nisi suasissem mihi
which are the most-important. For, unless I-had-persuaded myself

ab adolescentiâ, præceptis multorum, que
from youth (upwards), by-the-precepts of many (masters), and

multis literis esse nihil in vitâ, magnopere
by much literary-study (that) there is nothing in life, greatly

expetendum, nisi laudem atque honestatem,
to be-sought-after, except praise and honesty [an

autem in persequendâ ea,
honourable name], but in following (the attainment of) these,

omnes cruciatus corporis, omnia pericula mortis atque
all tortures of-the-body, all the dangers of death and

exsilii, esse ducenda parvi; nunquam
of exile, are to be held as of small (account); never

objecissem me pro vestrâ salute in tot ac tantas
had-I-exposed myself for your safety in so many and so-great

dimicationes, atque in hos quotidianos impetus
contests, and in these daily attacks

profligatorum hominum. Sed omnes libri sunt pleni,
of profligate men. But all books are full,

voces sapientium plenæ, vetustas
the voices of-the-wise are full (of the maxims of philosophy), antiquity

plena exemplorum; omnia quæ jacerent in
(is) full of examples all which might-have-lain in

tenebris, nisi lumen literarum accederet.
darkness, unless the light of literature had-approached (them)

Quàm multas imagines fortissimorum virorum
How many images [delineations] of the bravest men

expressas, non solum ad intuendum, verum etiam ad
delineated, not only to be contemplated, but also to

imitandum, et Græci et Latini scriptores
be imitated, 'have both the Greek and Latin writers

reliquerunt nobis; quas ego, semper preponens
'left us; which I, always placing

mihi in administrandâ republica,
before me in conducting the republic [in administering public

conformabam meam mentem et animum ipsâ
affairs], moulded my mind and soul by this

cogitatione excellentium hominum.
contemplation of excellent men.

7. Quispiam quæret; quid? fuerunt illi ipsi
'Should any one 'inquire; what? were those same

summi viri, quorum virtutes proditæ sunt
illustrious men, whose virtues have-been-handed-down (to us)

literis, eruditi istane doctrinâ, quam tu effers
in books, instructed in-this-same learning, which you extol (by your)

laudibus. Est difficile confirmare hoc de omnibus;
praises. It is difficult to-affirm this of all,

sed tamen est certum, quid respondeam.
but yet this is certain, which I-may-answer (thereto).

Ego fateor multos homines fuisse excellenti
I confess (that) many men have-been with distinguished

animo ac virtute, et sine doctrinâ, propè
minds and virtue, and without learning, as-if-nearly

divino habitu naturæ ipsius, extitisse per
by-the-divine disposition of nature itself, have-become of

se ipsos et moderatos et graves. Adjungo
themselves both discreet and important (men). I add

etiam illud sæpius naturam, sine doctrinâ
also this (that) more-often nature, without learning

valuisse ad laudem atque virtutem, quàm doctrinam
has-availed for fame and virtue, than learning

sine naturâ. Atque ego
without nature [without a good natural disposition]. And I

contendo idem, cum quædam ratio, que
contend at-the-same (time), when a certain method, and

conformatio doctrinæ accesserit ad eximiam atque
modelling of learning accedes to an excellent and

illustrem naturam, tum illud
illustrious nature [natural disposition], then (that) that

nescio quid præclarum ac singulare
I-know-not what brilliant and extraordinary (in the character)

solere existere; ex hoc numero esse hunc
is-accustomed to-take-place; of this number was that

divinum hominem Africanum, quem nostri patres
divine man Africanus, whom our fathers

viderunt; ex hoc C. Lælium L. Furium,
saw; of this (number was) C. Lælium (and) L. Furius,

moderatissimos et continentissimos homines; ex hoc
most-discreet and continent men; of this

fortissimum virum, M. Catonem,
(number was also that) most-vigorous man, M. Cato,

illum senem, et doctissimus illis temporibus,
that old man [the elder], and the-most-learned in-those times.

qui profectò si nihil adjuvarentur literis
who (all) indeed if 'they 'had not 'been-aided by literature

ad percipiendam que colendam virtutem, nunquam
in understanding and cultivating virtue, 'would never

contulissent se ad studium earum.
'have-applied themselves to the study of them [literature].

Quod si hic tantus fructus non ostenderetur,
Even if this so-great advantage 'should not 'be-made-apparent,

et si delectatio sola peteretur ex his studiis, tamen,
and if delight only is sought from these studies, however,

ut opinor, judicaretis hanc adversionem animi
as I think, you-would-judge this employment of-the-mind

humanissimam ac liberalissimam. Nam ceteræ
most-human and liberal. For other

sunt neque omnium temporum,
(occupations) are (proper) neither (for) all times,

neque ætatum, neque locorum; hæc studia
nor (for all) ages, nor (for all) places; these studies

alunt adolescentiam, oblectant senectutem, ornant
foster youth, delight old-age, adorn

secundas res, adversis præbent perfugium ac
prosperity, in adversity they offer a refuge and

solatium, delectant domi, non impediunt
a comfort, they-delight (us) at-home, 'they 'do not ʰhinder (us)

foris, pernoctant cum nobis, peregri-
abroad, they-pass-the-night with us, they-accompany-us-in-

nantur, rusticantur.
our-journeys, they-pass-the-time-with-us-in-the-country.

8. **Quòd si** ipsi possemus neque attingere
Although if we-ourselves could neither attain-to

hæc, neque gustare nostro sensu,
these, nor taste (them) with-our senses [nor enjoy them],

tamen deberemus mirari ea, etiam cum videremus
however we ought to admire them, even when we-see

in aliis. Quis nostrûm fuit tam agresti ac
(them) in others. Who of-us was (of) so rude and

duro animo, ut nuper morte Roscii non
insensible a mind, as lately at-the-death of-Roscius not (to)

commoveretur? Qui, mortuus esset cum
have-been-moved? Who (though he), died when (he was)

senex, tamen propter excellentem artem
an old-man, yet on-account-of (his) excellent art

ac venustatem, videbatur omninò
and the beauty (of his performance), appeared altogether (as if he)

debuisse non mori. Ergo ille tantum motu
ought not to die. Therefore (when) he only by-the-motion

corporis conciliarat sibi, a nobis
of (his) body [by his gestures] had gained for himself, from us

omnibus, amorem, nos negligemus incredibiles
all, (our) love, 'should we ʰneglect the incredible

motus animorum, que celeritatem ingeniorum?
movements of-the-mind, and the-celerity of talents?

Quoties, judices, vidi ego hunc Archiam, (enim
How-often, O judges, 'have I ʰseen this Archias, (for

utar vestrâ benignitate, quoniam tam diligenter
I-will-use your kindness, since you so attentively

attenditis me, in hoc novo genere dicendi), quoties
listen to-me, in this novel kind of pleading), how-often

vidi ego hunc, cum scripsisset nullam literam,
'have I 'seen him, when he-had-written not (even) a letter,

dicere ex tempore magnum numerum optimorum
to recite extempore a great number of the best

versuum, de iis ipsis rebus, quæ tum
verses, concerning the very same affairs, which 'were then

agerentur! quoties revocatum dicere eandem
'transacting! as-often-as he-was-recalled to-repeat the same

rem, commutatis verbis atque sententiis!
thing (he did it), with changed words and sentences!

Quæ vero scripsisset accuratè que cogitate,
That indeed which he-had-written accurately and with-reflection,

vidi ea sic probari, ut
I-have-seen them 'to-be so 'approved, that 'they (seemed as if)

pervenirent ad laudem veterum scriptorum.
they-had-attained to the praise of ancient writers [to the praise

Ego non diligam hunc?
bestowed on ancient writers]. 'Shall I not 'love this (man)?

non admirer? non putem
not admire (him)? 'may-I not 'think (that I ought)

defendendum omni ratione? Atqui,
to defend (him) by all means (in my power)? Moreover,

sic accepimus a summis que eruditissimis
'we-have so 'learned from most-eminent and most-learned

hominibus studia et doctrina ceterarum rerum
men, (that) the studies and science of other things

constare et præceptis et arte, poëtam valere
consists both in-precepts and art, (that) the poet prevailed

naturâ ipsâ, et excitari viribus
(as such) by nature itself, and (that) he-was-excited by-the-vigour

mentis, et inflari quasi
of (his) mind, and (that) he-was-breathed-into [inspired] as-if

quodam divino spiritu. Quare suo jure ille
by-some divine spirit. Wherefore by-his-own right 'does this

noster Ennius appellat poëtas sanctos, quod
our Ennius ¹call poets holy, because

videantur esse commendati nobis quasi aliquo dono
they-seem to-be recommended to us as-if by-some gift

atque munere deorum. Igitur, judices, hoc nomen
and present of-the-Gods. ¹Let then, O judges, ¹his ¹name

poëtæ sit sanctum apud vos, homines humanissimos,
of poet ¹be sacred with you, men (of) most cultivated

quod nulla barbaria unquam
(minds), which (name of poet) no barbarous (nation) ever

violavit. Saxa et solitudines respondent voci;
violated. Rocks and deserts reply to-the-voice

immanes bestiæ sæpe flectuntur atque
(of the poet); savage beasts ¹are often ¹turned aside and

consistunt cantu; nos, instituti optimis rebus,
stand-still by song; we, formed to-the-best things [we who

non moveamur voce
have received the best education], ¹may not ¹we-be-moved by-the-voice

poëtarum? Colophonii dicunt Homerum esse suum
of the poets? The Colophonians say (that) Homer was their

civem, Chii vindicant suum, Salumnii
citizen, the Chians claim (him as) their (citizen), the Salumnians

repetunt, Smyrnæi verò confirmant esse
reclaim (him), the Smyrnians indeed assert (that) he-was

suum, itaque etiam dedicaverunt delubrum
theirs, (and) therefore also they-have-dedicated a temple

ejus in oppido; permulti alii præterea
of .. in (their) town; a-great-many other (places) besides

pugnant atque contendunt inter
fight and contend among

se.
themselves (for the honour of his birth-place).

9. Ergo expetunt alienum, quia fuit poëta,
Therefore they-claim a stranger, because he-was a poet

etiam post mortem; nos repudiamus hunc
even after (his) death; shall we repudiate this (Archias)

vivum, qui est noster, et voluntate et legibus?
alive, who is ours, both by (his) free will and by (our) laws?

præsertim cum olim Archias contulerit omne
especially   when   heretofore Archias contributed all (his)

studium atque omne ingenium, ad celebrandum
zeal   and   all (his) talents, to   celebrating

gloriam que laudem Romani populi? Nam et
the glory and praise of-the-Roman people? For also

adolescens attigit Cimbricas res,
when) a-young-man he-touched-on the Cimbrican affairs [on the wars

et fuit jucundus   illi C.
with the Cimbri], and was agreeable to [was in favour with] that C.

Mario ipsi, qui videbatur durior ad hæc
Marius himself, who seemed (to be) very-insensible to such

studia. Neque enim est quisquam tam aversus a
studies. Nor indeed is there any one so averse to

Musis qui non facile patiatur eternum præconium
the Muses who 'would not readily 'suffer the eternal panegyric

suorum laborum mandari versibus. Aiunt
of his labours to-be-committed to verse. They-say (that)

Themistoclem, illum summum virum Athenis, dixisse,
Themistocles, that greatest of men in Athens, had said,

cum quæreretur ex eo, quod acroama, aut cujus
when it-was-inquired of him, what player, or whose

vocem, libentissimè audiret; "ejus a quo
voice, 'he-would most-willingly 'hear; "his by whom

sua virtus optimè prædicaretur." Itaque
his virtue [exploits] 'might-be best 'celebrated." Therefore

lle Marius, item eximiè dilexit L. Plotium,
this (same) Marius, also greatly loved L. Plotius,

cujus ingenio putabat ea, quæ gesserat,
'by whose 'talents he thought that, which he-had-performed,

posse celebrari. Vero totum Mithridaticum bellum,
could-be celebrated. But all the Mithridatic war,

magnum atque difficile, et versatum in multâ
great and difficult (as it was), and carried-on in much

varietate terrâ que mari, expressum est ab
diversity (of success) by-land and by-sea, has-been-related by

hoc; qui libri illustrant non modo
this (Archias); which books (of poetry of his) shed-lustre-on not only

L. Lucullum,   fortissimum   et   clarissimum   virum,
L. Lucullus, (that)   most-brave   and   distinguished   man,

verum   etiam   nomen   Romani   populi.   Enim
but   also (on)   the name   of-the-Roman   people.   For

Romanus populus, Lucullo imperante, aperuit Pontum
'the Roman   people,   Lucullus commanding,   'laid-open   Pontus

vallatum quondam, et   regiis   opibus, et naturâ
defended   hitherto,   both by-the-royal resources, and by-the-nature

ipsâ   regionis;   exercitus Romani   populi,   eodem
itself of-the-country;   the army   of the Roman   people,   the same

duce,   non   maximâ   manu   fudit
(Lucullus) being general,   'with no   'very large   force   dispersed

innumerabiles copias Armeiorum; est   laus   Romani
countless   forces   of Armenians; it-is the glory of-the-Roman

populi,   amicissimam   urbem   Cyzicenorum,
people, (that)   the-most-friendly   city   of-the-Cyziceni,

consilio   ejusdem   esse ereptam atque
by the (wise) counsels of this-same (Lucullus) was   delivered-from   and

servatam   ex   omni regio   impetu,   ac   ore
preserved   from   every   royal   attack,   and from-the-mouth

ac   faucibus totius   belli;
and   jaws   of the whole   war [from the perils of a destructive war];

semper   feretur et   prædicabitur
(the glory) 'will always   be related and   celebrated (as peculiarly

nostra,   L. Lucullo   dimicante,   cum classis
our-own,   L. Lucullus   fighting (as our general), when   the fleet

hostium   depressa,   ducibus   interfectis,   et
of-the-enemy   was sunk,   the commanders (thereof) being slain,   and

illæ incredibilis navalis   pugna   apud   Tenedus;
that   incredible   naval   battle   at   Tenedos; (these)

sunt   nostra   tropæa,   nostra   monumenta,   nostri
are   our   trophies,   our   monuments,   our

triumphi.   Quare   quorum ingeniis
triumphs.   Therefore (I say that those men) 'by whose   'talents

hæc feruntur,   ab
these things)   are-diffused [are spread out among the people],   by

eiis   fama   Romani   populi   celebratur.   Noster
them 'is the glory of-the-Roman   people   'celebrated.   Our-own

Ennius fuit carus superiori Africano; itaque
Ennius was dear to the elder African (Scipio); therefore

etiam is putatur esse constitutus e marmore
also he is-supposed to-have-been constituted of marble

in sepulcro Scipionum.
[to have been sculptured in marble] on the sepulchre of-the-Scipios.

At ejus laudibus certè non solùm ipsi, qui
But 'by his 'praises certainly not only those, who

laudantur, sed etiam nomen Romani populi
are-praised, but also the name of-the-Roman people

ornatur. Cato, proavus hujus
is honoured. Cato, the-great-grandfather of this (Cato, here present,)

tollitur in cœlum; magnus honos adjungitur rebus
is extolled to the skies; great honour is attached to-the-affairs

Romani populi. Denique, omnes illi Maximi,
of-the-Roman people. In-fine, all the Maximi,

Marcelli, Fulvii, decorantur, non sine
the Marcelli, (and) the Fulvii, are honoured, not without

communi laude nostrûm omnium.
the common praise of-us all.

10. Ergo nostri majores receperunt illum,
Therefore our ancestors received him [Ennius],

qui fecerat hæc, hominem
who had-done this (who had written on these subjects) a man (of)

Rudinum in civitatem; nos ejiciemus
Rudiæ in (their) city (as a citizen); 'shall we 'reject

hunc Heracleensem de nostrâ civitate,
this Heraclean [Archias] from our citizenship, (a man)

expetitum multis civitatibus, autem in hac
sought by many cities, but in this (our city)

constitutum legibus?
constituted (a citizen) 'by (our) 'laws?

Nam si quis putat minorem fructum gloriæ
For if any one thinks that a smaller harvest of glory

percipi ex Græcis versibus, quàm ex Latinis,
is-to-be-obtained from Greek verses, than from Latin verses,

vehementer errat; propterea quòd Græca leguntur
he greatly errs; because that Greek (works) are read

in   fere omnibus gentibus, Latina   continentur
among almost   all   nations,   Latin (works) are confined

suis   finibus,   exiguis   sane.   Quare
to-their-own limits, (and these) small-enough without-doubt. Wherefore

si   eæ   res,   quas   gessimus   definiuntur
if   these things,   which we-have-performed   are-bounded (only)

regionibus   orbis   terræ,   debemus
by-the-regions of-the-circle of-the-earth [by the whole world], we-ought

cupere,   quò   tela   nostrarum   manuum
to desire (that), whither   the weapons   of our   hands

pervenerint,   eodem   gloriam   que
may-have-reached, (that into) the same (place) (our) glory   and

famam penetrare ;   quòd cum hæc   sunt
renown   'should (also) 'penetrate; because while these (things) are

ampla   ipsis   populıs, de   quorum   rebus   scribitur,
illustrious to those   people,   of   whose   affairs   it-is-written

tum   certè, hoc est
[whose exploits are the subjects of writing], then certainly, this   is

maximum incitamentum,   et periculorum
the greatest   incitement (to the encountering), both   of dangers

et laborum iis, qui dimicant de vitâ,   causâ
and of labours to those, who   fight   for   life, (and) the cause

gloriæ. Quam multos scriptores suarum rerum
of glory.   How   many   writers   of his   exploits 'is

ille magnus Alexander dicitur habuisse cum se !
the   great   Alexander   'said   to-have-had   with him !

Atque is tamen, cum adstitisset ad tumulum Achillis
And   he   yet,   when   he-stood   at   the grave of Achillis

in   Sigeo inquit, "O fortunate adolescens,
on (the promontory of) Sigeum said,   "O fortunate   young-man,

qui inveneris Homerum præconem tuæ vırtutis.''
who may-have-found a Homer   the panegyrist of thy   fame."

Et vere : nam nisi illa Ilias   extitisset, idem
And truly :   for   if   that   Iliad 'had (not) 'existed,   the same

tumulus, qui contexerat ejus corpus, etiam nomen,
grave,   which   covered   his   body,   even   the name

obruisset.   Quid ?   nonne hic   noster
(thereof), would-have-perished.   What ?   'did not   this   our-own

Magnus,   qui,   cum   adæquavit   fortunam
great (Pompey),   who,   when   he-equalled (his)   fortune

     virtute   donavit   Theophanem
'by (his) 'virtue (and valour)   grant   Theophanes

Mitylenæum, scriptorem suarum rerum   civitate
the Mitylenæan, the historian of his deeds the-rights-of-citizenship

in concione   militum? et illi nostri fortes viri, sed
in an assembly of-the-soldiers? and those our   brave men, but

rustici ac milites commoti quâdam dulcedine gloriæ,
rustics and soldiers moved by a certain charm of glory,

approbaverunt illud magno clamore, quasi participes
approved   it by a great shout,   as-if participants

ejusdem laudis? Itaque credo si Archias   non
of-the-same praise? Therefore I suppose if Archias 'had not

esset Romanus civis legibus, ut potuisset non
'been a Roman citizen by-the-laws, that 'he-could   not

    perficere   donaretur
'have brought (it) to-pass   (that) he should-be-presented

    civitate   ab aliquo imperatore!
with-the-rights-of-citizenship by   some commander (of ours)!

Cum Sulla donaret Hispanos et   Gallos,
When Sylla granted the Spaniards and the Gauls (the rights of

         credo   repudiasset   hunc petentem!
citizenship), I suppose he would-have refused him   petitioning

        quem   nos   vidimus in
(for the citizenship)! whom [Sylla] we (ourselves) have-seen in

concione, cum malus poëta de   populo
a-public-assembly, when a bad poet from (among) the people

subjecisset ei libellum, quòd fecisset epigramma,
had presented him a petition, because he-had-made an epigram

       in eum, tantummodo alternis longiusculis
[a short poem], on him,   only   in alternate somewhat-longer

versibus,   statim
verses [in alternate hexameters and pentameters], (that he) immediately

jubere præmium tribui ei,   ex iis rebus, quas
ordered a present to-be-given to him, of those things, which

    tunc vendebat, sub ea   conditione,
'he-was then 'selling,   under that condition, (that)

ne **scriberet quid** **postea.** **Qui**
ne-should-not write any-thing hereafter. (Would not he), whe

duxerit **sedulitatem** **mali poëtæ, tamen dignam**
had-thought the industry of-a-bad poet, yet worthy (of)

aliquo præmio, **expetisset** **ingenium et**
some reward, have-sought-out (to honour) the talents and

virtutem et copiam in scribendo hujus ? **Quid**
ability and copiousness in writing of this (Archias) ? What

neque impetravisset **a suo**
could-he neither 'have-obtained (the freedom of the city) from his

familiarissimo **Q. Metello Pio, qui donavit**
most intimate (friend) Q. Metello Pius, who had-granted

multos civitate, neque per se
many the-rights-of-citizenship, neither by himself [by his own request]

neque per Lucullos ? qui **præsertim usque**
nor by Luculli ? who [Metellus] especially so

eò cuperet scribi **de suis rebus,**
greatly desired to-be-written-on concerning his affairs, [to have his

ut etiam dederet suas aures
deeds commemorated] that 'he also gave his ears [attention]

poëtis natis Cordubæ, **sonantibus quiddam**
to poets born at Cordova, (though) uttering something

pingue atque peregrinum.
dull and barbarous.

11. Neque enim est hoc dissimulandum, quod
Nor indeed is that to-be-dissembled, which

potest non obscurari; sed ferendum præ nobis;
can not be-concealed; but is-to-be-brought before us

omnes trahimur studio
[but must be openly avowed] (that) 'we all 'are-drawn-on by-a-desire

laudis, et quisque optimus **ducitur**
of praise, and each best (person) [the best of us] 'is led

maximè gloriâ. Philosophi ipsi, etiam illis
chiefly by-glory. Philosophers themselves, also in-those

libellis, quos scribunt de gloriâ contemnendâ,
books, which they-write about glory to-be-despised,

inscribunt suum nomen ;
on the contempt of glory] inscribe their names (in the books) ;

in eo ipso,   in quo despiciunt prædicationem que
in the same (case) in which they-despise   praise   and

nobilitatem volunt   prædicari   de se,   ac   se
renown   they-wish to be mentioned themselves, and themselves

nominari.   Quidem
named. [They desire to become notorious, and to be talked of].   Indeed

Decimus Brutus, ille summus vir et imperator,
  Decimus Brutus,   that   great   man and   commander,

exornavit   aditus   suorum   templorum   ac
adorned   the approaches of his   temples   and

monumentorum carminibus Attii sui   amicissimi.
monuments   with-the-verses of Attius his most-intimate-friend.

    Jam vero, ille Fulvius, qui bellavit cum Ætolis,
(And) even also, that Fulvius, who fought with the Ætolians,

Ennio   comite,   non dubitavit consecrare
Ennius being (his) companion, 'did not   'hesitate   to-consecrate

manubias Martis Musis.   Quare   imperatores,
the spoils   of-Mars to-the-Muses. Wherefore (when)   generals,

in quâ urbe propè armati,
in any city nearly armed, [almost with arms in their hands],

coluerunt nomen poëtarum, et delubra Musarum,
revered   the name of poets, and the temples of-the-Muses,

in eâ   togati judices debent non abhorrere a
in this (city) civil judges ought not to-be-averse to the

honore Musarum et a salute poëtarum.
honour of-the-Muses and to the safety of-poets.

    Atque, ut   faciatis   id   libentius,   jam
    And,   that you-may-do that the-more-willingly, 'I-will now

judices, indicabo me vobis,   et
O judges, 'declare myself to you [reveal my feelings to you], and

confitebor vobis quodam   de   meo amore gloriæ,
I-will-confess to you something concerning my   love of glory,

fortasse nimis acri, verumtamen honesto.   Nam hic
perhaps   too eager, but-yet   honourable. For this

          attigit atque inchoavit   versibus
(Archias) touched-on and   has-begun (to celebrate) 'in (his) 'verses

res,   quas   nos gessimus in nostro consulatu,
the deeds, which we have-performed in our   consulship,

simul cum vobis, pro salute hujus urbis, atque
together with you, for the safety of this city, and

imperii, et pro vitâ civium, que pro universâ
the empire, and for the life of-the-citizens, and for the entire

republica; quibus auditis, quòd visa est mihi
republic; which (verses) being heard, because it appeared to me

magna et jucunda res, hortatus sum hunc ad
a great and agreeable subject, I encouraged him to

perficiendum. Enim virtus desiderat nullam aliam
complete (it). For virtue desires no other

mercedem laborum que periculorum, præter hanc
reward of labours and dangers, except that

laudis et gloriæ; quâ quidem judices detractâ,
of praise and renown; which indeed O judges being-taken-away,

quid est, quod in hoc tam exiguo, et tam brevi
what is there, that in this so small, and so short

curriculo vitæ, exerceamus nos in tantis
a course of life, (that) we-should-exert ourselves in such

laboribus? Certe si animus præsentiret nihil in
labours? Certainly if the mind did-forebode nothing as respects

posterum, et si regionibus, quibus spatium vitæ est
the future, and if in-the-limits, in which the space of life is

circumscriptum, terminaret omnes suas cogitationes
circumscribed, it-should-bound all its thoughts

iisdem, nec frangeret se tantis
by-the-same, 'it would not break itself (down) by-such-great

laboribus, neque angeretur tot curis que
labours, neither would-it-be-tormented with-so-many cares and

vigiliis, neque toties dimicaret de vitâ ipsâ.
watchings, nor so-often would-it-contend for life itself.

Nunc quædam virtus insidet in quoque optimo, quæ
Now a certain virtue resides in every good-man, which

concitat animum noctes et dies stimulis gloriæ,
excites the mind night and day by-the-stimulus of glory,

atque admonet, commemorationem nostri
and reminds (it), (that) the remembrance of our

nominis esse non dimittendam cum tempore
name is not to-be-sent-away with the time of (our)

vitæ,   sed   adæquandam
life, [our name will not perish with our life], but   is-to-be-made-equal

cum omni posteritate.
with   all   posterity. [Will be transmitted to the latest posterity.]

12.   An vero omnes videamur esse tam parvi
    'Do-we then indeed   all   'appear   to be 'of such 'little

animi,   qui versamur in republica,
mind, [so narrow minded,] who are occupied in the republic, [with

              atque in his periculis que laboribus vitæ,
affairs of state,]   and in these dangers and labours of life,

ut cum usque ad extremum spatium   duxerimus
that when even to the extreme space (of life) we-have-drawn

nullum tranquillum atque otiosum spiritum,
no   tranquil   and   peaceful   breath, (that)

arbitremur omnia moritura simul cum nobis?
we-should-think all things are-to-perish together with us?

An, cum multi summi homines   studiosè
And-whether, when many   great   men   'have carefully

reliquerint statuas et imagines simulacra non
left-behind   statues and images representations not

animorum, sed corporum, debemus non   multò
of-the-mind, but of-the-body, 'ought not 'we much-more

malle relinquere   effigiem nostrarum virtutum
to-prefer to-leave-behind (us) the effigy of our   virtues

ac   consiliorum   expressam   et   politam
and 'of (our) deliberations   expressed   and elaborated

summis   ingeniis? Ego vero arbitrabar, omnia,
by-the-greatest geniuses?   I indeed thought, (that) all,

quæ gerebam, jam tum in gerendo,
which I-was-performing, already then in performing (them), (that)

me spargere ac disseminare   in sempiternam
I   was scattering and disseminating (them) for   the eternal

memoriam orbis   terræ.
recollection of the circle of-the-earth. [To be perpetually remembered

                Sive hæc   vero
throughout the whole world.] Whether this (remembrance) indeed

abfutura est a meo sensu post mortem, sive, ut
will-be-absent from my perception after death, or, as

sapientissimi homines putaverunt,   pertinebit   ad
the-most-wise   men   have-thought,   it-will-appertain   to

aliquam partem mei. Nunc certe quidem delector
some   portion of myself. Now   truly   indeed   I am delighted

quâdam   cogitatione que spe.
with-some-such   thought   and hope.

Quare, judices, conservate hominem   eo pudore,
Wherefore, O judges,   preserve   a man (of) such   modesty

         quem   videtis   comprobari
(in his merit as Archias), which (merit) you-see   approved

tum   dignitate   amicorum, tum etiam
as-well by-the-dignity [high rank] 'of his 'friends,   as   also

    vetustate ;   autém   ingenio
by-the-long-continuance (of their friendship);   but (his)   talent

   tanto   quantum   convenit   existimare id, quod
being as great   as   it-may-be-accorded to appreciate   it,   which

videatis   esse   expetitum ingeniis summorum
you-may-see, to-have-been   sought   by-the-talents of-the-greatest

hominum ;
men ; [his talents were highly estimated by illustrious men of the greatest

              causa   vero   ejusmodi, quæ
talents themselves,] (his) cause   indeed (is one) of this kind, which

comprobetur   beneficio   legis,   auctoritate
may-be-established   by-the-benefit   of-the-law,   by-the-authority

    municipii, testimonio Luculli,   tabulis
of (his) 'municipality, by-the-testimony of-Lucullus, (and) by-the-registers

Metelli. Quæ   cum   sint   ita,
of Metellus. Which (things) when they-may-be so, [which being so,]

petimus   a   vobis,   judices,   si   debet   esse qua
we-entreat of   you,   O judges,   if   there should   be   any

commendatio non modo humana, verum etiam divina
commendation   not   only   human,   but   also   divine

in   tantis   negotiis, ut   accipiatis   eum sic in
in   such-great   affairs,   that you-would-receive him   so   in

vestram fidem,   ut   videatur   esse levatus
your   faith, [protection,] that he-may-seem   to be   relieved

vestrâ humanitate, potius quàm violatus
by-your   kindness,   rather   than   injured 'by (your)

acerbitate, qui semper ornavit vos, qui
severity, (he) who 'has always 'adorned you, who (has celebrated)

vestros imperatores, qui res
your commanders, who has (commemorated) the-things

gestas Romani populi, qui etiam profitetur
performed [the exploits] of-the-Roman people, who also promised

se esse daturum aeternum testimonium laudum,
(that) he is to give an eternal testimony of praises,

his nostris recentibus, que vestris domesticis
in-these our recent, and your domestic

periculis, que qui est eo numero, qui
dangers, and who is in that number, (of poets), who 'have

semper sunt habiti atque dicti sancti apud omnes.
always 'been-held and called holy among all (nations).

Quae de causâ dixi pro meâ
Which (things) in relation (to) the cause I-have-related according to my

consuetudine, judices, breviter que simpliciter, confido
custom, O judges, briefly and simply, (and) I trust

ea probata esse omnibus, quae
(that) those (things) have-been-approved by all (of you), which

locutus sum non consuetudine fori, neque judiciali,
I-have-spoken not in accordance with-the-bar, nor judicial

et de ingenio hominis, et communiter
(practice), both concerning the talents of-the-man, and in-general

de ipsius studio, ea, judices, spero esse
respecting his studies, these (things), O judges, I-hope to-have-been

accepta in bonam partem; certe scio
received in good part; ' I certainly 'know (they) (will be)

ab eo, qui exercet judicium.
by him, who exercises judicature. [Who presides at this trial.]

ORATIO
THE ORATION

M. TULLII CICERONIS,
OF M. TULLIUS CICERO,

PRO

FOR

M. MARCELLO.
M. MARCELLUS.

~~~~~~~~~~

1. HODIERNUS dies, conscripti patres, attulit
This   day,   conscript   fathers,   has-brought

finem   diuturni silentii,   quo
an end [has made an end] 'of (my) 'long   silence, in which

his   temporibus eram usus,   non
in these   times   I-have-made-use-of, [have indulged in,] not

aliquo   timore,   sed partim   dolore,   partim
from-any   fear,   but   partly   from-sorrow,   partly

veracundiâ; que idem initium   dicendi,
from-modesty; and at-the-same-time the commencement of saying,

meo pristino more, quæ vellem, que quæ sentirem.
in-my ancient manner, what I-might-wish, and what I-might-think

      Enim nullo modo possum præterire tacitus
(on affairs). For in-no wise can-I pass-over   silent

tantam masuetudinem, tam inusitatam que inauditam
such-great humanity,   such   unusual   and unheard-of

clementiam, tantum modum   omnium rerum, in
clemency,   such-great moderation (in) all   things, in

summâ   potestate,   denique,
the highest   power, [when possessed of unlimited power,] in-fine,

tam incredibilem ac pæne divinam sapientiam. Enim
such incredible and nearly divine   wisdom.   For

M. Marcello   reddito,   conscripti   patres,   vobis   que
M. Marcellus   being-restored, O conscript   fathers,   to you   and

reipublicæ,   puto   non solum illius vocem   et
to-the-republic, I-think (that) not only his voice and

auctoritatem,   sed   etiam   meam   conservatam   ac
authority,   but   also   mine   is preserved   and

restitutam,   et   vobis   et   reipublicæ.
restored,   both   to-you   and   to-the-republic.

Enim   dolebam,   conscripti   patres,   et   vehementer
For   I grieved,   O conscript   fathers,   and   'was vehemently

angebar,   cum   viderem   talem   virum,   in eâdem
'distressed,   when   I-saw   such   a man, (who was)   in the same

causâ,   in   quâ   ego   fuissem,   non   esse   in   eâdem
cause,   in-which   I   had-been,   not   to-be   in   the same

fortunâ: nec poteram
fortune : [not enjoying the same good fortune with myself,]   nor   could-I

persuadere   mihi,   nec   ducebam   esse fas
persuade   myself,   nor   did-I-think   that it was right   (that)

me   versari   in nostro veteri curriculo, illo æmulo
I   should-be-engaged in   our   old   career,   he   the rival

atque   imitatore   meorum   studiorum   ac   laborum
and   imitator   of-my   studies   and   labours (and)

quasi   quodam   socio   et   comite   distracto   a   me.
as-it-were   an   associate and companion   being-torn   from   me,

Et   ergo,   C. Cæsar,   aperuisti   mihi   consuetudinem
And therefore, O C. Cæsar, you-have-opened   to-me   the habits

meæ   pristinæ   vitæ,   interclusam   et
of-my   former   life,   (which)   were-closed-on (me),   and

sustulisti   quasi   aliquod   signum   omnibus   his
you-have-raised   as (it were)   a   standard   for-all   those

ad   sperandum   benè   de   omni republica.
(here present) to   hope   well concerning the entire   republic

Enim   intellectum est   mihi,   in   multis,   et
For   it-was-made-apparent   to me,   in   many (instances), and

maxime in me ipso,   sed paulo antè   omnibus,
principally in my myself, (and) but a little   before (now)   to all

cum   concessisti   M. Marcellum   senatui
here present), when   you-granted   M. Marcellus   to-the-senate

que Romano populo, præsertim commemoratis
and to-the-Roman people, especially (after) having-made-mention

offensionibus, te anteferre auctoritatem hujus
(of his) offences, (that) you would-prefer the authority of this

ordinis, que dignitatem reipublicæ, vel tuis
order, [the senate] and the dignity of-the-republic, either to-your

doloribus vel suspicionibus.
resentments or suspicions.

Ille quidem hodierno die cepit maximum
He (Marcellus) indeed to-day received the greatest

fructum omnis anteactæ vitæ, cum summo
reward of all (his) past life, as-well by-the-unanimous

consensu senatûs, tum præterea tuo gravissimo
consent of the senate, as moreover in your [Cæsar's] most-solemn

et maximo judicio. Ex quo profectò intelligis,
and supreme judgment. From this indeed you (may)

quanta sit laus in beneficio
understand, how-great is the renown (to you) in (this) benefit

dato, cum sit tanta
conferred, [by granting Marcellus this kindness] when there is so-much

gloria in accepto. Ille vero est fortunatus,
glory (to him) in receiving (it). He indeed is fortunate,

ex salute cujus non pæne minor lætitia
from the safety of whom not scarcely less joy

pervenerit ad omnes, quàm ventura sit ad ipsum.
will accrue to all, than may arrive to himself.

Quod quidem
[Than he himself may feel, when he hears it.] Which (favour) indeed

contigit ei meritò, atque optimo jure. Enim
has-happened to-him deservedly, and with-the-best right. For

quis est præstantior illo aut nobilitate,
who is more-excellent (than) he either in nobility (of birth),

aut probitate, aut studio optimarum
or probity, or the zealous (cultivation) of-the-most-liberal

artium, aut innocentiâ, aut ullo genere
arts, or in purity-of-life, or in any kind

laudis.
of-praiseworthy-actions.

2. Tantum flumen ingenii est nullius,
Such a stream of genius is of-no-one, [no one possesses

tanta vis tanta copia dicendi
such a flow of genius,] such power and such copiousness of-speaking

aut scribendi nullius, quæ, non dicam
or of-writing (has) no-one, which, 'I-will not 'say

exornare, sed C. Cæsar possit
to-embellish, but (even) O C. Cæsar (that) he-might-be-able

enarrare tuas res gestas. Tamen affirmo (et tua
to-relate your exploits. However I assert (and with your

pace dicam hoc,) nullam laudem esse
permission I-will-say this,) (that) no renown is

ampliorem in his, quàm eam, quam
more-glorious in these (exploits) than that, which

consecutus es hodierno die. Soleo sæpe ponere
you-have-acquired this day. I-am-accustomed often to place

ante oculos, que libenter usurpare id
(this) before (my) eyes, and willingly to-maintain it

crebris sermonibus, omnes res gestas nostrorum
in frequent conversations, (that) all the deeds of-our

imperatorum, omnes exterarum gentium, que
commanders, all (those) of foreign nations, and

potentissimorum populorum, omnes clarissimorum
of-the-most-powerful people, all (those) of-the-most-celebrated

regum, posse conferri cum tuis, nec magnitudine
kings, can-be-compared with yours, neither in-the-greatness

contentionum, nec numero præliorum, nec varietate
of-the-contests, nor in-the-number of-the-battles, nor in-the-variety

regionum, nec celeritate conficiendi, nec
of-the-countries, nor in-the-celerity of-performing, nor

dissimilitudine bellorum ; nec vero
in-the-diversity (of character) of-the-wars; nor indeed (that)

disjunctissimas terras potuisse peragrari
the-most-widely-separated countries could-have been-travelled-over

citiùs passibus cujusquam, quàm, non
more-rapidly by the-footsteps of-any-one, than, 'I-will not

dicam,   lustratæ sint   cursibus,   sed
'say,   may-have-been-passed-through   by-(your)-marches,   but

    victoriis.
by-(your)-victories.

    Quæ   quidem nisi ego   fatear   esse
    Which (things) indeed unless I   should confess (that) they-are

ita magna, ut   vix   mens   aut cogitatio cujusquam
so   great,   that scarcely the mind   or imagination   of-any-one

possit capere ea,   sim   amens;   sed tamen
sould comprehend them, I-would-be devoid-of-reason;   but   yet

sunt alia   majora. Nam   quidam   solent
there-are other (things) greater.   For   some   are-accustomed

extenuare   verbis   bellicas laudes, que
to-depreciate by (their) words [by their remarks] military   praises,   and

detrahere eas   ducibus,   communicare
  to-detract those (praises) from-the-generals, (and)   to share (them

cum   multis,   ne   sint
with   the many, [with the soldiers,] (so that) they 'may not   'be

propriæ   imperatorum. Et certe, in   armis
the peculiar (right) of-the-commanders. And certainly, in military-affairs

virtus   militum, opportunitas locorum,
the bravery of-the-soldiers,   the opportunity of-the-places, [advantage of

       auxilia sociorum, classes   commeatus juvant
position,] the assistance of allies,   fleets (and)   supplies   help

multum;   vero Fortuna vindicat sibi   maximam
much;   but   Fortune   claims for herself (in war) the greatest

partem,   quasi   suo jure;   et   quidquid
part   (of success),   as   her-own right;   and   whatever

est gestum   prosperè,   ducit   id   pæne omne
has-been-done successfully, she-considers it   almost   all

suum.
er-own (work).

    At vero, C. Cæsar, habes neminem socium hujus
    But truly,   O C. Cæsar, you-have no-one (as) a partner of this

gloriæ, quam es adeptus paulo antè.   Totum
glory,   which you-have-obtained a little before. [Just now.]   All

hoc, quantumcunque est, (quod   certe   maximum),
this,   how-(great)-soever it is, (and which certainly (is) very great),

est totum, inquam, tuum. Centurio decerpit nihil ex
\s all, I-say, yours. The centurion plucks nothing from

ista laude sibi, præfectus nihil, cohors
this renown for himself, the prefect (of cavalry) nothing, the cohort

nihil, turma nihil. Quin etiam
(of infantry) nothing, the troop (of cavalry) nothing. Nay even

Fortana, illa ipsa domina humanarum rerum, non
Fortune, that same mistress of-human affairs, does not

offert se in societatem istius gloriæ,
present herself in the society of-this glory (as a participant thereof),

cedit tibi; fatetur esse totam et propriam
she cedes (all) to you; she confesses (that) it is all and peculiarly

tuam. Enim nunquam temeritas commiscetur cum
yours. For never ¹is rashness ¹mingled with

sapientiâ, nec casus admittitur ad consilium.
wisdom, nor ¹is chance ¹admitted to the-counsels (of prudence).

3. Domuisti gentes barbaras immanitate,
    You-have-conquered nations barbarous ¹by (their) ¹ferocity,

innumerabiles multitudine, infinitas locis,
countless ¹in (their) ¹numbers, immense (as respects) space,

abundantes omni genere copiarum; sed tamen
abounding in all kinds of-resources; but yet

vicisti ea, quæ habebant naturam et
you-conquered those (things), which had the nature and

conditionem, ut possent vinci; enim est
condition, that they-might be-conquered; for there-is

nulla vis tanta, quæ possit non debilitari que
no strength so-great, which may not be-weakened and

frangi ferro ac viribus. Vincere animum, cohibere
broken by-arms and force. To-conquer the mind, to-repress

iracundiam, temporare victoriam, non modo extollere
anger, to-temper victory, not only to-raise-up

jacentem adversarium præstantem nobilitate, ingenio
a prostrate foe excelling in-noble-birth, talents

virtute, sed etiam amplificare ejus pristinam
(and) virtue, but also to-enlarge his former

dignitatem; qui faciat hæc, ego non comparo eum
dignity; who does this, I ¹do not ¹compare him

cum summis viris, sed judico simillimum
with the-most-illustrious men, but think (him as) most

Deo.
like to God.

Itaque, C. Cæsar, illæ tuæ bellicæ laudes
Therefore, O C. Cæsar, those your warlike praises

celebrabuntur quidem non solum nostris literis atque
will-be-celebrated indeed not only in-our literature and

linguis, sed pæne omnium gentium; neque
language, but (in that) 'of almost 'all nations; nor

unquam ulla ætas conticescet de tuis laudibus. Sed
'will ever any age 'be-silent about your praise. But

tamen res ejusmodi, nescio quomodo, etiam cum
yet things of-this-kind, I-know-not how, even when

leguntur, videntur obstrepi clamore
they-are-read, appear to-be-overpowered (in noise) by-the-shouts

militum, et sono tubarum. At vero, cum
of-the-soldiers, and by-the-sound of-the-trumpet. But indeed, when

aut audimus, aut legimus aliquid factum
either we-hear, or read (that) something has-been-done

clementer, mansuete, juste, moderate, sapienter,
clemently, humanely, justly, moderately (and) wisely,

(præsertim in iracundiâ, quæ est inimica
(especially in anger, which is inimical 'to (prudent)

consilio, et in victoriâ, quæ naturâ est insolens et
'counsel, and in victory, which by nature is insolent and

superba); quo studio incendimur, non modo in
haughty); with what ardour are-we-inflamed, not only in

res gestas, sed etiam in fictis, ut
things (actually) performed, but even in fictitious (things), that

sæpe diligamus eos, quos nunquam vidimus!
often we-love those, whom 'we-have never 'seen!

Vero te, quem intuemur præsentem, cujus
But you, whom we-behold (here) present, whose

mentem que sensus cernimus eos, ut
mind and feelings we-perceive them (to be such), that

quidquid fortuna belli reliquum fecerit reipublicæ,
all-that the fortune of war may-have-left to-the-republic,

velis   id   esse   salvum,   quibus
you-wish that to-be   safe (and secured to the republic), with-what

laudibus efferemus ?   quibus studiis prosequemur ?
praises   shall-we-extol (you)? with-what zeal   shall-we-follow

        quâ   benevolentiâ   complectemur ?
(you)?   with-what   affection   shail-we-embrace (you)?

Parietes hujus curiæ, me dius fidius
The (very) walls of this senate-house, may Jupiter help me [most as-

        (ut videntur mihi) gestiunt agere gratias tibi,
surely] (as they seem to me) exult   to return thanks to you,

quod   brevi   tempore illa   auctoritas
because in-a-short   time   that   authority (of the senate)

futura sit,   in   et   his suis
will-hereafter-be, [will be restored] in both these their [the senators']

sedibus   suorum majorum.
seats,   (and that) of their   ancestors.

4. Equidem cum viderem modo cum vobis
    Indeed   when   I saw   just-now with you [senators]

lacrymas C. Marcelli, optimi   viri, et præditı
the tears   of C. Marcellus, a most-excellent man, and endowed

commemorabili pietate,   memoria omnium
with-recommendable affection (for his brother), the recollection of all

Marcellorum obfudit meum pectus. M. Marcello
the Marcelli   gushed over my   heart.   M. Marcello

conservato, tu   reddidisti suam dignitatem etiam
being-preserved, you [Cæsar] have restored their dignity   even

            quibus   mortuis ; que vindicâsti
(to those Marcelli) who   are-dead ; and you-have-saved

nobilissimam familiam, jam redactam ad paucos
a-most-noble   family,   now reduced   to   few

        pæne   ab interitu. Tu igitur jure
(in number) nearly from perishing. You therefore with-right

antepones hunc diem tuis maximis et innumerabilibus
will-prefer   this day to your greatest and   countless

gratulationibus. Enim hæc res est propria
congratulations.   For   this affair is the peculiar (right)

Cæsaris unius ; ceteræ gestæ, te   duce,
of Cæsar alone   other deeds, you being the general, (though)

illæ magnæ quidem, sed tamen
they (were) great indeed, but yet (were performed)

multo que magno comitatu. Autem tu
with a numerous and great train (of associates). But you

es idem et dux . et comes hujus rei;
are at-the-same-time both general and associate of this affair

quæ quidem est tanta, ut
(of pardoning Marcellus); which indeed is so-great, that (though

ætas allatura sit finem tuis tropæis que monumentis,
age may-bring an end to your trophies and monuments,

(enim est nihil factum opere aut manu
(for (there) is nothing made by labour or by the hand (of man)

quod aliquando vetustas non conficiat
which some-time-or-another length-of-time 'may not 'dissipate

et consumat); at vero hæc tua justitia et lenitas
and consume); but yet-indeed this your justice and lenity

animi quotidie florescet magis, ita ut
of mind 'will every day 'become more 'celebrated, so that

quantum diuturnitas detrahet tuis operibus,
as much as-length-of-time will-detract from your deeds,

tantum afferat laudibus. Et quidem
so-much may-it-add (to your) glory. And indeed

viceras omnes ceteros victores civilium
as-you-may-have-surpassed all other conquerers (in) the civil

bellorum jam ante æquitate et
wars now before [that have happened before now] in equity and

misericordiâ, vero hodierno die vicisti te ipsum
mercy, but this day you-have-surpassed yourself.

Vereor, ne hoc, quod dicam, possit non perinde
I-fear, lest that, which I-say, may not equally-as-well

intelligi auditu,
be understood by the hearing, [by those only hearing it mentioned],

atque ipse sentio cogitans. Videris
as I-myself feel (it, when) reflecting (thereon). You-appear

vicisse victoriam ipsam, cum remisisti
to-have-conquered victory herself, when you-have-remitted

victis ea, quæ illa erat adepta.
to-the-conquered those things, which she had obtained (for you).

Nam cum conditione victoriæ ipsius omnes
For when by-the-conditions of victory self 'we all (who were'

victi jure occidissemus,
conquered 'might by right 'have-fallen (by the sword, or been ruined

sumus conservati judicio tuæ
in our estates), we-have-been-preserved by-the-judgment of your

clementiæ. Recte igitur ūnus
clemency. [By your merciful decision.] Rightly therefore (you) alone

es invictus, a quo etiam conditio que vis victoriæ
are unconquered, by whom even the conditions and power of victory

ipsius devicta est.
self have-been-conquered.

5. Atque conscripti patres, attendite quàm late
And O-conscript fathers, observe how far

hoc judicium C. Cæsaris pateat; enim omnes,
this decision of-C. Cæsar may extend; for all, 'we,

qui sumus compulsi ad illa arma,
who 'were compelled '(to) that (civil) war (to take up arms),

nescio quo misero que funesto fato
I-know-not by-what miserable and fatal destiny

reipublicæ, etsi tenemur aliquâ culpâ humani
of-the-republic, although we-are-charged with some fault of-human

erroris, certe liberati sumus a scelere. Nam,
error, 'we certainly 'are liberated from crime. For,

cum, vobis deprecantibus, sconservavit M. Marcellum
when, you entreating, he preserved M. Marcellus

reipublicæ; reddidit memet mihi, et iterum
to-the-republic (also); he restored me to-myself, and once-more

reipublicæ, nullo deprecante,
to-the-republic, no-one entreating (for me), (he also restored)

reliquos amplissimos viros et sibi ipsis et
those-other illustrious men both to themselves and 'to (their)

patriæ; quorum et frequentiam et dignitatem
country; whose both numerous-concourse and dignity

videtis in hoc ipsa consessu. Ille non induxit
you see in this same assembly. He 'has not 'brought (any)

hostes in curiam; sed judicavit,
enemies into the-senate-house (by this); but he-has-decided (that),

bellum   esse   susceptum   a   plerisque   potius
the war   was   undertaken   by   the-most (of them)   rather

ignoratione   et   falso   atque
from-want-of-knowledge (of his real intentions) and from a false   and

inani   metu,   quàm cupiditate aut   crudelitate.
groundless   fear (of him),   than from cupidity   or   from-the-cruelty

In quo bello quidem semper   putavi
(of revenge).   In which war   indeed   'I always   'have-thought

de   pace   audiendum,   que semper
(that proposals) respecting peace ought-to-be-listened-to, and 'I always

dolui   non modo pacem,   sed orationem etiam
grieved (that) not   only   peace,   but   the entreaties   even

civium flagitantium   pacem repudiari. Enim ego
of citizens earnestly-begging (for) peace should-be-rejected.   For   I

unquam secutus sum   neque   illa, nec ulla
never   followed [took a part in]   either (in) these,   or   any

civilia   arma; que semper mea consilia fuerunt socia
civil   war;   and always   my   counsels   were-associated

pacis et   togæ,   non
(with) peace and the-gown,   [civil affairs and pursuits,]   not (with)

belli atque armorum.   Secutus sum hominem
war   and   arms.   I-followed   the man [Pompey]

privato officio,   non   publico;   que
from (a sense of)   private   duty,   not   public;   and

tantum   fidelis memoria   grati animi valuit
so-great   'did the faithful remembrance of a grateful mind   'prevail

apud me, ut   non modo   nullâ cupiditate,
over   me, that (there was) not   only (through)   no   desire

sed quidem ne   spe, prudens
(of advantage), but   indeed   not (even through) hope,   prudent

t sciens ruerem ad voluntarium interitum.
nd knowing I-rushed-on to   voluntary   destruction.

Quòd quidem meum consilium fuit
And   indeed   my   views   were (on this subject) (not)

minime obscurum. Nam et in hoc ordine,
in-the-least dissembled.   For also in   this   order (of the senate),

rê integrâ,   dixi multa
the thing being entire, [the war not having yet broken out], I-said   much

de   pace; et in bello ipso sensi eadem,
concerning peace; and in the war itself 'I-was-of the same 'opinion,

etiam cum periculo mei capitis. Ex quo nemo
even with the-risk of-my life. From which no-one

erit jam tam injustus existimator rerum, qui
'would now 'be so unjust a judge of-things, who

dubitet, quæ fuerit Cæsaris voluntas de
might-doubt, what may-have-been Cæsar's intentions respecting

bello, cum statim censuerit auctores pacis
the war when 'he immediately 'thought (that) the advisers of peace

conservandos, ceteris fuit iratior.
ought-to-be-preserved, (but) with-the-others he-was more-irritated.

Atque fortasse id minus mirum tum, cum exitus
And perhaps it (was) less strange then, when the-result

esset incertus, et fortuna belli anceps; vero
might-be uncertain, and the fortune of-war doubtful; but (he)

qui, victor, diligit auctores pacis, is profecto
who, a conqueror, loves the advisers of peace, he certainly

declarat se maluisse non dimicare, quàm
declares (that) he would-rather not have-fought, than

vincere.
have conquered. [That he would always have preferred peace to civil war.]

6. Atque sum quidem testis hujus rei
And I am indeed a witness (as respects) this thing

M. Marcello. Enim nostri sensus, ut semper
for M. Marcellus. For our opinions, as 'they always

congruebant in pace, sic etiam tum in bello. Quoties
'agreed in peace, so even when in war. How-often

ego vidi eum, et cum quanto dolore,
'have I 'seen him, and with what great grief,

extimescentem cum insolentiam certorum hominum,
dreading as-well the insolence of certain men

tum etiam ferocitatem victoriæ ipsius! Quò,
as also the ferocity of victory self! Wherefore,

C. Cæsar, tua liberalitas debet esse gratior
O C. Cæsar, your liberality ought to be the-more-agreeable

nobis, qui vidimus illa. Enim jam
to us, who have-seen those (things). For now

causæ
the causes (of the two parties, namely, that of Pompey and Cæsar, 'are

non sunt comparandæ   inter   se,   sed
not   'to-be-compared   (or discussed) among themselves, but

                              vitoriæ.   Vidimus
(the use that would be made) of victory (by each, may be). We-have seen

tuam victoriam terminatam   exitu   præliorum;
your   victory   terminated with-the-result 'of (your) 'battles;

          non vidimus gladium vacuum vaginâ, in urbe.
'we-have not   'seen   the sword   unsheathed,   in the city.

Cives,   quos amisimus,   vis Martis perculit eos
The citizens, whom we-have-lost, the force of Mars 'struck them

                    non irâ   victoriæ;   ut nemo
'down [they fell in battle] not by-the-fury of victory; so-that no-one

debeat dubitare quin C. Cæsar, si   posset   fieri,
ought   to doubt but-that C. Cæsar, if it-could-have been-done,

   excitaret   multos ab inferis; quoniam conservat
would-have-raised many from the dead; since   he-preserves

ex eâdem   acie   quos potest. Vero
from that-same army (of Pompey) (those) whom he-can.   But

        alterius partis,   dicam nihil amplius,
(as respects) the other party (of Pompey), I-will-say nothing more,

quàm (id quod   omnes verebamur)   victoriam
than (that which 'we all   'feared) (that) victory

futuram fuisse   nimis   iracundam. Enim   quidam
would-have-been   too   revengeful. For   some

minabantur non modo   armatis,   sed
threatened   not only (their) armed (opponents), but

interdum etiam   otiosis;
sometimes also (those who were) quiet, (and took no part in the

      dicebant   cogitandum esse,   nec quid
contest); they-said (that) it-was-to-be-considered, not what

quisque sensisset, sed ubi   fuisset;   ut quidem
each-one might-think, but where he-had-been; that indeed

immortales Dii videantur mihi (etiamsi   expetiverint
the immortal Gods seem   to me (even-though they-may-have

      pœnas   a Romano populo,   ob   aliquod
inflicted punishment on the Roman people, on-account-of some

delictum, qui excitaverint tantum et tam luctuosum
offence, who stirred-up so-great and so mournful a

civile bellum) vel jam placati, vel aliquando
civil war) 'are either now 'appeased, or at-length

satiati, contulisse omnem spem salutis
satiated, (and that) they-have-brought all (our) hope of safety

ad clementiam et sapientiam victoris.
to (depend on) the clemency and wisdom of-the-conqueror.

Quare gaude isto tuo tam excellenti bono;
Wherefore rejoice in-this your so excellent a privilege;

et fruere cum fortunâ et gloriâ, tum etiam
and enjoy as well (your) fortune and glory, as also (your)

naturâ, et tuis moribus; ex quo quidem
kind-disposition, and your amiable-manners; from which indeed

est maximus fructus que jucunditas sapienti.
there is the greatest fruit and pleasure to-the-wise-man.

Cum recordabere tua cetera,
When you-call-to-your-recollection your other (actions of life),

etsi persæpe congratulabere virtuti,
although you 'will very-often 'congratulate (yourself on your) valour,

tamen plerumque tuæ felicitati.
yet often (you will have to thank) your good-fortune.

Quoties cogitabis de nobis, quos voluisti esse
As-often-as you-shall-think of us, whom you-have-wished to be

salvos in republicâ simul cum te, toties
safe in the republic together with yourself, so-often

cogitabis de tuis maximis beneficiis,
you-will-think of your very-great favours (bestowed on us),

toties de incredibili liberalitate, toties
so-often-will-you-think of (your) incredible liberality, so-often

de tua singulari sapientiâ; quæ audebo dicere
of your unexampled wisdom; which I-will-venture to say (are)

non modo summa bona, sed nimirum vel
not only (your) greatest goods, but certainly even (your)

sola. Enim tantus est splendor in verâ laude,
only. For so great is the splendour in true praise,

tanta dignitas in magnitudine animi et
so great (is the) dignity in greatness of mind and

consilii, ut hæc videantur esse donata a virtute,
of counsel, that these appear to-be-given by virtue,

cetera commodata a fortunâ. Noli igitur
the others confided by fortune. Do-not therefore

defatigari in conservandis bonis viris lapsis,
become-wearied in preserving good men fallen,

præsertim non cupiditate, aut aliquâ pravitatate,
especially not by cupidity, or any depravity

sed opinione officii, fortasse stulta,
(of disposition), but by a sense of duty, perhaps foolish, (but)

certe non improba, et quâdam specie
certainly not wicked, and by-a-certain appearance (of duty)

reipublicæ. Enim est non ulla culpa tua, si aliqui
to-the-republic. For it is not any fault (of) yours, if some

timuerunt te; que contra summa laus,
feared you; and on-the-contrary (it is your) greatest praise

quòd plerique senserunt timen-
that the-most have-become-sensible (that) you-were (not)

dum fuisse minime.
to-have-been-feared in-the-smallest (degree).

7. Vero nunc venio ad tuam gravissimam querelam,
But now I come to your most-heavy complaint,

et atrocissimam suspicionem; quæ est providenda,
and severe suspicion; which is to-be-guarded-against,

non magis tibi ipsi, quam cum omnibus civibus,
not the more for-you yourself, than also for-all the citizens,

tum maxime nobis, qui sumus conservati a
then more-especially for-ourselves, who have-been preserved by

te; quam etsi spero esse falsam,
you; which (suspicion) though I-hope (that it) is false,

tamen nunquam extenuabo verbis. Enim
yet 'I-will never 'extenuate (it) by (my) words. For

tua cautio est nostra cautio; ut si
your caution (for yourself) is our caution; (so) that if

pecandum sit in alterutro, malim videri
it-may-be-erred in on-either (side), I-would-rather seem-to-be

nimis timidus, quàm parum prudens. Sed
too timid, than too-little prudent. [imprudent.] But

quisnam est iste tam demens? ne   de tuis?
who   is this-one so senseless? whether (is he) of   your-own

tametsi qui sunt magis tui,   quàm
(friends)? and-yet who are   more   your (friends), than (those)

quibus insperantibus   tu reddidisti salutem?   an
to whom without-hoping-for-it you have-restored safely? or-any

ex   eo numero, qui fuerunt unà cum te?
from-among that number, who had-been together-with you (in the

Est non credibilis   tantus furor
war)?   It-is not credible (that there should be) such madness

in ullo, ut,   quo   duce   sit
in any-one, that (the general), through which general he may-have

adeptus summa   omnia,   non anteponat
attained the height (of) all (his wishes), 'he-should not   'prefer

hujus   vitam suæ. At si tui   cogitant
this (general's) life to-his-own. But if your (friends) think (or plan)

nihil   sceleris,   cavendum est,
nothing of wickedness (against you), I-suppose-it-must-be-cared-for,

ne   inimici   quid.   Qui?
.est (your) enemies (might do) any-thing (against you). Who (are they)?

Enim omnes, qui fuerunt   aut amiserunt
For   all, who were (your enemies), 'have either   'lost

vitam suâ pertinaciâ, aut retinuerunt
(their) lives by-their obstinacy, or they-preserved (them)

tuâ   misericordiâ; ut aut nulli de   inimicis
by-your mercy;   so-that either none of (your) enemies

supersint, aut,   qui superfuerunt sint
remain,   or (those), who have-remained are (your)

amicissimi.
most-devoted-friends.

Sed tamen, cum sint in animis hominum tantæ
But however, as there are in the minds of men so many

latebræ,   et tanti   recessus,   augeamus
hiding-places, and so-many (secret) recesses, let-us-increase

sane tuam suspicionem, enim   simul   augebimus
then your suspicion, for at-the-same-time we-shall-increase

diligentiam.   Nam quis est, tam
(your) diligence (and circumspection). For who is there, so

ıgnarus omnium rerum, tam rudis in
ignorant of all things, so unskilled in (the affairs of)

republica, tam nihil cogitans unquam nec
the republic, so thoughtless (as) never (to reflect) either

de suâ salute, nec de communi, qui 'does
about his-own safety, or about the common (safety), who 'does

non intelligat suam contineri tuâ salute
not 'understand (that) his-own (safety) is comprised in-your safety

et ex tuâ vitâ unius pendere omnium ?
and (that) on your life alone depends (the lives) of all ?

Equidem, cogitans de te (ut debeo) dies que noctes,
In truth, thinking of you (as I ought) day and night,

extimescc duntaxat humanos casus,
I fear only (those) human accidents (to which all are

et incertos eventus valetudinis, et
subject), and the uncertain events of-health, and

fragilitatem communis naturæ; que doleo
the weakness 'of (our) 'common nature; and I-grieve (that)

cum respublica debeat esse immortalis, eam
while the republic ought to be immortal, (that) it

consistere in animâ unius mortalis. Vero si ad
depends on the life of-one mortal (man). But if to

humanos casus, que incertos eventus
human accidents (of life), and the uncertain events

valetudinis, accedit consensio sceleris que
of health, there-is-added the conspiracy of crime and

insidiarum, quem Deum credamus posse opitulari
treachery, then what God might-we-think could assist

reipublicæ, si cupiat.
the republic, (even) if he-desire (to do so).

S. Omnia, quæ, C. Cæsar, sentis jacere perculsa
All things, which, O C. Cæsar, you perceive to lie knocked-down

atque prostrata ımpetu belli ipsius, (quod fuit
and prostrated by-the-violence of war itself, (which was

necesse) sunt excitanda tibi;
necessarily so) (all these) are to-be-raised-up by you;

judicia constituenda
the-tribunals-of-justice are-to-be-established (on their ancient footing)

fides revocanda, libidines comprimendæ,
confidence is-to-be-restored, licentiousness is-to-be-repressed,

soboles propaganda; omnia quæ jam dilapsa,
population is-to-be-increased; all-things, which now fallen-to-pieces,

fluxerunt, vincienda sunt
(are fast perishing and) passing away, are-to-be-bound (together and

severis legibus. Fuit non recusandum,
reinstated) by severe laws. It-was not to-be-denied (that),

in tanto civili bello, que tanto ardore
in so-great a civil war, and in-so-great an excitement

animorum et armorum, quin
of mind and of arms, (in civil contests), but that (violently)

quassata, respublica, quicunque fuisset eventus
shaken, the republic, whatever might-be the event

belli, perderet multa et ornamenta
of-the-war, would-lose much both as (respects) the ornaments

dignitatis et præsidia suæ stabilitatis; que uterque
of (its) dignity and the guards of its stability; and each

dux faceret multa armatus, quæ idem
general would-have-done many-things (while in) arms, which he

prohibuisset fieri, togatus.
would-have-forbidden to-be-done, (when) clothed with the toga, (the

Omnia quæ vulnera belli curanda sunt
dress of peace). All which wounds of war are-to-be-cured

tibi; quibus nemo præter te potest mederi.
by you; which no-one except you can heal.

Itaque invitus audivi illam tuam præclarissimam
Therefore (with) regret I heard that your very-celebrated

et sapientissimam vocem, "Vixi satis diu vel
and very-wise saying, "I-have-lived sufficiently long either

naturæ vel gloriæ." Satis fortasse si vis
for-nature or for glory." Sufficiently (long) perhaps if you-wish

ita naturæ; etiam addo si placet gloriæ;
(it to be) so for-nature; also I-add if it-pleases (you) for-glory;

at (quod est maximum) certe parum
but (what is (of) the greatest (importance), certainly (but) little

patriæ. Quare omitte, quæso
(long enough) for (your) country. Wherefore give-up, I-pray (you!

istam prudentiam doctorum hominum in contemnendâ
this   wisdom   of learned   men   in   despising

morte; noli esse sapiens nostro periculo. Enim
death; do not be   wise   at-our   risk.   For 'it-has

sæpe venit ad meas aures, te dicere istud idem
often 'come to my ears, (that) you say this same

    nimis crebro, te vixisse satis
(thing) too often, that-you have-lived sufficiently (long,

tibi. Credo; sed tum
for-yourself. I believe (you are of this mind); but then (only)

audirem id, si viveres tibi soli, aut si
would-I-listen (to) it, if you-lived for yourself alone, or if

etiam natus esses tibi soli. Nunc, cum tuæ
also you-were-born for yourself alone. (But) now, when your

res gestæ complexæ sint salutem
deeds   have-embraced (and are identified with) the safety

omnium civium, que cunctam
of all the citizens, and (the same may also be said of) the entire

rempublicam; tantum abes a perfectione
republic;   'you-are so-very 'distant from the completion

maximorum operum, ut nondum jeceris
of (your) greatest works, that 'you-have not-as-yet 'laid

fundamenta quæ cogitas. Tu
the foundations (thereof) which you-may-think (you have). Will you

hìc definies modum tuæ vitæ non
here limit the measure of-your life not as respects the

salute reipublicæ, sed æquitate animi? Quid
safety of-the-republic, but the equanimity of your mind? What

si istud est ne quidem satis
if that (portion of your life passed) is not indeed sufficient

tuæ gloriæ? cujus, quamvis sis sapiens,
for-your glory? of which (glory), although you-be a-wise-man,

non negabis, te esse avidissimum.
'you will not 'deny, (that) you are very desirous.

Igitur inquies, ne parum magnam gloriam
Therefore you-ask, (is it) but little (of) great   glory

relinquemus? Immo
we-shall-leave (behind us, should our life now terminate)? Truly

vero satis aliis, quamvis multis; tibi uni parum
indeed enough for-others, however numerous; for-you alone (too) little.

Enim quidquid est, quamvis sit amplum,
For whatever is (your glory), although it-may be ample,

id certe est tum parum, cum est aliquid
it certainly is then little, when there-is something

amplius. Quod si, C. Cæsar,
greater (of glory, that may be obtained). Because if, O C. Cæsar,

hic futurus sit exitus tuarum immortalium rerum,
this were-to-be the result 'of your immortal achievements,

ut, adversariis devictis, relinqueres rempublicam
that, (your) enemies being conquered, you-would-leave the republic

in eo statu, in quo nunc est; vide, quæso, ne
in that state, in which 'it now 'is; see (to it), I-beg-you, lest

tua divina virtus sit habitura plus admirationis
your divine virtue may-hereafter-have more of-admiration

quàm gloriæ; siquidem gloria est illustris ac
than of-glory; since glory is illustrious and

pervagata fama multorum et magnorum meritorum,
wide-spread renown of-many and great services (done),

vel in suos, vel in patriam, vel in omne
either to one's (friends), or to one's country, or to the whole

genus hominum.
race of-men.

9. Igitur hæc est pars reliqua tibi, hic
Therefore this is the part (that) is left to-you, this

actus restat, in hoc elaborandum est ut
act remains (to be performed), in this exertion-is-to-be-made that

constituas rempublicam, que eâ
'you-may-(firmly) 'establish the republic, and this (republic)

compositâ, tu in primis perfruare
'being (thus) 'settled, you (may be) among the first to enjoy ('t)

cum summâ tranquillitate et otio; tum, cum
the greatest tranquillity and leisure; then, when

et solveris quod debes
'you-have both 'discharged the duty which you-owe 'to (your)

patriæ, et expleveris naturam ipsam satietate
country, and may-have-filled nature herself with satiety

vivendi   **dicito si voles,**
of living [and shall have attained to a good old age] say if you-wish,

te vixisse satis diu. Enim quid omnino est
(that) you have-lived sufficiently long.   For what after-all is

hoc ipsum diu, in quo est aliquid extremum,
this same long (living), in which there is something the last

quod cum venit, omnis
(and which must have an end), which when it-arrives,   all

præterita voluptas est pro nihilo, quia postea
past   pleasure is for nothing, because after-that

futura est nulla? Quanquam iste animus tuus
there will be nothing?   Although that mind (of) yours

nunquam contentus fuit his angustiis, quas
never   was-content with-those narrow (limits), which

natura dedit nobis ad vivendum; que semper
nature has-given us to live (in); and always

flagravit amore immortalitatis.
was-inflamed with-the-love of-immortality.

Nec vero hæc tua vita ducenda est, quæ
Nor truly 'is this your life 'to-be-considered (as that), which

continetur corpore et spiritu. Illa, illa, inquam
is-contained in-the-body and spirit.   That, that, I-say

est tua vita, quæ vigebit memoriâ omnium
is your life, which will-flourish in-the-memory of all

sæculorum; quam posteritas alet, quam æternitas
ages;   which posterity will-cherish, which   eternity

ipsa semper tuebitur. Huic oportet
itself 'will always 'preserve. For this (existence) it-behoves (that)

tu inservias, huic ostentes te;
you exert (yourself), for-this you-will-show yourself (in your

quæ quidem jampridem habet multa
true glory); (a life) which indeed long-since has many-things

quæ miretur; nunc etiam expectat, quæ
which may-be-admired; now also it-looks-for (that), which

laudet. Certe posteri obstupescent,
may-receive-praise. Certainly posterity will-be-amazed, (when)

audientes et legentes imperia
bearing, and reading (of) (your various) commands

provincias, Rhenum, Oceanum, Nilum,
the provinces, the Rhine, the Ocean, the Nile, (your)

innumerabiles pugnas, incredibiles victorias,
innumerable battles, (your) incredible victories, (your)

innumera monumenta, tuos triumphos. Sed, nisi
countless monuments, (and) your triumphs. But, unless

hæc urbs stabilita erit tuis consiliis et institutis,
this city is-firmly-settled by your counsels and laws,

tuum nomen modo tum vagabitur longe atque
your name 'will only then 'be-spread-out far and

late; quidem non habebit stabilem sedem et
wide; (but) indeed 'it will not 'have a stable abode and

certum domicilium. Etiam erit inter
certain domicile (to dwell in). Also there-will-be among

eos qui nascentur, sicut fuit inter nos,
those who (hereafter) will-be-born, as there-was among ourselves,

magna dissensio, cum alii efferent tuas res gestas
great dissension, while some will-raise your exploits

laudibus ad cœlum, alii fortasse requirent aliquid,
with praises to heaven, others perhaps will-require something

que id vel maximum, nisi
(more), and that even the-greatest-of-all, unless

restinxeris incendium civilis belli salute
you-shall-have-extinguished the conflagration of civil war by-the-safety

patriæ; ut illud videatur fuisse
of-(your) 'country; (so) that the-former may-appear to-have-been (the

fati, hoc consilii. Igitur
work) of fate, this (the latter the work of your wise) counsel. Therefore

servi etiam iis judicibus, qui multis seculis
have-regard also to-those judges, who many ages

pòst judicabunt de te, et quidem, haud scio an
hereafter will decide concerning you, and indeed, perhaps

incorruptius, quàm nos; nam judicabunt, et
more-unbiassedly, than we (can); for they-will-judge, both

sine amore et sine cupiditate, et rursus
without affection and without cupidity, and (also) again

sine odio et sine invidiâ. Autem etiam si
without hatred and without envy. But also if (all)

id   non tunc pertinebit ad te
this 'should not   then   'affect   to you (hereafter, w.en dead)

(ut quidam falso putant);   certe nunc pertinet
'as   some   falsely suppose); 'it certainly now 'behoves (you)

te esse talem,   ut nulla
'that) you be   such, [conduct yourself in such a manner], that   no

oblivio   unquam   obscuratura sit   tuas
oblivion   'shall ever (hereafter)   'obscure   your

laudes.
praises.

10. Voluntates civium fuerunt diversæ, que
The inclinations of-the-citizens were   diverse, and (their)

sententiæ distractæ,   enim   non
opinions   distracted (and divided in the civil war); for 'we did not

solum dissidebamus   consiliis et studiis, sed etiam
only   'differ   by (our) counsels and wishes, but   also

armis et castris.
by-arms and camps (and took different sides in the military operations).

Autem erat quædam obscuritas,   erat
But   there-was some   obscurity (in the affair), there-was

certamen inter   clarissimos duces ;
a contest between the-most-celebrated generals (Cæsar and Pompey);

multi dubitabant, quid esse optimum ;
many   doubted,   what   might-be best (to be done, for the in-

multi quid   expediret   sibi ;
terest of the republic); many what might-be-expedient for-themselves;

multi quid   deceret ;   etiam nonnulli
many what might-be-becoming (for them to do); also   some

quid   liceret.
what it-might-be-allowed (for them to do for their own private interest):

Respublica   perfuncta est hoc misero que
The republic 'has (at last) 'gone-through this miserable and

fatali   bello ; is   vicit,   qui   non
fatal (civil) war; he has-conquered, who 'would not

inflammaret suum odium fortunâ,
'inflame   his hatred by success (or make use of good

                    sed   leniret
fortune as a means of revenge),   but   would-mitigate (it)

bonitate ;   nec,   qui,   omnes   quibus
by kindness (and clemency);   nor,   who,   all (those)   with whom

    iratus esset   judicaret,   etiam
he-had-been-displeased (and offended) would-he-deem (them),   also

eosdem   dignos   · exsilio   aut   morte.   Arma
the same (as)   worthy (of)   exile   or   death.   Arms

    posita   ab aliis,   ab   aliis   erepta sunt.
were-laid-down   by some,   from   others   they-were-taken.   (That)

civis   est   ingratus   que   injustus,   qui   liberatus
citizen   is   ungrateful   and   unjust,   who   having-been-freed

    periculo   armorum,   tamen   retinet   armatum
from-the-dangers   of war,   yet   retains   a hostile

animum ;   ut   etiam   ille   sit   melior,
mind ;   (so) that   also   he   is   better (and more excusable),

qui cecidit in acie,   qui profudit   animam   in causâ.
who   fell   in battle,   who   lost   (his)   life   in the cause.

Enim   quæ   potest   videri   pertinacia   quibusdam,
For   that-which   may   appear   obstinacy   in some,

eadem   aliis   constantia.   Sed jam   omnis
the same   in-others (may appear) constancy.   But   now   all

dissentio   fracta est   armis,   et   exstincta
dissension   has-been-crushed   by-arms,   and   extinguished

    æquitate   victoris ;   restat,   ut omnes   velint
by-the-justice   of-the-conqueror;   it-remains,   that   all   may-desire

unum,   qui modo habent   non solum
one   (and the same thing),   who indeed may-have   not   only

aliquid   sapientiæ,   sed etiam   sanitatis.   Nisi,
any-thing   of wisdom,   but   also   soundness-of-mind.   Unless,

Cæsar,   te   salvo,   et   manente   in   istâ
O Cæsar,   you   being-safe,   and   remaining   in   this (same)

sententiâ,   quâ   cum   antea   vel   tum   hodie
opinion,   which   as   (well) heretofore   as   moreover   to-day

       maxime   usus es,
'you-have more-especially   'made-use-of, [in the same opinions you have

                  possumus   non   esse   salvi.
always declared yourself to be of]   'we-can   not   be   safe.

Quare   omnes, qui volumus hæc   esse salva,
Wherefore (we) all,   who   wish   these (things) to-be   safe,

et hortamur et obsecramus te ut consulas
both exhort and entreat you that you consult (your)

vitæ, ut tuæ saluti; que omnes
life, that (you would consult) your safety; and 'we all

pollicemur tibi (ut etiam loquar pro aliis,
'promise you (that 'I-may also 'speak for others,

quod ipse sentio de me), quoniam putas
that-which I-myself feel as respects myself), because you-think

aliquid subesse, quod
there 'is something (formed against you) 'concealed, which

cavendum sit, non modo excubias et
it-may-be-necessary-to-guard-against, not only watches and

custodias, sed etiam oppositus nostrorum
sentinels, but also (we promise) the opposition of our

laterum et corporum.
sides and bodies (as ramparts against your enemies).

11. Sed unde oratio orsa est terminetur in
But whence (my) speech began let-it-end in

eodem.
the same (place). [Let my speech end with the same expressions of thanks,

Omnes, C. Cæsar, agimus maximas
that it began with.] 'We all, O C. Cæsar, 'return great

gratias tibi; habemus etiam majores.
thanks to-you; we-have also (yet) greater (thanks that we

Nam omnes sentiunt idem;
cannot express). For all feel the same (thing)

quod potuisti sentire ex precibus et
which you-might-have perceived from the entreaties and

lacrymis omnium. Sed, quia est non necesse
tears of all. But, because it-is not necessary

omnibus stantibus dicere; certe
for all standing up to declare (their feelings and opinions); certainly

volunt dici a me, cui est quodammodo
they-wish (them) to-be-expressed by me, to whom it-is in-some-sort

necesse, et quod volunt, et quod decet,
necessary (to say), both what they-wish, and what is-proper,

et id, quod intelligo debere præcipue fieri a me,
and that, which I consider ought principally to-be-done by me

(M. Marcello reddito a te huic ordini
(M. Marcello being-restored by you to this order (of the senate)

que Romano populo et reipublicæ). Nam sentio
and the Roman people and to-the-republic) For I-feel (that

omnes lætari, non ut de salute unius solum, sed ut
all rejoice, not as for the safety of one alone, but as

de communi salute omnium ; atem quod est
for the common safety of all; but which is (a proof

summæ benevolentiæ (quæ fuit semper nota
of the greatest affection (which was always known

omnibus me erga illum, ut vix cederem
to all, (that) I (had) towards him, that scarcely did-I-yield

C. Marcello optimo et amantissimo fratri, quidem
to C. Marcellus his most excellent and affectionate brother, indeed

præter eum nemini), cum præstiterim id sollicitudine,
except him to no one), as I-showed this 'by (my) 'solicitude,

curâ, labore tamdiu quamdiu
'by (my) 'care, (and) 'by (my) 'exertion as-long as

dubitatum est de illius salutate, certe debeo
it-was-doubted respecting his safety, I certainly ought

præstare hoc tempore liberatus
to show (my affection) at-this time (when) freed

magnis curis, molestiis, doloribus.
from great cares, troubles, (and) sufferings (respecting him).

Itaque, C. Cæsar, sic ago gratias, ut me
Therefore, O C. Cæsar, I thus return thanks, that I being

non solum conservato a te omnibus rebus, sed
not only preserved by you in-all things, but

etiam ornato, tamen ad tua innumerabilia merita
also honoured, however to your innumerable kind acts

in me unum, (quod arbitrabar posse non jam
to me alone, (which I-thought could not even-now

fieri), hoc tuo facto
be made) (greater), by this your act (of pardoning M. Marcellus)

maximus cumulus accesserit.
the greatest crowning-favour has acceded.

ORATIO

THE ORATION

M. TULLII CICERONIS,
OF M. TULLIUS CICERO,

PRO

FOR

MANILIA LEGE.
THE MANILIAN LAW.

~~~~~~~~~~

1. QUANQUAM conspectus vester frequens
Although   the sight (of) **your**   numer. us (assembly)

semper est visus mihi, Quirites, multo
has always 'appeared   to-me,   O Romans, (by) much

jucundissimus,   autem hic locus amplissimus
the-most-agreeable (sight), moreover this place the-most-dignified

ad agendum,   ornatissimus ad dicendum;
to   treat (with you), (and) the-most-honourable to   speak (in);

tamen, hoc aditu laudis, qui semper maxime
however, from-this avenue to praise, which 'was always especially

patuit, cuique optimo,   non mea
'open, to each distinguished (and excellent man), not   my

voluntas, sed meæ rationes vitæ susceptæ ab
will,   but   my   rules   of life   adopted   from

ineunte ætate   prohibuerunt me. Nam
the commencing age (of my career) 'held me 'back.   For

cum antea, per ætatem, auderem nondum
when heretofore, on-account-of (my) age, I dared not-yet

attingere auctoritatem hujus loci, que statuerem,
aspire   to-the-dignity of-this place, and 'I-sat (it) 'down,

nihil oportere afferi huc nisi
(that) nothing ought to-be-brought to-this-place unless (it)

perfectum ingenio elaboratum industriâ; putavi
were-perfected by talent (and) elaborated by industry; 'I (therefore)

omne meum tempus transmittendum
'thought (that) all my time was-to-be-given-over

temporibus amicorum. Ita neque fuit hic locus
to-the-affairs of-my-friends. Also neither was this place

unquam vacuus ab iis, qui defenderent vestram
ever unoccupied by those, who might-defend your

causam; et meus labor versatus caste que
cause (and interests); and my labour employed faithfully and

integre in periculis privatorum, est consecutus
honestly in the dangers of private (individuals), has-obtained

amplissimum fructum ex vestro judicio.
the-most-ample reward from your judgment (and opinion,

Nam cum propter dilationem
favourably pronounced for me). For when on-account-of the adjournment

comitiorum, renuntiatus sum ter, primus
of-the-comitia, I-was-declared (elected) three-times, (as) first

prætor cunctis centuriis, facile intellexi,
prætor by-all the centuries, 'I readily 'understood (from this),

Quirites, et quid judicaretis de me, et quid
O-Romans, both what you-might-judge of me, and what

præscriberetis aliis. Et nunc, cum sit tantùm
you-might-prescribe to others. And now, when there-may-be so-much

auctoritatis in me, quantùm vos voluistis
of authority (and influence) in me, as you have-willed

esse honoribus mandandis; et
(that) there be by-honours assigned (to me, by you)· and

tantùm facultas ad agendum,
so much capacity (and fitness) for treating-with-you (and addressing

quantùm prope quotidiana exercitatio dicendi
you), as almost the daily exercise of speaking

potuit afferre vigilanti homini, ex usu
could bring to an industrious man, from the practice (of the)

forensi; et certe si est quid auctoritatis in
bar; and certainly if there is any-thing of-authority in

me, utar eâ apud eos, qui dederunt eam
me, I-will-use it before those, who conferred this (authority)

mihi; et si etiam possum consequi quid dicendo,
on me; and if also I can effect any-thing by speaking,

ostendam potissimum iis, qui quoque
I will-display (it) the-most-especially to-those, who also

censuerunt suo judicio fructum
have-thought by-their (favourable) opinion (and suffrages, that) a-reward

tribuendum esse ei rei. Atque video,
ought-to-be-given (me) for-this thing. And I-see, (that),

illud in primis, lætandum esse mihi jure,
that in particular, 'ought-to rejoice me by-right,

quòd in hac insolitâ ratione dicendi mihi, ex
that in this unusual mode of-speaking for-me, (and) from

hoc loco, talis causa oblata est, in quâ oratio
this place, such a cause is offered (to me), in which an oration

potest deesse nemini. Enim dicendum est de
could fail no-one. For it-is-to-be-discoursed about

singulari que eximiâ virtute Cn. Pompeii; hujus
the-singular and eminent virtue of Cn. Pompey; of-this

orationis est difficilius invenire exitum quàm
discourse it-is more-difficult to-find the termination than

principium. Ita non tam copia,
the commencement. Therefore not so-much copiousness (or diffusion),

quàm modus in dicendo quærendum est.
as (a restricted) mode in speaking is-to-be-sought-for.

2. Atque ut mea oratio proficiscatur inde,
Ar.1 that my oration may-proceed-from thence,

unde omnis hæc causa ducitur; grave et
whence all this affair is-derived; a serious and

periculosum bellum infertur vestris vectigalibus
dangerous war is-waged against-your revenues

atque sociis a duobus potentissimis regibus,
and allies by two most-powerful kings,

Mithridate et Tigrane, quorum alter relictus,
Mithridates and Tigranes, of-whom the one being-left

alter lacessitus,
(to himself and unmolested), the other provoked (by your attacks),

arbitrantur   occasionem   oblatum esse   sibi   ad
think   (that) an opportunity   is-offered   to-them   to

occupandum Asiam. Literæ   quotidie afferuntur
occupy   Asia.   Letters 'are   daily   'brought

ex   Asiâ Romanis   equitibus,   honestissimis viris,
from   Asia   to Roman   knights,   most-honourable   men,

quorum   magnæ   res   occupatæ, in
of, whom [belonging to whom] great sums-of-money employed,   in

exercendis   vestris   vectigalibus,   aguntur;   qui,
collecting   your   revenues,   are-at-stake;   who

pro   necessitudine,   quæ est mihi, cum illo
on-account-of the-intimate-connexion, which is   with-me, with that

ordine   detulerunt ad
order (of knight, from which I have myself sprung) brought   to

me   )   causam reipublicæ,
(and entrusted) me (with the task of pleading) the cause of-the-republic,

que pericula suarum   rerum;   Bithyniæ, quæ
and the dangers of their (private) fortunes;   in Bithynia, which

est nunc vestra provincia,   complures
is   now   your   province,   (it is said that)   many

vicos exustos esse;   regum Ariobarzanis, quod
villages have-been-burnt; (that) the kingdom of Ariobarzanes,   which

finitimum est   vestris   vectigalibus,   esse totum in
borders-on   your   tributaries,   is   entirely in

potestate hostium;   Lucullum,   gestis   magnis
the power of-the-enemy; (that) Lucullus, having-performed   great

rebus, discedere ab   eo   bello;   huic,   qui
exploits, is retiring from   that   war; (that)   to-him,   who

successerit   non   satis paratum esse
may-succeed (Lucullus) 'it has not 'been sufficiently   'provided

ad administrandum tantum bellum;   unum
for   conducting   so-great   a war; (that) one person [Pom.

deposci atque expeti ab omnibus sociis et
pey] is-demanded   and   required by   all   allies and

civibus   imperatorem   ad   id   bellum;   hunc
citizens (as) the commander   for   that   war;   (that)   this

eundem unum metui ab hostibus, præterea
same individual is-feared by the enemy, (and) besides (him)

neminem.
no-one.

Videtis quæ sit causa
You-see what may-be the case (and the nature of the affair before

nunc, considerate quid sit agendum. Videtur
you); now, consider what is-to-be-done. It-seems

mihi primum dicendum esse de genere
to-me (that) first mention-ought-to-be-made of the nature

belli, deinde de magnitudine, tum de
of-the-war, afterwards of (its) magnitude, (and) then of

imperatore diligendo. Genus belli est ejusmodi,
the commander to-be-chosen. The nature of-the-war is of-that-kind,

quod debeat maxime excitare atque inflammare
which ought very-greatly to-excite and to-inflame

vestros animos ad studium persequendi;
your minds to the zealous-desire of-carrying (it) on (to a suc-

in quo gloria Romani populi
cessful conclusion); in which the glory of-the-Roman people

agitur, quæ tradita est vobis a majoribus,
is-staked, which has-been-handed-down to you by (your) ancestors,

cum magna in omnibus
(which glory of your ancestor) when (it was) great in all

rebus, tum summa in militari re; salus
things, (was) then the greatest in military affairs; the safety

sociorum atque amicorum agitur, pro quâ vestri
of-our-allies and friends is-at-stake, for which your

majores gesserunt multa magna et gravia bella;
ancestors have-waged many great and serious wars;

certissima et maxima vectigalia Romani populi
the most-sure and greatest revenues of-the-Roman people

aguntur; quibus amissis, requiretis
are-at-stake; which being-lost, you-will-require (and miss

et ornamenta pacis, et subsidia belli; bona
both the ornaments of peace, and the subsidies of war; the property

multorum civium aguntur, quibus consulendum est
of many citizens is-at-stake, for-which care-is-to-be-taken

a vobus, et causâ ipsorum et
by you, both for the sake of-those-interested and (for the sage)

reipublicæ.
of the republic.

3. Et quoniam semper fuistis appetentes
   And because 'you always have-been seekers

gloriæ, atque avidi laudis præter ceteras gentes,
of glory, and eager of praise beyond (all) other nations,

illa macula, suscepta superiore Mithridatico bello,
that stain, received in-the-former Mithridatic war,

delenda est vobis, quæ jam insedit penitus
is-to-be-effaced by-you, which (stain) now has-settled deep

atque inveteravit in nomine
and 'established (itself) 'by-length-of-time on the name

Romani populi; quòd is qui, uno
of-the-Roman people; that he (Mithridates) who, in-one (and the

die, in totâ Asiâ, in tot civitatibus,
same) day, in all Asia, in so-many cities (and states)

denotavit uno nuntio, atque significatione
designated by-a-single messenger, and by-the-signification (or order)

unâ literarum Romanos cives
alone of-a-letter (he carried with him) Roman citizens

trucidandos que necandos, non modo adhuc
to-be-butchered and put-to-death, not only as-yet

suscepit ullam pœnam dignam scelere;
has-he-(not)-received any punishment commensurate with-the-crime;

sed jam regnat, tertium et vicesimum annum
but 'he now 'reigns, (in the) three and twentieth year

ab illo tempore; et regnat, ita ut
from that time (of the massacre); and he-reigns, so that 'he-does

non velit occultare se Ponto, neque latebris
not 'pretend to-hide himself in-Pontus, nor in-the-lurking-places

Cappadociæ, sed emergere e patrio
f Cappadocia, but (he seeks) to-emerge from (his) hereditary

regno, atque versari in vestris
kingdom, and to-carry-on (his warlike operations) among your

vectigalibus, hoc est in luce. Asiæ.
tributaries, that is in (open day) light (and view of all) Asia

Etenim adhuc, vestri imperatores ita contenderunt
For until-now, your generals 'have so 'contended

cum illo rege, ut reportarent ab
with that king, that (they may be said to) have carried off from

illo insignia victoriæ, non victoriam. L. Sulla
him the-tokens of victory, (and) not victory (itself). L. Sylla

triumphavit de Mithridate, L. Murena triumphavit,
triumphed over Mithridates, L. Murena triumphed

duo fortissimi viri, et summi imperatores;
(over him), two most-valiant men, and the greatest commanders;

sed triumpharunt ita, ut ille, pulsus que superatus,
but they triumphed so, that he, repulsed and defeated,

regnaret. Verumtamen laus est tribuenda illis
still reigned. But-indeed praise is to-be-given to-those

imperatoribus quod egerunt; venia danda,
generals (for) what they did; pardon is-to-be-granted,

quod reliquerunt; propterea quòd respublica
for what they-left-undone; because that the republic

revocavit Sullam ab eo bello in Italiam, Sulla
recalled Sylla from that war to Italy, (and) Sylla

Murenam.
(recalled) Murena.

4. Autem Mithridates contulit omne reliquum
But Mithridates employed all the intervening

tempus, non ad oblivionem veteris belli, sed ad
time, not in the oblivion of-the-old war, but in

comparationem novi; qui, posteaquam
the preparing of a new (war); who, after-that

ædificasset que ornasset maximas classes, que
ae-had-built and equipped very-great fleets, and

comparasset permagnos exercitus, ex quibuscunque
assembled very-large armies, from whatever

gentibus potuisset, et simulasset se
nations he-could, and pretended (that) he (was about

inferre bellum Bosporanis, suis
to wage war against-the-inhabitants-on-the-Bosphorus, his

finitimis; misit legatos ac literas, usque in
neighbours; he-sent ambassadors and letters, even unto

Hispaniam ad eos duces, cum quibus tum
Spain   to those leaders, with whom 'we-were then

gerebamus bellum; cum ut bellum gereretur
'waging   war;   so that the war might-be-carried-on

terrâ que mari, in duobus disjunctissimis, que
by-land and by-sea, in two widely-separated, and

maxime diversis locis, uno consilio
very greatly dissimilar places, with one (and the same) plan

a binis copiis hostium, vos districti
(of operation) by two armies of-the-enemy, (so that) you occupied

ancipiti contentione dimicaretis de imperio.
by-a-double contest might-have-to-fight for the empire (itself)

Sed tamen periculum alterius partis, Sertorianæ
But however the danger of-the-other part (namely), the Sertorian

atque Hispaniensis, quæ habebat multo plus
and Spanish (danger), which had much more

firmamenti ac roboris, depulsum est divino consilio
stability and strength, was-warded-off by-the-divine wisdom

ac singulari virtute Cn. Pompeii; in alterâ parte,
and singular valour of Cn. Pompey; on the other part

res ita administrata est a L. Lucullo,
(in Asia), the affair 'was so 'managed by L. Lucullus,

summo viro, ut illa magna atque præclara
a-most-distinguished man, that those great and brilliant

initia gestarum rerum videantur esse tribuenda,
beginnings 'of (his) 'exploits may-seem to be attributed,

non ejus felicitati, sed virtuti, autem hæc
not 'to his 'good-fortune, but 'to (his) 'valour, but these

extrema, quæ nuper acciderunt,
latter (reverses), which lately have-happened, (may seem to be attri

non culpæ, sed fortunæ. Sed de
buted), not (to any) fault (of his), but (to bad) fortune. But of

Lucullo dicam alio loco, et ita dicam
Lucullus I-shall-speak in-another place, and 'I shall so 'speak (of him)

Quirites, ut videatur, neque vera laus
O Romans, that it-may-seem, (that) neither true praise

detracta ei nostrâ oratione, neque falsa
has-been-taken-from him by-our oration, nor false (praise)

afficta esse   De   dignitate atque gloriâ
to-have-been-bestowed (on him). Concerning the-dignity   and   the-glory

vestri imperii, quoniam is est exorsus meæ
of-your   empire,   as   that   is   the beginning   of my

orationis, videte, quem   animum   putetis
oration,   consider,   what (feelings of) mind   you-may-think

suscipiendum vobis.
ought-to-be-entertained by-you.

5. Vestri majores   sæpe gesserunt bella
Your   ancestors 'have often   'waged   wars (on account

mercatoribus ac naviculariis   injuriosiùs
of their)   merchants   and seafaring-men 'having-been too-injuriously

tractatis; tandem, quo   animo debetis vos esse,
'treated;   in-fine, in-what (state of) mind   ought   you to-be,

tot millibus Romanorum civium necatis,
so-many thousands   of Roman   citizens being-slain, (by an order

uno nuntio, atque   uno   tempore? Vestri
carried) by-one messenger,   and (all) at-the-same   time?   Your

patres voluerunt   Corinthum, lumen totius Græciæ,
ancestors resolved (that)   Corinth,   the light of-all   Greece,

extinctum   esse   quòd   legati
should-be   extinguished (and destroyed) because (your) ambassadors

erant superbiùs appellati; vos patiemini eum regem
were   too-haughtily   addressed; you   suffer   that   king

esse inultum, qui necavit legatum   Romani populi,
to-be unpunished, who murdered an ambassador of the Roman   people,

consularem,   excruciatum vinculis ac
(and he of) consular-dignity, (after being)   tortured   by chains and

verberibus, atque omni   supplicio? Illi
scourging,   and   all (kinds of) punishments?   They (your

non   tulerunt   libertatem
ancestors)   'did not   'suffer   the liberty   (and privileges)

Romanorum civium imminutam;   vos negligetis
of Roman   citizens to-be-infringed;   'will you   'neglect

vitam ereptam?   Illi
(to avenge) the-life   taken   (from your ambassador)?   They

persecuti sunt jus   legationis
avenged   the right, (and privileges) of-an-embassy (when)

violatum   verbo;   vos relinquetis   legatum
violated (only) by-a-word; 'will you 'leave (unavenged) an ambassador

interfectum, omni   supplicio? Videte, ne, ut
put-to-death,   by-all (kinds of)   torture?   See-to-it, lest, as

fuit pulcherrimum   illis, relinquere vobis tantam
it was a-most-illustrious (thing) for-them, to-leave to you so-great

gloriam   imperii;   sic   sit
a glory   of-empire   (and such great renown);   so   it-may-be

turpissimum   vobis, non   posse   tueri   et
a-most-shameful (thing) for-you, not to-be-able to defend and

conservare, id, quod   accepistis.   Quid,
to preserve,   that, which you-have-received (from them).   What

quòd   salus   sociorum   vocatur, in
(shall I say of this), that the safety of-the-allies is-placed in

summum periculum ac discrimen? Rex Ariobarzanes,
the greatest danger   and   hazard?   King Ariobarzanes,

socius atque amicus Romani   populi,   expulsus est
the-ally and   friend of-the-Roman people,   has-been-driven

regno; duo reges imminent toti Asiæ,
'from (his) 'kingdom; two kings threaten all Asia, (who are)

non solum inimicissimi vobis, sed etiam vestris sociis
not   only   most-hostile to-you, but also to-your allies

atque amicis; autem omnes civitates, cuncta Asia
and   friends;   but   all   the cities, entire Asia

atque Græcia,   propter   magnitudinem   periculi,
and   Greece, on-account-of the magnitude   of-the-danger,

coguntur expectare   vestrum auxilium;
are-forced   to-expect   (and wish for)   your   assistance;

arbitrantur   neque   audent   deposcere certum
they-think (that) neither dare-they request a certain

imperatorem,   a   vobis, cum
(particular) commander, [namely, Pompey,] from you, when

præsertim vos miseritis alium, neque   posse
especially you have-sent another, nor (suppose that) they-could

facere id, sine   summo periculo.
do   it, without the greatest danger (from the commander just

Vident et sentiunt hoc idem,   quod
appointed). They-see and feel   this same (thing), which

vos esse unum virum, in quo sint omnia
you (do, that) there-is one man, in whom are all

summa, et eum esse
the highest (qualities, for carrying on the war), and (that) he is

prope, (quo etiam carent ægriùs),
near, (for which also they-desire (him) the-more-impatiently),

ipso adventu cujus, atque nomine
by-this-self-same arrival of-him, and 'by (his) 'name,

tametsi ille venerit ad maritimum bellum,
although he came to a maritime war (against the pirates),

tamen intelligunt impetus hostium esse
yet they perceive (that) the attacks of-the-enemy were

repressos ac retardatos. Hi rogant vos
repressed and retarded. These (allies and friends) entreat you

tacite, quoniam
silently, because (through fear of offending the commander of the pro

non licet loqui libere, ut
vince) 'it-is not 'allowed (them) to speak freely (and openly), that

quoque existimetis se sicut dignos
'you-would also 'consider them as worthy of your

socios ceterarum provinciarum, quorum
favours, as are the allies of-other provinces, whose

salutem commendetis tali viro: atque
safety you-may-have-confided to such a man (as Pompey): and

hoc etiam magis, quàm ceteros, quòd
for-this (reason) also the-more-so, than the others (are), because

mittimus homines ejusmodi in provinciam cum
we-send men of-that-sort into this province with (military

imperio, ut etiam si defendant
and civil) authority, (so) that though if they-defend (them)

ab hoste, tamen ipsorum adventus in urbes
from the enemy, yet their arrival among the towns

sociorum non differant multum ab hostili
of-the-allies 'does not 'differ much from a hostile

expugnatione. Audiebant hunc antea, nunc
capture. They-heard (of) him before, new

vident præsentem, tantâ
they-see (him) present (among them), (a man) of-so-much

temperantiâ, tantâ mansuetudine, tantâ humanitate,
moderation,   of-so-much   mildness,   of-so-much   humanity

ut ii videantur esse beatissimi, apud quos
that those   seem   to be   the-most-fortunate,   among   whom

ille commoratur diutissime.
he   sojourns   the-longest-time.

6. Quare, si vestri majores, propter socios,
Wherefore, if   your   ancestors,   on account (of their)   allies

ipsi lacessiti nullâ injuriâ, gesserunt
(although) themselves   provoked   by no   injury,   waged

bella cum Antiocho, cum Philippo, cum Ætolis,
wars   with   Antiochus,   with   Philip,   with   the Ætolians,

cum Pœnis; quanto studio convenit
with   the Carthaginians;   with-what   zeal (therefore)   does-it-become

vos, provocatos injuriis, defendere salutem
you,   provoked   by injuries,   to-defend   the-safety 'of (your)

sociorum, unâ cum dignitate vestri imperii,
'allies,   together   with   the dignity   of-your   empire;

præsertim cum agatur de vestris maximis
especially   when (the thing) agitated (is)   about   your   greatest

vectigalibus? Nam vectigalia
(and most productive)   revenues?   For   the revenues

ceterarum provinciarum, Quirites, sunt tanta
of-the-other   provinces,   O Romans,   are (only)   so-great

ut possimus vix esse contenti ad
that   we-can   scarcely   be   content (with them, as sufficient) for

tutandas provincias ipsas; Asia vero est tam
defending   the provinces   themselves;   Asia   indeed   is   so

opima et fertilis, ut facile antecellat omnibus
fertile   and productive,   that (it) easily   excels   all (other)

terris, et ubertate agrorum, et varietate
countries,   both   by-the-richness 'of (its) 'soil,   and   by-the-variety

fructuum, et magnitudine pastionis, et
'of (its) 'fruits,   and   by-the-extent 'of (its) 'pastures,   and

multitudine earum rerum, quæ exportantur. Itaque,
by-the-multitude of-those   things,   which may-be-exported.   Therefore,

Quirites, hæc provincia vobis, si vultis
O Romans,   this   province (belonging) to-you,   if   you-wish

sustinere, et utilitatem belli,
to sustain (and defend), both (its) usefulness (in time) of war,

et dignitatem pacis, est non modò
and (its) dignity (and ornament in time) of peace, is not only

defendenda calamitate, sed etiam a
to-be-defended (by you) 'from (all) 'calamity, but also from

netu calamitatis. Nam in ceteris rebus, cum
(even) the fear of calamity. For in other things, when

calamitas venit, tum detrimentum accipitur; at
(any) calamity arrives, then damage is received; but

in vectigalibus non solum adventus mali, sed etiam
in revenue-affairs not only the arrival of-evil, but also

metus ipse, affert calamitatem. Nam cum copiæ
the fear itself (of it), brings calamity. For when the forces

hostium non longe absunt, etiam si nulla
of-the-enemy 'are not far 'distant, (and) also if no

irruptio sit facta, tamen pecora relinquuntur,
inroad be made, however the flocks are-abandoned,

agricultura deseritur, navigatio mercatorum
agriculture is-deserted, the navigation (and commerce) of-merchants

conquiescit. Ita neque ex portu,
ceases-to-be-active. So (that) neither from port (duties on exports

neque ex decumis, neque
and imports), nor from the tithes (on agricultural produce), nor

ex scripturâ potest vectigal conservari.
from the pasturage-tax could (any) impost be preserved

Quare sæpe fructus totius anni
(or obtained). Wherefore often the produce of-an-entire year

amittitur uno rumore periculi, atque uno
is-lost by-a-single rumour of danger, and by-the-mere

terrore belli. Tandem, quo animo
fear of war. In-fine, in-what (state of) min

existimatis aut eos esse, qui pensitant vectigalia
do-you-think (that) either those are, who pay duties

nobis, aut eos qui exercent atque
to-us, or those who (make it their business to) collect and

exigunt, cum duo reges cum maximis copiis
exact (them), when two kings with very-large forces are

prope adsint? Cum una excursio equitatûs possit
nearly 'present? When one incursion of-cavalry may

perbrevi tempore, auferre vectigal totius
in-a-very-snort time, carry off the revenue of-the-whole

anni? Cum publicani arbitrentur, se
year? When the-farmers-of-the-revenue may-think, (that) they

habere magno periculo maximas familias,
maintain at-a-great risk very-great companies (of slaves),

quas habent in saltibus, quas in agris,
which they-have in the-forests, which (they have) in the-fields,

quas in portubus, atque custodiis?
which (they have) in the harbours, and in-the-custom-houses?

Ne putatis, vos posse frui illis rebus, nisi
Whether do-you-think, (that) you can enjoy those things, unless

conservaveritis eos, qui sunt fructui vobis (ut
you-preserve those who are (thus) useful to-you (as

dixi antea), non solum liberatos calamitate, sed
I-said before), not only freed from calamity, but

etiam formidine calamitatis?
also from-the-dread of calamity?

7. Ac illud quidem ne negligendum est vobis,
And that indeed 'is not 'to-be-neglected by you,

quod ego proposueram mihi extremum,
which I had-proposed to-myself (as) the-last-thing (to be men

cum essem dicturus, de genere belli,
tioned), when I-might (come) to-speak, concerning the kind of-war,

quod pertinet ad bona multorum
(namely, that) which appertains to the property of-many

Romanorum civium; quorum, Quirites, pro
Roman citizens; of whose (interest), O Romans, in

vestrâ sapientiâ, ratio
your wisdom, a sentiment of regard (for their interests) 'is

diligenter habenda est vobis. Nam et
especially 'to-be-had by you. For also

publicani, et honestissimi et ornatissimi
the-farmers-of-the-revenue, both honourable and accomplished

homines, contulerunt suas rationes et copias in
men, have-transferred their means and wealth into

illam provinciam; res et fortuna quorum
that province; the property and fortune of these

ipsorum debent esse, per se, curæ
same (men) ought to-be, on-their-own-account, (an especial) care

vobis Etenim si, semper duximus
to you. For if, (as) 'we-have always 'supposed

vectigalia esse nervos reipublicæ; certe
the revenues to-be the sinews of-the-republic; 'we certainly

diceremus esse recte, eum ordinem,
'may-be-said to be right, (when we assert, that), that order

qui exercent illa, esse
(of men, the equites), who follow-the-business-of-collecting them, are

firmamentum ceterorum ordinum. Deinde, gnavi
the support of-the-other orders. In-the-next-place, active

et industrii homines ex ceteris ordinibus,
and industrious men from the other orders, (that)

partim ipsi negociantur in Asiâ, quibus, absentibus,
partly themselves traffic in Asia, who, being absent,

debetis consulere; partim habent magnas
you-ought to-take-care of; (and who) partly have great

pecunias suas, et suorum collocatas
sums-of-money (both) their-own, and (that) of-their-friends, placed

in eâ provinciâ. Igitur erit vestræ humanitatis,
in that province. Therefore it-will-be (a part) 'of your 'humanity,

prohibere magnum numerum eorum civium calamitate;
to-shield a great number of-those citizens from misfortune;

sapientiæ, videre calamitatem
(it will be a part of your) wisdom, to-perceive (that) the misfortune

multorum civium posse non esse sejunctam a
of-many citizens can not be separated from (that of)

republica. Etenim illud primum, refert parvi,
the republic. For that at-first, it-avails little, (that)

vos recuperare postea, victoriâ, vectigalia amissa
you recover hereafter, by-a-victory, the revenues lost

publicanis Neque enim, erit facultas
by-the-farmers-thereof. Nor also, will-there-be the means

iisdem redimendi,
with-these-same (farmers of the revenue) 'of (again) 'contracting-to-

propter calamitatem,
collect-the-revenue, on-account-of the calamity (of losing their property)

neque   voluntas aliis,   propter timorem.
nor (will there be any) desire to others, on-account-of the fear

            Deinde,   quod   eadem Asia, atque iste
(of the risks).   Next,   that-which this-same Asia,   and   this

idem   Mithridates docuit nos   initio   Asiatici
very-same Mithridates   taught   us in-the-beginning of the Asiatic

belli ; id quidem   debemus   certe   retinere
war ;   that indeed we-ought certainly to retain 'in (our)

memoriâ docti calamitate.   Nam scimus   tum,
'memory   taught by calamity.   For we-know (that) then,

cum permulti amiserant magnas res, fidem concidisse
when very-many had-lost   large fortunes, credit   fell

Romæ,   solutione   impeditâ.   Enim multi
at Rome,   the payment (of debts) being hindered.   For   many

possunt non amittere   rem atque fortunas in unâ
can   not lose (their) property and fortunes in   a

civitate, ut   non trahunt plures, cum   se,   in
city,   that 'they-do not 'draw many, with themselves, into

eandem calamitatem.   A   quo
the same   calamity (of loss of property and fortune). From which

periculo,   prohibete   rempublicam, et credite mihi
misfortune, do-you-defend   the republic,   and   believe   me

(id quod   ipsi   videtis),   hæc fides, atque
(that which you-yourselves perceive) (to be so), these credits,   and

hæc ratio   pecuniarum, quæ versatur Romæ,
this rate (and state) of-money-affairs, which are-practised at Rome,

quæ   in foro, implicata est cum illis
which (are also practised) in the forum, are-bound-up with those

Asiaticis   pecuniis,   et
Asiatic   sums of money (belonging to citizens of Rome),   and

cohæret.   Illa   possunt non
cling (to them). Those (sums of moneys, invested in Asia), can   not

ruere,   ut hæc,   labefactata
fall (and be lost), (but) that these (money affairs in Rome), being shaken

eodem   motu,   non concidant.   Quare
by-the-same motion, would not   fall (with them). Wherefore

videte, num vobis dubitandum sit incumbere
consider, if you ought-to-doubt to-apply-yourselves

omni studio ad id bellum, in quo gloria vestri
with-all zeal to that war, in which the glory of-your

nominis, salus sociorum maxima vectigalia,
name, the safety 'of (your) 'allies, (your) greatest revenues,

fortunæ plurimorum civium, cum
(and) the fortunes of many citizens, with

republicâ defendantur.
the republic are defended (and protected).

8. Quoniam dixi de genere belli,
Because I-have-spoken concerning the nature of-the-war, 'I

nunc dicam pauca de magnitudine.
now 'will-say a few (words) concerning (its) magnitude.

Enim hoc potest dici; esse genus belli
For this may be-said (of it); (that it) is a kind of-war

ita necessarium, ut sit gerendum; esse
so necessary, that it-is (absolutely) to-be-waged; (that) it-is

non ita magnum, ut sit pertimescendum. In quo,
not so great, that it-may-be-greatly-feared. In which,

est maxime loborandum, ne forte ea
it-is principally to-be-sought-for (by me), lest by-chance those-things

videantur vobis esse contemnenda, quæ
may-seem to-you to-be despised, which 'are

diligentissime providenda sunt. Atque ut omnes
most-diligently 'to-be-provided-against. And that all

intelligant, me impertire L. Lucullo tantum
may-understand, (that) I grant to L. Lucullus so-much

laudis, quantum debeatur forti viro, et sapientissimo
of praise, as is due to-a-brave man, and to-a-very-wise

homini, et magno imperatori; dico, eju
man, and to-a-great general; I-say, (that) 'on hi

adventu, maximas copias Mithridates fuisse ornatas
arrival, the-very-great forces of-Mithridates were equipped

atque instructas, omnibus rebus; que
and supplied, with-all things (necessary for the war); and

urbem Cyzicenorum clarissimam Asiæ, que
(that) the town of-the-Cyzicenians the-most-celebrated of Asia, and

amicissimam nobis, obsessam esse ab rege ipso,
the-most-friendly to-us, was-besieged by the king himself,

maximâ mvltitudine, et vehementissime
with-a-very-great multitude (of troops) and most-violently

oppugnatum, quam L. Lucullus liberavit
assaulted, which (town) L. Lucullus relieved

summis periculis obsidionis, virtute, assiduitate
from-the-greatest dangers of-a-siege, 'by (his) 'valour, perseverance

consilio; ab eodem imperatore
(and wise) counsel; (and that) by the same general (Lucullus)

magnam et ornatam classem superatam esse atque
a large and well-equipped fleet was-defeated and

depressam, quæ, inflammata studio
sunk, which, inflamed with-an-eager-desire (of vengeance),

raperetur ad Italiam Sertorianis ducibus;
was-hurried-on towards Italy by Sertorian leaders;

præterea
[officers belonging to Sertorius's party in Spain]; moreover (that)

magnas copias hostium deletas esse multis
large forces of-the-enemy were-destroyed in-many

præliis; que Pontum patefactum esse nostris
battles; and (that) Pontus was-opened to-our

legionibus, qui ante clausus esset Romano populo,
legions, which before had-been-shut to-the-Roman people,

ex omni aditu; Sinopen atque Amisum, in
on al' (its) approaches; that Sinope and Amisus, in

quibus oppidis, erant domicilia regis ornata atque
which towns, were the palaces of-the-king adorned and

referta omnibus rebus; que permultas ceteras urbes
filled with-all things; and very-many other towns

Ponti et Cappadociæ captas esse, uno aditu
of-Pontus and of-Cappadocia were-taken, 'by (his) 'mere approach

atque adventu; regem spoliatum patria
and arrival; (that) the king deprived 'of (his) 'paternal

atque avito regno, contulisse se supplicem ad
and ancestral kingdom, betook himself a suppliant to

alios reges, atque ad alias gentes; atque omnia
other kings, and to other nations; and (that) all

hæc   gesta esse,   sociis   Romanı   populi   salvis,
this   was-performed,   the allies of-the-Roman people being-safe,

atque vectigalibus   integris.   Opinor
and   the revenues being entire (and undiminished). I-think

hoc   esse   satis laudis; atque ita,
'that' this   is   enough of-praise;   and so (delivered),

Quirites, ut vos intelligatis hoc   L. Lucullum
O Romans, that you may-understand this (that) L. Lucullus

laudatum esse similiter,   ex hoc loco   a
has-been-praised in-like-manner, from this place [the rostrum] by

nullo istorum, qui obtrectant huic legi atque
none of-those, who object   to-this law   and

causæ.
cause (of giving the command to Pompey).

9. Fortasse   nunc   requiretur, quemadmodum
Perhaps 'it-will now 'be-asked,   how

cum hæc sint ita,   magnum bellum possit esse
when these-things are so, (that) a great war   can   be

reliquum.   Cognoscite,   Quirites; cnim
left (for us to wage). Know (then) O Romans; for

hoc videtur quæri non sine causâ. Primum
this seems to-be-asked not without reason.   First

Mithridates sic profugit ex suo regno, ut illa Medea
Mithridates so fled from his kingdom, as that Medea

dicitur quondam profugisse ex eodem Ponto;
is-said once to-have-fled from this-same Pontus;

quam, prædicant, in fugâ dissipavisse membra
whom, they-say, in (her) flight had-strewed-about the limbs

sui fratris, in iis locis, qua   parens
of-her brother, in those places, where (her) father

persequeretur se, ut dispersa collectio eorum,
might-follow-after her, that the dispersed collection of them,

que patrius mœror retardaret celeritatem
and paternal grief might-retard the celerity

persequendi.   Sic Mithridates fugiens,
of (his) 'pursuing (her). Thus Mithridates flying,

reliquit in Ponto omnem   maximam vim auri
eft in Pontus all (that) very-great abundance of-gold

atque   argenti,   que   omnium   pulcherrimarum
and   of-silver,   and   of-all   (those) most-beautiful

rerum, quas   et   acceperat   a   majoribus, et
things, which both he-had-inherited from (his) ancestors,   and

      ipse   congesserat   in   suum regnum,
(which) he-himself had-collected-together in   his   kingdom,

direptas, superiore bello, ex totâ Asiâ. Dum
plundered, in-the-former war, from all Asia.   While

nostri diligentius colligunt omnia hæc,   rex
our-men diligently   collect   all these-things, the king

ipse   effugit   e   manibus. Ita   mœror
himself escaped out-of (their) hands.   So (as)   grief

retardavit illum   in studio persequendi, (so)
retarded   him (the father of Medea), in the ardour of-pursuing, (so)

hos   lætitiâ.   Tigranes,
these (our soldiers were retarded) by-the-delight (of plunder). Tigranes,

Armenius rex, excepit hunc in illo   timore et
the Armenian king, received him   in this (his) alarm   and

fugâ, que confirmavit   diffidentem suis rebus, et
flight, and he-encouraged (him) despairing of-his affairs, and

erexit   afflictum   que recreavit   (him)
¹cheered (him) ¹up afflicted (and cast down), (and) he-solaced   (him)

perditum.   In cujus regnum, posteaquam
ruined,   (with new hopes). In whose kingdom,   after

J. Lucullus venit cum exercitu, plures gentes etiam
L. Lucullus arrived with the army, many nations   also

concitatæ sunt contra nostrum imperatorem. Enim
were-excited   against   our   general.   For

metus injectus erat iis nationibus, quas Romanus
fear   was-inspired into those nations,   whom   the Roman

populus   nunquam putavit, neque   lacessendas
people   ¹had never   ¹thought, either (of)   harassing

bello, neque tendandas.   Erat etiam   alia
y-war,   or (of) attempting (to do so). There-was also another

gravis atque vehemens opinio, quæ pervaserat   per
grave   and   vehement   opinion, which had-prevailed through

animos barbararum gentium,   nostrum exercitum
he minds of-the-barbarous   nations, (that)   our   army

esse adductum in eas oras causâ diripendi
was led into those countries, for-the-purpose of despoiling

locupletissimi, et religiosissimi fani. Ita multæ
a-very-rich, and much-revered temple. So many

atque magnæ nationes concitabantur, quodam
and great nations were-excited (against us), by-some

novo terrore ac metu. Autem etsi noster exercitus
new terror and fear. But although our army

ceperat urbem ex regno Tigranis, et usus erat
had-taken a town in the kingdom of Tigranes, and had-obtained

secundis prœliis, tamen commovebatur
successful battles, however moved

nimiâ longinquitate locorum, ac desiderio
by-the-very great distance of-the-places, and by-the-desire

suorum.
of their (friends and home, to which they wished to return). 'I-will

Non jam dicam plura hic; enim illud fuit extremum,
not now 'say more here; for this was the extreme

ut magis maturus reditus quæreretur, ex
(point, so) that a more speedy return was-sought-for, from

iis locis a nostris militibus, quàm longior processio.
those places by our soldiers, than a farther advance

Autem Mithridates et confirmarat
(desired.) But Mithridates 'had both revived (the confidence of)

suam manum, et juvabatur
nis-own (immediate) band (of followers), and he-was-aided

eorum, qui collegerant
(and strengthened, by the assistance) of-those, who had assembled

se ex ejus regno, et magnis
themselves (together) from his (own) kingdom, and by great

adventitiis copiis multorum regum et nationum.
adventitious forces of-many kings and nations.

Jam accepimus hoc solere fere fieri sic,
We-have already 'understood that it usually mostly happens so,

ut afflictæ fortunæ regum, facile alliciant ad
that the fallen fortunes of-kings, easily entice on-account-of

misericordiam opes multorum, que maxime
pity (for them) the assistance of-many, and most-especially

eorum, qui sunt aut reges, aut vivunt in
of-those, who are either kings, or (who) live unde.

regno ; quòd regale nomen videatur iis,
a-kingly-government; because the-royal name appears te-them,

esse magnum et sanctum. Itaque, victus,
to-be great and sacred. Therefore, (though) conquered

potuit efficere tantum, quantum unquam
he-could effect so-much (more), than 'he ever

ausus est optare incolumis. Nam
'dared to-hope-for (when) safe, (and in prosperity). For

cum recipisset se in suum regnum, fuit non
when he-had-returned to his kingdom, he-was not

contentus eo ; quod acciderat ei
content (to remain quiet) there; (for) this had-happened to-him

præter spem, ut posteaquam
beyond (his) hopes, that after-that

pulsus erat ; unquam attin
he-had-been-driven (out of his-kingdom); he-should-ever touch

geret illam terran, sed fecit impetum
that country (with his foot again), but he-made an attack

in vestrum clarum atque vitorem exercitum. Sinite
on your renowned and conquering army. Allow

me, Quirites, hoc loc (sicut poëtæ solent, qui
me, O Romans, in-this place (as the poets used (to do), who

scribunt Romanas res), præterire nostram
wrote (verses) on-Roman affairs), to pass-over our

calamitatem ; quæ fuit tanta, ut non nuntius ex
calamity ; which was so-great, that not a messenger from

prœlio, sed rumor ex sermone
the battle (field), but rumour through the conversation (of men)

afferret eam ad aures L. Luculli.
brought this (news of our calamity) to the ears of L. Lucullus.

Hìc in illo ipso malo, que gravissimâ offensione
Here in this same misfortune, and 'in (this) 'most-grievous disaster

belli, L. Lucullus, qui tamen potuisset fortasse
of-the-war, L. Lucullus, who yet might perhaps

mederi, ex parte iis incommodis, coactus vestro
have-remedied, in part those disasters, compelled by-your

jussu, quòd putavistis veteri exemplo,
command, because you-thought, in accordance with-ancient example

modum statuendum diuturnitati imperii,
(and principles), a term was-to-be-set (to) long-continued command,

dimisit partem militum, qui jam confecti erant
he-discharged a part of-the-soldiers, who now had-completed

stipendiis, partem tradidit Glabrioni.
(their term-of-service, a part he-delivered-over to-Glabrio (his

Prætereo multa consultò; sed vos
successor). I-pass-over many-things on-purpose; but you

perspicitis ea conjecturâ. Putetis
may-perceive them by-conjecture. You-may-consider (therefore)

quantum illud bellum factum, quod potentissimi
how-important that war is-made, which most-powerful

reges conjungant, agitatæ nationes
kings unite-in, (which) agitated (and irritated) nations

renovant, integræ gentes suscipiant,
renew, (which) the entire people-of-a-country undertake, (and of

vester novus imperator accipiat,
which war) your new commander [Glabrio] receives

vetere exercitu pulso.
(the command), the old army being repulsed.

10. Videor mihi fecisse satis multa verba,
It seems to-me (that) I-have-made enough many words,

quare hoc bellum
[that I have spoken enough,] (to show you) why this war

esset genere ipso necessarium, magnitudine
might-be 'from (its) 'nature itself necessary, 'from (its) 'magnitude

periculosum; videatur restat, ut
dangerous; it seems (that) it remains, that

dicendum esse, de imperatore diligendo ad id
mention-ought-to-be-made, about the commander to-be-selected for this

bellum, ac præficiendo tantis rebus.
war, and the entrusting (him with) such great affairs.

Utinam, Quirites, haberetis tantam copiam
I-wish, O Romans, that-you-had so-great an abundance

fortium atque innocentium virorum, ut hæc vobis
of-brave and honest men, that this your

deliberatıo   esset   difficilis   quemnam
deliberation   would-be   difficult   (in determining)   whom

    putaretis   potissimum   præficiendum
you-might-consider   most-especially   (proper)   to-be-entrusted

    tantis   rebus,   ac   tanto   bello.   Vero   nunc
with-such-great affairs,   and   with-so-great   a war.   But   now

cum   sit   Cn. Pompeius   unius,   qui   superarit
when   there is   Cn. Pompey   alone,   who   may-have-excelled

gloriam   non modo   eorum   hominum,   qui nunc sunt,
the glory   not   only   of those   men,   who   now   are,

sed etiam   memoriam   antiquitatis,   virtute;
but   also   the-remembrance (of the men) of-antiquity,   by (his) courage

              quæ   res   est,   quæ   possit facere
(and merits);   what   thing   is   (there then),   which   can   occasion

dubium   animum   cujusquam,   in hac causâ?   Enim ego
a doubt   in-the-mind   of-any-one,   in   this   case?   For

existimo sic,   in summo imperatore,   has   quatuor
consider   thus, (that) in   a great   general,   these   four

res   oportere   inesse,   scientiam militaris
things are-necessary (for him) to-be-possessed-of, the-science   of military

rei,   virtutem,   auctoritatem,   felicitatem.
affairs,   válour,   the authority   (of renown), (and)   good-fortune

Quis   igitur   fuit   aut   unquam   scientior,
Who   therefore   was   either   ever   more-skilled (in military affairs),

aut   debuit   esse   hoc   homine?   qui   e   ludo,
or   ought   to-have-been (than) this   man?   who   from school,

atque disciplinâ   pueritiæ,   profectus est ad exercitum
and   the instruction 'of (his) 'youth,   went   to   the army

    patris,   atque in   disciplinam
'of (his) 'father,   and   for (the purpose of receiving)   instruction (in)

militiæ;   maximo   bello,
military affairs; (there being then) a-very-great   war,   [the social war,]

atque acerrimis hostibus;   qui   extremâ
and   most-active   enemies;   (he,) who   (thus)   at the close (of his)

pueritiâ fuit miles   summi   imperatoris,   ineunte
boyhood   was a soldier of-a-consummate   commander,   on entering

              adolescentiâ,   ipse   imperator   maximi
(the age of) a-young-man, (was) himself the commander of-a-very-great

exercitûs ; qui   sæpius   conflixit   cum   hoste,
army;   who 'had more often   'fought   with (the public)   foe.

quàm   quisquam   concertavit   cum   inimico,
than   any-one   had-contended   with (a private)   enemy.

gessit   plura   bella,   quàm   ceteri   legerunt,
had-waged   more   wars,   than   others   had-read-of,

confecit   plures   provincias,   quàm   alii
had-settled-the-affairs (of) more   provinces,   than   thers

concupiverunt ;   cujus   adolescentia   erudita est   ad
had-longed-for ;   whose   youth   was-trained   to

scientiam   militaris   rei   non   præceptis   alienis,
the knowledge   of-military   affairs   not   by-the-precepts (of)   others,

sed   suis   imperiis,   non   offensionibus belli,
but   'by his   'commands (of armies),   not   by-the-disasters   of war,

sed   victoriis,   non   stipendiis,   sed   triumphis.
but   by-victories.   not   by-campaigns,   but   by-triumphs.

Denique,   quod   genus   belli   potest   esse,   in quo
In-fine,   what   kind   of-war   can   there-be,   in which

fortuna   reipublicæ   non   exercuerit   illum ?
the-good-fortune   of-the-republic 'may not   'have-exercised   him,

Civile,
(and given him an opportunity, to display his abilities)? The civil (war),

Africanum,   Transalpinum,   Hispaniense,
the African (war),   the Transalpine (war),   the Spanish (war),

mixtum   ex civitatibus   atque ex
a mixed (war, composed) of   states (revolted from Rome), and   of

bellicosissimis nationibus, servile,   navale bellum,
the most-warlike   nations,   the servile (war), the-naval   war

varia et diversa genera, et bellorum
(against the pirates), various and diverse   kinds,   both   of wars

et hostium,   non solum gesta ab hoc uno,
and of enemies,   'were not   only   'waged by this   one (man),

sed etiam confecta ;   declarant   esse
but   also   terminated (successfully);   they-assert (that) there is

nullam rem positam   in militari usu, quæ
no   thing laid-down (or established) in   military practice which

possit fugere scientiam hujus viri.
could   escape the knowledge of-this   man.

11. Vero jam, quæ oratio potest inveniri par
But   now,   what   language   can   be-found equal

virtuti Cn. Pompeii? quid est, quod
to-the (military) 'virtue of-Cn. Pompey? what is there, which

quisquam possit afferre aut dignum illo, aut novum
any-one   can   announce either   worthy   of-him,   or   new

vobis, aut inauditum cuiquam? Enim neque sunt
to you,   or   unheard-of by-any-one?   For   neither   are

illæ solæ virtutes imperatoris, quæ vulgo
those the only   virtues   of-a-commander, which 'are commonly

existimantur, labor in negotiis, fortitudo
'considered (as such), (namely), industry in   business,   fortitude

in periculis, industria in agendo, celeritas in
in   danger,   energy   in   acting,   rapidity   in

conficiendo, consilium in providendo;
executing, (wise)   counsel   in   foreseeing, (and providing against

quæ sunt tanta in hoc uno quanta
events); which (all) are so-great in this one (man) as

non fuerunt in omnibus reliquis imperatoribus, quos
never   were   in   all   other   commanders,   whom

aut vidimus, aut audivimus. Italia est testis
'we-have either 'seen,   or   heard-of.   Italy   is a witness

quam, L. Sulla ipse, ille victor, confessus est,
(of this), which, L. Sulla himself, that conqueror,   confessed,

liberatam virtue et subsidio hujus. Sicilia
was-delivered by-the-valour and assistance of him. [Pompey.]   Sicily

est testis, quam cinctam undique multis
is   a witness,   which   surrounded on-all-sides by-many

periculis, explicavit, non terrore belli, sed
dangers,   he-delivered,   not by-the-terror of-war, but

celeritate consilii. Africa est
by-the-celerity 'of (his) 'deliberations (and operations). Africa   is

testis, quæ oppressa magnis copiis
witness, which oppressed (and overwhelmed) by-the-great   forces

hostium, redundavit sanguine eorum ipsorum.
of-the-enemy, the country overflowed with-the-blood of-these   same

Gallia est testis, per quam, iter in
(enemies). Gaul   is   a-witness, through which, a road into

Hispaniam patefactum est nostris legionibus,
Spain was-opened for-our legions,

internecione Gallorum. Hispania est testis, quæ
by-the-massacre of-the-Gauls. Spain is a-witness, which

sæpissime conspexit plurimos hostes superatos,
very-often has-seen (our) many enemies overcome,

que prostratos ab hoc. Italia est sepius et
and prostrated by this (man). Italy is often and

iterum testis, quæ cum premeretur tetro,
again a witness, which when it-was-hard-pressed by-the-disgraceful,

que periculoso servili bello, expetivit auxilium ab
and dangerous servile war, requested aid from

hoc absente; quod bellum attenuatum est atque
him absent; which war was-weakened and

imminutum expectatione Pompeii, adventu
diminished by-the-expectation of Pompey, 'by (his) 'arrival (it)

sublatum ac sepultum. Vero jam omnes
was-done-away-with and buried. But now all

oræ, atque omnes exteræ gentes ac nationes,
the coasts, and all foreign people and nations,

denique omnia maria, tum universa, tum in
in-fine all the-seas, as-well collectively, as in

singulis, omnes sinus atque portus, testes. Enim
particular, all the bays and harbours, (are) witnesses. For

quis locus, toto mari, habuit aut tam
what place, in-all (the Mediterranean) sea, had either so

firmum præsidium, ut esset
strong a protection, (and was so strongly fortified), that it-might-be

tutus, aut fuit tam abditus, ut
safe (from the attacks of the pirates), or was so concealed, that

lateret? Quis navigavit, qui
it-might-be-hidden (from them)? Who made-a-voyage, by-sea, that did

non committeret se, aut periculo mortis, aut
not 'expose himself, either to-the-danger of death, or

servitutis, cum mari navigaretur, aut hieme, aut
of slavery, when the sea was-to-be-navigated, either in-winter, or

referto prædonum? Quis unquam
full of pirates (in summer)? Who ever

arbitraretur   hoc   tantum   bellum,   tam
sould-have-supposed   (that)   this   so-great   a war,   so

turpe,   tam vetus,   tam   late   dispersum,   posse
disgraceful,   so   old, (and)   so   widely   dispersed,   could

confici,   aut   ab   omnibus   imperatoribus   uno
be-terminated,   either   by   all   the generals   in-one

anno, aut ab uno imperatore omnibus annis?
year,   or by one   general   in-all   the years (of his life).

Quam provinciam   tenuistis   liberam a prædonibus,
What   province   have-you-kept   free   from   pirates,

per   hosce   annos? quod   vectigal fuit
through   these-here (late) years?   what (source of)   revenue   was

tutum   vobis?   quem socium   defendistis?   cui
safe   for-you?   what   ally   have-you-defended?   to-whom

fuistis   præsidio   vestris   classibus? quàm
were-you   a guard   (and defence)   with-your   fleets?   how

multas   insulas   existimatis   esse   desertas? quàm
many   islands   do-you-suppose   to-have-been   deserted?   how

multas urbes sociorum   aut   relictas   metu,
many   cities   of-the-allies   'have either   'been-left   through-fear,

aut captas prædonibus?
or   captured   by-the-pirates?

12. Sed quid 'ego commemoro longinqua?
But   why   'do I   'make-mention-of   distant (things).

Hoc fuit quondam,   fuit   proprium   Romani
This   was   formerly,   (this) was   the peculiarity   of-the-Roman

populi   bellare   longe   a   domo,   et   defendere
people   to-carry-on-war   far   from   home,   and   to protect

fortunas sociorum,   propugnaculis   imperii,
the fortunes   'of (their) allies,   by-all-the-defences-and-arms   of-the-empire,

non   sua tecta   Ego dicam,
(and) not (to contend for)   their   houses (and homes).   I   say,   (that)

mare,   per   hosce   annos,   fuisse   clausum vestris
the sea,   during   these-latter   years,   has-been   closed   to-your

sociis,   cum   nostri   exercitus   nunquam
allies,   when   our   (own)   armies   'have   never

transmiserint   a   Brundisio, nisi   summâ
'crossed-over   (the sea)   from   Brundisium,   unless   in-the-depth (of)

hieme ?   Querar   qui, ab exteris
winter ?   May-I (not) complain, (when those) who, from foreign

nationibus venirent ad vos, captos, cum   legati
nations   were-coming to you, were-captured, when the ambassadors

Romani populi   redempti sint ?   dicam
of-the-Roman people had-to-be-ransomed ? may-I (not) say, (that)

mare   fuisse   non   tutum   mercatoribus,   cum
the sea   was   not   safe   for-the-merchants,   when

duodecim   secures   pervenerint   in
the twelve   axes   (of two prætors)   had-come   into

potestatem prædonum ?   Commemorem Cnidum aut
the power   of-the-pirates ? Need-I-mention Cnidus   or

Colophonem, aut Samum, nobilissimas urbes, que
Colophon,   or   Samos,   most-noble   cities,   and

innumerabiles alias   captas esse,   cum
innumerable   others (all)   captured (by the pirates), when

sciatis vestros portus, atque eos portus, quibus
you know your-own harbours, and those harbours, from-which

ducitis vitam et spiritum,
you-draw life and breath, [from which you derive the means of

            fuisse in potestate prædonum ? An vero,
sustenance,] were   in the power of-the-pirates ? Or indeed,

ignoratis   celeberrimum   portum Caietæ.
are-you-ignorant (that) the-very-celebrated harbour of Caieta,

atque   plenissimum   navium,   direptum esse   a
and (then)   very-full   of-ships,   was-plundered   by

prædonibus,   prætore inspectante ? Autem
the pirates,   a (Roman) prætor looking-on ?   But

        ex Miseno liberos ejus ipsius,   qui
(that also) from Misenum the child of-that same (person), who

antea   ibi   gesserat bellum cum prædonibus,
before 'had there 'waged   war with   the pirates,

sublatos esse a prædonibus ? Nam quid   ego
was carried-off by the pirates ? For why 'may I (not)

querar   Ostiense incommodum, atque illam labem
complain (of) the Ostian   disaster,   both   that   stain

atque ignominiam reipublicæ, cum, vobis prope
and   ignominy of-the-republic, when, you almost

inspectantibus, ea classis, cui consul Romani
looking-on, that fleet, over-which a consul of-the-Roman

populi præpositus eset, capta atque oppressa est
people was-placed, was-taken and destroyed

a prædonibus? Pro immortales dii! Ne potui.
by-the-pirates? By the immortal Gods! How could

incredibilis, ac divina virtus unius hominis
he incredible, and divine virtue (and courage) of-one man

affere tantam lucem reipublicæ
[Pompey] bring such-great light (and safety) to-the-republic.

tam brevi tempore, ut vos, qui modo videbatis
in so 'short a time, that you, who not-long-since saw

classem hostium ante ostium Tiberinum
the fleet of-the-enemy before the mouth (of the) Tiber

nunc audiatis esse nullam navem prædonum
now hear (that) there-is no ship of-the-pirates

intra ostium Oceani? Atque
within the straits of-the Ocean? [within the straits of Gibralter?] And

quanquam videtis quâ celeritate, hæc
although you-see with-what rapidity, these (things)

gesta sint, tamen non prætereunda sunt
may-have-been-done, however 'they-are not 'to-be-passed-over

a me, in dicendo. Enim quis unquam, aut
by me, in (my) discourse. For who ever, either

studio obeundi negotii, aut consequendi
with-the-desire of transacting business, or of-seeking-after

quæstus, potuit, tam brevi tempore, adire tot
gain, could, 'in so 'short a time, visit so-many

loca, conficere tantos cursus, quam
places, (and could have) performed such (long) voyages, as

celeriter impetus belli navigavit,
rapidly (as) the impetuosity of war navigated (the deep),

Cn. Pompeio duce? qui, mari nondum
Cn Pompey being leader? who, the sea 'not (being as) 'yet

tempestivo ad navigandum, adiit Siciliam,
in-a-proper-state for navigation, sailed (to) Sicily,

exploravit Africam; inde venit cum classe
explored (the coast of) Africa; thence he-came with the fleet

Sardiniam, atque munivit hæc tria frumentaria
to Sardinia, and he fortified these three granaries

subsidia reipublicæ, firmissimis præsidiis que classibus.
of the republic, with-very-strong garrisons and with-fleets.

Inde cum recepisset se in Italiam, duabus Hispaniis
Thence when he-had-returned into Italy, the two Spains

et Cisalpinâ Galliâ confirmatâ præsidiis ac
and Cisalpine Gaul being-strengthened by-garrisons and

navibus, item missis navibus in oram Illyrici
by-ships, also having-sent ships unto the coast of the Illyrican

maris, et in Achaiam que omnem Græciam.
sea, and unto Achaia and all Greece,

adornavit duo maria Italiæ maximis classibus
he-furnished the two seas of Italy with-very-large fleets

que firmissimis præsidiis; autem ipse adjunxit
and very-strong garrisons; but he-himself added

totam Ciliciam ad imperium Romani populi,
all Cilicia to the empire of-the-Roman people,

undequinquagesimo die, ut profectus est Brundisio;
on-the-forty-ninth day, after he-had-left Brundisium;

omnes prædones, qui, ubique fuerunt, 'were
all the pirates, who, in-whatever-place they-were,

partim capti sunt que interfecti, partim dediderunt
partly 'captured and killed, partly they-surrendered

se imperio ac potestati hujus unius.
themselves to-the-command and power of this one (man).

Idem Cretensibus,
[They unconditionally surrendered to Pompey.] Also to-the-Cretans,

cum misissent legatos que deprecatores ad
(who) when they-had-sent ambassadors and intercessors to

eum, in Pamphyliam usque non ademit
him, to Pamphylia, 'he-even did not 'take-from (them)

spem deditionis, que imperavit
the hope (of receiving their) submission, and he-commanded

obsides. Ita Cn. Pompeius extremâ
(them to give) hostages. Thus Cn. Pompey at-the-end (of)

hieme apparavit, ineunte vere, suscepit,
winter prepared for, at-the-commencement (of) spring, undertook,

mediâ   æstate   confecit,   tantum **bellum**
~y-the-middle of summer   terminated, (this) so-great   a war (of)

tam diuturnum, tam longe que late dispersum, quo
such long-duration, so   far   and wide spread-out, by which

bello omnes gentes ac nationes premebantur.
war   all   people and nations   were oppressed.

13. Hæc virtus   imperatoris,   **est**
    This   virtue   (and talent of this) commander,   is

divina atque incredibilis. Quid?   ceteræ
divine   and   incredible. What? (his) other (virtues)

quas paullo ante cœperam commemorare, quantæ
which a little before I-began   to mention,   how-great

atque quam multæ sunt? enim non solum   virtus
and   how numerous they-are? for not only the virtue

            bellandi   querenda est in summo atque
and talent) of-carrying-on-war are-required in a great and

perfecto imperatore, sed sunt multæ eximiæ artes
perfect   commander, but there are many eminent qualities

administræ que comites hujus   virtutis.
the-hand-maids and companions of this (military) virtue (and talent).

Ac primùm,   quanta   innocentia   debent
And firstly,   how-much   honesty   (and purity) ought

imperatores esse? deinde quanta temperantia in
commanders to-have? then how-much   moderation   in

omnibus rebus?   quanta   fides,
all   things? how-great the-faith (and confidence that may

            quantâ   facilitate? quanto
be placed in them), how-very (easy of) access?   how-great (their)

ingenio?   quanta   humanitate?
genius (and good disposition)? how-great (their)   humanity?

quæ   breviter consideremus, qualia   sint
which (qualities) 'let-us briefly   'consider,   how they-may-be

n   Cn. Pompeiio. Enim omnia
im, (or may be appropriate to), Cn. Pompeius.   For   all

sunt summa,   Quirites, sed ea possunt
are (of) the highest (degree in him), O Romans, but these may

magis cognosci atque intelligi, ex contentione
better be known and understood, from comparison (with

aliorum, quam ipsa per sese. Enim quem
others, than they by themselves. For whom

possumus putare aliquo in numero
can-we reckon in-any (manner) among the number

imperatorum, in cujus exercitu, veneant
of-generals, in whose army, they-may-sell

centuriatus, atque venierint? quid
the-office-of-centurion, and may-have-sold (it)? how (can we suppose

hunc hominem cogitare magnum, aut amplum,
that) that man thinks (in) a great, or (in) a noble,

de republicâ, qui aut
and lofty (manner) concerning the republic, who 'may-have either

diviserit pecuniam depromptam ex ærario
'distributed the money taken-out from the-public-treasury

ad administrandum bellum, magistratibus, propter
to carry-on the war, among the magistrates, on-account-of

cupiditatem provinciæ, aut,
a desire (to retain the command) 'of (his) 'province, or,

propter avaritiam, reliquerit Romæ, in
on-account-of avarice, may-have-left (the money) at Rome, at

quæstu? Vestra admurmuratio, Quirites, facit,
interest? Your murmurs, O Romans, make (it appear),

ut videamini agnoscere, qui fecerint hæc; autem
that you-seem to-recognise, who may-have-done this; but

ego nomino neminem; quare nemo poterit irasci
I mention no-one; wherefore no-one may get-angry

mihi, nisi qui ante voluerit confitere
(with) me, unless (he) who beforehand might-wish to-confess

de se. Itaque quis
concerning himself, (that he has committed such faults). Therefore who

ignorat quantas calamitates, nostri exercitus
is ignorant how-many calamities, our armies

ferant, quocunque ventum sit,
may-have-brought, in-whatever-place (they may) arrive,

propeter hanc avaritiam imperatorum?
on-account-of this avarice, (and rapacity) 'of (our) 'generals?

Recordamini itinera, quæ, per hosce annos,
Recollect the marches, which, during these-latter years.

nostri imperatores fecerunt in Italiâ,   per   agros
our   commanders   made   in Italy,   through lands

atque   oppida   Romanorum   civium,   tum
and   towns   of Roman   citizens,   then you-will)

facilius   statuetis, quid existimetis fieri   apud
the-more-easily 'determine, what you-may-think is-done among

exteras   nationes. Utrum   arbitramini,   per
foreign   nations.   Whether do-you-think, (that) during

hosce annos, plures urbes hostium   deletas esse
these-latter years, more   towns of-the-enemy have-been-destroyed

armis vestrorum militum,   an civitates sociorum
by-the-arms of-your   soldiers,   or cities of (your) allies

in   hibernis?   Enim neque potest
in   the winter-quarters (of your soldiers)? For neither can

is   imperator continere exercitum, qui   non
that commander restrain (his) army,   who 'does not

continet se ipsum;   neque   esse severus in
'restrain himself;   nor can he be   strict   in

judicando,   qui   non vult   alios esse
judging (of others), who 'does not 'wish (to have) others to-be

severos judices in se.   Hìc miramur hunc
strict   judges   over himself. Here let-us-admire this

hominem,   tantum   excellere   ceteris, cujus
man,   [Pompey,] so-much excelling (all) others, whose

legiones pervenerunt sic   in Asiam, ut
legions arrived (in that state of discipline) in Asia, that

non modo   manus   tanti exercitûs, sed
not only (not) the hand (of any one) of-so-great an army, but

ne quidem vestigium dicatur   nocuisse cuiquam
not even the footstep may-be-said to-have-injured any

pacato?   Vero jam, quotidie sermones ac
peaceable (person)? But now,   daily   reports and

literæ perferuntur,   quemadmodum   milites
letters are-brought (to us),   how   the soldiers

hibernent.   Non   modo   vis
conduct-themselves-in-winter-quarters. Not only (that) force

affertur nemini, ut faciat   sumptum in
is 'applied to-no-one, that he-should-make expense in (maintaining)

militem ; sed ne quidem permittitur cuiquam
a soldier ; but this is not even allowed to any one

cupienti. Enim nostri majores voluerunt,
wishing (to do so). For our ancestors desired, (that)

in tectis sociorum atque amicorum, esse
in the-houses 'of (our) 'allies and friends, (there ought) to-be

perfugium hiemis, non avaritiæ,
a refuge (from the severity) of-winter, not (a place) of-rapacity.

14. Age vero, considerate qualis sit
But now, consider what may-be (his)

temperantia in ceteris rebus. Unde putatis
moderation in other things. Whence do-you-suppose

inventum illam tantam celeritatem, et tam
originated that so-great celerity, and such

incredibilem cursum? Enim non eximia
incredibl (expeditious) voyages? For no extraordinary

vis remigum, aut quædam inaudita
strength (or skill) of-the-rowers, or any (hitherto) unheard-of

ars gubernandi, aut aliqui novi venti,
skill of-steering-a-vessel, or any new winds, (that)

pertulerunt illum tam celeriter in ultimas
carried him so swiftly unto the-most-distant

terras: sed eæ res, quæ solent remorari ceteros
lands: but those things, which used to retard other

non retardarunt; avaritia non
(commanders) 'did not 'retard (him); avarice 'did not

devocavit ab instituto cursu ad aliquam
'call (him) 'away from (his) intended route to any

prædam, non libido ad voluptatem, non amœnitas
plunder, no lust to pleasure, no charms

ad delectationem, non nobilitas
(of a place enticed him) to the enjoyment (of it), no renown

urbis ad cognitionem, denique,
of-a-city (induced him) to become-acquainted (with it), in-fine,

non labor ipse ad quietem. Postremo
not labour itself to (indulge in) repose. Lastly

signa et tabulas, que cetera ornamenta Græcorum
the statues and pictures, and the other ornaments of Greek

oppidorum, quæ ceteri arbitrantur
towns, which other (commanders) suppose

tollenda esse, ille quidem existimavit, ea
might-be-taken-away, he indeed thought, (that) they

ne visenda sibi. Itaque nunc quidem,
they-ought not 'to-be-seen by-him. Therefore now indeed,

omnes in his locis intuentur Cn. Pompeium, sicut
all in those places look-upon Cn. Pompey, as

aliquem non missum ex hac urbe, sed
some-one not sent from this city, but (as one)

delapsum de cœlo; nunc denique incipiunt credere
descended from heaven; now at-length they-begin to-believe

fuisse quando homines Romanos,
(that) there-had-been once (such) men (among) the Romans,

hac abstinentiâ; quod jam
(thus distinguished) by that moderation; which (until) now

videbatur incredibile exteris nationibus, ac falsô
appeared incredible to foreign nations, and falsely

proditum memoriæ. Nunc splendor vestri
transmitted to-the-memory (of posterity). Now the splendour of your

imperii lucet illis gentibus. Nunc, non sine
empire shines (on) these nations. Now, not without

causâ, intelligunt, suos majores tum, cum
reason, they-understand, (that) their ancestors then, when

habeamus magistratus hac temperantiâ,
we-had magistrates (distinguished) by such temperance,

maluisse servire Romano populo, quàm imperare
would-rather serve the Roman people, than command

aliis. Jam vero, aditus ad eum privatorum
others. Now indeed, access to him (by) private-persons

dicuntur esse ita faciles, ita liberæ,
is-said to-be so easy, and so unrestrained (are)

querimoniæ de injuriis aliorum, ut is, qui
the complaints of the injuries of others (received), that he, who

excellit principibus dignitate, facilitate,
excels the-first-and-highest (of men) in dignity, in affability,

videatur esse par infimis. Jam quantum
seems to-be on-a-par with-the-lowest. Now how-much

valeat   **consilio, quantum**   **gravitate**
he-prevails 'by (his wise) 'counsel, how-much 'by-the °weight

et copiâ dicendi, in quo ipso, inest
and copiousness of (his) speaking, in which same, there-exists

quædax imperatoria dignitas, vos, Quirites,
a certain commanding dignity, (which) you, O Romans,

sæpe cognoscitis, in hoc ipso loco. Vero
often experience, in this same place. [The forum.] But

quantam putatis ejus fidem existimari inter
how-great do-you-think his (good) faith was-estimated among

socios, quam hostes omnium gentium
the allies, which the enemies of-all nations [the pirates]

judicarint sanctissimam? Jam tantâ
may-have-judged (to be) most-sacred? Now by-such-great

humanitate est, ut sit difficile dictu, utrum
humanity it is (so), that it-may-be difficult to-say, whether

hostes timuerint ejus virtutem magis,
the enemy may-have-feared his valour more, (when)

pugnantes, an dilexerint mansuetudinem
fighting, or have-loved (his) mildness (more, when they

victi. Et quisquam dubitabit, quin
were) conquered. And 'will any-one 'doubt, but-that

tantum bellum transmittendum sit, huic
so-great a war (as the Mithridatic) may-be-entrusted to-him,

qui videatur natus esse quodam divino consilio
who may seem to-have-been-born by-some divine counsel

ad conficienda omnia bella nostræ
to the (successfully) finishing all the wars of our (present)

memoriæ?
recollection (and time)?

15. **Et quoniam auctoritas valet multum, quoque**
    And because great-reputation avails much, as-well

in administrandis bellis, atque in militari imperio,
in carrying-on war, as in military command,

certe est dubium nemini, quin ea re,
there certainly is (no) doubt to-any-one, but-that in-this affair,

ille idem imperator possit plurimum. Autem quis
that same commander can-do much. But who

ignorat,   vehementer pertinere ad administrand**a**
is ignorant, (that) it strictly   belongs   to   the conducting

  bella, quid   hostes,   quid socii existiment de
(of) war, what the enemy, what the allies may think about

vestris imperatoribus,   cum sciamus,   homine**s**
your   commanders,   when we-know, (that   me**n**

commoveri   in tantis rebus, ut aut
are-moved (and excited) in such-great affairs, that **e**ithe**r**

contemnant aut metuant, aut oderint aut ament,
they-may-despise or fear, or may-hate or love (them),

non minus opinione et famâ, quàm aliquâ certâ
not   less by-opinion and by-report, than by-any certain

ratione?   Quod nomen igitur fuit unquam
reason (and grounds)? What name therefore was   ever

  clarius   in   orbe terrarum? cujus
more-celebrated (than Pompey's) in   the world?   whose

res gestæ   pares?   id quod maxime
exploits (have been) equal (to his)? (and) that which most-greatly

facit   ad   autoritatem;   de quo homine
contributes to his authority (and dignity); of what   man

    vos fecistis tanta   et tam præclara judicia?
'have you 'made · so-great and so   illustrious judgments?

An vero   putatis   esse usquam ullam
Or indeed do-you-think (that) there-was any-where   any

oram tam desertam, quo fama illius diei
region so   deserted, in-which the renown of-that day 'may

non pervaserit; cum universus Romanus populus,
not 'have-penetrated; when the-entire Roman   people,

  foro   referto, que omnibus templis repletis,
the forum being-full, and all the temples being-filled,

ex quibus hic locus potest conspici, depoposcit sibi
from which this place might be-seen, demanded for themselves

Cn. Pompe**i**um unum,   imperatorem ad commun**e**
  Cn. Pompey   alone, (as) commander for the commo**n**

bellum omnium gentium?   Itaque,
war   of-all   nations? [The war against the pirates?] Therefor**e**

ut non dicam plura, neque confirmem exemplis
'hat 'I-may not . 'say more, nor   confirm by-the-example**s**

aliorum, quantùm auctoritas valeat in
of others, how-much authority prevails (and has influence) in

bello; exempla omnium egregiarum rerum
war; the examples of-all eminent exploits

sumantur ab eodem Cn. Pompeio; die
are-to-be-taken from this-same Cn. Pompey; on-the-day

quo, qui præpositus est maritimo bello a vobis
in-which, he was-placed-over the maritime war by you as

imperator, repente tanta vilitas annonæ
commander, suddenly so-great a cheapness of provisions

consecuta est, ex summâ inopiâ et caritate
followed, from the greatest want and dearness

frumentariæ rei, spe unius
of corn, by-the-hope (and confidence placed in) one

hominis, et nomine quantam
man, and (by-the renown of his) name 'such (cheapness) 'as

vix diuturna pax potuisset efficere, ex summâ
scarcely a long peace could-have effected, from the greatest

ubertate agrorum. Jam, calamitate in
fertility of-the-fields. Yet-now-more, the (great) calamity in

Ponto acceptâ, ex eo prœlio, de quo paullo
Pontus being-sustained (by us), by that battle, of which a little

ante, invitus admonui vos, cum socii
before, 'I unwilling 'admonished you, when (our) allies

pertimuissent, opes que animi hostium
were-greatly-alarmed, (when) the powers and spirits of-the-enemy

crevissent, provincia haberet non satis
had-increased, (when) the province had not a sufficiently

firmum præsidium; amisissetis Asiam, Quirites,
strong defence; you-might-have-lost Asia (then), O Romans,

nisi fortuna Romani populi divinitus
unless the good fortune of-the-Roman people 'had providentially

attulisset Cn. Pompeium, id ipsum temporis, ad
'brought Cn. Pompey, at-that same time, into

eas regiones. Adventus hujus et continuit
those regions. The arrival of-this (man), both checked

Mithridatem inflammatum insolitâ victoriâ, et
Mithridates flushed with-unwonted victory and

retardavit   Tigranem   minitantem   Asiæ,   magnis
retarded   Tigranes   threatening   Asia,   with-great

copiis.   Et   quisquam   dubitabit,   quid
forces.   And   'will   any-one   'doubt,   what

perfecturus sit   virtue,   qui perfecerit
he-may-accomplish 'by (his) 'virtue (and bravery), who has-accomplished

tantùm   auctoritate?   aut quàm facile
so-much 'by (his) 'authority (and reputation)?   or   how   easily

conservaturus sit   socios   et   vectigaliâ,
'will (not) 'he-preserve   (our)   allies   and   revenues,

imperio   atque   exercitu,   qui
by (his) 'command (and authority)   and   'by (his) army,   who

defenderit   ipso   nomine ac rumore?
has-defended (them) by-his-very   name   and   renown?

16. Vero age,   illa res   declarat quantam
But come, 'does (not) this thing 'declare   how-great

auctoritatem ejusdem hominis apud   hostes
(was) the authority of-this-same   man   among   the enemies

Romani   populi,   quòd   ex   locis   tam
of-the-Roman   people, (namely,)   that   from   places   so

longinquis, que tam diversis,
distant,   and so   different (in their institutions, and far from

tam brevi tempore omnes   dediderunt
one another), 'in so 'short a time   all   had-surrendered

se   huic unì?   quòd legati Cretensium,
themselves to this   one (man)?   that the ambassadors of-the-Cretans,

cum   esse   in eorum insulâ noster imperator que
when there was in   their   island   our   commander   and

exercitus,   venerunt   ad Cn. Pompeium, in prope
army,   came   to   Cn. Pompey,   unto   nearly

ultimas   terras,   que dixerunt,
the-most-distant countries (of the world),   and   said,   (that

omnes civitates Cretensium velle   dedere   se
all   the cities   of-the-Cretans wished to-surrender themselves

ei?   Quid   iste idem Mithridates?   nonne
to-him? What (did) this   same   Mithridates (do)? 'did-he not

misit legatum ad eundem Cn. Pompeium usque in
send an ambassador to   the same   Cn. Pompey   even   to

Hispaniam? eum quem Pompeius semper
Spain? he whom Pompey 'has always

judicavit legatum; ii, quibus erat semper
'considered (as) an ambassador; those, to-whom it-was always

molestum, esse potissimum
an annoyance, that (this ambassador) 'should-be more especially

missum ad eum, maluerunt judicari
'sent to him, [Pompey,] would-rather (have him) to be thought

speculatorem, quàm legatum. Potestis jam
a spy, than an ambassador. You-may now

igitur, Quirites, constituere quantùm existimetis
therefore, O Romans, determine how-much you may think

hanc auctoritatem amplificatum, multis
that this authority (and influence) augmented, by-many

rebus gestis postea, que vestris magnis
exploits afterwards (performed), and by-your great

judiciis,
(and solemn) judgments (and opinions expressed in his favour),

valituram esse apud illos reges, quantùm apud
will-avail with those kings, (and) how-much with

exteras nationes.
foreign nations.

Est reliquum, ut dicamus pauca et timide,
It remains, that we-may-say a few (words) and timidly,

de felicitate, quam nemo potest præstare,
concerning good-fortune, which no-one may show,

de se ipso,
(or ought to boast of) of himself (as being his own case), (but which)

possumus meminisse et commemorare de altero,
we-may remember and commemorate of another,

sicut est æquum homini de potestate deorum.
as it-is proper for-man (to speak) of the power of-the-gods,

Enim ego sic existimo
(and their disposal of affairs). For I thus think (and am of

imperia sæpius mandata esse, atque
opinion), (that) commands 'have oftener 'been-confided, and

exercitus commissos Maximo, Marcello, Scipioni,
armies entrusted to Maximus, to-Marcellus, to-Scipio,

Mario, et ceteris magnis imperatoribus, non solum
to-Marius, and to-other great commanders, not only

    propter virtutem, sed etiam
on-account-of (their) valour (and military skill), but also

    propter fortunam. Enim profectò quibusdam
on-account-of (their) good-fortune. For indeed to-some

summis viris, quædam fortuna fuit, divinitus,
very-great men, a certain good-fortune was, by-the-favour-of-heaven,

adjuncta ad amplitudinem et gloriam, et ad
added to (their) grandeur and glory, and for

bene gerendas magnas res; autem de
successfully performing great exploits; but concerning

    felicitate hujus hominis, de quo nunc
the-good-fortune of-this man, of whom 'we-are now

agimus, utar hac moderatione dicendi,
discoursing. I-will-make-use-of that moderation (in) speaking,

non ut dicam, fortunam positam esse in illius
not that I-may-say, (that) fortune was-placed in his

potestate, sed ut videamur meminisse præterita,
power, but that we-may-seem to-have-remembered past-things,

    sperare reliqua ne aut
(and) to hope (well for those that) remain (to come) nor either (that)

nostra oratio videatur esse invisa
our speech may-appear to be (arrogant, or) displeasing

immortalibus diis, aut ingrata.
to-the-immortal gods, or ungrateful (for what has been done).

Itaque non prædicaturus sum, Quirites, quantas
Therefore 'I am not 'going-to-declare, O Romans, what-great

res gesserit domi que militæ, terrâ que mari,
affairs he-achieved at-home and in war, by-land and by-sea,

que quantâ felicitate; ut semper, non modo
and with-what-great good-fortune; that always, not only

cives assenserint ejus voluntatibus, socii
the citizens assented (to) his will, the allies

obtemperarint, hostes obedierint, sed etiam
yielded (to him), the enemies obeyed (him) but also

venti que tempestates obsecundarint. Hoc
the winds and weather favoured (him). This I-wil'

brevissime dicam   unquam   fuisse
very-briefly say (that) never (in any place) had (any one been

tam impudentem, qui tacitus auderet optare
found) so presumptuous, who silently might-dare to-wish-for

tot, et tantas res, a immortalibus diis,
so-many, and such-great things, from the immortal gods,

quot et quantas immortales dii detulerunt ad
as-many and as-great (as) the immortal gods have-granted to

Cn. Pompeium. Quod ut sit proprium ac
Cn. Pompey. Which that it-may-be a peculiar and

perpetuum   illi, Quirites, debetis velle
perpetual (favour and privilege) to-him, O Romans, you-ought to-wish

et optare, (sicuti facitis), cum causâ communis
and to-entreat, (as you-do), as-well for-the-sake of-the-common

salutis atque imperii, tum   hominis
safety and of-the-empire, as (for the sake) of-the-man

ipsius.
himself.

Quare, cum et bellum sit ita necessarium, ut
Wherefore, when both the war is so necessary, that

possit non negligi; ita magnum, ut
it-can not be-neglected; so great, that

sit administrandum accuratissime; et cum possitis
it-is-to-be-conducted most carefully; and when you-can

præficere ei imperatorem, in quo sit eximia
place-over it a commander, in whom there-is the-most-excellent

scientia belli, singularis virtus,   clarissima
knowledge of-war, uncommon bravery (and talent), illustrious

auctoritas, egregia fortuna; dubitabitis,
authority, (and) eminent good-fortune; will-you-doubt,

Quirites, quin conferatis hoc tantum boni,
O Romans, but-that you-may-confer this so-great a good,

quod oblatum est, et datum vobis a immortalibus
which is offered, and given to-you by the immortal

diis in conservandum atque amplificandum
gods for preserving and aggrandising

rempublicam?
the republic?

17. Quod si Cn. Pompeius esset   privatus,   hoc
    Even if Cn. Pompey   were a private-person, at this

tempore Romæ; tamen is diligendus erat ad tantum
time   in-Rome; yet he ought-to-be-selected for so-great

bellum,   atque mittendus.   Nunc; cum
a war,   and   to-be-sent (to carry it on.) Now; when

ad   ceteras   summas   utilitates,   quoque hæc
to   the other   eminent   advantages,   also   this

opportunitas adjungatur, ut   adsit   in   iis
opportune-circumstance may-be-added, that he-is-present in these

ipsis locis, ut habeat exercitum,   ut possit
same countries, that he has an army (with him), that he-can

statim   accipere   ab eis, qui habent;
immediately receive   reinforcements from those, who   have

quid   expectamus, aut   cur   non,
(armies there); what do-we-wait-for, or why 'do-we not,

immortalibus diis   ducibus, committimus
the immortal   gods   (being our) leaders,   'commit

quoque hoc bellum regium eidem,   cui
also   this war of-the-kings to-the-same (person), to-whom

cetera   commissa sunt, cum summa
the other (wars in those countries) are committed, with the greatest

salute   reipublicæ ?
advantage to-the republic ?

At enim Q. Catulus clarissimus vir amantissimus
But indeed Q. Catulus a most-illustrious man (and) most attached

reipublicæ,   affectus   vestris amplissimis
to-the-republic, (and one) affected (honourably) by-your very-considerable

beneficiis; que item, Q. Hortensius   præditus
favours;   and also, Q. Hortensius (a man) endowed

summis ornamentis honoris, fortunæ, virtutis,
with-the-highest ornaments of honour, of fortune, of virtue, (and)

ingenii,   dissentiunt ab hac   ratione.
of talent, (both) dissent from this (my) opinion (of giving the

Ego confiteor,   quorum
command to Pompey).   I   confess, (that)   their

auctoritatem, multis locis, valuisse plurimùm apud
authority,   on-many occasions, has-prevailed very-much with

vos, et oportere   valere;   sed in hac causâ, tametsi
you, and ought,   to-prevail;   but in this cause, although

cognoscitis,   auctoritates   fortissimorum
you-know,   (that) the authority and opinions   of-the-most-brave

et clarissimorum virorum   contrarias,
and most-illustrious   men (are) contrary   (and different from

           tamen,   omissis   autoritatibus,
one another), however,   omitting   the authority (of opinions),

possumus exquirere veritatem,   re ipsâ,
we-can inquire-into   the truth, by (examining) the affair itself,

et   ratione; atque hoc   facilius,   quod
and (by the aid of) reason;   and this the-more-easily, because

omnia ea,   quæ adhuc   dicta sunt   a me,
all   those (things), which as-yet have-been-said by me,

idem   isti   concedunt esse vera, et
these here-same (persons) concede   to-be   true, and (that)

bellum esse necessarium, et magnum,   et
the war   is   a necessary, and a great (one), and (that)

omnia summa   esse   in Cn. Pompeio
all   the highest (qualifications) are-to-be (found) in   Cn. Pompey

uno.   Quid igitur   Hortensius ait? "Si omnia
only.   What therefore 'does Hortensius 'say?   " If   all (power)

tribuenda sint   uni,   Pompeium unum
is-to-be-conferred-on one (person), (that) Pompey   alone

esse dignissimum;   sed   tamen,   non
is   the-most-worthy (of it); but however, (that) 'it-is not

oportere deferri omnia   ad unum."   Ista
'proper   to-grant all   (power) to one   (person)."   This

oratio   jam   obsolevit,
argument   'has now   'become-obsolete, (and has no force),

    refutata   multò magis re, . quàm verbis. Nam
having-been-refuted, much more by-facts, than by-words. For

tu idem, Q. Hortensi, dixisti multa, graviter que
you the-same, Q. Hortensius, have-said much, forcibly and

ornate,   pro   tuâ summâ copiâ, ac singulari
eloquently, according-to your very-great fluency, and uncommon

facultate dicendi, et in senatu, contra   fortem
talent (in) speaking, both in the senate, against (that) courageous

virum A. Gabinium, cum is promulgasset legem, **de**
man   A. Gabinius,   when he-had-proposed the law, about

constituendo uno imperatore contra prædones; **et**
constituting   one commander against the-pirates; and

ex hoc ipso loco,   item fecisti verba permulta
from this very-same place, 'you also 'spoke verba much

contra eam legem. Quid? tum, per immortales
against that law. What now? then, by the immortal

deos! si tua auctoritas valuisset apud Romanum
gods! if your authority had-prevailed with the Roman

populum plus, quam salus Romani populi ipsius,
people more, than the safety of-the-Roman people itself,

vera causa,   teneremus
(and) the true cause (and interest of the republic), would-we-possess

hanc gloriam, atque hoc imperium orbis terræ?
this glory,   and   this command of-the-world?

An   hoc tum videbatur tibi esse imperium,
Whether 'did this then 'appear to-you to-be dominion,

cum legati, prætores que quæstores Romani
when the ambassadors, prætors and questors of-the-Roman

populi capiebantur? cum prohibebamur
people were-made-captives? when hindered (and cut off)

commeatu   et privato, et publico, ex
from-supplies (of provisions) both private, and public, from

omnibus provinciis? cum omnia maria   ita clausa
all   the provinces? when all the seas 'were so 'closed

nobis, ut possemus jam neque obire privatam,
to us, that we-could at-that-time neither transact private,

neque publicam rem transmarinam?
nor   public business beyond-the-seas?

18. Quæ civitas   fuit unquam antea,
    What city (or state) was there ever heretofore, **I-do**

non dico Atheniensium, quæ dicitur quondam
not say of-the-Athenians, who it-is-said formerly

tenuisse satis late   mare, non
held a sufficiently extensive (command of) the sea, not

Carthaginiensium, qui valuerunt permultum,
of-the-Carthaginians, who prevailed very-much,

classe, que maritimis rebus, non Rhodiorum,
with (their) 'fleet, and maritime affairs, not of-the-Rhodians,

quorum navalis disciplina, et gloria remansit,
whose naval discipline, and naval renown has-remained,

usque ad nostram memoriam: quæ civitas
even to our memory (and time): what state

unquam antea, tam tenuis, quæ insula
(was there) ever heretofore, so feeble, (and) what island

tam parva, quæ non defenderet suos portus, et
so small, which 'could not 'defend its harbours, and

agros, et aliquam partem regionis, atque
fields, and some portion 'of (its) 'territory, and

maritimæ oræ per se ipsa? At Hercle, aliquot
maritime coast by itself (alone)? But by-Hercules, for-some

continuos annos, ante Gabiniam legem, ille Romanus
successive years, before the Gabinian law, that Roman

populus, cujus nomen permanserat
people, whose name (and renown) has-remained (as)

invictum in navalibus pugnis, usque ad
unconquered in naval battles, even to (within)

nostram memoriam, caruit magnâ,
our memory, have-felt-as-if-deprived-of a great,

ac multò maximâ parte, non modò utilitatis,
and (of) much the greatest part, not only of-what-is-useful,

sed dignitatis atque imperii;
[namely, the revenues,] but 'of (their) 'dignity and 'of (their) 'empire;

nos, quorum majores classe superarunt regem
we, whose ancestors 'by (their) 'fleet conquered king

Antiochum que Persen, que omnibus navalibus
Antiochus and Perses, and in-all naval

pugnis vicerunt Carthaginienses, homines
engagements defeated the Carthagenians, men

exercitatissimos in maritimis rebus, que paratissimos,
most-skilled in maritime affairs, and well-provided

ii poteramus, in
(with every thing relating thereto), we (the same) could, in

nullo loco, esse jam pares prædonibus; nos, qui
no place, be now equal to-the-pirates; we, who

antea non modò habebamus Italiam tutam, **sed**
heretofore not only kept Italy safe, bu!

poteramus præstare omnes socios, in ultimis
we-could show all (our) allies, in the-most-distant

oris, salvos autoritate nostri imperii; **tum,**
coasts. to-be-safe by-the-authority of-our empire; then,

cum insula Delos, tam procul a nobis, posita
when the island of-Delos, so far-distant from us, situated

in Ægeo mari, quo omnes commeabant
in the Ægean sea, in-which all (merchants) assembled

cum mercibus atque oneribus,
with the gains (of their commerce), and the freights (of their ships),

parva sine muro, referta divitiis,
(though) small (and) without walls, (and) filled with-riches, (yet)

timebat nihil; iidem carebamus non modò
it-feared nothing; (but) even-we are-deprived-of not only

provinciis, atque maritimis oris
(the intercourse) with-the-provinces, and the sea coasts

Italiæ, ac nostris portubus, sed etiam jam
of-Italy, and our harbours, but also now (even)

Apiâ viâ; et his temporibus, magistratus
from-the-Apian road; and in-these times, a magistrate

Romani populi non pudebat ascendere in hunc
of-the-Roman people 'was not 'ashamed to-come-up into this

ipsum locum, cum vestri majores
very-same place, [the rostra,] when your ancestors

reliquissent eum vobis ornatum nauticis exuviis,
had-bequeathed it to you adorned with naval trophies,

et spoliis classium. (against the pirates, on Pompey).
and the spoils of fleets, (and address you against conferring the command.

19. Romanus populus, Q. Hortensi, existimavit,
The Roman people, O Q. Hortensius, considered,

te et ceteros, qui erant in eâdem sententiâ,
that you and the others, who were of the same opinion,

dicere ea, quæ sentiebatis, bono animo;
spoke that, which you-thought, with-a-good (and sincere) mind;

sed tamen idem Romanus populus, in
but however the same Roman people, in (an affair concerning

communi salute, maluit obtemperare suo dolori,
the common safety, preferred to-obey their own painful-feelings

quàm vestræ auctoritati. Itaque
(of fear and shame), than (to yield) to-your authority. Therefore

una lex, unus vir, unus annus, non modò
one law, one man, [Pompey,] one year, not only

liberavit nos, illâ miseriâ ac turpitudine; sed
delivered us, from-that misery and infamy; but

etiam effecit, ut aliquando videremur omnibus
also caused, that once (again) we-might-appear to-all

gentibus ac nationibus, vere imperare terrâ que
people and nations, really to-command by-land and

mari. Quo etiam videtur mihi indignius
by-sea. For which 'it also 'appears to-me more-unworthy

obtrectatum esse adhuc, dicam Gabinio
that-opposition-should-have-been-made hitherto, shall-I-say to Gabinius

anne Pompeio, an utrinque? (id quod est verius),
or to-Pompey, or to-both-of-them? (that which is more-likely)

ne A. Gabinius legaretur,
lest A. Gabinius might-be-chosen-a-lieutenant (of Pompey), (though)

Cn. Pompeii, expetenti ac postulanti. Utrum
Cn. Pompey (himself), desiring and requesting (it). Whether

ille, qui postulat legatum ad tantum bellum, est
he, who requests a lieutenant for so-great a war, it-is

non idoneus, qui impetret quem velit, cum
not proper, (that) he should-obtain whom he-wishes, when

ceteri eduxerint ad expilandos
other (commanders) have-taken-out (with them) to pillage

socios, que diripiendas provincias, legatos, quos
the allies, and plunder the provinces, the lieutenants, whom

voluerunt; an debet ipse, cujus lege
he desired; whether ought he, [Gabinius,] 'by whose law

salus ac dignitas constituta est,
'safety and dignity has-been-placed (on a sure basis),

Romano populo, atque omnibus gentibus esse
for-the-Roman people, and for-all nations is to-be

expers gloriæ
prevented from participating in, and) (be) deprived of-the-renown

imperatoris,   atque   ejus   exercitûs,   qui
of the-commander,   and   of-his   army,   which

constitutus est   ipsius   consilio   atque
was-constituted (and appointed) 'by his   'counsel   and

periculo ?   An   C. Falcidius, Q. Metellus, Q. Cælius
'at (his) 'risk ? Whether C. Falcidius,   Q. Metellus,   Q. Cælius

Latiniensis,   Cn. Lentulus,   omnes   quos   nomino,
Latiniensis,   Cn. Lentulus,   all   whom   I mention

causâ honoris,   cum fuissent tribuni
for-the-cause of-honour, [out of respect,] when they-had-been tribunes

plebis,   proximo anno,   potuerunt
of-the-people, in the   next   year (after their tribuneship), could

esse legati ;   in   hoc Gabinio uno, sunt
be lieutenants ; in (opposition to) this Gabinius alone, are

tam diligentes, qui deberet præcipuo jure
(people) so   active,   who ought by-an-especial right

esse etiam, in hoc bello, quod geritur Gabiniâ
to-be also, in this war, which is-carried-on by-the-Gabinian

lege,   in hoc imperatore,   atque   exercitu,
law, (and) under this commander, [Pompey,] also in (this) army,

quem constituit per vos ipse ?   de
which he-constituted through yourselves (by your suffrages) ? about

legando quo,   spero consules relaturos ad
'appointing whom 'a-lieutenant, I-hope the consuls will-refer (it) to

senatum.   Qui si   dubitabunt,
the senate (for their favourable action). Who if they-should-hesitate,

aut gravabuntur, ego memet profiteor relaturum ;
or be-reluctant,   I myself declare (that) I-will-refer

neque   inimicum edictum
(the matter to them) ; neither 'shall the inimical   edict

cujusquam,   Quirites, impediet me, quo
of-any-one (of the consuls), O Romans, 'hinder me, that no

minus, fretus vobis, defendam vestrum jus
the less, relying on-you, I-should-defend   your   right

que beneficium ;   neque audiam quidquam,
and   favour (conferred) ; neither will-I-listen (to) any-thing,

præter intercessionem ;   de
except the interposition [veto] (of the tribunes) : concerning

quâ (ut arbitror), istι ipsi,   qui minantur,
which (as I-think),   these same (persons) who threaten (opposition),

    etiam atque etiam considerabunt, quid   liceat.
will again and   again   'consider,   what may-be-allowed

            Quidem   meâ   sententiâ,   Quirites,
(to them to do). Indeed   in-my   opinion,   O Romans,

A. Gabinius unus   adscribitur,   socius
A. Gabinius   alone is-to-be-enrolled, (as) an associate (in sub-

            Cn. Pompeio   maritimi belli, que
ordinate command) for Cn. Pompey (in) the maritime war,   and

rerum gestarum ;   propterea quod alter
  the exploits (thereof);   because that the one [Gabinius]

detulit   id   bellum suscipiendum vestris suffragiis
gave   that   war   to-be-undertaken by-your   suffrages

uni ;   alter   delatum, que susceptum,
to-one (man), [Pompey;] the other having-received, and undertaken,

confecit.
finished (it).

    20. Reliquum est,   ut   videatur
        It remains,   as   it-appears, (that something)

dicendum esse,   de   auctoritate   et   sententiâ
is-to-be-said,   concerning the authority and   opinion

Q. Catuli ; qui cum quæreret ex vobis, si poneretis
of Q. Catuli ; who when he-inquired of you, if you-place

omnia   in Cn. Pompeio uno, si   quid
all   (your trust) in Cn. Pompey alone, if any-thing

factum esset de eo, in quo essetis habituri   spem ;
should-happen him, in whom would-you-place (your) trust;

          cepit magnum fructum suæ virtutis
he [Catulus] 'received a great   reward for-his virtue

ac dignitatis, cum   omnes, prope unâ voce,
and dignity, when 'you all, nearly with-one voice,

dixistis,   "vos habituros esse   spem in ipso."
'said,   (that "you would-place (your) hope in himself."

Etenim   est talis vir, ut sit nulla res
for   'he [Catulus] 'is such a man, that there is no   thing

tanta ac tam difficilis, quam ille possit non et
so-great and so difficult, that he   can   not both

regere consilio, et tueri integritate,
direct (it) by (his) 'counsel, and defend (it) 'by (his) 'integrity,

et conficere virtute. Sed in hoc ipso
and accomplish (it) 'by (his) 'valour. But in this same (case)

vehementissime dissentio ab eo, quòd, quo
'I most-vehemently 'differ from him, because, by-how-much

minus certa, ac minus diuterna, est vita hominum,
less certain, and less lasting, is the life of man,

hoc magis, respublica debet frui vitâ
by-so-much the more, the republic ought to-make-use-of the life

atque virtute summi hominis, dum licet per
and talents of-an-illustrious man, while it-is-allowed by

immortales deos. At enim nihil
the immortal gods (to do so). But indeed (you may say) 'let nothing

novi fiat contra exempla atque instituta
new 'be-done contrary to the examples and practices

majorum. Non dico hoc loco, nostros
'of-our-'ancestors. 'I-will not 'say in-this place, (that) our

majores in pace semper paruisse consuetudini,
ancestors in peace always conformed to usage, (and)

in bello utilitati, semper
in war to-utility (and expediency), (that) 'they always

accommodasse rationes novorum
'accommodated plans (resulting from their) new

consiliorum, ad novos casus temporum; non
deliberation, to new emergencies of-the-times; 'I-will not

dicam, duo maxima bella, Punicum
'mention, (that) two very-great wars, the (third) Punic (with Carthage)

et Hispaniense esse confecta, ab uno
and the Spanish were-carried-through (successfully), by one

imperatore, duas potentissimas
commander, [the younger Scipio,] (that) two most-powerful

urbes, Carthaginem atque Numantiam, quæ maxime
cities, Carthage and Numantia, which very-much

minitabantur huic imperio, esse deletas, ab eodem
threatened this (our) empire, were destroyed, by the same

Scipione; non commemorabo, nuper
o; 'I-will not 'remind-you, (that) some-short-time-since

visum esse   **ita**   **vobis que vestris patribus, ut**
it-seemed   equally proper   to-you and   to-your   fathers,   that

spes   **imperii**   **poneretur**   **in C. Mario uno,**
the hopes   of-the-empire   should-be-placed   in   C. Marius   alone, (so)

ut idem   **administraret bellum cum Jugurthâ,**
that   the same [Marius] should-conduct   the war   with   Jugurtha,

idem   **cum Cimbris,**   **idem cum Teutonis;**
the same (person) with   the Cimbri, (and) the same   with   the Teutoni?

recordamini in   **ipso Cn. Pompeio,**   **in**
recollect   in (the case of) this same   Cn. Pompey,   as-respects

quo Q. Catulus vult nihil novi constitui, quàm
whom   Q. Catulus   wishes   nothing   new   to-be-adopted,   how

multa nova   **sint**   **constituta**
many   new (things) may-there have-been-adopted (in Pompey's favour)

summâ   **voluntate Q. Catuli.**
with-the-highest approbation of Q. Catulus.

21. Enim quid   **tam novum,**   **quàm privatum**
    For   what (was) so   new, (as) that   a private

adolescentulum   **conficere**   **exercitum**   **difficile**
young-man   should-levy   an army   in-a-critical

tempore republicæ? confecit;   **præesse huic?**
time   of-the-republic?   he-did-levy (it);   to command   it?

præfuit;   **gerere**   **rem**   **opitime**
he-did-command (it); (and) to-carry-through the affair most-successfully,

suo   **ductu?**   **gessit.**
by-his-own guidance, (and in person)?   he-did carry it through (success-

     Quid   **tam præter consuetudinem, quàm**
fully).   What (can be) so   contrary   to-usage,   than (for)

imperium atque exercitum dari   **peradolescenti**
command   and   an army   to-be-given   to-a-very-young

homini, cujus ætas   **longe abesset a**   **senatorio**
man,   whose   age   'was far   'distant from   the senatorial

gradu?   **Siciliam, atque**
degree? [from the age required for a senator?] 'to-have Sicily,   and

Africam, permitti   **que administrandum bellum**
Africa   'to be confided (to him), and   to carry on   the war

in ea? Fuit in his provinciis
in   them?   He-was   in   these   provinces   (distinguished)

singulari   innocentiâ,   gravitate,   virtute;
by (his) ¹uncommon   honesty,   dignity,   (and) valour

confecit maximum bellum in Africâ,   deportavit,
he-terminated a-very-great   war   in Africa, (and) brought-back,

victorem exercitum. Quid vero tam inauditum,
(his) victorious   army.   What indeed so   unheard-of,

quàm Romanorum equitem   triumphare?
as-that   a Roman   knight   should-have-a-triumph-granted

At eam rem quoque Romanus populus, non
(to him)?   But this thing   also   the Roman   people,   not

modo vidit, sed etiam putavit   visendam,   et
only   saw,   but   also   thought (that) it-ought-to-be-seen, and

celebrandam omni   studio. Quid tam inusitatum,
celebrated   with-all   zeal.   What   so   unusual,

quàm ut,   cum   essent   duo   clarissimi   que
than   that,   when   there were   two   most-illustrious   and

fortissi consules,   Romanus   eques   mitteretur
most-brave   consuls, (that)   a Roman   knight   should-be-sent

ad   maximum,   que formidolosissimum bellum
to (carry on) a very-great,   and   most-dangerous   war

pro consule?   Missus est. Quo tempore quidem,
for   the consul? (Yet) he-was-sent. At which   time   indeed,

cum esset   nonnemo in senatu, qui diceret,
when there-was   an individual in   the senate, who   said,   (that)

privatum hominem oportere non   mitti   pro consule;
a private   man   ought   not to-be-sent for   the consul;

dicitur;   L. Philippus dixisse,
[as proconsul] it-is-said; (that) L. Philippus   said (on the occasion),

"suâ sententiâ se   non mittere illum pro
(that) "in-his   opinion   he ¹would not   ¹send   him   for

consule, sed pro   consulibus." Tanta   spes
the consul, but   for (both) the consuls."   So-great ¹was the hope

constituebatur in   eo   bene   gerendæ
¹placed   in   him ¹of well ¹conducting (the affairs of)

reipublicæ, ut munus duorum consulum committeretur
the republic,   that the office of-the-two   consuls   might-be-entrusted

virtui   unius adolescentis. Quid
to-the-valour (and talents) of-one   young-man.   What (is there)

tam singularis, quàm ut, ex senatusconsulto,
so extraordinary, as that, by a decree-of-the-senate,

solutus legibus, fieret
being-freed from the laws (fixing the age for holding office), he-was-made

consul, ante quàm licuisset, per leges, capere
consul, before that it-was-allowed, by the-laws, (for him) to-hold

ullum alium magistratum? Quid tam incredibile
any other magistracy? What so incredible

quàm ut iterum, Romanus eques
as that a-second-time, a Roman knight

triumpharet, ex
should-have-the-honour-of-a-triumph-awarded-to-him, by

senatusconsulto? quæ nova
a-decree-of-the-senate? whatever new (or unusual precedents)

constituta sunt, in omnibus hominibus, post
have-been-established, in (the case of) all (other) men, since

memoriam hominum, ea sunt non tam multa,
the memory of-man, (all) these are not so many,

quàm hæc, quæ vidimus in hoc uno homine.
as those, which we-see in this one man. [Pompey.]

Atque hæc tot exempla, tanta ac
And these so-numerous examples (of dispensation), so-great and

tam nova, profecta sunt in eundem hominem
so novel, have-originated in (favour of) this-same man

a auctoritate Q. Catuli, atque a
[Pompey] from the authority of Q. Catuli, and from (that)

ceterorum amplissimorum hominum ejusdem
of other illustrious men of-the-same

dignitatis.
dignity.

22. Quare videant, ne sit periniquam, et
Wherefore let-them-see-to-it, lest it-may-be very-unjust, and

non ferendum, illorum auctoritatem,
not to-be-borne-with, (that) their authority (and opinion),

de dignitate Cn. Pompeii,
respecting the dignity (and elevation) of Cn. Pompey, (which dignity)

semper comprobatam esse a vobis, vestrum
has always 'been-approved-of by you, (that) your

judicìum de eodem homine, que auctoritatem
judgment concerning the same man, and the authority

Romani populi improbari ab illis; præsertim,
of-the-Roman people should-be-blamed by them; especially,

cum Romanus populus, jam suo jure, possit
when the Roman people, (now) in-their-own right, can

defendere suam auctoritatem in hoc
defend their authority (and opinion), as respects this

homine, vel contra omnes, qui dissentiant; proptcrea
man, even against all, who may-dissent; because

quòd, iisdem istis reclamantibus, vos delegistis
that, these very-same objecting, you selected

illum unum ex omnibus, quem præponeretis
him alone from all, whom you-might-place-over

bello prædonum. Si vos fecistis hoc temere, et
the war (with) the pirates. If you did this rashly, and

parum consuluistis reipublicæ; recte
(but) little consulted (the interests) of the republic; rightly 'did

isti conantur regere vestra
these (persons here present) 'endeavour to-regulate (and guide) your

studia suis consiliis; autem sin vos tum
wishes (and resolves) by-their counsels; but if you then

vidistis plus in republica;
saw more (deeply) into (the interest of) the republic (than they did);

vos, his repugnantibus, per vosmet ipsos attulistis
(if) you, these opposing, by yourselves have-conferred

dignitatem huic imperio, salutem orbi terrarum;
dignity to-this empire, (and) safety to-the-circle of-the-earth;

aliquando isti principes
[the world]; (so that) at-length these chiefs (of the senate)

fateantur, et sibi, et ceteris,
may-confess, (that it is necessary) both for-themselves, and others

parendum esse auctoritati universi Romani populi
to-obey the authority of-the-entire Roman people.

Atque in hoc Asiatico bello, et regio,
And in this Asiatic war, and regal (war with the kings),

non solum illa militaris virtus, quæ est singularis in
not only that military talent, which is eminent in

Cn. Pompeio,   sed quoque multæ aliæ et
Cn. Pompey (is required),   but   also   many   other and

magnæ virtutes   animi requiruntur. Est
great   virtutes (and qualities) of-the-mind   are-required.   It-is

difficile,   vestrum imperatorem ita versari, in
difficult,   (that) your   commander   'be so 'employed,   in

Asiâ,   Cilicia. Syriâ,   que regnis interiorum
Asia,   Cilicia,   Syria,   and in-the-kingdoms of-the-interior

nationum, ut cogitet nihil aliud, quàm   de
nations,   that he-may-think-of nothing else,   than   concerning

hoste, ac de laude. Deinde etiam, si sunt
the enemy, and concerning renown.   Then,   also,   if there-are

    qui   moderatiores   pudore   ac
(those) who   (are)   more-held-in-restraint   by-shame   and

   temperantiâ,   tamen nemo arbitratur   eos
the-control-of-themselves,   yet   no-one   thinks (that) they

esse tales, propter multitudem cupidorum
are   such, on-account-of the multitude   of-covetous (and rapacious)

hominum. Est difficile dictu, Quirites, in quanto
men.   It-is   difficult   to-say,   O Romans,   in   what-great

odio   simus apud exteras nationes,
hatred (and unpopularity) we-are among   foreign   nations,

   propter   injurias ac   libidines eorum, quos
on-account-of the injuries and (wicked) licentiousness of-those,   whom

missimus ad eas,   per hos   annos cum imperio.
we-have-sent to those (nations) during these (late) years with command.

Enim quod fanum putatis, in illis terris
For   what   temple do-you-think, in those countries, (has-been)

  religiosum   nostris magistratibus, quam
religiously-sacred (in the eyes of)   our   magistrates,   what

civitatem   sanctam, quam   domum
city   (has been held)   sacred,   what (private)   house

fuisse satis clausam ac munitam? locupletes ac
has-been sufficiently shut   and   fortified?   rich   and

copiosæ urbes   jam requiruntur,   quibus
opulent   cities   'are now   'sought-for, against which (some)

causa   belli inferatur, propter cupiditatem
cause (or pretext) of war may-be-alleged, on-account-of   the desire

deripiendi.   Libenter disputarem hæc
of plundering (them).   'I-would willingly   'discuss   these (things)

coram, cum Q. Catulo et Q. Hortensio, summis et
publicly, with   Q. Catulus and   Q. Hortensius, most eminent and

clarissimis viris; enim noverunt vulnera sociorum·
illustrious   men;   for they-have-known the wounds of-the allies;

vident eorum calamitates; audiunt   querimonias.
they-see their   calamities;   they-hear (their)   complaints.

Putatis   vos mittere exercitum contra hostes
Do-you-think (that) you   send   an-army   against   the enemy

pro   sociis, an   simulatione
for (the protection of your) allies, or-rather under-the-pretence (of act-

      hostium,   contra socios atque
ing against) enemies, (really to act) against   allies   and

amicos? quæ civitas est in Asiâ, quæ possit
friends?   what   city   is there in   Asia,   which   can

capere   animos, ac   spiritus,
comprehend (or satisfy) (the greedy) mind, and (rapacious)   spirit,

non modo imperatoris, aut legati, sed   unius
not only of-a-commander, or of-a-legate, but (even) of-a-single

tribuni militum?
tribune of-the-soldiers?

    23. Quare, etiam si habetis quem, qui, signis
      Wherefore, also   if you-have any-one, who, the standards

collatis,   videatur posse
being collected, [the battle having commenced] may seem to-be-able

superare regios exercitus; tamen nisi erit idem,
to-overcome the royal   armies;   however, unless he-be   one,

qui possit cohibere se a pecuniis sociorum,
who   can   restrain himself from the money of-the-allies,

qui   manus, oculos,   animum,
who (can restrain) (his) hands, (his) eyes, and (his)   mind,

      ab eorum conjugibus ac liberis, qui
and desires) from their   wives   and children, who

      ab ornamentis fanorum, atque
(can restrain them) from the ornaments of-the temples,   and

oppidorum, qui   ab auro que regia
of-the-towns. who (likewise can keep them) from the gold, and roya.

gaza;   non erit idoneus, qui mittatur ad
treasures; 'he-will not 'be a-proper-person, who may-be-sent to

Asiaticum que regium bellum. Putatis,   ecquam
the Asiatic and royal war. Do-you-think, (that) any

civitatem pacatam fuisse, quæ sit locuples?
city has-been-subdued, which may-be rich? (or

ecquam   esse locupletem, quæ videatur istis
any (city that) is rich, which may-seem to these

     pacata esse? Maritima ora, Quirites,
(commanders) to-be-subdued? The sea coast, O Romans,

requisivit Cn. Pompeium, non solum propter
requested Cn. Pompey, not only on-account-of

gloriam militaris rei, sed etiam propter
the renown 'of (his) 'military exploits, but also on-account-of

continentiam animi. Enim,
the moderation 'of (his) 'mind. For, (the people inhabiting the sea

   videbat, Romanum populum non locupletari
coast) saw, (that) the Roman people 'were not 'made-richer

quotannis, publicâ pecuniâ, præter paucos;
from-year-to-year, by-the-public money, except a few;

   nos neque assequi quidquam aliud,
(and that) 'we neither 'attained any-thing else,

nomine classium, nisi ut, detrimentis
by-the-name 'of (our) 'fleets, unless that, injuries (and losses)

accipiendis, videremur affici majore
being-sustained, we-might-seem to-be-affected with greater

turpitudine. Nunc, quâ cupiditate,
disgrace. Now, with-what cupidity (to obtain money),

quibus jacturis,   quibus
with-what bribery, (made to influential persons), with-what

conditionibus,   homines
engagements, (entered into for the obtaining command), men

profisciscantur in provincias, isti ignorant
go to the provinces, are-these-here ignorant-of

videlicet, qui non arbitrantur omnia
forsooth, who 'do not 'think (that) all (command)

deferenda esse ad unum? Quasi vero, videamus
is-to-be-conferred on one? As if-indeed, 'we-might (not) 'perceive

Cn. Pompeium esse magnum, cum suis virtutibus,
Cn. Pompey to-be great, as-well by-his-own virtues,

tum etiam vitiis alienis. Quare nolite dubitare,
as also by-the-vices (of) others. Wherefore do-not doubt,

quin credatis omnia huic uni, qui, inter
but-that you-may-entrust all to-this one (man), who, for

tot annos, unus inventus sit, quem socii
so-many years, 'has alone 'been-found, whom the allies

gaudeant venisse in suas urbes cum exercitu.
rejoice (to see) come into their towns with an army.

Quod si, Quirites, putatis hanc causam
But if, O Romans, you-think this cause, (of giving the sole

confirmandam auctoritatibus;
command to Pompey), ought-to-be-confirmed by authorities;

vobis est auctor, P. Servilius, vir
you-have (as) adviser-of-the-measure, P. Servilius, a man

peritissimus omnium bellorum, que maximarum
most-experienced (in) all the wars, and (in) the greatest

rerum: cujus res gestæ tantæ, terrâ que mari,
affairs: whose exploits so-great, by-land and sea,

exstiterunt, ut, cum deliberetis de bello,
have-excelled (so much), that, when you-deliberate concerning war.

nemo debeat esse vobis gravior
no-one ought to-be (considered) by-you (as) a-more-weighty

auctor: est C. Curio præditus vestris
adviser-in-this-measure: there is C. Curio endowed with your

summis beneficiis, summo ingenio et prudentiâ,
highest favours, with-the-greatest talent and prudence,

que gestis maximis rebus; est Cn. Lentulus,
and having-performed the greatest exploits; there-is Cn. Lentulus,

in quo, omnes cognovistis, pro vestris
in whom, 'you all ¹ have-known, by-reason-of your

amplissimis honoribus, esse summum
most ample honours, there is the greatest (wisdom of)

consilium, summam gravitatem; est
counsel, (and) the greatest weight (of character); there is

C. Cassius, integritate, virtute,
C. Cassius, (distinguished by his) integrity, virtue, (and)

singulari constantiâ.   Quare videte,
uncommon   constancy (and perseverance). Wherefore see (then)

num videamur posse respondere orationi illorum,
whether we-appear to-be-able to-reply to-the-speech of-those,

qui dissentiunt,   auctoritatibus horum.
who dissent-from (us), by-the-authorities of-these (men mentioned).

24   Quæ   cum sint ita, C. Manili,   primum
Which things when they-are so, O C. Manili, in-the-first-place,

laudo, que vehementissime comprobo et istam tuam
I praise, and most-vehemently approve both this your

legem, et voluntatem,   et sententiam;
law, and the purpose (intended by it), and the opinion

           deinde hortor te, ut, Romano
(respecting the commander); next I-exhort you, that, the Roman

populo auctore,   maneas   in
people approving (and abetting), you-may-remain (steadfast) in (your)

sententiâ, neve   pertimescas   vim, aut minas
opinion, nor (that) you-may-fear the violence, or threats

cujusquam.   Primum, arbitror,   esse   satis
of-any-one. In-the-first-place, I-believe, (that) there is enough

perseverantiæ animi in te; deinde cum videamus
of-perseverance of-mind in you; next, when we-see

tantam multitudinem   adesse,   cum tanto studio,
so-great a multitude assembled-here-present, with so-great zeal

        quantam   nunc videmus   iterum
(for the cause), as-much-as 'we now   'see   a second time

       in   præficiendo   eodem homine;
(displayed) in appointing-to-command the-same man; [Pompey;]

quid est, quod dubitemus, aut   de   re
what is there, that we-may-doubt, either concerning the affair

aut de facultate   perficiendo.   Autem ego,
or of the power (of) accomplishing it. But   1,

quidquid est in me studii, consilii, laboris, ingenii,
whatever is in me of-zeal, of-counsel, of-industry, of-talent,

quidquid   possum   hoc   beneficio Romani
whatever I-am-able-to-do by-this kindness of-the-Roman

populi,   atque hac   prætoriâ
people (in bestowing office on me), and by-this prætorian

potestate, quidquid
power, (I am possessed of), whatever (I am able to do)

auctoritate, fide, constantiâ ;
'by (my) 'authority, credit, constancy, (and perseverance in the cause);

polliceor ac defero omne id tibi et
I-promise and offer all this, (both) to-you [Manilius] and

Romano populo, ad conficiendam hanc rem.
to-the-Roman people, for the accomplishing this affair.

Que testor omnes deos, et eos maxime, qui
And I-call-to-witness all the-gods, and those most-especially, who

præsident huic loco que templo, qui maxime
preside over-this place and temple, (and) who especially

perspiciunt mentes omnium eorum, qui adeunt ad
see-into the minds of-all those, who go to

Rempublicam, me neque
the Republic, [who apply themselves to public affairs,] (that) I neither

facere hoc rogatu cujusquam, neque quò
am doing this at-the-request of-any-one, nor because

putem per hanc causam conciliari gratiam
I-may-think, by this cause, to-conciliate the favour

Cn. Pompeii mihi, neque quò quæram ex
of Cn. Pompey for-me, nor because I-may-seek from

amplitudine cujusquam, aut præsidia
the dignity (or elevated rank) of-any-one, either protection

mihi periculis, aut adjumenta honoribus ·
for-myself in-dangers, or aids (in acquiring) honours

propterea quod, tecti innocentiâ, facile
therefore that, shielded by innocence, 'we-will easily

repellemus pericula, ut oportet hominem præstare ;
'repel dangers, as it-becomes a man to-do;

autem consequemur honores, neque ab uno,
but we-will-obtain honours, neither from one (person),

neque ex hoc loco, sed illâ nostrâ eadem
nor from this place, but by-that our same

laboriosissimâ ratione vitæ,
most-laborious course of-life (we have heretofore pursued),

si vestra voluntas feret. Quamobrem,
if your (kind) wishes sustain (and favour me). Wherefore.

quidquid   susceptum est,   in   hac   causâ   mihi,
whatever   has-been-undertaken,   in   this   cause   (by) me,

Quirites,   confirmo   me   suscepisse   id   omne
O Romans,   I-assure (you, that)   I   undertook   it   all,

    causâ   reipublicæ; que tantum   abest,
for-the-cause (and interest) of-the-republic ; and so-much is-it therefrom,

ut   videar   quæsisse   mihi   aliquam bonam
that I-may-seem   to-have-sought   for-myself   any   good

gratiam,   ut,   etiam   intelligam,
offices (or favours of others),   that,   'I also   understand,   that)

suscepisse   multas   simultates   partim   obscuras,
I-have-become   many   enmities   partly   hidden,

partim apertas,   non necessarias
partly   open, (enmities) not   necessary (to be incurred by)

mihi,   non   inutiles   vobis.   Sed ego   statui,
me, (but) not   without-use   to-you.   But   I   determined, (that)

oportere me   præditum   hoc   honore,
it behoved   me   invested   with-this   honour (of the prætorship),

    affectum, Quirites,   vestris   tantis   beneficiis,
(and)   affected,   O Romans,   by-your   so-many   favours,   (that)

vestram   voluntatem,   et   dignitatem   reipublicæ,   et
your   will,   and   the dignity   of-the-republic,   and

salutem   provinciarum atque   sociorum,   præferre
the safety   of-the-provinces   and   of-the-allies,   were-to-be-preferred

omnibus   meis   commodis et   rationibus.
to-all   my-own   advantage   and   affairs (and interests).

ORATIO
THE ORATION

M. TULLII CICERONIS,
OF M. TULLIUS CICERO,

PRO
FOR

L. MURENA.
L. MURENA

---

1. Quæ deprecatus sum a immortalibus diis,
That-which I-entreated from the immortal gods,

judices, more que instituto majorum,
O judges, (according to) the usage and institutions 'of (our) 'ancestors,

illo die, quo auspicato, comitiis
on-that day, on-which the-auspices-were-taken, 'I, in the comitia

centuriatis, renuntiavi L. Murenam consulem;
centuriata, 'declared L. Murena consul (elect);

ut ea res eveniret bene
(namely), that that affair (of the election) might-eventuate advantageously

atque feliciter mihi que meo magistratui, populo,
and happily to-me and to my magistracy, to-the-nation,

que plebi Romanæ: precor eadem ab eisdem
and people of-Rome: I-pray-for the-same-thing of the same

immortalibus diis, ob obtinendum consulatum
immortal gods, on entering-upon the consulship (by)

ejusdem hominis, unà cum salute,
the same man, together with (his personal) safety (and privileges),

et ut vestræ mentes atque sententiæ consentiant
and that your minds and opinions may agree

(242)

cum   voluntatibus   que   suffragiis   Romani   populi,
with   the wishes   and   suffrages   of the-Roman   people,

que   ea   res   afferat   vobis,   que
and (that) this affair (of your agreement) may-bring to-you,   and

Romano   populo,   pacem, tranquillitatem, otium, que
to-the-Roman   people,   peace,   tranquillity,   ease,   and

concordiam.   Quòd si illa solemnis precatio
concord.   For   if that   solemn   prayer (offered up in

comitiorum,   consecrata   consularibus
the assembly) of-the-comitia,   hallowed   by-consular

auspiciis, habet tantam vim,   et religionem in
auspices,   has   so-great a power, and religious-effect in

se,   quantam   dignitas   reipublicæ   postulat;
it,   as   the dignity of-the-republic   requires;

idem   ego sum precatus, ut quoque   eis
at-the-same-time I   prayed,   that   also to-these-same

hominibus, quibus hic consulatus datus esset, me
men,   to-whom this consulship had-been-granted, I

rogante,   ea   res
(presiding over the assembly, and) asking (their opinion), the same thing

eveniret   fauste,   feliciter,   que prospere.
might-turn-out auspiciously,   happily,   and prosperously.

Quæ   cum   sint   ita,   judices, et cum omnis
Which-things when they-are so, O judges, and when   all

potestas immortalium deorum   aut translata sit ad
the power of-the-immortal gods   'is either 'transferred to

vos, aut certe communicata cum vobis, idem consul
you, or certainly   shared   with you, the same consul

commendat eum   vestræ fidei,   qui
recommends him (Murena) to-your faith (and protection), who

antea commendavit   immortalibus diis; ut   et
before had-recommended (him) to-the-immortal gods; so-that (he) both

declaratus consul voce ejusdem   hominis,
declared   consul by-the-voice of-the-same   man,   (Cicero)

et   defensus,   tueatur   beneficium
and   defended (by the same), he-may-watch-over   the favours

Romani populi,   cum vestrâ salute, atque
of-the-Roman people, (together) with   your   safety, and (that)

omnium civium. Et quoniam in hoc
of-all the citizens. And because in (the discharge of) this

officio, studium
duty (which I have undertaken, of defending Murena), the zeal

meæ defensionis, atque etiam ipsa susceptio
of my defence (of him), and even the-very undertaking

causæ, reprehensa est ab accusatoribus;
of-the-cause (itself), has-been-reprehended by the accusers;

antequam instituo dicere pro L. Murenâ,
(therefore) before I-commence to plead for L. Murena,

dicam pauca pro me ipso; non quò,
I-will-say a few (words) respecting my self; not because,

defensio mei officii sit potior
the defence of-my duty (in this cause) may-be preferred (as of more

mihi, quidem in hoc tempore, quàm
importance) to-me, even at this time, than (the defence)

salutis hujusce, sed ut, meo facto
of-the-safety of-this-same (person); but that, my acts (in this case)

probato vobis, possim majore auctoritate,
being-approved by-you, I-may-be-able with-greater authority

propulsare impetus inimicorum, ab
(and weight), to-repel the-attacks 'of (his) 'enemies, upon

hujus honore, famâ, que omnibus fortunis.
his honour, fame, and all (his) fortunes.

2. Et primum, respondebo M. Catoni,
And in-the-first-place, I-will reply to M. Cato, (who is

dirigenti vitam ad certam normam
in the habit of) regulating life according-to a certain rule

rationis, et diligentissime perpendenti momenta
of-reason, and diligently weighing the value

officiorum omnium, de meo officio.
of-the-duties of-all, concerning my-own duty (in this cause).

Cato negat, fuisse rectum me et
Cato denies, (that) it-was right (or proper, that) I both

consulem, et latorem legis
consul, and (also) proposer of-the-law (against)

ambitûs, et tam severe
bribery-and-improper-influence to-obtain-office, and 'having so severely

gesto consulatu,
and strictly 'discharged (the duties of) the consulship, 'should (in the

attingere, causam
slightest degree) 'touch, (or have any thing to do with) the cause

L. Murenæ. Cujus reprehesio vehementer movet
of L. Murena. Whose reprehension vehemently moves

me, ut non solum probem
(and excites) me, so that not only 'I-may (explain and) 'prove

~obis, judices, rationem mei facti
to-you, O judges, the reason of-my action (and conduct), (and)

quibus debeo maxime, verum etiam ut
to-whom I-ought especially (to do so), but also that (I ought

Catoni ipsi, gravissimo atque
to do the same) to Cato himself, a most-respectable and

mtegerrimo viro. A quo tandem, M. Cato, est
upright man. By whom in-fine, O M. Cato, is-it

æquius, consulem defendi, quam a consule?
more-just, (that) a consul should-be-defended, than by a consul?

Quis, in republica, potest, aut debet esse conjunctior
Who, in the republic, can, or ought to-be more-united

mihi, quàm is, cui respublica traditur, a me uno,
to-me, than he, to-whom the republic is-delivered, by me alone,

sustinenda, sustentata meis magnis laboribus et
to-be-sustained, having-been-upheld by-my great labours and

periculis? Quòd si, in iis rebus repetendis,
dangers? For if, in those things demand-is-made-for-recovery,

quæ sunt mancipi, is debet præstare periculum
which are warranted-property, he ought to-incur the risk

judicii, qui obligavit se nexu,
of-a-trial, who has-bound himself by-the-obligation (of warranting the

profectò etiam rectius, in judicio consulis
vale), certainly also more-justly, in the trial of a consul

designati, is consul potissimum, qui declaravit
elect, that consul most-especially, who declared (him)

sonsulem, debebit esse auctor beneficii
consul, ought-to-be the guarantee (for him) of-the-favours

Romani populi, que defensor periculi.
of-the-Roman people, and (his) defender (in case) of danger.

Ac, si, ut in nonnullis civitatibus solet fieri,
And, if, as in some states it-is-the-custom to-be-done,

patronus huic causæ constitueretur
an (advocate or) patron for-this cause should-be-appointed

publice, is potissime daretur
publicly (by the authorities), he 'would most-especially 'be-assigned

defensor, affecto honore, qui,
as-a-defender, to-the-one-invested with-the-honour (of office) who,

præditus eodem honore, afferret non
endued with-the-same honour (of office himself), might-bring no

minus auctoritatis, quàm facultatis ad dicendum.
less authority, than ability to (his) pleading.

Quod si, ii, qui jam invehuntur ex alto
For if, those, who now are-brought (by the winds) from the high

in portum solent præcipere summo
(sea) into the harbour are-accustomed to-give with-the-greatest

studio, solventibus portu, et rationem
care, (those) leaving the harbour, both an-account

tempestatum, et prædonum, et locorum;
of-the-storms, and of-the-pirates, and of (the dangerous) places;

quod natura fert, ut faveamus eis, qui
because nature impels (us), that we-favour those, who

ingrediantur eadem pericula, quibus nos
are-about-to-undergo the same dangers, which we

perfuncti sumus: quo animo tandem
have-gone-through: in-what (state of) mind 'is-it then

oportet me esse, jam prope videntem terram,
'proper (that) I should-be, now near seeing land,

ex magâ jactatione, in
after a great tossing (on the stormy sea of public life), as-respects

hunc, cui, video, esse subeundas maximas tempestates
him, who, I-see, is-about encountering the greatest storms

reipublicæ? Quare si est boni consuli,
of-the-republic? Wherefore if it-is (the part) of-a-good consul,

non solum videre, quid agatur, verum etiam
not only to-see-to, what 'is (now) 'doing, but also

providere, quid futurum sit; ostendam,
to-foresee, what may-hereafter-be (the state of affairs); I-will-show

alio **loco,** **quantum** **intersit** **communis** **salutis,**
in-another place, how-much it-interests the common safety

esse **duos** **consules,** **in** **republica**
(that) there-should-be two consuls, in the republic

kalendis Januariis, **Quod** **si** **est**
on-the-kalends-of-January. [On the first of January.] Which if it-is

ita, **non** **tam** **officium debuit** **vocare** **me**
so, not so-much (my) duty ought to-call-on me (to defend)

fortunas **hominis** **amici,** **quam** **respublica**
the fortunes of-a-man (my) friend, as (that) the republic

consulem **ad** **defendendam** **communem**
(should call on) the consul to defend the common

salutem.
safety.

3. **Nam** **quòd** **tuli** **legem** **de** **ambitu,**
For that I-proposed the law concerning bribery,

certe **ita tuli,**
(and corrupt means of obtaining office), 'I certainly 'did so 'propose (it),

ut **non abrogarem eam,** **quam** **tulerim**
that 'I-might not 'abrogate that (law), which I-had-proposed

jampridem mihimet ipsi **de** **defendendis**
long-since to-my-own self, concerning defending (and warding

periculis **civium. Etenim si** **confiterer**
off) the dangers of (my) fellow citizens. For if I-were-to-confess

largitionem esse factum, que defenderem id,
(that) bribery was committed, and should-defend it, (as)

esse **recte factum,** **facerem** **improbe,**
'having-been rightly 'done, I-would-act unjustly (and reprehen-

etiam si alius **tulisset** **legem : vero cum**
sibly), even if another (person) had-proposed the law: but when

defendam, **nihil commissum esse** **contra**
I maintain, (that) nothing has-been-done (by Murena) against

legem, quid est, quòd latio **legis** **impediat**
the law, what is-there, that the proposing of-the-law should-hinder

meam defensionem ? **Negat** **esse**
my defence (of him)? He (Cato) denies (that) it-is

ejusdem **severitatis,**
(in consonance with) the same severity (and strictness).

expulisse urbe Catilinam molientem
to-have-expelled from-the-city Catiline plotting

exitium reipublicæ intra mœnia, verbis
the destruction of-the-republic, within the walls (thereof), by-words,

et pene imperio, et nunc dicere pro
and almost by-command, and now to-plead the cause of

L. Murenâ. Autem ego semper libenter egi has
L. Murena. But I 'have always willingly 'acted those

partes lenitatis et misericordiæ, quas natura ipsa
parts of-mildness and of-compassion, which nature herself

docuit me: non vero appetivi illam personam
has-taught me: 'I-did not indeed 'seek-for that character

gravitatis que severitatis, sed, impositam mihi
of-rigour and of-severity, but, being imposed on-me

ab republica, sustinui, sicut dignitas
(as a duty) by the republic, I-sustained (it), as the dignity

hujus imperii postulabat, in summo periculo
of-this empire required, amid the greatest danger

civium. Quod si tum, cum respublica desiderabat
of-the-citizens. And if then, when the republic required

vim et severitatem, vici naturam, et fui
force and severity, I-conquered (my) nature, and was

tam vehemens quàm cogebar, non quàm volebam:
as rigorous as I-was-forced-to-be, not as I-wished:

nunc, cum omnes causæ vocent me ad misericordiam,
now, when all motives call me to compassion,

atque ad humanitatem, quanto studio tandem debeo
and to humanity, with-what ardour then ought-I

servire meæ naturæ que consuetudini?
to-indulge my nature and habits (inclined to humane, and

At de officio meæ defensionis,
friendly feelings)? But concerning the duty of-my defence

ac de ratione tuæ accusationis,
of Murena), and concerning the motives of-your accusation

etiam fortasse erit nobis dicendum
(of him), (there) also perhaps will-be (occasion) for-us to-speak

in aliâ parte orationis.
in another part of-the-oration.

Sed, judices, conquestio Ser. Sulpicii, sapientissimi
But, O judges, the complaint of Ser. Sulpicius, a most-wise

atque ornatissimi hominis, commovebat me non
and most-accomplished man, moved me no

minus, quam accusatio Catonis: qui dixit
less, than the accusation of Cato: who [Sulpicius] said

ferre gravissime et acerbissime, me
(that he) bore very-heavily and very-bitterly, (that) I

oblitum familiaritatis que
having-forgotten (the claims) of-long-acquaintance and

necessitudinis defendere causam
of-intimate-and-binding-friendship was-defending the cause

L. Murenæ contra se. Ego cupio, judices, satisfacere
of-L. Murena against him. I desire, O judges, to-satisfy

huic, que adhibere vos arbitros. Nam cum
him, and employ you as umpires (between us). For when

est grave, accusari vere in amicitiâ, tum,
it-is a serious (thing), to-be-accused truly in friendship, so,

etiam si falsò accuseris, est non negligendum.
even if 'you-be falsely 'accused, it-is not to-be-neglected.

Ego Ser. Sulpici confiteor, et me debuisse tibi,
I O Ser. Sulpicius confess, (that) both I owed you,

in tuâ petitione, omnia
in your application (and canvass for the consulship), all (my)

studia atque officia, pro nostrâ necessitudine,
zeal and (good) offices, according-to our intimate-friendship,

et arbitror præstitisse.
and I-think (that) I-have-performed (the same, by giving all the assist

Defuit nihil a me
ance in my power). There-lacked nothing on my (part, to assist)

tibi petenti consulatum, quod postulandum esset, au
you soliciting the consulship, that could-be-required, either

ab amico, aut a gratiosso, aut
from a friend, or from a favoured (and influential person), or

a consule. Illud tempus abiit; ratio
from the consul. That time has-gone-by; the motive (of action)

mutata est. Existimo sic, sic persuadeo mihi,
is-changed. I-think so, and so persuade myself, ('that'

me debuisse tibi tantum   contra honorem
I owed you as-much (assistance) against the advancemen

L. Murenæ,   quantum tu ausus sis
of-L. Murena (to the consulship), as you might-venture

postulare a me;   contra salutem,
to require-of from me; (but that) against (his personal) safety,

debere nihil. Neque enim, si tum adfui tibi,
I-owe (you) nothing. Nor indeed, if 'I then 'stood-by you,

cum peteres consulatum, debeo idcirco nunc, cum
when you-sought the consulship, ought-I for that reason now, when

petas Murenam ipsum, esse adjutor
you-seek (to injure) Murena himself, to-be (your) assistant

eodem pacto. Atque hoc non modo non
by-the-same agreement. And this not only 'is not

laudari, sed potest ne quidem concedi, ut,
'to-be-praised, but can not indeed be-conceded, that,

nostris amicis accusantibus, non defendamus
our friends accusing, 'we-might not 'defend

etiam alienissimos.
even the-greatest-strangers.

4. Autem, judices, est et vetus, et magna
But, O judges, there-is both an old, and great

amicitia cum Murenâ mihi, quæ non
friendship with Murena (and) me, which (friendship) 'shall not

idcirco obruetur a Ser. Sulpicio, in dimicatione
for-such-reason 'be-overwhelmed by Ser. Sulpicius, in a capital

capitis, quòd ab eodem
trial, (involving all the civil rights of Murena), because by the same

superata est in contentione
(Sulpicius, this friendship) was-overcome in a contest (for)

honoris. Quæ causa si esset non,
the honour (of office). Which motive (of friendship), if it-were not

tamen vel dignitas hominis,
(in existence), yet either the dignity (and high rank) of-the-man,

vel amplitudo ejus honoris, quem adeptus est,
or the-great-dignity of-his office, which he-has obtained,

inussisset mihi summam famam superbiæ
would-have-branded me (with) the greatest stigma of-pride

que crudelitatis, si repudiassem causam tanti
and of-cruelty, if I-had-repudiated a cause of-so-much

periculi, hominis amplissimi, et suis ornamentis
danger, of-a-man most-distinguished, both by-his-own honours

et Romani populi. Neque enim licet
and (by those) of-the-Roman people. Neither indeed is-it-allowed

mihi jam, neque est integrum, ut non
me now, nor is-it wholly-in-my-power, that 'I-should not

impertiam meum laborem, sublevandis
'impart my labour (and assistance), in-alleviating

periculis hominum. Nam cum tanta præmia
the dangers of-men. For when such-great rewards

data sint mihi pro hæc industria,
have-been-given to-me, for this industry (in defending others),

quanta antea nemini;
as before-this (have been conferred) on-none (for like services),

deponere labores, per quos ceperis ea,
to-desist-from labours, by which you-obtained those (honours),

cum adeptus sis, esset hominis,
when you-have-obtained (them), would-be (the part) of-a-man,

et astuti et ingrati. Si quòd licet
both cunning and ungrateful. If however it-would-be-allowed (for me)

desinere, si, te auctore, possum,
to-desist (from my labours), if, you being the adviser, I-might (do so),

si nulla turpitudo inertiæ, nulla superbiæ,
if no disgrace (or reproach) of-indolence, none of-arrogance,

nulla culpa inhumanitatis suscipitur; ego
no fault of-inhumanity is-incurred (thereby); I (would)

vero libenter desino. Sin autem fuga laboris
indeed willingly desist. But if the shunning of-labour

coarguit desidiam, repudiatio supplicum superbiam,
proves idleness, the rejection of-suppliants (proves) arrogance,

neglectio amicorum improbitatem;
(and) the neglect of-friends (proves) worthlessness; (and)

nimirum hæc causa est ejusmodi, quam nec
indeed this cause is of-that-kind, which neither

industrius, nec misericors, nec officiosus possit
an industrious, or merciful, or obliging (man) can

deserere. Atque hujusce rei, Servi,   facillime
abandon.   And   of this thing, O Servius, 'you-may very-easily

ceperis conjecturam de tuo ipsius studio
'form   an opinion, from your own pursuits (as a lawyer).

Nam si putas necesse tibi, etiam respondere
For if you-think-it necessary for-you, also to-give-legal-advice

adversariis tuorum amicorum, consulentibus   de
to-the-enemies of-your   friends,   consulting (you) respecting

jure; et si existimas turpe, te   advocato,
the law; and if you think (it) shameful, you having been counsel,

                            illum ipsum,
(and given your advice and opinion), (that) the   same (person),

contra quem   veneris, cadere   causa;
against whom 'you (now) 'appear, should-lose (his) cause;

 noli   esse tam injustus, ut, cum tui fontes
resolve-not to-be so unjust. that, when your springs

            pateant vel tuis inimicis,
(of legal knowledge) are-open, even to-your enemies, (that)

    putas   nostros   rivulos oportere esse
you-would-think (that) our (small) rivulets ought to-be

clausos etiam amicis. Etenim si   familiaritas
closed,   also 'to (our) 'friends. For-indeed, if (my) long-friendship

    tua removisset me ab hoc causâ, et si hoc idem
(for) you had-removed me from this cause, and if this same

accidisset Q. Hortensio, M. Crasso, clarissimis
had-happened to Q. Hortensius, to M. Crassus, most-distinguished

viris,   si item ceteris, a
men, (and engaged in this case for Murena), if also to-others, by

quibus intelligo tuam gratiam   magni
whom I-know your favour and (esteem) 'is greatly

æstimari; consul designatus   non haberet
prized;   the consul elect   'would not 'have

defensorem, in eâ civitate, in quâ nostri majores
a defender, in that city, in which our ancestors

voluerunt   unquam   deesse   patronum
'had-resolved that never should-there-be-wanting a patron

        nemini   infimo. Ego ipse
and defender to-any-one, (even of) the lowest-degree. myself

vero, judices, existimarem me nefarium, si
Indeed, O judges, would-consider myself a-wicked-man, if

defuissem amico, crudelem, si
I-were-wanting to (my) friend, a-cruel-man, if (I were wanting)

misero, superbum si consuli.
to-one-in-distress, an-arrogant-man, if (I were wanting) to-the-consul

Quare quod dandum est amicitiæ, larg
Wherefore whatever is-to-be-conceded to-friendship, will-be freely

dabitur a me, ut agam cum te, Servi, non
given by me, so-that I-will-act with you, O Servius, in no

secus, ac si esset meus frater, qui est carissimus
otherwise than if (it) were my brother, who is most-dear

mihi, in isto loco. Quod
to me, (stood) in this same place (that you are). Whatever

tribuendum est officio, fidei, religioni,
is-to-be-yielded to-duty, to (good) faith, (and) to-religion,

moderabor id ita, ut meminerim, me dicere
I-will regulate it so, that I-may-remember, (that) I am-pleading

pro amici periculo, contra studium
for (the safety) of-a-friend in-danger, against the attacks of (another)

amici.
friend.

5. Intelligo, judices, fuisse tres partes
I-understand, O judges, (that) there-were three parts

totius accusationis, et unam earum
of-the-entire accusation, and (that) one of-them

versatam esse, in reprehensione vitæ,
has-been-taken-up, in the censure (of his mode of) life,

alteram in contentione
the other in contesting (his claims, on account of his not being of

dignitatis, tertiam in criminibus
the proper rank and) dignity, (and) the third with the crimes

ambitûs. Atque harum trium
of-bribery (and corruption in the election). And of-these three

partium, illa prima, quæ debeat esse gravissima,
parts, that first, which ought to-have-been the-most-grave,

fuit ita infirma et levis, ut magis lex
was so weak and trifling, that rather the law, (respecting)

quædam   accusatoria coëgerit illos dicere aliquid,
certain (forms of) accusation,   forced   them to-say something,

de   vitâ L. Murenæ, quàm   vera facultas
concerning   the life of L. Murena,   than (any) real   power

maledicendi.   Enim Asia   objecta est
of-criminating (him).   For   Asia has-been objected (to him as a

          quæ   non expetita est ab hoc ad
reproach) which 'was not   'sought   by him, for (the purpose

          voluptatem   et   luxuriam,   sed
of indulging in)   pleasure   and   luxury,   but which

peragrata in militari labore. Qui si   adolescens,
he-traversed in military   duty.   Who if (when) a-young-man,

suo   patre   imperatore,   non meruisset;
his-own father   being commander,   'he-had not   'served

          videretur, aut timuisse hostem, aut
(in the army); he-would-seem, either to-have-feared the enemy,   or

imperium patris, aut repudiatus   a parente.
the command of-his-father, or to-have-been-repudiated by his parent.

An   cum   filii   prætextati
Whether when   the sons, (under 17 years, and) wearing-the-prætexta

triumphantium soleant potissimum sedere in   equis;
of-those-triumphing   used   especially   to-sit on the horses

          fugiendum fuit   huic decorare
(drawing the triumphal car); was-it-to-be-avoided (by) this one, to adorn

triumphum   patris   militaribus donis,
the triumph 1of (his) 1father, 'with (his own) 'military   rewards,

ut,   rebus gestis communiter,
so-that, by-exploits performed   together,   (it might be said that)

pæne triumpharet simul cum   patre? Hic
'he nearly 'triumphed together 'with (his) 1father? This (man)

vero, judices, et fuit in Asiâ, et fuit magno
then, O judges, both was in Asia, and was a great

adjumento fortissimo viro suo parenti in periculis,
assistance to-the-very-brave man his father in   dangers,

solatio   in   laboribus, gratulationi   in
a comfort (to him) 'in (his) 'labours, a congratulation (to him) in

victoriâ. Et, si Asia habet quandam suspicionem
victory.   And, if Asia has   a certain   suspicion

luxuriæ. non   unquam vidisse Asiam, sed
of luxury, not (that) ¹he ever   ¹saw   Asia,   but (that)

vixisse continenter in Asiâ, laudandum est. Quamobrem
he-lived temperately in Asia, is-to-be-praised. For-which-reason

nomen   Asiæ   fuit non objiciendum Murenæ,   ex
the name of-Asia was not to-be-objected to Murena, from

quâ laus constituta est   familiæ, memoria
which renown was constituted (and arose) ¹for (his) ¹family, a memorial

        generi,   honos et gloria   nomini: sed
¹for (his) ¹race, (and) honour and glory ¹to (his) ¹name: but

aliquod flagitium ac   dedecus   aut susceptum
some   debauchery and scandalousness (was) either   acquired

      in Asiâ, aut   deportatum ex Asiâ. Vero
(by him) in Asia, or (when) brought   from Asia. But

meruisse stipendia   in eo bello,
to-have-earned pay [to have served in the army] in that war,

quod tum Romanus populus gerebat, non modò
which then the Roman   people   waged, not only

maximum, sed etiam solum, fuit
the greatest, but also the only-one, was (a proof) ¹of (his)

virtutis: libentissime meruise,   patre
¹valour: ¹to-have-most-willingly ¹served (in the army, his) father

imperatore,   pietatis: finem
being commander, ¹of (his filial) ¹piety: (that) the termination ¹of (his

        stipendiorum fuisse victoriam ac triumphum
¹military)   services   was the victory, and triumph

        patris,   felicitatis. Idcirco
¹of (his) ¹father, (and which was a proof) ¹of (his) ¹good-fortune. Therefore

quidem in hisce rebus, est nihil loci maledicto,
indeed in these things, there-is no room for-censure,

quod laus occupavit omnia.
because praise has-taken-up all (the place).

6. Cato appellat L. Murenam saltatorem. Si
Cato calls L. Murena a dancer. If (this is)

vere objicitur,   est maledictum vehementis
truly objected (to him), it-is the reproach of-a-violent

accusatoris; sin falso   maledici conviciatoris.
accuser; but-if falsely (it is that) of-a-slanderous calumniator.

Quare cum sis istâ auctoritate,
Wherefore when you are (of) such authority (and weight of character),

debes non, M. Cato, arripere maledictum ex
you-ought not, O M. Cato, to-snatch calumny out-of

trivio, aut ex aliquo convivio
the-cross-streets, (where idlers meet), or from some carousal

scurrarum, neque temere vocari consulem Romani
of-buffoons, nor rashly to-call the consul of-the-Roman

populi saltatorem : sed conspicere, quibus vitiis
people a dancer : but to-consider, with-what vices

præterea sit necesse eum affectum esse,
besides it-may-be necessary (that) he should-be-affected,

cui istud possit vere objici. Enim fere nemo
to-whom this may-be truly objected. For almost no-one

saltat sobrius, nisi forte insanit; neque
dances, (when he is) sober, unless perhaps he-is-crazy; neither

in solitudine, neque in moderato atque honesto
in solitude, nor in a moderate and decent

convivio. Saltatio est extrema comes tempestivi
feast. Dancing is the last companion of-prolonged

convivii, amœni loci, multarum
feasting, of-pleasant (and luxurious) places, (and) of-many (voluptuous)

deliciarum. Tu arripis id mihi, quod
pleasures. You catch-at that, (it seems to) me, which (it)

est necesse omnium vitiorum esse
is necessary (that) of-all vices (it should) be

postremum : relinquis illa, quibus
the last : you-leave those (things unnoticed), which

remotis, hoc vitium potest non omnino esse.
being-removed, this vice can not at-all exist.

Nullum turpe convivium, non amor, non
No disgraceful feasting, no improper love, no

comissatio, non libido, non sumptus
revelling, no lust, no extravagance-in-expenditure

ostenditur. Et, cum ea non reperiantur,
is-shown. And, when those (things) 'are not found,

quæ habent nomen voluptatis, que quæ sunt vitiosa:
which have the name of-pleasure, and which are vicious; (he)

in quo potes non reperire luxuriam ipsam, in eo
in whom you-can not find luxury itself, in him

putas te reperturum umbram luxuriæ?
do-you-think (that) you will-find the shadow of-luxury?

Potest nihil igitur dici in vitam L. Murenæ?
Can nothing therefore be-said against the life of L. Murena?

Inquam nihil omnino, judices. Consul designatus
I-say nothing at-all, O judges. The consul elect 'is

sic defenditur a me, ut nulla fraus,
thus (and on those grounds) 'defended by me, that no fraud,

nulla avaritia, nulla perfidia, nulla crudelitas, nullum
no avarice, no perfidy, no cruelty, no

petulans verbum ejus proferatur. Habet
lascivious word of-his can-be-brought-against (him). It-is

bene: fundamenta defensionis jacta sunt. Enim
well: the foundations of-the-defence are-laid. For

nondum defendimus bonum virum, atque
we-are not-as-yet 'defending a good man, and

integrum hominem, nostris laudibus, quibus postea
upright man, by our praises, which hereafter

utar, sed prope confessione inimicorum.
I-will-make-use-of, but almost by-the-confession 'of (his) 'enemies.

7. Quo constituto, aditus ad
Which (first part) being-established, the approach to

contentionem dignitatis, quæ fuit
the contest (respecting his) dignity (and rank), which was

altera pars accusationis, est facilior mihi.
the second part of-the-accusation, is more-easy for-me.

Video esse in te, Ser. Sulpici, summam
I-see (that) there-is in you, O Ser. Sulpicius, the highest

dignitatem generis, integritatis, industriæ, que
dignity of-birth, of-integrity, of-industry, and

omnium ceterorum ornamentorum, fretum quibus,
of-all other accomplishments, relying on-which,

est par aggredi ad petitionem consulatûs.
it-is proper (for you), to-attempt to apply (for) the consulship.

Cognosco ista esse paria in
I-know that-these-same (virtues and endowments) are equally-so in

L. Murenâ, atque ita paria, ut neque ipse poterit
L. Murena, and so equal, that neither he-himself could-be

vinci dignitate, neque
surpassed in-dignity (and worth by you), nor 'can-he (Murena)

superarit te dignitate. Contempsisti genus
'surpass you in-dignity. You-have-despised the family

L. Murenæ; extulisti tuum. Quo loco, si
of L. Murena; you-have-extolled your-own. On-which subject, if

sumis hoc tibi, nisi qui sit patricius,
you-assume this to-yourself (to assert), except he who is a patrician,

neminem esse natum bono genere; facis, videatur,
no-one is born of-a-good family; you-act, it-would-seem,

ut rursus plebes sevocanda in Aventinum.
that again the people were-to-be-called-out to the Aventine hill.

Autem sin sunt amplæ et honestæ plebeiæ
But if there-are distinguished and honest plebeian

familiæ; et proavus, et avus
families; (and indeed) both the great-grandfather, and grandfather

L. Murenæ fuerunt prætores, et pater, cum
of-L. Murena were prætors, and (his) father, when

triumphasset amplissime atque honestissime
he-had-triumphed most-splendidly and honourably (for exploit

ex præturâ, hoc reliquit huic
performed) in (his) prætorship, (and) thereby left to-him

faciliorem gradum adipiscendi
a-more-easy step [and thereby prepared the way for him] of-obtaining

consulatûs, quod is jam debitus patri
the consulship, because it 'was already 'due to-the-father

petebatur a filio. Vero tua nobilitas, Ser. Sulpici,
was-sought by the son. But your nobility, O Ser. Sulpicius,

tametsi est summa, tamen est notior
although it-is (of the) highest (order), yet it-is more-known

literatis hominibus et historicis, vero obscurior
to-literary men and historians, but less-known

populo et suffragatoribus. Enim pater fuit
to-the-people and to-the-voters. For (your) father was

equestri loco; avus celebratus nullâ
in-the-equestrian rank; (your) grandfather was-celebrated by no

illustri laude. Itaque non ex recenti sermone
illustrious reputation. Therefore not from the modern discourse

hominum, sed ex vetustate annalium est memoria
of-men, but from the antiquity of-annals is the remembrance

tuæ nobilitatis eruenda. Quare ego soleo
of-your nobility to-be-extracted. Wherefore I am-accustomed

semper aggregare te in nostrorum numerum, quod,
always to-associate you in our number, because

cum esses filius Romani equitis virtute que
when you-are the son of-a-Roman knight, 'by (your) 'virtue and

industriâ perfecisti, tamen
industry, you-have-attained (such reputation, that) yet

putarere dignus summâ amplitudine:
you might-be-thought worthy of-the-highest honours (of the state):

nec unquam visum est mihi esse minus virtutis
nor 'did-it ever 'seem to-me to-be less of-virtue

in Q. Pompeio, novo homine, et fortissimo viro,
in Q. Pompeius, a new man, and a-most-brave man

quàm in nobilissimo homine, M. Æmilio. Etenim
than in (that) most-noble man, M. Æmilius. For

est ejusdem animi atque ingenii, tradere
it-is (a part) of-the-same mind and talent, to-transmit

suis posteris, quod Pompeius fecit, amplitudinem
to-his posterity, which Pompeius did, the greatness (and honour)

nominis, quam non acceperat;
of-a-name, which 'he had not 'received (from his parents)

et, ut Scaurus, renovare, virtute prope
and, like Scaurus, to-renew, 'by (his) 'virtue, the nearly

intermortuam memoriam sui generis.
extinct remembrance of-his family.

8. Quanquam ego jam putabam, judices,
Although I heretofore did-think, O judges, (that it)

perfectum esse meo labore, ignobilitas
had-been-brought-about by-my exertion, (that) want-of-nobility

generis ne objiceretur multis fortibus viris; qui
of-birth 'might not 'be-objected to-many brave men; who

jacebant, non modò commemorandis
remained-neglected, not only (when) mentioning (and pointing out)

Curiis, Catonibus, Pompeiis, illis antiquis,
the Curii, the Catoes, the Pompeii, those ancient,

fortissimis viris, novis hominibus, sed his
most-brave-men, (and) new men, but these

recentibus, Mariis, Didiis, et Cæliis. Cum ego
modern-ones, the Marii, the Didii, and the Cælii. When I

vero, tanto intervallo, refregissem
indeed, so-great an interval (of time having elapsed), had-broken

ista claustra nobilitatis, ut aditus ad consulatum
these barriers of-nobility, so-that access to the consulship

posthac, non pateret magis nobilitati, quàm
hereafter, 'might not 'be-open more to-nobility, than

virtuti, sicut fuit apud nostros majores:
to-virtue (and merit), as it-was with our ancestors: 'I-did

non arbitrabar, cum consul designatus, ex vetere et
not 'think, when the consul elect, of an old and

illustri familiâ, defenderetur filio Romani
illustrious family, was-defended by-the son of-a-Roman

equitis, consule, accusatores dicturos esse
knight, (he being) consul, (that) the accusers would-say-any thing

de novitate generis. Etenim accidit mihi
concerning newness of family. For it-happened to-me

ipsi, ut peterem, cum duobus patriciis,
myself, that I-sought-for (the consulship), with two patricians

altero improbissimo atque audacissimo,
(against me), the one a most-worthless and most-audacious (man),

altero modestissimo, atque optimo viro: tamen,
the other a most-modest, and most-excellent man: however,

superavi Catilinam dignitate, Galbam gratiâ.
I-overcame Catiline in-dignity, (and) Galba in-favour.

Quod si id deberet esse crimen novo
Because if this ought to-have-been (alleged as) a crime to-a-new

homini, profecto neque inimici, neque invidi
man, certainly neither enemies, nor envious-persons

defuissent mihi. Omittamus
would-have-been-wanting to-me (on the occasion). Let-us-omit

igitur dicere de genere, dignitas
therefore saying (any thing) concerning birth, the dignity

cujus est magna in utroque : videamus
of-which is great in each (candidate,: let-us-look

cetera.
to-the-rest.

"Petit quæsturam unà, et ego
'He (Murena) 'sought the quæstorship together (with me), and I

factus sum prior." Est non
was-made the first" (in order, says Sulpicius). It-is not (necessary

respondendum ad omnia. Enim neque fugit
to-reply to every-thing. For neither does-it-escape

quemquam vestrûm, cum multi pares
(the observation of) any-one of-you, when many equal

dignitate fiant, autem unus solus possit
in-dignity are-designated (for office), but one alone can

obtinere primum; ordinem dignitatis et
obtain the first (place); (for that) the order of-dignity and

renuntiationis esse non eundem; propterea quod
of-announcement is not the same; because that

renuntiatio habeat gradus, autem
the announcement (of the election) may-have degrees, but

dignitas sit persæpe eadem omnium.
the dignity may be (considered) very-often (as) the same (for) all.

Sed quæstura utriusque fuit propemodum
But the quæstorship of-each (of you) was nearly (of)

pari momento sortis. Hic habuit,
equal importance (as assigned by) lot. This-one [Murena] had,

Titiâ lege, tacitam et quietam provinciam:
by-the-Titian law, a still and quiet province:

tu illam Ostiensem, cui, cum
you [Sulpicius] had that Ostian (province), at-which, when

quæstores sortiuntur, solet etiam
the quæstors draw-lots, it-is-customary also (for the by-standers)

acclamari; non tam gratiosam et
to-shout-out (in derision); (a province) not so pleasant and

illustrem, quàm negotiosam et molestam. Nomen
illustrious, as full-of-care and troublesome. The name

utriusque consedit in
of-each (of you) settled-down in (your)

quæsturâ.   Enim sors dedit
quæstorship, (and was not heard out of it).   For   chance gave

vobis   nullum campum, in quo   virtus posset
you (both)   no   field,   in which (your) virtue might

excurrere que   cognosci. Spatium temporis
come-forth and (make itself) be-known. The space of-time

reliqui,   vocatur   in
remaining, (after the quæstorship was passed), is called into

contentionem. Tractatum est   dissimillimâ ratione
contest.   It-was-managed in-a-very-different manner

ab utroque.
by   each.

9. Servius secutus est, hìc cum nobis, hanc
   Servius   followed,   here with   us,   this

urbanam militiam respondendi,   scribendi,
city   warfare of-answering (legal questions), of-writing,

          cavendi,   plenam sollicitudinis ac
of-giving-legal-caution-and-advice, full   of-solicitude and

stomachi;   didicit   civile jus: vigilavit multum;
chagrin;   he-studied the civil law: he-watched much;

laboravit; fuit præsto multis;
he-laboured; he-was present for-many; [he was to be seen by all;]

perpessus est   stultitiam multorum; pertulit
he-suffered-much (from) the folly of-many; he-bore (with)

arrogantiam; exsorbuit difficultatem: vixit ad
arrogance;   he-overcame difficulties: he-lived at

arbitrium aliorum, non ad suum.   Magna
the will   of-others, not at his-own. (There is) great

laus, et   grata hominibus,   unum hominem
praise, and (a thing) pleasing to-men, (that) one   man

elaborare, in eâ scientiâ, quæ sit profutura
should-labour, in that science, which may-be advantageous

multis. Quid   Murena   interea?   Fuit
to-many. What (was) Murena (doing) in-the-mean-time? He-was

legatus L. Lucullo, fortissimo et sapientissimo
a lieutenant to L. Lucullus, a most-brave and   most-wise

viro,   summo   imperatori; in quâ legatione
man, (and) great   commander;   in which lieutenancy

duxit   exercitum;   contulit   signa,
he-commanded   an army;   he-brought-together   the standards; [he

conseruit   manum;
engaged in battle;]   he-joined   hand; [he fought hand to hand;]

fudit   magnas copias   hostium;   cepit   urbes
he-routed   great   forces   of-the-enemy;   he-took (several) towns

partim   vi,   partim obsidione;   sic   obiit   istam
partly   by-force,   partly   by-besieging;   'he so 'traversed   this

Asiam refertam,   et eandem   delicatam,
Asia   filled   (with luxuries), and that-same (so) voluptuous,

ut reliquerit in eâ, neque vestigium avaritiæ, neque
that   he-left   in it, neither   a trace   of-avarice,   nor

luxuriæ; in maximo bello   sic versatus est, ut
of-luxury; in a-very-great war   'he-was so   'employed,   that

hic   gesserit   multas   et   magnas   res,   sine
he   performed   many   and   great   exploits, without

imperatore,   imperator   nullam   sine
the commander, (but) the commander (performed)   none   without

noc. Atque   loquar   hæc,   quanquam L. Lucullo
him.   And (as) I-mention these-things, notwithstanding   L. Lucullus

præsente, tamen,   ne videamur, propter
being present,   yet,   (that) 'we-may not   'seem,   on-account-of

nostrum   periculum,   habere   licentiam   fingendi
our   danger,   to-have   a license   of fiction

concessam   ab ipso, omnia sunt testata   publicis
granted   (to us) by himself,   all   are   verified   by-the-public

literis;   quibus L. Lucullus impertit
despatches (of that commander); in-which   L. Lucullus   imparts

tantum   laudis,   quantum neque ambitiosus, neque
so-much   of-praise,   as   neither   an ambitious,   nor

invidus   imperator   debuit   tribuere   alteri   in
envious   commander   ought   to-have-granted   to-another   in

communicandâ   gloriâ.   Est   summa   honestas,
participating   (his) glory.   There-is the greatest   honesty,

summa   dignitas in utroque;   quam ego si
the greatest dignity   in   each-one (of you); which   I   if

liceat   mihi per Servium, ponam in pari atque
it-is allowed   to-me by Servius,   will-place in the-like   and

eâdem laude. Sed non licet. Agitat
in-the-same (degree of) praise. But 'it-is not allowed. He-agitates

militarem rem; insectatur totam hanc legationem;
military affairs; he-attacks all this lieutenancy

putat consulatum esse
(of Murena); he-thinks, (that) the consulship is (an office requiring)

assiduitatis, et harum quotidianarum operarum.
industry, and these daily labours.

Inquit, "mihi fueris tot annos apud exercitum?
He-says, "were-you not so-many years with the army?

non attigeris forum? tamdiu
did-you ever 'set-foot (in) the forum? 'were-you (not) so-long

abfueris? et cum venris, longo intervallo,
absent? and when you-return, (after) a long space-of-time,

contendas cum iis, qui habitarunt in
will-you-contend with those, who (may be said to) dwell in

foro, de dignitate?" Primum
the-forum, about dignity (and merit)?" First (as respects)

ista nostra assiduitas, Servi, nescis quantum
this our assiduity, O Servius, you-know-not how-much

fastidii interdum afferat hominibus, quantum
disgust 'it sometimes 'occasions men, and-how-much

satietatis. Expediit mihi quidem
satiety. It disembarrassed (and helped) me indeed

vehementer, gratiam esse
exceedingly, (that) the favour (I had won by my conduct) was

positam in oculis. Sed tamen
placed before the eyes (of my countrymen). But however

superavi satietatem mei
I-overcame the satiety of-myself, (occasioned by my frequent appear

meo magno labore, et tu fortasse
ance), by-my great labour (and exertions), and you perhaps

idem: verum tamen desiderium
(have done) the-same-thing: but however the desire

obfuisset nihil
(of hearing us, occasioned by absence), 'might-have-been no 'injury

utrique nostrûm. Sed, hoc omisso, ut,
to-either of-us. But, this being-passed over, that,

revertamur ad contentionem   studiorum
we-may-return to   the contest (and comparison) 'of (our) 'studies

          atque   artium; quî potest
(and habits), and 'of (our) professions; to-whom can 'there-be (any)

dubitari, quin ad adipiscendum consulatum, gloria
'doubt,   but-that for   obtaining   the consulship, the renown

militaris rei   afferat multo plus
of military exploits may-bring much more (of claim thereto, as re-

          dignitatis,   quàm   civilis juris?
spects)   dignity (and merit), than (that) of-the-civil law?

Tu vigilas de nocte, ut   respondeas
You watch at night, that you-may-give-answers (and advice)

tuis consultoribus: ille,   ut   perveniat
to-your   clients: he (does the same), that he-may-arrive

maturè   cum   exercitu,   eo,   quò
early,   with   his army,   in that place, whither

     intendit.   gallorum exsuscitat te,
he-is-directing-his-march. (The crowing) of-the-cocks awakes you,

cantus buccinarum   illum. Tu instituis
the sound of-the-trumpets (awakes) him. You arrange (the manner

          actionem,   ille instruit
of conducting) a case (in law), he draws-up (an army in)

  aciem;   tu   caves,   ne   tui consultores
order-of-battle; you take-care, lest your   clients

capiantur,   ille ne urbes aut castra.
be-taken (unawares), he, lest the towns or the camps (may be

    Ille tenet et scit, ut copiæ hostium
taken). He understands and knows, how the forces of-the-enemy

arceantur   tu, ut   aquæ pluviæ;
may-be-kept-back (from doing harm), you, how   the rains

                    ille exercitatur
(and inundations, may be kept back, from doing harm); he is occupied

in propagandis finibus;   tu in regendis:
in extending the boundaries (of the empire); you in regulating

          ac nimirum (enim quod
(the boundaries of private estates): and assuredly   (for   what

sentio,   dicendum est),   virtus   militaris   rei
I-think,   must-be-said),   the excellence   of-military   art

præstat   omnibus ceteris.
rpasses (that of)   all   others.

10. Hæc   peperit   nomen
      (It is) this   (military skill, that)   has-produced   a name

Romano   populo,   hæc   æternam   gloriam
for-the-Roman people,   this (has produced) eternal   glory

huic   urbi;   hæc   coëgit   orbem terrarum parere
for-this   city;   this-same has-forced the whole   world   to-obey

huic imperio: omnes urbanæ   res,   omnia hæc nostra
this   empire: all   city   affairs,   all   these   our

præclara   studia,   et hæc forensis   laus
noble   studies (and pursuits), and this   forensic reputation

et industria   latent,   in   tutelâ   et præsidio
and   industry   lie-sheltered, under the defence and   protection

bellicæ virtutis.   Atque   simul   suspicio   tumultûs
of warlike virtue.   And   as-soon-as a suspicion of-a-tumult

increpuit, illico   nostræ artes
is reported, immediately our   arts (of eloquence and pleading)

conticescunt.
become silent.

Et quoniam videris mihi osculari   istam
And   because you-seem to-me to-kiss   (and fondle)   this

scientiam juris,   tanquam   tuam   filiolam,
science   of-the-law,   as-if   (it were) your little-daughter,

nor. patiar te versari in tanto errore, ut
I will not 'suffer you to-be under so-great an error, that

arbitrere istud, nescio   quid, quod   didicisti
you should-think this, I-know (not) what, which you-have-learned

tanto opere, esse aliquid præclarum. Ego semper
with so-much labour, to-be something eminent.   I   always

judicavi te dignissimum   consulatu,   et   omni
'udged   you most-worthy of-the-consulship, and of-every

honore,   aliis virtutibus, continentiâ, gravitate,
honour,   by-other virtues, 'by (your) 'moderation,   gravity

justitiâ, fide,   omnibus   ceteris
ıustice, good-faith, (and) by-all (your) other (virtues) 'I-will

Non quidem dicam, quod didicisti civile jus,
not indeed 'say, (that) because you-have-learned the civil law,

perdidisti operam ; sed dicam illud,
you-have-lost (your) labour ; but I-will-say this, (that)

esse, in illâ disciplinâ, nullam
there-is, in that knowledge (of the civil law), no

munitam viam ad consulatum. Enim omnes artes,
sure way to the consulship. For all the arts

quæ conciliant studia Romani populi nobis,
which conciliate the good-will of-the-Roman people to-us

debent habere, et admirabilem dignitatem, et
ought to-have, both an admirable dignity, and

pergratum utilitatem.
very-agreeable usefulness.

11. Summa dignitas est, in iis, qui
The highest dignity (and esteem) is, in those, who

antecellunt militari laude ; enim omnia quæ sunt
excel in-military renown ; for all-things which are

in imperio, et in statu
in the empire, (or connected with it), and in the state (and condition)

civitatis, putantur defendi et firmari ab
of-the-government, are-considered to-be-defended and strengthened by

iis ; etiam summa utilitas ; siquidem
them ; (there is) also the greatest usefulness (in them) ; since

eorum consilio, et periculo possumus
'by-their 'counsel, and the dangers (they incur), we-can

perfrui, cum respublica, tum etiam nostris
enjoy, as-well the republic, as also our (private)

rebus. Etiam illa facultas dicendi est gravis, et
property. Also that talent of-speaking is important, and

plena dignitatis, quæ sæpe valuit in deligendo
full of-dignity, which often has-availed (much) in electing

consule, posse permovere consilio atque oratione,
a consul, to-be-able to-move by counsel and oratory,

mentes, et senatûs, et populi, et eorum, qui
the minds, both of-the-senate, and of-the-people, and of-those, who

judicant res. Consul quæritur, qui,
judge (and decide) affairs. A consul is-required, who, (by his eloquence)

dicendo,　　　nonnunquam　comprimat　tribur.icios
in-speaking,　'may　　sometimes　　'repress　　tribunician

furores, qui flectat concitatum populum, qui resistat
excesses, who may-sway the excited people, who resists,

　　　　　　　　　　largitioni.　　　　　Non
(and opposes himself against) bribery-and-corruption.　(It is)　not

mirum, si　ob　　hanc facultatem　homines,
strange,　if on-account-of this　talent, (that)　men, (who were)

non　nobiles,　sæpe　consecuti sunt　consulatum:
not　noble,　often　have-obtained　the consulship:

præsertim cum hæc eadem　res　pariat plurimas
especially　when this　same　thing procures　many

gratias,　　　　　firmissimas amicitias, maxima
favours, (and great influence),　the firmest friendships, the greatest

studia,　　　　　Quorum, Sulpici,　est
zeal, (and good feeling towards us). Of-which, O Sulpicius, there-is

nihil, in isto vestro artificio.　Primum,　quæ
nothing, in this　your　profession.　In-the-first-place,　what

dignitas potest esse in tam tenui scientiâ? Enim
dignity　can-there-be in so　slender a science?　For

sunt parvæ res,　prope occupatæ in singulis
they-are small affairs,　nearly taken-up with　single

literis,　atque　interpunctionibus　verborum.
letters,　and　the punctuation　of-words.

　Deinde, etiam si, apud nostros majores,　fuit
In-the-next-place, even if, among　our　ancestors, there-was

quid admirationis in isto studio,　　id, vestris
any-thing of-admiration in this study (of yours), it,　your

mysteriis enuntiatis, est totum contemptum et
mysteries being-revealed, is altogether despised and

abjectum. Pauci quondam sciebant,　　posset
degraded.　Few formerly knew, (whether) it-might

agi lege, necne.　　　　　　　Enim
be-done by-law, or-not. [Whether they might go to law, or not.]　For

vulgò　　habebant non fastos.　Qui
generally (the people) had　no calender. (Those) who

consulebantur erant in magnâ potentiâ: a quibus
were-consulted were in great　power:　from whom

etiam dies petebantur, tanquam a
also   days (of consultation) were requested,   as   by

Chaldæis. Quidam scriba inventus est,
the Chaldæan-astrologers. A certain scribe (or writer) was-found,

Cn. Flavius, qui confixerit oculos cornicum,
Cn. Flavius (by name), who might-have-pierced the eyes of crows,

et proposuerit
who could deceive the cunning ones,] and (who) exposed

populo fastos ediscendos singulis diebus, et
to the people a calender to-be-learned for-each day, and

compilarit, ab cautis jureconsultis ipsis,
(thus) pilfered, from the subtle lawyers themselves,

eorum sapientiam. Itaque illi irati,
their-own science. Therefore they [the lawyers] enraged,

quòd veriti sunt, ne, ratione dierum
because they were afraid lest, the order of-the-days (for going to law),

pervulgatâ et cognitâ, posset agi lege,
being-published and known, (that people) might go to-law,

sine suâ operâ, composuerunt quasdam
without their assistance, they composed (and invented) certain

notas, ut ipsi interessent in
(legal) forms, that they 'might (necessarily) 'be-present in

omnibus rebus.
all affairs.

12. Cum hoc posset fieri bellissime
When this may have-been-done very-well,

"Sabinus fundus est meus;" "immo
(as thus): "The Sabine farm is mine;" "indeed (it is)

meus;" deinde judicium:
mine;" (rejoins the opponent); then judgment (is given): (the

noluerunt. Inquit
lawyers) would not (agree to this mode of procedure). Says-one,

"fundus, qui est in agro, qui vocatur Sabinus."
"the farm, which is in the country, which is-called the Sabine."

Verbose satis. Cedo, quid postea; Ego aio eum
Verbosely enough. Well, what next; I say that (farm)

esse meum, ex jure Quiritium." Quid tum?
is mine, according to-the-law of-the-Romans." What then?

"Ego voco te ex jure, inde ibi manu
"I call you out-of-court, from that-place-there, to-contend

consertum." Ille, unde petebatur,
with-me." He, when it-was-demanded, [the defendant]

habebat non, quid responderet huic, tam
had not, what (wherewith) he-might-reply to-this-one, so

loquaciter litigioso. Idem jureconsultus transit
verbosely litigious. The-same lawyer (now) crosses-over,

modo Latini tibicinis; inquit:
in-the-manner of-a-Latin flute-player; and-says: (from-that-place-there),

"unde tu vocasti me ex jure manu consertum,
"whence you called me out of court, to contend with (me),

inde ibi ego revoco te." Interea, ne
from thence I (now) call you." In-the-mean-time, lest

Prætor putaret se pulchrum ac
the Prætor should-think himself (to be) an excellent and

beatum, atque
lucky (person), [should have too good an opinion of himself], and

ipse loqueretur aliquid suâ sponte,
should himself 'say something of-his-own accord,

carmen compositum est ei quoque, cum
a set-form-of-words is-composed for-him also, when

absurdum ceteris rebus, tum vero in illo.
absurd in-other things, so indeed in this.

"Utrisque, suis superstitibus, dico, istam
"To-each, their witnesses-being-present, I-say, (that) this

viam, inite viam," ille sapiens
(is) the way, proceed on-the-way," that wise (lawyer)

aderat præsto, qui doceret inire
was-present at-hand, who might-show (how) to-proceed

viam. "Redite viam." Redibant eodem
on-the-way. "Return on-the-road." They-returned with-the-same

duce. Credo hæc, tum jam videbantur
leader. I-believe (that) these-things, even then, appeared

ridicula apud illos barbatos: homines,
ridiculous, among these bearded (personages): (these) men,

cum constitissent rectè, atque in
when they-had-placed (themselves) properly, and in

loco,   juberet   abire;   ut   statim
a place,   sheuld-be-ordered   to-go-away; that they might immediately

redirent   eodem,   unde   abissent.
return   to-the-same-place,   whence   they-had-gone.

Omnia illa   fucata sunt   iisdem   ineptiis.
All   these (legal forms)   are-tainted   with-these-same   follies

" Quando   conspicio   te   in   jure,"   et   hæc:
" When   I-behold   you   in   law,"   and   these,

" Aune   tu   dicis   vindicaveris
" Or-   'do you   'say (this for appearance) or have you sustained

causa?"   quæ   dum   occulta erant,   qui
the cause?"   which   while   they-were-kept-secret; (those) who

tenebant   ea   necessariò   petebantur
held   those (secrets) were   necessarily   sought-for,

ab cis :   vero   postea   pervulgata,
by those, (having law suits): but   afterwards having-been-divulged,

atque   jactata   in   manibus   et
and   thrown (about) in   hands, [and well handled] and

excussa,   reperta sunt   inanissima   prudentiæ,
examined,   they-were-found (to be) most-devoid   of-sense

autem plenissima fraudis et stultitiæ. Nam cum
but   very-full   of-fraud   and   folly.   For   when

permulta   præclarè   constituta essent
very-many things   'were   admirably   'established

legibus,   ea   pleraque   corrupta sunt   ac
by-the-laws,   'they-were   mostly   'corrupted   and

depravata   ingeniis   jureconsultorum.   Omnes
depraved   by-the-ingenuity   of-the-lawyers.   All

mulieres,   propter   infirmitatem   consilii,
women,   on-account-of   the weakness   'of (their) 'judgment,

    majores voluerunt   esse   potestate   tutorum :
(our) ancestors   resolved   should-be in-the-power of-guardians;

hi   invenerunt genera tutorum, quæ
these (lawyers) found-out   classes of-guardians, which (classes)

continerentur   potestate   mulierum.   Illi
might-be-contained (or held) in-the-power   of-the-women.   They

     noluerunt   sacra   interire :
(our ancestors) did-not-wish   the sacred-family-rites   to-die-out

ingenio   horum   senes
by-the-ingenuity of-these (lawyers) old-men, (who had no children.)

reperti sunt   ad   faciendas   coëmptiones,
were-found   for   making   (fictitious) purchases   (of the

                  causâ   interimendorum   sacrorum.
family estates), for-the-purpose   of destroying   the-sacred-rites,

                Denique, in omni civili jure
entailed on such estates). In-fine, in   all   the civil law

            reliquerunt   æquitatem,
they [the lawyers] abandoned   equity,   (and the spirit of the

            tenuerunt   verba   ipsa: ut,
laws), (and only) held-on, (literally to) the words themselves: as

        quia in libris alicujus,   invenerant
(for instance), because in the books of-some-lawyer, they-had-found

id nomen,   causâ   exempli, putarunt
that name (Caia), by-reason (of giving an) example, they-thought

      omnes mulieres, quæ   facerent
(that) all   women,   who might-contract (matrimony by the

              coëmptionem, vocari Caias. Jam quidem
ceremony of) co-emption, were called Caia.   Yet   indeed

illud solet videri mihi mirum,   tot   tam
that   used   to-seem to-me strange, (that) so-many (and) so

ingeniosos,   per   tot   annos   etiam   nunc
ingenious-persons, through so-many years, (and) even   now

potuisse   non   statuere, utrum   oporteret   dici
would   not   determine, whether it-might-best be-said

tertium   diem,   an   perendinum: judicem,   an
the third day,   or the-day-after-to-morrow: judge,   or

arbitrum; rem, an litem.
arbiter;   the action, or the suit.

    13. Itaque (ut dixi)   nunquam fuit
       Therefore (as I-have-said), there never   was (any)

consularis dignitas in ista scientiâ; quæ   tota
consular   dignity,   in this science; which altogether

constaret   ex fictis que commenticiis rebus;
consists   of fictitious and   imaginary   things; (and)

vero multò minores gratiæ.   Enim
certainly much   fewer   favours (can be obtained by it). For

quod patet omnibus, et est æque promptum
that-which is-open to-all, and is equally free

mihi et meo adversario, id potest nullo pacto
to-me and to-my adversary, it can in-no manner,

esse gratum. Itaque jam
(be considered) to-be a favour. Therefore ¹you-have now

perdidistis non modò spem collocandi beneficii,
¹lost not only the hope of-conferring a benefit,

sed etiam illud quod aliquandi
but also that (consideration) which ¹you for-a-certain-time

fuit " licet consulere."
¹had, (of being respectfully asked) " is-it-allowed (me) to consult (you)."

Nemo potest existimari sapiens in
No one can be-considered wise, (who is only skilled) in

eâ prudentiâ, quæ neque valet quidquam extra
that knowledge, which neither is-worth any-thing without

Romam usquam, neque Romæ, rebus pro-
Rome any-where, nor in Rome, during-the-vacation-of-

latis. Nemo potest ideo haberi peritus,
the-courts. No-one can therefore be-considered skilled,

quod in eo, quod omnes
(above other, in the civil law), because in that which all

sciunt, possunt nullo modò discrepare
know (equally well), they-can in no wise differ

inter se. Autem res non ideo putatur
among themselves. But a thing ¹is not therefore ¹thought

difficilis, quod continetur, et per paucis et
difficult, because it-is-contained, both in a few and

minime obscuris ¹iteris. Itaque si moveritis
by-no-means obscure writings. Therefore if you-excite

mihi, homini vehementer occupato, stomachum,
me, a man excessively occupied, (to) anger,

triduo profitebor me esse jureconsultum.
in-three-days I-will-profess myself to-be a lawyer

Etenim, quæ aguntur de scripto,
For (those things) which are transacted by writing,

sunt omnia scripta; neque est tamen
have all (their) written forms; nor is there indeed

quidquam scriptum tam anguste, quo ego
any-thing, written so abbreviatedly, that I

possim non addere, "de qua re agitur;"
can not add, "about what thing is-it-the-question;"

autem quæ consuluntur respondentur
but these-things (about which) advice-is-asked, are-answered

minimo periculo. Si responderis id, quod
with-very-little risk. If you-answer that, which

oportet; videare respondisse idem, quod
is-right; you-may-seem to-have-answered the same, that

Servius; sin aliter; videare etiam
Servius (would); but-if otherwise; you-may-seem also

nosse et tractare controversum jus. Quapropter
to-know, and (how) to-handle the controversial law. Wherefore

non solum est illa militaris gloria anteponenda
not only is that military renown to-be-preferred

vestris formulis atque actionibus, verum etiam
to-your (legal) forms and actions, but also

consuetudo dicendi longe et multum antecellit
the habit of speaking, far and much excels

isti vestræ exercitationi, ad
this your practice (of the law), for (obtaining)

honorem. Itaque plerique videntur mihi,
the honour (of office). Therefore many seem to me,

initio multò maluisse
in-the-commencement (of their public life) 'to-have much 'preferred

hoc: post, cum potuissent non
this (practice of eloquence): afterwards, when they-could not

assequi id, potissimum delapsi sunt
succeed-in it, 'they-have mostly 'fallen-back

istuc. Ut aiunt
there-where-you-are, (to the practice of the law). As they say

n Græcis artificibus, eos esse auloedos,
especting Greek musicians, (that) those are flute-players

qui potuerint non fieri citharoedi: sic
who could not become players-on-the-harp: thus

videmus nonnullos, qui potuerunt non evadere
we-see some, who could not become

•ratores, eos devenire **ad** studium juris.
orators, (that) they betake-themselves to the study of-the-law

Magnus labor dicendi,
Great (is) the labour, (in acquiring eminence, in public) speaking,

magna res, magna dignitas, autem
great (is) the thing (itself), great (its) dignity, but

summa gratia. Etenim
great (is) the favour, (and influence connected with it). For

a vobis quædam salubritas
from you (lawyers) a certain (degree of) health [safety]

petitur, ab iis, qui dicunt, salus
is sought, (but) from those, who plead [from the orators] safety

ipsa. Deinde vestra responsa atque
itself (is sought). Next your answers and

decreta et sæpe evertuntur dicendo, et sine
decisions are, both often overturned by-eloquence, and without

defensione oratoris possunt non esse
the defence of-the-orators they-could not be (established on a)

firma; in qua, si satis
firm (basis); in which (art of oratory), if 'I-had-made sufficient

proecissem dicerem parcius de ejus
'progress (myself) I-might-have-spoken more-sparingly of its

laude: nunc dico nihil de me, sed de iis, qui
praise: now I-say nothing of myself, but of those, who

sunt, aut fuerunt magni dicendo.
are, or were great in-speaking.

14. Sunt duæ artes, quæ possunt locare homines
There are two professions, which can place men

in amplissimo gradu dignitatis; una
in the-most-exalted degree of-dignity (and consideration); the one

imperatoris altera boni oratoris. Enim
(that) of-a-commander, the other (that) of-a-good orator. For

ab hoc ornamenta pacis retinentur; ab illo
by this (last), the ornaments of-peace are-preserved; by the former,

pericula belli repelluntur. Tamen ceteræ virtutes
the dangers of-war are-repelled. However other virtues

ipsæ valent multùm per se, justitia,
(and merits) themselves avail much of themselves, as justice,

fides, pudor temperantia; quibus, omnes
good-faith, modesty, temperance; in which, all

intelligunt te, Servi, excellere: sed nunc
know, (that) you, O Servius, excel: but now

disputo de studiis dispositis
I-am-arguing of (those) pursuits disposed, (and calculated)

ad honorem, non de insitâ virtute
for (obtaining) the honour (of office), not of the innate virtu

cujusque. Omnia ista studia nobis excutiuntur
of-each-one. All these pursuits for-us are-dashed

de manibus, simul atque aliquis novus motus
from (our) hands, as-soon as any new movement

cœpit canere bellicum. Etenim,
(or commotion) begins to-sound the warlike (signal). For,

ut ingeniosus poëta, et valde bonus auctor ait,
as an-ingenious poet, and very excellent writer says,

prœliis promulgatis, "pellitur e medio," non
battles being-announced, "there-is-driven from among-us," not

solum ista vestra verbosa simulatio prudentiæ, sed
only this your verbose imitation of-prudence, but

etiam illa domina ipsa rerum, "sapientia; res
also that mistress herself 'of (all) 'things, "wisdom; every thing

geritur vi; orator spernitur," non solum
is-done by-violence; the orator is-despised," not only

odiosus in dicendo, ac loquax, verum
the disagreeable-one in speaking, and the wordy-one, but-indeed

etiam "bonus; horridus miles amatur;" vero
also "the good-one; the rough soldier is-beloved;" indeed

totum vestrum studium jacet. Inquit,
all your pursuits lie-neglected. He says, (men)

"repetunt rem, non ex jure manu consertum,
"redress (their) affairs, not by a process of law,

sed mage ferro." Quod si est ita, Sulpici,
but rather by-the-sword." Which if it-is so, O Sulpicius,

forum cedat castris, otium militiæ, stilus
the forum must-yield to-the-camp, tranquillity to-war, the pen

gladio, umbra soli; denique,
to-the-sword, the shady (retreat to exposure) to-the-sun; in-fine,

ea res sit prima in civitate, propter quam civitas
that thing is the first in a state, through which the state

ipsa est princeps omnium. Verum Cato
itself is the chief of-all (states). But Cato (endeavours to)

demonstrat nos facere nimium magna
show, (that) we make too great (an affair of this)

nostris verbis; et oblitos esse, omne
by-our discourse; and, (that we) have-forgotten, (that) all

illud Mithridaticum bellum gestum esse,
that Mithridatic war was-waged, (as it were)

cum mulierculis. Quod ego existimo, judices,
with women. Which I believe (to be), O judges,

longe secus: que de eo disseram pauca;
far otherwise: and about this I-will-say something; (and but

enim neque causa continetur
little), for neither 'is (my) cause (properly) 'contained

in hoc.
in this.

Nam, si omnia bella, quæ gessimus, cum
For, if all the wars, which we-have-carried on with

Græcis, contemnenda sunt, triumphus
the Greeks, are-to-be despised, (then) 'let the triumph

M. Curii de rege Pyrrho derideatur; F. Flaminini
of M. Curii over king Pyrrhus 'be derided; (that) of F. Flamininus

de Philippo; M. Fulvii de Ætolis;
over Philip; (that) of M. Fulvius over the Ætolians; (that)

L. Paulli de rege Perse; Q. Metelli de
of L. Paullus over king Perses; (that) of Q. Metelli over

Pseudophilippo; L. Mummii de Corinthis;
the false Philip; '(that) of L. Mummius over the Corinthians;

sin hæc bella fuerunt gravissima, que victoriæ
but-if these wars were very-important, and the victories

eorum bellorum gratissimæ; cur Asiaticæ
of-these wars (were) most-acceptable (to us); why 'are the Asiatic

nationes, atque ille hostis contemnitur a
nations, and that enemy (Mithridates) 'despised by

te? Atqui video ex monumentis veterum rerum
you? But I-see, from the records of-ancient transactions

Romanum populum gessisse, vel maximum
(that) the Roman people carried-on, indeed a-very-great

bellum cum Antiocho; L. Scipio victor cujus belli
war with Antiochus; L. Scipio the conqueror, in this war,

partita gloria cum Publico fratre, ille,
shared the glory (thereof) with Publicus (his) brother, he,

Africâ oppressâ, ferebat præ se,
(Publicus Scipio), Africa being-conquered, bore before himself,

quam laudem, cognomine ipso, hic
this renown, by-the-surname itself (of Africanus), this (L. Scipio)

assumpsit eandem sibi ex nomine Asiæ.
assumed the-same (renown) to-himself from the name of-Asia.

In quo bello quidem, egregia virtus M. Catonis
In which war indeed, the rare virtue of M. Cato,

tui proavi enituit; quò ille, cum esset,
your great-grandfather shone-forth; and-as he, when he-might-be,

ut ego statuo mihi, talis, qualem video te esse,
as I set-it-down to myself, the same, as I-see you to-be,

nunquam profectus esset, si
would never 'have-gone (to that war), if

arbitraretur bellandum esse cum mulierculis. Neque
he thought it-was-to-fight with women. Neither

vero, cum senatus egisset P. Africano, ut
indeed, when the senate had-arranged-with P. Africanus, that

proficisceretur legatus fratri; cum ipse, paullo
he-would-go (as) lieutenant 'to (his) 'brother; when he, a little

ante, Hanibale expulso ex Italiâ, ejecto ex
before, Hannibal being-driven from Italy, ejected from

Africâ, Carthagine oppressâ, liberasset rempublicam
Africa, (and) Carthage conquered, had delivered the republic

maximis periculis, nisi putaretur illud
from-the-greatest dangers, unless it-was-thought (hat) that

bellum grave et vehemens.
war (was) a serious and violent-one.

15. Atqui si consideraris diligenter, quid
But if you-consider carefully, what

Mithridates potuerit, et quid effecerit, et
Mithridates might-have-done, and what he-accomplished, and

qui vir fuerit, nimirum antepones hunc
what (kind of) a man he-was, 'you-will assuredly 'prefer this

regem, omnibus regibus, cum quibus Romanus
king, to-all the kings, with whom the Roman

populus gessit bellum; quem, L. Sulla, non rudis
people have-waged war; whom, L. Sylla, no rude

imperator, ut dicam nihil aliud,
(or inexperienced) commander, that I-may-say nothing else,

maximo et fortissimo exercitu, excitatum
with-a-very-large and very-powerful army, having-excited-him

pugnâ, invectum bello in totam
(by a lost) battle, and) having-attacked (him) by-war in all

Asiam, dimisit cum pace; quem L. Murena,
Asia, left (him) in peace; whom L. Murena,

pater hujusce vehementissime que
the father of this (Murena) 'having most-violently and

vigilantissime vexatum, reliquit, ex magnâ parte
vigilantly 'harassed, left, for the great part

repressum, non oppressum; qui rex sumptis aliquot
checked, (but) not reduced; this king, having-taken some

annis sibi, ad confirmandas rationes et copias,
years to-himself, to strengthen (his) affairs and forces,

ipse tantum invaluit, opibus que
he so re-established (himself), 'by (his) 'resources and

conatu, ut putaret se conjuncturum Oceanum
efforts, that he-thought, (that) he might-unite the Ocean

cum Ponto, copias Sertorii cum suis.
with the Black Sea, the forces of-Sertorius (in Spain) with his-own.

Ad quod bellum, duobus consulibus missis,
To which war, two consuls being-sent,

ita, ut alter persequeretur
in this-manner, that, (while) the one pursued

Mithridatem, alter tueretur Bithyniam;
Mithridates, the other should-defend Bithynia;

calamitosæ res alterius, et terrâ et mari,
the calamitous affairs of-one-of-them, both by-land and sea,

vehementer auxerunt et opes et nomen regis:
greatly increased both the means and renown of-the-king:

vero tantæ exstiterunt res L. Luculli, ut neque
out so-great were the exploits of-L. Lucullus, that neither

majus bellum possit commemorari, neque gestum
a greater war can be-mentioned, nor one-waged

majore consilio et virtute. Nam cum impetus
with-more (wise) counsel and valour. For when the force

totius belli constitisset ad mœnia Cyzicenorum,
of-all the war had-centered against the walls of-the-Cyzicenians,

que Mithridates putasset, eam urbem fore
and Mithridates had-thought, (that) that town would-be

sibi januam Asiæ, qua effractâ et revulsâ, tota
for-him the door of-Asia, which broken-down and destroyed, all

provincia pateret, omnia
the (Roman) province (of Asia) would-be-open (to him), all

hæc perfecta sunt ab Lucullo ut urbs
these-things were-(so)-accomplished by-Lucullus that the town

fidelissimorum sociorum defenderetur, et omnes
of-the-most-faithful allies was-defended, and all

copiæ regis consumerentur diuturnitate
the forces of-the-king were-consumed by-the-long-duration

obsessionis. Quid? arbitraris, illam navalem
of-the-siege. What? do-you-think, (that) that naval

pugnam ad Tenedum, commissam mediocri certamine,
battle at Tenedos, was-fought with-a-slight contest,

et parvâ dimicatione, cum classis hostium, inflata
and small combat, when the fleet of-the-enemy, inflated

spe atque animis, peteret Italiam contento
with-hope and courage, sought Italy with-a-strained

cursu, acerrimis ducibus?
(and rapid) course, (and) with-most-ardent (and active) leaders?

Mitto prœlia; prætereo oppugnationes oppidorum.
I omit the battles; I-pass-over the storming of-towns.

Aliquando tandem, expulsus regno, tamen
When in-fine, expelled 'from (his) 'kingdom, yet

tantùm valuit consilio atque auctoritate, ut,
so did-he-prevail by (his) 'counsel and authority, that

adjuncto   se   rege   Armeniorum, renovarit
having united   himself   with-the-king of-the-Armenians, he-renewed

novis   opibus   que copiis.
(the contest) with-new resources and   forces.

16. Ac, si   mihi nunc dicen
    And, if 'it-were (necessary) for-me now   'to-

dum esset,   de   rebus   gestis   nostri exercitûs
speak,   concerning the things performed (by) our   army

que imperatoris, possem commemorare plurima et
and   general,   I-might   relate   many, and

maxima prœlia. Sed   non agimus id.
great   battles.   But 'we-are not 'doing that, (nor is

Dico hoc: si hoc bellum, si hic
it our object). I-say this: if this war,   if this

hostis, si ille rex contemnendus fuisset, neque
enemy, if that king were-to-have-been-despised, neither

senatus, et Romanus populus putasset
'would the senate, and Roman people 'have-thought, (that)

suscipiendum   tantâ curâ, neque gessis-
it-was-to-be-undertaken with-so-much care, nor would-they

set   tot annos, neque
have-waged (the war) for-so-many years, nor (would there have

tanta gloria L. Lucnlli: neque verœ
been) such-great glory (to) L. Lucullus; nor indeed

Romanus populus, tanto studio, detulisset
would the Roman people, with-such-great zeal, 'have-offered

ad Cn. Pompeium curam conficiendi
(and entrusted) to Cn. Pompey the care of-finishing

ejus belli; ex omnibus cujus pugnis, quæ
this war; of all his (Pompey's) battles, which

sunt innumerabiles, vel acerrima videtur mihi
are innumerable, yet the-most-violent seems to-me

illa, quæ commissa est cum rege, et pugnata
that, which he-engaged-in with the king, and fought

summâ contentione. Cum ille   eripuisset se
with-the-greatest ardour. When he (Mithridates) had-escaped

ex qua pugnâ, et confugisset Bosporum, quò
from that battle, and had-fled to-the-Bosphorus, whither

exercitus posset non adire; etiam in extremâ
an army could not approach; also in (his) extreme

fortunâ et fugâ retinuit tamen regium nomen.
fortune and flight he-retained however the royal name.

Itaque Pompeius ipse possesso
Therefore Pompey himself having-obtained-possession (of his)

regno, hoste pulso, ex omnibus oris,
kingdom, (and) the enemy being-driven, from all (his) regions,

ac notis sedibus, tamen posuit tantum
and known places (and resorts), however he-placed so-much

in animâ unius, ut cum
(importance) in the life of-one-man, that when he (Pompey)

possideret omnia, quæ ille tenuerat
possessed all, which he (Mithridates) had-possessed

adierat speraret victoriâ;
might-have-made-claim-to, (or) might-have-hoped-for by (his) victory;

tamen non judicarit, bellum confectum
however 'he did not 'think (that) the war was-finished

antequam expulit illum vitâ. Tu, Cato,
before-that he-had-deprived him of-life. 'Do you, O Cato,

contemnis hunc hostem, cum quo, tot imperatores
'despise this enemy, with whom, so-many commanders

gesserunt bella per tot annos tot
have-waged wars through so-many years (and through) so-many

prœliis? vita cujus expulsi et ejecti
battles? (and 'was not) the life of-him 'expelled and ejected

æstimata est tanti, ut,
(from his kingdom) esteemed of-so-much-importance, that,

ejus morte nunciatâ, tum denique
his death being-announced, then at-length (only)

arbitraremur bellum confectum? Igitur in hoc
we-thought the war was-finished? Therefore in this

bello, defendimus L. Murenam, legatum
war, we-maintain (that) L. Murena, (as a) lieutenant

cognitum esse fortissimi animi summi
was-known (as a man of) of-the-greatest courage of-the-greatest

consilii maximi laboris; et hanc
counsel (and skill, and also) of-the-greatest industry; and (that) this

ejus operam   habuisse non minus dignitatis
his   performance (and services) have   no   less   a claim

                    ad adipiscendum consulatum, quàm
(founded on merit) for   obtaining the consulship, than

hanc nostram forensem industriam.
this   our   forensic industry.

17. "At enim in petitione   praeturae Servius
     "But indeed in the soliciting of-the-praetorship Servius

renuntiatus est   prior."   Ne
was-announced   (as) the first," (or highest on the list). What,

    vos pergitis agere cum populo ex syngraphâ
'are you proceeding to-deal with the people as-if-on a bond

            ut, quem locum   honoris,
or written contract), so-that, whatever place (or rank) of-honour,

         semel dederit cuipiam,   eundem
'they-may once 'have-given to-any-one, the same (rank:

debeat   reliquis honoribus?   Enim
they-ought (to confer on him) in-other honours (of office)? For

quod fretum, quem Euripum putatis habere
what strait, what Euripus do-you-think has

tot   motus,   tantas,   tam varias agitationes
so-many movements, so-great, (and) such varied agitations

fluctuum,   ratio   comitiorum
of (its) waves, as the manner (and nature) of-the-comitia 'may (not)

habet quantas perturbationes et quantos
'have equally-great perturbations and equally-great (swellings

            aestus? Unus dies   intermissus,
and tossings of) tides? A single day having-been-discontinued,

aut nox   interposita,   saepe perturbat omnia;
or a night having-been-interposed, often disturbs every-thing;

et parva aura rumoris nonnunquam commutat
and the small breeze of-rumour sometimes changes

totam opinionem. Saepe etiam sine ullâ apertâ
the entire opinion. Often also without any open

causâ   fit   aliud, atque existimamus,
cause the thing-terminates otherwise, than we-supposed

        ut nonnunquam etiam populus admiretur
(it would), so-that sometimes even the people wonder

factum esse ita: quasi vero   ipse   non
(that) it-was-done so: as-if indeed they-themselves 'had not

fecerit.   Nihil   est   incertius   vulgo,
'done   (it). Nothing is more-uncertain (than) the common-people,

nihil   obscurius   voluntate hominum, nihil
nothing   more-obscure (than) the wishes of-men,   nothing

fallacius   totâ ratione   comitiorum.
more-fallacious (than) the whole order (and nature) of-the-comitis

                    Quis   arbitratus est,
(and the result of their elections). Who would-have-supposed, (that)

L. Philippum   summo ingenio, operâ, gratiâ,
L. Philippus (a man of the) greatest talent, industry, favour,

        nobilitate posse superari a M. Herennio?
(and)   nobility   could be-overcome by M.   Herennius?

Quis   Q. Catulum   antecellentem
Who (thought that) Q.   Catulum (a man)   excelling

humanitate, sapientiâ, integritate   a
in-humanity,   wisdom, (and) integrity (would be beaten) by

Cn. Mallio? quis   M. Scaurum, hominem
Cn. Mallius? who (thought that) M.   Scaurus,   a man

    gravissimum,   egregium   civem,
of-great-weight-of-character, a-most-excellent   citizen, (and

fortissimum senatorem   a
most-intrepid   senator, (would be beaten, at the election,) by

Q. Maximo? Non modo putatum esset   horum
Q. Maximus?   Not only was-it-thought (that) of-these-things

nihil   fore   ita, sed cum quidem esset
nothing would-happen so,   but when indeed   it-was

factum, potuit ne intelligi, quare factum esset ita.
done,   it-could not be-understood, why it-was-done   so.

Nam ut tempestates sæpe commoventur aliquo
For   as   storms   often are-excited   by-some

certo signo cœli,   sæpe   improviso
certain sign of-the-heavens, (so also) often 'they-are suddenly

concitantur ex nullâ certâ ratione,   ex aliquâ
'put-in-motion from no   certain reason, (or) from   some

obscurâ causâ: sic, in hac populari tempestate
obscure   cause: so,   in this popular   tempest

comitiorum   **sæpe**   **intelligas,**   **quo**   **signo**
of-the-comitia   'you-may often   'know,   by-what   sign

commota sit ;   **sæpe**   **causa**   **est**   **ita**
it-may-have-been-set-in-motion ;   (but) often   the cause   is   so

obscura,   **ut**   **videatur**   **excitata esse**   **casu.**
obscure,   that   it-may-seem   to-have-been-excited   by-chance.

18.   **Sed**   **tamen,**   **si**   **ratio**   **reddenda est,**   **duæ**
  But   however,   if   a reason   must-be-given,   two

res   **vehementer**   **desideratæ sunt**   **in**
things   were most-particularly   wanting,   in (soliciting)

præturâ,   **quæ**   **ambæ**   **profuerunt**   **Murenæ**   **in**
the prætorship,   which   both   were-of-advantage   to-Murena,   in

consulatu: una   **exspectatio**   **muneris,**
(soliciting) the consulship: the one (was) the expectation of-public-shows,

quæ   **creverat, et**   **nonnullo**   **rumore,**   **et**   **studiis**
which   had-increased, both   by-certain   rumours,   and   by-the-zeal

que   **sermonibus**   **competitorum:**   **altera,**   **quod**
and   conversation   'of (his)   'competitors: the other,   that

ii,   **quos**   **habuerat in**   **provinciâ ac**   **legatione**
those, whom   he-had   in   the province and   legation,   (as)

testes   **omnis, et**   **suæ**   **liberalitatis et**   **virtutis,**
witnesses   of-all, both   of-his   liberality   and 'of (his) 'virtue,

nondum decesserant.   **Fortuna reservavit**
'had not-yet   'left   (the province).   Fortune   had-reserved

utrumque horum   **ei**   **ad**   **petitionem**   **consulatûs.**
each   of-them for-him for (his)   seeking-for   the consulship.

Nam   **et**   **exercitus**   **L. Luculli,**   **qui**   **convenerat**
For   both   the army   of-L. Lucullus,   that   had-assembled

ad   **triumphum,**   **idem**   **fuit**   **præsto**   **comitiis**   **L.**
for   the triumph,   the same   was   present at-the-comitia of-L.

Murenæ;   **et amplissimum**
Murena, (to assist him in obtaining the consulship); and the most-splendid

munus,   **quod**   **desiderabat**   **petitio**   **præturæ,**
public-shows,   which   were-wanting in-seeking-for the prætorship,

restituit   **præturâ.**   **Num**
he-replaced, (by giving them; 'in (his) 'prætorship.   Whether 'do

hæc   **videntur**   **tibi**   **parva**   **adjumenta**   **et**
these-things 'appear   to-you   trifling   aids   and

subsidia   consulatûs?   Voluntas militum?
assistances (for obtaining) the consulship? (Is) the good-will of-the-soldiers

          quæ   cum   valet   per   se
(a trifle)? which   as   it-avails   by   itself 'on-account-of (its)

multitudine,   tum   gratiâ   apud   suos,
'numbers,   as-also 'by (their) 'influence   among   their-own

          tum   vero   in   declarando   consule
(connexions),   so   indeed   in   electing   a consul,

          habet   etiam   multum   auctoritatis
(the army) has   also   much   authority   (and weight

apud   universum   Romanum   populum.   Suffragatio
with   the entire   Roman   people.   (Is)   the vote

militaris?   enim   consularibus   comitiis
of-the-military (a trifle)?   for   in-the-consular   comitia

imperatores   deliguntur   non   interpretes
commanders   are-elected   not   interpreters (and expounders)

verborum.   Quare   gravis   est
of-words   (and legal forms).   Therefore   weighty (and influential)   is

illa   oratio,
that   speech,   (of the soldier to the by-standers, at the comitia),

"recreavit   me   saucium,   donavit   me
"he-took-care-of   me   wounded,   he-gave   me (a share of)

præda;   hoc   duce,   cepimus   castra
the booty;   under-this   leader,   we-took   (that) camp, (and)

contulimus   signa;   nunquam   iste   imposuit
fought   (that) battle;   never   'did this-general   'impose

plus   laboris   militi,   quàm   ipse   sumpsit
more   labour   on-the-soldier,   than   he   was-willing-to-undergo

sibi;   cum   fortis,   tum   felix   etiam."
himself;   as   brave (as he was),   so   fortunate (he) also (was)."

Quanti   putas   hoc   esse   ad
How-much   do-you-think   (that)   this   is (of use) to   (gain)

famam,   ac   voluntatem   hominum?   Etenim   si
renown,   and   the good-will   of-men?   For   if

          religio   est   tanta   illis   comitiis,
(the feeling of a) religious (superstition) is   so-great   in-those   comitia,

ut   semper   adhuc   omen
that   alway   (even)   to-the-present (time),   the omen (of the century)

præerogativum   valuerit,
that-by-lot-voted-first, 'had (a great) 'influence (on the result of the elec-

quid   est   mirum,   in   hoc   famam
tion), what is (then) wonderful, (that) in this-man the renown

felicitatis que sermonem   valu-
'of (his) 'good-fortune, and the discourse (of his soldiers) should-have-

isse ?
availed (so much)?

19.   Sed, si ducis hæc   leviora, quæ
        But, if you-think these-things too-trifling, which (yet)

sunt   gravissima, et   anteponis hanc urbanam
are   the most-important, and (if) you-prefer these   city

suffragationem militari,   noli valde contemnere
votes   to-the-military (votes), do-not too-much despise

elegantiam hujus ludorum, et magnificentiam
the elegance of-his   shows, and   the magnificence 'of (his)

scenæ ;
scenes, (and theatrical exhibitions, as given for the gratification of the

quæ   admodum   profuerunt huic.
people); which 'were greatly   'advantageous to-him

Nam quid   ego
(in procuring the favour of the people). For   what 'shall I

dicam,   populum ac vulgus   imperitorum
'say,   (but that) the people, and the multitude of-ignorant-men

magnopere delectari ludis ?
'are   greatly   'delighted with-games (and public shows)?

Est minus mirandum : quanquam id est
(Which) is less to-be-wondered-at : although it is

satis huic causæ; enim comitia sunt
sufficient for-this cause; for the comitia are (composed

populi   ac multitudinis. Quare si magnificentia
of-the-people and of-the-multitude. Wherefore if the magnificence

ludorum   est   voluptati   populo
of-games (and public shows) is   a pleasure to-the-people,

est non   mirandum,   eam profuisse
it-is not to-be-wondered-at, (that) it was-of-service

L. Murenæ apud populum. Sed si nosmet ipsi,
to-L. Murena with the people. But if we ourselves,

qui   et impedimur negotiis ab   omni
who 'are both 'hindered by-business from (taking part in) all

delectatione, et in   occupatione ipsa, possumus
amusements,   and in (that) occupation   itself,   we-can

habere multas alias delectationes, tamen oblectamur
have   many other   amusements,   however   are-delighted

et ducimur   ludis;   quid tu   admirer
and are-attracted by-shows-and-games; why 'are you (then) 'astonished

de indoctâ multitudine?   L. Otho, fortis vir,
at the ignorant   multitude?   L. Otho,   a brave man,

meus   necessarius   restituit   equestri   ordini
my   intimate-acquaintance   restored   to-the-equestrian   order

non solum   dignitatem, sed etiam   voluptatem.
not only (its)   dignity,   but also (its)   pleasure,

                                        Itaque hæc
(by the seats assigned to it at the public games). Therefore this

lex, quæ pertinet ad   ludos,   est omnium
law, which relates   to the public-games-and-shows, is   of-all

gratissima,   quòd honestissimo ordini
the most-agreeable (and acceptable), because to-a-most-honourable order

restitutus est, cum   splendore,   quoque
is-restored,   with the splendour (of their rank),   also

fructus   jucunditatis. Quare ludi, crede
the enjoyment 'of (their) 'pleasure. Therefore games, believe

mihi, delectant homines, etiam illos, qui dissimulant,
me,   delight   men,   as-well those, who   dissimulate

                            non solum eos,
(and pretend, not to be delighted therewith), as not   only those,

qui fatentur;   quod ego sensi
who confess (they are pleased therewith); which I experienced

in mea petitione.   Nam nos quoque
in my application (for the consulship). For we   also

habuimus   scenam   competitricem. Quòd
had   a theatrical-decoration   as-a-competitor. And-though

si ego   ædilis feceram trinos ludos,   tamen
if I, (who when) ædile   gave the triple games, 'was however

commovebar   ludis Antonii;   putas
moved   (and alarmed) by-the-games of-Antonius; do-you-think,

istam ipsam argenteam scenam hujus
(that) this same silver scene of-this (man Murena),

quam irrides, nihil adversatam tibi, qui casu
which you-deride, 'was nothing 'against you, who by-chance

feceras nullos? Sed sane omnia
¹(never) gave 'any (games)? But indeed 'let all

hæc sint paria; forensis opera sit par militari
these 'be equal; 'let forensic labour 'be equal to-military

urbana suffragatio sit par militari;
'let the civic vote 'be equal to-the-military; 'let (those,

fecisse magnificentissimos ludos sit idem,
who) have-given the most-magnificent games 'be the same,

et unquam fecisse nullos: quid?
as (those who) 'have never 'given any: what (then)?

ne existimas nihil interfuisse
'do-you 'think there 'was nothing 'present (of difference)

inter tuam sortem, in ipsâ prætturâ, et
between your lot, in that-same prætorship, and (that)

istius?
of-this-man [Murena]?

20. Sors hujus fuit ea, quam omnes tui
The lot of him [Murena] was that, which all 'we your

necessarii optabamus tibi, dicendi juris;
friends 'wished for-you, (namely, that) of deciding the law

in qua, magnitudo negotii
(and dispensing justice); in which, the greatness of-the-business

conciliat gloriam, largitio æquitatis
procures renown, (and) the liberality of-equitable-decision (procures)

gratiam: in qua sorte, sapiens prætor, qualis
favour: in which lot (of office), a wise prætor, as

hic fuit, vitat offensionem
his (man) [Murena] was, avoids (giving) offence

æquabilitate decernendi, adjungit benevolentiam
by-the-uniform-justice of-his-decisions, he-unites benevolence

lenitate audiendi.
by-indulgent-affability of-listening (to complaints). (This is a)

Egregia provincia, et apta ad
most excellent province, and adapted for (obtaining)

consulatum, in qua laus æquitatis, integritatis.
the consulship, in which the praise of-justice, of-integrity,

facilitatis, ad extremum concluditur
of-affability (may be obtained, and which) at last is-terminated

voluptate ludorum. Quid tua sors?
by-the-pleasure of public-plays. What (was) your lot?

tristis, atrox; questio peculatûs,
a gloomy, (and) harsh-one; inquiry-into embezzlement-of-public-money,

ex alterâ parte, lacrimarum et squaloris, ex
on the-one side, (full) of tears and squalid-appearance, on

alterâ, plena catenarum, atque
the-other (side), full of-chains (and imprisonments), and

indicum. Judices cogendi inviti,
of informers. Judges are-to-be-forced-to-sit 'against (their) will, (and)

retinendi contra voluntatem; scriba damnatus,
to-be-detained against (their) will; a scribe was-condemned,

totus ordo alienus:
the whole order (was, in consequence), alienated (from him)

gratificatio Sullana
the-bounty of Sylla (from the public treasury to his followers)

reprehensa; multi fortes viri, et prope
is condemned (and reversed); many brave men, and nearly (a great)

pars civitatis offensa est; lites severe
part of-the-city are offended; damages 'are severely

æstimatæ; cui placet obliviscitur,
'assessed; (he) to whom it-gives-pleasure forgets-it, (but he)

cui dolet, meminit. Post emo tu noluisti
to-whom it-gives pain, remembers-it. In-fine you would-not

ire in provinciam. Possum nor
go to the province (assigned to you). I can no

reprehendere id in te, quod probavi in me ipso
reprehend that in you, which I-approved in my self

et prætor et consul.
both (when) prætor and consul, (by not going to the provinces assigned

Sed tamen provincia attulit multas bonas
to me). But however the province brought many excellent

gratias L. Murenæ, cum optimâ existimatione
favours for-L. Murena, with the greatest reputation

Proficiscens habuit delectum in Umbriâ;
Journeying-thither he-had a levy-of-troops in Umbria; (the state of)

respublica dedit ei facultatem liberalitatis;
the republic gave to-him the power of-being-liberal (and indul-

usus quâ, adjunxit
gent, as respects the levy); having-made-use of-which, he-united

multas tribus sibi, quæ conficiuntur
many tribes to-himself (in interest), which are-constituted

municipiis Umbriæ. Autem in Galliâ ipsâ,
by-the-municipalities of-Umbria. But in Gaul itself,

perfecit æquitate que diligentiâ, ut nostri
he-accomplished 'by (his) 'equity and diligence, that our

homines exigerunt pecunias jam desperatas. Tu
men recovered money already despaired-of. You

interea fuisti Romæ, silicet præsto
in-the-mean-time were at-Rome, without-doubt (to be) near (and aiding)

amicis. Fateor; sed tamen cogita
'to (your) 'friends. I-confess (all this); but however think-on

iliud, studia nonnullorum amicorum solere
this, (that) the zeal of-some friends is-accustomed

minui in eos, a quibus intelligant
to-be-diminished towards those, by whom they-understand (that)

provincias contemni.
provinces are-despised.

21. Et quoniam, ostendi, judices, fuisse
And because, I-have-shown, O judges, (that) there-was

parem dignitatem in Murenâ atque in
equal dignity (and worth) in Murena and in

Sulpicio, ad petitionem consulatûs, disparem
Sulpicius, in (their) claims of-the-consulship, (but) unequal

fortunam provincialium negotiorum; jam dicam
good-fortune of-provincial affairs; I-may now say (it)

apertiùs, in quo meus necessarius Servius fuerit
more-openly, in what my intimate-friend Servius may-have-been

infe ior, et dicam ea,
inferior, (as a candidate for the consulship), and I-may-say these-things,

vobis audientibus, tempore
vos listening, the time (and occasion of the election

jam amisso, quæ sæpe dixi ipsi soli,
'having now 'passed, which 'I often 'said to-himself alone,

re   integrâ.   Persæpe
the business (of the election) being-undetermined. 'I-have very often

dixi tibi, Servi,   te   nescire   petere
'told you, O Servius, (that) you know-not-how to-solici-

consulatum et in iis rebus ipsis,   quas
the consulship: and in those things themselves, (respecting) which

videbam te, et agere et dicere, magno et
I-saw   you, both act   and speak, with-a-great and

forti animo, solitus sum dicere tibi,   te videri
courageous mind, I-used   to-say to-you, (that) you seemed

mihi magis   fortem senatorem, quàm sapientem
to-me more (like) an intrepid senator, than a prudent

candidatum. Primum terrores et minæ accusandi,
candidate.   In-the-first-place the terrors and threats of impeaching

                                      quibus tu
(those candidates, who might be suspected of bribery), which you

solebas uti quotidie,   sunt   fortis viri,
used   to-use daily, (may) be (the part) of-an-intrepid man;

sed et avertunt opinionem populi   a   spe
but both turn-away the opinion of-the-people from (any) hope

       adipiscendi,   et debilitant studia
(on his part) of obtaining (office), and weaken the zeal

amicorum. Nescio quo pacto hoc fit semper;
'of (his) 'friends. I-know-not by-what means it is always (so);

neque animadversum est in uno aut altero,
neither has-it-been-observed in one or two (candidates),

sed jam in pluribus;   simul atque candidatus
but already in many; (that) as-soon-as a candidate

visus est meditari accusationem,   videatur
seems to-meditate impeachment (of candidates), it-appear

ut   desperasse   honorem.   Quid ergo?
that (he) has-despaired (of) the honour (of office). What then?

       non   placet   persequi injuriam acceptam?
'is-it not agreeable to prosecute an injury received?

Immo   vehementer   placet; sed est aliud
Indeed 'it-is exceedingly 'agreeable; but there is a differenc

tempus petendi, **aliud** persequendi.
time for soliciting (the consulship), a different (time) for prosecuting

Ego volo petitorem, præsertim
(candidates). I require (that) a candidate, especially

consulatûs, magnâ spe, magno animo,
for-the-consulship, (should be of) great hope, of-great courage,

deduci, et in forum, et in campum,
and be-accompanied, both into the forum, and into the Campus Martius.

magnis copiis: inquisitio
by-a-great assemblage (of friends): the-inquiry-into-the-conduct

candidati, prænuntia repulsæ, non placet mihi;
of-a-candidate, the announcer of-a-repulse, 'does not 'please me;

non comparatio testium potius, quàm suffragatorum;
neither the procuring of-witnesses rather, than of-voters;

non minæ magis, quàm blanditiæ; non
neither threats more, than blandishments; neither (angry

declamatio potius, quàm persalutatio
declamations (against bribery) rather, than saluting

præsertim cum jam,
(the people by name, and soliciting votes); especially when now

hoc novo more omnes
in-this new manner (of soliciting votes), all

concursent domos fere omnium,
the candidates go-round among-the-houses 'of nearly 'all (the citizens),

et ex vultu candidatorum faciant, quantum
and from the countenance of-the-candidates they-make-out, how-much

quisque videatur habere animi et facultatis.
each-one may-seem to-have (of hope) spirit, and of-means

"Tu ne vides illum tristem?
(for the contest). "'Do you not 'see that sad-looking (man)?

demissum? jacet, diffidit,
(that) dejected (one)? he-is-down, he-doubts-his-chance,

abjecit hastas." Hic
he-has-thrown-away his spears (and given up the day)." This

rumor serpit: "tu scis illum cogitare
rumor spreads-abroad: "do you know (that) he is-thinking-of

accusationem? inquirere
an impeachment (of the candidates) (that) he-is-inquiring

in   competitores?   quærere   testes"
in (relation to his)   competitors?   (that) he-is-seeking-for witnesses?

Faciam   alium,   quoniam   hic   ipse
I-will-make another (my candidate),   because   this-one   himself

desperat sibi."   Intimi   amici   ejusmodi
  despairs   (of success)." The intimate   friends   of-this-kind

candidatorum debilitantur,   deponunt
  of-candidates   are-debilitated (and dispirited), they-remit-in (their)

studia,   aut abjiciunt rem testatam;
zeal (for him), or   give-up   the thing evident (to all as hopeless);

aut reservant suam operam et gratiam, judicio
or   reserve   their   aid   and   influence,   for-the-trial

et accusationi.
and   accusation.

22.   Accedit   eòdem,   ut,   etiam   candidatus
       It-happens   likewise,   that,   even   the candidate

ipse, possit non ponere   totum animum, atque
himself, can   not   place   (his) entire   mind,   and

omnem suam curam, operam, que diligentiam in
all   his   care,   labour,   and   diligence   in

petitione.   Enim cogitatio accusationis adjun-
soliciting   (office). For   the thought of impeachment is-added-

gitur,   non   parva   res,   sed   nimirum maxima
thereto,   not   a small   affair,   but   assuredly   the greatest

omnium. Enim est magnum,   te comparare
of-all.   For   it-is a great-thing, (that) you   prepare

ea,   quibus possis exturbare hominem a
those-things, by-which you-can   expel   a man   from

civitate,   præsertim
the state, (and deprive him of the rights of citizenship),   especially

          non   inopem, neque   infirmum; qui
(one, who is) not   destitute,   nor   weak;   who

defendatur,   et per se,   et per suos,
can-defend-himself, both by himself, and by his-own (friends),

et etiam vero per alienos.   Enim   omnes
and even indeed by strangers.   For   'we   all

concurrimus ad propulsanda pericula; et   qui
hasten   to   repel   danger;   and 'we, who

sumus non aperte inimici, in periculis
'are not openly enemies, (and) in the danger

capitis præstamus
of-capital-punishment, (either of life, or loss of citizenship), offer

officia et studia amicissimorum, etiam
the duties and zeal of-the-most-friendly (relations), even

alienissimis. Quare ego expertus molestiam
to-the-greatest-strangers. Whereas I-having-experienced the trouble

et petendi, et defendendi, et accusandi,
both of-soliciting (office), and of-defending, and of-accusing,

sic intellexi; in petendo
'I-have thus 'understood, (and formed my opinion); (that) in seeking

esse acerrimum studium; in
(for office) there-is the most-ardent zeal (required); in

defendendo officium; in accusando
defending (a person) duty (and faithfulness); in accusing

laborem. Itaque statuo
(and impeaching) labour (and industry). Therefore I-maintain

sic, ut posse nullo modò fieri, ut
(it to be) thus, that it-can in-no wise be-done, that

idem diligenter adornet, atque
the same (person) 'can diligently 'prepare (materials), and

instruat accusationem, et petitionem
arrange (them) for-an-accusation (or impeachment), and for-a-soliciting

consulatûs. Pauci possunt sustinere unum,
(for) the consulship. Few can sustain the one (part),

nemo utrumque. Tu existimasti, cum deflexises
no-one both. 'Did you 'think, when you-turned-aside

te de curriculo petitionis, que transtulisses
from the career of-seeking-office, and transferred (your)

animum ad accusandum, te posse satisfacere
mind to impeachment, (that) you could satisfy

utrique negotio? Vehementer
(the requirements) for-both affairs? (If you did) 'you greatly

errasti. Enim quis dies fuit, posteaquam
erred. For what day was-there, after-that

ingressus es in istam denuntiationem
you-entered on this announcement (of your intention)

accusandi, quem　　tu　　　non　total consumpseris
of-impeaching, which　you 'did not　altogether　　consume

in istâ ratione?
In　this　employment (of procuring materials, for an impeachment)?

23.　　Flagitasti　　legem　　　ambitûs, quæ
You-earnestly-demanded a law (against) bribery,　which

　　　non　deerat tibi. Enim erat Calpurnia
(law) 'was not 'wanting to-you. For　there-was the Calpurnian

scripta　　severissime.　　Gestus mos est, et
(law) written (in) very-severe (terms).　In-compliance, both

　　tuæ　voluntati et dignitati.
'with your　'wish　and　dignity, (a new law, respecting bri-

　　　　　Sed　tota　illa　lex　　fortasse
bery, was passed).　But　all　that　law 'might　perhaps

armasset tuam accusationem　　　si haberes
'have-armed your　impeachment (with new terrors) if　you-had

　　reum　nocentem;　vero　refragata est
an accused-person really-guilty;　but-indeed　it-was-opposed-to (and

　　　　　　petitioni.　　Gravior
injurious) 'to (your) 'seeking (the consulship). More-severe

pœna　　　efflagitata est　tuâ voce, in plebem;
punishment was-earnestly-demanded by-your voice, against the people

animi　　tenuiorum　commoti;　exsilium　in
the minds of-the-lower-orders were-alarmed;　banishment against

nostrum　ordinem;　　　senatus concessit
our　(senatorial) order (for bribery);　the senate　acceded

tuæ　postulationi, sed non libenter　constituit
to-your　request,　but　not　willingly did-they-establish

duriorem conditionem communi fortunæ,
a severer　condition　for-the-common fortune, (of the order

　　　te　　auctore.　　Pœna addita est
of senators), you (being) the author (thereof). Punishment was-added

excusationi　　　　morbi, voluntas multorum
to-excuses　　(on account) of-sickness, the good-will　of-many

　　　　offensa, quibus aut　　laborandum est,
(towards you) was-hurt, by-whom either business-is-to-be-performed

　　　contra　commodum　　valetudinis
(in the courts),　contrary　to-the-state (of their)　health

aut incommodo morbi, etiam ceteri fructus
or to-the-inconvenience of-sickness, also the other advantages

vitæ relinquendi. Quid ergo? quis tulit
of-life are-to-be-relinquished. What then? who proposed

hæc? Is, qui paruit auctoritati senatûs,
these-things? He, who obeyed the authority of-the-senate, (and)

tuæ voluntati: denique is tulit, qui
your wish: in-fine he proposed (it), who 'di

mimime probarat. Existimas illa,
not-at-all 'approve (it). Do-you-think (that) these, (following

quæ, meâ summâ voluntate,
propositions of yours), which, with-my highest approbation,

frequens senatus repudiavit, mediocriter
a full senate rejected, 'was (only) slightly

adversata esse tibi?
'opposed-as-a-hinderance to-you (in the affair of the consulship)?

Flagitasti confusionem suffragiorum,
You-earnestly-demanded the confused (mingling) of-the-votes

prorogationem legis Maniliæ, æquationem
(of the centuries), an extension of-the-law of-Manilia, an equalizing

gratiæ, dignitatis suffragiorum. Honesti
of-the-influence, (and) rank of-suffrage. Honourable

homines, atque gratiosi in suis vicinitatibus, et
men, and of-influence in their neighbourhood, and

municipiis tulerunt graviter, pugnatum esse
municipalities took-it ill, (that) they-should-be-opposed

a tali viro, ut omnes gradus et dignitatis et
by such a man, so-that all degrees both of-rank and

gratiæ tollerentur, idem
of-influence should-be-taken-away (from them), 'you, the same-person,

voluisti judices esse editicios,
'desired the judges to-be chosen (by the parties in the suit)

ut occulta odia civium, quæ nunc continentur
so-that the secret hatreds of-citizens, which 'are now contained

tacitis discordiis, erumperent in
(within the bounds of) private animosities, may-break-out against

fortunas cujusque optimi. Omnia hæc
the fortunes of-any very-great (person). All these-things

muniebant   viam   accusandi   tibi,   obsæpiebant
fortified   the way   of-impeaching   for-you,   (but) they-obstructed

adipiscendi.
(that) of-obtaining   (the consulship).

Atque   ex   omnibus   illa   maxima   plaga
And   from   all   (which)   that   very-great   wound

injecta est tuæ petitioni,   me non tacente,
was-given to-your   seeking   (the consulship),   I   not being-silent,

de   quâ   multa   gravissime dicta sunt ab
about which many-things 'were very-severely   'said   by (that)

ingeniosissimo   et   copiosissimo   homine   Hortensio.
very-talented   and   very-fluent   man   Hortensius.

Quò   etiam   durior   locus   datus   mihi   dicendi;
Wherefore also   a more-difficult   task   is-given to-me of-speaking;

ut,   cum   ante   me,   et   ille   dixisset,   et
as,   when   before   me,   both   he   had-spoken,   and (likewise)

M.   Crassus,   vir   et   summâ   dignitate,   et
M.   Crassus,   a man   both (of) the greatest   dignity,   and

diligentiâ,   et   facultate   dicendi;   ego   in extremo,
diligence,   and   talent   in-speaking;   I   in the last-place,

non   agerem   aliquam   partem
(and concluding), 'will not   'treat   any   (particular)   part

causæ,   sed   dicerem   de   totâ   re,
of-the-cause,   but   may-speak   concerning   the whole   affair,

quod   videretur   mihi.   Itaque   versor
what   might-seem (proper) to-me.   Therefore I-am- (now) occupied

fere in iisdem rebus, et, quoad possum, judices,
nearly with the same   subjects, and, as-much-as   I-can,   O judges,

occurro   vestræ   sapientiæ.
I-help   your   wisdom,   (in coming to a decision).

24.   Sed tamen,   Servi,   quam   securim   putas
But   however, O Servius,   what   axe   do-you-think

te   injecisse,   tuæ   petitioni
(that)   you   laid,   (to cut off the success of)   your   seeking

cum   tu   adduxisti   Romanum
(for the consulship), when   you (by your conduct)   had-brought the Roman

populum   in   eum   metum,   ut   pertimesceret
people   into   that (state of)   apprehension, that they-greatly-feared

ne Catilina fieret consul, dum tu comparares
lest Catiline might-be-made consul, while you were-preparing

accusationem, depositâ atque abjectâ
an impeachment, having-given-up and thrown-aside (your)

petitione? Etenim videbant te inquirere,
application (for the consulship)? For they-saw you inquiring-for

tristem ipsum, amicos
(witnesses, and proofs of bribery), sad yourself, (and your) friends

mœstos; animadvertebant observationes, testifica-
dejected; they-noticed the precautions, the deposi-

tiones, seductiones testium, secessionem
tions, the taking-aside of-witnesses, the going-apart (and consultation)

subscriptorum; quibus rebus
of-the-subscribers, (who abetted the impeachment); by-which things

certe, vultus ipsi candidatorum solent
certainly, the countenances themselves of-the-candidates used

videri obscuriores; Catilinam inter-
to-appear more-clouded (and dejected); (that) Catiline in-the-mean-

ea alacrem atque lætum, stipatum choro
time (was) active and cheerful, densely-accompanied by-a-band

juventutis; vallatum indicibus atque sicariis;
of-young-men; surrounded by-informers and assassins;

inflatum cum spe militum tum
inflated with the hope (of the assistance) of-the-soldiers, as-also

promissis mei collegæ, quemadmodum ipse
the promises of-my colleague, as he-himself

dicebat; circumfluentem exercitu Arretinorum et
said; encompassed by-an-army of-Arretinian and

Fesulanorum colonorum, quam turbam, ex
Fesulanian colonists, which crowd, (composed) of

dissimillimo genere, homines distinguebant
very-different materials, (those) men very-remarkable (who)

perculsi calamitate temporis Sullani. Ipsius
were-ruined by-the-calamity of-the-times of-Sylla. His

vultus erat plenus furoris; oculi
[Catiline's] countenance was full of-fury; (his) eyes

sceleris; sermo arrogantiæ sic ut consulatus
of-wickedness; (his) speech of-arrogance so that the consulship

videretur ei jam exploratus, et conditus domi.
might-seem to-him (as) now certain, and laid-up at-home

Contemnebat Murenam;
(to be used when required). He-despised Murena;

numerabat Sulpicium suum accusatorem, non
he-counted Sulpicius (amongst) his accusers, not

competitorem; denuntiabat vim ei;
(as his) competitor; he-announced violence to-him;

minabatur reipublicae.
he-threatened the republic.

25. Quibus rebus, qui timor sit injectus omnibus
By-which things, what fear was-excited in-all

bonis, que quanta desperatio reipublicae, si
good (men), and what-great desperation of-the-republic, if

ille factus esset, nolite velle a me
he should-be-made (consul), do-not require of me

commoneri; vosmet ipsi recordamini
that-it-be-adverted-to; you yourselves remember (all this)

cum vobis. Enim meministis, cum voces illius
among yourselves. For you-remember, when the expressions of-that

nefarii gladiatoris percrebuissent, quas dicebatur
wicked gladiator [Catiline] had-spread-abroad which it-was-said

habuisse in domesticâ concione, cum negasset
he-delivered in a private meeting, when he-may-have-denied

fidelem defensorem miserorum posse inveniri
(that) a faithful defender of-the-unfortunate could be-found,

nisi eum, qui ipse, esset miser;
unless (that) he, as himself [Catiline], might-be unfortunate

saucios et miseros opertere non credere
(that) the injured and unfortunate ought not to-trust,

promissis integrorum et fortunatorum; quare
to-the-promises of-the-uninjured and fortunate; wherefore

qui vellent replere consumpta
those) who desire to-replenish (their) exhausted (fortunes, and)

recuperare erepta, spectarent
to-recover (that, which) has-been-taken (from them), let-them-see-to-it,

quid ipse deberet, quid possideret, quid
what any-one-himself may-owe, what he-may-possess, what

auderet;   oportere eum, qui futurus esset
ne-might-dare (to do); (that) it-behoved him, who   was-to be

dux   et   signifer   calamitosorum, esse minime
the leader and standard-bearer of-the-unfortunate, to-be   little

timidum, et   valde calamitosum.
fearful,   and (to have undergone) great   calamities (and mis-

        Igitur tum, his rebus auditis,
fortunes). Therefore then, these things being-heard (and ascertained),

meministis   senatusconsultum fieri, me referente,
you-remember (that) a decree-of-the-senate was-made, I   moving

        comitia   ne haberentur postero die,
(it), (that) the comitia 'should not   'be-held on-the-next day,

ut possemus agere de his rebus in senatu.
that we-might consult about these things in the senate.

Itaque postridie, frequenti   senatu, excitavi
Therefore next-day, (in) a full (meeting of) the senate, I-called-on

Catilinam, atque jussi eum, si quid vellet,
Catiline,   and I-requested him, if 'he so 'desired,

dicere   de his rebus, quæ
to say (something in explanation) concerning these things, which

allatæ essent ad me. Atque ille, ut semper fuit
were-reported to me. And he, as 'he always 'was

apertissimus,   non purgavit se,
very-open   (in his declarations), 'did not 'clear himself

        sed indicavit atque induit.
(of the charge) but openly-owned (them) and took-them-on-himsel-

Enim tum dixit,   esse duo corpora
For then he-said, (that) there-were two bodies (in)

reipublicæ, unum debile, infirmo capite; alterum
the republic, the one weak, with-a-weak head; the other

firmum, sine capite; huic, cum meritum esset
strong, without a head; to-this (last), as it-had-deserved

ita de se,   non defuturum caput,
so (well) of himself, 'there-should not 'be-wanting a head, 'while

se vivo. Frequens senatus congemuit,
he 'was-alive. A full senate groaned (at hearing this),

        decrevit, tamen neque satis severe pro
(and) passed-a-decree, however not sufficiently severe fo-

indignitate rei. Nam erant partim,
the indignity of-the-affair. For (some) 'were partly

ideo non fortes in decernendo, quia timebant
therefore not severe in 'deciding, because they-feared

nihil; partim, quia timebant. Tum erupit
nothing; (others) partly, because they-feared. Then he-rushed

e senatu, triumphans gaudio, quem omnino
from the senate, triumphing with-joy, who altogether

non oportuerat exire illuc vivum;
'ought not 'to-have-been-allowed to-depart thence alive ·

præsertim cum ille idem, paucis diebus
especially when this same (Catiline), a few days

ante, in eodem ordine, respondisset
before, in this-same order (of the senate), had-replied

Catoni, fortissimo viro, minitanti ac denuntianti
to-Cato, a most-valiant man, threatening and announcing

judicium, si quod incendium excitatum esset
a capital-trial, (that) if any conflagration should-be-kindled

in suas fortunas, se non restincturum id
against his fortunes, (that) he 'would not 'extinguish it

aquâ sed ruinâ.
by-water but by-ruin.

26. Commotus tum his rebus, et quòd sciebam
Moved then by-these things, and because I knew

jam tum homines conjuratos deduci in
(that) already then men banded-together were-led into

campum a Catilinâ cum gladiis,
the Campus Martius by Catiline (armed) with swords, 'I (also)

descendi in campum cum firmissimo præsidio
'went-down into the campus with a strong guard

fortissimorum virorum, et cum illâ latâ que insigni
of-very-brave men, and with that broad and conspicuous

loricâ, non quæ tegeret me (etenim sciebam,
breast-plate, not that-it might-defend me, (for I-knew, (that)

Catilinam non solere petere latus aut
Catiline 'was not 'used to-aim at the sides or

ventrem, sed caput et collum), verum
me 'fore-part-of-the-body, but at the head and neck), but

ut omnes boni animadverterent, et cum
that all good (citizens) might-notice (it), both when

viderent consulem in metu, et periculo,
they-might-perceive the consul in fear, and in-danger, (and)

id quod est factum, concurrerent ad meum
that which was-done, (that) they-would-assemble to my

præsidium que opem. Itaque cum putarent te,
protection and assistance. Therefore when they-thought you,

Servi, remissiorem in petendo,
O Servius, (to be) more relax in seeking-for (the consulship), (and)

viderent Catilinam inflammatum, et spe et
saw Catiline inflamed, both with-hope and

cupiditate, omnes, qui cupiebant depellere illam
desire, all (those), who desired to-repel that

pestem ab republica, statim contulerunt se ad
pest from the republic, immediately went-over to

Murenam. Autem consularibus comitiis, magna
Murena. But in-the-consular comitia, (of) great-importance,

est repentina inclinatio voluntatum, præsertim cum
is a-sudden turn of-will, especially when

incubuit ad bonum virum, et ornatum
it-rests-on (and is inclined) to a good man, and provided

multis aliis adjumentis petitionis. Qui
with-many other aids (in) seeking (the consulship). Who

cum honestissimo patre atque majoribus,
is (he was) of-a-most-worthy father and ancestors,

adolescentiâ modestissimâ,
was distinguished) by-a-youth (of) much-modesty (and self-control),

legatione clarissimâ, præturâ probatâ
in (his) 'lieutenancy greatly-distinguished, 'in (his) 'prætorship approved

jure, gratâ in munere, in provinciâ
legal-affairs, acceptable in his public shows, in (his) province

ornatâ; diligenter petisset,
every-thing required-being-supplied; he-diligently sought (the con-

et ita petisset ut neque cederet
sulship), and so sought (it), that 'he neither 'yielded to (those

minanti, neque minaretur cuiquam;
threatening (him), nor did-he-threaten any-one:

mirandum est   subitam   spem   Catilinæ
is-it-to-be-wondered-at (that) the sudden hope of-Catiline

adipiscendi   consulatus   fuisse   magno   adjumente
of-obtaining   the consulship   was   a-great   aid

nuic?
to-him?

Est   nunc   ille   tertius   locis   mihi   orationis
There is   now   that   third   part for-me of (my)   speech

de   criminibus   ambitûs,   perpurgatus   ab   iis,
concerning   the crimes   of-bribery,   fully-cleared-up   by those,

qui   dixerunt   ante   me,   retractandus   a
who   have-spoken before me, (but which) is-again-to-be-gone-over by

me,   quoniam Murena voluit   ita; in quo loco
me,   because   Murena wished (it to be) so; in which place

respondebo   Postumio   meo   familiari,
I-will-reply   to-Postumius   my   intimate-friend, (and)

ornatissimo   viro,   de   indiciis
most-accomplished   man,   concerning   the discoveries

divisorum,   et   de   pecuniis
of-the-distributors-of-bribes,   and   concerning the sums-of-money

deprehensis;   ingenioso et bono
seized   (in their hands); 'to (that) 'talented and good

adolescenti,   Ser. Sulpicio,   de   centuriis
young-man,   Ser. Sulpicius,   concerning   the centuries

equitum; M. Catoni, homini excellenti in omni
of-the-knights; to-M. Cato, a man excelling in every

virtute,   de   ipsius accusatione,   de
virtue,   concerning   his accusation,   respecting

senatusconsulto,   de   republica.
the-decree-of-the-senate, (and) respecting the republic.

27. Sed prius, conquerar   pauca   de
But first, I-may-complain (of) a few-things respecting

fortunâ L. Murenæ, quæ   repente moverunt
(the hard) fortune of-L. Murena, which 'have suddenly 'excited

meum animum. Nam cum   sæpe antea, judices,
my   mind. Now as 'I-have often heretofore, O judges,

et ex miseriis aliorum, et ex meis quotidianis
both from the miseries of-others, and from my   daily

curis que laboribus, judicarem eos homines fortunatos,
cares and labours, ¹judged those men fortunate,

qui, remoti a studiis ambitionis, secuti sunt otium
who, remote from the pursuits of-ambition, have-sought-after ease

ac tranquillitatem vitæ: vero tum in his tantis,
and tranquillity of-life: but moreover in these so-great

que tam improvisis periculis L. Murenæ, sum ita
and so unexcited dangers of-L. Murena, I-am so

affectus animo, ut queam non satis miserari,
affected ¹in (my) ¹mind, that I-can not sufficiently commiserate,

neque communem conditionem nostrûm omnium,
neither the common condition of-us all,

neque eventum que fortunam hujus;
nor the lot and fortune of-this (man, Murena);

qui, primum, dum conatus est adscendere unum
who, firstly, when he-attempted to-ascend one

gradum dignitatis, ex continuis honoribus
degree (higher in) dignity, from the continued honours

familiæ que majorum, venit in periculum,
(of office) ¹of (his) ¹family and ancestors, gets in danger,

ne amittat ea, quæ relicta sunt,
lest he-may-lose those (honours), which have-been-left (him by his

quæ parta sunt ipso; deinde,
ancestors), (and) those-which were-obtained by-himself; then

propter studium novæ laudis,
on-account-of (his) pursuit of-new praise (and honours of office),

etiam adducitur in discrimen veteris
¹he also ¹is-led into danger (of losing his) ancient

fortunæ. Quæ cum sint gravia, judices,
fortune. Which as they-may-be serious (things), O judges,

tum illud est acerbissimum, quod habet eos
yet that is harshest, that he-has those

accusatores, qui non odio inimicitiarum
as-accusers, who (are) not (induced) by-the-hatred of-animosities

ad accusandum, sed qui studio accusandi
to accuse, but who ¹in (their) ¹zeal of-accusing

descenderunt ad inimicitias. Nam, ut omittam
have-descended to enmities. For, that I-may-omit

Servium Sulpicium, quem intelligo, permotum
Servius Sulpicius, whom (as) I-understand, was-moved

non injuriâ L. Murenæ,
(and urged to action) not 'by (any) 'injury (received from) L. Murena,

sed contentione honoris; Cn. Postumius
but in-a-contest for-the-honours (of office); Cn. Postumius

amicus paternus accusat, ut ipse ait
friend (of) the family accuses (him, and) as he-himself says

vetus vicinus ac necessarius, qui protulit
an old neighbour and acquaintance, who has-produced

complures causas necessitudinis, potuit commemorare
many instances of-friendship, (but) could remember

nullam simultatis; Ser. Sulpicius accusat,
none of-hatred; Ser. Sulpicius (the younger) accuses (him),

sodalis filii, cujus ingenio
(and who is) the companion 'of (his) [Murena's] son, 'by whose 'talents

omnes necessarii paterni debebant esse
all the friends (of his) father ought to-be (made)

munitiores; M. Cato accusat, qui quanquam
more-secure; M. Cato accuses, (him), who though

unquam fuit, nulla re, alienus a Murenâ,
'he never 'was, in-any thing, estranged from Murena,

tamen natus erat nobis, in hac civitate, eâ
yet he-was-born among-us, in this city, under-such

conditione, ut ejus opes et ingenium deberent
circumstances, that his assistance and talents ought

esse præsidio multis, etiam alienissimis,
to-be a protection to-many, even to-the-greatest-strangers, (and)

vix exitio cuiquam inimico. Igitur
scarcely the ruin (of) any (personal) enemy. 'I-will therefore

primum respondebo Postumio, qui, nescio quo pacto
first 'reply to-Postumius, who, I-know-not why

videtur mihi, candidatus prætorius
seems to-me, (being as he is) a candidate (for the) prætorship

in consularem, quasi desultorius
(to run) against the consular (competitor), like-as-if a-vaulter-on-horses

incurrere in quadrigarum curiculam. Si cujus
were-to jump into a-four-horse chariot. If his

competitores deliquerunt nihil, concessit eorum
competitors   had-been-wanting in-nothing, he-yielded to-their

dignitati, cum destitit petere; autem
worth,   when he-desisted from-seeking (the prætorship); but

sin aliquis eorum largitus est, amicus
if any-one of-them had-been-guilty-of-bribery, a friend

expetendus est, qui potius persequatur alienam
is-to-be-sought, who 'would rather 'prosecute another's

injuriam, quam suam. * * *
injury,   than his-own. * * *

28. Nunc venio ad M. Catonem, quod est
'I now 'come to M. Cato, (and) this is

firmamentum ac robur totius accusationis, qui
the support and strength of-the-whole accusation, who

tamen est ita gravis et vehemens accusator, ut
however is so severe and vehement an accuser, that

pertimescam multo magis ejus auctoritatem
I-fear   much more his authority (and weight

quam criminationem. In quo
of character), than (his) accusation. As-respects this

accusatore, judices, ego primum deprecabor
accuser,   O judges, I 'shall in-the-first-place 'earnestly-entreat

illud, illius dignitas ne quid
(of you) this, (that) his [Cato's] dignity 'may not (be of) any

noceat L. Murenæ, ne quid expectatio
'injury to-L. Murena, nor any (his) expectation

tribunatûs, ne quid splendor et gravitas
of-the-tribuneship, nor any (his) splendour and solidity-of-character

totius vitæ; denique ea bona
'of (his) 'whole life; in-fine (that) those qualities (and ad-

M. Catonis, quæ ille adeptus est, ut
vantages) of-M. Cato, which he has-obtained, that

posset prodesse multis, ne obsint huic
he-might be-useful to-many, 'may not 'be-an-injury to him

soli. L. Africanus fuerat bis consul, et deleverat
alone. L. Africanus had-been twice consul, and had-destroyed

duos terrores hujus imperii Carthaginem que
the two (great) terrors of-this empire Carthage and

Naumantiam, cum accusavit L. Cottam. Erat in
Numantia, when he-accused L. Cotta. There-was in

eo summa eloquentia, summa fides, summa
him the most-perfect eloquence, the greatest good-faith, the greatest

integritas, auctoritas tanta quanta Romani
integrity, (his) authority (was) as-great as-that of-the-Roman

populi, in imperio ipso, quod tenebatur
people, in the empire itself, which was-defended (and preserved)

illius operâ. Sæpe audivi majores natu
'by his 'exertion. 'I-have often 'heard old-men

dicere hoc, hanc eximiam dignitatem
say this, (that) this very-great dignity (and authority)

accusatoris plurimum profuisse L. Cottæ.
of-the-accuser 'was (of) very-great 'advantage to-L. Cotta.

Sapientissimi homines, qui tum judicabant illam
The very-wise men, who then judged this

rem, noluerunt quemquam ita cadere in
cause, did-not-wish (that) any-one 'should so lose-his-cause in

judicio, ut videretur abjectus nimiis
court, that it-might-seem he-was-borne-down by-the-too-great

viribus adversarii. Quid? Non ne Romanus
power 'of (his) 'adversary. What-then? 'Did not the Roman

populus (nam traditum est memoriæ) eripuit
people (for it-is-preserved-in (our) memory) 'deliver

Ser. Galbam tuo proavo, M. Catoni, fortissimo
Ser. Galba from-your great-grandfather, M. Cato, a very-brave

atque florentissimo viro, incumbenti ad ejus
and very-distinguished man, (who was) bent on 'his

perniciem. Semper in hac civitate, et universus
destruction. Always in this city, both the entire

populus, et sapientes judices, ac prospicientes in
people, and wise judges, and looking-for into

posterum, restiterunt nimis magnis opibus accu-
the future, have-resisted the too great power of-ac-

torum. Nolo accusator afferat potentiam
cusers. I-do-not-wish (that) an accuser should-bring power

in judicium, non aliquam majorem vim,
to the trial, nor any greater force (than common,

non excellentem auctoritatem,   **non nimiam**
nor   excelling   authority   (and character), nor   too-great

gratiam. Omnia hæc valeant   **ad salutem**
influence.   All   these are-of-avail (and to be used) for   the safety

innocentium, ad opem impotentium, ad auxilium
of-the-innocent, for the assistance of-the-weak,   for   the aid

calamitosorum: vero in periculo, et in pernicie
of-the-unfortunate :   but   in   danger,   and in   the ruin

civium, repudientur.   **Nam si quis forte**
of citizens, they-are-to-be-rejected.   For   if   any-one by-chance

dicet hoc, Catonem non fuisse descensurum
should-say this, (that)   Cato   'would not have   descended

ad accusandum, nisi prius
to   accuse,   unless 'he-had previously (examined into, and)

judicasset de causâ; instituet,
'formed-a-judgment (and opinion) concerning the cause; it-will-establish

judices, iniquam legem, et miseram conditionem
O judges,   an unjust   law,   and a miserable   condition

periculis hominum, si existimabit, judicium
for-the-dangers of-men,   if   it-be-held, (that) the judgment

accusatoris in reum oportere valere
of-the-accuser against the defendant   ought   to-have-force (against

pro aliquo præjudicio.
him)   like   some   legal-precedent.

29. Ego, Cato, audeo non, propter singulare
I,   O Cato,   dare   not, on-account-of the singular (great)

judicium mei animi de tuâ virtute, vituperare
opinion   (formed in) my   mind   of your   virtue,   censure

tuum consilium; forsitan possim, in
your   determination (in this case); perhaps   I-may-be-able,   in

nonnullâ re conformare et leviter emendare.
some   things   to-mould   and   slightly   to-amend (it).

"**Non peccas multa,**" **inquit ille senior magister**
"You-do not 'offend much,"   said   that   aged   instructor

fortissimo viro; "**sed, si peccas possum regere**
to-a-very-brave man ;   "but, if   you-do-offend   I-can   rule

te."   **At ego verissime dixerim,**
you (and set you right)." But   I   may most-truly   'say,   (that)

te peccare nihil, neque in ullâ re esse **te**
you offend (in) nothing, nor (that) in any thing are you

hujusmodi, ut videare potius corrigendus,
of-that-nature, that you-may-seem rather (to require) to-be-corrected,

quàm leviter inflectendus. Enim natura ipsa
than 'to-be gently 'put-right. For nature herself

finxit te ad honestatem, gravitatem, temperantiam,
formed you for honesty, gravity, temperance,

magnitudinem animi, justitiam, denique ad omnes
greatness of-mind, justice, (and) in-fine for all

virtutes, magnum et excelsum
(those) virtues, (that constitute) a great and distinguished

hominem. Istuc accessit doctrina
man. To-this acceded a system-of-doctrines (and precepts)

non moderata, nec mitis, sed, ut videtur mihi
not moderate, nor mild, but, as it-seems to-me

paullo asperior, et durior, quàm aut veritas aut
somewhat harsher, and more-severe, than either truth or

natura patiatur. Et quoniam hæc oratio non
nature may-allow. And because this speech 'is not

habenda est nobis, aut cum imperitâ multitudine,
to-be-delivered (by) us, either before an ignorant multitude,

aut in aliquo conventu agrestium, disputabo paullo
or in some assemblage of-rustics, I-will-discourse somewhat

audacius de studiis humanitatis, quæ sunt
more-boldly concerning the studies of-polite-literature, which are

nota et jucunda et mihi et vobis. Scitote,
known and agreeable both to-me and you. Know (then),

judices, hæc divina et egregia bona, quæ
O judges, (that) those divine and admirable qualities, which

videmus, in M. Catone, esse ipsius propria.
we-see, in M. Cato, are his peculiar-property.

Quæ nonnunquam requiremus, omnia ea sunt
What 'we sometimes 'reprehend, all such are

non a naturâ, sed a magistro.
(derived) not from nature, but from (the instruction of) a master.

Enim fuit quidam vir summo ingenio,
For there-was a certain man (of) the greatest talents, (named)

Zeno, æmuli   cujus inventorum
Zeno, the admirers (and followers) of-whose discoveries (and doctrines)

nominantur Stoici. Hujus sententiæ et præcepta
are called Stoics. His opinions and precepts

sunt ejusmodi: sapientem nunquam moveri
are of-this-sort: (that) the-wise-man 'is never 'moved

gratiâ; nunquam ignoscere delicto cujusquam;
by-favours; (that) 'he never 'forgives the-crime of-any-one;

neminem esse misericordem, nisi stultum et
(that) no one is merciful, unless a fool and

levem; non esse viri neque
a trifler; (that) 'it-does not 'belong-(to)-a-man (to allow himself) either

exorari, neque placari; sapientes solos
to-be-intreated, or to-be-propitiated; (that) the wise only

esse formosos, si sint distortissimi;
are beautiful, though they-may-be the-most-distorted (in person);

si mendicissimi, divites; (that)
(that) if (they are) the-poorest-beggars, (yet they are) rich; (that)

si serviant servitutem, reges; autem
if they are in slavery, (yet they are) kings; but

dicunt, nos, qui sumus non sapientes, esse
they-say, (that) we, who are not wise, are

fugitivos, exsules, hostes, denique insanos;
fugitives, exiles, enemies, in-fine mad-men; (they say that)

omnia peccata esse paria; omne delictum esse
all sins are equal; (that) every offence is

nefarium scelus; nec eum delinquere
a nefarious crime; nor (that) he 'does (not) 'offend

minus, qui gallum gallinaceum, cum fuerit
less, who (killed) a cock, when there was

non opus, quàm eum, qui suffocavit patrem;
no necessity, than he, who suffocated (his) father; (that)

sapientem opinari nihil, poenitere
the-wise-man believes nothing (till fully convinced), (that) he-repents

nullius rei, falli in nullâ re, nunquam
of no thing, (that) he-is-deceived in no thing, (that) he never

mutare sententiam.
changes (his) opinion.

30. Ingeniosissimus homo, M. Cato, arripuit hæc,
The most-talented   man,   M. Cato,   adopted   these

                 inductus   eruditissimis
opinions and doctrines of Zeno), induced-thereto by-the-most-learned

auctoribus;   neque   causâ   disputandi,
writers;   (and this) not for-the-purpose of-disputing (about them)

ut magna pars,   sed vivendi ita.
as the great part (of men do), but of-living as (they prescribe).

         Publicani   petunt   aliquid ? "Cave
'Do the farmers-of-the-revenues 'petition-for any-thing? "Take-care

gratia   habeat   quidquam   momenti."
(lest) influence   have   any-thing   of-weight (with you)."

Aliqui miseri et calamitosi   veniunt
'Do some miserable and unfortunate (persons) 'come   (to you)

supplices ?   "Fueris   sceleratus et nefarius,
as suppliants? "You-will-be   a wicked   and   criminal (man),

si feceris quidquam, adductus misericordiâ."
if you-do any-thing,   induced   by-mercy."   'Does

Aliquis fatetur   se pecasse,   et petit veniam
any-one confess (that) he has-done-wrong, and asks-for pardon

ejus delicti ? "Ignoscere facinus est nefarium."
(for) his   offence?   "To-pardon   crime   is   wicked."

At delictum est leve. "Omnia peccata sunt paria."
But the fault is trifling.   "All   offences   are   equal."

Dixisti   quidpiam ? "Est fixum et statutum."
Have-you-said any-thing?   "It is   fixed and determined."

      Non ductus   esre,   sed opinione.
'You-were   not   induced by-the-thing (itself), but by-supposition.

"Sapiens opinatur nihil."   Errasti   in aliquâ
"A wise-man supposes nothing." You-may-have-erred in   some

re.   Putat   maledici.
thing. He-considers (himself) to-be-calumniated (by this remark).

Illa sunt   nobis, ex hac disciplinâ. "Dixi
Those are (the results) for-us, from this   doctrine.   "I-said

in senatu,   me delaturum nomen consularis
in   the senate, (that) I   would-announce the name of-a-consular

candidati."   Dixisti   iratus.
candidate   (for impeachment)." (But) you-said (it when) angry.

" Nunquam, inquit, sapiens irascitur." At
"Never, says-he, 'does a wise-man 'get-angry." But

causâ temporis,
(it may have been said) by-reason (of some peculiar) circumstance,

inquit, " est improbi hominis fallere
he-replies, "it-is (the part) of-a-dishonest man to-deceive

mendacio; est turpe mutare sententiam;
by-a-falsehood; it-is shameful to-change (one's) opinion; (to allow

exorari, scelus; misereri,
one's self) to-be-entreated, is a crime; (and) to-pity, (is)

flagitium." Autem illi nostri (enim
infamy." But those our (masters and teachers) (for

fatebor, Cato, me quoque in adolescentiâ,
I-will-confess, O Cato, (that) I also in (my) youth,

diffisum meo ingenio, quæsisse adjumenta
diffident (of) my-own talents, sought the assistance

doctrinæ, illi nostri, inquam,
of-the-doctrine (of philosophers), those our (teachers), I-say,

a Platone et
(who derived their doctrine, and principles) from Plato and

Aristotele, moderati et temperati
Aristotle, (and who were) moderate and temperate

homines, aiunt, gratiam aliquando valere
men, say, (that) favour 'does sometimes 'have-an-influence

apud sapientem; boni viri
with a-wise-man; (that it is the part) of-a-good man

misereri, esse distincta genera
to-pity, (that) there-are distinct kinds (and degrees)

delictorum, et dispares pœnas; esse
of-crimes, and different (grades of) punishments; (that) there-is

locum ignoscendi apud constantem
a place for-forgiveness (even) with a firm-and-determine

hominem; sapientem ipsum, sæpe opinari
man; (that) the-wise-man himself, often forms-an-opinion (about)

aliquid, quod nesciat; nonnunquam
something, that he-does-not-know (for certain); (that) 'he sometimes

irasci; eundem exorari et placari;
gets-angry; (that) he the-same may-be-entreated and propitiated'

quod   interdum   dixerit,   si   sit
that-which 'he-may-have   occasionally   'said,   if   it-should-be

rectius   ita,   mutare ;   aliquando decedere
more-proper   so,   he-changes ;   'he sometimes   'recedes

de   sententiâ ;   omnes virtutes   moderatas esse
from (his) opinion ;   (that)   all   virtues   are-to-be-regulated

quadam   mediocritate.
by a certain (degree of) moderation.

31. Si, Cato, cum istâ   naturâ,
     If,   O Cato,   with   this (good) natural-disposition, (which

        qua   fortuna detulisset te   ad hos
you possess,) any (good)   fortune   had-brought   you   to   these

magistros, tu   non quidem esse melior vir,
instructors,   you 'would not   indeed   'have-been a better   man,

nec   fortior,   nec temperantior, nec justior (neque
nor   more-brave,   nor   more-temperate,   nor   more-just   (nor

enim potes esse) sed paullo propensior ad lenitatem.
indeed can-you be)   but   a little   more-inclined to   lenity

      Non accusares   adductus nullis inimicitiis,
'You-would not   'accuse (when) led-thereto by-no   animosities,

     lacessitus nullâ injuriâ, pudentissimum
(or)   provoked   by-no   injury,   a most-modest   (and worthy)

hominem, præditum   summâ   dignitate atque
man,   endowed   with-the-highest dignity-of-rank   and

honestate ;   putares   cum   fortuna posuisset te
integrity ;   you-might-think when   fortune   had-placed   you

atque L. Murenam in custodiâ ejusdem anni,
and   L.   Murena   in the guardianship of-the-same   year,

     te conjunctum esse cum hoc   vinculo
(that) you   were-united   with   him 'by (the political)   'ties

reipublicæ ;   quod   dixisti   atrociter   in   senatu,
of-the-republic ; that-which you-said   so-severely   in   the senate,

       aut non dixisses,   aut   seposuisses
'you-would either not   'have-said,   or   would-have-put-it-aside,

          aut   interpretarere   in
(and not applied it to him), or   would-have-explained   (it)   in

mitiorem partem. Ac   te ipsum (quantum ego
'milder   manner. And (that) you yourself (as-much-as   I

opinione auguror) nunc et concitatum
'in (my 'opinion (may) predict) now both excited

quodam impetu animi, et elatum vi naturæ
by-a-certain impulse of-the-mind, and elated by-the-force of-nature

atque ingenii, et flagrantem recentibus studiis
and of-genius, and inflamed by-the-recent studies

præceptorum usus jam flectet,
of-the-precepts (of the Stoics), experience 'will at-some-time 'bend,

dies leniet, ætas mitigabit. Etenim isti ipsi,
time soften, (and) age render-milder. For these same,

vestri præceptores et magistri virtutis, videntur
your preceptors and instructors (in) virtue, seem

mihi protulisse fines officiorum, paullo longius,
to-me to-have-carried the limits of-duty, a little farther,

quàm natura vellet; ut cum, animâ, contendissimus
than nature requires; so-that when, in-mind, we-had-striven

ad ultimum, tamen consisteremus
(to reach) to the ultimate (limits), yet we-should-stop-short

ibi, ubi oportet. "Ignoveris nihil."
there, where it-is-proper (to do so). "Pardon nothing" (you say).

Immo aliquid, non omnia.
Indeed (truly) something (may be pardoned, but) not all.

"Feceris nihil causâ gratiæ." Immo resistito
"Do nothing by-reason of-favour." Yes-indeed resist

gratiæ cum officium et fides postulabit. "Sis
favour, (but only) when duty and good-faith will-require-it. "Be

ne commotus misericordiâ." Etiam, in dissolvenda
not moved by-pity." Certainly, in relaxing

severitate; sed tamen est aliqua laus
(proper) severity; but yet there-is some praise (for)

humanitatis. Permaneto in sententiâ. Vero,
humanity. Abide in (your) opinion. True,

nisi alia melior vicerit sententiam.
unless another better (opinion) should-prevail-over (your) opinion.

Ille Scipio fuit hujuscemodi, quem
The (great) Scipio was (a man) of-this-kind, (to) whom 'it-caused

non pœnitebat facere idem, quod tu; habere
no 'regret to-do the same, that you (do); (and) to-have

eruditissimum, et pæne divinum hominem domi;
a most-learned, and nearly divine man 'in (his) 'house;

cujus oratione et præceptis, quanquam erant
'by whose 'discourse and precepts, although they-were

ista eadem, quæ delectant te, tamen non
the very same, which (so) delight you, yet 'he-was not

factus est asperior, sed (ut accepi a senibus),
'made more-austere, but (as I-have-heard from old-men),

lenissimus. Quis vero comior,
most-mild. Who indeed (was) more-civil-and-obliging, (than)

C. Lælio? quis jucundior ex isto
C. Lælius? who more-agreeable, (than he, though formed) by these

eodem studio? quis gravior sapientior
same studies (that you are)? who more-grave (and) wise

illo? Possum dicere hæc eadem de
(than) he? I-can say these same (things) concerning

L. Philo, de C. Gallo; sed deducam te
L. Philus, (and) concerning C. Gallus; but I-will-conduct you

jam tuam domum. Ne existimas quemquam fuisse
now to-your-own home. Do-you-think any-one was

commodiorem, comiorem, moderatiorem ad omnem
milder, more-obliging, more-moderate as-respects all

rationem humanitatis, Catone tuo pro-
the relations of-humanity (and life), (than) Cato your great-

avo. Cum vere que graviter diceres de
grandfather. When 'you truly and gravely 'spoke of

præstanti virtute cujus, dixisti te habere
of-the-eminent virtue of-this (man), you-said (that) you had

domesticum exemplum ad imitandum. Illud quidem
a domestic example to imitate. That indeed

est exemplum propositum tibi domi; sed
is an example offered to-you 'in (your own) 'family; but

tamen similitudo illius naturæ potuit
however the resemblance of-his nature (and endowments) could

magis pervenire ad te, qui ortus es ab illo,
more-easily arrive to you, who are-descended from him,

quam ad unumquemque nostrûm; vero illud
than to any-one of-us; but that

exemplar   tam   propositum   mihi   ad imitandum,
example   'is as-much   'offered   to-me   for   imitation,

quàm tibi.   Sed, si   adsperseris   illius   comitatem
as   to-you.   But, if you-would-have-mingled his   obliging-civility

et facilitatem,   tuæ gravitati   que severitati, ista
and   affability, (with) your   gravity   and   severity,   those

quidem   non   erunt   meliora,   quæ   nunc
(things)   indeed   'will not   'be   better,   which   now

sunt optima, sed certe   jucundius
are   excellent,   but   certainly (will become) more-agreeable (when)

condita.
seasoned.

32.   Quare, ut revertar ad id, quod   institui,
    Wherefore, that I-may-revert to that, which I-had-proposed,

tolle   mihi   nomen Catonis e causâ ;   remove
take-away   for-me   the name   of-Cato from the cause ;   remove

ac   prætermitte   auctoritatem,   quæ   in   judiciis
and   make-no-mention-of   authority,   which   in   trials

debet, aut   valere nihil, aut   valere ad salutem ;
ought, either   to-avail nothing, or (ought) to-avail   for   the safety

congredere cum me criminibus   ipsis.
(of the accused) ;   attack   with me   the crimes   themselves

Quid   accusas,   Cato ?
(that he is charged with).   What   do-you-accuse-him-of,   O Cato.

quid affers in judicium ? quid arguis ?   Accusas
what do-you-bring to   trial ?   what do-you-prove ? Do-you-accuse

ambitum ?   Non defendo.   Reprehendis
(him of)   bribery ?   'I-do not   'defend (bribery).   You-reprehend

me, quod defendam idem, quod   punierim
me,   that   I-defend   the same, which   I-would-have-punished

lege.   Punivi ambitum, non innocentiam
by-a-law (of my proposing). I-punished bribery,   not   innocenc

Vero ambitum ipsum, accusabo vel cum   te,   si
But   bribery   itself,   I-will-accuse even with yourself, if

voles.   Dixisti   senatusconsultum fac-
you- desire (it).   You-have-said   (that)   a decree-of-the-senate   was-

tum esse, me referente,   " si   corrupti
made,   I   proposing-it, (as thus)   "if (persons) corrupted

mercede   issent   obviam candidatis, si
by-recompense [bribery] should-go-out   to-meet the candidates, if

conducti   sectarentur,   si locus
hired-persons attend-and-follow (them), if a place (were given free)

    vulgo   tributim   gladiatoribus, et
to-the-common-people by-tribes (in shows of) the gladiators, and

item, si prandia data essent   vulgo,
also, if dinners were-given to-the-common-people, (this would

    videri factum contra Calpurniam legem."   Ergo
all) seem   done against the Calpurnian law."   Therefore

senatus ita judicat,   hæc   videri   facta
the senate so decided, (that) these (things) seemed to-have-been-done

contra legem, si facta sint ; decernit, quod   est
against the law, if they-were-done; it-decreed, what there-is

nihil opus,   dum   morem gerit   candidatis.
no occasion-for, while it-complied-with-the-wishes (of the) candidates.

Nam factum sit, nec ne,   vehementer quæritur.
For (if) done,   or not, 'is vehemently 'questioned.

Si factum sit, quin sit contra legem, nemo potest
If it-is-done, but-that it-is contrary to-the-law, no-one can

dubitare. Est igitur ridiculum,   relinquere id
doubt.   It-is therefore ridiculous,   to-leave   that

incertum, quod est dubium ; quod potest esse
uncertain, which is doubtful; that-which can   be

dubium nemini,   id judicare.   Atqui
a doubt to-no-one, that determine (and decide on). But-now

id   decernitur, omnibus candidatis postulantibus :
that (decree) was-passed, all the candidates asking-for-it :

ut   ex   senatusconsulto,   possit neque
so-that from   the-decree-of-the-senate,   it-can   neither

intelligi   cujus   intersit,   neque
be-understood 'for whose 'advantage, or interest it-might-be,   nor

contra quem   sit.   Quare doce   illa
against whom   it-might-be.   Therefore show (that) that

commissa esse a L. Murenâ ;   tum   egomet
was-done   by   L. Murena ;   then   I-myself

concedam tibi   commissa esse contra legem.
will-concede to-you (that) it-was-done contrary to-law.

33. "Multi prodierunt obviam decedenti de
"Many went-out to-meet-him returning from (his)

provinciâ, petenti consulatum." Solet fieri.
province, seeking the consulship." It-is-the-custom to-do-so.

Autem eccui non proditur revertenti?
But to-whom 'do (persons) not 'go-out-to-meet returning

Quæ multitudo ista fuit!" Primùm,
(from abroad)? What a multitude this was!" In-the-first-place,

si possim non reddere rationem istam tibi; quid
if I-can not explain this to-you; what

habet admirationis, multos prodisse obviam
is-there wonderful, (that) many (persons) went-out to-meet

tali viro advenienti, consulari candidato? Quod
such a man coming, (as) a consular candidate? Which

nisi factum esset, videretur magis mirandum.
unless it-had-been-done, would-seem the more to-be-wondered-at.

Quid? si etiam addam illud, quod non abhorret
What-then? if 'I also 'add this, which is not contrary

a consuetudine, multos rogatos esse? num sit
to custom, (that) many were-invited? whether is-it

aut criminosum, aut mirandum, in civitate quâ
either criminal, or to-be-wondered-at, in a city (in) which

rogati soleamus venire deductum filios
'we, (when) 'asked are-accustomed to come to-escort the sons

hominum infimorum, prope de
of-men of-the-lower-order, (when candidates), nearly when

nocte, sæpe ex ultimâ
yet night, [at early dawn of day], often from the extreme (part of)

urbe, in eâ homines esse non gravatos
the city, (that) in that men are not burdened (when)

prodire tertiâ horâ in Campum
they-go-forth at-the-third hour [nine o'clock] into the Campus

Martium, præsertim, rogatos nomine talis
Martius, especially, (when) invited in-the-name of-such

viri? Quid? Si omnes societates
a man (as Murena)? What? If all the societies (of knights

venerunt, ex numero quorum, mult.
had-come (to meet him), out-of the number of-whom, many

sedent hìc judices? quid? si multi homines nostri
sit here (as judges? what? if many men of-our

honestissimi ordinis? quid? si illa
most-honourable order (had gone)? what? if that

officiossima tota natio candidatorum, quæ
most officious (body) the whole nation of-candidates, which

patitur neminem introire in urbem non
suffers no-one to-enter into the city not

honeste? denique si
in-an-honourable-way, (had gone out to meet him)? in-fine if

accusator, noster Postumius ipse, venit obviam
the accuser, our Postumius himself, had-come to-meet-him

cum bene magnâ catervâ suâ;
with a very large crowd (of) his (followers and dependants);

quid habet ista multitudo admirationis?
what has this multitude of admiration, (or what that may

Omitto clientes, vicinos
excite our surprise)? I-omit (his) clients, (his) neighbours,

tribules, totum exercitum Luculli, qui venerat,
those-of-his-tribe, the whole army of-Lucullus, which had-come,

per eos dies ad triumphum; dico hoc,
on those days to the triumph; I-say this, (that)

gratuitam frequentiam in isto officio,
a voluntary concourse (of friends) in such kind-offices, 'was

unquam defuisse, non modò dignitati ullius, sed
never 'wanting, not only to-the-dignity of-any-one, but

ne quidem voluntati. "At multi sectabantur."
not even to-his-wish. "But many followed-him."

Doce, mercede; concedam esse
Show, (that it was) for-reward; (and) I-will-concede it-to-be

crimen. Hoc quidem remoto, quid
a crime. This (reward) indeed being-removed, what

reprehendis?
do-you-find-fault-with?

34. "Quid opus est, inquit, sectatoribus?"
"What need is-there, says-he, (of) followers?"

Tu quæris id a me, quid opus sit eo,
Do you ask that of me, what need may-there-be in-that

quo semper usi sumus? Homines tenues
which 'we-have always 'practised? Men (of) humble-rank

habent unum locum aut promerendi beneficii
have the only opportunity 'of either 'conferring a favour

in nostrum ordinem aut referendi, in
on our order or of-returning (a benefit received), in

hanc operam, atque assectationem
this aid (give us), and (this) attendance (on us),

nostris petitionibus. Neque enim potest fieri,
in-our seeking-for-office. Neither indeed could (it) be-done,

neque postulandum est a nobis, aut ab Romanis
nor is-it-required from us, or from the Roman

equitibus, ut sectentur candidatos suos
knights, that they-should-accompany the candidates their

necessarios, totos dies; si nostra domus
particular-friends, for-whole days (together); if our house

celebratur a quibus, si interdum
is-frequented by them, [the senators and knights,] if sometimes

deducimur ad forum, si honestamur uno
we-are-escorted to the forum (by them), if we-are-honoured with

spatio basilicæ, videmur diligenter
a turn (round the portico) of-some-basilica, we-seem (to be) diligently

observari et coli; ista assiduitas
respected and honoured; this assiduity (in attendance)

est tenuiorum amicorum, et non
is (the part) 'of (our) 'humble friends, and (who are) not

occupatorum, quorum copia non solet
occupied (with business), whose assistance 'is not 'used

deesse bonis et beneficis. Noli igitur, Cato,
to be-wanting to-the-good and beneficent. Do-not therefore, O Cato,

eripere hunc fructum officii inferiori generi
take-away this benefit of-duty from-the-inferior class

hominum; sine eos, qui sperant omnia a nobis,
of-men; allow those-men, who hope all from us.

ipsos quoque habere aliquid, quod possint
themselves also to-have something, which they can

tribuere nobis. Si erit nihil, præter ipsorum
give us. If there-were nothing, except their

suffragium, est tenue; si, ut suffragentur, valent
vote, it-is trifling; if, that they-aid-us, they-can-avail

nihil gratiâ. Ipsi denique, ut solent
nothing 'by (their) influence. They in-fine, as they-are-accustomed

loqui, possunt non dicere pro nobis, non
to-say, can not plead for us, (can) not

spondere, non vocare suam domum
go-security (for us), (can) not invite (us) to-their houses

atque petunt omnia hæc a nobis, neque
and they-ask all these (things) of us, nor

putant posse compensari, quæ consequuntur
do-they-think (that) they-can compensate, that-which they-receive

a nobis ullâ aliâ re, nisi suâ operâ.
from us in-any other way, unless 'by (this) 'their assistance

Itaque restiterunt et Fabiæ legi,
(and attendance). Consequently they-resisted both the Fabian law,

quæ est de numero sectatorum,
which is concerning the number of-followers, (that might be al-

et senatusconsulto, quod
lowed to attend a candidate,) and the decree-of-the-senate, which

factum est, L. Cæsare consule. Enim est nulla
was-passed, L. Cæsar being-consul. For there-is no

pœno, quæ possit excludere observantiam
punishment, which can exclude (or prevent) the regard

tenuiorum ab hoc vetere instituto
of-the-lower-classes from this ancient custom 'of (showing their)

officiorum. "At spectacula data sunt
'duty-and-zeal (for a candidate). "But shows were-given

vulgo tributim, et vocati ad
to-the-common-people by tribes, and they-were-invited to

prandium." Etsi hoc, judices, non omnino
dinner." Although this, O judges, 'was not at-all

factum est a Murenâ, autem factum est ab ejus
'done by Murena, but was-done by his

amicis more et modo; tamen admonitus
friends in-accordance-with-custom and mode; however admonished'

re ipsa, Servi, recordor quantum
by-the-thing itself, O Servius, I-remember how-much-of [how many

punctorum, hæ quæstiones, habitæ in senatu,
votes, these discussions, had in the senate,

detraxerint nobis. Enim quod tempus fuit, aut
may-have-taken from-us. For what time was-there, either

nostrâ memoriâ, aut nostrorum patrum, quo
in-our memory, or (that) of-our fathers, in-which

hæc sive est ambitio, sive liberalitas,
this (same thing), either be-it ambition, or liberality,

fuerit non, ut locus daretur, et in circo,
was not, that a place (or seats) might-be-given, both in the circus,

et in foro amicis et tribulibus?
and in the forum 'to (one's) 'friends and those-of-one's-own-tribe?

Primum hæc homines tenuiores qui nondum
First these men (of) the-lower-classes, who 'had not-yet

assequebantur a suis tribulibus vetere
'obtained from their tribe's-men in-accordance-with-old

instituto. * * *
custom. * * *

35. * * * **Præfectum** fabrum
* * * (That) the præfect, (or chief) of-the-artificers

semel dedisse locum suis
(or military workmen) once gave a place (or seats) to-his

tribulibus: quid statuent in primarios viros,
tribe's-men: what will-they-decide as-respects eminent men,

qui compararunt totas tabernas in circo, causâ
who have-prepared entire booths in the circus, for-the-use

tribulium? Item omnia hæc, Servi,
of (their) tribe's-men? Also all these, O Servius, (accusa-

crimen sectatorum, spectaculorum, prandiorum,
tions of) the crime of-followers, of-shows, of-dinners,

conjecta sunt a multitudine in tuam nimiam
are-attributed by the multitude to your too-great

diligentiam; in quibus tamen Murena
diligence (and scrupulousness); in which however Murena

defenditur ab auctoritate senatûs. Enim quid?
is-defended by the authority of-the-senate. For what?

Num senatus putat crimen prodire obviam?
Does then the senate 'think (it' a crime to-go-out to-meet (any one)?

"**Non**; **sed** **mercede.**"   Convince.   Num
"No;   but (if) for-a-reward, (it does)."   Prove-it.   Does

multos **sectari?**   "**Non;**
(the senate think it a crime, that) many   follow?   "No,

sed **conductos.**"   Doce.
but (it does, if they)   are-hired."   Show, (that Murena has done

Num   **dare** **locum** **ad**
this).   Does (the senate condemn) giving a place (or seats) to

spectandum?   **aut** **invitare** **ad** **prandium?**
see   (the shows)? or to-invite to dinner?

Minime;   "**sed** **vulgo** **passim.**"   Quid
Not-in-the-least; "but to-the-multitude without-distinction." What

est **vulgo?**   "**Universos.**"   Non
is to-the-multitude? "The entire-collection (of citizens)."   Not

igitur, si L. Natta, adolescens summo loco,
therefore, if L. Natta, a young-man (of) the highest rank,

qui, et videmus quo animo jam sit,
who, both we-see (of) what (disposition of) mind 'he now 'may-be,

et qualis vir sit futurus, voluit esse
and what (kind of) man he-may-be hereafter, wished to-be

gratiosus, in centuriis equitum, et ad hoc
in-favour, with the centuries of-the-knights, both for this

officium necessitudinis,   et ad tempus
duty of-friendship, (and relationship,) and for the time

reliquum id erit fraudi, aut,   crimini
to-come, 'will this 'be a crime, or, (cause of) accusation

ejus vitrico; nec, si Vestalis virgo, propinqua
'to his step-father; nor, if a Vestal virgin, a relation

et necessaria hujus   concessit suum locum
and friend of-this (Murena) gave-up her place

gladiatoribus huic,   non illa et fecit pie,
in the-gladiatorial-exhibitions to-him, 'did not 'she then 'act kindly

et hic remotus est a culpâ. Omnia hæc
and he [Murena] is-removed from censure.   All these-things

sunt officia necessariorum,   commoda
are the duties of-friends, the convenience-and-gratification

tenuiorum,   munia candidatorum.
of-the-lower-classes, (and) the privileges of-candidates

At enim Cato agit cum me austere
But indeed Cato acts (and argues) with me austerely,

et Stoice. Negat esse verum, allici
and like-a-Stoic. He-denies (that) it-is proper, to-conciliate

benevolentiam cibo; negat judicium hominum
good-will by-food; he-denies (that) the judgment of-men

oportere corrumpi voluptatibus in
ought 'to-be (influenced, or) 'corrupted by-pleasures in

mandandis magistratibus. Ergo
confiding (any of) the magistracies (to candidates). Therefore,

causâ petitionis, si quis vocat ad cœnam,
in-the-case of-seeking-office, if any-one invites to supper,

condemnetur. "Quippe," inquit, "tu
he-may-be-condemned. "For-now-indeed," says-he, 'do "you

petas mihi summum imperium, tu
'seek (I would ask) the highest command, (do) you (seek)

summam auctoritatem, tu gubernacula
the greatest authority, (do) you (seek) the helm

reipublicæ, fovendis sensibus hominum, et
of-the-republic, by-pampering the senses of-men, both

deleniendis animis, et adhibendis voluptatibus?
by-soothing the minds, and by-administering pleasures?

Utrum," inquit, "petebas lenocinium a
Whether," says-he, "did-you-ask the-station-of-a-pimp from

grege delicatæ juventutis, an imperium orbis terrarum
a herd of-effeminate young-men, or the command of-the-world

a Romano populo?" Horribilis oratio sed (our)
from the Roman people?" A horrid speech but (our)

usus, vita, mores, civitas ipsa
customs, (our modes of) life, (our) manners, the state itself

respuit eam. Tamen neque 'did
rejects (and refutes) this. However neither 'did

Lacedæmonii, auctores istius vitæ atque
the Lacedæmonians, the authors of this (your mode) of-life and

orationis, qui accumbant quotidianis epulis in
of-speaking, who recline to (their) daily meals on

robore, neque verò Cretes, nemo quorum
hard-oak (benches), nor indeed the Cretans, no-one of-whom

unquam gustavit cubans, retinuerunt suas
ever tastes (any thing) reclining, preserve their

respublicas melius, quàm Romani homines qui
republics better, than the Roman people who

dispertiunt tempora voluptatis que laboris :
set-apart times (for) pleasure and (times for) labour :

quorum alteri deleti sunt uno
of-these the-one [the Cretans] were-destroyed (as a nation) by-one

adventu nostri exercitûs; alteri
invasion of-our army; the other [the Lacedæmonians]

conservant suam disciplinam que leges, præsidio
preserve their discipline and laws, by-the-protection

nostri imperii.
of-our empire.

36. Quare, Cato, noli reprehendere nimium
Wherefore, O Cato, do-not reprehend ¹with too

severâ oratione instituta majorum, quæ res
severe a speech the customs ¹of (our) ¹ancestors, which the thing

ipsa, quæ diuternitas
itself, (in the flourishing state of our affairs), which the long continuance

imperii comprobat. Fuit ex eodem
¹of (our) ¹empire has-shown-to-be-good. There-was of the same

studio, eruditus vir apud nostros
study, [school of the stoics], a learned man among our

patres, homo et honestus et nobilis, Q. Tubero.
fathers, a man both honest and noble, Q. Tubero

Is, cum Q. Maximus daret epulum
(by name). He, when Q. Maximus gave a solemn-feast

Romano populo nomine sui patrui Africani,
to-the-Roman people in-memory ¹of his ¹uncle Africanus,

rogatus est a Maximo, ut sterneret triclinium,
was-requested by Maximus, that he-should-cover the couch,

cum Tubero esset filius
[prepare a banqueting place], as Tubero was the son

sororis ejusdem Africani. Atque ille
of-the-sister of-the-same Africanus. And he

eruditissimus homo, ac Stoicus, stravit
a most-learned man, and a Stoic, covered (means

Punicanos lectulos   hœdinis pelliculis, et
Carthagenian couches with 'little goats' 'skins, and

exposuit vasa   Samia; quasi vere mortuus
set-out vessels (of) Samian-earthenware; as-if indeed the dead

cynicus Diogenes honestaretur, et non mors
cynic Diogenes were-honoured, and not the death

divini hominis Africani; quem, cum Maximus
of (that) 'divine man Africanus; whom, when Maximus

audaret ejus supremo die egit
praised on his last day [day of his death] he-gave

gratias immortalibus diis, quòd ille vir
thanks to-the-immortal gods, because that man [Africanus] 'was

potissimum natus esset, in hac republica; enim
more-especially 'born, in this republic; for

fuisse necesse, imperium terrarum
it-was a necessary (consequence, that) the empire of-the-world

esse ibi, ubi ille esset. In
must-be there, where he might-be (as a citizen). At

celebrandâ morte hujus, Romanus
the celebrating (of) the obsequies of-this man, (Africanus), the Roman

populus tulit graviter hanc perversam sapientiam
people 'were much 'displeased at-this perverse wisdom

Tuberonis. Itaque integerrimus homo, et
of Tubero. Therefore (he, Tubero,) a most-honest man, and

optimus civis, cum esset nepos
most-excellent citizen, (and) also-though-he-was the grandson

L. Paulli, filius, ut dixi, sororis P. Africani,
of-L. Paullus, the son, as I-said, of-the-sister of P. Africanus, (yet)

dejectus est præturâ his
he-lost (his election, when a candidate for the) prætorship, by-these

hœdinis pelliculis. Romanus populus odit
'little goat 'skins. The Roman people hate

privatam luxuriam, diligit publicam magnificentiam,
private luxury, (and) love public magnificence,

non amat profusas epulas, multò minus
'they-do not 'love profuse banquets, much less

sordes et inhumanitatem. Distinguit
sordidness and meanness. 'They distinguish (between)

rationem   officiorum   ac   temporum,   vicissitudinem
the relations   of-duties   and   of-occasions,   the vicissitudes

laboris   ac   voluptatis.   Nam   quod   ais   mentes
of-labour   and   of-pleasure.   For   that   you-say   the minds

hominum   oportere   allici   nullâ   re   ad
of-men   ought   to-be-induced   by-no   thing (else)   in

mandandum magistratum,   nisi   dignitate;
conferring   magistracy,   except   by-dignity   (and worth);

hoc   tu   ipse,   in   quo   est   summa   dignitas,
this   you   yourself,   in   whom   there-is   the greatest   dignity (and worth),

non   servas.   Enim   cur   rogas   quemquam,   ut
'do not   'observe.   For   why   do-you-ask   any-one,   that

studeat   tibi,   ut   adjuvet   te?   Tu
he-should-take-care (of)   your-interest,   that   he-should-help   you?   You

rogas   me,   ut   præsis   mihi,   ut   ego
ask   me,   that   you-may-be-placed-over   me,   that   I

committam   me   tibi.   Quid   tandem?   Oportet,
may-commit   myself   to-you.   What   then?   Is it-proper,

me   rogari   istuc   abs te,   an   te
(that) I   be-asked   this   by-you,   or (that) you (be asked it)

potius   a   me,   ut   suscipias   laborem   que
rather   by   me,   that   you-should-undertake   labour   and

periculum   pro   meâ   salute?   Quid?   quod   habes
perils   for   my   safety?   What?   that   you-have

nomenclatorem?
a nomenclator?   [a slave, who accompanied his master, and whispered

In   eo   quidem   fallis   et
the names of the citizens to him.]   In   this   indeed   you-mislead and

decipis.   Nam   si   est   honestum
deceive.   For   if   it-is   an honourable (and praiseworthy thing),

tuos   cives   appellari   nomine   abs te,
(that) your   fellow-citizens   should-be-addressed   by-name   by   you,

est   turpe   eos   esse   notiores   tuo   servo,
it-is   shameful, (that) they   should-be   better-known   to-your   slave,

quàm   tibi.   Sin   si   etiam   noris,
than   to-yourself.   But   if   also   you-might-have-known (them),

tamen   appellandi   sunt   per
∵   (if through custom)   'they-are (only)   'to-be-addressed   through

monitorem, cur petis
the suggestion of your) prompter, why do-you-ask (the name)

ante, quàm insusurravit? aut quid, cum
before, than he-has-whispered-it-to-you? or why, when

admoneris, tamen salutas ita, quasi noris
you-are-reminded, yet you-salute (them) so, as-if you-had-known

tute? quid posteaquam designatus es, salutas
(them) well? why after you-are-elected, do-you-salute

multò negligentius? Si dirigas omnia hæc
so-much more-negligently? If you-regulate all these (things)

ad rationem civitatis recta sunt, sin velis
according to-the-usages of-the-state they-are-right, but-if you-wish

perpendere ad præcepta disciplinæ
to-weigh (them) according-to the precepts 'of (your) discipline

reperiantur pravissima. Quare
(and sect) they-may-be-found (to be) very-bad. Wherefore

nec isti fructus ludorum gladiatorum conviviorum
neither these enjoyments of-games of-gladiators of-banquets

non eripiendi Romanæ plebi, omnia quæ
'are not 'to-be-taken from-the-Roman people, all which

nostri majores comparaverunt;
our ancestors prepared, (and instituted for their gratifi-

nec est ista benignitas adimenda candidatis,
cation); nor is this kindly-feeling to-be-taken-from the candidates,

quæ significat liberalitatem magis quàm largitionem.
which indicates liberality more than bribery.

87. At enim respublica adduxit te ad
But indeed (the interest of) the republic led you to

accusandum. Credo, Cato, te venisse isto
accuse. I-believe, O Cato, (that) you came with-this

animo et eâ opinione. Sed tu laberis
mind and with-this opinion. But you fall

imprudentiâ. Quod ego facio,
by-imprudence (you act imprudently, and err). That-which I do,

judices, facio cum gratiâ amicitiæ atque dignitatis
O judges, I-do for the sake of-the-friendship and of-the-worth

L. Murenæ, tum clamo atque testor me facere
of-L. Murena, then I-proclaim and attest (that) I do-it

causâ   pacis,   otii,   concordiæ,   libertatis,
for-the-cause of-peace,   of-tranquillity,   of-concord,   of-liberty,

salutis,   denique   vitæ   nostrûm omnium.   Audite,
of-safety,   in-fine   of-the-lives   of-us   all.   Hear,

audite,   judices,   consulem,   dicam   nihil
hear,   O judges,   (your)   consul,   I-will-say   nothing

arrogantius,   dicam tantum   cogitantem
arrogantly,   'I-will (only) 'say   so-much (that I)   thinking

de   republica, totos dies atque noctes.
about the republic,   entire   days   and   nights, (may be allowed to

                              L. Catilina   non despexit
say, with propriety and moderation). L. Catiline 'did not   'despise

atque   contempsit   rempublicam   usque   eo,   ut
and   contemn   the republic   so   far,   that

arbitraretur   se   oppressurum   hanc   civitatem,
he-thought   (that) he   could-reduce   this   city.

eâ   copiâ,   quam   eduxit   cum   se.   Contagio
with-that force,   which   he-led-out   with him. The contagion

illius sceleris patet latius   quàm quisquam putat;
of-that crime spreads more-widely than   any-one   supposes;

pertinet   ad   plures.   Intus,   intus,   inquam
it-belongs   to   many.   Within,   within,   I-say   (that)

Trojanus   equus est;   a quo,   me consule,
the Trojan   horse   is;   by which,   I being-consul, 'you-will

nunquam dormientes   opprimemini.   Quæris
never   sleeping (be surprised and) 'be-oppressed.   You-ask

a me quid ego metuam Catilinam.   Nihil;
of me   why   I   fear   Catiline.   (I fear) nothing (of him);

et   curavi   ne quis metueret;
and   I-have-taken-care (that)   no   one   might-fear   (any thing);

sed   illius   copias,   quas   video   hic,   dico   esse
but   his   forces,   which   I-see   here,   I-say   are

metuendas;   nec est nunc exercitus L. Catilinæ,
to-be-feared,   nor   is   now   the army   of-L.   Catiline,

tam   timendus, quàm isti, qui dicuntur deseruisse
so-much to-be-feared,   as   these-here, who   are-said to-have-deserted

illum exercitum.   Enim   non deseruerunt, sed
that   army   For 'they-have not   deserted,   but

relicti ab illo in speculis atque insidiis, restiterunt
being-left by him as out-posts and ambuscades, remained

in capite atque in nostris cervicibus. Hi
against (our) heads and against our necks. These

volunt et integrum consulem, et bonum imperatorem,
wish both an honest consul, and good commander,

et naturâ et fortunâ conjunctum cum
(one, who is) both by-nature and by-fortune united with

salute reipublicæ, deturbari vestris sententiis,
the safety of-the-republic, to-be-overthrown by-your decision,

dejici de præsidio urbis, et de
(so as) to-be-removed from the protecting of-the-city, and from

custodiâ civitatis. Quorum ferrum et audaciam,
the guardianship of-the-state. Whose weapons and audacity,

ego, judices, rejeci in campo, debili-
I, O judges, have-repulsed in the Campus-Martius, I-have-intimi-

tavi in foro, sæpe etiam compressi
dated (them) in the forum, (and) 'have often also 'repressed

meæ domi ; si vos tradideritis
(their attempts on me) in-my-own house; if you will-have-given-up

his alterum consulem consecuti erunt
to-them the one-of-the-two consuls they-will-have-obtained

plus multò vestris sententiis, quàm suis gladiis.
much more by-your votes, than by-their swords.

Magni interest, judices, esse duo
It-is of-great 'consequence, O judges, (that) there-should-be two

consules in republica kalendis Januariis,
consuls in the republic on-the-kalends of-January [first of January],

id quod ego perfeci, multis repugnantibus.
that which I have-accomplished, many striving-against-it.

Nolite arbitrari mediocribus consiliis, aut usitatis
Do-not think (that) by-moderate counsels, or the usual

viis, aut * * * Non improba lex, non perniciosa
ways, or * * * No bad law, no pernicious

largitio non aliquod malum aliquando auditum
bribery, not any evil at-any-time heard-of

quæritur reipublicæ. Consilia inita sunt
is-sought-for against-the-republic. Plans have-been-entered-into

in   hac   civitate,   judices,   delendæ   urbis,
in   this   city,   O judges,   of-destroying   the town,

trucidandorum civium, extinguendi Romani nominis.
of-massacring   the citizens, of-extinguishing the Roman   name.

Atque   hæc,   cives,   cives inquam, (si est fas
And   these-things, citizens, citizens I-say, (if it-is rig

eos   appellari   hoc   nomine), et cogitant et
(that) they be-called by-this name), both think and

cogitaverunt de suâ patriâ; ego quotidie occurro
have-thought against their country; I daily counteract

consiliis   horum.   Debilito   audaciam,
the plans of-these-men. I-weaken (their) audacity, (and)

resisto   sceleri.   Sed moneo vos, judices,
resist   (their) wickedness. But I-admonish you, O judges;

meus consulatus est jam   in   exitu: nolite
my   consulship is now (nearly) in (its) termination: do-not

subtrahere mihi   vicarium   meæ dili-
take-from   me one-who-is-to-supply-my-place (in) my   dili-

gentiæ;   nolite   eum adimere,
gence,   (and care for the republic); do-not 'take him   'away,

cui cupio tradere rempublicam incolumem,
to-whom I-desire to-give-over the republic   safe.

defendendam ab his tantis periculis.
to-be-defended from these so-great dangers.

38. Atque   non videtis, judices, quid   aliud
And   'do-you not 'see, O judges, what other evil

accedat ad hæc mala? Te, te, Cato, appello;
accedes to these evils? You, you, O Cato, I-address;

nonne prospicis tempestatem tui anni?
do-you not foresee the storm of-your-own year

jam enim hesternâ concione perniciosa
(of tribuneship)? now indeed in-yesterday's assembly the pernicious

vox tribuni designati, tui collegæ, intonuit; contra
voice of-a-tribune elect, your colleague, sounded-forth; against

quem tua   mens   multùm,   omnes
whom your-own mind and foresight (provided) much, (also) 'did all

boni providerunt, qui vocaverunt te ad
good-men 'provide-against who requested you to

petitionem   tribunatûs.   Omnia,   quæ
be-a-candidate   (for)   the tribuneship.   All,   which

agitata sunt   per hoc
have-been-agitated (and plotted against the Republic) for these (last)

triennium, jam scitis   esse   ab eo tempore,
three-years,   as   you-know to-have-been from that   time,

quo   consilium initum   a L. Catilinâ et Cn.
a-which   the plot was-entered-into by   L. Catiline and Cn.

Pisone interficiendi senatûs, erumpunt in hos dies,
Piso   of massacring the senate, break-out in these days,

in hos menses, in hoc tempus. Qui locus est,
in these months, in this   time.   What place is-there,

judices, quod tempus, qui dies, quæ nox, cum ego
O judges, what time, what day, what night, that   I

non   eripiar   atque evolem ex insidiis ac
'am not 'snatched-from and   escape from the snares and

mucronibus istorum,   non solum meo   consilio,
swords   of-these-men,   not only by-my-own   counsel

sed etiam multò magis divino ?
(and precaution), but indeed much more-so by-divine (counsel

Neque   isti volunt me   interfici
and providence)?   Nor do these-men 'wish me   to-be-killed

meo nomine,   sed demovere
on-my-own name, [on my own individual account,] but   to-remove

vigilantem consulem de   præsidio reipublicæ ;
a vigilant   consul   from the guardianship of-the-republic;

nec   minus vellent, Cato, tollere te quoque,
nor 'do-they the less 'wish, O Cato, to-remove you   also,

si possent, aliquâ ratione ; id quòd, crede mihi,
if they-could, by-any means;   that which, believe   me

et agunt et   moliuntur.   Vident,
(they are) both attempting and endeavouring-to-effect).   They-see

quantùm sit in te animi, quantùm ingenii,
how-much there-is in you of-courage, how-much of-talent,

quantùm   auctoritatis,   quantùm præsidii
how-much of-weight-of-character, how much of-protection (for,

reipublicæ ; sed cum   viderint   tribunitiam vim
the republic;   but when they-have-perceived the tribunitian power

spoliatum consulari auctoritate, et auxilio, tum
deprived of-the-consular authority, and assistance, then

arbitrantur, se facilius oppressuros
they-think, (that) they 'will the-more-easily 'oppress (and over-

te inermem et debilitatum. Nam non
some) you defenceless and weakened. For 'they-do not

timent, ne consul sufficiatur.
'fear, lest (another) consul should-be-substituted (in place of

Vident te fore in
Murena, should he be condemned). They-see (that) you will-be in

potestate tuorum collegarum; sperant Silanum,
the power of-your colleagues; they-hope (that) Silanus.

clarum virum, sine collegâ, te sine consule,
an illustrious man, without a colleague, you without a consul,

rempublicam sine præsidio, posse objici sibi.
the republic without a protection, may-be exposed to-them

In his tantis rebus, que in
(in their attacks on it). In these such-great affairs, and in

tantis periculis est tuum, M. Cato, qui natus es
such-great dangers it-is your part, O M. Cato, who are-born

non mihi, non tibi, sed patriæ, videre quid
not for-me, not for-yourself, but 'for your 'country, to-see what

agatur retinere adjutorem, defensorem, socium
may-be-done to-retain an assistant, defender, (and) associate

in republica, consulem, consulem non cupidum,
in the republic, (as) consul, a consul not ambitious,

(quod hoc tempus maxime
(or desirous of change), (which this (present) time greatly

postulat) constitutum fortunâ ad amplexandum
requires) formed 'by (his) 'fortune to embrace

otitum; scientiâ ad gerendum
(and enjoy) ease and leisure; with-the-knowledge to carry-on

bellum; animo et usu ad quod negotium
war; of-mind and experience for any business

velis.
you may-wish.

89. Quanquam, omnis potestas hujusce rei
Although, all the power of-this affair

sita est in vobis, judices; vos in hac causâ
is-placed in you, O judges; you in this cause

tenetis, vos gubernatis totam rempublicam. Si
hold, you govern the whole republic. If

L. Catilina cum suo consilio nefariorum hominum,
L. Catiline with his council of-infamous men.

quos eduxit cum se, posset judicare de nas
whom he-took-out with him, could judge concerning this

re, condemnaret L. Murenam; si posset
affair, he-would-condemn L. Murena; if he-coul.

interficere occideret. Enim rationes illius
'put (him) 'to death, he-would-kill (him). For the plans of-this-man

petunt, ut respublica orbetur auxilio;
require, that the republic should-be-deprived 'of (its proper) 'assistance,

ut copia imperatorum contra suum
that the number-and-power of-the commanders opposed (to) his

furorem minuatur; ut major facultas detur
fury may-be-diminished; that greater power may-be-given

tribunis plebis, adversario depulso,
to-the-tribunes of-the-people, (his) opponent (Murena) being-rejected,

concitandæ seditionis ac discordiæ.
for the purpose) of-exciting sedition and discord

Igitur honestissimi atque sapientissimi viri,
Therefore the most-honourable and most-wise men,

delecti ex amplissimis ordinibus,
selected from the highest orders, (of the state, for judges in

nè judicabunt idem, quod ille
this case,) 'will not 'judge the same, as that

importunissimus gladiator, hostis reipublicæ,
most-dangerous gladiator [Catiline], the enemy of-the-republic,

judicaret? Credite mihi, judices, in hac causâ,
would-judge? Believe me, O judges, (that) in this case,

non solùm feretis sententiam de
'you not only 'pronounce judgment on (the safety)

L. Murenæ, etiam verùm de vestrâ salute.
of-L. Murena, (but) also indeed on your-own safety

Venimus in extremum discrimen; est nihil jam,
We-have-come into extreme danger; there-is nothing now,

unde   nos   reficiamus,   aut   ubi   lapsi
whence we   may-repair (our strength), or   where   fallen

resistamus.   Non   solùm   auxilia,   quæ   habemus
we-may-resist.   Not   only   the resources,   which   we-have

non   minuenda,   sed   etiam   nova,   si   possit
'are   not 'to-be-diminished, but   also   new-ones,   if   it-can

fieri   comparanda.   Enim   hostis   est   non   apud
e-done   are-to-be-procured.   For the enemy is   not   on

Anienem,   quod,   Punico   bello   visum est   gravissi-
the Anio,   which, in-the-Punic war   appeared   the most-grievous-

mum,   sed   in   urbe,   in   foro   (immortales   dii !
thing,   but   in   the city, in the forum   (O immortal   gods!

potest   hoc   dici   sine   gemitu ;)   etiam   est
can   this   be-said   without   a sigh ;)   also   there-is [are]

non-nemo   hostis   in   illo   sacrario   reipublicæ,
some   enemies   in   this   sanctuary   of-the-republic,

inquam   non nemo in   curiâ   ipsâ.   Dii
I-say   (there are) some   in the senate-house itself. 'May the gods

faxint, ut meus collega,   fortissimus vir,   armatus,
grant,   that my colleague, a most-brave man, 'may,   armed,

opprimat   hoc   nefarium   latrocinium Catilinæ ;   ego
'suppress   this   nefarious   armed-robbery of-Catiline ;   I

togatus,   vobis que   omnibus bonis   adjutoribus,
a civilian,   you and   all   good (men) being-assistants

discutiam et comprimam   consilio hoc periculum.
will-dispel and   crush   'by (my) 'counsel this   danger.

quod conceptum,   respublica   parturit.   Sed
which   conceived (in it), the republic is-about-to-bring forth. But

quid   tandem fiet,   si   hæc,   elapsa de nostris
what 'will in-fine 'happen, if these-things, escaped from   our

manibus,   redundarint,   in   eum   annum, qui
hands,   should-make-their-appearance in   that   year,   which

consequitur?   Erit   unus consul, et is non
follows   (this)?   There-will-be (only) one consul, and he   not

occupatus in   administrando   bello,   sed   in
occupied in   conducting   warlike-affairs, but   in

sufficiendo   collegua.   Jam   qui
procuring the-election-of-a-colleague, (in the consulship). Now those-who

impedituri sint hunc * * * illa immanis pestis,
will-hinder him * * * that enormous pest,

importuna, prorumpet, quâ poterit; et jam
dangerous, will-break-forth, where it-can; and already

minatur Romano populo; repente advolabit in
it-is-threatening the Roman people; suddenly it-will-fly to

suburbanos agros; furor versabitur in castris, timor
the suburban districts; fury will-prevail in the camp, fear

in curiâ, conjuratio in foro, exercitus in
in the senate-house, conspiracy in the forum, an army in

Campo, vastitas in agris; autem in omni
the Campus-Martius, devastation in the country; but in every

sede ac loco metuemus flammam que ferrum.
habitation and place we-fear the fire and the sword.

Quæ jamdiu comparantur, omnia
These things), which 'are for-a-long-time 'prepared, all

ista eadem, si respublica ornata erit suis
these same, if the republic should-be-provided 'with her (proper)

præsidiis, facile comprimentur; et consiliis
'defences, 'will easily 'be-repressed; both by-the-counsels

magistratuum, et diligentiâ privatorum.
of-the-magistrates, and by-the-diligence of-private-persons.

40. Quæ, judices, cum sint ita, primum,
Which-things, O judges, as they-are so, in-the-first-place,

causâ reipublicæ, qua nulla res debet esse
for-the-sake of-the-republic, (than) which no thing ought to-be

potior cuiquam, moneo vos pro meâ summâ
dearer to-any-one, I-admonish you on-account-of my very-great

diligentiâ in rempublicam et
diligence (and zeal) in (the affairs of) the republic and (well)

cognita vobis, pro consulari auctoritate
known to-you on-account-of (my) consular authority

hortor, pro magnitudine periculi obtestor,
I-exhort (you), on-account-of-the-greatness of-the-danger I-entreat

ut otio, ut paci, ut saluti, ut
(you), that for-tranquillity, that for-peace, that 'for (your) 'safety, tha

vestræ vitæ et, ceterorum civium, consulatis,
for-your life and (that), of-the-rest of-the-citizens, you-would-consult

deinde ego, adductus officio defen-
(and take measures); next I, induced by-the-duty of-a-de-

soris et amici, oro atque obsecro, judices,
fender, and of-a-friend, do-pray and entreat, O judges,

vestram fidem, ut ne obruatis recentem
your good-faith, that 'you-do not overwhelm the recent

gratulationem miseri hominis, L. Murenæ, et
felicitations of-a-distressed man, L. Murena, and

confecti cum morbo corporis, tum dolore animi,
afflicted with disease of-body, as-well-as with distress of-mind,

novâ lamentatione. Modò ornatus maximo
by-a-new (cause of) lamentation. Just honoured with-the-greatest

beneficio Romani populi, videbatur fortunatus,
favour of-the-Roman people, he-seemed-to-be fortunate,

quòd primus attulisset consulatum in
because 'he first 'had-brought (the honour of) the consulship into

veterem familiam, primus in antiquissimum
an old family, (and) first into a most-ancient

municipium; nunc idem sordidus
municipality ; now the same-person (of) squalid-appearance, (on

squalore, confectus morbo, perditus
account of his), neglected-dress, afflicted with-sickness, spent

lacrymis ac mœrore, est vester supplex, judices,
with-tears and sorrow, is your suppliant, O judges,

obtestatur vestram fidem, implorat misericordiam,
he-invokes your good-faith, he-implores (your) compassion,

intuetur vestram potestatem, ac vestras opes.
he-earnestly-looks to-your power, and to-your might.

Nolite, per immortales deos, judices, privare eum
Do-not, by the immortal gods, O judges, deprive him

hac re, qua putavit, se fore honesti-
of-that thing, by-which he-thought, (that) he would-become more-hon-

orem, etiam ceteris honestatibus ante
oured, (but) also of-other honours, (which he had) before

partis, atque omni dignitate que fortunâ. Itaque
obtained, and of-all (his) dignity and fortune. Therefore

ita, judices, L. Murena orat atque obsecrat vos,
so, O judges, 'does L. Murena 'pray and entreat you.

si injuste læsit neminem; si violavit
(that) if 'he-has unjustly 'injured no-one; if he-has-offended

aures ve voluntatem nullius; si, ut levissime
the ears or desires of-no-one; if, as 'I-may most-moderately

dicam, fuit odio nemini, nec domi nec
'say, he-was (a cause of) hatred to-no-one, neither at-home nor

militiæ, sit apud vos locus modestiæ
in-war, may-there-be with you an asylum (for) moderation

sit perfugium demissis hominibus,
may-there-be (with you) a refuge for-dejected men,

sit auxilium pudori. Spoliatio
may-there-be (with you) encouragement for-modesty. The depriving

consulatûs debet, judices, habere magnam miseri-
of-the-consulship ought, O judges, to-excite great compas-

cordiam. Enim unà cum consulatu omnia
sion (in you). For together with the consulship all-things

eripiuntur. Vero, his temporibus, consulatus
are-taken-away. Indeed, in-these times, the consulship

ipse potest habere nullam invidiam.
itself can have no envy. [The consulship is not

Enim objicitur concionibus sedi-
to be envied.] For (the consul) is-exposed to-the-harangues of-the-

tiosorum, insidiis conjuratorum, telis Ca-
seditious, to-the-plots of-conspirators, (and) to-the-weapons of-Ca-

tilinæ; denique opponitur solus ad omne periculum,
tiline; in-fine it-is-opposed alone to every danger,

atque ad omnem invidiam. Quare, judices,
and to all (kinds of) unpopularity. Wherefore, O judges,

non video quid invidendum sit Murenæ, aut
'I-do not 'see what may-be-envied (in) Murena, or

cuiquam nostrûm, in hoc præclaro consulatu.
any-one of-us, in this distinguished (office of) consulship

Vero quæ sunt miseranda, ea
But (those things) which are to-be-commiserated (in it), these

versantur ante mihi oculos, et vos potestis videre
are-present before (my) eyes, and you may see

et perspicere.
and clearly-perceive (them).

41. Si (quod omen Jupiter avertat!)
If (which omen 'may Jupiter 'avert!)

afflixeritis hunc vestris sententiis, quò
you-should-condemn this-man by-your sentence, whither 'will

miser vertet se? domumne? ut eam
the-miserable-man 'turn himself? home? that that

imaginem clarissimi viri, sui parentis, quam
image of-a-most-illustrious man, his parent, which

paucis diebus ante, conspexit laureatam, in
a few days before, he-had-beheld crowned-with-laurels, for

suâ gratulatione, videat eandem deformatam
his congratulation, he-may-see the same (now) disfigured

ignominiâ que lugentem? an ad matrem, quæ
with-ignominy and in-mourning? whether to (his) mother, who

misera modo osculata suum filium con-
wretched (woman) 'had just 'kissed her son (as) con-

sulem, nunc cruciatur et sollicita est, ne paullo
sul, now tormented and agitated, lest a little

post conspiciat eundem spoliatum omni dignitate?
after she-may-behold him deprived of-all (his) dignity

Sed quid ego appello matrem aut
(and honours)? But why 'do I 'mention mother or

domum, quem nova pœna legis privat, et domo
home, whom the new penalty of-the-law deprives, both of-home

et parente, consuetudine que conspectu omnium
and parent, (and) of-the-intercourse and sight of-all

suorum. Igitur miser ibit
his (relations and acquaintances). Therefore the miserable-man will-go

in exsilium? Quo? ne ad partes Orientis, in
into exile? Where? whether to the parts of-the-East, in

quibus fuit multos annos legatus, et duxit
which he-was for-many years a lieutenant, and led (and

exercitus, et gessit magnas res? At
commanded) armies, and performed great things? But

habet magnum dolorem reverti eodem cum
it-occasions great sorrow to-return to-the-same-place with

ignominiâ, unde decesseris cum honore. An
ignominy, whence you-had-departed with honour. But

abdet se in contrariam partem terrarum, ut
should-he-hide himself in a different part of-the-earth, as

Transalpina Gallia, quem nuper libentissime viderit
Transalpine Gaul, whom lately 'it most-willingly 'saw

cum summo imperio, videat eundem
(invested) with supreme power, (now) may-see the same-person

lugentem, mœrentem exsulem? In eâ provinciâ
mourning, grieving (and) an exile? In that province

porro, quo animo, adspiciet suum fratrem,
moreover, with-what state-of-mind, would-he-behold his brother,

C. Murenam? qui erit dolor hujus? qui
C. Murena? what will-be the grief of-this-one? [Murena] what

mœror illius? quæ lamentatio utriusque?
the sadness of-that-one? [his brother] what the lamentation of-both?

autem quanta perturbatio fortunæ, atque sermonis,
but what an alteration of-fortune, and of-speech,

quòd, in locis quibus paucis diebus ante, nuntii
that, in the places in-which a few days before, messengers,

que literæ celebrassent, Murenam esse factum
and letters had-joyfully-announced, (that) Murena was-made

consulem, et unde hospites atque amici concur-
consul, and whence (his) guests and friends had-

rerint Romam gratulatum, repente eo accedat
flocked to-Rome to-congratulate (him), suddenly there arrives

ipse nuntius suæ calamitatis? Quæ
the same messenger (with the news) of-his calamity? Which-things

si sunt acerba, si misera, si
if they-are harsh, if (they are) miserable, if (they are)

luctuosa, si alienissima a vestrâ mansuetudine
lamentable, if (they are) most-foreign to your clemency

et misericordiâ, judices, conservate beneficium
and mercy, O judges, preserve (for him) the favour

Romani populi; reddite
of-the-Roman people, (that they have conferred on him); restore

consulem reipublicæ; date hoc pudori
the consul to-the-republic; grant this to-the-modesty

ipsius, date mortuo patri, date
of-the-man-himself, grant (it) 'to (his) 'dead father, grant (it) 'to (his'

generi et familiæ, date etiam Lanuvio honestissimo
kindred and family, grant (it) also to-Lanuvium a most-honourable

municipio, quod vidistis frequens que
municipality, (the inhabitants of) which you-have-seen thronging and

mœstum in totâ hac causâ. Nolite avellere a
sad in all this cause. Do-not tear from

patriis sacris Junonis Sospitæ, cui est necesse
the paternal sacrifices of-Juno Sospita, to-whom it-is necessary

omnes consules facere, domesticum et suum
(for) all consuls to-sacrifice, her-domestic and her

potissimum consulem. Quem ego, si commendatio
most-especial consul. Whom I, if (my) recommendation

habet quid momenti, aut mea confirmatio
have any weight, or my strong-assurance (any)

auctoritatis, consul, judices, ita commendo consulem,
authority, (I) consul, O judges, so recommend the consul

ut promittam et spondeam, futurum esse
(elect), that I-promise and will-answer-for-him, (that) he-will-be

cupidissimum otii, studiocissimum
most-desirous of-tranquillity (in public affairs), most-anxious

bonorum, acerrimum contra seditionem,
(for the welfare) of-good-men, most-active against sedition,

fortissimum in bello, inimicissimum huic conjurationi,
most-brave in war, most-inimical to-this conspiracy

quæ nunc labefactat rempublicam.
(of Catiline), which now shakes the republic.

ORATIO
THE ORATION

M. TULLII CICERONIS,
OF M. TULLIUS CICERO,

PRO
FOR

Q. LIGARIO.
Q. LIGARIUS.

1. **MEUS propinquus**, Q. Tubero, detulit ad te,
My relation, Q. Tubero, has-brought before you,

C. Cæsar, novum, et ante hunc diem, inauditum
O C. Cæsar, a new, and before this day, unheard-of

crimen, Q. Ligarium fuisse in Africâ; que C.
crime, (that) Q. Ligarius was in Africa; and C.

Pansa, vir præstanti ingenio, fretus fortasse
Pansa, a man (of) excellent talent, trusting perhaps (to)

eâ familiaritate, quæ est ei cum te,
that familiarity, which is to-him with you, [familiarity, that

ausus est confiteri. Itaque nescio
exists between you,] has-ventured to-confess-it. Therefore I-know-not

quò vertam me. Enim veneram paratus,
where I-may-turn myself. For I-had-come prepared,

quum tu neque scires id per te, neque potuisses
as you neither knew it of yourself, nor could-have

audire aliunde, ut abuterer tuâ ignoratione
heard (it) any-where, that I-might-abuse your ignorance

ad salutem miseri hominis. Sed quoniam quod
or the safety of-a-miserable man. But because that-which

latebat, diligentiâ inimici investigatum est,
was-concealed, by-the-diligence 'of (his) 'enemy has-been-discovered,

confitendum est, ut opinor; præsertim quum meus
it-must-be-confessed, as I-suppose; especially when my

necessarius Pansa fecerit, ut id esset non jam
friend Pansa has-acted (so), that it would not now

integrum; que controversiâ omissâ, omnis
be-in-my-power (to deny it); and controversy being-omitted, all

oratio conferenda est ad tuam misericordiam
(my) speech must-be-addressed to your mercy

quâ plurimi conservati sunt, quum impetravissent
by-which many have-been-preserved, when they-had-besought

a te non liberationem culpæ, sed veniam
from you not a release (from) crime, but pardon (for)

errati. Igitur, Tubero, habes, quod est maxime
error. Therefore, O Tubero, you-have, what is greatly

optandum accusatori, confitentem reum; sed
to-be-wished-for (by) an accuser, a confessing defendant; but

tamen confitentem hoc, se fuisse in eâ parte,
however confessing this, (that) he was in that part,

quâ te, quâ tuum patrem, virum
[Africa,] in-which you, (were), in-which your father, a man

dignum omni laude. Itaque est prius necesse
worthy (of) all praise (was). Therefore it-is first necessary

confitemini de vestro delicto, quàm
(that) you-confess your-own fault, than (that)

reprehendatis ullam culpam Ligarii.
you-may-reprehend any fault of-Ligarius.

Enim Q. Ligarius, quum esset nulla suspicio
For Q. Ligarius, when there-was no suspicion

belli, profectus est in Africam, cum C. Considio,
of-war, went to Africa, with C. Considius,

legatus; in quâ legatione, probavit se ita,
as-lieutenant; in which lieutenancy, he-proved himself so,

et civibus et sociis, ut Considius,
(acceptable), both to-the-citizens and to-the-allies, that Considius,

decedens provinciâ, posset non satisfacere
(on) departing from-the-province, could not have-satisfied

hominibus, si **præfecisset** alium **quemquam**
the people, if he-had-placed any other-whatever (over)

provinciæ Itaque **Ligarius** quum diu **recusans**
the province. Therefore Ligarius when (by) long refusing

profecisset nihil, **invitus** accepit provinciam;
he-had-accomplished nothing, against-his-will he-accepted the province;

cui præfuit sic in pace, ut ejus integritas ac
over-which he-presided so in peace, that his integrity and

fides esse gratissima, et civibus et sociis
good-faith were most-acceptable, both 'to (our) 'citizens and allies

Subito bellum exarsit; quod
On-a-sudden the war, (between Pompey and Cæsar) broke-out; which

qui erant in Africâ audierunt
(war) those-who were in Africa heard-of (its actually)

geri, ante quàm parari.
being-waged, before (they heard) that preparations-were-made (for it).

Quo audito, partim inconsideratâ cupiditate,
Which being-heard, partly by-inconsiderate zeal,

partim quodam cæco timore, quærebant
partly (on account of) some blind fear, they-sought-for

aliquem ducem, primò salutis, post
some-one (as) leader, at-first, (indeed, for the sake) of-safety, afterwards

etiam sui studii; quum Ligarius spectans
also (led by) their-party zeal; when Ligarius looking

domum, cupiens redire ad suos,
(towards) home, (and) desiring to-return to his (relations and

passus est se implicari nullo negotio.
friends), suffered himself to-be-implicated in-no (such) business.

Interim P. Atius Varus, qui prætor obtinuerat
In-the-mean-time P. Atius Varus, who (as) prætor had-obtained

Africam, venit Uticam; statim concur
Africa, (as his province,) came to-Utica; immediately there-was-

sum est ad eum. Atque ille arripuit imperium,
a-flocking to him. And he seized on-the-command,

non mediocri cupiditate, si illud potuit esse
'with no moderate 'cupidity, if that could be

imperium, quod deferebatur ad privatum, clamore
command, which was-conferred on a private-person, by the clamour

imperitæ multitudinis, nullo publico
of-an-ignorant mob, (and having the sanction of) no public

consilio. Itaque Ligarius, qui cuperet effugere
council. Therefore Ligarius, who desired to-avoid

omne tale negotium, conquievit paulum adventu
all such affairs, rested for-a-while by-the-arrival

Vari.
of-Vari.

2. Adhuc, C. Cæsar, Q. Ligarius vacat omni
To-this-point, C. Cæsar, Q. Ligarius is-free from-all

culpâ. Egressus est domo non modò
blame. He-left home not only, (for the purpose of

ad nullum bellum, sed ne quidem ad minimam
joining) in no war, but not indeed with the least

suspicionem belli; profectus legatus
suspicion (of embarking in any) war; he-went (as) a lieutenant

in pace, ita gessit se in pacatissimâ
in (time of) peace, 'he so 'conducted himself in a most-peaceable

provinciâ, ut expediret ei pacem
province, that it-advantaged him (that) peace (should continue)

esse. Profectio certe debet non
to-be. (His) departure (from Rome) certainly ought not

offendere tuum animum; num igitur remansio?
to-offend your mind; then-why therefore (his) remaining

Multò minus; nam profectio habuit
(in Africa)? Much less; for (his) going-thither had

non turpem voluntatem, etiam remansio
no discreditable intent, (so) also (his) remaining (there was)

honestam necessitatem. Ergo hæc duo tempora
au honest necessity. Therefore these two periods

carent crimine: unum, quum profectus est legatus;
are-free from-reproach: the one, when he-went (as) lieutenant

alterum quum efflagitatus a provinciâ præpositus est
the other when being-importuned by the province he-was-placed-over

Africæ. Tertium tempus, est quo post
Africa. The third period, is (that) in-which after

adventum Vari restitit in Africâ: quod si est
the arrival of-Varus he-remained in Africa: which if it-is

criminosum est crimen necessitatis, non voluntatis.
criminal   is   a crime of-necessity,   not   of-will.

An   ille, si potuisset ullo modo evadere, maluisset
Whether he, if   he-could in-any manner have-escaped, would-rather

esse Uticæ, quàm Romæ, cum P. Atio,   quàm
be   at-Utica, than   at-Rome, with P. Atius (rather), than

cum   concordissimis   fratribus, cum
with   (his)   most-united   (and beloved) brothers,   with

alienis,   quàm cum   suis?   Quum
strangers (rather),   than   with his-friends-and-relations? When (his)

legatio   ipsa fuisset plena desiderii ac
government (in Africa) itself   was   full   of-regret and

sollicitudine, propter quendam incredibilem amorem
solicitude,   on-account-of some   incredible   affection

         fratrum, potuit hic esse   æquo   animo,
(for his) brothers, could   he be in-an-easy-state (of) mind,

distractus a   fratribus, discidio belli?   Igitur,
separated   from (his) brothers, by-the-discords of-war? Therefore,

Cæsar, habes adhuc nullum signum, in Q. Ligario,
O Cæsar, you-have as-yet   no   sign,   in Q. Ligarius.

alienæ   voluntatis   a   te.   Animadverte,
of-an-unfriendly disposition   towards you.   Observe,

ego quæso   quâ   fide   defendam causam
I   entreat (you) with-what confidence (in you) I-defend the cause

cujus;   prodo meam, O admirabilem clementiam,
of-this-man; (and) declare my-own, O   admirable   clemency,

atque   decorandum laude omnium, præadicatione,
and (worthy) to-be-celebrated by-the-praise of-all,   by-proclamation,

literis   que monumentis! M. Cicero defendit
by-written-records and   monuments!   M. Cicero   defends

         alium   apud te,   fuisse non in ea
(and pleads for) another before you, (who) was   not   in that

voluntate,   in qua confitetur
disposition   (of mind against you), in which he-confesses (that)

se ipsum fuisse, nec extimescit tuas tacitas
he himself was,   nor does-he-dread your   silen*

cogitationes, nec reformidat quid occurrat
thoughts,   nor does-he-fear   what   may-occur

tĭbi,   de   se ipso,   audienti   de
to-you. concerning himself, (while) hearing, (what he is pleading) for

alio
another.

3. Vide, quàm   non reformidem!
        See,   that 'I-am not   'afraid   (to express my

                vide quanta   lux   tuæ liberalitatis,
opinion before you)! see   how   the light of-your   liberality

et sapientiæ   oboriatur   mihi   dicenti   apud te!
and wisdom   rises   on-me speaking   before you!

contendam   voce quantùm   potero,   ut Romanus
I-will-raise   (my) voice as-much-as I-shall-be-able, that the Roman

populus exaudiat hoc.   Bello   suscepto,
people   may-hear   it.   The war   being-undertaken,

Cæsar,   etiam   ex magnâ   parte   gesto,
) Cæsar,   also   for a great   part (already) carried-on,

coactus nullâ vi,   judicio ac voluntate
constrained by-no force, 'from (my own) 'judgment and free-will

profectus sum   ad   ea   arma,   quæ   sumpta erant
    I-went   to those arms,   which were-taken-up

contra te.   Apud quem
against you. [I joined the armies opposed to you.] Before whom

igitur dico hoc?   Nempe apud eum, qui quum
then   do-I-say this?   Indeed before him,   who   when

        sciret hoc,   tamen antequam vidit   me,
(though) he-knew this,   yet   before   he-saw   me

reddidit   reipublicæ: qui misit literas ad me
restored (me) to-the-republic: who sent letters to me

ex Ægypto, ut essem idem, qui fuissem; qui,
from Ægypt,   that I-might-be the same, which I-had-been; who,

quum ipse esset unus   imperator, in toto
when   he-himself was   the one (sole) commander, in the entire

imperio Romani populi, passus est me esse alterum;
empire of-the-Roman people,   suffered me to-be the other;

a   quo,   hoc ipso C. Pansâ   perferente
from whom [Cæsar], this   same C. Pansa (came)   bringing

mihi hunc nuntium   tenui   concessos
me   this   message (that) I-might-retain the conceded (faces of a

laureatos,   quoad   putavi
successful commander) wreathed-with-laurel, as long-as I-thought

tenendos; qui tum denique putavit
(proper), (that) they-might-be-kept; who then at-last thought

se   reddere mihi salutem, si dedisset
(that) he (did not properly) 'grant me' safety, unless he-gave

eam spoliatam nullis ornamentis. Vide quæso,
it despoiled of-no honours-and-dignities. See, I-pray

Tubero, ut, qui non dubitem dicere de
(you), O Tubero, that (I), who 'do not 'hesitate to-speak concerning

meo facto, audeam de Ligarii. Atque
my-own actions, may-dare (to speak) of (those) of-Ligarius. And

dixi hæc propterea de me, ut
I-have-said these-things on-that-account concerning myself, that

Tubero ignosceret mihi quum dicerem eadem
Tubero may-pardon me when I-say the same-things

de se; cujus industriæ que gloriæ ego
concerning himself; whose industry and renown I

faveo, vel propter propinquam cognationem,
applaud, either on-account-of (our) near relationship,

vel quòd delector ejus ingenio que studiis,
or because I-am-pleased 'with his 'talents and zeal,

vel quòd existimo laudem adolescentis pro-
or because I-think (that) the praise of-a-young-man (my) re-

pinqui, etiam redundare ad aliquem fructum
lation, also redounds to some advantage (of)

meum. Sed quæro hoc: quis putat esse crimen,
my-own. But I-ask this: who thinks (it) to-be a crime,

fuisse in Africâ? Is nempe, qui et ipse
to-have-been in Africa? (Why) he indeed, who both himself

voluit esse in eâdem Africâ, et queritur, se
wished to-be in the same Africa, and complains, (that) he

prohibitum a Ligario; et certe congressus est
was-prohibited by Ligarius; and (who) certainly assembled

armatus contra Cæsarem ipsum. Quid
(with others) armed against Cæsar himself. What

enim, Tubero, ille tuus destrictus gladius agebat
indeed, O Tubero, 'did that 'your drawn sword 'do

in acie Pharsalia? cujus latus ille mucro
in the battle (of) Pharsalia? whose side 'was that sword

petebat? qui erat sensus tuorum
(of yours) 'aimed-at? what was the meaning (and intent) of-your

armorum? quæ tua mens, oculi, manus ardor
arms? what your mind, eyes, hands, (and) ardour

animi? quid cupiebas? quid optabas? Urgeo
of-soul? what did-you-desire? what did-you-wish? (But) I-am-urging

nimis; adolescens videtur commoveri: revertar
too-strongly; the young-man seems to-be-moved: I-will-return

ad me; fui in armis in iisdem.
to myself; I-was (also) in arms in the same (cause).

4. Autem quid aliud, Tubero, egimus, nisi,
But what else, Tubero, are-we-in-want-of, unless,

ut quod hic potest, nos posse-
that which he [Cæsar] can-do, (in acts of clemency,) we might-be-

mus? Quorum impunitas igitur, Cæsar, est
able-to-do? Whose impunity therefore, O Cæsar, is

laus tuæ clementiæ, oratio eorum ipsorum,
the praise of-your clemency, 'shall the speech of-these same-men,

acuet te ad crudelitatem? Atque in
(the accusers,) 'stir you 'up to cruelty? And in

hac causâ, Tubero, equidem desidero nonnihil,
this cause, O Tubero, 'I indeed 'miss in-some-degree,

etiam tuam prudentiam, sed multò magis tui
not-only your prudence, but much more (that) of-your

patris; quòd homo quum excellens
father; because (this) man (your father) when excelling

ingenio, tum etiam doctrinâ, non
'by (his) 'talents, as also 'by (his) 'learning, 'did not

viderit, quod genus causæ hoc esset; nam si
'see, what kind of-cause this might-be; for if

vidisset, maluisset agi a te
he-had-perceived (it), he-would-rather (that it) were-conducted by you

quovis modo profectò, quàm isto.
in-any (other) manner indeed, than in-this (of yours).

Arguis fatentem; est
You-accuse (one) confessing (what you allege against him); (this) is

non satis; accusas eum, qui habet causam, aut ut
not enough; you-accuse him, who has a cause, either as

ego dico, meliorem quàm tu; aut ut tu
I say, better than you (have); or as you

vis parem. Hæc admirabilia: sed quod
will-have-it equal. These-things (are) strange: but what

dicam est simile prodigii. Ista accusatio habet
I-am-about-to-say is like a prodigy. This accusation has

non eam vim, ut Q. Ligarius condemnetur,
not that force (and object), that Q. Ligarius should-be-condemned,

sed ut necetur. Nemo, Romanus civis,
but that he-should-be-killed. No-one, a Roman citizen, (ever)

egit hoc ante te. Isti externi mores
did this before you. These foreign manners (are accustomed)

incitari odio usque ad sanguinem,
to-be-excited by-hatred even to (spilling) blood, (and are the

aut levium Græcorum aut immanium
manners) either of-fickle Greeks or of-ferocious

barbarorum. Nam quid aliud agis?
barbarians. For what else are-you-doing? (that) 'he-may

ne sit Romæ? ut careat domo?
not 'be in-Rome? that he-may-be-deprived of-home? (that) 'he-may

ne vivat cum optimis fratribus, ne cum hoc
not 'live with (his) most-excellent brothers, nor with this

T. Broccho avunculo, ne cum ejus filio, suo
T. Brocchus (his) uncle, nor with his son, his

consobrino, ne cum nobis? ne sit in
cousin, nor with us? (that) 'he-may not 'be in (his)

patriâ? Est num? potest num carere omnibus
country? Is-it then-so? can-he then want all

his magis, quàm caret?
these-things more, than 'he-does (actually now) 'want (them)?

prohibetur Italiâ, exsulat. Ergo tu vis non
he-is-prohibited from-Italy, he-is-an-exile. Therefore you wish not

privare hunc patriâ, quâ caret,
to-deprive him 'of (his) 'country, which 'he-is (already) 'deprived-of,

sed vitâ. At ne quisquam egit isto modo
but (of his) life. But not any-one acted in-this manner (in)

istud   apud eum lictatorem
this (accusation of yours) (even) before that   dictator   [Sylla

quidem, qui multabat morte omnes, quos oderat.
indeed, who punished with-death all,   whom he-hated.

Ipse jubebat   occidi, nullo postulante;
He-himself ordered (them) to-be-killed, no-one   soliciting (it); 'he

etiam invitabat præmiis;
even   'invited by-rewards, (the commission of these murders)

quæ crudelitas tamen, vindicata est, aliquot annis
which cruelty however, was-avenged,   some   years

post ab hoc eodem,   quem tu vis nunc
after by this same (person), [Cæsar] whom you desire now

esse crudelem.
to-be   cruel.

    5. Ego vero, inquies non postulo istud.
      I indeed, you-say 'do not   'ask   this, (the death

                Mehercule, Tubero, existimo ita.   Enim
of Ligarius).   By-Hercules, O Tubero, I-think so.   For

novi te, novi vestrum patrem, novi   domum
I-know you, I-know   your   father, I-know (your) family

que nomen; studia virtutis, humanitatis
and name; the love of-virtue, of-humanity (and politeness)

doctrinæ   plurimarum atque optimarum
of the-learning (and science) of-many and most-excellen:

artium,   vestræ familiæ ac generis,
arts   (and sciences), (for which) your race and   family

            sunt nota mihi. Itaque   certò scio,
(are distinguished), are known to-me. Therefore 'I certainly 'know,

      vos   non petere sanguinem. Sed
(that) you 'do not 'seek for-blood.   But 'you (the accusers)

attenditis parum.   Enim   res
'attend   little (to the consequences of this). For the affair

             spectat eo, ut   non videamini
(of the prosecution) tends to-that, that 'you-do not   'seem

esse contenti, eâ   poenâ, in quâ Q. Ligarius
to-be satisfied, with-that punishment, in which Q.   Ligarius

sit.   Quæ alia   igitur prætei
may be [may have received]. What other (punishment) therefore except

mortem est? Enim si est in exsilio, sicut
death is-there? For if he-is in exile, as 'he (actually)

est, quid amplius postulatis? an ne
'is, what more do-you-ask-for? whether (that) 'he-may not

ignoscatur? Hoc vero multò acerbius, que
'be pardoned? This (would be) indeed much more-harsh, and

multò durius. Pugnabis ne impetremus id,
much harder. Will-you-strive-against, lest we-should-obtain that,

quod nos domi petimus precibus
which we 'at (his) 'house [Cæsar's] asked-for with-entreaties, (and)

lacrymis, strati ad pedes, non fidentes
tears, having-thrown-ourselves at (hic) feet, not confiding

tam nostræ causæ, quàm hujus humanitati?
so-much to-our-own cause, as 'to his 'humanity?

et irrumpes in nostrum fletum? et prohibebis
and do-you-break-in upon our tears? and will-you prohibit

nos jacentes ad pedes, voce supplicum?
us lying at (his) feet, (to speak) with-the-voice of-suppliants?

Si quum faceremus hoc domi, quod
If when we-were-doing this at-the-house (of Cæsar), which 'we

et fecimus et, ut spero, fecimus non frustra,
both 'did-do and, as I-hope, we-did (it) not in-vain,

tu repente irrupisses, et cœpisses clamare:
'you-had suddenly 'broke-in (upon us), and had-commenced to-cry-out

"C. Cæsar, cave ignoscas, cave te
"O C. Cæsar, take-care that-you-forgive, take-care 'how) you

misereat fratrum obsecrantium pro salute
take-compassion on-brothers supplicating for the safety

fratris;" nonne exuisses omnem
of-a-brother;" 'would-you not 'have-divested (yourself of) all

humanitatem? Quantò durius hoc,
humanity? How-much-more (disagreeable and) hard (than) this

quod nos petimus domi, id
(is it, that) what we petitioned-for 'at (his) 'house, (that) the same

oppugnari a te in foro? te tollere
should-be-opposed by you in the forum? (that) you should-take-away

perfugium misericordiæ multorum in tali miseriâ?
the refuge of-mercy of-many in such misery?

Plane dicam, Cæsar, quod sentio. Si in hac
'I-will openly 'say, O Cæsar, what I-think. If in this

tuâ tantâ fortunâ, lenitas non esset tanta,
your so-great fortune, (your) lenity 'had not 'been so-great,

quantam tu per te, per te, inquam, obtines
as you of yourself, of yourself, I-say, possess

(intelligo, quid loquar), ista victoria redundaret
(I-understand, what I-say), this victory would-abound

acerbissimo luctu. Enim quàm
with-the-most-distressing mourning (and grief). For as

essent multi de victoribus, qui vellent te
there-may-have-been many of the victors, who wished you

esse crudelem, quum etiam reperiantur
to-be cruel, so also 'may-there (not) 'be-some-found

de victis? quàm multi, qui,
among the conquered, (who wish the same thing)? as many, who,

quum vellent ignosci nemini a
when they-desire (that) pardon-should-be-granted to-no-one by

te, impedirent tuam clementiam, quum etiam ii,
you, would-impede your clemency, so also those,

quibus ipse ignovisti, nolint te esse
whom you-yourself had-pardoned, do-not-wish you to-be

misericordem in alios? Quòd si possemus probare
merciful to others? For if we-could prove

Cæsari, Ligarium fuisse non omnino in Africâ;
to-Cæsar, (that) Ligarius was not at-all in Africa;

si vellemus esse saluti
should-we-have-desired to-be (the means of procuring) the safety (of an)

calamitoso civi, honesto et misericordi mendacio,
unfortunate citizen, by-a-well-meant and commiserating falsehood,

tamen non hominis, in tanto discrimine
yet 'it-would not 'be (the part) of-a-man, in such-great hazard

et periculo civis, refellere et redarguere nostrum
and danger of-a-citizen, to-refute and reprehend our

mendacium; et si esset alicujus, certe
falsehood; and if there-might-be any-one, 'it-would certainly

non esset ejus, qui fuisset in eadem
not have-been (the part) of-him (to do so), who had-been in the same

causâ et fortunâ. Sed tamen aliud nolle,
state and condition. But however it-is-one-thing not-to-wish,

Cæsarem errare, aliud nolle mise-
(that) Cæsar should-err, another not-to-wish (that) he-should-be-mer-

reri. Tunc diceres "Cæsar, cave
ciful. Then (in the first case) you-would-say "O Cæsar, beware

credas; fuit in Africâ; tulit arma
(how) you-believe (this); he-was in Africa; he-bore arms

contra te." Nunc quid dicis? Cave
against you." Now what do-you-say? Beware (how)

ignoscas." Hæc vox est nec hominis,
you-pardon." This language is neither (the part) of-a-man

nec ad hominem; qui utitur
(to utter), nor (to be addressed) to a man; (and) he-who makes-use

quâ apud te, C. Cæsar, citius abjiciet suam
of-it before you, O C. Cæsar, 'will sooner 'throw-off his-own

humanitatem, quàm extorquebit tuam.
humanity, than (that) he-will-extort yours (from you).

6. Ac primus aditus, et postulatio
And the first opening (of the case), and declaration

Tuberonis fuit hæc, ut opinor, se velle dicere
of-Tubero was this, as I-suppose, (that) he wished to-speak

de scelere Q. Ligari. Non dubito, quin
of the crime of-Q. Ligarius. 'I-do not 'doubt, but-that

admiratus sis, vel quòd quisquam afferret
you-were-surprised, either that any-one had-brought-forward

de nullo alio, vel quod is, qui fuisset in
(this) against no other-person, or that he, who had-been in

eadem causâ, vel
the same cause (and condition himself, should bring it forward), or

quidnam novi sceleris. Tu
(that he should bring forward) something of-a-new crime. Do you

vocas illud scelus, Tubero? cur? Enim illa causa
call that a crime, O Tubero? why-so? For that cause

adhuc caruit isto nomine. Alii
[of Pompey] as-yet had-been-free-from this name. Some

appellant errorem; alii timorem; qui
call (it) an error; others (call it) fear; those-who (judge

durius, spem, cupiditatem, odium, pertinaciam;
more-harshly (call it), hope, cupidity, hatred, pertinacity;

qui gravissime temeritatem; adhuc, præter
those-who (judge) most-severely (call it) temerity; as-yet, except

te, nemo scelus. Ac quidem mihi,
you, no-one (has called it) a crime. And indeed (it appears) to-me

s_ proprium et verum nomen nostri mali quæritur
if a proper and true name of-our misfortune is-required

videtur quædam fatalis calamitas incidisse, e
it-seems (as if) some fatal calamity had-fallen-upon, and

occupavisse improvidas mentes hominum: ut nemo
occupied the improvident minds of-men: so-that no-one

debeat mirari, humana consilia superata esse
ought to-wonder, (that) human counsels were-overcome

divinâ necessitate. Liceat esse miseros;
by-divine necessity. May-it-be-allowed (us) to-be miserable;

quamquam, hoc victore, possumus
although, this-man [Cæsar] (being) conqueror, we-can

non esse; sed non loquor de nobis; loquor
not be (so); but 'I-do not speak of ourselves; I-speak

de illis, qui occiderunt. Fuerint
concerning those, who fell (in battle). They-may-have-been

cupidi, fuerint irati,
ambitious, they-may-have-been under-the-influence-of-passion-and-anger,

fuerint pertinaces; vero liceat Cn. Pompeio
they-may-have-been obstinate; but let Cn. Pompey

mortuo, liceat multis aliis carere crimine
(who is) dead, let many others be-free-from the crime

sceleris, furoris, parricidii. Quando quisquam
of-wickedness, of-rage, (and) of-parricide. When 'has any-one

audivit hoc ex te, Cæsar, aut quid aliud tua
'heard this from you, O Cæsar, or what else 'did your

arma voluerunt, nisi propulsare
arms, (and military exploits,) 'intend, unless to-repel

contumeliam a te? quid ille tuus invictus
insult-and-injury from yourself? what 'did that your invincible

exercitus egit, nisi tueretur suum jus, et
army 'intend, unless-that it-might-defend its rights, and

tuam dignitatem? Quid? tu, quum **cupiebas**
your dignity? What? you, when you-were-desirous (that)

esse pacem, ne agebas id, ut
there-should be peace, whether you-acted so, that

conveniret tibi cum sceleratis, an ut
you-might-come-to-terms-of-agreement with the wicked, or that

cum bonis civibus? Vero, Cæsar, tua
(it might be) with good citizens? Indeed, O Cæsar, your

maxima merita in me non certe viderentur
very-great favours to me 'would not certainly 'have-appeared

mihi tanta, si putarem me conservatum a
to-me so-great, if I-had-thought, (that) I was-preserved by

te ut sceleratum. Autem quomodo tu
you as a wicked-person. But how 'would you

meritus esses bene de republica, quum voluisses,
'have-merited well of the republic, if you-had-desired,

tot sceleratos esse dignitate
(that) so-many wicked (men) be (continued) in (their) dignity

incolumi? Tu, Cæsar,
(and honours, without having them) impaired? You, O Cæsar,

initio, existimavisti illam secessionem,
in-the-beginning, thought that (affair) a secession,

non bellum; neque hostile odium, sed civile
not a war; nor a hostile hatred, but civil

dissidium; utrisque cupientibus rempublicam
dissension; men-on-both-sides desiring the republic

salvam, sed partim consiliis, partim
(to be) safe, but partly 'with (good) 'intentions, partly

studiis, aberrantibus a communi utilitate.
'through (party) 'zeal, wandering from the general welfare.

Dignitas principum erat pæne par;
The dignity of-the-leaders [Pompey and Cæsar] was nearly equal;

fortasse eorum qui sequebantur non par:
perhaps (the dignity) of-those who followed (was) not equal:

causa tum dubia, quòd erat aliquid in
the cause (was) then doubtful, because there-was something in

utrâque parte, quod posset probari; nunc ea
each party, that might be-approved-of; now that

judicanda est melior, quam etiam dii
is-to-be-judged the better (cause), which even the gods

adjuverunt. Vero, tuâ clementiâ cognitâ,
assisted (and favoured). But your clemency being-known,

quis non probet eam victoriam, in quâ nemo
who 'does not 'approve-of that victory, in which no-one,

occiderit nisi armatus?
may-have-fallen unless (he were) armed?

7. Sed, ut omittam communem causam,
But, that I-may-omit the general cause,

veniamus ad nostram utrum
let-us-come to our (particular cause of Ligarius), whether

tandem existimas fuisse facilius, Tubero,
in-fine do-you-think (it) to-have-been easier, O Tubero, (that)

Ligarium exire ex Africâ, an vos
Ligarius (should) depart from Africa, or (that) you (should)

non venire in Africam? Ne poteramus,
not arrive in Africa? But could-we (avoid doing so),

inquies, quum senatus censuisset? Si consulis
you-say, when the senate had-decreed-it? If you-consult

me, nullo modo. Sed tamen
me, (I say you could) in-no way (avoid doing so). But however

idem senatus legaverat Ligarium.
the same senate had-sent-as-lieutenant Ligarius (into Africa).

Atque ille paruit, eo tempore, [before the civil war,]
And he obeyed, at-that time,

quum erat necesse parere senatui; vos paruistis
when it-was necessary to-obey the senate; (but) you obeyed

tunc, quum nemo paruit, qui noluit.
then, [during the civil war,] when no-one obeyed, who did-not-wish

Reprehendo igitur? Vero minime; enim neque
Do-I-blame (you) therefore? Not in-the-least; for neither

licuit vestro generi, nomini, familiæ, disciplinæ,
was-it-allowed 'to your 'race, name, family, and education,

aliter. Sed non concedo hoc, ut
(to do) otherwise. But 'I-do not 'grant this, that (those)

rebus quibus gloriemini in vobis, easdem
things which you-glory-of in yourselves, (that) the same-things

reprehendatis in aliis. Sors Tuberonis
you-should-blame in others. The lot of Tubero [the father, for the

conjecta est ex consulto senatûs,
command of a province,] was-drawn by a decree of-the-senate,

quum ipse non adesset, etiam
when he-himself 'was not 'present, (and when) 'he-was also

impediretur morbo; statuerat excusare.
hindered by-sickness; he-had-determined to excuse (himself).

Ego novi hæc propter necessitudines omnes,
I knew these-things on-account-of the intimacies (of) all-kinds,

quæ sunt mihi cum L. Tuberone.
which are (peculiar) to-me with L. Tubero.

Eruditi unà domi, contubernales
We-were-instructed together at-home, (we were) mess-mates (in)

militiæ, post affines, denique in omni
war, afterwards connected-by-marriage, in-a-word during all

vitâ familiares, etiam magnum vinculum,
life familiar-acquaintances, also (that) great bond

quòd semper usi sumus
(of union existed between us), because 'we-were always 'devoted (to)

iisdem studiis. Scio igitur Tuberonem
the-same studies (and pursuits). I-know therefore, (that) Tubero

voluisse manere domi; sed quidam ita agebat
desired to-remain at-home; but a certain-person so acted

ita opponebat sanctissimum nomen
and urged, (and) 'gave such 'force to-the-most-sacred name

reipublicæ, ut etiamsi sentiret aliter, tamen
of-the-republic, that although he-might-think otherwise, however

posset non sustinere pondus ipsorum verborum.
he-could not sustain the weight of-his words.

Cessit auctoritati amplissimi viri, vel potius
He yielded to-the-authority of-a-most-distinguished man, or rather

paruit. Profectus est unà cum iis, causa
he-obeyed (him). He-departed together with those, the cause

quorum erat una; fecit tardius
of-whom was one-and-the-same (with his); he-made a slow

iter. Itaque venit in Africam jam
journey. Therefore he-arrived in Africa (when) already

occupatam. **Hinc oritur** crimen in
occupied. Hence originates (the charge of) crime against

Ligarium, vel potius ira; nam si est
Ligarius, or rather (of) anger (against him); for if it-is

ullum crimen voluisse, est non minus magnum
any crime to-have-wished, it-is no less a great

vos voluisse obtinere Africam
crime) (that) you wished to-obtain (possession of) Africa

arcem omnium provinciarum, natam ad
the citadel of-all the provinces, (a country) fitted-by-nature to

gerendum bellum contra hanc urbem, quàm
carrying-on war against this city, than (that)

aliquem maluisse se. **Atque**
any-one else might-have-wished (to obtain it for) himself. And

tamen is aliquis non fuit Ligarius.
though this some-one 'might not 'have-been Ligarius

Varus dicebat se habere imperium; certe
Varus said (that) he had the command; 'he certainly

habebat fasces. Sed, quoquo modo illud habet
had the fasces. But, in-whatever manner that may-hold

se, quid valet hæc vestra querela?
itself, [however that may be], what avails this your complaint

"**Non** recepti sumus in provinciam.'
(that) "'We-were not 'received in the province."

Quid si essetis? Ne tradituri fuistis eam
What if you-had-been? Would-you-have-delivered it (up)

Cæsari, an retenturi contra Cæsarem?
to-Cæsar, or have-held (it) against Cæsar?

8. Vide, Cæsar, quid licentiæ, vel potius audaciæ,
See, O Cæsar, what licence, or rather audacity

tua liberalitas det. Si Tubero responderit,
your liberality gives (us). If Tubero should-reply, (that)

suum patrem traditurum fuisse tibi Africam, quò
his father would-have-delivered-up to-you Africa, whither

senatus que sors miserat, non
the senate and the lot (he drew) had-sent (him), 'I-shall not

dubitabo, apud te ipsum cujus interfuit,
hesitate, before you yourself, (O Cæsar,) whose interest-it-was

eum facere id, reprehendere ejus consilium
(that) he should-do this, to-reprove his intention

gravissimis verbis. Enim non si
with-the-most-severe words For (it does) not (follow, that) if

ea res fuisset grata tibi, esset etiam
this thing may-have-been acceptable to-you, (that) it-should also

probata. Sed jam omitto totum hoc; non
be-approved (by you). But 'I now 'omit all this; not

tam ne offendam tuas patientissimas aures,
so-much lest I-might-offend your most-patient ears,

quàm Tubero ne videatur facturus fuisse,
as-that Tubero 'might not 'seem to-have-been-about-to-do,

quod nunquam cogitavit. Igitur veniebatis
that-which 'he never 'contemplated (doing). Therefore you-came

in provinciam Africam, unam ex
(and attempted to enter) into the province (of) Africa, the one of

omnibus, maxime infestam huic
all (others) the most-greatly inimical (to the results of) this

victoriæ; in qua erat
victory (of Pharsalus); in which (country of Africa) there-was

potentissimus rex, inimicus huic causæ,
a-most-powerful king, opposed to-this cause (of Cæsar),

voluntas, aliena, firmi
the disposition (of the people of the province) hostile, firm (and

atque magni conventus.
determined), and large assemblages (of Roman citizens, opposed

Quæro, quid facturi fuistis. Quamquam
to Cæsar). I-ask, what would-you-have-done. Yet

dubitem, quid facturi fuistis, quum videam,
may-I (not) 'doubt, what you-would-have-done, when I-see,

quid feceritis? Prohibiti estis ponere pedem in
what you-have-done? You-were-prohibited to-set a foot i

vestrâ provinciâ, et prohibiti cum summâ injuriâ.
your province, and prohibited with the greatest injustice.

Quomodo tulistis id? Ad quem detulistis
How did-you-bear this? To whom did-you-carry

querelam injuriæ acceptæ? Nempe
the complaint of-the-injury (and injustice) received (by you)? Why

ad eum,   cujus auctoritatem   secuti
to   him [Pompey]   whose   authority (and command) being-followed

veneratis in   societatem
(and acknowledged) you-had-come   to (his)   party (and associates)

belli.   Quòd   si   veniebatis in   provinciam
(in) the war.   Because   if   you-came   into   the province

causâ   Cæsaris,   profectò venissetis   ad
for-the-cause of-Cæsar,   'you-would certainly   'have-gone   to

eum,   exclusi   provinciâ.   Venistis   ad
him,   (when) excluded   from-the-province.   (But) you-came   to

Pompeium.   Quæ   querela   ergo   est   apud
Pompey.   What   complaint therefore   is (that to make) before

Cæsarem, quum accusetis eum, a quo queramini,
Cæsar,   when   you-accuse   him,   of whom you-complain,

vos   prohibitos   gerere   bellum
(that) you   were-prohibited (by him, from) carrying-on   war

contra Cæsarem ?   Atque quidem in   hoc   licet
against   Cæsar ?   And   indeed   in this-thing, it-is-granted

per me,   vel cum mendacio, gloriemini, si
by   me (that), though with   a falsehood,   you-may-boast,   if

vultis,   vos tradituros fuisse provinciam Cæsari.
you-please, (that) you would-have-delivered the province   to-Cæsar.

Etiamsi   prohibiti estis   a Varo et a quibusdam
Even-if   you-had-been-prohibited by Varus and by   some

aliis ; ego tamen confitebor,   culpam esse Ligarii,
others;   I   however   confess,   (that) the fault   was of-Ligarius.

qui privaverit vos occasione   tantæ laudis.
who   deprived   you of-the-opportunity of-so-much   praise.

9. Sed vide, quæso, Cæsar, constantiam
But   see, I-pray-you, O Cæsar,   the constancy 'of (this)

ornatissimi   viri L. Tuberonis ; quam quamvis, ego
'most-accomplished man L.   Tubero;   which   although,

ipse   probarem, ut   probo,   tamen   non
myself   might-approve,   as   I-do-approve, however 'I-would not

commemorarem,   nisi cognovissem   eam virtutem
·have-mentioned   (it), unless   I-had-known, (that) that   virtue

solere laudari a   te in primis.   Quæ constantia
used   to-be-praised by you   especially   Which   constancy

igitur fuit unquam tanta, in ullo homine?
therefore was (it) ever so-great, in any man?

constantiam dico? nescio an possim
constancy do-I-say? I-know-not whether I-might (not)

melius dicere patientiam. Enim quotus quisque
better say patience. For what individual

fecisset istud, ut in civili dissensione,
would-have-done this-thing, that in civil dissensions,

rediret ad eos ipsos, a quibus non
he-should-return to those same, by whom 'he-had not

esset receptus, etiam esset rejectus cum crudelitate.
'been-received, (and) even was-rejected with cruelty.

Cujusdam magni animi, atque
(This would be the act) of-some great mind, and

ejus viri, quem nulla contumelia, nulla vis,
of-that man, whom no contumely, no force,

nullum periculum possit depellere, de susceptâ
no danger could drive, from (his) adopted

causâ, que propositâ sententiâ. Enim ut
cause, and formed opinion. For although

cetera fuissent paria Tuberoni cum Varo,
other-things may-have-been equal to-Tubero with Varus,

honos, nobilitas, splendor, ingenium, quæ fuerunt
honour, nobility, splendour, (and) talent, which were

nequaquam; hoc certe præcipuum
by-no-means (equal); this (was) certainly the particular (advantage)

Tuberonis, quòd venerat in suam provinciam cum
of-Tubero, that he-had-come in his province with

justo imperio ex consulto senatûs.
a just (and legal) command (derived) from a decree of-the-senate.

Hinc prohibitus non ad Cæsarem,
Hence (when) prohibited (he did) not (go) to Cæsar,

ne iratus; non domum,
lest (he might appear) to-be-angry (with his party; and) not home,

ne iners; non in aliquam
lest (he might seem to be) inactive; not to any (other

regionem, ne videretur condemnare illam causam,
country, lest he-might-seem to-condemn that cause,

quam   secutus est: venit in Macedo
which 'he-had (adopted and) 'followed: he-came to Macedo-

niam, ad Cn. Pompeii castra, in eam ipsam causam,
nia, to Cn. Pompey's camp, for that same cause,

a quâ rejectus erat cum injuriâ. Quid? quum
fron. which he-had-been-rejected with injury. What? when

ista res nihil commovisset animum ejus, ad
this thing 'had not-at-all 'moved the mind of-him, to

quem veneratis, credo fuistis   langui-
whom you-had-come, I-believe (that) you-were (excited) by-a-more-lan-

diore studio in causâ; eratis tantummodo in
guid zeal for the cause; you-were only in

præsidiis,   vero animi abhorrebant a
garrisons (and camps), but (your) minds became-estranged from

causâ; an   ut fit   in civilibus
the cause; or, (was it so,) as is-done [as is the case] in civil

bellis, nec in vobis magis quàm in reliquis;
wars, nor in you more than in the rest; (that,

enim omnes tenebamur studio vincendi.
indeed 'we-are all 'possessed with-the-desire of-conquering

Fui semper equidem auctor pacis; sed tum
I-was always indeed the advocate of-peace; but then (I-was

serò; enim erat   amentis, cogitare pacem,
too-late; for it-was (the part) of-a-madman, to-think (of) peace.

quum videres   aciem. Omnes,
when you-saw (the armies drawn up) in-order-of-battle. All

  inquam, volebamus vincere; tu certe præcipue,
(of us), I-say, wished to-conquer; you indeed especially,

qui venisses in eum locum, ubi   esset
who had-come into that place, where 'it-would (necessarily) 'be

tibi pereundum, nisi vicisses; quanquam,
for-you (that you) must-perish, unless you-had-conquered; however,

ut res nunc habet se,   non
as the thing now has itself [as things now are], 'I do not

dubito, quin anteponas hanc salutem
doubt, but-that you-prefer this (present) safety (of yours'

illi victoriæ.
to-that victory.

10. Ego non dicerem hæc, Tubero, si aut
I-would not say these-things, O Tubero, if either

pœniteret vos vestræ constantiæ,
it-repented you [if either you repented] of-your constancy,

aut Cæsarem sui beneficii. Nunc
or Cæsar of-his benefits, (conferred on you). 'I now

quæro, utrum persequamini vestras injurias,
ask, whether you-are-seeking-to-redress your-own injuries,

an reipublicæ? Si reipublicæ; quid
or (those) of-the-republic? If of-the-republic; what

respondebitis de vestrâ perseverantiâ, in illâ
will-you-reply concerning your perseverance, in that

causâ? si vestras videte, ne
cause (of Pompey)? if your-own (cause) see, lest

erretis, qui putetis, Cæsarem fore
you-may-be-mistaken, who may-think, (that) Cæsar would-be

iratum vestris inimicis, quum ignoverit suis.
angry with-your enemies, when he-has-forgiven his-own.

Itaque, num videor tibi esse occupatus
Therefore, whether do-I-seem to-you (O Cæsar) to-be-occupied

in causâ Ligarii? num dicere de
with the cause of-Ligarius? whether (do I seem) to-speak concerning

ejus facto? Quidquid dixi volo referri
his action (and conduct)? Whatever I-said I-wish to-be-referred

ad unam summam vel humanitatis, vel
to one principal-thing (that) either 'of (your) 'humanity, or

clementiæ, vel misericordiæ. Egi
clemency, or mercy. I-have-conducted-and-pleaded

multas causas, et quidem cum te, Cæsar, dum
many causes, and indeed with you, O Cæsar, while

ratio tuorum honorum tenuit te in foro;
the course of-your honours kept you in the forum; (but)

certe nunquam hoc modo. "Ignoscite, judices;
certainly never in-this manner. "Pardon, O judges,

erravit; lapsus est; non putavit; si unquam
he-has-erred; he-has-fallen; 'he-did not 'think; if ever

posthac." Sic solet agi apud
hereafter." Thus it-is-usual to-act (and plead) with

parentem; ad judices, "ncn fecit,
a parent; (but) to judges (thus), "'he-did not do-it, 'he-did

non cogitavit; testes falsi, crimen
not 'think-of-it; the witnesses (are) false, the crime (he is accused

fictum." Dic, Cæsar, te esse judicem de
of is) fictitious." Say, O Cæsar, (that) you are a judge of

facto Ligarii; quære, in quibus præsidiis
he acts of-Ligarius; ask, in what garrisons and camps)

fuerit. Taceo; ne quidem colligo
he-may-have-been. I-am-silent; 'I-do not indeed 'collect

hæc, quæ fortasse etiam valerent apud judicem:
those proofs, which perhaps also might-avail before a judge:

"profectus legatus ante bellum, relictus in
"he-went a lieutenant before the war, (and was) left in

pace, oppressus bello, in eo ipso non
peace, (but) overtaken by-war, in that same (war) he was not

acerbus totus tuus animo ac studio."
a severe (opponent), (but) altogether yours in-mind and good-will."

Sic solet agi ad judicem;
Thus it-is-usual (for the pleadings) to-be-carried-on before a judge;

sed ego loquor ad parentem. Erravit, fecit
but I am-speaking to a parent. He-has-erred, he-acted

temere, pœnitet, configio ad tuam clementiam,
rashly, he-repents, I-take-refuge in your clemency,

peto veniam delicti; oro, ut ignoscas.
I-beg pardon (for) (my) offence; I-pray, that you-pardon (me).

Si nemo impetravit,
If no-one has-obtained (such favours of you), (it would be)

arroganter; si plurimi, tu idem
arrogant (in me, thus to address you); (but) if many, you the same

fer opem, qui dedisti spem. An non sit
bring assistance, who have-given hope. May not there-be

causa sperandi Ligario, quam sit etiam locus
cause of-hoping to-Ligarius, when there-may-be also a place

mihi apud te, deprecandi pro altero? Quamquam
for-me before you, of-soliciting for another? Although

spes causæ est neque posita in hac
the hope 'of (this) 'cause is neither placed in this

oratione, nec in studiis eorum, qui tui
oration, nor in the zeal of-those, who (are) your

necessarii, petunt a te pro
intimate-acquaintances, (and who) entreat of you for

Ligario.
Ligarius. [Who ask pardon of you for Ligarius.]

11. Enim vidi, et cognovi, quid maxime
For I-have-seen, and known, what 'you principally

spectares, quum multi laborant pro salute
'look-to, when many exert-themselves for the safety

alicujus: causas rogantium esse
of-any-one: (that) the cases (of those) entreating-you were

gratiosiores apud te, quàm vultus;
more-acceptable to you, than (their) faces; (and that)

neque te spectare quàm is esset tuus
neither 'do you 'consider how-much he may-be your

necessarius, qui oraret te, sed quàm
intimate-friend, who entreats you, but how-much (he is the friend

illius, pro quo laboraret. Itaque tu quidem
of-him, for whom he-exerts-himself. Therefore you indeed

tribuis tuis ita multa, ut illi interdum
grant to-your (friends) so much, that they sometimes

videantur mihi beatiores, qui fruantur tuâ liberalitate,
seem to-me richer, who enjoy your liberality,

quàm tu ipse, qui concedas tam multa illis.
than you (are) yourself, who give-up so much to-them

Sed tamen video, ut dixi, causas
But however I-perceive, as I-said (before), (that) the cases

plus valere apud te quàm preces,
(themselves) 'have more 'weight with you than entreaties,

que te moveri maxime ab iis quorum
and (that) you are-moved most-especially by those whose

dolorem, in petendo, videas justissimum.
affliction, in petitioning, you-perceive (to be) the truest.

In conservando Q. Ligario, tu quidem facies
In preserving Q. Ligarius, you indeed will-do (what

gratum multis tuis necessariis; sed
will be) agreeable to-many (of) your intimate-friends; but

quæso   considera   hoc,   quod
I-entreat (you)   consider   this (affair carefully), (and) which

soles.   Possum   proponere
(you-are-accustomed-to-do).   I-can   place-before-you (as suppliants

fortissimos viros, Sabinos   probatissimos
for Ligarius) the most-brave men,   Sabines   the-most-approved-of

tibi,   que   totum   Sabinum   agrum,
(and esteemed) by-you,   and   also the whole   Sabine .   district

florem Italiæ,   robur reipublicæ.   Nosti
the flower of-Italy, (and) the strength of-the-republic. You-have-known

homines optime ; animadverte mœstitiam et dolorem
the men   well ;   observe   the sadness   and   grief

omnium   horum.   Vides   lacrimas   que   squalorem
of-all   these.   You-see   the tears   and   neglected-dress

hujus   T. Brocchi ipsius et   filii,   de   quo
of-this-here T. Brocchus himself and 'of (his) 'sons, concerning whom

non   dubito   quid   existimes.   Quid   dicam
'I-do not 'doubt   what   you-may-think.   What shall-I-say

de   fratribus?   Noli,   Cæsar,   putare
concerning (his)   brothers?   Do-not, O Cæsar,   think (that)

nos   agere   de   capite   unius ;
we   are-pleading about the capital-punishment of-one-individual ;

aut   tres Ligarii sunt retinendi   tibi in civitate,
either three   Ligarii   are to-be-retained (by) you in   the city,

aut   tres   exterminandi   ex   civitate.   Quodvis
or   three   are-to-be-banished   from   the city.   Any

exsilium est   optatius   his,   quàm   patria,
banishment is   more-desirable to-these,   than (their) country,

quàm   domus,   quàm   dii penates,   illo
than (their) home,   than (their) household-gods,   that (other)

uno   exsulante.   Si   faciunt   fraterne,
one   (being)   exiled.   If   they-act   fraternally,

si   pie,   si   cum   dolore,   horum
if   piously,   if   with   grief,   'may   their

lacrimæ moveant te,   pietas moveat,
tears   'move   you, 'may (their) piety   'move (you), 'may

germanitas moveat;   illa   tua   vox
'(their) fraternal-relationship 'move (you) ; 'may that your expression

valeat, quæ vicit. Enim audiebamus te dicere
prevail, which conquered. For we-heard you say (that)

nos putare omnes adversarios, nisi qui essent
we thought all (to be) enemies, unless those-who were

cum nobis; te omnes tuos, qui
with us; (but that) you (looked upon) all (as) your-friends, who

essent non contra te. Ne igitur vides hunc
were not against you. 'Do-you not therefore 'see this

splendorem omnium, hanc domum Brocchorum,
splendour of-all (the knights), this family of-the-Brocchi,

hunc L. Marcium, C. Cæsetium, L. Confidium,
this L. Marcius, C. Cæsetium, (and) L. Confidium,

omnes hosce Romanos equites, qui adsunt,
all these-here Roman knights, who are-present,

veste mutatâ, viros non solum notos tibi, verum
in-mourning-apparel, men not only known to-you, but

etiam probatos? Fuerunt cum te.
also approved (and esteemed by you)? They-were with you.

Atqu. irascebamur his, requirebamur hos
And we-were-angry with-them, we-missed them (from

nonnulli etiam minabantur his. Igitur
among us), some also were-threatened by-them. Therefore

conserva suos tuis; ut quemadmodum
preserve their (friends) with-yours; tha' whereas

cetera, quæ dicta sunt a te,
the other-things, which have-been-said by you, (have been found to be

sic hoc reperiatur
true), so this (saying of yours above me..ioned) may-be-found (to be

verissimum.
most-true.

12. Quòd si posses perspicere penitus
For if you-could 'see intimately 'int.

concordiam Ligariorum, judicares omnes
the concord of-the-Ligarii, you-would-think (tnat) all

fratres fuisse cum te. An potest quisquam
the brothers were with you. Whether can any-one

dubitare, quin, si Q. Ligarius potuisset esse in
doubt, but-that, if Q. Ligarius could-have-been in

Italiâ, fuisset futurus in eadem sententiâ, in qua
Italy, he-would-have-been of the same opinion, in which

fratres fuerunt? Quis est, qui non
(his) brothers were? Who is-there, who 'may not

noverit conspirantem consensum, pæne
'have-known the agreeing harmony (and dispositions), almost

conflatum horum, in hac prope
melted-together-into-one of-these (brothers), in this nearly

fraternâ æqualitate? qui non sentiat hoc,
fraternal equality? who 'does not 'feel this, (that)

quivis prius futurum fuisse, quàm ut hi
any-thing 'would sooner 'be-about-to-happen, than that these

fratres diversas sententias, que sequerentur
brothers (would be of) different opinions, and would-follow

fortunas? Igitur omnes
the fortunes (of different parties)? Therefore all (the brothers)

fuerunt cum te voluntate: unus abreptus est
were with you in-good-will: one was-forced-away

tempestate; qui si fecisset id consilio, esset
by-adverse-circumstances; who if he-had-done it by-design, would-be

similis eorum, quos tamen tu voluisti esse salvos.
like those, whom however you wished to-be safe.

Sed ierit ad bellum, discesserit non solùm
But if-he-may-have-gone to war, he-departed not only

a te, verùm etiam a fratribus, hi
from you, but also from (his) brothers, these [his brothers]

tui orant te, Equidem, quum
your-friends entreat you, (for his pardon). Indeed, when

interessem omnibus tuis negotiis, teneo memoriâ
I-was-mixed-up in-all your affairs, I-remember

qualis T. Ligarius, urbanus quæstor fuerit tum
how T. Ligarius, the city quæstor 'was then

erga te et tuam dignitatem. Sed est
'disposed towards you and your dignity. But it-is (of)

parum me meminisse hoc; spero
small (account for) me to-have-remembered this; I-hope (that)

te etiam, qui soles oblivisci nihil nisi
you also, who are-accustomed to-forget nothing unless

mjurias, quonian hoc   **est**
injuries,   because   this (forgetfulness of injuries) is   (a part) ¹of

animi, quoniam   **etiam tui ingenii,**
(your) mind,   because   (it is a part)   also   of-your disposition,

reminiscentem te recordari aliquid   **de**
calling-to-mind   (that) you   would-remember   something   concerning

illo quæstorio officio hujus, etiam de quibusdam
the quæstor   office   of-that-man, so-also concerning   some

aliis quæstoribus. Igitur hic T. Ligarius, qui tum
other   quæstors.   Therefore this T. Ligarius, who   then

nihil aliud egit, (enim   neque divinabat
¹had nothing else ¹in-view, (for   ¹he-did not   ¹foresee

hæc),   nisi ut judicares eum
these) (present circumstances), unless that you-might-judge him (to be)

studiosum tui, et bonum virum, nunc supplex
devoted   to-you, and   a good   man,   now   a suppliant

petit salutem fratris a te. Quum admonitus
begs-for the safety of-a-brother from you.   When being-reminded

officio hujus,   dederis quam,
of-the-services of-him (T. Ligarius), you-will-have-granted this   (his

utrique his   condonaveris
safety),   to-both   these (suppliant brothers), you-will-have-restored

tres optimos et integerrimos fratres, non solùm
three most-excellent and most-irreproachable brothers,   not   only

sibi ipsos, neque his tot, ac talibus
to-themselves, neither to-these so-many, and   such   (esteemed)

viris, neque nobis   necessariis, sed etiam
men,   nor   to-us (his) particular-acquaintances, but   also

reipublicæ. Igitur fac, quod fecisti nuper in
to-the-republic.   Therefore do, that-which you-did   lately   in

curiâ,   de nobilissimo et clarissimo homine,
the senate-house, for   a most-noble   and most-illustrious   man,

nunc idem in foro, de   optimis,
[M. Marcellus,] now the same in the forum, for these-most-excellent,

et huic omni frequentiæ, probatissimis fratribus.
and to-this entire crowded-assembly, most-approved-of   brothers.

Ut concessisti illum   senatui, sic da hunc
As   you-granted him [Marcellus] to-the-senate, so   give this-one

populo, cujus voluntatem
[Ligarius] to-the-people, whose good-will (and affections) 'you

semper habuisti carissimam; et si ille dies fuit
always 'held most-dear; and if that day was

gloriosissimus tibi, gratissimus Romano populo;
most-glorious to-you, (it was) most-agreeable to-the-Roman people;

noli obsecro, C. Cæsar, dubitare quærere
do-not I entreat (you), O C. Cæsar, hesitate to-seek

similem laudem illi gloriæ quàm sæpissime. Nihil
a similar praise to-that glory, as often-as-possible. Nothing

est tam populare quàm bonitas; nulla le tuis
is so popular as kindness; none of your

plurimis virtutibus est nec admirabilior, nec
many virtues is either more-admirable, or

gratior misericordiâ; enim homines
more-acceptable, (than your) mercy; for men

accedunt propius ad deos nullâ re, quàm
approach nearer to the gods in-no-thing (more), than

dando salutem hominibus. Nec tua fortuna habet
in-giving safety to-men. For your fortune has

nihil majus, quàm ut possis, nec natura
nothing greater, than that you-can, nor (your) nature (any thing

melius, quàm ut velis servare quàm plurimos.
better, than that you-wish to-save as many (as you can,

Causa forsitan postulat longiorem orationem,
The cause (itself) perhaps may-require a longer speech,

certe tua natura breviorem. Quare, quum
(but) certainly your nature a shorter-one. Therefore, as

arbitrer esse utilius te ipsum loqui,
I-think it-to-be more-useful (that) you yourself should-commune

quam me aut quemquam
(with yourself), than (that) I or any-one-else (should speak)

cum te, jam faciam finem;
with you, 'I-shall now 'make an end (of my discourse); 'I-shall

tantùm admonebo te, si dederis salutem illi
only 'remind you, (that) if you-give safety to-him

absenti, te daturum omnibus his præsentibus.
absent, (that) you will-give-it to-all those present.

ORATIO
THE ORATION

M. TULLII CICERONIS,
OF M. TULLIUS CICERO,

PRO
FOR

REGE DEIOTARO.
KING DEIOTARUS

1. QUUM in omnibus gravioribus causis, C. Cæsar,
Though in all more-important causes, O C. Cæsar,

initio dicendi soleam vehe-
in-the-beginning 'of (my) 'discourse I-may-be-accustomed (to be) more

mentius commoveri, quàm videatur vel usus,
violently agitated, than it-may-seem (that) either practice,

vel mea ætas postulare, tum in hac causâ
or my age requires, yet in this cause (especially)

multa ita perturbant me, ut quantum studii mea
many-things so disturb me, that as-much of-zeal (as) my

fides afferat mihi ad defendendum
good-faith, (and promise,) may-induce me to defend

salutem regis Deiotari, tantum facultatis
the safety of-king Deiotarus, so-much 'of (my) 'power 'does (my)

timor detrahat. Primum dico pro
fear 'deprive (me of). In-the-first-place I-am-pleading for

capite que fortunis regis; quod ipsum etsi non
the life, and fortunes of-a-king; which-thing itself although not

iniquum, duntaxat in tuo periculo
unjust (or improper), at-least in your danger, (or any thing

tamen est ita inusitatum, regem
affecting your interest,) however it-is so unusual-a-thing, for-a-king

esse reum capitis, ut ante hoc tempus
to-be a defendant in-a-capital-crime, that before this time,

non sit auditum. Deinde nunc
[1]it-has not [1]been heard-of. In-the-next-place I-am now

cogor defendere contra atrocissimum
compelled to-defend against (the accusation of) the most-atrocious

crimen, eum regem, quem antea solebamus cum
crime, that king, whom heretofore we-used, with

cuncto senatu ornare, pro ejus perpetuis meritis
all the senate to-honour, for his uninterrupted services

in nostram rempublicam. Accedit, ut
towards our republic. (And to this) is-added, that

conturber crudelitate alterius accusatorum,
I-am-disturbed by-the-cruelty of-one of-the-accusers, (and)

indignitate alterius. Crudelis Castor, ne dicam
by-the-baseness of-the-other. O cruel Castor, not (to) say

sceleratum et impium! qui, nepos, adduxerit
wicked and impious! who, a grandson, has-brought (his)

avum in discrimen capitis, que intulerit
grandfather in danger [1]of (his) [1]life, and brought

terrorem suæ adolescentiæ ei,
the terror of-his youth to-him, [and caused his grandfather

cujus senectutem debebat tueri
to fear him quite a youth,] whose old-age he-ought to-defend

et tegere, que duxerit commendationem
and protect, and (who) has-derived the commendation [1]of (his)

ineuntis ætatis ab impietate et scelere; impulerit
[1]early age by impiety and wickedness; he-impelled

servum avi, corruptum præmiis, ad
the slave [1]of (his) [1]grandfather, corrupted by-bribes, to

accusandum dominum, abduxerit a
accuse (his) master, (and) he-led-him-away from

pedibus legatorum.
the feet of-the-ambassadors [and took him from the service of the am-

Autem quum videbam os,
bassadors of the King]. But when I-saw the countenance

quum audiebam verba   fugitivi accusantis
when   I-heard   the words 'of (this) 'runaway   accusing   (his)

dominum, et   absentem   dominum,   et   dominum
master,   and   an absent   master,   and   a master

amicissimum nostræ reipublicæ,   non   tam   dolebam
most-friendly   to-our   republic,   not so-much did-I-grieve-at

afflictam   regiam   conditionem,   quàm   extimescebam
the afflicted   royal   condition,   as   I-feared

de   communibus fortunis.   Nam quum
concerning the common   fortunes [general safety].   For   when

more   majorum,   ne liceat   de
according-to-the-usage of-our-ancestors, 'it-is not 'allowed as-respects

servo   quæri   in   dominum, quidem
a slave, (that) he-be-examined against (his)   master,   even

tormentis, in quâ quæstione   dolor   possit
by-torture, in which examination (by torture) pain   might

elicere veram vocem   etiam ab   invito;
elicit   the true   word [the truth] even from the unwilling;

servus   exortus est, qui solutus   accuset
(but here) a slave   rose-up,   who unrestrained   accuses

eum,   quem   in   equuleo   posset   non
him,   whom   on   the rack   he-could   not

appellare.
make-mention-of (accuse).

2.   Etiam illud   interdum,
Also   that (which I am now going to mention) sometimes,

C. Cæsar, perturbat me;   quod   tamen,   quum
O C. Cæsar,   disquiets   me;   which   however,   as

recognovi te penitùs, desino timere; enim   re
I-have-known you well,   I-cease to-fear;   for in-principle

est iniquum, sed tua sapientiâ   fit   æquissimum.
it-is   unjust,   but by-your wisdom it-becomes   most-just.

Nam dicere apud eum de facinore, contra cujus
For   to-plead   before him of   a crime, against whose

vitam,   arguare   inisse   consilium facinoris,
life,   you-may-be-accused to-have-entered-into a plan   of-crime,

si   consideres   per   se ipsum,   est   grave;
if   you consider (this) by   itself,   it-is (a)   serious

enim est fere nemo, qui
(and unpleasant affair); for there-is almost no-one, who (being)

judex sui periculi, non præbeat se æquiorem
judge of-his-own danger, 'does not 'show himself more-favourable

sibi, quam reo. Sed, Cæsar, tua præstans
to-himself, than to-the-defendant. But, O Cæsar, your excellent

que singularis natura minuit hunc metum
and singular (good) natural-disposition diminishes this fear

mihi; enim non timeo tam, quid tu
(in) me; for 'I-do not fear so-much, what you (may judge)

de Deiotaro, quam intelligo, quid velis
concerning Deiotarus, as I-understand, what you-wish (that)

ceteros judicare de te. Etiam
others judge of you, (as an impartial judge). 'I-am also

moveor insolentiâ loci ipsius, quod dico
moved by-the-unusualness of-the-place itself, that I-plead

tantam causam, quanta nulla unquam
such (and so great) a cause, as never yet

versata est in disceptatione, intra domesticos
was in dispute, [on trial,] within domestic

parietes, dico extra conventum et
walls, I-plead without the assembly (and out of court), and

eam frequentiam, in quâ studia oratorum
(without) that numerous-assemblage, on which the exertions of-orators

solent niti: in tuis oculis, tuo ore
are-accustomed to-depend: (it is) in your eyes, your countenance

que vultu acquiesco; intueor
and face (alone, that) I-am-pleased (and cease to fear); I-behold

te unum; omnis mea oratio spectat ad te unum.
you alone; all my speech (is) directed to you alone

Quæ sunt gravissima mihi ad spem obtinendæ
Which-things are most-weighty for-me for the hope of-obtaining

veritatis, ad motum animi, et ad omnem
he truth, (but) for the excitement of-the-mind, and for all

impetum dicendi que contentionem leviora.
the force of-speaking and controversy lighter (and em-

Enim si, C. Cæsar, dicerem hanc causam
barrassing). For if, O C. Cæsar, I-were-to-plead this cause

in foro, te **eodem** audiente **et disceptante,**
in the forum, you the same hearing and deciding,

quantam alacritatem concursus
what alacrity (and excitement) 'would the concourse

Romani populi afferret mihi! Enim quis civis
of-the-Roman people 'bring to-me! For what citizen

non faveret ei regi, omnem cujus ætatem
'would not 'favour that king, all whose life

meminisset esse consumptam in bellis Romani
he-would-have-remembered to-have-spent in the wars of-the-Roman

populi? Spectarem curiam, intuerer forum,
people? I-would-see the-senate-house, I-would-look-over the forum,

denique testarer cœlum ipsum. Sic quum
in-fine 'I-might-call heaven itself 'to-witness. Thus when

recordarer beneficia et immortalium deorum,
I-might-have-recalled the kindness both of-the-immortal gods,

et Romani populi, et senatûs in regem
and of-the-Roman people, and of-the-senate towards king

Deiotarum, posset nullo modo oratio deesse mihi.
Deiotarus, there-could in-no wise a speech be-wanting to-me.

Quoniam parietes faciunt quæ
(And) because the walls (of the house) make these-things

angustiora, que actio maximæ causæ
more-narrow (and difficult), and the pleading of-a-great cause

debilitatur loco, est tuum, Cæsar, qui sæpe
is-weakened by-the-place, it-is your (part), O Cæsar, who 'have often

dixisti, pro multis, referre ad te ipsum, quid
pleaded for many, to-refer to your self, what 'may

nunc sit mihi animi; quo facilius quum
now 'be my state-of-mind; whereby the more-easily as-well

tua æquitas tum diligentia audiendi
your justice as (your) diligent-attention (in) listening

minuat hanc meam perturbationem. Sed antequam
may-lessen this my embarrassment. But before

dico de accusatione ipsâ, dicam
I-say (any thing) concerning the accusation itself, I-shall-say

pauca de spe accusatorum. Qui quum
a few-words concerning the hope of-the-accusers. Who when

videantur, nec ingenio, nec usu
they-may-seem, neither 'by (their) 'talents, nor by practice

atque exercitatione rerum valere,
and experience (in) affairs (of this kind) to-be-of-any-account,

tamen non venerunt ad hanc causam sine
yet 'they-did not 'come to this cause without

aliquâ spe, et cogitatione.
some hope, and reflection (on the subject).

3. Non erant nescii, te iratum
'They-were not 'ignorant, (that) you were-

fuisse regi Deiotaro; meminerant illum
angry (with) king Deiotarus; they-had-remembered (that) he

affectum quibusdam incommodis et detrimentis,
suffered some inconveniences and losses,

propter offensionem tui animi; que
on-account-of the displeasure of-your mind (towards him); and

quum cognoverant te iratum huic,
when they-had-known (that) you were-angry (with) him,

tum esse amicum sibi; que quum
as-well-as (that you) were friendly to-themselves; and when

dicerent apud te ipsum de tuo periculo,
they spoke with you yourself (privately) concerning your danger,

putabant, ut fictum crimen facile insideret
they-thought, that a fictitious crime would easily lodge

in exulcerato animo.
(and fix itself) in a sore, (and irritated) mind.

Quamobrem, Cæsar, libera nos primum hoc metu,
Wherefore, O Cæsar, deliver us first from-this fear,

per fidem et constantiam, et per tuam
by (your) good-faith and firmness, and by your

clementiam, ne suspicemur ullam
clemency, (so that) we-may not suspect, (that) any

partem iracundiæ residere in te. Oro te per
portion of-anger remains in you. I-entreat you by

istam dexteram, quam hospes porrexisti
that right-hand (of yours), which 'you a guest 'reached-forth

regi Deiotaro hospiti; istam dexteram, inquam,
to-king Deiotarus (your) host; that right-hand, I-say,

non tam firmiorem in bellis, nec in prœliis,
(which is) not even more-firm in wars, or in battles,

quam in promissis et fide. Tu voluisti inire
than in promises and in-good-faith. You have-chosen to-enter

domum, et tu renovari vetus
(his) house, and you (desired) to-renew (your) old

hospitium; ejus dii penates
bond-of hospitality-and-friendship; his household-gods

acceperunt te; aræ que foci regis Deiotari
have-received you; the altars and hearths of-king Deiotarus

viderunt te amicum et placatum. Quum, Cæsare,
have-seen you friendly and appeased. As, O Cæsar,

soles facile exorari, tum
you-are-accustomed 'to-be easily 'entreated (to forgive), so

exorari semel;
(you are used) to-be-entreated, (and to forgive) once (and for ever);

nemo unquam, inimicus, placavit te,
no-one ever, (being) an-enemy, appeased you, (and became

qui senserit resedisse ullas
reconciled to you), who might-perceive (that) there remained any

reliquias simultatis in te. Quamquam cui
rest of-resentment in you. However to-whom 'have

tuæ querelæ cum Deiotaro inauditæ sunt?
your complaints (and expostulations) with Deiotarus 'been-unheard-of?

Tu nunquam accusavisti illum ut hostem, sed ut
You never accused him as an-enemy, but as

amicum, parum functum officio, quod
a friend, but little discharging the duty (of friendship), because

fuisset propensior in amicitiam Cn. Pompeii quam in
he-was more inclined to the friendship of-Cn. Pompey than to

tuam. Tamen dicebas te daturum fuisses
your-friendship. Yet you-said (that) you would-have-granted

veniam cui ipsi rei, si tantum misisset
pardon for-this same thing, if 'he-had only 'sent

auxilia Pompeio, vel si etiam filium,
assistance to-Pompey, or if even (he had sent) (his) son (to him),

ipse usus esset excusatione ætatis.
'had he-himself 'made-use (of) the excuse 'of 'his) 'old-age.

Ita quum liberares eum maximis rebus,
So-that when you-acquitted him (of) the principal things,

relinquebas perparvam culpam amicitiæ.
you-left (only) the-very-small blame (respecting his) friendship

Itaque non solùm non animadvertisti in eum,
Therefore not only 'did-you not 'punish him,

sed liberavisti omni metu, agnovisti
but you-released (him) from-all fear, you acknowledged

hospitem, reliquisti regem.
the-bond-of-hospitality, (and) you-left (him) a king.

4. Enim neque ille progressus
For neither (did) he proceed (in this affair)

odio tui, sed lapsus est communi errore.
through-hatred of-you, but he-fell (into) the common error

Is rex, quem senatus sæpe appellavisset
(of us all). This king, whom the senate 'had often 'called

hoc nomine honorificentissimis decretis, que qui,
by-this title in-the-most-honourable decrees, and who

quum ab adolescentiâ duxisset illum ordinem
as 'he-had from (his) youth 'considered that order

gravissimum que sanctissimum,
(of the senate) the most-respectable and most-sacred,

perturbatus est iisdem rebus, quibus nos,
was-perplexed (and led astray) by-the-same things, by-which we,

nati in mediâ republicâ, que semper versati.
born in the midst (of) the republic, and always residing-therein,

homo longinquus et alienigena.
(were), (though he was) a man (living) far-off and a foreigner.

Quum audiret arma sumpta auctoritate
When he-heard (that) arms had-been-taken by-the-authority

consentientis senatûs; rempublicam datam
of-the-consenting senate; (that) the republic was-given

defendendam consulibus, prætoribus, tribunis plebis,
to-be-defended by-the-consuls, the prætors, the tribunes of-the-people,

nobis imperatoribus, move-
(and) to-us (who had received the title of) imperator, he-was-

batur animo, et vir, amicissimus huic imperio.
troubled in-mind, and a man, most-friendly to-this empire.

extimescebat de salute Romani populi, in qua
feared-greatly for the safety of-the-Roman people, in which

etiam videbat suam esse inclusam; tamen
also he-perceived (that) his-own (safety) was-included; however

in summo timore arbitrabatur esse sibi
in the greatest fear he-thought (it) to-be (best) for-himself

quiescendum. Vero maxime perturbatus est,
to-remain-quiet. But 'he-was greatly 'distressed.

ut audivit consules profugisse ex Italiâ, que
when he-heard (that) the consuls had-fled from Italy, and

omnes consulares (enim sic nuntiabatur ei),
all (those of) consular-rank (for so it-was-announced to-him),

cunctum senatum, totam Italiam effu-
(also) the entire senate, (and that) all Italy was-

sam esse; enim via patebat ad Orientem, talis
dispersed; for the road was-open to the East, for-such

nuntiis et rumoribus, nec ulli veri
messengers and reports, nor 'did any true (accounts)

sequebantur. Audiebat nihil de tuis conditio-
'follow. He-heard nothing concerning your propo

nibus, nihil de studio concordiæ et pacis,
sitions, nothing concerning (your) desire of-concord and of-peace

nihil de conspiratione certorum hominum
nothing concerning the conspiracy of-certain men

contra tuam dignitatem. Quæ quum essent ita,
against your dignity. Which-things when they-were so,

tamen tenuit se usque eò, quoad
yet-however he-kept himself (quiet) till that (time), that

legati que literæ venerunt ad eum a Cn.
ambassadors and letters came to him from Cn

Pompeio. Ignosce, ignosce, Cæsar, si rex Deiotarus
Pompey Pardon, pardon, O Cæsar, if king Deiotarus

cessit auctoritati ejus viri, quem nos omnes
yielded to-the-authority of-that man, whom we all

secuti sumus; ad quem quum dii atque homines
have-followed; on whom when gods and men

congessissent omnia ornamenta, tum tu ipse
have-heaped all honours, so-also you yourself (have

plurima et maxima.   Enim neque,
conferred) many and very-great (favours on him). For neither,

si tuæ res gestæ attulerunt obscuritatem laudibus
if your deeds have-brought obscurity to-the-praise

ceterorum,   idcirco amisimus memoriam
(and renown) of-others, 'have-we therefore 'lost the remembrance

Cn. Pompeii. Quis ignorat quantum ejus nomen
of-Cn- Pompey. Who is-ignorant how-great his name

fuerit, quantæ opes,   quanta
(and renown) was, how-great (his) power (and influence), how-great

gloria in omni genere bellorum, quanti honores
(his) glory in all kinds of-wars, how-great the honours

Romani populi, quanti senatûs,
(received from) the Roman people, how-great (from) the senate.

quanti tui? Ille tantô vicerat superiores
how-great (from) yourself? He so-much surpassed (his) predecessors

gloriâ,   quantô tu præstitisti omnibus.
in-glory (and renown), as you have-excelled all-men.

Itaque admirantes numerabamus bella, victorias,
Therefore admiring we-counted the wars, the victories,

triumphos, consulatus Cn. Pompeii; tuos possumus
the triumphs, the consulships of-Cn. Pompey; (but) yours we-can

non enumerare.
not count.

5. Ad eum igitur rex Deiotarus venit, hoc
To him therefore king Deiotarus came, in-this

misero que fatali bello, quem antea adjuverat
miserable and fatal war, whom before he-had-assisted 'in (his)

justis hostilibus bellis, cum quo erat conjunctus
'regular foreign wars, with whom he-was united

non solùm hospitio, verùm etiam
not only by-the-bonds-of-hospitality, but also

familiaritate, et venit vel rogatus, ut amicus,
by-familiar-acquaintance, and he-came either asked, as a friend,

vel arcessitus, ut socius, vel evocatus, ut is qui
or requested, as an ally, or called-out, as one who

didicisset parere senatui; postremô venit ut ad
had-learned to-obey the senate; in-fine he-came as to

fugientem, non ut ad insequentem, id est ad
one-flying, not as to one-pursuing, that is to

societatem periculi, non ad victoriæ. Itaque,
the companionship of-danger, not to (that) of-victory. Therefore,

prœlio Pharsalico facto, discedit a
the battle (of) Pharsalicus being-determined, he-departed from

Pompeio; noluit persequi infinitam
Pompey; he-did-not-wish to-follow endless (and uncertain)

spem; duxit satisfactum esse vel officio,
hopes; he-considered (that) he-had-discharged either (his) duty,

si debuerat quid, vel errori, si
if he-owed any, or (had atoned for) error, if

nescierat quid; contulit se domum, atque, te
he-had-mistaken any-thing; he-returned home, and, you

gerente Alexandrinum bellum, paruit tuis
carrying-on the Alexandrine war, he-consulted your

utilitatibus. Ille sustentavit exercitum Cn. Domitii,
interests. He supported the-army of-Cn. Domitius,

amplissimi viri suis tectis et copiis;
a-most-illustrious man in-his houses and 'with (his) 'means; [he gave

ille misit pecuniam
quarters and supplies to his army;] he sent money

Ephesum ad eum, quem tu delegisti ex omnibus
to-Ephesus to him, whom you had-selected from all

tuis fidelissimum et probatissimum; ille
your (friends, as) the-most-faithful and most-esteemed; he

iterum, ille tertio dedit pecuniam, quâ
a second-time, he a third-time gave money (to him), which

uterere ad bellum, auctionibus
you-might-use for the war, public-sales (of his property)

factis; ille objecit suum corpus periculo, fuit cum
being-made; he exposed his person to-danger, he-was with

te in acie contra Pharnacem, que dixit tuum
you in battle against Pharnaces, and he-considered your

hostem esse suum. Quæ quidem, Cæsar,
enemy to-be his. Which-things indeed, O Cæsar,

accepta sunt ... te in eam partem, ut
were accepted by you in that (good) part, that

affecetis   eum   amplissimo   honore,   et
you rewarded   him   with-the-most-ample   honours,   and

nomine   regis.   Is igitur, non modò liberatus a
with-the-name   of-king.   He therefore, not   only   freed   by

te   periculo,   sed etiam ornatus   amplissimo
you from-danger, but   also   invested (by you) with-the-most-ample

honore,   arguitur,   voluisse   interficere te   suæ
honours,   is-accused, to-have-desired   to-kill   you   in-his-own

domi.   Quod tu,   nisi   judices   eum furiosissimum,
house.   Which you,   unless you-suppose him   a-most-furious

        potes   non   profectò   suspicari.   Enim ut
(madman)   can   not   at-all   suspect.   For that

omittam,   tanti   sceleris   fuerit   cujus,
I-may-omit, [of] how-great   a crime   it-would-have-been   of-him,

in   conspectu   penatium   deorum,   necare
in   the-sight 'of (his) 'household   gods,   to-kill

hospitem ;   tantæ   importunitatis cujus extinguere
a-guest ;   [of] how-great   the audacity   of-him to-extinguish

clarissimum   lumen   omnium   gentium,   atque   omnis
the brightest   light   of-all   nations,   and   of-all

memoriæ ;   tantæ   ferocitatis   cujus   non
remembrance ; [of] how-great   the ferocity   of-him   not

extimescere   victorem   orbis terrarum ;   tam
to-fear   the conquerer   of-the-world ;   'of the so

inhumani   et   ingrati   animi   cujus   inveniri
'inhuman   and   ungrateful   mind   of-him (as) to-be-found

tyrannum   in   eo,   a   quo   appellatus esset   rex ;
a tyrant   towards him, by whom   he-was-called   king ;

ut   omittam   hæc,   tanti   furoris   fuit
that   I-may-omit   these-things, [of] how-great   the frenzy   would-be

hujus,   excitare   contra   se   unum   omnes   reges,
of-him,   to-excite   against   himself   alone   all   the kings,

quorum   erant   multi   finitimi,   omnes   liberos
of-whom   there-were   many   'on his 'frontiers,   all   free

populos,   omnes   socios,   omnes   provincias,   denique
people,   all   the allies,   all   the provinces,   in-fine

arma   omnium ?   Quonam modo   ille
the arms   of-all-people ?   How   'would he

distractus esset,   cum   regno,   cum   domo,
'have-been-at variance,   with (his) kingdom,   with (his) house,

cum   conjuge,   cum   carrissimo filio, non
with (his)   wife,   (and) with (his) beloved   son,   not

modò   perfecto   tanto   scelere, sed etiam
only   having-accomplished   so-great   a crime,   but   even

   cogitato ?
having-thought-of-it?

6. At,   credo   inconsultus et temerarius homo
But,   I-suppose   the inconsiderate and   rash   man

non videbat hæc.   Quis consideratior
'did not   'see these-things. (But) who   more-considerate (than)

illo ? quis   tectior ?   quis prudentior ? Quamquam
he?   who more-circumspect? who more-prudent?   Though

hoc loco puto,   Deiotarum defendendum non
in-this place I-think, (that) Deiotarus   is-to-be-defended   not

tam   ingenio et prudentiâ, quàm
so-much 'for (his) 'talents and   prudence,   as   'for (his)

fide,   et   religione   vitæ.   Probitas
'good-faith, and religious-conscientiousness of-life. The-probity

hominis est nota tibi, C. Cæsar,   mores   noti,
of-the-man is known to-you, O C. Cæsar, (his) manners are-known

   constantia   nota.   Cui   porro,
(to you, his) constancy   is-known (to you). To-whom   moreover,

qui   modò audivit nomen Romani populi   non
who 'has only   'heard the name of-the-Roman people   'is not

integritas,   gravitas,   virtus,   fides   Deiotari
the honesty,   weight-of-character,   virtue, (or) good-faith of-Deiotarus

audita est ? quod facinus igitur posset nec cadere
'known ?   which crime therefore could   neither happen

in imprudentem hominem, propter metum præsentis
to   an imprudent   man,   on-account-of the fear   of-present

exitii,   nec in   facinorosum,   nisi idem esset
destruction, nor to the-most-wicked-man, unless the-same were

amentissimus, id confingitis   cogitatum esse   ab
the most-foolish, this you-suppose to-have-been-thought-on   by

homine   minime stulto. At quam   non
a man   (not in) the least foolish. But this (you present) not

modò non credibiliter, sed quidem ne
only not in-a-credible-manner, but indeed not (even

suspiciose! Quum inquit,
in-a-suspicious-manner! When 'he, the accuser, 'says, (that)

venisses in castellum Luceium, et devertisses
you-had-come to the castle Luceium, and you-had-turned-aside

domum regis tui hospitis, erat quidam
to-the-palace of-the-king your host, there-was a certain

locus, in quo erant ea composita quibus rex
place, in which were those arranged-things which the king

constituerat munerare te. Volebat ducere
had-determined to-offer-as-presents to-you. He-desired to-conduct

te huc a balneo, priusquam
you thither (on coming) from the-bath, before

accumberes. Enim erant ibi armati
you-reclined-at-table. For there-were there there armed-men

collocati in eo ipso loco, qui interficerent te.
stationed in that same place, who were-to-have-killed you.

En crimen, en causa, cur fugitivus
Behold the accusation, behold the reason, why a runaway

servus accuset regem dominum. Ego mehercules,
slave should-accuse the king (his) master. I by-Hercules,

Cæsar, initio, quum ista causa delata est ad
O Cæsar, in-the-beginning, when this cause was-brought to

me, perculsus sum hac suspicione, Phidippum,
me, was-struck with-this suspicion, (that) Phidippus,

medicum, regium servum, qui missus esset cum
the physician, (and) royal slave, who had-been-sent with

legatis, corruptum esse ab isto adolescente
the ambassadors, had-been-corrupted by this young-man.

Subornavit medicum indicem;
He-has-suborned (thought I) the physician (as) an informer; he-will

videlicet finget aliquod crimen veneni. Etsi longe
certainly 'invent some crime of-poison, Although far

a veritate, tamen res non
from the truth, yet the affair (of my conjecture) 'was not

multùm abhorrebat a consuetudine
much 'opposed to, (or at variance) (with) the-usual-practice

criminandi.   Quid   ait   medicus?   Nihil   de
of-accusing.   What   says   the physician?   Nothing   about

veneno.   At primò id potuit   fieri   occultius
poison.   But firstly it   could   have-been-done   more-secretly

in potione,   in   cibo;   deinde   etiam
in drink,   (or) in   food;   next   also   (it could have)

fit   impunius,   quod quum factum est, potest
been-done more-impunibly,   because   when   it-is-done,   it-can

negari.   Si interemisset te palam,   convertisset
be-denied.   If   he-had-killed   you openly,   he-would-have-brought

in   se   non solùm   odia   omnium gentium,   sed
on himself   not   only   the hatred   of-all nations,   but

etiam   arma;   si   veneno, ille quidem potuisset
also   (their)   arms;   if   by-poison,   he   indeed   could

nunquam   celare   numen   Jovis
never   have-concealed (this deed from) the divinity of-Jupiter

hospitalis,   fortasse   celasset
(the God of) hospitality, (though) perhaps   he-might-have-concealed

homines.   Igitur quod   et potuit conari
(it from) men.   Therefore that-which 'he both 'might attempt

occultius, et efficere cautius,   non credidit
more-secretly, and execute more-cautiously,   'he-did not   'confide

id tibi, et callido medico, et, ut putabat, fideli
it to-you, both a skilful physician, and, as he-thought, faithful

servo?   noluit celare   te   de
slave?   (but) would-not conceal (from) you (his designs) respecting

armis,   de   ferro,   de   insidiis?   At quàm
arms,   respecting swords, (and) respecting ambuscades?   But   how

festive   crimen   contexitur!   Tua   fortuna,
finely   'is the accusation 'put-together!   Your   good-fortune,

inquit, eadem, quæ semper,   servavit te;
says-he, the same, which always (did, now also)   saved   you;

negavisti,   te velle tum inspicere.
you-disavowed, (that) you wished then to examine (the presents).

7. Quid   postea?   an   Deiotarus   continuò
What   afterwards? whether   did Deiotarus   immediately

dimisit   exercitum,   re
dismiss   (his)   army,   the affair (of assassinating)

non   illo tempore perfectâ? erat nullus alius
not 'being at-that time   'completed? was-there no   other

locus insidiandi? At dixeras,   te rediturum
place of-forming-ambuscades? But you-said, (that) you would-return

eodem   quum cœnavisses; itaque fecesti.
to-the-same-place when you-had-supped; therefore you-did (it)

Fuit   magnum   retinere armatos, ut
Was-it (such) a great   (thing) to-retain the armed-men, as

collocati fuerant, unam horam aut duas
they-had-been-stationed, one hour or two (hours longer)

eodem loco? Quum fuisses,
in-the-same place? When you-had-been, [When you had spent

    comiter et jucunde in convivio, tum
your time,] cheerfully and agreeably at the banquet, then

isti illuc, ut dixeras. In quo loco cognovisti
you-went there, as you-had-said. In which place you-perceived

Deiotarum   talem erga te, qualis rex Attalus
Deiotarus (to be) the same towards you, as king Attalus

fuit in P. Africanum; cui, ut legimus scriptum,
was towards P. Africanus; to-whom, as we-read (it) recorded,

misit magnificentissima dona, ex Asiâ usque ad
he-sent most-magnificent   presents, from Asia even to

Numantiam; quæ   Africanus accepit, exercitu
Numantia;   which Africanus accepted, the army

inspectante, quod quum Deiotarus præsens
looking on, which when Deiotarus present (and in person)

fecisset et regio animo et more, tu discessisti
had-done both with-a-royal mind and manner, you departed

in   cubiculum. Obsecro,   Cæsar, repete
to (your) sleeping-apartment. I-beseech (you), O Cæsar, recall

memoriam illius temporis, pone illum diem ante
the remembrance of-those times, place that day before

  oculos, recordare   vultus   hominum
(your) eyes, remember the countenances of-the-men

intuententium te, atque admirantium. Num quæ
looking-on you, and admiring (you). Now what

trepidatio? num qui tumultus? num   quid
the trepidation? now what the tumult? was-there any-thing (done)

nisi moderate, nisi quiete, nisi ex disciplinâ
unless moderately, unless quietly, unless by the-regulation

gravissimi et sanctissimi hominis? Igitur
of-a-most-dignified and most-venerable man? Therefore

quid causæ potest excogitari, cur voluerit
what [of] reason can be-imagined, why did-he-wish

occidere te lotum, noluerit
to-kill you after-having-bathed, (but) did-not-wish (to kill you)

cœnatum? Inquit distulit in posterum
after-having-supped? 'He, says (the accuser), 'put-it-off to the next

diem, ut quum ventum esset in castellum
day, that when he-had-come to the castle (of)

Luceium, ibi perficeret cogitata. 'I-do
Luceius, (that) there he-might-accomplish (his) designs. 'I-do

Non video causam mutandi loci; sed tamen
not 'see the reason of-changing the place; but however

res acta est criminose. Quum,
the affair was brought-forward in-a-criminating-manner. When,

inquit dixisses te velle vomere
'he (the accuser) says (that) you-had-said, (that) you desired to-vomit

post cœnum, cœperunt ducere te in
[take an emetic] after supper, they-began to-lead you to

balneum; enim ibi insidiæ erant.
the bath-room; for there the ambuscades (of soldiers) were (placed).

At illa eadem fortuna tua servavit te;
But that same good-fortune (of) yours saved you; (for

dixisti malle in cubiculo.
you-said (that) you-preferred (doing it) in (your) sleeping apartment.

Dii perduint te, fugitive! es non
'May the gods 'destroy you, O runaway (slave)! you-are not

modò ita nequam et improbus, sed etiam fatuus et
only so wicked and corrupt, but also a fool and

amens; quid? ille posuerat ænea signa in
senselessly (stupid); what? 'had he 'placed brazen statues in

insidiis, quæ possent non transferri e balneo
ambush, which could not be-transferred from the bath-room

in cubiculum? Habes crimen
into (his) sleeping-apartment? You-have (the whole) accusation

insidiarum; enim dixit nihil amplius;   horum
of-ambuscades; for he-said nothing more; of-all-these-things

inquit eram conscius. Quid tum? erat ille ita
he-says I-was privy. What then? was he so

demens, ut dimitteret a se eum, quem
senseless, that he-should-send from himself him, (to) whom

haberet conscium tanti sceleris? Etiam
he-had (intrusted) the knowledge of-so-great a crime? Also (that)

mitteret Romam, ubi sciret   et
he-should-send (him) to Rome, where he-might-know (that) both

suum inimicissimum nepotem esse, et C. Cæsarem,
his inimical grandson was, and C. Cæsar,

cui fecisset insidiis? præsertim quum is
for whom he-had-placed ambuscades? especially when he

esset unus, qui posset judicare de
(Phidippus) was the only-one, who could give-testimony concerning

se absente? Et inquit, conjecit meos fratres in
himself absent? And says he, he-threw my brothers into

vincula, quod erant conscii.
prison, because (they also) were acquainted (with the affair).

Igitur quum vinciret eos, quos habebat cum se,
Therefore when he-bound those, whom he-had with himself,

mittebat te solutum Romam. qui scires eadem,
he-sent you unbound to-Rome, who know the-same-things

quæ dicis illos scire?
which you-say (that) they know?

8. Reliqua pars accusationis fuit duplex;
The remaining part of-the-accusation was twofold;

una regem fuisse semper in speculis,
the one (that) the king was always in the-watch-towers, (on

quum animo esset alieno a te; altera
the look-out), as in-mind he-was estranged from you; the other

eum comparasse magnum exercitum contra
that) he had-assembled a great army against

te. De exercitu dicam breviter, ut cetera.
you. Concerning the army I-shall-speak briefly, as the rest.

Rex Deiotarus nunquam habuit eas copias, quibus
King Deiotarus never had these forces, with-which

posset inferre bellum Romano popゝlo; sed
he-could wage war against the Roman people; but (only

quibus tueretur suos finos ab
those) by which he-might-protect his territories from

excursionibus et latrociniis, et mitteret auxilia
incursions and armed-robbery, and might-send auxiliaries

nostris imperatoribus. Atque quidem antea poterat
to-our commanders. And indeed formerly he-could

alere majores copias; nunc potest vix tueri
maintain greater forces; now he-can scarcely support

exiguas. At misit ad Cæcilium, nescio
very-small (forces). But he-sent to Cæcilius, I-know-not

quem; sed conjecit eos, quos misit ın vincula,
whom; but he-threw those, whom he-had-sent into prison,

quod noluerunt ire. Non quæro quàm
because they-would-not go. 'I-do not 'inquire how

verisimile sit, regem aut habuisset non
likely it-may-be, (that) the king either had not

quos mitteret, aut eos, quos misisset,
those-whom he-might-send, or (that) those, whom he-had-sent,

non paruisse; aut qui fuissent non
(should) not have-obeyed; or those-who were not

audientes dicto, in tantâ re, eos
obedient, in so-great an-affair, (that) they (should)

potius vinctos quàm necatos. Sed tamen
rather be-put-in-prison than killed. But however

quum mittebat ad Cæcilium, utrum nesciebat
when he-was-sending to Cæcilius, whether he-did-not-know

illam causam victam esse, an putabat
(that) the cause (of Pompey) was-defeated, whether did-he-think

istum Cæcilium magnum hominem? quem profectò
this Cæcilius (to be) a great man? whom certainly,

is, qui optimè novit nostros homines, contemneret,
he, who well knew our men, would-have-despised

vel quia nosset vel quia non nosset.
either because he-knew (him), or because 'he-did-not 'know (him).

Addit etiam illud, non misisse optimos
He adds also this, he-had-not 'sent the best

equites ;   credo,   Cæsar,
cavalry   (to Cæsar);   I-believe,   O Cæsar,   (that they were)

nihil   ad   tuum   equitatum ;   sed   misit
nothing (as compared) to   your   cavalry ;   but   he-sent

delectos ex iis, quos habuit.   At   nescio
the best   of those, which he-had.   But I-know-not (says he)

quem   ex   eo   numero   judicatum
whom [what particular one] of   that   number (was) a condemned

servum.   Non
slave.   [A person sentenced to slavery for his crimes.]   'I-do not

arbitror;   non audivi;   sed in eo, etiam si
'believe (it);   'I-have 'not 'heard-of (it); but   in   this,   even   if

accidisset,   arbitrarer   fuisse nullam culpam
it-had-happened,   I-may-believe (that) it-was   no   fault

regis.
of-the-king.

9. Autem quomodo   animo alieno a te?
    But   how   (was he) in-mind alienated from you?

                   Credo speravit
(or in what respect was he inimical to you)? I-believe   he-hoped, (that)

exitus   Alexandreæ   fore   difficiles   tibi,
the departure   from Alexandria   would-be   difficult   to-you,

propter   naturam regionum,   et   fluminis. At
on-account-of   the nature of-the-place, and of-the-river.   But

eo ipso tempore dedit pecuniam,
at-that same   time   he-gave   money (to your officers, and)

aluit   exercitum;   defuit in
'supplied (your) army 'with the necessaries of life; he-was-wanting in

nullâ re   ei,   quem
nothing,   (as respects supplying, and assisting)   him,   whom

præfeceras Asiæ; fuit presto   non
you-had-placed-over Asia: he-was ready (in aiding you)   not

solium ad hospitium, sed etiam ad periculum,
only   as-respects hospitality, but also as-respects   danger,

atque ad aciem. Africanum bellum secutum est;
and   as-respects battle. The African   war   followed;

       graves   rumores   de   te; qui etiam
(there were) distressing   rumours   concerning you; which   also

excitaverunt illum furiosum Cæcilium. Que
excited   that furious   Cæcilius. In what

animo fuit tum rex? qui
disposition-of-mind was then the king? who

auctionatus sit que maluerit spoliare sese,
sold-his-goods-at-public-sale, and preferred to-deprive himself,

quam   non subministrare tibi pecuniam.
than (that) 'he-might not 'supply you (with) money,

At eo ipso tempore, inquit   mittebat
But at-that same time, says (the accuser) he-sent (persons)

Nicæam que Ephesum, qui exciperent Africanos
to Nicæa and Ephesus, who might-catch-up the African

rumores, et celeriter referrent ad se.
rumours, and speedily report (them) to himself.

Itaque quum nunciatum esset ei,   Domitium
Therefore when it-was-announced to-him, (that) Domitius

periisse naufragio,   te circumsidere in
had-perished by-shipwreck, (and that) you were-besieged in

castello, dixit de Domitio Græcum versum
a fortress, he-recited concerning Domitius a Greek verse (of)

eâdem sententiâ, quâ nos hebemius Latinum,
the-same import, in-which we have (it in) Latin,

Pereant amici, dum unà inimici intercidant.
Let friends perish, when together (with them our) enemies may fall

Quod ille, si esset inimicissimus tibi, tamen
Which he, if he-had-been the-most-inimical to-you, yet 'would

nunquam dixisset; enim ipse mansuetus,
never 'have-said; for he-himself is-mild, (but)

versus immanis. Autem qui poterat esse amicus
the verse ferocious. But how could-he be a friend

Domitio, qui esset inimicus tibi? Porro cur
to-Domitius, who was inimical to-you? Moreover why

esset inimicus tibi, a quo, quum vel
should-he-be inimical to-you, by whom, when even

potuisset interfici lege belli,
he-might-have-been put-to-death by-the-laws of-war,

meminisset, et se et suum filium
he-might-have-remembered, (that) both himself and his son

constitutos esse regem ? Quid deinde ? quò
were constituted kings ? What next ? whither 't *~~a~~* (this)

furcifer progreditur ? Ait Deiotarum
scoundrel 'go ? He-says (that) Deiotarus (was so)

elatum hac lætitiâ
elated by-this joy (of the news of your reverses, that)

obruisse se vino que saltavisse
he-overloaded himself with-wine [became drunk] and (that) he-danced

nudum, in convivio. Quæ crux potest afferre satis
naked at the banquet. What cross could bring sufficient

supplicii huic fugitivo ? quisquam
punishment to-this runaway (slave)? 'did any-one

unquam vidit Deiotarum saltantem aut ebrium ?
ever 'see Deiotarus dancing or drunk '

Omnes virtutes sunt in illo rege, quod abitror
All virtues are in that king, which I-think (that)

te, Cæsar, non ignorare, sed præcipue singularis
you, O Cæsar, are not ignorant-of, but especially a singular

et admiranda frugalitas; etsi
and to-be-admired frugality (and temperance); although

scio non solere regem laudari hoc
I-know (that) 'it-is not 'usual (that) a king be-praised by this

verbo. Hominem dici frugi habet non
word (frugality). (That) a man is-called frugal has not

multum laudis in rege; fortem, justum,
much of-praise in a king; (to be called) brave, just,

severum, gravem, magnanimum, largum, beneficum,
grave, dignified, magnanimous, profuse, beneficent,

liberalem, hæc sunt regiæ laudes; illa est privata.
liberal, these are royal praises; that other is a private

Quisque accipiat ut volet; ego
(virtue). Each-one may-receive (this) as he-pleases; I

tamen judico frugalitatem, id est, modetiam et
however esteem frugality, that is, moderation and

temperantiam, maximam virtutem. Hæc
temperance, (as) the greatest virtue. This-frugality

perspecta est, et cognita, ab ineunte ætate,
has-been-perceived, and known, from (his) early-commencing age,

quum a cunctâ Asiâ, tum a nostris magistratibus
as-well by all Asia, as by our magistrates

que legatibus, tum ab Romanis equitibus, qui
and ambassadors, as by the Roman knights, who

negotiati sunt in Asiâ. Ille quidem ascendit ad hoc
may-have-trafficked in Asia. He indeed attained to this

regium nomen multis gradibus officiorum erga
royal name by-many degrees of-services towards

nostram rempublicam; sed tamen quidquid
our republic; but however whatever

vacabat a bellis Romani populi jungebat cum
leisure-he-had from the wars of-the-Roman people he united with

nostris hominibus consuetudines, amicitias,
our people (in cultivating) intercourse, friendships,

res que rationes, ut non
(and) the affairs and relations (of business), so-that [1]he-was not

solùm haberetur nobilis tetrarches, sed etiam
only [1]held-to-be an illustrious tetrarch, but also

optimus paterfamilias, et diligentissimus
a most-excellent father-of-a-family, and a most-industrious

agricola et pecuarius. Is igitur, qui,
agriculturist and rearer-of-cattle. [1]Did-he then, who, (when)

adolescens, nondum præditus tantâ gloriâ,
a young-man, (and) not-yet endowed with-so-much renown,

fecerit nihil nisi severissime et gravissime,
had-done nothing unless most-seriously and gravely, (being held)

eâ existimatione, que eâ ætate saltavit?
in-that esteem, and at-that age [1]dance?

10. Debeas, Castor, potius imitari mores que
You-ought, O Castor, rather to-imitate the manners and

disciplinam tui avi, quàm maledicere
discipline of-your grandfather, than to-calumniate

optimo et clarissimo viro ore fugitivi.
a-most-excellent and illustrious man by-the-mouth of-a-fugitive

Quòd si habuisses avum saltatorem,
(slave). But-even if you-had-had a-grandfather a dancer,

neque   eum   virum,   unde   exempla   pudoris
and-not   that   man,   whence [in whom] examples of-honour

que pudicitiæ   peterentur,   tamen   hoc maledictum
and   modesty   might-be-sought, however this   calumny

minime conveniret   in   illam ætatem.   Quibus
did very-little   'agree   with   that   age.   With-which

studiis   ille   imbuerat   se
studies (and pursuits) he   had-imbued (and accustomed) himself

ab incunte ætate non saltandi, sed, ut uteretur
from early age   not of-dancing, but, that he-might-use (his)

armis   bene,   ut   equis
weapons   well,   (and)   that   (he might manage his) horses

optime;   tamen   cuncta   ea   defecerant
in-the-best-manner; however   all   these-things   failed

illum jam,   exactâ   ætate. Itaque quum plures
him   now,   'in (his) 'old   age.   Therefore when   several

sustulerunt Deiotarum in   equum, solebamus
had-placed   Deiotarus   on (his) horse,   we-used

admirari quòd senex   posset hærere in eo. Vero
to-admire   that the-old-man could   stick on it.   But

hic adolescens,   qui in Ciliciâ fuit meus
this   young-man, (Castor), who in Cilicia was   my

miles, in Græciâ   commilito; quum equitaret, in
soldier, in Greece (my) fellow-soldier; when   he-rode,   in

illo nostro exercitu cum suis delectis equitibus,
that   our   army   with his   select   cavalry,

quos   pater miserat unà cum eo ad Pompeium,
which (his) father had-sent together with him   to   Pompey,

quos concursus solebat facere! quàm   jactare
what   courses   he-used to-make!   how   he-used-to-vaunt

se!   quàm   ostentare!   quàm   concedere
himself!   how   to-display (himself)!   how   to-concede

nemini, in illâ causâ   studio et cupiditate!
to-no-one, in that cause (of Pompey) in-zeal and   ardour!

Vero quum, exercitu   amisso,   ego, qui
But   when,   the army (of Pompey) being-lost,   I,   who (was)

semper auctor pacis, post proelium Pharsalicum,
always   an advocate of-peace, after the battle (of)   Pharsalia,

fui suasor non deponendorum armorum, sed
was the adviser not of-laying-down arms, but

abjiciendorum; potui non adducere
of-'throwing (them) 'away; (yet) I-could not bring

hunc ad meam auctoritatem,
him (Castor) to my authority, [induce him to adopt my

quòd ipse et ardebat studio ipsius
opinion,] because he-himself both was-ardent in-zeal (for) that-same

belli, et arbitrabatur satisfaciendum
war, and he-thought, (that) he-ought-to-satisfy (the wishes of his)

patri. Felix ista domus, quæ non solùm
father. Fortunate (is) this family (of yours), which not only

lepta sit impunitatem, sed etiam licentiam
has-obtained impunity, but also the license

accusandi; calamitosus Deiotarus, qui accusetur
of-accusing (others); unfortunate Deiotarus, who is-accused

ab eo, qui fuerit in iisdem castris, non
by him, who was in the same camp (with him), not

modò apud te, sed etiam a suis. Potestis
only before you, but also by his-own (relations). Could

non vos, Castor, esse contenti vestrâ secundâ
not you, O Castor, be content with-your good

fortunâ, sine calamitate
fortune, without (bringing) calamity (on your)

propinquorum?
relations?

11. Sane, sint inimicitiæ,
'There-may, without-doubt, 'be enmities (between you),

quæ debebant non esse; enim rex Deiotarus
which ought not to-have-been; for king Deiotarus

evocavit vestram abjectam et obscuram familiam,
called-forth your low and obscure family,

e tenebris in lucem. Quis antea audivit
from darkness into light. Who (ever) before heard (of)

tuum patrem, qui esset, quàm
your father who he-might-be, than (till he heard)

cujus gener esset? Sed quamvis ingrate et
whose son-in-law he-was? But although ungratefully and

impie   repudiaretis   nomen   necessitudinis,
impiously you-may-have-repudiated the name 'of (your) 'relationship,

tamen   poteratis   genere   inimicitias
however   you-might-have   conducted (your)   animosities

more   hominum, non insectari
After-the-manner of-men,   not to-prosecute (him, your grandfather)

ficto   crimine, non expetere   vitam,   non
with-false   crime,   not   to seek   (his) life,   (and) not

arcessere   capitis.   Esto ;   quoque
to-arraign   (him) for-a-capital-offence.   Be-it-so ;   let also

hæc acerbitas, et magnitudo odii concedatur ;   ne
this   bitterness, and   greatness of-hatred be allowed ; ought it

adeo, ut omnia jura vitæ, que communis
(to be allowed) so-far, that   all   rights of-life, and   of-common

salutis, atque etiam humanitatis   violentur ?
safety,   and   also   of-humanity   are-to-be-violated ?

Sollicitare servum verbis, corrumpere   spe   que
To-solicit   a slave by-words, to-corrupt (him) by-hopes   and

promissis, abducere   domum,   armare   contra
promises,   to entice (him) from-home, to-arm him   against

dominum, hoc est indicere nefarium bellum, non
(his)   master,   this   is to-declare a wicked   war,   not

uni   propinquo, sed   omnibus   familiis. Nam
against-one relation,   but   against-all   families.   For

ista   corruptela   servi,   si   non   modò
this   corruption   of-slaves, if   'it-should not   only

impunita fuerit, sed etiam approbata   a   tantâ
'be-left-unpunished,   but   also   be-approved   by   so-great

auctoritate,   nulli parietes, nullæ
an-authority   (as this tribunal of yours),   no   walls,   no

leges, nulla jura custodient nostram salutem. Enim
laws,   no   rights will-protect   our   safety.   For

ubi id,   quod est intus,   atque   nostrum,
when that, which is within (our houses), and   (is)   ours,

potest   evolare   impune,
'namely, our slaves,] (that) it-should-be-able to-come-forth impunibly,

que pugnare contra nos, servitus   fit in
and   fight   against   us,   slavery 'is (then) 'made into

dominatu, et dominatus in servitute.
mastership, and mastership into slavery. [The slave becomes

        O tempora,   O mores!
master, and the master slave.] O the times, O the manners!

Cn. Domitius, ille, quem nos, pueri, vidimus
Cn. Domitius, he, whom we, (when) boys, saw (as'

consulem censorem pontificem maximum,
consul censor (and) pontifex maximus, [chief pontiff,]

quum tribunus plebis vocasset M. Scaurum
when (he was) tribune of-the-people he-had-called M. Scaurus

principem civitatis in judicium populi, que
a-chief-man of-the-state on trial (before) the people, and

servus Scauri venisset ad eum clam domum, et
a slave of Scaurus had-come to him secretly, at-his-house, and

dixisset, se delaturum esse crimina in
said, (that) he would-bring accusations against (his)

dominum, jussit hominem prehendi, que
master, he-ordered the man to-be-apprehended, and

deduci ad Scaurum. Vide quid intersit;
to-be-taken-back to Scaurus. See what the-difference-is;

etsi inique comparo Castorem cum Domitio; sed
although unjustly I-compare Castor with Domitius; but

tamen ille remissit servum inimico, tu
however he sent-back the slave 'to (his) 'enemy, you

abduxisti ab avo; ille noluit
have-led-away (the slave) from (your) grandfather; he would-not

audire incorruptum, tu corrupisti; ille
listen (to the slave) unbribed, you bribed (one); he

repudiavit servum adjutorem contra dominum,
rejected a slave (as) assistant against (his) master,

tu etiam adhibuisti accusatorem.
you even made-use-of (one, as) an accuser (of his master).

   An semel iste corruptus est a
But-was-it-only once (that) this (slave) was-corrupted by

vobis? Nonne quum productus esset,
you? Was-it-not-so (that) when he-had-been-brought-forth,

et quum fuisset cum te, refugit ad legatos?
and when he-was with you, he-fled-back to the ambassadors?

Nonne etiam venit ad hunc Cn. Domitium? Nonne
Did-he-not also come to this Cn. Domitius? Did-he-not

confessus est audiente hoc Ser. Sulpicio,
confess in-the-hearing (of) this Ser. Sulpicius,

clarissimo viro, qui tum casu cœnabat apud
a most-illustrious man, who then by-chance was-taking-supper with

Domitium, et hoc T. Torquato, optimo adolescente
Domitius, and this T. Torquatus, a-most-excellent young-man

se corruptum esse a te, tuis
(also present, that) he was-bribed by you, (and) by-your

promissis impulsum in fraudem.
promises impelled to dishonesty (and treachery).

12. Quæ est ista tam impotens, tam crudelis,
What is this so unrestrained, so cruel,

tam immoderata inhumanitas? idcirco
so immoderate inhumanity (of yours)? was-it-for-this

venisti in hanc urbem, ut corrumperes jura,
that-you-came to this city, that you-might-corrupt the laws,

et exempla hujus urbis,
(institutions), and examples (and manners) of-this city,

que inquinares humanitatem nostræ
and that-you-might pollute the humanity of-our

civitatis domesticâ immanitate? At
city, 'by your 'domestic (Asiatic) ferocity? But

quàm accute crimina collecta! Blesamius,
how ingeniously (your) charges have-been-collected! Blesamius,

inquit, (enim nomine ejus optimi viri,
says he (the accuser), (for by-the-name of-this very-excellent man,

nec ignoti tibi, maledicebat tibi), solebat scribere
nor-not unknown to-you, he-calumniated you), used to-write

ad regem, te esse in invidiâ,
to the king, [Deiotarus,] (that) you were unpopular, (that you)

existimari tyrannum; statuâ positâ,
were-considered a tyrant; (that your) statue being-placed,

inter reges, animos hominum
among (the ancient) kings (of Rome), the minds of-men 'were

vehementer offensos; non solere tibi
vehemently 'offended; (that) 'it-was not 'usual for you

plaudi.   Nonne, Cæsar, intelligis,
to-be-applauded. 'Do-you not, O Cæsar, 'understand, (that)

hæc   collecta esse ab istis   ex urbanis
these-things were-collected by these-fellows from the town

sermunculis   malevolorum ?   Blesamius
gossip   of-evil-disposed-persons ? 'would Blesamius

scribere   Cæsarem   tyrannum ? Enim
write (that) Cæsar (was) a tyrant ? Perhaps

viderat   capita multorum civium ;
he-had-seen the heads of-many citizens (exposed); (or)

multos vexatos, verberatos, necatos, jusu Cæsaris;
many ill-treated, scourged, killed, by-the-order of-Cæsar;

multas domos afflictas et eversas ;   forum
(or) many houses ruined and destroyed ; (or) the forum

refertum armatis militibus.   Quæ
filled with-armed soldiers. The things-which 'we-have

semper sensimus in civili victoriâ, ea   non
always experienced in civil victory, those 'we-did not

vidimus, te   victore. C. Cæsar, es, inquam,
see, you (being) victor. 'You, O C. Cæsar, 'are, I-say,

solus in cujus victoriâ nemo ceciderit, nisi
the only-one by whose victory no-one fell, unless

armatus.   Et quem nos
armed. [With arms in his hands.] And (him) whom we

liberi, nati in summâ   libertate Romani
free-men, born in the highest (and fullest) liberty of-the-Roman

populi, ducimus non modò non tyrannum, sed etiam
people, consider not only no tyrant, but even

clementissimum in victoriâ, potest is videri tyrannus
most-clement in victory, can he appear a tyrant

Blesamio qui vivit in regno ? Nam de statuâ,
to Blesamius who lives in a monarchy? For concerning the statue,

quis queritur, unâ præsertim, quum videat tam
who complains, about-one especially, when he-may see so

multas ? Valde enim est invidendum ejus statuis,
many? Greatly indeed is it-to-be-envied 'to-his 'statues,

              cujus   tropæis   non
are his statues to be envied,] whose trophies 'we-do not

invidimus. Nam si locus affert invidiam, nullus
envy. For if the place excites envy, no

est quidem clarior ad statutem
(place) is indeed more-conspicuous for a statue (than)

Rostris. Sed de plausu, quid
the Rostra. But concerning (public) applause, what

respondeam? qui nec unquam desideratus est a
shall I-reply? which 'has not ever 'been-desired by

te, et nonnunquam, hominibus obstupefactis,
you, and sometimes, men being-astonished

compressus est admiratione ipsâ,
(at your great deeds), it-has-been-repressed by-admiration itself,

et fortasse eò prætermissus, quia nihil vulgare
and perhaps therefore omitted, because nothing vulgar

potest videri dignum te.
could appear worthy of-you.

13. Arbitror nihil prætermissum a me, sed
I-think (that) nothing has-been-omitted by me, but

aliquid reservatum ad extremam partem causæ.
something is-reserved to the extreme part of-the-cause.

Autem id est aliquid, ut mea oratio plane
But this is something, that my speech 'will clearly

reconciliet te Deiotaro; enim non jam metuo,
'reconcile you to Deiotarus; for 'I-do not now 'fear,

ne tu succenseas illi; vereor illud, ne
lest you may-be-angry (with) him; (but) I-fear that, lest

suspicere, illum aliquid succensere
you-may suspect, (that) he 'is somewhat 'angry (with)

tibi, quod, crede mihi, Cæsar, abest longissime;
you, which, believe me, O Cæsar, is-distant most-far

enim quid retineat per te meminit,
(from him); for what he-retains through you he-remembers,

non quid amiserit; neque arbitratur, se
not what he-has-lost; neither does-he-think, (that) he

multatum a te; sed quum existimares,
has-been-punished by you; but as you-may-have-thought, (that)

multa tribuenda esse tibi multis, quominus
many things had-to-be-given (by) you to-many-people, at-least-that

non recusavit sumeres ea a se, qui
'he-did not object that-you took those things from him, who

fuisset in alterâ parte. Etenim si
had-been in the other party (that of Pompey). For if

Antiochus ille magnus, rex Asiæ posteaquam
Antiochus the great, king of Asia after-that

devictus a L. Scipione jussus esset
he-was-conquered by L. Scipio (and) had-been-commanded, (only

regnare tenus Tauro, que
to-reign (over the country) as-far-as (Mount) Taurus, and

amisisset omnem hanc Asiam, quæ est nunc
had-lost all that (part of) Asia, which is now

nostra provincia, solitus est dicere, benigne
our province, was accustomed to-say, (that) 'it-was kindly

factum sibi a Romano populo, quod liberatus
'done to-him by the Roman people, because being-freed

nimis magnâ procuratione
'from-the too 'great care (of a large kingdom)

uteretur regni modicis terminis, potest
he-might-enjoy a kingdom (of) moderate extent, (so) can

Deiotarus multò facilius consolari se. Enim
Deiotarus much more-readily console himself. For

ille sustulerat multam furoris, hic
he [Antiochus] had-sustained the penalty of-fury, this-one [Deiotarus]

erroris. Tu tribuisti, Cæsar, omnia Deiotaro,
of (his) 'error. You granted, O-Cæsar, every-thing to Deiotarus,

quum concessisti, et ipsi et filio regium
when you-conceded, both to-him and (his) son the royal

nomen. Hoc nomine retento
name. [Title of king.] This title (of king) being-retained

atque servato, putat nullum beneficium
and preserved, he (considers, that) no benefi

Romani populi, nullum judicium
(or kindness) of-the-Roman people, no judgment (or decree)

senatûs de se imminutum; est animo
of-the-senate concerning him has-been-diminished; he is (in) mind

magno et erecto, nec unquam succumbet
great and courageous. nor 'will-he ever 'succumb

inimicis, ne quidem fortunæ. Arbitratur se
to-enemies, nor even-indeed to-fortune. He-thinks (that) he

et peperisse multa ante factis, et
'has both 'acquired much before by-his deeds, and (that he

habere in animo atque virtute,
has (it) in (his) mind and 'in (his) 'power (to do more),

quæ possit nullo modo amittere. Enim quæ fortuna,
which he-can by-no means lose. For what fortune,

aut quis casus, aut quæ tanta injuria
or what accident, or what so-great injustice (or injury)

possit delere decreta omnium imperatorum
could efface the decrees of-all (our) commanders

de Deiotaro? Enim ornatus est ab omnibus
respecting Deiotarus? For he-has-been-honoured by all

iis, qui, posteaquam per ætatem, potuit esse in
those, who, after-that by (his) age, he-could be in

castris, gesserunt bella, in Asiâ, Cappadociâ, Ponto,
camps, carried-on wars, in Asia, Cappadocia, Pontus,

Ciliciâ, Syriâ. Vero judicia senatûs de
Cilicia, (and) Syria. But-indeed the decrees of-the-senate concerning

illo, tam multa, que tam honorifica,
him, (which are) so many, and so honourable, (and)

quæ consignata sunt publicis literis, que
which are-consigned to-the-public records, and

monumentis Romani populi, quæ vetustas
monuments of-the-Roman people, which 'will length-of-age

unquam obruet aut quæ oblivio tanta
ever 'obliterate or which 'will oblivion so-much-as

delebit? Quid dicam de ejus virtute?
deface? What shall-I-say concerning his valour?

de magnitudine animi, gravitate,
concerning (his) 'greatness of-mind, gravity, (and)

constantiâ? quæ omnes docti atque sapientes
constancy? which all learned and wise (men)

dixerunt esse summa, quidam etiam sola bona,
have-said to-be the greatest, some also the only good

que his, virtutem contentam esse, non modò ad
and by-these, that virtue was-sufficient, not only for

vivendum bene, sed etiam ad beate. Ille
living well, but also for (living) happily. He

reputans hæc, et cogitans dies que noctes,
reflecting on-these-things, and thinking days and nights (thereon),

non modò, non succenset tibi, (enim esset
not only, 'is-he not 'displeased (with) you, (for he-would-be

non solum ingratus, sed etiam amens), verum
not only ungrateful, but even mad), but-indeed

refert omnem acceptam tranquillitatem, et quietem
refers all the received tranquillity, and quiet

senectutis, tuæ clementiæ
'of (his) 'old-age, to-your clemency.

14. Quum quidem antea fuit quo
When indeed heretofore he-was in-this (state of)

animo, tum, non dubito, quin tuis literis,
mind, then, 'I-do not 'doubt, but-that by-your letter,

exemplum quarum legi, quas dedisti huic
a copy of-which I-have-read, (and) which you-gave to-this

Blesamo, Terracone, ad eum, etiam erexerit
Blesamus, at Terraco (in Spain), for him, 'he also 'cheered

se magis, que abstraxit ab omni
himself 'up the more, and withdrew (his mind) from all

sollicitudine. Enim jubes sperare bene,
anxiety. For you-tell (him in that letter) to-hope well,

et esse bono animo: quod scio, te
and to-be (of) good courage: which I-know, (that) you 'are

non solere scribere frustrà; enim memini
not 'accustomed to-write in-vain; for I-remember (that)

te scribere ad me fere iisdem verbis, que me,
you wrote to me nearly the same words, and (that) I,

tuis literis, jussum esse, non frustrà, sperare bene.
in-your letter was told, not in-vain, to-hope well.

Equidem laboro causâ regis Deiotari,
'I indeed 'exert-myself in-the-cause of-king Deiotarus,

cum quo respublica conciliavit mihi amicitiam,
with whom the republic united me (in) friendship,

voluntas utriusque conjunxit hospitium,
will-and-inclination of-both joined (us in) the bond-of-hospitality,

consuetudo attulit familiaritatem, vero ejus magna
intercourse brought-on familiarity, but his great

officia, et in me et in meum exercitum,
zeal-and-good-offices, both to me and to my army,

effecerunt summam necessitudinem; sed quum
produced the-greatest-degree (of) intimate-friendship; but when

laboro de illo, tum de multis amplissimis
I-exert-myself for him, as-also for many illustrious

viris, quibus oportet, ignotum esse a
men, to-whom it-is-proper, (that) pardon-should-be-extended by

te semel, nec tuum beneficium
you once-for-all, nor is your favour (or pardon granted)

vocari in dubium, nec sempiternam
to-be-called in doubt, nor (so that) perpetual

sollicitudinem hærere in animis hominum, nec
anxiety should-fasten in the minds of-men, or

accidere ut quisquam eorum incipiat
that-it-should-happen, that any-one of-those might-commence

timere te, qui semel liberati sint a te timore.
to-fear you, who 'have once 'been-liberated by you from-fear.

Debeo non, C. Cæsar, quod solet fieri, in
I-ought not, O C. Cæsar, which it-is-usual to-do, in

tantis periculis, tentare, ecquonam modo dicendo
such-great dangers, to-attempt, if-by-any mode of speech

possim commovere tuam misericordiam. Est nihil
I-could move your compassion. There-is-no

opus; solet occurrere ipsa
need (of this); (your compassion) is-used to-come-forth itself

supplicibus, et calamitosis, evocata oratione
for-the-suppliants, and unfortunate-persons, called-forth by-the-oration

nullius. Propone tibi duos reges,
of-no-one. Place-before yourself two kings, [Deiotarus and his son],

et contemplare in animo, quod potes non
and contemplate in (your) mind, which you-can not

oculis. Profectò dabis misericordiæ,
with (your) 'eyes. 'You-will certainly grant to-compassion,

quod denegavisti iracundiæ. Multa sunt
that-which you-have-denied to-anger. Many are

monumenta tuæ clementiæ, sed maxime
the-monuments of-your clemency, but more-especially

incolumnitates eorum, quibus dedisti salutem.
the security of-those, to-whom you-have-given safety

Quæ si sunt gloriosa,
Which (monuments of clemency) if they-are glorious, (when conferred

in privatis, multò magis
on persons) in private-life, 'they-will-be much more

commemorabuntur in regibus. Regium nomen
'praised (when conferred) on kings. The royal name

fuit semper sanctum in hac civitate; regum
was always holy in this city; (but that) of kings (our)

sociorum et amicorum sanctissimum.
allies and friends most-holy.

15. Quod nomen hi reges timuerunt ne
Which title (of kings) these kings feared lest

amitterent, te victore; vero retentum,
they-might-lose, you being-victorious; but (which title) being-retained,

et confirmatum a te, confido etiam
and confirmed by you, I-trust (that they) also

tradituros esse suis posteris. Hi regii legati
will-transmit (it) to-their posterity. These royal ambassadors

tradunt tibi sua corpora, pro salute suorum
surrender to-you their persons, for the safety of-their

regum; Hieras et Blesamius, et
kings; (these ambassadors are) Hieras and Blesamius, and

Antigonus, jamdiu noti tibi que nobis omnibus,
Antigonus, long-since known to-you and us all,

que Dorylaus præditus eâdem fide et virtute,
and Dorylaus endowed with-the-same good-faith and virtue;

qui nuper missus est ad te legatus cum
who lately has-been-sent to you as-an-ambassador with

Hierâ, quum amicissimi
Hiera, when (as they were ambassadors) of-the-most-friendly

regum, tum etiam, ut spero, probati tibi. Exquire
of-kings, so also, as I-hope, approved-of by-you. Inquire

de Blesamio, numquid scripserit ad regem contra
of Blesamius- if-ever he-wrote to the king against

tuam   dignitatem.   Hieras   quidem   suscipit
your   dignity.   Hieras   indeed   takes-on-himself

omnem causam,   et   illis criminibus
the entire   cause   (of the king), and (as respects) those   charges

               supponit   **se**   **reum**   **pro rege;**
(against Deiotarus) he-substitutes himself as defendant for the king

implorat   **tuam memoriam,**   **quâ**   **vales**
implores   (the aid of)   your   memory,   in-which you-excel

plurimum;   **negat**   **se unquam decessisse pedem**
so-much;   he-denies (that) he   ever   stepped

a te,   **in tetrarchiâ Deiotari; dicit,**
from you, (while) in   the tetrarchy of-Deiotarus; he-says, (that)

se fuisse præsto tibi in primis finibus,
he   was   present to-you on   the first frontier, [that he met you,

                que prosecutum usque
on your first entrance into the country,]   and   followed-you   even

ad ultimos;
to   the last (frontiers); [and accompanied you, till you left the country;]

       se fuisse cum te, quum exisses e balneo;
(that) he   was   with you,   when you-came-out from the-bath;

           quum cœnatus inspexisses illa
(also he was with you) when   having-supped   you inspected those

munera,   **quum in cubiculo recubuisses;**
presents,   (and) when   in   your-chamber, you-had-lain-down;

que   **postridie se præbuisse eandem assiduitatem**
and (that) the-next-day he   had-shown   the same   attention

tibi. Quamobrem,   **si**   **quid**   **eorum**   **quæ**
to-you.   Wherefore,   if   any   of-those (charges) which

     objecta sunt,   **cogitatum sit,**
have-been-brought-against   (Deiotarus)   may-have-been-thought of,

      non recusat, quin judices id suum
he-does not   'refuse,   but-that   you-judge   it (to be)   his

facinus. Quocirca, C. Cæsar, velim existimes,
crime.   Therefore,   O C. Cæsar,   I-wish you-may-consider, (that)

hodierno die, tuam sententiam importaturam esse
to-day,   your   sentence   will-bring-on   (these)

regibus aut miserrimam pestem, cum summo
kings   either the-most-miserable   ruin,   with the greatest

dedecore,   aut   incolumem   famam,   cum   salute,
disgrace,   or   uninjured   fame,   with   safety,

   quorum alterum   est   crudelitatis illorum
of-which the-first-sentence   is   (the part)   of-the-cruelty   of-those

           optari,   alterum   tuæ
(accusers of Deiotarus)   to-wish-for,   the other (is the part) of-your

clementiæ conservare.
clemency   to preserve.

ORATIO
THE ORATION

M. TULLII CICERONIS,
OF M. TULLIUS CICERO,

PRO
FOR

T. ANNIO MILONE.
T. ANNIUS MILO.

~~~~~~~~~~

1. Etsi vereor, judices, ne sit
Although I am apprehensive, O judges, lest it-may (be considered)

turpe, incipientem dicere pro fortissimo
shameful, ('n one) beginning to-speak for a very-brave

viro, timere, que minimè decet, quum
man, to-show-fear, and 'it-is in-no-way 'becoming, when

T. Annius ipse magis perturbatur salute
T. Annius himself 'is more 'disturbed for-the-safety

reipublicæ, quàm de suâ, me posse non
of-the-republic, than for his-own. (that) I can not

affere ad ejus causam parem magnitudinem
bring to his cause equal greatness (and command)

animi, tamen hæc nova forma novi judicii
of-mind, however this new form of-an-unusual (kind) of-tria

terret oculos, qui, quocunque incidunt
terrifies (my) eyes, which, wherever they-fall

requirunt consuetudinem fori, et pristinum
equire [miss] the usual-customs of-the-forum, and the ancient

morem judiciorum. Enim vester consessus
'orm (and usage, of-tribunals. For your session, [seats,]

non cinctus est coronâ, ut
(O judges), 'is not 'surrounded by-a-circle (of citizens), as

solebat; non stipati sumus usitatâ
it-used-to-be; (and) 'we-are not 'densely-environed by-the-usual

frequentiâ; nec illa præsidia
crowd (of hearers); nor those guards (of soldiers)

quæ cernitis pro omnibus templis, etsi
which you-see before all the temples, although

collocata sunt contra vim, tamen
they-are-stationed-there against violence, yet

non afferunt aliquid oratori, ut
'they-do not 'bring any (encouragement) to-the-speaker, as

in foro et in judicio; quamquam
(the people) in the forum and in the courts-of-justice; although

septi sumus salutaribus et necessaris præsidiis,
we-are-surrounded by-salutary and necessary guards,

tamen quidem possimus ne non timere sine aliquo
yet indeed we-can not fear without some

timore. Quæ si
fear. [We cannot divest ourselves of all fear.] Which (things) if

putarem opposita Miloni, cederem
I-thought (that) they-were-opposed to-Milo, I-would-give-way

tempori, judices, nec existimarem esse locum
to-the-times, O judges, nor would-I-deem (that) there-was place

orationi inter tantam vim armorum. Sed
for-an-oration among so-great a force of-arms. But

consilium Cn. Pompeii sapientissimi et justissimi
the prudent-counsels of-Cn. Pompey a most-wise and just

viri recreat et reficit me, qui profectò nec
man encourages and reassures me, who certainly 'would not

putaret suæ justitiæ, quem
'think (it a part) of-his justice, (that the persons) whom

tradidisset reum sententiis judicum,
he-had-given-over as-a-defendant (to receive) the sentence of-the-judges,

dedere eundem telis
(that) they had-surrendered the same-person to-the-weapons

militum; nec sapientiæ, armare
of-the-soldiers; nor (a part) 'of (his) 'wisdom, to-arm

publicâ auctoritate, temeritatem concitatæ multitudinis.
with-public authority, the rashness of-an-excited multitude.

Quamobrem illa arma, centuriones, cohortes
Wherefore those arms, (those) centurions, (those) cohorts

non denuntiant periculum, sed præsidium nobis,
do not 'announce danger, but protection to-us,

neque solùm hortantur ut simus
nor 'do-they alone 'exhort (us) that we-should-be

quieto, sed etiam ut magno
in-a-calm (state of mind), but also that (we should be) in-a-great

animo; neque modò pollicentur
state of) mind [courageous]; nor 'do-they only 'promise

auxilium meæ defensioni, verùm etiam silentium.
assistance to-my defence, but also silence.

Verò reliqua multitudo, quæ quidem est
But the remaining multitude, which indeed is (composed)

civium, est tota nostra;
of-citizens, is altogether ours, (and favourable to our cause);

neque quisquam eorum, quos videtis intuentes
neither any-one of-those, whom you-see looking-on

undique, unde aliqua pars fori potest adspici,
from-every-place, whence any part of-the-forum can be-seen,

et expectantes exitum hujus judicii, quum non
and waiting the issue of-this trial, when 'he-does not

favet virtuti Milonis, tum putat
(only as much) 'favour the virtue of-Milo, as-that he-thinks

decertari hodierno die, de se, de suis
it-to-be-contended to-day, concerning himself, concerning his

liberis, de patriâ, de
children, concerning (his) country, (and) concerning (his own)

fortunis.
fortunes.

2. Unum genus est adversum, que infestum nobis
One class is adverse, and hostile to-us

eorum, quos furor P. Clodii pavit rapinis, et
of-those-people, whom the fury of-P. Clodii has-fed by-rapine, and

incendiis et omnibus publicis exitiis; qui etiam
conflagrations and by all public disasters; who even

nisternâ   concione   incitati sunt,   ut   præirent
by-yesterday's harangue   were-incited,   that they-should-dictate

vobis   voce,   quid   judicaretis.   Clamor
to-you 'by (their) 'clamour, what you-were-to-decide. The shouts

quorum, si forte   fuerit qui, debebit admorere
of-these-men, if perchance there-should-be any, ought to-admonish

vos, ut retineatis eum civem,
you, that you-should-retain him a citizen, (in the country, by a

          qui semper neglexit illud genus
sentence of acquittal), who always neglected that class

hominum, que   maximos clamores, pro vestrâ
of-men, and (their) very-great outcries, for your

salute. Quamobrem adeste animis,
safety.   Wherefore be-present in mind [be of good courage],

judices, et deponite   timorem, si habetis quem.
O judges, and lay-aside (all) fear, if you-have any.

Nam si unquam potestas fuit vobis
For if ever the power was to-you [if you ever had the

        judicandi   de bonis et fortibus
power] of-judicially-deciding concerning good and brave

viris, si unquam de civibus   meritis bene,
men, if ever concerning citizens (who have) deserved well

        si denique unquam locus datus est
(of their country), if in-fine ever an opportunity was-given

delectis viris amplissimorum ordinum,   ut
to-chosen men of-the-most-illustrious orders (in the state), that

declararent   re   et   sententiis,
they-declare (and show) by-the-affair-itself, and 'by(their)'votes-as-judges,

sua studia erga fortes et bonos cives, quæ
their good-will towards brave and good citizens, which

        sæpe significassent   vultu et
they-have often 'signified 'by (their) 'countenance and

verbis, vos profectò hoc tempore habetis omnem
words, you certainly at-this time have all

eam potestatem, ut statuatis,   utrum nos, qui
that power, that you-may-determine, whether we, who

    semper dediti fuimus vestræ auctoritati,
'have always 'been-devoted to-your authority 'are

miseri,   semper   lugeamus,   an,   diu
miserable-men, always   'to-mourn,   or,   'having for-a-long-time

vexati   a   perditissimis   civibus,   aliquando
'been-harassed by   most-abandoned   citizens,   at-length

recreemur   per vos, ac per
we-may-be-restored-to (our former state of safety) by   you, and by

vestram fidem,   virtutem que sapientiam.   Enim
your   good-faith,   virtue   and   wisdom.   For

quid,   judices, laboriosius, quid magis sollicitum,
what (condition), O judges, more-harassing, what more   vexatious,

magis   exercitum,   potest   dici   aut fingi, nobis
more   trying,   can   be-said or imagined, for-us

duobus, qui adducti   ad rempublicam,
two,   who induced (to devote ourselves) to   the republic,

spe   amplissimorum præmiorum, possumus non
by-the-hope of-most-honourable   rewards,   can   not

carere   metu   crudelissimorum   suppliciorum ?
be-free-from   the fear   of-the-most-cruel   punishments ?

Equidem semper putavi tempestates et procellas,
Indeed   'I always 'thought (that) the storms and   tempests,

duntaxat in illis fluctibus   concionum
at-least   in those agitations (and tumults) of-public-assemblies

subeundas esse   Miloni, quia semper senserat
were-to-be-encountered (by) Milo, because 'he always 'was-in-favour

pro bonis contra improbos; vero in judicio, et in
of   the good against   the bad ;   but   in a court, and in

eo consilio, in quo   amplissimi viri   ex
such a council, in which the-most-honourable men (selected) from

cunctis ordinibus   judicarent,
all   the orders (of men in the state, sit as judges and)   decide,

nunquam   existimavi,   inimicos   Milonis
'I-have never   'thought,   (that) the enemies   of-Milo

habituros esse ullam spem ad exstinguendam, non
would-have   any   hope to   destroy,   not

modò   salutem, sed etiam   infringendam
only   (his) safety, but even (to)   weaken (or diminish

gloriam, per tales viros   Quanquam in hac
his) glory, by such men   Although   in this

causâ, judices, non abutemur tribunatu T.
cause, O judges, [1]we-will not [1]misuse the tribuneship of-T.

Annii, que omnibus rebus gestis pro salute
Annius, and all (his) deeds performed for the safety

reipublicæ, ad defensionem hujus
of-the-republic, for (the purpose of) defence (in) this

criminis. Nisi videritis oculis,
accusation. Unless you-may-have-seen [1]with (your own) [1]eyes, (that)

insidias factas a Clodio Miloni, nec depre-
ambuscades were-laid by Clodius (against) Milo, nor shall-we-

caturi sumus, ut condonetis nobis hoc crimen,
entreat (you), that you-pardon us this crime,

propter multa præclara merita in rempublicam;
on-account-of (our) many eminent services for the republic;

nec postulaturi, ut, si mors P. Clodii fuerit
nor shall-we-request (of you), that, if the death of-P, Clodius was

vestra salus, idcirco assignetis eam virtuti
your safety, that-therefore you-should-attribute it to-the-courage

Milonis, potius quàm felicitati Romani populi.
of Milo, rather than to-the-good-fortune of-the-Roman people.

Sin illius insidiæ fuerint clariores
But-if his [Clodius's] ambuscades will-be (made) clearer (than)

hac luce, tum denique obsecrabo que obtestabor
this light (of day), then in-fine I-entreat and supplicate

vos, judices, si amisimus cetera, ut saltem
you, O judges, (that) if we-have-lost (all) the rest, that at-least

hoc relinquatur nobis. ut liceat defendere
this may-be-left to-us. that it-may-be-allowed (us) to-defend

impune vitam ab audaciâ que telis
with-impunity (our) life from the audacity and weapons

inimicorum.
of-our-enemies.

3. Sed antequam venio ad eam orationem,
But before I-come to that (part of) the speech,

quæ est propria vestræ quæstionis,
which is properly your inquiry. (and which especially

ea videntur, refutanda esse,
belongs to this trial), those-things seem (necessary) to-be-refuted.

quæ sæpe jactata sunt et in senatu ab
which ¹have often ¹been-brought-forth both in the senate by (our)

inimicis, et in concione ab improbis, et
enemies, and in the assembly-of-the-people by bad-men, and

paulo ante ab accusatoribus, ut, omni
a little before (this) by (our) accusers, so-that, all

errore sublato, possitis plane videre rem quæ
error being-removed, you-may plainly see the affair which

veniat in judicium. Negant esse fas ei intueri
may-come on trial. They-deny that-it-is right for-him to-see

lucem, qui fateatur hominem occissum esse a
the light, who confesses (that) a man has-been-killed by

se. In qua urbe tandem stultissimi homines
him. In what city then ¹do most-foolish men

disputant hoc? Nempe in eâ, quæ primum
¹dispute about-this? Namely in that-city, which first

vidit judicium de capite M. Horatii,
saw a trial for life (namely that) of-M. Horatius,

fortissimi viri, qui, civitate nondum liberâ,
a most-brave man, who, the city ¹being not-yet ¹free,

tamen liberatus est comitiis
(but under the kingly government,) yet was-acquitted by-the-comitia

Romani populi, quum fateretur sororem
of-the-Roman people, although he-confessed (that his) sister

interfectam esse suâ manu. An est quisquam,
was-killed by-his-own hand. Or is-there any-one,

qui ignoret hoc, quum quæratur de
who may-be-ignorant of-this, when inquiry-is-made concerning

homine occiso, aut solere negari
a man, (who has been) slain, either it-is-usual for-it-to-be-denied

omninò factum esse, aut defendi
altogether (that) it-has-been-done, or for-it-to-be-defended (because)

factum esse recte et jure? Nisi vero existimatis
it-was-done rightly and lawfully? Unless indeed you-think

P. Africanum fuisse dementem, qui, quum
(that) P. Africanus was out-of-his-mind, who, when

interrogaretur in concione, a C. Carbone,
he-was-asked in an assembly-of-the-people, by C Carbo,

tribuno plebis seditiose, quid sentiret
a tribune of-the-people in-a-factious-manner, what he-thought

de morte T. Gracchi, responderit videri
of the death of-T. Gracchus, replied (that) he-seemed-to-be

jure cæsum. Enim neque posset ille
rightly killed. For neither could that (distinguished)

Servilius Ahala aut P. Nasica, aut L. Opinius, aut
Servilius Ahala or P. Nasica, or L. Opinius, or

C. Marius, aut, me consule, senatus
C. Marius, or, I (being) consul, the senate (itself)

haberi non nefarius, si esset nefas
be-considered (as) not wicked, if it-was unlawful (that)

sceleratos cives interfici. Itaque, judices, non
criminal citizens be-put-to-death. Therefore, O judges, not

sine causâ doctissimi homines prodiderunt memoriæ
without reason most learned men have-transmitted to-memory

hoc, etiam fictis fabulis, eum, qui necavisset
this, even in-fabulous stories, (that) he, who had-killed

matrem causâ ulciscendi patris,
(his) mother for-the-purpose of-avenging (his) father's (death),

sententiis hominum variatis, libe-
the opinions of-men (who were his judges) being-divided, he-was-

ratum, non solùm divinâ sententiâ, sed etiam
acquitted, not only by-divine opinion, but even

sapientissimæ deæ. Quod si
(by that) of-the-most-wise goddess [Minerva]. Because if (the laws of)

duodecim tabulæ voluerunt nocturnum furem
the twelve tables allowed a nocturnal robber

interfici impune quoquo modo, autem
to-be-killed with-impunity in-any manner, but (one who robbed)

diurnum, si defenderet se telo; quis
in-the-day-time, (only) if he-defended himself with-a-weapon; who

est, qui quoquo modo quis interfectum sit,
is-there, who in-whatever manner any-one may-be-killed,

putet puniendum, quum videat
may-consider that-he-ought-to-be-punished, when he-sees (that)

aliquando gladium porrigi nobis ab legibus ipsis
sometimes a sword is-presented to-us by the laws themselves

ad occidendum hominem
to kill a man.

4. Atqui si est ullum tempus
But if there-is any time (or occasion, that)

hominis necandi jure, quæ sunt multa,
a man might-be-killed with-right, (and) which are many,

certe illud est non modò justum, verùm etiam
certainly that is not only just, but also

necessarium, quum illata vis defenditur vi.
necessary, when offered violence is-resisted by-violence.

Quum militaris tribunus, in exercitu C. Marii,
When a military tribune, in the army of-C. Marius, (and

propinquus ejus imperatoris, eriperet pudicitiam
a relation of-that commander, attempted violence

militi, interfectus est ab eo
(on the person of) a soldier, he-was-killed by him (the soldier)

cui afferebat vim. Enim probus adolescens
to-whom he-offered violence. For the virtuous youth

maluit facere periculose, quàm perpeti turpiter.
chose-rather to-act dangerously, than suffer shamefully

Atque ille summus
[he preferred incurring danger, to dishonour]. And that illustrious

vir liberavit hunc, solutum scelere, periculo.
man (Marius) delivered him, absolved from-crime, from-danger.

Vero quæ injusta nex potest inferri insidiatori,
But what unjust death can be-inflicted on-the-waylayer

et latroni? Quid nostri comitatus,
and robber? What 'do our escorts (on a journey),

quid gladii volunt? quos certe non
what (do our) swords 'mean? which certainly 'it-would not

liceret habere, si nullo pacto liceret
be-allowed (us) to-have, if 'it-were in-no manner 'allowed

uti. Igitur, judices, hæc est non scripta,
to-use (them). Therefore, O judges, this is not a written

lex, sed nata, quam non didicimus,
law, but a natural-law, which 'we-have not 'learned.

accepimus,   legimus,   verùm   arripuimus,
received   (by tradixion, or)   read,   but   have-taken,

hausimus,   expressimus   ex   naturâ   ipsâ,   ad
imbibed   (and)   extracted   (it) from   nature   herself,   (in)

quam   non docti,   sed   facti,
which [1]we-were not [1]instructed,   but (for which) we-were-made, [1]we-are

non   instituti sumus,   sed   imbuti   ut   si
not   [1]taught   (it),   but   are-imbued (with it), so-that,   if

nostra vita   incidisset   in aliquas   insidias, si in
our   life should-be-endangered (by)   any   snares,   if (by)

vim,   et   in   tela   aut   latronum   aut
violence,   and   (by)   the weapons   either   of-robbers   or

inimicorum,   omnis ratio   salutis expediendæ   esset
of-enemies,   every means   of-saving-life   would-be

honesta.   Enim   leges   silent
honourable.   For   the laws   are silent, (and inoperative, in contests)

inter   arma,   nec   jubent   se
with   arms   (in hand),   nor   (do the laws)   command (that) they

exspectari, quum   ei   qui   velit   exspectare
be-waited-for,   when   on-him who   might-wish   to-wait   (for the en-

injusta   pœna   luenda sit,
forcement of the laws)   an unjust   punishment   might-be-inflicted,

ante quàm   justa   repetenda.
before   that   a just-one   might-be-demanded, (or obtained by him).   [A

great calamity, or even death, might be inflicted, before the law could be

Etsi   lex   ipsa   persapienter,   et quodam-
enforced.]   Although the law   itself   very-wisely,   and   in-some-

modo   tacite   dat   potestatem   defendendi,   quæ
measure   tacitly   gives   the power   of-defending,   which   (does)

non   hominem   occidi,   sed   vetat   esse
not   (allow, that)   a man   be-killed,   but   forbids (any one)   to-be

cum telo   causâ   occidendi hominis;
with a weapon [to have a weapon]   for-the-purpose   of-killing   a man;

ut,   quum   causa,   non   telum
so-that,   as   the cause (of carrying a weapon),   not   the weapon (itself)

quæretur,   qui   esset usus   telo,   causâ
is-inquired-into,   be-who   made-use   of-a-weapon,   for-the-purpose

defendendi **sui,** **judicaretur** **habuisse** **telum**
of-defending himself, would-be-judged to-have-had the weapon

non **causâ** **occidendi hominis.** **Quapropter,**
not for-the-purpose of-killing a man. Wherefore,

judices, **hoc maneat in causâ ;**
O judges, 'let this 'remain in the cause [let this be an established

enim **non** **dubito,** **quin**
principle in this cause] ; for 'I-do not 'doubt, tha

probaturus sim **meam defensionem vobis,**
I-shall-prove (and make good) my defence before-you,

si **memineritis id, quod potestis non oblivisci**
if you-remember that, which you-can not have-forgotten

insidiatorem **posse interfici**
(that) a waylayer (and plotter against one's life) may be-slain

jure.
lawfully.

5. Sequitur illud, **quod sæpissime**
There-follows that, [the next thing is], which 'is very-often

dicitur a(b) inimicis Milonis, **senatum judicasse**
'asserted by the enemies of-Milo, (that) the senate had-judged

cædem in qua P. Clodius occisus est,
(that) the slaughter in which P. Clodius was-killed,

factam esse contra rempublicam. Vero illam
was-done against the republic. But that (act of Milo)

senatus comprobavit, non solùm suis sententis, sed
the senate approved, not only by-their votes, but

etiam **studiis.** **Enim quoties illa**
also 'by (their) 'zeal (in his favour). For how-often 'has that

causa acta est a nobis in senatu ? quibus
cause been-pleaded by us in the senate ? with-what

assensionibus universi ordinis ? **quam**
assenting-approbations of-the-whole order (of the senate)? (and) tha

nec tacitis, nec occultis ? **Enim quando frequen-**
neither silent, nor concealed? For when in-a-very-

tissimo senatu **quatuor, aut summùm quinque,**
full senate (only) four, or at-most five,

inventi sunt, qui non probarent causam Milonis.
were-found, who 'did not 'approve the cause of-Milo.

Illæ intermortuæ conciones hujus ambusti tribuni
Those lifeless harangues of-that scorched tribune

plebis declarant, quibus meam potentiam
of-the-people show (that), in-which (harangues) my power

quotidie invidiose criminabatur, quum
(and influence) ¹is daily invidiously ¹found-fault-with, when

diceret, senatum decernere non quod sentiret,
he-says, (that) the senate decrees not what it-might-think

sed quod ego vellem. Quæ quidem si
but what I might-wish. Which indeed if

appellanda est potentia potius, quam mediocris
it-is-to-be-called power rather than a moderate

auctoritas, aut propter magna merita
authority (or influence), either on-account-of great services (done)

in rempublicam in bonis causis, aut nonnulla gratia
for the republic in good causes, or some favour

apud bonos, propter hos meos officiosas
(and credit) among the good, on-account-of these my serviceable

labores; sane appelletur ita,
(and obliging) labours; well-then let-it-be-called so,

dummodo nos utamur eâ pro salute bonorum
provided we use it for the-safety of-the-good

contra amentiam perditorum. Vero etsi est non
against the madness of-the-wicked. But although it-is not

iniqua, tamen senatus nunquam putavit
an unjust (investigation), yet the senate never thought

hanc quæstionem constituendam. Enim
(that) that investigation ought-to-be-instituted. For

erant leges, erant quæstiones, vel de
there-were laws, there-were inquisitions, either concerning

cæde, vel de vi; nec mors P. Clodii
murder, or concerning violence; nor ¹did the death of-P. Clodius

afferebat tantum mœrorem ac luctum senatui, ut
¹bring such-great grief and mourning to-the-senate, that

nova quæstio constitueretur.
a new (and particular) inquisition should-be-instituted (by them).

Enim potestas decernendi judicium de illo
For (when) the power of-ordering a trial concerning that

incesto stupro cujus erepta esset senatui,
sacrilegious crime of-his [Clodius] was-taken (from) the-senate;

quis potest credere, senatum putasse
who can believe, (that) the-senate had-thought-of

constituendum novum judicium, de ejus
constituting a new (and special) trial, concerning his

interitu? Cur igitur senatus decrevit,
death? Why therefore 'has the senate 'decreed, (that)

incendium curiæ, oppugnationem ædium
the burning of-the-senate-house, the attack on-the-house

M. Lepidi, hanc ipsam cædem factum esse contra
of-M. Lepidus, (and) this same murder was-done against

rempublicam? Quia nulla vis, in liberâ civitate,
the republic? Because no violence, in a free state,

unquam suscepta est inter cives, non contra
'has ever 'occurred among citizens, (that is) not against

rempublicam. Enim illa defensio contra vim est
the republic. For that defence against violence is

non unquam optanda, sed nonnunquam est
not ever to-be-desired, but sometimes it-is

necessaria. Nisi vero aut ille dies, quo
necessary. Unless indeed either that day, on-which

T. Gracchus cæsus est, aut ille quo Caius, aut
T. Gracchus was slain, or that on-which Caius was, or

arma Saturnini, etiamsi oppressa sunt e
the arms of-Saturninus, although repressed on-the-part-of

republica, tamen non vulnerarunt
the republic, yet 'they-have not wounded (or injured)

rempublicam.
the republic.

6. Itaque ego ipse decrevi, quum constaret
Therefore I myself voted, when it-was-evident

cædem factam esse in Appiâ, non
(that) the murder was-committed on the Appian (way), (that) not

eum, qui defendisset se, fecisse contra
he, who had-defended himself, acted against

rempublicam; sed, quum inessent insidiæ et
the republic: but, as there were snares and

vis   in   re,   reservavi   crimen judicio,   notavi
violence   in the-affair,   I-reserved   the guilt for-trial,   I-admitted

rem.   Quod   si   licuisset,   per illum furiosum
the deed.   Because   if   it-had-been-allowed,   by   that   furious

tribunum,   senatui   perficere   quod   sentiebat,
tribune,   to-the-senate   to-perfect   what   it-thought,

haberemus   nullam   novam   quæstionem.   Enim
we should-have-had   no   new   inquisition.   For

decernebat, ut   quæreretur   veteribus
it-decreed,   that (the affair) should-be-investigated   according-to-old

_egibus,   tantummodo   extra
(and established) laws,   only   out-of (the usual)

ordinem.   Sententia   divisa est,   nescio
order.   The proposition (or resolve) was-divided,   I-know-not

quo   postulante;   enim   est   nihil
by-whom (it was)   moved   (to do so);   for   it-is   not

necesse   me   proferre   flagitia omnium.   Sic
necessary   for-me   to-bring-forward   the infamy of-all.   So

reliqua   auctoritas senatûs
the remaining   authority of-the-senate (to act on the entire proposition)

sublata est,   emptâ   intercessione.
was-taken-away,   by-the-bought   veto   (of a tribune). (Oh)-

At enim Cn. Pompeius suâ   rogatione
but indeed   Cn. Pompey   by-his   bringing-a-law before-the-people

judicavit,   et   de   re,   et de causâ; enim
pronounced-judgment, both concerning the fact, and the cause;   for

tulit   de   cæde, quæ facta esset
he-brought-forward (a law) concerning the murder, which was-committed

in Appiâ viâ,   in   qua   P. Clodius occisus est.
on the Appian way,   in   which   P. Clodius   was-slain.

Quid   ergo   tulit?   Nempe   ut
What   therefore   did-he-bring-forward?   Namely   that

quæreretur.   Porro quid   quærendum est?
it-should-be-investigated.   But   what   is-to-be-inquired-into?

Ne   factum sit? At   constat.   A quo?   At
Whether   was-it-done? But (that) is-evident.   By whom?   But that

paret.   Igitur   vidit etiam   in   confessione
is-manifest   'He therefore   saw   even   in   the confession

facti, tamen defensionem juris posse
of-the-fact, (that) yet a defence of-the-right could

suscipi. Quod nisi videsset,
be-maintained. Because unless he [Pompey] might-have-perceived,

eum, qui fateretur, posse absolvi, quum
(that) he, who confessed, might be-acquitted, when

videret nos fateri, neque unquam jussisset
he-saw (that) we confessed, neither would-he ever have-ordered

quæri, nec dedisset vobis hanc tam
(the affair) to-be-tried, nor would-he-have-given you that so

salutarem literam in judicando, quam
salutary letter (of acquittal) in pronouncing-judgment, as

illam tristem. Cn. Pompeius
(likewise) that sad-one (of condemnation). Cn. Pompey

videtur vero mihi, non modò judicasse nihil
seems indeed to-me, not only to-have-adjudged nothing

gravius contra Milonem, sed etiam statuisse,
unfavourable against Milo, nor even to-have-ordained,

quid oporteret vos spectare in
what it-might-be-proper (that) you should-look-to in

judicando. Nam, qui non
forming (your) judgment. For, he-who (did) not (inflict)

pœnam confessioni, sed dedit
punishment (after) confession, but. gave (the cause for trial and)

defensionem, is putavit, causam
defence, 'he (certainly) 'thought, (that) the cause

interitûs quærendam, non interitum.
of-the-death was-to-be-inquired-into, not the death (itself).

Jam ipse profectò dicet illud, ne quod
Now he-himself 'will certainly 'tell (us) that, whether what

fecit suâ sponte, putarit tribuendum
he-did (of) his-own accord, he-might think, ought to-be-attributed

Publio Clodio, an tempori.
to-Publius Clodius, or to-the-times.

7. Nobilissimus vir suæ domæ, propugnator
The-most-illustrious man of-his family, the-defender

senatûs, atque quidem illis temporibus, pæne
of-the-senate, and indeed in-those times, almost

patronus,   avunculus   hujus   nostri   judicis,
the patron (thereof),   the uncle   of-this   our   judge,

fortissimi   viri M. Catonis,   M. Drusus tribunus
the most-brave man   M. Cato,   M. Drusus   a tribune

plebis   occisus est.   Populus   nihil   consultus
of-the-people was-killed.   The people 'were not 'consulted

de   ejus morte, nulla quæstio decreta est
concerning his death,   no   inquisition was decreed

senatu. Quantum luctum fuisse in hac urbe,
the senate. What mourning was-there in this city, (as)

accepimus a nostris patribus, quum illa nocturna
we-have-heard from our fathers, when that nocturnal

vis illata esse P. Africano,   quiescenti
violence was-offered to-P. Africanus, [when he was killed] reposing

suæ domi? quis   non tum gemuit? quis   non
in-his house? who 'did not then 'groan? who 'did not

arsit dolore,   quem omnes cuperent   esse
'burn with grief, whom   all   desired   to-be

immortalem, si posset fieri, ejus mortem esse
immortal,   if it-could be-so, (that) his death was

ne quidem necessariam   exspectatam?
not indeed a necessary (and) expected (one)?

                              Num
[That his death was not even a natural one?] Whether 'there-was

igitur ulla quæstio lata est,   de   morte
therefore any inquiry 'brought-forward, concerning the death

Africani? Certe nulla; quid ita? Quia   clari
of-Africanus? Certainly none; why so? Because illustrious

homines   non necantur alio facinore,
men   'are not 'killed by-one crime,   (and)

obscuri alio
obscure-men by-another. [The crime is the same, in killing an illustrious

                              Intersit
man, as in killing an obscure one.] Grant (that) there-may-be-a-difference

inter dignitatem   vitæ summorum atque
in   the dignity (and worth) of-life of-the-highest   and

infimorum; quidem mors illata per scelus
of-the-lowest; indeed death inflicted by crime

teneatur   et   iisdem   pœnis   et
is-held   (amenable) both   to-the-same punishments and

legibus.   Nisi forte   erit magis
laws (for all classes of men). Unless perchance it-were a greater

parricida,   si qui necaverit consularem patrem,
parricide, [crime,] if one should-kill a consular father,

quàm si quis   humilem, aut   mors
than if one (should kill) an humble-citizen, or (that) the death

P. Clodii   erit   eo   atrocior,   quod is
of-P. Clodius should-be in-that the-more-atrocious, because he

interfectus sit in monumentis suorum majorum.
may-have-been-killed among the monuments of-his ancestors.

                          Enim hoc   sæpe
[On the Appian way, which they made.] For this 'is often

dicitur istis;   proinde quasi ille
'said, by-these (advocates of Clodius); consequently as-if that

            Appius Cæcus muniverit viam, non
(celebrated) Appius Cæcus had-constructed the road, not (that)

populus uteretur qua, sed   ubi   sui posteri
the people might-use it, but (that) there (on it) his posterity

latrocinarentur impune. Itaque quum, in istâ
might-rob   with impunity. Therefore when, in this

eâdem Appiâ viâ, P. Clodius occidisset M. Papirium,
same   Appian way, P. Clodius had-killed M. Papirius,

ornatissimum · Romanum equitem, illud facinus fuit
a most-accomplished Roman knight, that crime was

non   puniendum; enim nobilis homo occiderat
not   to-be-punished; for a noble man had-killed

Romanum equitem, in suis   monumentis;
a Roman   knight, among his (family) monuments;

nunc nomen   ejusdem   Appiæ   quantas
now   the name of-that-same Appian (road) what

tragœdias excitat!   Quæ,   antea
tragedies does-it-excite! (This same road) which, (when) heretofore

imbuta est, cruentatâ cæde honesti atque
it-was-wet with-the-bloody murder of-an-honourable and

innocentis viri silebatur, eadem nunc crebò
innocent   man was-not-mentioned, the same 'is now often

usurpatur   posteaquam   sanguine
'mentioned   after-that   (it has been wet)   with-the-blood

latronis   et parricidæ. Sed quid   ego commemoro
of a-robber and parracide.   But why 'do I   'mention

illa?   Servus P. Clodii comprehensus est, in
those-things?   A slave of-P. Clodius   was arrested,   in

templo Castoris, quem ille collocaret   ad
the temple of-Castor, whom he had-placed there for-the-purpose

interficiendum Cn. Pompeium;   sica   extorta est
of-killing   Cn. Pompeius;   the dagger   was wrested

de   manibus, confitenti;   postea   Pompeius
from (his)   hands,   he-confessing;   after-this   Pompey

caruit   foro,   caruit   senatu,
was-wanting (absent) from the forum, was absent from the senate,

caruit   publico;   texit   se   januâ
was-absent from the public; he-protected himself 'by (his) 'doors

ac parietibus, non jure legum que   judiciorum.
and walls,   not by-the-right of-laws and (power) of-tribunals.

Num quæ   rogatio   lata,   num quæ nova
Now what motion-for-a-law was-offered, or what   new

quæstio decreta est? Atqui, si res,   si   vir,
inquisition was-decreed? But, if the thing (itself), if the man,

si ullum tempus   fuit dignum,
if any   time (or occasion) was   worthy (of an extraordinary

           certe hæc fuerunt omnia, in illâ causâ,
investigation), certainly these were   all, in that cause,

summa.   Insidiator   erat collocatus in foro,
the greatest. The concealed-assassin was   placed   in the forum,

atque in ipso vestibulo senatûs;   autem mors
and in the very vestibule of-the-senate; but   death

parabatur ei viro, in cujus vitâ salus   civitatis
was-prepared for-that man, on whose life the safety of-the-state

nitebatur; porro,   eo tempore reipublicæ, quo,
depended;   moreover, at-that   time of-the-republic, in-which

si ille   unus occidisset, non solùm hæc
if he (though only) one   had-fallen,   not alone   this

civitas, sed omnes gentes concidissent. Nisi vero,
state   but   all   nations   had fallen.   Nor indeed

quia   res   non   perfecta est,   fuit   non
because the thing ¹was not ¹accomplished, it-was not

punienda;   proinde   quasi   exitus   rerum,   non
to-be-punished; consequently as-if the result of-things, not

consilia   hominum   vindicentur   legibus. Minus
the-intentions of-men were-to-be-vindicated by-the-laws. Less

dolendum fuit,   re   non   perfectâ,   sed
would-have-to-be-grieved-for, the thing not being-accomplished, but

nihilominus certe   puniendum.   Quoties, judices,
nevertheless certainly it-ought-to-be-punished. How-often, O judges,

ego ipse effugi ex   telis   P. Clodii et
have I myself ¹escaped from the weapons of-P. Clodius and

ex ejus cruentis manibus? ex quibus, si vel mea
from his bloody hands? from which, if either my

fortuna,   vel   reipublicæ   non servasset
good-fortune, or (that) of-the-republic ¹had not ¹saved

me, qui tandem   tulisset   quæstionem   de
me, who in-fine would-have-moved-for an inquisition concerning

meo interitu.
my   death.

8. Sed   sumus   stulti, qui audeamus conferre
But   we-are   foolish, who ¹are to compare

Drusum, qui   Africanum, Pompeium,   mosmet
Drusus, who (also) Africanus, Pompey, (or) we

ipsos cum P. Clodio. Illa fuerunt tolerabilia;
ourselves with P. Clodius. Those-things were to be-borne-with;

nemo potest ferre mortem P. Clodii   æquo
(but) no-one can bear the death of-P. Clodius with-undisturbed

animo. Senatus   luget,   equester   ordo
mind. The senate mourns, the equestrian order

mœret,   tota   civitas   confecta est
is-afflicted-with-grief, the whole state weighed-down

senio   municipia   squalent,
ith-the-languor-of-old-age, the municipalities are-in-mourning,

coloniæ   afflictantur,   denique agri ipsi
the colonies are-afflicted-with-grief, in-fine the fields themselves

desiderant tam beneficum,   tam   salutarem,   tam
miss   so   beneficent, so   useful,   so

mansuetum civem.   Ea fuit non causa, judices,
mild   a citizen.   This was not the reason, O judges,

profectò fuit non, cur Pompeius censeret
certainly it-was not, why Pompey thought (that a law)

quæstionem ferendum sibi; sed,
for-a-special-inquiry-and-trial should-be-moved-for (by) him; but,

sapiens homo atque præditus altâ, et
(being) a wise man and endowed with a profound, and

quodam divinâ mente, vidit multa; illum
a certain divine mind, he-saw many-things (that) he

fuisse inimicum sibi, Milonem
(Clodius) had-been an enemy to-him, (but) Milo

familiarem; in communi lætitiâ omnium, si
an intimate-friend; in the general joy of-all, if

ipse etiam gauderet, timuit ne fides
he-himself also should-rejoice, he-feared lest confidence (in his)

reconciliatæ gratiæ videretur infirmior;
reconciliation (with Clodius) might-seem more-weak;

etiam vidit multa alia, sed maxime illud,
he also saw many other-things, but especially this, (that)

quamvis atrociter ipse tulisset, tamen
however severe (the law) he-himself may-have-proposed, yet (that)

vos judicaturos fortiter. Itaque delegit e
you would-decide fearlessly. Therefore he-has-selected from

florentissimis ordinibus lumina ipsa.
the most illustrious ranks the lights themselves (of the state, for

Neque verò, quod nonnulli dictitant, in
judges). Nor indeed, as some often-say, in

legendis judicibus secrevit meos amicos.
selecting the judges has-he-separated (and passed by) my friends.

Enim neque justissimus vir cogitavit hoc,
For neither 'has (this) most-just man 'thought this,

neque, in legendis bonis viris, potuisset assequi
nor in selecting good men, could-he have-accomplished

id, etiamsi cupisset. Enim mea gratia
that, even-if he-had-wished. For my favour (and influence)

non continetur familiaritatibus,
'is not 'limited (to my) intimacies, [intimate friends,]

quæ possunt non patere late, propterea quòd
which can not extend far, because that (our

consuetudines victûs possunt non esse cum
habits of-social-living can not be with

multis ; sed, si
many, (and necessarily restricts us to few social companions); but, if

possumus quid, possumus
we-can (effect) any thing (by our influence), we-can (do it only)

ex eo, quòd respublica conjunxit nos cum
through this, that the republic has-united us with

bonis ; ex quibus, quum ille legeret
the good; from-among whom, when he [Pompey] had-selected

optimos viros, que arbitraretur id maxime
the best men, and he-thought (that) this greatly

pertinere ad suam fidem,
appertained to his credit, (and the confidence placed in him),

potuit non non legere studiosos mei.
he-could not but select (those) favourably-disposed (to) me.

Quod vero voluit te L. Domiti maxime præesse,
That indeed he-wished you O. L. Domitius especially to-preside,

huic quæstioni, quæsivit nihil aliud, nisi
over-this investigation, he-sought-of nothing else, unless

justitiam, gravitatem, humanitatem, fidem.
justice, dignity, humanity, and good-faith.

Tulit ut
He [Pompey] brought forward (in his law) that (the president) 'should

necesse esset consularem ; credo, quod
necessarily 'be a man-of-consular-dignity ; I-believe, because

ducebat esse munus principum
he-thought (that) it-was the duty of-the-higher-orders

resistere et levitati multitudinis et
to-oppose-themselves both to-the-fickleness of-the-multitude and

temeritati perditorum. Potissimum creavit
to-the-rashness of-the-profligate. Above-all he-selected

te ex consularibus. Enim, jam ab
you from-among those-of-consular-rank. For, already from (your)

adolescentiâ,   dederas   maxima   documenta,
youth,   you-had-given   the greatest   proofs,

quàm   contemneres populares insanias.
how-much   you-despised   popular   madness.

9. Quamobrem, judices, ut aliquando veniamus
Wherefore,   O judges, that   at-length   we-may-come

ad   causam   que   crimen,   si   neque   omnis
to   the cause   (itself) and the accusation, if   neither   all

confessio   facti   est inusitata, neque   quidquam
confession of-the-deed   is   unusual,   nor   (that) any-thing

judicatum est   a   senatu,   de   nostrâ causâ,   aliter
was-determined   by the senate, about   our   cause,   otherwise

ac   nos vellemus, et   lator   legis   ipse,   quum
than   we   wished,   and the proposer of-the-law himself,   when

esset   nulla   controversia   facti,   tamen
there-was   no   dispute   (concerning) the deed,   however

voluit   esse   disceptationem   juris,
desired   that-there-should-be   a discussion   of-the-lawfulness,

    et judices   electi,   que   is   præpositus
(thereof), and   judges being-chosen, and   he   appointed-to-preside

quæstioni,   qui   disceptet   hæc   juste   que
over-the-investigation,   who   would-decide these-things justly   and

sapienter, reliquum est, judices, ut   debeatis   jam,
wisely,   it-remains,   O judges, that   you-ought   now,

quærere   nihil   aliud,   nisi   uter   fecerit
to-inquire   into-nothing   else,   unless   which-one   laid

   insidias   utri.   Quod   quò   possitis
snares-and-ambushes   for-the-other.   Which   that   you-may

facilius   perspicere   argumentis,
the-more-easily   perceive   (what relates)   to-the-argument,

quæso   attendite diligenter, dum   breviter expono
I-entreat (you) attend   carefully,   while 'I   briefly   'explain

vobis   rem gestam. Quum   P. Clodius   statuisset
to-you   the occurrence.   When   P. Clodius   had-determined

vexare   rempublicam   omni   scelere   in
to-harass   the republic   by-all   (kinds of) wickedness   in (his)

præturâ,   que   videret   comitia
prætorship,   and (as)   he-saw   (that) the comitia (for electing officers)

ita   tracta esse   anno   superiore,   ut
'had-been so-long 'delayed in-the-year before,   tha

posset   non gerere præturam multos menses,   qui
he-could   not   hold the prætorship many   months,   he-who

non spectaret gradum honoris, ut ceteri,   sed
did not   regard   the degree of-honour, as others (did), but

et vellet effugere   L. Paullum, civem
also he-wished to-avoid (having) L. Paullum, a citizen (endowed)

singulari virtute,   collegam, et   quæreret
with singular virtue, (for his) colleague, and (as) he (also) desired

integrum annum ad dilacerandam rempublicam,
an entire   year   to   dilacerate   the republic,

subitò reliquit suum annum, que transtulit sese
suddenly he-gave-up his   year,   and transferred himself

in proximum annum, non, ut fit   aliquâ
into   the next   year,   not, that it-was-done through-any

religione,   sed, ut haberet, quod ipse dicebat,
religious-scruples, but, that he-might-have, as he   said,

plenum atque integrum annum, ad gerendam
a full   and   entire   year,   for discharging

præturam, hoc est ad evertendam rempublicam.
the prætorship, that is for   overturning   the republic.

Occurrebat ei,   suam præturam futuram
It-occurred   to-him, (that) his   prætorship   would-be

mancam ac debilem, Milone   consule; porro
lame   and weak,   Milo   (being) consul; moreover

videbat   eum fieri consulem summo
it-seemed, (that) he would-be-made consul with-the-greatest

consensu Romani populi. Contulit se ad ejus
unanimity of-the-Roman people. He betook himself to his

competitores, sed ita, ut   ipse solus
[Milo's] competitors,   but so, that he-himself-alone

gubernaret totam petitionem, etiam illis invitis;
might-rule   the entire   canvass,   even they being-unwilling;

ut sustineret, ut dictitabat tota comitia suis
that he-sustained, as 'he often-'said, the whole comitia on-his

humeris. Convocabat tribus, interponebat   se;
shoulders. He-convoked the tribes,   he-interposed   himself;

conscribebat novam Collinam   delectu
he-formed   a-new   Colline (tribe) by-the-enrolment-of-the

perditissimorum   civium.   Quanto   ille
most-worthless   citizens.   As-much-as   he [Clodius]

       miscebat,   tanto   magis   hic
threw-things-into-confusion, so-much the more this-one [Milo]

convalescebat   in dies.   Ubi   homo
gained-strength (from day) to day. When the-man (Clodius)

paratissimus ad omne facinus vidit,   fortissimum
most-ready   for every crime saw, (that) the-most-brave

virum,   suum inimicissimum   certissimum
person (Milo), his greatest-enemy (was) most-certain (to be)

consulem, que   intellexit   id   sæpe
consul,   and   he-understood (that) this   'was often

declaratum esse, non solum sermonibus,   sed etiam
'declared,   not only by-the-conversation, but also

suffragiis Romani populi, cœpit agere palam, et
by-the-votes of-the-Roman people, he-began to-act openly, and

aperte dicere,   Milonem   occidendum esse.
plainly to-say, (that) Milo   must-be-killed.

    Deduxerat   ex Apennino agrestes et barbaros
He-had-brought-down from the Apennines rustic and barbarous

servos, quos videbatis, quibus depopulatus erat
slaves, whom you-saw, with-whom he   ravaged

publicas silvas, que vexarat Etruriam. Res   erat
the public forests, and harassed Etruria. The affair was

minime obscura. Enim dictitabat palam,
by-no-means concealed. For he-often-said openly, (that)

consulatum posse non   eripi   Miloni
the consulship 'could not 'be-taken-from Milo (but that his)

vitam posse. Hoc sæpe significavit in senatu;
life   could. This 'he often 'hinted in the senate;

dixit   in   concione;   quin etiam
he-said (it openly) in the-public-assemblies-of-the-people; but also

respondit M. Favonio, fortissimo viro, quærenti ex
he-replied to-M. Favonius, a very-brave man inquiring of

eo   qua spe   fureret,   Milone vivo,
him with-what hope he-thus-gave-way-to-his-fury, Milo being-alive,

respondit   triduo,   aut summum quatriduo,
he-answered (that) in three-days, or   at-most   in-four-days, (that)

illum periturum esse ; quam vocem ejus, Favonius
he   would-be-dead ;   which expression of-his,   Favonius

detulit statim   ad hunc M. Catonem.
related immediately to   this   M. Cato, (here present as judge).

10.   Interim,   quum Clodius sciret, (enim neque
     In-the-mean-time,   when   Clodius   knew,   (for   neither

erat difficilis scire),   esse   sollemne,
was-it difficult   to-know-it), (that) there-was   a yearly,

legitimum   necessarium iter Miloni Lanuvium,
legitimate (and)   necessary   journey for Milo to-Lanuvium,

ante XIII diem Kalendis Februarias
before the XIII   day   of-the Kalends of-February [18th of January]

ad prodendum flaminem,   quòd Milo erat dictator
to   nominate   the priest,   because Milo   was   dictator

Lanuvii, ipse   subitò   pridie   profectus est
of Lanuvium, he (Clodius) suddenly, on-the-day-before, proceeded-from

Româ, ut collocaret insidias ante suum fundum
Rome,   that he-might-place ambuscades before his   farm

Miloni (quod intellectum est re).   Atque ita
for Milo   as   was-understood by-the-thing (itself). And he-so

profectus est,   ut relinqueret turbulentam
  departed   (from Rome), that   he-left   a turbulent

  concionem,   in qua ejus furor desideratus est,
assemblage-of-people, in which his violence   was-missed,

   quæ habita est illo ipso die, quam
(and) which was-held on-that same day, which 'he-would

nunquam reliquisset, nisi voluisset obire
never   'have-left, unless he-wished to-go (and make

  locum que tempus   facinoris. Autem
use of) the place and   time (for committing) a crime.   But

Milo, quum fuisset in senatu eo die, quoad
Milo, when he-had-been in   the senate that day, until

senatus   dimissus est, venit domum; mutavit
the senate   was-dismissed,   came   home ; he-changed (his)

calceos et vestimenta; commoratus est paulisper,
shoes   and   dress ;   he-waited   a little,

(ut fit), dum uxor comparat se,
(as (is usually) done), while (his) wife 'gets herself 'ready,

deinde profectus id temporis, quum jam Clodius
then he-departed (at) that time, when already Clodius

potuisset redire, si quidem venturus erat Romam,
might have-returned, if indeed he-was-to-return to Rome,

eo die. Clodius obviam fit ei,
on-that day. Clodius meets him, (he Clodius being)

expeditus, in equo, nullâ rhedâ, nullis
unencumbered, on horseback, with-no carriage, with-no

impedimentis, nullis Græcis comitibus, ut solebat,
baggage, with-no Greek attendants, as he-used

sine uxore, quod fere nunquam,
(to-have), without (his) wife, which (was) almost never

quum hic insidiator, qui apparasset
(the case), when this waylayer, [Milo,] who had-prepared

illud iter, ad faciendam cædem, veheretur
that journey, for-the-purpose-of committing murder, was-drawn

in rhedâ cum uxore, pænulatus
in a carriage with (his) wife, (and was) enveloped-in-a-travelling-cloak,

et magno impedito, et muliebri ac delicato
and with great baggage, and with-an-effeminate and delicate

comitatu ancillarum, que puerorum. Fit obviam
cortege of-maid-servants, and of-boys. He-meets

Clodio ante ejus fundum, fere undecimâ horâ,
Clodius before his farm, about the eleventh hour,

aut non multo secus. Statim complures faciunt
or not much from-it. Immediately many make

impetum in hunc cum telis, de superiore loco;
an attack on him with missiles, from the higher place,

adversi occidunt rhedarium; autem
the opponents kill the driver (of his carriage); but

quum hic, rejectâ pænulâ, desiluisset
when he, having-thrown-off (his) cloak, had-jumped

de rhedâ, que defenderet se acri
from-the-carriage, and defended himself with-a-courageous (and

animo, illi, qui erant cum Clodio.
vigorous) mind, those, who were with Clodius

eductis   gladiis,   partim   recurrere   ad
having-drawn (their) swords,   some-of-them   ran-back   to

rhedam,   ut   adorirentur   Milonem   a   tergo,
the chariot,   that   they-might-attack   Milo   in   the-rear,

partim,   quòd   putarent   hunc   jam
some-of-them,   because   they-thought (that)   he   'was already

interfectum, incipiunt cædere ejus servos, qui erant
slain,   begin   to-kill   his   slaves,   who were

post,   ex   quibus,   qui   fuerunt   præsenti
behind,   from-among   whom,   those-who   had   presence (of)

animo,   et   fideli   in   dominum,
mind   (and resolution), and   were faithful to (their) master,   'were

partim   occisi sunt, partim,   quum   viderent
part-of-them   'slain,   a part,   when   they-saw (that)

pugnari   ad   rhedam,   prohiberentur
there-was-a-fight   at   the carriage,   (and)   were-prohibited from

succurrere   domino,   audirent   ex   Clodio
succouring   (their)   master,   (when) they-heard   from   Clodius

ipso   Milonem occisum, et putarent re
himself, (that)   Milo   was-killed, and   believed the thing (to be)

verâ,   servi   Milonis fecerunt   id   (enim dicam
true,   the servants   of-Milo   did   that   (for   I-speak

aperte, non   causâ   derivandi criminis,
openly,   not for-the-purpose   of shifting   the blame (from Milo to

sed   ut factum est),
nis servants),   but (that the affair may be stated) as   it-was-done),

domino   nec   imperante,   nec   sciente,   nec
(their)   master neither   commanding,   nor   knowing,   nor

præsente,   quod   quisque   voluisset   suos
being-present,   which   each-one (of us) might-have-wished   his

servos facere, in tali re.
servant   to-do,   in   such an affair.

11. Hæc,   judices,   gesta sunt,   ita   sicut
    These-things, O judges,   have-been-done,   just   as

exposui;   insidiator   superatus est;   vis
I-have-stated (them); the-waylayer   was-overcome;   violence

victa   vi,   vel potius audacia   oppressa est
was-defeated by-violence, or   rather   audacity   was-put-down

virtute. Dico nihil, quid respublica
by-valour   I-say   nothing,   (about) what   the republic

consecuta sit, nihil, quid vos
may-have-gained,   nothing,   (about) what   you   (may have gained),

nihil, quid omnes boni.
nothing,   (about) what   all   good-men   (may have gained, by this

    Sane id prosit nihil Miloni, qui
event).   But-indeed 'let that 'be   no   'advantage   to Milo,   who

natus est hoc fato, ut quidem potuerit ne servare
is born   to-this   fate,   that   indeed   he-could   not   save

se, quin unâ, servaret
himself,   but-that   together   (and at the same time),   he-saved

rempublicam que vos. Si id potuit non fieri
the republic   and   you.   If   this   could   not   be-done

jure, habeo nihil, quod defendam. Sin et
with right,   I-have   nothing,   that   I-may-defend.   But-if   both

ratio præscripsit hoc doctis, et necessitas
reason   has-prescribed   this   to-the-learned,   and   necessity

barbaris, et mos gentibus, et etiam natura
to-barbarians,   and   custom   to-nations,   and   also   nature

feris belluis, ut semper propulsarent omnem
to-wild beasts,   that 'they-might always   'repel   all

vim quacunque ope possent, a corpore,
violence,   by-whatever   means   they-could,   from (their)   body

a capite, a suâ vitâ, potestis non
from (their) head,   (and) from   their   life,   you-can   no

judicare hoc improbum facinus, quin
adjudge   this (to be)   a wicked   deed,   but-that

    simul judicetis, omnibus, qui inciderint
at-the-same-time   you-decide,   for-all,   who   may-have-fallen

in latrones, pereundum esse, aut illorum
among   robbers,   (that)   they-must-perish,   either   'by their

    tellis, aut vestris sententiis. Quòd si
[the robber's] 'weapons,   or   by-your   sentences.   Because if

putasset ita, certe fuit optabilius
he-had-thought   so,   'it certainly   'would-have-been   more-desirable

Miloni, dare jugulum P. Clodio,
for Milo.   to-offer   (his)   throat   to-P. Clodio,   (which)

petitum   ab illo non semel, neque tum
had-been-sought by him not once, nor then

primùm, quàm jugulari a vobis, quia
for-the-first-time, than to-be-strangled by you, because 'he-had

non tradidisset se illi jugulandum. Sin nemo
not 'delivered himself to-him to-be-killed. But-if no-one

vestrum sentis ita, jam illud venit in judicium,
of-you thinks so, now this comes in judgment, (and is a

non, ne occisus sit,
subject of inquiry for the judges), not, whether he-may-have-been-killed,

quod fatemur; sed jure, an injuriâ;
which we-confess; but (whether it was done) justly, or unjustly;

quod, in multis causis sæpe quæsitum est.
which, in many causes, 'has often 'been-inquired-into.

Constat insidias factas esse, et id
It-is-evident (that) snares and ambuscades were laid, and this

est, quod senatus judicavit, factum contra
is, what the senate has-determined, was-done against

rempublicam; ab utro factæ sint, est
the republic; by which-of-the-two they-might-have-been-laid, is

incertum. De hoc igitur latum est
uncertain. Concerning this therefore it-has-been-moved (and or-

ut quæreretur. Et ita senatus
dered) that it-should-be-inquired-into. And so the senate

notavit rem, non hominem, et Pompeius
disapproved the-thing, not the man, and Pompey

tulit quæstionem de jure, non
has-brought-forward the inquiry concerning the lawfulness, not

de facto.
concerning the fact (itself).

12. Igitur numquid aliud, venit in
Therefore is-there-any other-thing, (that) comes in

judicium, nisi uter fecerit insidias
judgment, unless which-one laid snares-and-ambuscades

utri? Profectò nihil; si hic
for-the-other? Indeed nothing-else; if this (Milo laid snares)

illi, ut ne sit impune; si
for-him (Clodius), 'let-it not 'be with impunity; if

ille   huic,   tum   nos   solvamur
he (Clodius laid snares) for-this (Milo), then   we   are-acquitted

scelere.
of-guilt.

Igitur   quonam   pacto   potest   probari,
Therefore   in-what   manner   can (it)   be-proved, (that)

Clodium   fecisse   insidias   Miloni?   Est   quidem
Clodius   had-laid   snares   for-Milo?   It-is   indeed

satis,   in   illâ   tam   audaci,   tam   nefariâ   belluâ,
sufficient,   in   that   so   audacious,   so   wicked   a monster,

docere,   magnam causam   ei
to-show, (that there was)   great   reason   for-him (to desire Milo's

           magnam   spem   propositam   in   morte
death, and)   great   hopes   were offered (him) by   the death

Milonis,   magnas   utilitates   fuisse.
of-Milo,   that great   advantages   would-have (resulted to him

       Itaque   illud   Cassianum,   "cui
thereby). Therefore   that (maxim of)   Cassius,   "to-whom

fuerit   bono,"   valeat   in   his
would-it-be   advantageous,"   may-have-authority   among   these

personis;   etsi   boni   impelluntur   nullo
persons;   although   the good   are-impelled   by-no

emolumento in   fraudem, improbi
advantage   in (committing)   a crime,   bad-men (are induced

      saepe   parvo.   Atqui,   Milone
to do so) often   by-a-small (advantage). But-then,   Milo

interfecto, assequebatur hoc, non modò, ut   esset
being-slain,   he-attained   this,   not   only, that he-might-be

praetor, non   eo   consule,   quc   posset facere
praetor,   not   with-such   a consul, under-whom he-could   commit

nihil sceleris,   sed etiam, ut   esset praetor,
nothing of-crime, [no crime,] but   also, that he-would-be praetor,

iis   consulibus, quibus si   non juvantibus,
those being-consuls,   who   if (they were) not   assisting (him),

at   certe conniventibus, speraret,   se   posse
at-least certainly   were conniving,   he-hoped, (that) he might-be-able

eludere   in   illis suis   cogitatis   furoribus;
to-elude (detection) in   those   his   contemplated   frantic-deeds:

cujus conatus illi, ut ipse ratiocinabatur,
whose attempts they, [the consuls], as he [Clodius] reasoned

nec cuperent reprimere, si possent,
(with himself), 'would not 'desire to suppress, if they-could,

quum arbitrarentur se debere ei
when they-considered (that) they were-indebted to-him

tantum beneficium, et si vellent,
for-such-a-great favour, and if they-wished (to repress them),

fortasse possent vix frangere audaciam
perhaps 'they-could 'scarcely crush the audacity

sceleratissimi hominis, jam corroboratam
of-a-most-wicked man, now confirmed

vetustate. An verò, judices, 'are
by-a-long-duration (of impunity). But indeed, O judges,

vos soli ignoratis, vos versamini
you alone ignorant (of all this), 'do you 'reside (as)

hospites in hac urbe? vestræ aures
strangers in this city? 'do your ears

peregrinantur neque versantur in hoc
'wander-and-pay-no-attention, nor are-they-practised in this

pervagato sermone civitatis, quas leges
common-and-wide-spread report of-the-city, what laws

(si nominandæ sunt leges, ac non faces
(if they-are-to-be-called laws, and not firebrands (for)

urbis, pestes reipublicæ) ille impositurus fuerit
the city, (and) pests of-the-republic) he would-have-imposed

nobis omnibus, atque inusturus? Exhibe
on us all, and indelibly-branded (on us all)? Produce

quæso Sexte Clodi, exhibe illud librarium
I-entreat-you Sextus Clodius, produce that book-case (containing)

vestrarum legum, quod aiunt, te eripuisse
your laws, which they-say, (that) you snatched

e domo, et ex mediis armis, que
from (your) house, and from the midst (of) arms, and

nocturnâ turbâ, extulisse tanquam
a nocturnal mob (threatening you), (and) bore (it) aloft as

Palladium, videlicet, ut posse deferre
a Palladium, for-the-purpose, that you-might-be-able to-carry

præclarum munus, atque instrumentum
the splendid present, and instrument-of-writing (for)

tribunatûs ad aliquem, si nactus esses, qui
the tribuneship, to some-one, if you-could-find (him), who

gereret tribunatum tuo arbitrio.
would-discharge-the-duties (of) the-tribuneship to-your wish.

An ille ausus esset facere mentionem hujus
Whether 'would he 'have-dared to-make mention of-this

legis, quam Sex. Clodius gloriatur, inventam
law, which Sex. Clodius boasts, (that) it-was-devised

a se, Milone vivo, ne dicam
by him, Milo being-alive, not I-may-mention (his) (being)

consule? De omnium nostrum—audeo non dicere
consul? Concerning all of-us —I dare not say

totum. Videte, quid ea lex habitura fuerit
all. See, what that law would-have-had

vitii cujus etiam reprehensio
of odiousness, (when the mere mention) of-which even (for) reprehension

est periculosa. Et quidem adspexit me illis
is dangerous. And indeed he-looked at-me with-those

oculis, quibus tum solebat, quum minabatur
eyes, with-which 'he then 'used-to-do, when he threatened

omnia omnibus. Lumen curiæ quippe
every-thing to all. This light of-the-senate-house indeed

movet me.
moves me.

13. Quid? tu putas, me iratum tibi,
What? do you think, (that) I am-angry with-you,

Sexte, cujus inimicissimum tu punitus es, etiam
O Sextus, whose greatest-enemy you have-punished, even

multò crudeliùs, quàm erat meæ
much more-cruelly, than it-would-be (the part) of-my

humanitatis postulare? Tu ejecisti domo
humanity to-require? You threw 'from (his) 'house

cruentum cadaver P. Clodii, tu abjecisti in
the bloody carcass of-P. Clodius, you 'cast (it) 'out to

publicum, tu reliquisti spoliatum maginibus,
he public. you left-it deprived (of ancestral) images,

exsequiis, pompâ, laudatione, semustilatum
of-funeral-rites, of-funeral-pomp, of-funeral-panegyric, half-burnt

    infelicissimis   lignis
'with (those) 'most unfortunate (pieces of) wood [the furniture of the

      dilaniandum   canibus,
senate chamber] (and) to-be-torn (and devoured) by dogs,

  nocturnis. Quare etsi fecisti nefarie,
that-prowl-about-at night. Wherefore although you-have-acted wickedly

tamen, quoniam exprompsisti tuam crudelitatem
however, because you-have-wreaked your cruelty

in meo inimico,   possum non laudare,
on my enemy, (though) I-can not praise (you),

certe debeo non irasci. [Demonstravi judices,
certainly I-ought not to-be-angry. [I have-demonstrated O judges,

quantum Claudii inter] fuerit, Milonem
how-much (as respects) Claudius it was] (his) interest, (that) Milo

 occidi. Nunc convertite animos vicissim ad
should-be-slain. Now turn (your) minds next to

Milonem. Quid intererat Milonis, Clodium
Milo. What was-the-interest of-Milo, (that) Clodius

 interfici? Quid erat cur Milo, non dicam
should-be-slain? What was-there why Milo, 'I-will not 'say

admitteret,   sed   optaret?
should commit (such a deed), but 'should (even) 'desire (it)? (But)

Clodius obstabat Miloni, in spe consulatûs.
Clodius was-an-obstacle to-Milo, in (his) hope of-the-consulship.

At, eo repugnante, fiebat;   immo verò
But, he opposing, he-was-made (to gain); moreover indeed

 fiebat   eò magis, nec utebatur me
he-was-made (to gain) so-much the more, nor did-he-use me

  meliore suffragatore, quàm Clodio
[nor was I] a better electioneerer (for him), than Clodius (was)

memoria, meritorum Milonis erga me que
the remembrance, of-the-services of-Milo towards me and

rempublicam, valebat apud vos, judices; nostræ
the republic, availed (much) with you, O judges; our

lacrimæ et preces, quibus ego sentiebam, vos
tears and entreaties, by-which I perceived, (that) you

tum mirifice moveri valebant; sed multò plus
'were then wonderfully 'moved were-of-avail; but much more

timor impendetium periculorum valebat. Enim
did the fear of-impending dangers 'avail. For

quis erat civium, qui proponeret sibi
who was-there of-the-citizens, who could-place-before himself

solutam præturam P. Clodii, sine maximo metu
the unrestrained prætorship of-P. Clodius, without the greatest fear

novarum rerum? Autem videbatis fore
of a revolution? But you-saw that it would-be

solutam, nisi is esset consul, qui auderet que
unrestrained, unless he were consul, who might-dare and

posset constringere eam. Quum universus Romanus
could restrain it. When the entire Roman

populus sentiret eum Milonem esse unum,
people perceived (that) this Milo was the only-one,

quis dubitaret, suo suffragio
(that could do this), who would-doubt, by his vote

liberare se metu, rempublicam periculo?
to-free himself from-fear, (and) the republic from-danger?

At nunc, Clodio remoto, est Miloni jam
But now, Clodius being-removed, it-is for-Milo now

enitendum, usitatis rebus, ut tueatur suam
to-exert-himself, by-the-usual means, that he-may-preserve his

dignitatem; illa singularis gloria, et concessa huic
dignity; that peculiar glory, and conceded to-him

uni, quæ quotidie augebatur frangendis
alone, (and) which 'was daily 'increased of-breaking (and

furoribus Clodianis, jam cecidit
frustrating) the mad-schemes (of) Clodius, 'has now 'fallen

morte Clodii. Vos adepti estis
(and ceased), by-the-death of-Clodius. You attained-to-this, (that)

ne metueritis quem civem; hic perdidit
'you-need not 'fear any citizen; he lost

exercitationem virtutis, suffragationem
(the occasion of) exercising (his) valour, votes

consulatûs, perennem fontem suæ gloriæ
(for) the-consulship, (and) the perpetual fountain of-his glory

Itaque   consulatus Milonis, qui, Clodio   vivo,
Therefore the consulship of-Milo, which, Clodius (being) alive,

poterat non labefactari,   denique,
could   not be-shaken, (or defeated, but now), in fine, (he being)

mortuo,   cœptus est   tentari.
dead,   it-has-been-commenced (for it) to-be-attempted. [they have

                         Igitur   mors   Clodii   non
commenced to prevent it.] Therefore   the death of-Clodius is not

modò nihil prodest Miloni, sed etiam obest.
only   no 'advantage to-Milo, but even is-an-injury (to him).

    At   odium valuit, fecit   iratus, fecit
But-then (his) hatred prevailed, he-did (it) enraged, he-did (it)

inimicus,   fuit   ultor   injuriæ,   punitor   sui
as an enemy, he-was the avenger of-injury, the avenger of-his

doloris. Quid? si   non   dico,   hæc fuerunt
griefs.   What? if I-do not say, (that) these-things were

majora in Clodio, quàm in Milone, sed maxima in
greater in Clodius, than in Milo,   but the greatest in

illo,   nulla   in   hoc?   quid   vultis
the former, (and) not-at-all in the latter? what   do-you-wish

amplius? Enim quid   Milo odisset Clodium,
more?   For   why (should) Milo have-hated Clodius,

segetem ac materiem suæ gloriæ, præter hoc civile
the cause and material of-his glory, except that civil

odium, quo odimus omnes improbos? Erat,
hatred, by-which we-hate all wicked-persons? There-was (reason)

ut ille   odisset   primùm
that he (Clodius) should-hate (Milo, for) firstly he [Milo, (was)]

defensorem meæ salutis, deinde   vexatorem
the defender of-my safety, next (as) the disturber (of his)

furoris,   dominatorem   suorum
fury,   (and) (as)   the master   (and repressor)   of-his

armorum, postremò etiam   suum accusatorem. Enim
arms,   finally   also (as) his   accuser.   For

Clodius quoad vixit fuit reus Milonis, Plotiâ
Clodius as-long-as he-lived was the accused of-Milo, by-the-Plotian

lege.
law. [On the accusation of Milo, Clodius was liable to be tried by the

Tandem   quo   aninio
Plotian law, against violence.]   In-fine   with-what   feelings

creditis   illum   tyrannum   tulisse   hoc ?
do-you-suppose (that)   that   tyrant   bore   this ?

quantum   illius odium, et, in injusto
how-great (do you suppose was)   his   hatred, and, in an unjust

homine,   etiam   quàm   justum
(and wicked)   man,   also   how   reasonable, (that this)

fuisse ?
was ?

14. Reliquum est jam,   ut ipsius natura,
It-remains   now, (to show) that   his   nature,

que consuetudo   defendat illum,   autem hæc
and   habits   may-defend that-one, [Clodius,] but   these

eadem coarguant   hunc.   Clodius
same-things may-accuse (and censure) this-one. [Milo.] Clodius (did)

nihil   unquam per vim, Milo   omnia   per vim.
nothing at-any-time by force, Milo (did) every-thing by force.

Quid? quum ego cessi: urbe,   vobis, judices,
What?   when I   departed from-the-city, you,   O judges,

mœrentibus, ne timui judicium?   non
mourning,   did-I fear a trial?   (was it) not (rather)

servos, non   arma, non   vim ? quæ
slaves,   not (rather) arms,   not (rather) violence ? what

igitur   fuisset   justa causa restituendi mei,
therefore might-have-been a just cause of-recalling me (from

nisi   ejiciendi
banishment), unless (the cause) of-throwing (me into banishment)

fuisset injusta ?   Credo   dixerat   diem mihi,
had-been unjust ?   I-suppose he-had-appointed a day for-me

irrogarat multam, intenderat
(for trial), (he had proposed) to impose a fine, he-had-threatened

actionem perduellionis, et   mihi   videlicet,
an action   of-treason,   and (by) me   forsooth, (your)

judicium timendum fuit, in causâ, aut malâ aut
judgment   was-to-be-feared, in a cause, either bad   or

meâ, non   et præclarissimâ et vestrâ.   Nolui
mine, not (as) both most-illustrious and yours.   I-did-not-wish

objici meos cives servatos, meis consiliis que
to-expose my citizens saved, by-my counsels and

periculis, armis servorum, et egentium civium,
dangers, to-the-arms of slaves, and of-needy citizens,

et facinorosorum, pro me. Enim vidi, vidi hunc
and of-the-wicked, for me. For I-saw, I-saw this

ipsum Q. Hortensius lumen et ornamentum
same Q. Hortensius (here) the light and ornament

reipublicæ, pæne interfici manu servorum, quum
of-the-republic, nearly killed by-a-band of-slaves, when

adesset mihi; in quâ turbâ C. Vibienus,
he-was-standing by-me; in which mob C. Vibienus,

senator, optimus vir, quum esset unâ cum
a senator, (and) most-excellent man, when he-was together with

hoc, ita mulcatus est, ut amiserit vitam.
him, 'was so 'beaten, that he-lost (his) life.

Itaque quando postea illa sica illius, quam
Therefore when after-that 'did that 'dagger of-his, which

acceperat a Catilinâ conquievit? Hæc
he-had-received from Catiline 'rest? This (dagger)

intentata est nobis; ego non passus sum huic
was-aimed at-us; [me] I 'can not 'suffer this

objici vos pro me; hæc insidiata est
to-be-thrust at-you for me; this (dagger) lay-in-wait

Pompeio, hæc cruentavit istam Appiam,
for-Pompey, this (dagger) stained-with-blood this Appian way,

monumentum sui nominis, nece Papirii; hæc,
the monument of-his name, by-the-murder of-Papirius; this,

hæc eadem, longo intervallo, rursus
this same (dagger), after-a long interval, 'was again

conversa est in me; nuper quidem, ut scitis,
'turned against me; lately indeed, as you-know,

pæne confecit me ad regiam.
it nearly killed me at the royal (house). [Palace of Numa.]

Quid simile Milonis? omnis cujus
What like (this in the conduct) of Milo? all whose

vis fuit semper hæc, P. Clodius ne
violence was always this, (that) P. Clodius 'might not

teneret civiatem oppressam   vi,
[1]hold   the city   oppressed   by-violence, [keep the city in con-

quum   posset   non detrahi   in
tinual fear of his violence,] since   he could   not   be-brought   to

judicium.   Quem si voluisset interficere,   quantæ
justice.   Whom if he-had-wished   to kill,   how-many

occasiones,   quoties,   qàm   præclaræ   fuerunt?
opportunities,   (how) often,   how   splendid   were-they?

Potuit   ne, quum   defenderet   domum, ac suos
Could-he   not, when   he-defended   (his)   house,   and his

penates deos, illo   oppugnante,   jure   ulcisci
household gods,   he (Clodius)   attacking,   have by-right avenged

se?   potuit ne,   egregio   civi,   et
himself?   could-he not (have done so), (that) excellent   citizen, and

fortissimo   viro P. Sestio suo   collegâ   vulnerato?
most-brave   man   P. Sestius   his   colleague   being-wounded?

potuit   ne   Q. Fabricio,   optimo   viro,
could-he   not (have done so)   Q. Fabricio,   a-most-excellent   man,

quum   ferret   legem,   ɑe   meo reditu,
when   carrying-through a law,   respecting   my   return (from banish-

pulso,   crudelissimâ cæde
ment),   being driven away   (by a mob),   (and) a-most-cruel   slaughter

factâ   in foro?   potuit   ne   domo   L.
being-made   in-the-forum?   could-he   not (have done so) the house of-L.

Cælii, justissimi que fortissimi prætoris,   oppugnatâ?
Cælius,   a most-just   and   most-brave   prætor,   being-attacked?

potuit   ne,   illo die, quum   lex   de
could-he   not (have done so), on-that day,   when   the law concerning

me   lata est?   quum   concursus   totius
me   was-passed?   when   the concourse (of the people)   of-all

Italiæ, quem mea salus concitarat,
Italy,   whom   my   safety   had-excited (and brought together),

libens   agnovisset   gloriam illius   facti
[1]would   willingly   [1]have-acknowledged the glory   of-that   deed (and)

ut etiamsi,   Milo   fecisset   id,   cuncta   civitas
that   although,   Milo   may-have-done   it,   the whole   state

vindicaret   eam laudem pro   sua.
would-have-claimed   that   praise   for   its-own.

15. At   quod   tempus   erat !
But   what   (a favourable) time   it-was ! (For)

Clarissimus   et fortissimus P. Lentulus   consul,
the-most-illustrious and most-brave P. Lentulus (was) consul,

inimicus Claudio,   ultor illius sceleris, propugnator
an enemy to-Claudius, the avenger of-his wickedness, the bulwark

senatûs,   defensor vestræ   voluntatis, patronus
of-the-senate, the defender of-your   will,   the patron

publici   consensûs,
(and promoter) 'of (that) 'public unanimity (for my return),

restitutor meæ   salutis; septem prætores, octo
the restorer of-my safety;   seven   prætors,   eight

tribuni plebis   adversarii illius,   defensores
tribunes of-the-people (being) adversaries of-him, (and) defenders

mei; Cn. Pompeius   auctor,   et dux mei
of-me; Cn. Pompey (being) the author, and leader of-my

reditûs   illius hostis, cujus gravissimam et
return (and) his enemy, whose most-dignified and

ornatissimam sententiam   de meâ salute, omnis
most-beautiful opinion concerning my safety, the entire

senatus   secutus est,   qui   cohortatus est
senate   adopted,   who [Pompey]   exhorted

Romanum populum, qui, quum fecit decretum
the Roman   people,   who, when he passed the decree

de   me Capuæ, ipse dedit signum cunctæ
concerning me at-Capua, he-himself gave the signal to-entire

Italiæ, cupienti, et imploranti ejus fidem,
Italy,   desiring, and imploring his good-faith (in my favour),

ut   concurrent   ad   restituendam
that they-should-assemble-together for-the-purpose-of restoring

me Romam; denique tum omnia odia   civium
me to-Rome; in-fine then all the hatred of-the-citizens

ardebant   in illum, desiderio mei;
was-strongly-excited against him, 'with-regret-at my 'absence;

quem   qui interemisset tum;   non
whom [Clodius] if any-one 'had-killed then; 'it-would not

cogitaretur   de ejus impunitate, sed de
nave-been-thought concerning his impunity, but about

præmiis Tamen Milo continuit
the rewards (to be conferred on him). However Milo restrained

se, et bis vocavit P. Clodium in judicium
himself, and twice summoned P. Clodius to a trial-in-court,

nunquam ad vim. Quid?
(but) never (challenged him) to deeds-of-violence. What?

Milone privato, et reo ad populum,
Milo being a private-person, and a defendant before the people,

P. Clodio accusante, quum impetus factus est in
P. Clodius being-the-accuser, when an attack was made on

Cn. Pompeium dicentem pro Milone, quæ occasio
Cn. Pompeius pleading for Milo, what an opportunity

non modò tum, sed etiam causa
not only (was there) then, but even a reason (for)

opprimendi? Nuper vero quum M.
surprising (and killing him)? Lately indeed when M.

Antonius attulisset summam spem salutis omnibus
Antonius had-brought the greatest hope of-safety to-all

bonis, que nobilissimus adolescens fortissime
good-men, and the-most-noble young-man 'had most-bravely

suscepisset gravissimam partem reipublicæ, atque
espoused the-most-responsible cause of-the-republic, and

teneret illam belluam, declinantem
when 'he (almost) 'held that wild-beast, avoiding

laqueos judicii, jam irretitam; qui
the snares of-the-tribunals, already entangled-in-his-nets; what

locus, quod tempus fuit illud, immortales
a place, what a time (and opportunity) was that, O immortal

dii? Quum ille fugiens abdidisset se in tenebras
gods? When he flying had-hid himself in the darkness

scalarum, fuit magnum Miloni
of-the-stairs, it (might) have-been a-great-thing for-Milo

conficere illam pestem, nullâ invidiâ suâ, vero
to-have-killed that pest, with-no odium (to himself), but

maximâ gloriâ Antonii. Quid? comitiis
with great glory (to) Antonius. What? in-the-comitis

in Campo, quoties fuit
(when voting) in the Campus Martius, how-often was

potestas,   quum
the power, [how often had Milo the opportunity of killing Clodius] when

ille   irrupisset   in   septa,
he   [Clodius]   had-broken   into   the-enclosures-for-voting, (and)

curavisset,   gladios   destringendos   lapides
had-taken-care,   (that)   swords   should-be-drawn   (and)   stones

jaciendos,   dein   subitò   perteritus   vultu
should-be-thrown,   then   suddenly   frightened   by-the-appearance

Milonis   fugeret   ad   Tiberim,   vos   et   omnes   boni
of-Milo   he-fled   to   the Tiber,   you   and   all   good-men

faceretis   vota,   ut   liberet   Miloni   uti
made   vows,   [prayed,]   that   it-would-please   Milo   to-make

suâ   virtute.
use-of-his   courage (and kill Clodius).

16. Igitur   quem   noluit   cum   gratiâ
    Therefore   whom   he-would-not (kill) with   the-approbation

omnium, voluit   hunc   cum   querelâ   aliquorum?
of-all,   would-he (kill) him   with   the disapprobation   of-some?

quem   ausus   est   non   jure,   quem
whom   he-dared   not (kill) lawfully, whom (he dared not kill) ⁴in

loco,   quem   tempore,
(a proper) ⁴place,   whom   (he dared not kill) at-an-opportune-time,

quem   impune,   non   dubitavit
whom (he dared not kill) with-impunity, ⁴would-he   not ⁴have-doubted

occidere   hunc   injuriâ,   iniquo   loco,   alieno
to-kill   him   unlawfully, in-an-improper   place,   at-an

tempore,   periculo   capitis   præsertim,   judices,
inopportune-time, with-danger   of-his-life   especially,   O judges,

quum   contentio   amplissimi   honoris,   et
when   the contest (for)   the greatest   honours (of the state)   and

dies   comitiorum   subesset;   quo   tempore
the day of-the-comitia [election] was-at-hand;   at-which   time

quidem (enim   scio   quàm   timida   ambitio   sit,   que
indeed   (for   I-know   how   timid   ambition   is,   and

quanta   et   quàm   sollicita   sit   cupiditas   consulatûs),
how-great   and   how   anxious   is   the desire of-the-consulship),

timemus   omnia   non   modò   quæ   possunt   palam
we-fear   every-thing   not   only   what   may   be openly

reprehendi, sed etiam quæ　　obscure cogitari,
'reprehended, but also what (may) 'be obscurely 'thought,

perhorescimus levem rumorem fictam fabulam,
we shudder-at idle rumours (and) false stories

intuemur ora atque oculos omnium. Enim
we-look-at the countenances and eyes of-all. For

nihil est tam molle, tam tenerum, aut tam fragile,
nothing is so soft, so tender, or so fragile,

aut flexibile, quàm voluntas que sensus civium
or flexible, as the good-will and feeling of-the-citizens

erga nos, qui non modò irascuntur improbitati
towards us, who not only are-provoked at-the-wickedness

candidatorum, sed etiam sæpe fastidiunt in factis
of-the-candidates, but also often become-disgusted with deeds

recte. Milo igitur, proponens sibi
(done) correctly (by him). 'Would Milo then, placing-before him

hunc speratum atque exoptatum diem Campi,
this hoped-for and desired day of-the Campus Martius,

confitens et ferens præ se
[day of the election,] confessing and bearing before himself

cruentis manibus, scelus et facinus, veniebat ad
with-bloody hands, (his) crime and wickedness, 'come to

illa augusta auspicia centuriarum? Quàm
those august auspices of-the-centuria? How

non credibile hoc in hôc! quàm non dubitandum
incredible is this in this-one! how indubitable

idem in Clodio, qui, Milone interfecto, putaret
(is) the same in Clodius, who, Milo being-slain, he-thought

se regnaturum! Quid?
(that) he would-resign! What (is to be said of that)?

quod, judices, est caput audaciæ, quis
which, O judges, is the head (and source) of-audacity, who

ignorat maximam illecebram peccandi esse
is-ignorant (that) the greatest enticement of-doing-wrong is

spem impunitatis? In utro igitur fuit hæc?
the hope of-impunity? In which-of-the-two therefore was this?

in Milone, qui est etiam nunc reus facti, aut
in Milo, who is even now a defendant (for a deed, either

præclari, aut certe necessarii, an in Clodio, qui
illustrious, or certainly necessary, or in Clodius, who

ita contempserat judicia que pœnam, ut
'has so 'despised courts-of-justice and punishment, that

nihil delectaret eum, quod esset aut fas per
nothing delighted him, which might-be either allowed by

naturam, aut liceret per leges? Sed quid ego
nature, or permitted by the-laws? But why 'do I

argumentor? quid disputo plura?
'bring-forward-arguments? why dispute (about so) many-things?

Appello te Q. Petili, optimum et fortissimum
I-appeal-to you, O Q. Petilius, a most excellent and most-brave

civem; te, M. Cato, testor; quos
citizen; 'I-call-on you, O. M. Cato, 'as witness; whom (both)

quædam divina sors dedit mihi judices. Vos
some divine chance has-given to-me (for) judges. You

audistis ex M. Favonio, Clodium dixisse
have-heard from M. Favonius, (that) Clodius said

sibi, et audistis, Clodio vivo,
to-himself, and you-heard (it), Clodius being (yet) alive, (that)

Milonem periturum triduo. Post tertium diem
Milo would-die in-three-days. On the third day

res gesta est, quam dixerat. Quum ille non
the affair took-place, which he-had-said. When he 'did not

dubitarit aperire, quid cogitaret, potestis vos
'hesitate to-make-known, what he-thought, can you

dubitare, quid fecerit?
doubt, what he-did?

17. Quemadmodum igitur dies non fefellit
How therefore 'did the-day not 'deceive

eum? equidem
him? [How was he so certain of the day?] 'I-have indeed

modò dixi erat nihil negotii
just 'explained (that) there-was nothing of-the-affair [no difficulty]

nosse stata sacrificia dictatoris Lanuvii. Vidit
to-know the stated sacrifices of-the-dictator of-Lanuvium. He-saw

esse necesse Miloni proficisci Lanuvium,
'that) it-was necessary for Milo to-go to-Lanuvium,

illo ipso die, quo profectus est. Itaque
on-that same day, on-which he-went. Therefore

antevertit. At quo die? Quo,
he-anticipated (Milo in his journey). But on-what day? On-that-day,

ut dixi ante, fuit insanissima
as I-have-said before, (on which) there was a most-furious

concio concitata ab ipsius mercenario
meeting-of-the-people stirred-up by his mercenary

tribuno plebis; quem diem, quam concionem,
tribune of-the-people; which day, which meeting,

quos clamores, ille nunquam reliquisset, nisi
which clamours, he-would never have-left, unless

approperaret ad cogitatum facinus. Ergo
he-were-hastening to (some) premeditated crime. Therefore

quidem ne causa itineris illi, etiam
(there was) indeed no cause of-a-journey for-him, (but) indeed

causa manendi; nulla facultas Miloni
a reason for-remaining (at home); (there was) no possibility for-Milo

manendi, exeundi fuit non solùm
remaining (in the city, but for) departing there-was not only

causa, sed etiam necessitas. Quid? si, ut
a reason, but also a necessity. What (moreover)? if, as

ille scivit, Milonem fore eo die in
he knew, (that) Milo would-be on-that day on (his)

viâ, sic Milo potuit ne quidem suspicari,
journey, so Milo could not indeed suspect, (that)

Clodium sic. Primum quæro, qui
Clodius (would be) so. In-the-first-place I-ask, who

potuerit scire? quod idem vos potestis non
could have-known (it)? which same-thing you could not

quærere in Clodio. Ut enim rogasset
have-asked respecting Clodius. For though he-might-have-asked

neminem alium, nise suum familiarissimum T.
no-one else, but his most-intimate-friend T.

Patinum, potuit scire illo ipso die,
Patinus, he-might have-known, (that) on-that same day,

esse necesse flaminem prodi a Milone, Lanuvii,
't-was necessary for-a-priest to-be-appointed by Milo, at Lanuvium,

dictatore.   Sed   erant   permulti   alii.   ex
(as) dictator (thereof). But there-were a-great-many others, from

quibus   posset   facillime   sire   id;   scilicet   omnes
whom   he-might   very-easily   learn   that;   namely   all

Lanuvini.   Unde   Milo   quæsivit   de   reditu
the Lanuvians. Where 'did Milo 'inquire about the return

Clodii?   Quæsierit   sane.   Videte, quid
of-Clodius? He-may-have-inquired without doubt. See,   what

largiar   vobis.   Etiam   corruperit   servum, ut
I-concede to-you.   Also (that) he may-have-bribed a slave,   as

Q. Arrius,   meus   amicus   dixit.   Legite   testimonia
Q. Arrius,   my   friend   said.   Read   the evidence

vestrorum   testium.   C. Cassinius Schola,
of-your   witnesses.   C. Cassinius Schola,   (of)

Interamnanus,   familiarissimus, et idem   comes
Interamna, (his) most-intimate-friend, and the same a companion

         Clodii,   cujus   testimonio Clodius
(and attendant) of-Clodius, whose   testimony   Clodius (had)

jampridem,   dixit,   P. Clodius fuerat
some-time-since (made use of), said, (that) P. Clodius   was

eadem   horâ   Interamnæ   et   Romæ,
at-the-same hour at-Interamna and at-Rome, (and that)

Clodium mansurum fuisse   illo   die in Albano,
Clodius   was-to-have remained on-that day in   Alba,

sed   subitò   nunciatum esse   ei,   Cyrum
but (that) suddenly it-was-announced to-him, (that) Cyrus

architectum   esse   mortuum;   itaque   repente
the architect   was   dead;   therefore (that he) at-once

constituisse   proficisci   Romam.   C. Clodius,   item
resolved   to-proceed   to-Rome.   C. Clodius,   also

      comes   P. Clodii, dixit hoc.
an accompanying-companion of-P. Clodius, said this (same).

18. Videte, judices,   quantæ   res confectæ sint
    See, O judges, how-many things are-determined

         his   testimoniis. Primùm, Milo
(and made manifest) by-these depositions. First,   Milo

certe   liberatur,   esse,
is certainly freed (from guilt), (for it is shewn) to-be, (that) he did

non profectus   eo concilio, ut insidiaretur
not   go (from Rome) with-that intention, that he-might-waylay

Clodio in viâ;   quippe;   si   non omnino
Clodius   on the road; certainly-indeed; since 'it-could not   at-all

erat   ille futurus   obvius ei. Deinde
'be (supposed, that) he   was-about (to) meet   him.   Next

(enim   non video, cur   non quoque agam
for   I-do not   'see,   why 'I-may not   also   'mention

neum negotium), scitis, judices,   fuisse,
my-own   affair),   you-know, O judges, (that) there-were (those),

qui dicerent, in   suadenda   hac rogatione
who   said,   in advocating-and-urging this   petition (and ac-

        cædem   factam esse   manu
tion against Milo, that) the murder   was-committed   by-the-hand

Milonis,   vero   consilio alicujus   majoris.
of-Milo,   but-indeed by-the-counsel   of-some   greater-personage.

     Abjecti   et perditi homines describebant
'Did (these) abandoned   and profligate   men   'describe

me videlicet   latronem ac   sicarium.   Hi
me   forsooth   (as) a robber   and   an assassin. Those-men

jacent,   suis   testibus, qui negant
lie prostrate, (and convicted) by-their-own witnesses, who   deny (that)

Claudium rediturum fuisse Romam   eo   die, nisi
Claudius   would-have   returned to-Rome on-that day, unless

audisset de Cyro. Respiravi;   liberatus sum;
he-had-heard-of Cyrus. I-breathed-again;   I-was-freed   (from

      non vereor, ne   videar   cogitasse
anxiety); 'I-do not   'fear, lest-that I-may-seem to-have-thought

quod   potuerim ne   quidem   suspicari. Nunc
that-which   I-could   not   indeed   have-suspected. Now

persequar   cetera.   Nam illud
I-will-proceed (with) the rest.   For   this (expression of theirs)

occurrit. Igitur Clodius   ne   quidem cogitavit
occurs.   Therefore Clodius   'did not   indeed   'think

de insidiis, quoniam fuit mansurus in Albano.
about snares,   because   he-was to-remain   in   Alba.

     Si quidem   non exiturus fuisset   e
[Granted] if   indeed   'he-was not   'to-have-departed from (his)

villâ   ad   cædem.   Enim   video,   (that
villa (in Alba) to (commit) a murder.   For   I-perceive,   (that

illum,   qui   dicatur   nuntiasse   de   morte
he,   who   is-said   to-have-brought-news   concerning the death

Cyri,   non   nuntiasse id,   sed   Milonem
of Cyrus,   'did not   'announce   it,   but   (that)   Milo

appropinquare. Nam   quid   nuntiaret   de
was-approaching.   For   what   might-he-announce   concerning

Cyro, quem Clodius proficiscens Româ, reliquerat
Cyrus, whom Clodius   departing   from-Rome,   had-left

morientem ?   Fui   unà ;   obsignavi
dying ?   I-was   together   (with them) ;   I-signed

testamentum   simul cum Clodio ; tamen 'he-had
the will   (as witness) together with   Clodius ;   but   'he-had

palam   fecerat   testamentum, et scripserat et
openly   'made   (his)   will,   and   left   both

illum et me   heredem. Quem   tertiâ   horâ,
him   and me   (his)   heirs.   Whom   at-the-third   hour,

  pridie,   reliquisset efflantem   animam,
the day-before,   he-had-left   breathing-out (his)   soul,   [at the

     denique   nuntiabatur   ei
point of death,]   'would-it in-fine   'have-been-announced   to-him

postridie   eum mortuum decimâ horâ ?
on-the-next-day (that)   he   died   at the tenth   hour ?

  19. Age,   sit   factum ita ;   quæ   causa
   Well then, let-it-be   done so ;   [be it so ;] what   reason

    cur   properaret   Romam ? cur   conjiceret
(was there) why   he-should-hasten   to-Rome ? why   should-he-throw

se   in   noctem ?   quid
himself   into   the night ? [why should he depart at nightfall ?] what

afferebat   causam festinationis ?
brought   (any) reason   of-hastening ? [what occasion of hurrying

    quod   erat   heres ?   Primùm   erat
was there ?] what-because he-was   heir ?   First   there-was

nihil,   cur   esset   opus   properato ; deinde, si
nothing, why there-should-be   need (of) hastening ;   next,   if

esset   quid,   quid   tandem   erat   quod posset
there-was   any,   what   indeed   was-there   that   could

consequi, eâ nocte, autem amitteret,
be-obtained, that night, which 'he-might (possibly) 'lose,

si venisset Romam mane postridie?
if he-had-come to-Rome early-in-the-morning on-the-next-day?

Atque ut illi nocturnus adventus ad urbem
And as for-him (Clodius) a nocturnal arrival in the city

fuit potius vitandus, quàm expetendus, sic fui
was rather to-be-avoided, than to-be-sought-for, so it-wa

Miloni quum esset insidiator si sciebat
for-Milo as he-was a waylayer (as you say) if he-knew

illum accessurum ad urbem noctu,
(that) he (Clodius) would enter the city by-night,

subsidendum, atque exspectandum fuit.
that-he-should-stop, and wait (for him).

Occidisset noctu in insidioso loco, et
He-would-have-killed [Clodius] by night in a suspicious place, and

pleno latronum; nemo non credidisset ei
full of-robbers; no-one 'would not 'have-believed him

neganti, quem omnes volunt esse salvum, etiam
denying (it), whom all wish to-be safe, even

confitentem. Primùm ille locus ipse, occultator
confessing (it). First that place itself, the hiding-place

et receptor latronum, sustinuisset crimen;
and receptacle of-robbers, would-have-borne the blame;

tum neque muta solitudo indicasset
for-then neither the mute solitude would-have-announced

Milonem, neque cæca nox ostendisset; deinde
Milo, nor the dark night have-shown-him; next

ibi multi violati ab illo,
in-that-place many (who) had-been-violently-used by him, (many who)

spoliati, expulsi
had-been-despoiled (by him), (many who) had-been-plundered (of their)

bonis; multi etiam timentes hæc caderent
goods (by him); many even fearing this would-fall

in suspicionem; denique tota Etruria citaretur
under suspicion; in-fine all Etruria would-have-been-cited

rea. Atque certe illo die, Clodius rediens
as defendants. And certainly on-that day, Clodius returning

Aricâ   devertit   ad se,   in Albanum.   Quòd ut
from Arica turned-aside to-his-house,   in   Alba.   Though as

Milo   sciret,   illum   fuisse   Aricæ,   tamen
Milo   might-know, (that) he   had-been   at Arica,   however

debuit   suspicari   eum,   etiamsi   vellet
he-ought   to-have-suspected, (that) he,   although he-might-wish

reverti   Romam   illo   die,   deversurum   ad suam
to-return   to Rome   on-that   day,   would-turn-aside   to   his

villam,   quæ   tangeret   viam.   Cur   neque
villa,   which   touched (on)   the road.   Why 'did-he neither

occurrit   ante,   ille   ne   resideret in
'meet   (him) before, (that) he 'might not   'be-seated   in (his)

villâ,   nec   subsedit,   in   eo   loco,   quo   ille
villa,   nor   lay-in-wait,   in   that   place,   where   he

venturus esset   noctu ?
was-to-come   by-night?

Video, judices,   adhuc omnia constare;
I-see, O judges, (that) thus-far all-things are-consistent; (that)

fuisse etiam   utile   Miloni   Clodium   vivere,
it-was   even   advantageous for-Milo (that) Clodius   should-live,

illi   interitum   Milonis
(but that) for-him   (Clodius)   the death   of-Milo (was)

optatissimum   ad   ea,   quæ   concupierat,
the-most-desirable (in respect) to those-things, which   he-had-coveted;

odium   illius   acerbissimus in   hunc,
the-hatred of-that-one (was) most-bitter   against this-one, [Milo],

nullum   hujus   in   illum,   (that)
(but there was) no-hatred of-this-one against that-one [Clodius], (that)

perpetuam   consuetudinem   illius
the constant   habits   (and occupation) of-that-one (was)

in vi inferenda, hujus   tantum in repellenda;
in deeds of-violence, of-this-one only   in   repelling (them);

mortem   ab   illo   Miloni, et palam
(that) death was-denounced by that-one to-Milo, and openly

prædictam,   nihil   unquam auditum
predicted,   (that) nothing (of the kind) 'was ever   'heard

ex Milone;   diem   profectionis   hujus
(coming) from   Milo;   (that) the day   of-departure   of-this-one

notum   illi,   reditûs   illius
was-known   to-that-one, (but that the day) of-return   of-that-one

ignotum fuisse   huic;   iter   hujus
was-unknown   to-this-one; (that) the journey of-this-one (was)

necessarium,   illius   etiam potius alienum;
necessary,   (but) of-that-one even rather inconvenient; (that)

hunc tulisse præ se,   se exiturum
this-one bore before himself, [openly declared,] that he would-leave

Româ illⁱ die,   illum   dissimulasse,   se
Rome on-that day, (but) that-one had-dissembled, (that) he

rediturum,   illo die;   hunc   mutasse
would-return (to-Rome), on-that day; (that) this-one 'had-changed (his)

consilium   nullius rei,
counsel   (in)   no   affair, [that Milo had in no wise altered the

                      illum   finxisse   causam
plan of his journey] (but) that-one had-feigned a reason (for)

mutandi consilii;   huic,   si   insidiaretur,
changing (his) plan; (that) to-this-one, if he-were-waylaying,

noctem prope urbem expectandum,   illi,
night   near the city was-to-be-waited-for, (but) to-that-one,

etiamsi   non timeret hunc, tamen nocturnum
although 'he might not 'fear this-one, yet   a nocturnal

accessum ad urbem fuisse metuendum.
approach to the city was   to-be-feared.

20.   Nunc videamus   id,   quod   est
     Let-us now   see   that, which is

caput,   utri, fuerit tandem ille
the-principal-thing, for-which-of-the-two, was really-in-fine that

locus ipse ubi congressi sunt, aptior ad insidias.
place itself where they-met, more-proper for ambuscades.

Vero, judices, id etiam dubitandum, et   diutius
But, O judges, 'is that even 'to-be-doubted, and (any) longer

cogitandum est? Ante fundum Clodii, in quo
to-be-considered? Before the-farm of Clodius, in which

fundo propter illas insanas substructiones,
farm on-account-of those foolish   foundations (and prepara-

                      facile   mille   valentium
tion of the ground for building), at-least a thousand   strong

hominum versabatur; edito atque excelso loco
men were-employed; on-the-raised and high ground

adversarii, Milo putarat se fore
'of (his) 'adversary, 'did Milo 'think (that) he would-be

superiorem, et ob eam rem,
superior, (or have a local advantage) and for that reason, 'had

potissimum elegerat eum locum ad pugnam? an
especially 'selected that place for a flight? or (that)

potius expectatus est in eo loco ab eo, qui
'he-was rather 'waited-for in that place by him, who

cogitarat facere impetum, spe.
had-thought to-make an attack, in-the-hope (and confidence)

ipsius loci. Res, judices, loquitur ipsa,
of-that-same place. The-thing, O judges, speaks (for) itself,

quæ semper valet plurimum. Si non audiretis
which always avails much. If 'you-had not 'heard-of

hæc gesta, sed videretis
these-things (as actually) performed, but had-seen (them)

picta, tamen appareret,
delineated-in-a-picture, yet-however it-would-appear,

uter esset insidiator, uter
which-of-the-two was the waylayer, which-of-the-two

cogitaret nihil mali, quum alter veheretur
might-be-thinking of nothing evil, when the one was-riding

in rhedâ, pænulatus, uxor sederet
in a carriage, having-on-a-cloak, (while his) wife sat

unâ. Quid horum non
together (with him). Which of-these-things (was) not

impeditissimum? vestitus, an vehiculum
the most-embarrassing? (his) dress, or (his) carriage

an comes? quid minus promptum ad
or (his) companion? what (is) less adapted for

pugnam, quam irretitus pænulâ, impeditus
fight, than being-entangled with-a-cloak, hampered

rhedâ, pæne constrictus esset uxore?
with-a-carriage, (and) nearly bound by (his) wife

Videte nunc illum, primùm
(clinging to him)? Behold now that-man, [Clodius,] at-first

egredientem e **villâ subitò; cur? vesperi;**
coming   from (his) villa   suddenly;   why?   it-was-evening,

quid est necesse? tarde; qui convenit,
why   is   it necessary?   slowly;   (with) what   propriety

præsertim id tempus? Devertit in Pompeii
especially   at-that   time?   He-turns-aside   to   Pompey's

villam, ut videret Pompeium? sciebat
villa,   that   he-might-see   Pompey?   he-knew (that)

esse in Alsiensi; ut perspiceret villam? fuerat
he-was   in   Alsiensis;   that   he-might-view   the villa?   he-had-been

in eâ millies; quid ergo erat? mora et
in   it   a thousand-times;   what   therefore   was-it?   delay   and

tergiversatio; dum hic veniret, noluit
evasion;   till   he (Milo)   came,   he-did-not-wish

relinquere locum.
to-leave   the place.

21. Age nunc, comparate iter expediti
Well   now,   compare the journey 'of (this) 'unencumbered

latronis cum impedimentis Milonis. Ille semper
robber   with   the hinderances   of-Milo.   He   always

antea cum uxore; tum sine
before-this-time (travelled) with   (his)   wife;   then (he was)   without

ea; nunquam nisi in rhedâ; tum in
her;   (and)   never   unless   in   a carriage;   (but) then   on

equo. Græculi comites
horseback.   (His) trifling-Greek attendants,   (who always accompanied

quocunque ibat, etiam quum properabat
him),   wherever   he-went,   even   when   he-was-hastening

in Etrusca castra; tum in comitatu
in the Etruscan   camp;   (but) then in (his)   retinue,   (there were)

nihil nugarum. Milo, qui nunquam, tum
no   triflers.   Milo,   who   never   (did so) then

casu ducebat uxoris symphoniacos pueros,
by-chance had-with-him (his)   wife's   music   boys,

et greges ancillarum. Ille, qui duceret semper
and crowds of-maid-servants.   He, [Clodius] who   had   always

cum se scorta, semper exoletos,
with   him   prostitutes   always (with him)   infamous-men, (and)

semper   lupas,   tum neminem, nisi ut
always   (with him) lewd-wom. n, then   none,   unless as

diceres,   esse   virum lectum a viro.
you-might-say, (that) there was   man   chosen   by man. [That

                                                    Cur
each man had selected his companion for a desperate enterprise.]   Why

igitur,   victus est?   Quia   viator   non semper
therefore, was-he-defeated? Because the traveller 'is not always

occiditur a latrone,   nonnunquam etiam   latro
'killed   by the robber, (but) sometimes   even the robber

           a viatore;   quia,   quamquam Clodius
(is killed) by the traveller; because,   although   Clodius

paratus   in imparatos, tamen
prepared   (had attacked those) unprepared,   yet   (it was)

mulier   inciderat in viros. Nec vero erat Milo
a woman (who) encountered men.   Nor indeed was   Milo

unquam sic non paratus contra illum,   ut
ever   so   unprepared   against   him (Clodius) that

           non esset   fere   satis paratus.
'he-might not 'be (said to be) nearly sufficiently prepared.

      Ille   semper   cogitabat,   et   quantum
(For) he   always   thought,   both   how-much

   interesset P. Clodii,   se   perire,   et
it-was-the-interest of-P. Clodius, (that) he (Milo) should-die, and

   quanto odio esset illi,
in-how-great hatred he-was to-him, [and how much Clodius hated him,]

et   quantum   ille auderet.   Quamobrem,
and   how-much   he   dared   (to do).   Wherefore,

nunquam projiciebat suam vitam, quam sciebat
'he never   'exposed   his   life,   which   he-knew

propositam maximis præmiis, et pæne addictam, in
was-exposed to-the-highest price, and nearly   sold,   in

periculum, sine   præsidio, et sine custodiâ.
danger,   without a protection, and without   a guard

Adde   casus, adde incertos exitus pugnarum,
Add   (to this) chance, add the uncertain result of-battles,

que communem Martem,   qui sæpe evertit
and the common-fortune-of-war, which often overthrows (him)

jam spoliantem, et exultantem, et
already despoiling, and exulting (over the enemy), and

perculit ab abjecto; adde inscitiam
drives (him) from (his) prostrate (foe); add the insufficiency

ducis oscitantis
of-a-commander (who has been made) listless (by having just)

pransi, poti, qui, quum reliquisset
dined, (and indulged in) drink, who, when he-had-left (his)

hostem interclusum a tergo, cogitavit nihil de
enemy cut-off in the rear, thought nothing about

ejus comitibus extremis, in
his attendants on-the-extreme (and surrounding parts), among

quos, incensos irâ, que desperantes vitam
whom, excited by-anger, and despairing (of) the life of (their)

domini, quum incidisset, hæsit in
master, when he-had-fallen, he-stuck-fast in, (and cou'd not

iis poenis, quas fideles servi
escape from) those punishments, which faithful slaves

expetiverunt ab eo, pro vitâ domini. Cur
sought of him, for the life 'of (their) 'master. Why

igitur manumisit eos? Metuebat scilicet,
therefore did-he manumit them? He-was-afraid forsooth,

ne indicarent, ne
lest-that they-might-give-information (against him), and that 'they-could

non perferre dolorem, ne cogerentur
not 'support pain, and-lest-that-they-would-be-forced

tormentis confiteri, P. Clodium occissum esse a
by-tortures to-confess, (that) P. Clodius was-killed by

servis Milonis in Appiâ viâ. Quid opus est
the slaves of-Milo on the Appian road. What need is there of

tortore? Quid quæris? Ne occiderit?
torture? What do-you-inquire-about? 'Was-he not 'killed?

Occidit. Jure an injuriâ? Nihil
He-was-killed. Lawfully or unlawfully? (This has) nothing

ad tortorem. Enim quæstio facti est in
(to do with) the torturer. For the-question of-that-fact (belongs to)

equuleo,   juris   in
the torture,   (the question)   of-the-lawfulness   (belongs to)

judicio.
the-courts-of-justice.

22. Quid   igitur   est   quærendum   in   causâ,
What   therefore (is)   to-be   investigated   in (his) cause,

agamus   id   hìc;   quod   vis   invenire
we-will-treat-of   it   here;   that-which   you-wish   to-find-out

tormentis,   fatemur   id.   Si   potius   vero   quæris id,
by-tortures,   we-confess   it.   If you   rather   indeed   inquire that,

cur   manu   miserit,   quàm   cur   effecerit
why he   manumitted   (his slaves,)   than   why   he-gave-them

parùm amplis præmiis,   necis   reprehendere
less   ample   rewards,   you-do-not-know (how) to-find-fault-with

factum   inimici.   Enim M. Cato, qui   semper
the act   of-an-enemy.   For   M.   Cato,   who   always (says)

omnia   constanter et fortiter, dixit   hic   idem, et
every-thing   with-firmness and forcibly,   said   this   same, and

dixit   in turbulentâ concione, quæ tamen placata est
he-said (it) in   a turbulent   assembly,   which however   was stilled

hujus   auctoritate,   qui defendissent
'by his   authority,   (that those slaves) who   had-defended

caput   domini,   fuisse   dignissimos,   non   solùm
the-life-of (their) master,   were   most-worthy,   not   only

libertate, sed etiam   omnibus præmiis.   Enim quod
of liberty,   but   also   (of)   all   rewards.   For   what

præmium est   satis   magnum   tam benevolis,   tam
reward   is   sufficiently   great   'for such   'well-disposed,   such

bonis,   tam   fidelibus   servis,   propter   quos   vivit?
good,   such   faithful   slaves,   through   whom   he-lives?

Etsi   id   quidem   est   non   tanti,   quàm
Although that   indeed   is   not   so-great (if we consider),   that

quòd propter   eosdem,   non satiavit mentem
because through   the same-slaves,   'he did-not   'satiate   the-mind

que oculis   crudelissimi   inimici,   sanguine
'and   eyes   of (his) most-cruel   enemies,   with (his) blood

  suis   vulneribus.   Quos   misi   manumisset,
and   his   wounds.   Whom   unless   he-had-manumitted,

conservatores domini, ultores sceleris,
the preservers 'of (their) 'master, the avengers of crime,

defensores necis, dedendi fuerunt etiam
the averters 'of (his) 'death, would-have-to-be-surrendered even

tormentis. Vero hic, in his malis, habet nihil,
to-tortures. But he, in these misfortunes, has nothing,

quod ferat minùs moleste, quàm, etiamsi
that he-bears less anxiously (than this,) that, although

quid accidat ipsi, tamen meritum præmium
any-thing might-happen to-himself, yet a merited reward

persolutum esse illis. Sed quæstiones,
had-been-conferred (on) them [the slaves]. But the examinations

quæ nunc habitæ sunt, in
(of the slaves by torture,) which have just now been-had, in

atrio Libertatis, urgent Milonem. De quibusdam
the hall of-Liberty, press-hard against Milo. From what

servis? Rogas? de P. Clodii, quis
slaves? Do-you-ask? from (the slaves) of P. Clodius, who

postulavit eos? Appius. Quis produxit? Appius.
demanded them? Appius. Who brought-them-forth? Appius.

Unde? Ab Appio. Boni dii! quid potest
Whence? From the-house-of Appius. Good gods! what can

agi severius? est nulla quæstio lege de
be-done more-severely? there-can-be no examination by-law (of)

servis in dominum, nisi de incestu, ut
slaves against (their) master, unless concerning incest, as

fuit in Clodium. Clodius accessit proxime
was the case (with) Clodius. Clodius has-approached most-nearly

deos, propius quàm tum, quum penetraret
to-the-gods, more-nearly than then, when he-had-penetrated

ad ipsos, de
unto them, [when he had violated the mysteries of Bona dea] concerning

morte cujus quæritur tanquam de
the death of-this-man an-investigation-is-had, as if concerning

violatis cærimoniniis. Sed tamen nostri majores
the violated sacred-rites. But however our ancestors

noluerunt de servo quæri in dominum,
would-not (allow) of a slave to-be-examined against (his) master,

non quia verum posset non inveniri, sed quia
not because the truth could not be-discovered, but because

videbatur indignum, et tristius
it-seemed improper, and more-sad (and distressing) to (their)

dominis, quàm morte ipsa. Quum quæritur de
'masters, than death itself. When an examination-is-made of

servo accusatoris in reum, potest verum
the slave of the accuser against the defendant, can the truth

inveniri? Vero age, quæ erat, aut qualis
be-discovered? But come, what was-it, or how (was)

quæstio? Heus tu, Rufio, causâ
the examination (conducted)? Holloa you, Rufio, for-the-sake

verbi cave, sis,
of-a-name [or example] take-care, if-you-please, (that) 'you-do (not)

mentiare. Clodius fecit insidias Miloni?
tell-a-lie. Did Clodius lay snares for Milo? (should the

fecit. Crux certa
slave answer) he-did. The cross (is) sure (to be his punishment, but

fecit nullas. Libertas sperata. Quid
should he say) he-laid none. Freedom is-to-hoped-for. What

certius hac quæstione. Subitò abrepti
(is) more-certain (than) this examination. They-are suddenly taken-off

in quæstionem, tamen separantur a ceteris, et
for an examination, however they-are-separated from others, and

conjiciuntur in arcas, ne quis possit colloqui
thrown into cells, lest any-one might speak

cum iis. Hi quum fuissent centum dies penes
with them. These when they-had-been a hundred days in the-power-of

accusatorem, producti sunt, ab eo ipso accusatore.
the accuser, are-brought-forward, by that same accuser.

Quid potest dici integrius hac quæstione?
What can be-said (to be) more-impartial (than) this examination?

Quid incorruptius?
What more-incorruptible?

23. Quod si nondum cernitis satis
Which if 'you-do not-yet 'see-this sufficiently (clear

quum res ipsa luceat, tot tam claris
when the thing itself is-manifest, by so-many such clear

argumentis que signis, recordamini, per
proofs and indications, recollect, (I entreat you) by

immortales deos; Milonem revertisse Romam,
the immortal gods; (that) Milo had-returned to-Rome,

purâ atque integrâ mente, imbutum nullo scelere,
with-a-pure and irreproachable mind, tainted with-no crime,

perteritum nullo metu, exanimatum nullâ con-
terrified with-no-fear, breathless-and-pale with-no con-

scientiâ; quæ fuerit celeritas ejus reditûs, qui
scientious-fear; what was the speed of-his return, who

ingressus in forum, curiâ ardente, quæ
entered into the forum, the senate-house being-on-fire, what

magnitudo animi, qui vultus, quæ oratio. Neque
greatness of-mind, what a countenance, what an oration. Nor

vero commisit se solùm populo, sed etiam
indeed did-he-commit himself alone to the people, but also

senatui, neque senatui modò, sed etiam publicis
to-the-senate, nor to-the-senate only, but also to-the-public

præsidiis et armis, neque his tantum, verùm etiam
guards and arms, nor to-these only, but-indeed also

potestati ejus, cui senatus commiserat totam
to-the-power of-him, to-whom the senate had-entrusted the entire

rempublicam, omnem pubem Italiæ, cuncta arma
republic, all the youths of-Italy, (and) all the arms

Romani populi; cui nunquam
(and forces) of-the-Roman people; to-whom 'he-would never

profectò tradidisset se, nisi confideret suæ
indeed 'have-given himself 'up, unless he-trusted to-his

causæ, præsertim, audienti omnia, metuenti
cause, especially (to him), hearing all, fearing

magna, suspicanti multa, credenti nonnulla. Magna
great-things, suspecting many, believing some. Grea

est vis conscientiæ, judices, et magna in utramque
is the power of-conscience, O judges, and great on both

partem, ut, qui
sides, (either of guilt or innocence) so that, those-who

commiserint nihil neque timeant, et qui
may-have-committed no (fault) do-not fear, and those-who

peccant, putent poenam semper versari
have-done-wrong, think (that) punishment 'is always 'present

ante oculos. Neque vero,
before (their) eyes [is always ready to overtake them]. Nor indeed,

sine certâ ratione, causa Milonis semper
without certain (and good) reason, 'was the cause of Milo always

probata est a senatu. Enim sapientissimi
'approved by the senate. For (these) most-wise

homines videbant rationem facti,
men saw the reason (and lawfulness) of-the-deed,

praesentiam animi, constantiam
the presence of mind, the constancy (and perseverance)

defensionis. Vero an, judices, obliti estis, illo
of defence. But 'have you, O judges, 'forgotten, the

nuntio necis Clodianae recenti, sermones
announcement of-the-murder (of) Clodius being-yet-recent, the language

et opiniones, non modò inimicorum, sed etiam
and opinions, not only 'of (his) 'enemies, but also

nonnullorum imperitorum? Negabant,
of some inexperienced (and ignorant persons)? They-denied,

eum rediturum esse Romam. Enim sive
(that) he [Milo] would-return to Rome. For if-that

fecisset illud, irato ac percito animo, ut
he-had-done that, in an angry and excited (state of) mind, that

incensus odio trucidaret inimicum, abitrabantur,
inflamed by-hatred he-had-killed (his) enemy, they-thought,

eum putasse mortem P. Clodii tanti,
(that) he would-consider the death of-P. Clodius of-so-much-account,

ut careret patriâ, aequo animo;
that he-might-want (his) country, with-an-equal mind; [that he would

quum explesset suum odium
contentedly go into banishment] since he-had-satiated his hatred

sanguine inimici; etiam sive voluisset liberare
by-the-blood of (his) enemy; also if he-had-wished to-liberate

patriam morte illius fortem
(his) country by-the-death of-that-man (Clodius, that he) a brave

virum non dubitaturum, quin, quum attulisset
man 'would not 'hesitate, but-that, when he-had-brought

salutem reipublicæ,   suo periculo, cederet   legibus
safety to-the-republic, by-his-own danger, he-would-submit to-the-laws

    æquo   animo;   auferret cum se sempiternam
with-a-resigned mind; (that) he-would-carry with himself   everlasting

gloriam;   relinqueret nobis fruenda haec,   quæ
glory;   (and) would leave   us   to-enjoy those-things, which

  ipse   servasset.   Multi etiam loquebantur
he-himself had-preserved (for us).   Many also   talked

    Catilinam, atque illa portenta
(concerning) Catiline,   and those monsters (of-his-party say

    "Erumpet,   occupabit   aliquem locum,
ing, that' "He-will-break-out, he-will-occupy   some   place,

    faciet bellum   patriæ." Miseros cives,
(that) he-may-make war (on his) country." O miserable citizens,

  interdum meritos optime de republica, in
(who) sometimes having-deserved most-well of the republic, in

quibus, homines non modò obliviscuntur præclarissimas
whom, men   not only forget the-most-renowned

res, sed etiam suspicantur   nefarias !
deeds, but even suspect (the most) nefarious (designs)!

Ergo illa fuerunt falsa; quæ certe exstitissent
Therefore those-things were false; which certainly would-have-been

vera, si Milo admisisset aliquid, quod posset non
true, if Milo had-committed any-thing, which he-could not

honeste que vere defendere.
honestly and truly defend.

24.   Quid?   ut sustinuit,   quæ
    (But) what (more? how) that he-bore (those charges), which

postea congesta sunt in eum quæ perculissent
afterwards were heaped on him which would-have-struck-down

quemvis, etiam conscientiâ mediocrium delictorum,
any-one, even with the consciousness of moderate offences,

immortales dii! sustinuit?   immo vero
immortal gods! did-he-bear (them)? yes indeed (it may

  ut contempsit, ac putavit pro nihilo;
be said) that he-despised-them, nd considered them as nothing;

quæ neque nocens maximo animo, neque
which neither a guilty-man with-the-most-resolute mind, nor

innocens, nisi fortissimus vir, potuisset negligere.
the innocent-man, unless a very-brave man,   could have-neglected.

Indicabatur   etiam multitudo scutorum, gladiorum,
It-was-intimated (that) even a-great-number of-shields,   of swords,

frenorum, que pilorum posse deprehendi, dicebant,
of-bridles,   and of-javelins could   be seized,   they-said,

esse nullum vicum,   nullum angiportum in
(that) there-was no   street, (or) no   alley   in

urbe, in quo   non   domus conducta esset
the city, in which 'there-was not   a house   'hired

Miloni;   arma   devecta   Tiberi in   villam
for-Milo; (that) arms were-carried-on the Tiber 'to (his) 'villa (of)

Oriculanam;   domus in Capitolino clivo referta
Oriculum;   (that his) house on the Capitoline hill was-filled

scutis;   omnia   plena   malleolorum
with-shields; (that) all   (places) were-full   of-fire-brands

comparatorum ad incendia urbis.   Hæc   nor
prepared   for the burning of-the city. These things were not

solùm delata, sed pæne credita, nec repudiata sunt
only reported, but nearly believed, nor were-they-repudiated

ante quàm   quæsita.   Equidem
[disbelieved] before   that   they-were-investigated. 'I   indeed

laudabam incredibilem diligentiam Cn. Pompeii; sed
'praised   the incredible   diligence of-Cn. Pompey;   but

dicam, ut   sentio, judices. Nimis multa
I-will-say, that (which) I think, O judges. Too many-things

coguntur   audire,
are-made-necessary to hear [too many things are required to be listened

neque possunt ii facere aliter, quibus tota
to], nor   can those do otherwise, to-whom the whole

respublica commissa est,   cui   fuerit etiam
republic   is entrusted,   to whom [Pompey] it-was   even

Licinius,   nescio   qui,
(necessary that a certain) Licinius, I-know-not who, (but)

popa,   de maximo circo,
a-servant-and-attendant-on-the-sacrifices, from the great   circus,

[where he kept an eating and drinking house for slaves, and low people]

audiendus fuerit;   **servos Milonis, factos**
should-be-heard;   (he stated, that)   slaves   of Milo,   made

ebrios   **apud**   **se,**   **confessos esse**   **sibi,**
drunk   at   his-house,   had-confessed   to-him, (that)

conjurasse   **de interficiendo Pompeio, dein**
they-had-conspired (together) about   killing   Pompey,   after

postea,   **se percussum esse gladio ab uno de illis,**
(which), (that) he   was-struck   with-a-sword by one of them,

ne   **indicaret.**   **Nuntiavit Pompeio in**
lest   he-might-give-information.   (This) he-announced to Pompey   at

hortos. Arcessor in primis. De sententiâ
(his) country-seat. I-am-called-for   especially.   By   the advice

amicorum defert rem ad senatum. Poteram
'of (his)   'friends   he-refers the affair to the senate.   I-could

non, non   **exanimari**   **metu, in tantâ suspicione**
not,   but be-nearly-frightened-to-death by fear, in such   a suspicion

illius custodis mei que patriæ, sed
(of the danger) of-that   guardian of-myself and   country,   but

mirabar tamen,   **credi**   **popæ,**
I-wondered however, that-credit-should-be-given to-the-sacrificial-servant,

confessionem servorum audiri,   **vulnus in**
(that) the confession   of slaves   should-be-heard, (that) the wound in

latere, quod videretur   **acii punctum,**
the side,   which   seemed   (to be given by)   the point of a needle

probari pro ictu gladiatoris. Verum, ut
should-be-taken for   the stroke   of-a-gladiator.   But-truly,   as

intelligo, Pompeius magis cavebat, quàm
I-understand,   Pompey 'acted more 'with precaution,   than

timebat,   **non**   **ea**   **solùm**   **quæ**
that-he-feared (anything), not   those-things   only   which

timenda erant, sed omnia,   **ne**
were-to-be-feared,   but   all-things (are to be guarded against), lest

vos timeretis aliquid.
you   may-fear   something [lest you may have cause for fear]

Nuntiabatur,   **domus C. Cæsaris, clarissimi et**
It-was-reported, (that) the house of C.   Cæsar,   a most-illustrious and

fortissimi viri, oppugnata per multas horas noctis.
most-brave   man, was-assailed during many   hours of-the-night

Nemo, tam celebri loco, audierat, nemo senserat;
No-one, in so conspicuous a place, had-heard (it), no-one perceived (it)

tamen audiebatur. Poteram non suspicari, Cn.
yet it-was-reported. I-could not suspect, (that) Cn.

Pompeium, virum præstantissimâ virtute timidum;
Pompey, a man of-most-distinguished courage (to be) timid

putabam nullam diligentiam nimiam,
(and) I-thought (that) no diligence (could be) too-great,

susceptâ totâ republica.
(in one) having-undertaken (the management of) the whole republic.

Nuper frequentissimo senatu, in
Lately in-a-very-full (meeting-of the) senate, (held) in

Capitolio, senator inventus est, qui diceret Milonem
the Capitol, a senator was found, who said (that) Milo

esse cum telo. Nudavit se
was with a weapon [was armed]. He-bared himself [by throwing

in sanctissimo templo, quoniam vita
back his clothes] in the-most-holy temple, because the life

et talis civis et viri, non faciebat fidem,
both of such a citizen and (such) a man, did not procure (him) credit,

ut, eo tacente, res loqueretur ipsa.
that, he being-silent, the thing might-speak (for) itself.

25. Omnia comperta sunt falsa atque insidiose
All-things have-been-found (to be) false, and insidiously

ficta; quum tamen etiam nunc Milo metuitur.
devised; yet however even now Milo is feared. 'We-do

Non jam timemus hoc crimen Clodianum,
not at-present 'fear this accusation (respecting) Clodius,

sed tuas, Cn. Pompei, (enim jam appello te, et
but yours, O Cn. Pompey, (for 'I now 'address you, and

eâ voce, ut possis exaudire me) tuas, tuas,
with-such a voice, that you-may hear me) your, your,

inquam, suspiciones perhorrescimus. Si times
I-say, suspicions we-shudder-at. If you-fear

Milonem, si putas hunc aut nunc cogitare
Milo, if-you-think (that) he either now meditates (any-

nefarie de tuâ vitâ, aut aliquando
thing) wickedly concerning your life, or that 'he-ever

molitum aliquid, si delectus
'attempted any-thing (against your life), if the-levying-of-troops

Italiæ, ut nonnulli tui conquisitores
(throughout) Italy, as some of-your agents-to-enroll-troops

dictitarunt; si hæc arma. si cohortes
have-frequently-asserted; if these arms. if (these) cohorts (in)

Capitolinæ, si excubiæ, si vigiliæ, si deleta
the Capitol, if (these) sentinels, if (these) watchmen, if the chosen

juventus, quæ custodit tuum corpus que domum,
youths, who guard your person and house,

armata est contra impetum Milonis; atque omnia
are-armed against an attack of-Milo; and all

illa sunt instituta, parata, intenta in hunc
those-things are instituted, prepared, (and) directed against this

unum, certe in hoc magna vis et
one (man), (there is) certainly in him a great power and

incredibilis animus, et vires atque opes indicantur
incredible courage, and forces and means are-indicated

non unius viri, si quidem et
not (in the possession) of-one man, if indeed both

præstantissimus dux, et tota respublica
the-most-eminent general, and the whole republic

armata est in hunc unum. Sed quis
is-armed against this one (man). But who (is there, that)

non intelligit, omnes partes reipublicæ, ægras
does not understand, (that) all the parts of-the-republic, feeble

et labantes, commissas esse tibi, ut sanares et
and tottering, were-committed to-you, that you-might-heal and

confirmares eas his armis? Quòd si locus
strengthen them by-these arms? That if an opportunity

datus esset Miloni profectò probasset tibi
had-been-given to-Milo 'he-had certainly 'proved to-you

ipsi, neminem hominem fuisse unquam
yourself, (that) no man was ever

cariorem homini, quàm te sibi; se
more-dear to-man, than you (were) to-himself; (that) he

unquam fugisse nullvm periculum pro tuâ
at any-time av ided no danger for (promoting) your

dignitate;   se sæpissime contendisse cum illâ
dignity;   (that) 'he had 'very-often   contended   with that

ipsâ teterrimâ peste, pro tuâ gloriâ; su'm
same   most-foul   pest,   for your   glory; (that) his

tribunatum, gubernatum tuis consiliis,
tribuneship,   governed   by-your   counsels,   (was directed)

ad meam salutem, quæ fuisset carissima tibi;
to   my   safety,   which was   most-dear   to-you; (that)

se   postea   defensum a   te,
he 'was afterwards 'defended   by   you,   (when he was)

in periculo   capitis,
in   danger   'of (his) 'life,   [of conviction for a capital offence,]

  adjutum   in petitione præturæ;
(that) he-was-assisted (by you) in   seeking   the prætorship; (that,

se semper sperasse habere duos amicissimos,
'he always   'hoped   to-have   two   most-friendly (to himself),

te   tuo beneficio,   me
you (on account of) your   benefits (conferred on himself), me (on ac-

  suo.   Quæ si   non
count of) his   (services, rendered to me). Which if 'he-had not

probaret, si ista suspicio   ita penitus inhæsisset,
'proved,   if   this   suspicion 'had so   deeply   'taken-root,

ut posset nullo modò   evelli,   si denique Italia
that it-could in-no wise   be-eradicated, if   in-fine   Italy

nunquam conquietura esset a   delectu,
'was   never   'to-rest   from (these) levies-of-soldiers.

urbs ab   armis, sine   clade   Milonis,
(nor) the city from   arms,   without the destruction   of-Milo,

næ   iste haud dubitans   cessisset
certainly   he   without   hesitating would-have-departed 'from his

patriâ, is, qui natus est   ita, et   consuevit
'country, he,   who 'was-born (to do) so, and was-accustomed-to-do

ita; tamen   antestaretur   te   Magne,
so;   however he-would-have-called-on   you (to witness) O Magnus,

  quod nunc etiam facit.
(that he was innocent), which 'he now   also   'does.

26. Vide, quàm varia, que commutabilis ratıo
  See,   how   various, and   changeable   the course

vitæ, quàm vaga que volubilis fortuna, quantæ
of-life, how uncertain and inconstant (is) fortune, what

infidelitates in amicitiis, quàm simulationes aptæ ad
faithlessness in friendships, what dissembling suited to

tempus, in periculis, quantæ fugæ proximorum,
the times, in dangers, what desertion of-relations-and-friends,

quantæ timiditates. Erit, erit profectò
what timidity. There-will-be, there-will-be certainly

tempus, et ille dies aliquando illucescet, quum
a time, and that day 'will at-some-time 'appear, when

tu, tuis rebus, ut spero, salutaribus, sed fortasse
you, your affair, as I-hope, being-prosperous, but perhaps

aliquo motu temporum communium (qui
by-some commotion of-the-times common (to them) (which

quàm crebro accidat, experti debemus
how often it-may-happen, 'we-experienced 'ought

scire) desideres et benevolentiam amicissimi,
to-know) you-may-want both the-good-will of-the-dearest-friend,

et fidem gravissimi hominis, et
and the good-faith of-a-most-dignified (and influential) man, and

magnitudinem animi unius fortissimi viri, post
the greatness of-mind of-one of-the-bravest men, since

homines natos. Quamquam
men were-born. [The bravest man that ever lived.] Although

quis credat hoc, Cn. Pompeium, peritissimum
who would-believe this, (that) Cn. Pompey, most-skilled

publici juris, moris majorum, denique
(in) public law, the customs 'of (our) 'ancestors, (and) in-fine

publicæ rei, quum senatus commiserit ei,
(in) public affairs, when the senate had-entrusted to-him,

ut videret "ne respublica caperet quid
that he-should-see "lest the republic should-receive any (thing of)

detrimenti" quo uno versiculo consules semper
injury" by-which one short-line the consuls 'were always

satis armati fuerunt, etiam nullis armis datis,
sufficiently 'armed, even no arms being-given

hunc exercitu, hunc
(to them), (that) he (having) an army (given him), (that) he 'having

delectu   dato,   exspectaturum
a levy-of-soldiers 'granted (him), would-wait

fuisse judicium, vindicandis consiliis ejus, qui
for the-decision-of-a-court, in-punishing designs-of-that man, who

tolleret vi judicia ipsa?   Satis
would-destroy by-force the courts themselves? It was sufficiently

judicatum est, a Pompeio, satis   ista
decided by Pompey, sufficiently-so (that) these-charges

falsò conferri in Milonem,   qui
were falsely 'brought against Milo, (and by Pompey), who

tulit legem, qua ut ego sentio opporteret
brought-forward the law, by-which as I think it-was-necessary

Milonem absolvi a vobis, ut omnes
(that) Milo should-be-acquitted by you, (and) as all

confitentur liceret.   Verò quòd
confess it-might-be-allowed (for him to be so). But as

sedet in illo loco, atque circumfusus illis copiis
he-sits in that place, and surrounded by-those forces

publicorum præsidiorum, satis declarat, se
of-public guards, 'he sufficiently 'declares, (that) he

non inferre terrorem vobis (enim quid minus
does not 'bring fear to-you (for what less

dignum illo, quàm cogere, ut vos condemnetis
worthy (of) him, than to-force (you), that you should-condemn

eum, in quem ipse posset animadvertere, et
him, on whom he-himself could inflict-punishment, both

more majorum, et suo jure) sed
according-to-the-customs 'of (our) 'ancestors, and by-his right) but

esse præsidio ut intelligatis
(that this) is for-a-guard (to you) that you-may-understand (that)

licere vobis judicare libere, quòd
it-is-allowed you to-pronounce-your-judgment freely, as

sentiatis, contra illam concionem histernam.
you-think, against that meeting (of) yesterday.

27. Nec verò judices, crimen Clodianum
Nor indeed 'does, O judges, the accusation concerning Clodius

movet me, nec sum tam demens, que tam ignarus
'move me, nor am-I so foolish, and so ignorant

atque expers vestri sensûs, quid sentiatis
and devoid (of knowledge) of-your opinion, what you-think

de morte Clodii. De qua, si nollem jam
concerning the death of-Clodius. Concerning which, if I-would-not now

ita diluere crimen, ut dilui, tamen
so do-away (with) the accusation, as I-have-done-away (with it), yet

liceret Miloni palam clamare impune, ac
it-would-be-allowed Milo openly to-exclaim with-impunity, and

gloriose mentiri: "Occidi, occidi, non Sp.
boastingly to-tell-an-untruth: "I-have-killed, I-have-killed, not Sp.

Mælium, qui levanda
Mælius, who (attempting, or) being-about-to-lower (the price of)

annona, que jacturis familiaris rei, quia
provisions, and at-the-expense 'of (his) 'private fortune, because

videbatur ampleti plebem nimis, incidit in
he-seemed (as) having-favoured the people too-much, he-fell under

suspicionem appetendi regni, non Ti. Gracchum,
suspicion of-seeking royalty-and-power, not Ti. Gracchus,

qui abrogavit magistratum collegæ per
who abrogated the magistracy (of his) colleague by

seditionem, interfectores quorum impleverunt orbem
sedition, the slayers of-whom filled the whole

terrarum gloriâ sui nominis; sed eum (enim
world with-the-renown of-their name; but him (for

auderet dicere, quum liberasset patriam
he-might-dare to-speak, since he-had-saved (his) country

suo periculo) cujus nefandum adulterium in
by-his-own danger) whose infamous adultery in

sanctissimis pulvinaribus, nobilissimæ feminæ
the-most-holy shrines, most-noble women

comprehenderunt; eum, cujus supplicio, senatus
detected; him, 'by whose 'punishment, the senate 'had

sæpe censuit, sollemnes religiones expiandas;
often 'decreed, (that) solemn religious-rites ought-to-be-expiated;

tum, quem L. Lucullus juratus, dixit se
aim, whom L. Lucullus having-sworn, said (that) he

comperisse, fecisse nefarium stuprum cum
had-discovered, (that) he-had-committed a nefarious incest with

germanâ sorore, habitis quæstionibus;   eum,
his-own   sister, having-had an examination (of her slaves); him.

qui   exterminavit,   armis   servorum,   civem,
who   had-driven-into-exile, by-the-arms of-slaves,   a citizer

           quem senatus, quem Romanus populus, quem
[Cicero],   whom the senate, whom the Roman people,   whom

omnes gentes judicarant   conservatorem urbis
all   nations had-judged (to be) the preserver of-the-city,

ac vitæ   civium; eum,   qui dedit   ademit
and of-the-life of-the-citizens; him,   who gave (and) took-away

regna,   partitus est orbem terrarum   cum
kingdoms, (and who)   divided   the world   with

quibus voluit; eum, qui, plurimis cædibus   factis
whom he-pleased; him, who, many murders being-committed

in foro, compulit domum   vi   et armis civem
in the forum, drove to-his-house by-force and arms a citizen

           singulari virtute et gloriâ;
[Pompey] (distinguished) 'by (his) 'singular bravery and renown

eum, cui nihil fuit unquam nefas, nec in facinore
him, to-whom nothing was ever forbidden, either in   crime

nec in   libidine; eum,   qui incendit ædem
or   in   lust;   him,   who set-fire to-the-temple

Nympharum, ut exstingueret publicam memoriam
of-the-Nymphs, that he-might-destroy the public   records

recensionis impressam publicis tabulis; eum denique,
of-the-census impressed on-the-public tablets; him   in-fine,

cui jam erat nulla lex, nullum civili jus, nulli
to-whom now there-was no law,   no   civil right, no

termini possessionum; qui petebat
boundaries of-possessions; who sought (to obtain possession of)

   fundos   alienos,   non   calumniâ
the landed-estates (of) others,   not by-the-quirks-and-chicanery

litium, non injustis   vindiciis   ac
of-law-suits, not by-unjust legal-processes-and-claims and 'by (unjust)

sacramentis, sed castris, exercitu,   inferendis
'oaths,   but by-camps, by-an-army, (and) advancing

signis;   qui conatus est pellere
the standards; [by military attacks] who endeavoured to-drive-from

possessionibus, armis que castris, non solum
(their) possessions, by-arms and camps, not only

Etruscos (enim penitùs contempserat eos), sed
the Etrurians (for 'he entirely 'despised them), but (also)

hunc P. Varium, fortissimum atque optimum civem
this P. Varius, a most-brave and most-excellent citizen

nostrum judicem; qui peragrabat
and) our judge (in this cause); who travelled-through

villas que hortos multorum cum architectis et
the villas and gardens of-many with architects and

decempedis; qui terminabat spem suarum
on-feet-measuring-rods; who bounded the hopes of-his

possessionum Janiculo et Alpibus; qui, quum
possessions by-the-Janiculum and the Alps; who, when

non impetrasset ab M. Paconio, splendido
'he-could not 'obtain from M. Paconius, an illustrious

et forti Romano equite, ut venderet sibi insulam
and brave Roman knight, that he-would-sell him the island

in lacu Prilio, repente convexit in eam insulam
in lake Prilius, suddenly conveyed to that island

lintribus materiem, calcem, cæmenta, arma,
in boats timber, lime, small-stones-for-building, and tools,

non dubitavit extruere ædificium in alieno,
'he-did not 'hesitate to-build a house on another-man's

que domino trans ripam inspectante; qui
(ground), and the proprietor on the opposite shore looking-on; who

huic T. Furfanio, cui viro? immortales
(dared to say) to this T. Furfanius, to-what a man? O immortal

dii; (enim quid ego dicam de
gods; (but why 'should I 'mention (any thing) concerning

mulierculâ Scantiâ, quid de adolescente
the woman Scantia, why (any thing) concerning the young-man

P. Apinio? utrique quorum minatus est mortem,
P. Apinius? both of-whom he-threatened (with) death,

nisi cessissent possessione hortorum sibi),
unless they abandoned the possession 'of (their) 'gardens to-himself),

sed ausus est dicere Furfanio si non dedisset
but he-dared to-say to-Furfanius (that) if 'he-did not 'give

sibi pecuniam, quantam poposcerat, se
him   money,   as-much-as   he-might-have-asked-for, (that) he

illaturum mortuum in ejus domum, quâ invidiâ
would-carry a dead-body in his house, by-which odium

conflagrandum esset tali viro huic;
'a flame (of indignation) 'would-break-out against-such a man (as) this;

qui dejecit Appium absentem fratrem, hominem
who turned Appius (his) absent brother, a man

conjunctum mihi fidissimâ gratiâ, de possessione
united to-me by-the-most-faithful friendship, from the possession

fundi; qui instituit ducere parietem sic per
'of (his) farm; who determined to-run a wall so through

vestibulum sororis, agere fundamenta
the vestibule 'of (his) 'sister's (house), (and) to-lay the-foundation

sic, ut non modò privaret sororem vestibulo,
so, that 'he not only 'deprived (his) sister (of her) vestibule,

sed omni aditu et limine."
but (of) all access (to) and entrance by the threshold (of her house)."

28. Quamquam hæc videbantur jam quidem
    Although thesa-things appeared then indeed (as)

tolerabilia, etsi æquabiliter irruebat
tolerable, although 'he equally 'attacked (and violently

in rempublicam, in privatos, in
rushed) (against) the republic, (against) private-persons, (against)

longinquas, in propinquas, in
those-at-a distance, against neighbours (and those near), against

alienos, in suos; sed nescio quomodo
strangers, (and) against his-own (relations); but I-know-not how

incredibilis patientia civitatis jam obduruerat
the incredible patience of-the-state 'had then 'become-hardened

et percalluerat usu. Vero quæ jam
and callous by-use. But (those things) which 'were already

aderant, et impendebant, quonam modo
'present, and impended (over you), in-what manner

potuissetis aut depellere aut ferre ea? Si ille
could-you either repel or bear them? If he

nactus esset imperium, omitto
had-obtained-possession (of) the empire, I-omit (and say nothing of our)

socios, exteras nationes, reges, tetrarchas; enim
allies, foreign nations, kings, and tetrarchs; for

faceretis vota,
you-would-have-made vows, [you would have wished] 'that-he-would

potius immitteret se in eos, quàm in vestras
rather 'have-turned (his) 'attention to them, than to your

possessiones, vestra tecta, vestras pecunias; pecunias
possessions, your houses, your money; money

dico? medius fidius, nunquam cohibuisset
do-I-say? may Jupiter help me, 'he-would never 'have-restrained

suas effrenatas libidines a liberis, et a
his unbridled lusts from (your) children, and from (your)

conjugibus. Putatis hæc fingi, quæ
wives. Do-you-think (that) these-things are-feigned, which

patent, quæ sunt nota omnibus, quæ tenentur?
are-evident, which are known to-all, which are-held (in

illum conscripturum fuisse, in
our memory)? (was it not, that) he was-about-to-raise, in

urbe, execitus servorum, per quos possideret totam
the city, armies of-slaves, by whom he-might-possess the entire

rempublicam, que privatas res omnium? Quamobrem,
republic, and the private fortunes of-all? Wherefore

si T. Annius tenens cruentum gladium clamaret,
if T. Annius holding a bloody sword had-cried-out:

"quæso cives adeste atque audite P.
"I-entreat (you) O citizens draw-near and hear (that) P.

Clodium interfeci; ejus furores, quos jam
Clodius has-been-killed; his furious-deeds, which heretofore

poteramus frenare nullis legibus, nullis judiciis,
we-could restrain by-no laws, by-no courts,

repuli a vestris cervicibus, hoc ferro et hac
I-have-repelled from your necks, by-this sword and by-this

dexterâ, ut per me unum, jus, æquitas, leges,
right-hand, that by me alone, right, equity, laws,

libertas, pudor, pudicitia manerent in civitate,"
liberty, modesty, (and) chastity remains in the city,"

vero timendum esset quonam modo
but it-would-have-to-be-feared (by Milo) in what manner

civitas ferret id! Enim nunc quis est,
'he city would-bear this (announcement)! For now who is-there,

qui non probet? qui non laudet?
who 'does not 'approve? who 'does not 'praise (what has been done)?

qui, post memoriam hominum, non et dicat et
who, since the memory of-man, 'does not both 'say and

sentiat T. Annium unum plurimum profuisse
think ' that) T. Annius alone 'did very-great 'service

reipublicæ, affecisse Romanum populum,
to-the-republic, (and) to-have-affected the Roman people,

cunctam Italiam, omnes nationes maximâ
all Italy, (and) all nations with-the-greatest

lætitiâ? Non queo judicare, quanta fuerit illa
joy? I am not 'able to judge, how-great may-have-been that

vetera gaudia Romani populi. Tamen nostra ætas
old joy of-the-Roman people. Although our age

jam vidit clarissimas victorias summorum
'has already 'seen the-most-celebrated victories of-the-greatest

imperatorum, nulla quarum attulit neque tam
commanders, (yet) none of-these-victories brought either such

diuturnam, nec tantam lætitiam. Mandate hoc
lasting, or such-great joy. Commit these

memoriæ, judices. Spero vos, que vestros liberos
to-memory, O judges. I-hope (that) you, and your children

visuros esse multa bona; in republica;
may-see many good-things (and happy days); in the republic;

in singulis iis, semper ita
as-respects each-one (of) these-things, 'you-will always so

existimabitis, P. Clodio vivo, visuros fuisse
'think, (that) P. Clodio being-alive, you-would-have-seen

nihil eorum. Adducti sumus in maximam spem, et
nothing of-them. We-have-been-led to the greatest hope, and

quemadmodum confido, verissimam, hunc ipsum
as I-confide, a most-true-hope, (that) this same

annum, hoc ipso summo viro consule,
year, this same eminent man (Pompey) (being) consul,

licentiâ hominum compressâ, cupiditatibus
the-licentiousness of-men being-repressed, (evil) desires

fractis,   legibus   et   judiciis
being broken-and-put-down,   the laws   and   courts 'being (fully

constitutis,   fore   salutarem
'established (in their authority),   that-it-would-be   a salutary (day)

civitati.   Est num quis igitur tam demens, qui,
for-the-state.   Is-there then any-one therefore so   foolish,   who,

arbitetur   hoc   potuisse   contingere,   P.
may think   that this   could   happen (or be obtained),   P.

Clodio   vivo?   Quid?   quod jus perpetuæ possessionis
Clodius being-alive? What?   what right of-perpetual   possession

potuissent   ea   habere, quæ tenetis   privata
could   those things   have,   which you-hold (as) private (property

atque   vestra,   furioso   homine   dominante?
and   your-own,   this frenzied   man   ruling?

29.   Non timeo, judices, ne inflammatus   odio,
      'I-do not   'fear, O judges, lest   inflamed   by-hatred,

mearum inimicitiarum, videar   evomere
(arising from) my-own   enmities,   I-may-seem to-vomit-forth

hæc   in   illum libentius, quam verius. Etenim
these-charges against him   more freely,   than   truly.   For

etsi   meum odium   debebat esse   præcipuum,
although   my hatred   (of him)   ought   to-be   a principal thing,

                       tamen
(on account of the many and great injuries he inflicted on me), yet-however

ille erat ita   communis hostis omnium, ut
he   was so-much the common enemy   of-all,   that (my own

      versaretur   pæne   æqualiter   in
hatred seemed)   to-be   nearly   equally (shared)   in

communi odio. Potest non   satis   dici, ne
the general   hatred.   It-can   not 'be sufficiently 'expressed, nor

quidem cogitari, quantum fuerit   sceleris in illo,
indeed   imagined, how-much there-was of-wickedness in him,

quantum   exitii.   Quin sic attendite,
how-much (there was) of-destruction-and- ruin. But thus pay-attention,

judices.   Nempe   hæc est   quæstio   de
O judges.   For-certainly   this   is   an-investigation   concerning

interitu P. Clodii.   Fingite   animis (enim nostræ
the death of-P. Clodius. Imagine 'in (your) 'minds (for   our

ogitationes sunt liberæ, et quæ volunt sic
thoughts are free, and that-which they-wish 'they so

intuentur, ut cernimus, ea quæ videmus),
contemplate, that we-distinguish-and-know those-things which-we-see),

fingite igitur cogitatione imaginem hujus
form therefore 'by (your) 'thoughts the image of-this

meæ conditionis, si possim efficere, ut
my condition, if I-could effect (this), tha

absolvatis Milonem, sed ita si P. Clodius
you-acquit Milo, but so and-provided-that P. Clodius

revixerit. Vultu quid extimuistis ?
should-again-live. By (your) countenance what have-you-feared ?

Quonam modo
[Why is fear depicted in your countenances.] In-what manner 'would

ille vivus afficeret vos, quos mortuus
he alive 'affect (and move) you, whom he-being-dead

percussit, inani cogitatione ?
'has (so) 'struck (and disturbed you) by-the-mere thought

Quid ? si Cn. Pompeius ipse, qui est ea
(of him) ? What ? if Cn. Pompey himself, who is such

virtute ac fortunâ, ut semper potuerit
by-courage and by-fortune, that 'he-was always 'able (to do)

ea, quæ nemo, præter illum, si is,
those-things, which no-one, except him, (could do), if he,

inquam, potuisset aut ferre questionem de
I-say, could either institute an investigation concerning

morte P. Clodii, aut excitare ipsum ab inferis,
the death of-P. Clodius, or raise him from the dead,

uterum putatis potius facturum fuisse ?
which-of-the-two do-you-think 'he-would rather 'have-done ?

Etiamsı propter amicitiam vellet evocare illum
Although on-account of-friendship he-might-wish to recall him

ab inferis, propter rempublicam non
from death, (yet) on-account of-the-republic 'he-would not

fecisset Igitur sedetis ultores ejus mortis,
'have-done (it). Therefore you-sit (as) avengers of-his death,

cujus vitam, si puteis, posse restitui per
whose life. if you-thought, (that) it-could be-restored by

vos, nolitis, et de ejus nece
you, you-would-not (restore it), and concerning his death

quæstio lata est, qui si posset
an investigation is instituted (by law), who if he could

revivescere eâdem lege, lex
revive by-the-same law, the law ¹would-have

nunquam lata esset. Ne ergo interfector
never ¹been-passed. ¹Should then therefore the slayer

hujus, si esset timeret pœnam, in confitendo,
of-this-man, if he-were-it, ¹fear punishment, in confessing,

ab iis, quos liberavisset? Homines Græci
from those, whom he-had-freed? The men (of) Greece

tribuunt honores deorum iis viris, qui
grant the honours of-the-gods to-those men, who

necaverunt tyrannos. Quæ ego vidi Athenis?
have-slain tyrants. What ¹have I (not) ¹seen at-Athens?

quæ in aliis urbibus Græciæ? quas divinas res
what in other cities of-Greece? what divine ceremonies

institutas talibus viris? quos cantus? quæ
have-been-instituted for-such men? what songs? what

carmina? Propè consecrantur et ad
odes? ¹They-are nearly ¹consecrated both to

religionem et memoriam immortalitatis.
religion and (to) the memory of-immortality. [They are

Vos non modò afficietis
almost honoured as gods.] (And) ¹do-you not only (not) ¹reward

conservatorem tanti populi, ultorem tanti
the preserver of-so-great a people, (and) the avenger of-such-a-great

sceleris nullis honoribus, sed etiam
crime with (any) honours, but ¹do-you even

patiemini rapi ad supplicium? Confiteretur,
¹suffer (him) to-be-carried-off to punishment? He-would-confess

confiteretur, inquam, si fecisset, et magno
he-would-confess, I-say, if he-had (done it), and with-a-great

animo et libente, se fecisse causâ
mind and willingly, (that) he had-done (it) for-the-sake

libertatis omnium, quod esset non modò
of-the-liberty of-all, which was not only

confitendum   ei   verùm   etiam
to-be-confessed   by-him   but-indeed   even

prædicandum.
to-be-proclaimed.

30. Etenim si   non negat id, ex quo   petit
    For   if [1]he-does not [1]deny it, from which he-seeks

nihil, nisi ut   ignoscatur,   dubitaret   fateri
nothing, unless that he-may-be-pardoned, would-he-hesitate to-avow

id,   ex quo etiam   præmia laudis petenda essent?
that, for which even the reward of-praise were-to-be-demanded?

nisi verò   putat   esse   gratius vobis,   se
unless indeed he-may-think (it) to-be more-grateful to-you, (that) he

fuisse   defensorem sui capitis,   quàm
[1]should-be the defender of-his-own life, than the (defender)

vestri;   quum   praesertim, in ea confessione si
of-you;   when   especially, in that confession, if

velletis   esse   grati,   assequeretur   amplissimos
you-desire to-be grateful, he-would-attain-to the-most-ample

honores;   si   factum   non   probaretur vobis,
honours;   if the deed [1]were not [1]approved-of by-you,

(quamquam qui poterat non   probari, cuiquam, sua
(however   who could not (but) approve, any-one, (for) his

salus)?   sed si   tamen   virtus
safety) (obtained through him)? but if however the virtue

fortissimi viri cecidisset   minus grata
of-a-very-brave man had-fallen-out (but) little agreeable [1]to (his fellow)

civibus,   magno que constanti animo cederet   ex
[1]citizens, [1]he with-a-great and constant mind [1]had-departed from

ingratâ vivitate. Nam quid esset ingratius, quàm
an ungrateful city. For what could-be more-ungrateful, than

ceteros lætari,   eum solum lugere,
(that) others should-rejoice, (and that) he alone should-grieve,

propter quem ceteri lætarentur? Quamquam semper
through whom others rejoice?   Although [1]we always

fuimus omnes hoc   animo,   in
[1]were all in-this mind (and opinion, that) in

opprimendis proditoribus   patriæ, ut quoniam
putting-down traitors [1]to (their) [1]country, that because

gloria futura esset nostra, quoque
the glory would-hereafter-be ours, (that) 'we should also

putaremus periculum et invidiam
'think (that) the danger and odium (would also be)

nostram. Nam quæ laus tribuenda esset mihi
ours For what praise would-have-been-given to-me

ipsi, quum ausus essem tantum in meo consulatu
myself, when I-had-dared so-much in my consulship

pro vobis ac vestris liberis, si quum conabar id,
for you and your children, if when I-undertook it,

arbitrarer me ausurum esse, sine meis maximis
I-thought (that) I might-attempt (it), without my greatest

dimicationibus? Quæ mulier non auderet
contests-and-struggles? What woman (that) 'would not 'dare

occidere sceleratum ac perniciosum civem, si
to-kill a wicked and pernicious citizen, if 'she-did

non timeret periculum? Invidiâ, morte, pœnâ
not 'fear the danger? Odium, death, punishment

proposita, qui nihilo segnius
being-placed-before (any one), (yet) he-who not-the-less tardily (for that)

defendit rempublicam, is vere putandus est vir.
defends the republic, he 'is truly 'to be-considered a man.

Est grati populi afficere præmiis cives,
It-is (the part) of-a-grateful people to-reward citizens, (who)

meritos bene de republica, fortis viri,
have-deserved well of the republic, (it is the part) of-a-brave man,

ne quidem moveri suppliciis, ut pœniteat
not even to-be-moved by-punishments, (so) that he-may-repent (that)

fecisse fortiter. Quamobrem T. Annius uteretur
he-acted bravely. Wherefore T. Annius may-make-use

eâdem confessione, qua Ahala, qua
(of) the same confession (and declaration), of-which Ahala, of-which

Nasica, qua Opimus, qua Marius, qua nosmet
Nasica, of-which Opimus, of-which Marius, of-which we

ipsi et si respublica esset grata
ourselves (have each made use of) (that) if the republic were grateful

lætaretur, si ingrata, tamen in gravi fortunâ
he-would-rejoice, if ungrateful, however in (his) adverse fortune

niteretur suâ conscientiâ.
he-would-rest (and depend) on his conscience (for support and consolation).

Sed, judices, fortuna Romani populi, et vestra
But, O judges, the good-fortune of-the-Roman people, and your

felicitas et immortales dii putant deberi sibi
happiness and the immortal gods think (that) they-owe him

gratiam hujus beneficii. Nec
[Milo] gratitude (for) this favour (of destroying Clodius). Nor

verò potest quisquam arbitrari aliter, nisi qui
indeed can any-one think otherwise, unless he-who

ducit esse nullam vim, ve divinum
thinks (that) there is no divine power, no divine

numen, quem neque magnitudo nostri
influence-and-providence, whom neither the greatness of-our

imperii, neque ille sol, nec motus Cœli que
empire, neither that sun, nor the motions of-the-heavens and

signorum, nec vicissitudines rerum, atque ordines
of-the-signs, nor the vicissitudes of-things, and (their) order

movent, neque id quod est maximum, sapientia
move, nor that which is the greatest, the-wisdom

majorum, qui, et ipsi sanctissime
'of (our) 'ancestors, who, and they-themselves most-holily

coluerunt sacra, qui cerimonias,
observed the sacred (institutions), who (also) the ceremonies-and-rites

qui auspicia, et prodiderunt
(of religion), who (also) the auspices, and transmitted (them)

nobis suis posteris.
to-us their posterity.

31. Est, profectò est illa vis, neque in
There-is, 'there certainly 'is that power, nor-only in

his corporibus, atque in hac nostrâ imbecillitate
these bodies, and in this our weakness

inest quiddam, quod vigeat et sentiat, et inest
there-is something-within, which is-vigorous and thinks, and is

non in hoc tanto tam præclaro
not [and it is also much more so] in this so-great so glorious

motu naturæ. Nisi forte idcirco   non putant
motion of nature. Unless perhaps for-that-reason ¹they-do ¬ot   ¹think

              quia apparet non, nec cernitur; proinde
(it to exist) because it-does-not-appear, nor is-seen; consequently

quasi possimus, aut plane videre,   aut sentire
as-if we could, either clearly see (our mind), or   feel

qualis,   ubi sit,   nostram **mentem**
what (it might be, or) where it might be, (that is) our   mind

ipsam, qua   sapimus, qua providemus, qua
itself, by-which we-are-wise, by-which we-have-foresight, by-which

agimus ac dicimus hæc ipsa.   Ea igitur
we-do and say those very-same-things. That therefore (is)

ipsa vis, quæ sæpe attulit huic urbi incredibiles
the same power, which often has-brought to-this city   incredible

felicitates atque opes;   extinxit   ac
prosperity and wealth (and power);   it-destroyed and

sustulit illam perniciem,   cui   primum
removed that calamity [of Clodius], to-whom (it)   first

injecit mentem,   ut auderet
threw-into (his) mind, [it first inspired Clodius] that he-should-dare

irritare vi, que lacessere ferro fortissimum
to-irritate by-violence, and to-attack with-the-sword a-most-brave

virum, que vinceretur ab eo, quem si vicisset,
man, and he-was-conquered by him, whom if he-had-conquered,

habiturus esset sempiternam impunitatem et
he-would-have-had uninterrupted impunity and

licentiam. Illa res perfecta est, judices, non humano
licentiousness. That thing was-accomplished, O judges, not by-human

consilio, ne quidem mediocri   immortalium
counsels, nor indeed by-the-ordinary (counsels) of-the-immortal

deorum. Mehercule Religiones ipsæ,   quæ
gods. By-Hercules the sacred-places themselves,   which

**viderunt illam belluam cadere, videntur,   se
saw that monster fall, seem, (that) they

**commovisse, et   retinuisse   suum jus
were moved, and to-have-maintained-and-defended their right

in illo. Enim jam imploro atque testor
over him. For ¹I now ¹implore and ¹call ea

vos, vos, inquam, Albani tumuli atque
you 'to-witness, you, I-say, O Alban mounts and

luci, que vos obrutæ aræ Albanorum sociæ
groves, and you O destroyed altars of-the Albans, the-associates

et æquales Romani populi, sacrorum, quas ille,
and equals of-the-Roman people, (in) the-sacred-rites, which he

praeceps amentia, sanctissimis lucis,
(and his) headlong folly, the-most-holy groves,

cæsis que prostratis, oppresserat
being-cut-down and prostrated, had-oppressed (and buried)

insanis molibus substructionum; tum vestræ aræ,
by (his) insane masses of-substructures; then your altars,

vestræ religiones viguerunt, vestra vis valuit,
(then) your religious-rites flourished, your power prevailed,

quam ille polluerat omni scelere, que tu, sancte
which he had-polluted with-every crime, and you, O sacred

Jupiter Latiaris, ex tuo edito monte, cujus locus,
Jupiter Latiaris, from your high mountain, whose lakes,

nemora, que fines ille sæpe macularat omni
groves, and boundaries he 'had often 'defiled by-every

nefario stupro et scelere, aliquando aperuisti
wicked lust and crime, 'have at-length 'opened (your)

oculos ad puniendum eum; vobis, vobis in vestro
eyes to punish him; to-you, to-you in your

conspectu, illæ seræ, sed tamen justæ, et debitæ
view, those late, but however just, and due

pœnæ solutæ sunt.
punishments have-been-paid (in atonement for such great crimes).

Nisi forte dicemus hoc etiam factum esse
Unless perhaps we-say (that) this also was-done

casu; ut ante sacrarium ipsum Bonæ Deæ, quod
by-chance; that before the shrine itself of Bona Dea, which

est in fundo T. Sestii, in primis honesti et
is in the-farm of T. Sestius, especially an honourable and

ornati adolescentis, ante ipsam Bonam Deam,
accomplished young-man, before that-same Bona Dea,

inquam, quum commisisset prœlium, acciperet illud
I-say, when he-had-begun the battle he-received that

primum vulnus, quo obiret teterrimam mortem,
first   wound, by-which he-died a most-shameful death.

ut videretur non absolutus, illo nefario judicio,
that he-seemed not acquitted, by-that iniquitous trial,

sed reservatus ad hanc insignem pœnam.
but reserved for this conspicuous punishment.

32 Nec vero non, eadem ira deorum
[Nor indeed not], and indeed the same anger of-the-gods

injecit hanc amentiam in ejus satellitibus, ut
excited this folly in his followers, that

abjectus amburetur, sine
he-was-thrown-out (after) he-was-half-burnt, without (ancestral)

imaginibus, sine cantu atque
images, without (a funeral) song and (without funeral)

ludis, sine exsequis, sine lamentis, sine
games, without funeral-rites, without lamentations, without

laudationibus, sine funere, oblitus cruore et luto,
praises, without a funeral, besmeared with-blood and mud,

spoliatus celebritate illius supremi
deprived of-the-solemn-concourse (and honours) of-that last

diei, cui etiam inimici solent cedere. Credo
day, to-which even enemies are-accustomed to-accede. I-believe

fuisse non fas formas
(that) it-was not allowed (by the will of the gods), (that) the-images

clarissimorum virorum afferre aliquid decoris
of-the-most-illustrious men could-bring any-thing of-ornament

illi teterrimo parricidæ, neque in ullo
(and honour) to-that most-foul parricide, nor in any

loco ejus mortem lacerari potius,
place (that) his death [his dead body] might-be-lacerated rather,

quam in quo vita damnata esset.
than in that-which his life had-been-condemned.

Medius fidius, fortuna Romani populi
May Jupiter help me, (but) the fortune of-the-Roman people 'did

jam videbatur mihi dura et crudelis, quæ
heretofore 'appear to-me hard and cruel, which

pateretur illum, tot annos insultare
suffered him, for-so-many years to-insult (and attack;

in hanc rempublicam. Polluerat sanctissimas
this republic. He-had-polluted the-most-holy

religiones stupro, perfregerat gravissima
religious-rites with (his) lust, he-had-broken the most-weighty

decreta senatûs, palam redemerat se a
decrees of-the-senate, 'he-had openly 'freed himself from

judicibus pecuniâ, in tribunatu, vexarat
the judges by-money, in (his) tribuneship, he-had-harassed

senatum, resciderat gesta, consensu
the senate, he-had-rescinded acts-passed, by-the-consent

omnium ordinum pro salute reipublicæ, expulerat
of-all the orders for the safety of-the-republic, he-had-expelled

me 'from (my) patriâ, diripuerat bona,
me 'country, he-had-plundered (my) property,

incenderat domum, vexarat meam
ne-had-burned (my) house, he-had-ill-treated my

conjugem, liberos, indixerat nefarium bellum
wife (and) children, he-had-declared a-wicked war

Cn. Pompeio, effecerat cædes magistratuum
against Cn. Pompey, he had-made slaughter of-magistrates

que privatorum, incenderat domum mei
and of-private-persons, he-had-burned the house of-my

fratris, vastarat Etruriam, ejecerat multos
brother, he-had-laid-waste Etruria, he-had-ejected many

sedibus ac fortunis; instabat, urgebat;
'from (their) 'homes and possessions; he-pressed, he-urged;

civitas, Italia, provinciæ, regna poterant non
the city, Italy, the provinces, the kingdom could not

capere ejus amentiam; leges jam
contain his folly; the laws 'were already

incidebabantur domi, quæ addicerent nos
'engraved (on brass) at-his-house, which were-to-subject us

nostris servis; erat nihil cujusquam,
o-our slaves; there-was nothing of-any-one, [belonging to any

quod quidem ille adamasset, quod non
one] which indeed he might-take-a-liking-to, which 'he-did not

putaret fore suum hoc anno. Nemo obstabat
'think would-be his this year. No-one was-an-obstacle

ejus cogitationibus,   præter Milonem.
to his   'thoughts   (and expectations), except   Milo.

Arbitrabatur   illum ipsum,   qui poterat
He-thought   (that) that same-person, [Pompey,] who   could

obstare,   novo   reditu
(resist, and) be-an-obstacle (to him), 'would by-the-late   return

in gratiam   quasi   devinctum ;
to   favour (and friendship) 'be as-it-were 'bound   (to him);

dicebat   potentiam Cæsaris esse suum ;
he-said (that) the power of-Cæsar was his ; the (good-will and)

animos   bonorum in meo casu contempserat,
minds   'of (all) 'good-men in my cause   he-despised ;

Milo   unus   urgebat
Milo (was) the only-one (that) pressed-hard (on him).

33. Hìc immortales dii, ut dixi supra, dederunt
Here the immortal gods, as I-have-said above,   gave

mentem   illo perdito ac   furioso,   ut
the mind 'to [inspired] 'that abandoned and furious-man, that

faceret insidias huic.   Illa pestis
he-should-lay snares for-this-man. [Milo.] That pest (and wicked

potuit non aliter   perire ;   nunquam
man) could not otherwise have-perished; (for) never would

respublica ulta esset illum suo   jure.
the republic have-punished him by-their-own right (and laws).

Senatus, credo, circumscripsisset   eum
The senate, I-suppose, would-have-circumscribed (and restrained) him

prætorem. Ne quidem quum   solebat
(when) prætor. Not-even indeed when it-was-accustomed

facere id,   profecerat   aliquid
to-do this (with the magistrates), had-it-accomplished any-thing

hoc   eodem,   in   privato.
(of the kind) with-this same-person, [Clodius] in   private-life.

An fuissent consules   fortes in coercendo
Whether 'would the consuls 'have-been vigorous in restraining

prætore ? Primùm, Milone occiso,   habuisset
the prætor? In-the-first-place, Milo-being-killed, he-would-have-had

suos consules ;   deinde   quis consul, in
his-own consuls ; in-the-next-place what consul, on

eo   prætore,   esset   fortis
this (Clodius) (being) prætor, would-have-been courageous (enough

    per quem   tribunum,   meminisset
to resist him), by whom (when) tribune, he-may-have-remembered,

   consularem virtutem esse crudelissime vexatam?
(that) the consular   dignity   was   most-cruelly   harassed?

Oppressisset omnia   possideret   teneret;
He-had-oppressed   all   (that) he-might-possess (and)   hold (all);

  novâ   lege, quæ inventa est apud eum, cum reliquis
by-the-new law,   which   was found   with   him,   with the other

Clodianis legibus,   fecisset   nostros servos suos
Clodian   laws,   he-would-have-made   our   slaves   his

libertos. Postremo, nisi immortales dii impulissent
freedmen.   Lastly,   unless   the immortal gods   had-impelled

in eam mentem,   ut   effeminatus homo
into that   mind, [had inspired him], that (he) an effeminate   man

   conaretur   occidere fortissimum   virum,   hodie
should-attempt   to-kill   a-most-brave   man,   to-day

   haberetis   nullam   rempublicam.   An   ille
you-would-have   no   republic.   Whether   he (as)

prætor, ille   verô   consul, si modô, eo   vivo,
prætor,   he   indeed (as) consul, if indeed, he being-alive,

hæc templa, atque mœnia ipsa potuissent stare
these   temples,   and   the walls themselves could-have   stood

tamdiu, et exspectare ejus consulatum, denique
so-long,   and   waited-for   his   consulship,   in-fine

     ille vivus fecisset nihil mali, qui mortuus
'would   he   alive 'have-done nothing bad, who   dead

incenderit curiam   uno   ex   suis satellitibus,
burned   the senate-house by-one from-among his   satellites,

Sex. Clodio   duce?   Quo   quid . miserius,
Sex. Clodius being-the-leader? Than-this what more-miserable,

quid   acerbius,   quid   luctuosius   vidimus?
what   more-grievous,   what more-lamentable   have-we-seen?

    Templum sanctitatis amplitudinis, mentis,
(That) the temple of-sanctity   of-dignity,   of-mind   (and

     publici   consilii,   caput   urbis,   aram
wisdom), of-public   counsels,   the head of-the-city, the altar

sociorum, portum omnium gentium, **sedem**
of-the-allies, the harbour of-all nations, the seat

concessam ab universo populo uni ordini
granted by the entire people to-one order (of the state),

inflammari, exscindi, funestari ? neque (that)
to-be-set-on-fire, to-be-destroyed, to-be-polluted? nor (that)

id fieri a(b) imperitâ multitudine, quamquam id
this was-done by a senseless mob, although this

ipsum esset miserum, sed ab uno? Qui
same would-have-been lamentable, but by one-person? Who

quum ustor pro mortuo ausus sit tantum,
when (only) a burner for the-dead may-have-dared so-much,

quid non ausus esset signifer pro
what 'would-he not 'have-dared (as) standard-bearer for

vivo? Potissimum abjecit in curiam,
the living? 'He above-all 'threw (him) into the-senate-house,

ut mortuus incenderet eam quam vivus
that dead he-might-set-on-fire that which alive

everterat. Et sunt, qui querantur
he-had-overthrown. And are-there (persons), who complain

de Appiâ viâ, taceant de
concerning (the affair on) the Appian road, (but) are-silent concerning

curiâ? et qui putent ab eo spirante
the-senate-house? and who may-think (that) against him breathing

forum potuisse defendi, cujus cadaveri
(and alive), the forum could have-been-defended, whose dead-body

curia non restiterit. Excitate, excitate
the senate-house 'could not 'resist. Resuscitate, resuscitate

ipsum, si potestis a mortuis. Frangetis
himself, if you-can from the-dead. Will-you-break

impetum vivi, cujus furias vix sustinetis
the-shock-of-him alive, whose violence 'you-can scarcely 'sustain

insepulti? Nisi vero sustinuistis
unburied? Unless indeed you-could-have-sustained (and resisted)

eos, qui concurrerunt ad curiam cum
those-men, who ran to the-senate-house with

facibus, cum falcibus ad Castoris,
torches, with scythes to (the temple) of-Castor, (and who)

volitarunt   **toto**   **foro**   **cum**   **gladiis.**   **Vidistis**
ran-through   the whole   forum   with   swords.   You-saw

Romanum   **populum**   **cædi,**   **concionem**
the Roman   people   slaughtered,   a meeting of the citizens

disturbari   **gladiis,**   **quum**   **silentio**   **M. Cœlius**
disturbed   by-swords,   when   in-silence   M. Cœlius

audiretur,   **tribunus**   **plebis,**   **vir**   **fortissimus**   **et**
was-listened-to,   a tribune   of-the-people,   a man   most-brave   both

in   **republica,**   **et**   **firmissimus**   **in**   **causâ**
in (the affair of) the republic,   and   most-firm   in the cause

susceptâ   **et**   **deditus**   **voluntati**   **bonorum, et**
undertaken (by him)   and   devoted   to the will   of-the-good, and

auctoritati   **senatûs, et**   **divinâ et**   **incredibili**   **fide,**
to-the-authority of-the-senate, and of divine and   incredible   fidelity

sive in hac   **invidiâ, sive**   **singulari**   **fortunâ**   **Milonis.**
either in   this   odium,   or   singular   fortune   of Milo.

34. Sed   **jam**   **satis**   **multa**   **de**
But   already sufficiently   enough (has been said) concerning

causâ,   **etiam**   **extra**   **causam, fortasse**
the cause (and)   also   beyond (or foreign) to-the-cause,   perhaps

nimis multa.   **Quid restat, nisi ut**   **orem**   **que obtester**
too   much.   What remains, unless that   I-pray   and   entreat

vos,   **judices,**   **ut**   **tribuatis**   **eam**   **misericordiam**
you,   O judges,   that   you-may-grant   that   mercy

fortissimo   **viro, quam**   **ipse**   **non implorat,**
to-a-most-brave   man,   which   he-himself 'does not   'implore,

ego,   **etiam, hoc**   **repugnante, et**   **imploro et**
(which) I,   even,   he   opposing,   both   implore   and

exposco? Nolite,   **si,**   **in**   **omnium**   **nostro**
demand ?   Do-not,   if,   in (the midst)   of all   our

fletu, adspexistis   **nullam**   **lacrimam**   **Milonis, si**
weeping,   you-saw   no   tear   of-Milo,   if (his)

vultum   **semper eundem, si**   **videtis**   **vocem, si**
countenance (is) always   the same,   if you-perceive (his) voice,   if

orationem stabilem,   **ac**   **non**   **mutatam,**
(his) discourse   steady,   and   not   changed   (or faltering),

minus   **hoc**   **parcere ei.**
(do not) the-less   on-this (account be inclined to)   spare   him.

Haud scio, an etiam multò
I-do not 'know, whether 'he-ought (not) even (so) much

magis adjuvandus sit. Etenim si in
the more 'to-be-assisted (on that account). For if in

gladiatoriis pugnis, et in conditione infimi generis
gladiatorial contests, and in the condition of-the-lowest classes

hominum atque fortunâ, etiam solemus
of-men and (lowest) fortune, 'we-are even 'accustomed

odisse timidos, atque supplices, et obsecrantes,
to-hate the timid, and suppliant, and (those) entreating,

ut liceat vivere; cupimus servare
that it-may-be-allowed (them) to-live; (but) we-wish to-save

fortes et animosos, et acriter offerentes
the brave and courageous, and (those) eagerly offering

se ipsos morti; que miseret nos magis eorum,
themselves to-death; and it-pities us most of them,

qui non requirunt
[we feel the greatest compassion for those] who 'do not 'ask-for

nostram misericordiam, quàm qui efflagitant illam,
our pity, than those-who entreat it,

quantò magis debemus facere hoc in fortissimis
how much more ought-we (not) to-do this for most-brave

civibus? Hæ voces Milonis, quas assidue audio,
citizens? These expressions of-Milo, which 'I continually 'hear

et quibus quotidie intersum,
and 'to (the utterance of) 'which 'I-am daily 'present,

quidem, judices, exanimant et interimunt me.
do indeed, O judges, 'discourage and overcome me.

"Valeant," inquit, "mei cives valeant;
"May-they-flourish," says-he, "may my citizens flourish (and fare well);

sint incolumnes, sint florentes, sint beati;
may-they-be safe, may-they-be prosperous, may-they-be happy;

hæc præclara urbs, que patria carissima mihi
may this illustrious city, and country most-dear to-me

stet, quoquo modo merita erit de me;
(long) 'stand, in-what-ever manner it-may-have-merited of me;

mei cives ipsi (quoniam non licet mihi
'may my fellow-citizens themselves (since 'it-is not allowed me

cum illis) perfruantur tranquillâ republica
(to enjoy it) with them) 'enjoy   a quiet   republic

sine me, sed tamen   per me; ego cedam
without me, but however (acquired) through me; I will-retire

atque abibo; si non licuerit mihi frui bonâ
and depart; if 'it-has not 'been-allowed me to-enjoy a-good

republica, ut carebo malâ, et primam
republic, at-least I-shall-be-absent-from a bad-one, and the first

civitatem tetigero, quam bene moratum et
city I-shall-have-arrived-at, which (is) well regulated and

liberam, in ea conquiescam. O frustra," inquit,
free, in that will-I-rest. O (how) vain," says-he,

"mei labores suscepti; O fallaces
are) "my labours (that I have) undertaken; O (how) fallacious

spes; O inanes meæ
(have been my) hopes; O (how) empty (have been) my

cogitationes! Ego quum tribunus plebis,
thoughts! I when (I was) tribune of-the-people,

republica oppressâ, dedissem me senatui,
the republic being-oppressed, had-devoted myself to-the senate,

quem acceperam exstinctum,
(the power of) which I-had-perceived (was nearly) extinguished,

Romanis equitibus, quorum vires
(I also had devoted myself) to the Roman knights, whose powers

erant debiles, bonis viris, qui abjecerant
were weak, (likewise) to-good men, who had-renounced

omnem auctoritatem armis Clodianis,
all authority (by reason of) the arms (of) Clodius,

putarem præsidium bonorum unquam
could-I-think (that) the protection (and-aid) of-the-good 'would ever

defuturum mihi? Ego quum (enim sæpissime
'be-wanting to-me? I when (for 'he very-often

loquitur cum me,) reddissem te patriæ,
'converses with me,) I-had-restored you (to your) country,

putarem in patriâ non futurum
could-I think (that) in (my) country 'there-would not 'be

locum mihi? Ubi nunc est senatus, quem
a place for-me? Where now is the senate, which

secuti sumus ? ubi illi Romani equites, illi," inquit,
we-have-followed ? where those Roman knights, those," says-he,

" tui ? ubi studia municipiorum ? ubi **voces**
" so much yours ? where the zeal of-the-municipal-towns ? where the **voice**

Italiæ ? ubi denique illa tua vox atque
of-Italy ? where in-fine (is) that your voice and (eloquence in)

defensio, M. Tulli, quæ fuit auxilio plurimis ?
defence, O M. Tullius, which brought assistance to-many ?

potest ne ea nihil opitulari mihi soli, qui
can then that-voice 'bring no 'assistance to-me alone, who

toties obtuli me morti pro te ?"
have-so-often offered myself to-death for you ?"

35. Nec vero, judices, hæc, ut ego
Nor indeed, O judges, (does he say) those-things, as I

nunc flens, sed loquitur hoc eodem vultu,
now (do) weeping, but he-speaks (them) with-this same countenance,

quo videtis. Enim negat,
with-which 'you (now) 'see (him). For he-denies, he (indeed

negat se fecisse, quæ fecerit civibus
positively) denies (that) he did, what he-performed for citizens

ingratis ; non negat
(who were) ungrateful ; 'he does not deny (that those things may

timidis et circumspicientibus omnia
have been done) for-the-timid and for-those-contemplating every

pericula. Commemorat plebem, et infimum
danger. He-states (that) the common-people, and the-lowest

multitudinem, quæ, P. Clodio duce,
multitude (or rabble), which, P. Clodius (being their) leader,

imminebat vestris fortunis, se fecisse
threatened your fortunes, (that) he had-acted-on (and so treated)

eam, quo vestrâ vitâ esset tutior, ut non
this-multitude, whereby your life might-be more-safe, so-that not

modò flecteret virtute, sed etiam
only he-bent (and ruled it) 'by (his) 'courage, but also

deleniret suis tribus patrimoniis ;
he-tamed (and won it) (by spending) his three patrimonies

nec timet, quum placaret
(left to him) ; nor does-he-fear, when he-may-have-pacified (and secured)

plebem   muneribus, ne non   conciliarit **vos**
.he common-people 'by (his) 'presents,   but-that he-would-conciliate you

singularibus meritis in rempublicam.   Dicit
'by-his   'singular   services in   the republic.   'He 'says

benevolentiam senatûs erga   se,   his   ipsis
(that)   the good-will of-the-senate towards himself, in-these same

temporibus,   sæpe esse perspectam,   se verò
times,   'has often been   'experienced, (that) he   indeed

ablaturum esse cum se vestras   occursationes,
   would-carry   with him your attentive-and-complimentary-calls,

studia,   sermones,   et   vestrorum ordinum
(your) zeal, (and) discourses, and (that) of-your   order

quemcunque cursum fortuna dederit.   Etiam
in whatever   route   fortune may-designate (for him). 'He also

meminit   vocem præconis modò defuisse sibi,
mentions (that) the voice of-the-herald alone was-wanting to-him

quam desiderarit minime, verò
(to be declared consul),   which   he-desired but-little, for-indeed

cunctis suffragiis populi quod unum cupierit,
(it was) by the entire   votes of-the-people which alone he-desired,

se   declaratum   consulem; nunc denique, si
(that) he had-been-declared   consul;   now   in-fine,   if

hæc   sint futura contra   se,   suspicionem
these-things may-be hereafter against him, (that)   the suspicion

facinoris, non   crimen   facti   obstare   sibi.
of-crime,   not   the crime of-commission would-stand-against him.

Addit hæc,   quæ sunt certe vera,   fortes et
He-adds these-things, which are certainly true, (that) brave and

sapientes viros non tam   solere   sequi
wise   men 'are not so-much 'accustomed to-follow (and seek after)

præmia factorum recte, quàm   facta ipsa
the rewards of-deeds done-well, as (to seek) the deeds themselves

bene;   se   fecisse nihil in   vitâ, nisi
done well · (that) he   had-done nothing in (his) life, unless

præclarissime si quidem   sit   nihil
(what was) most-honourable if   indeed there-may-be nothing

præstabilius   viro,
[there is any thing] better,   (or more preferable) for-a-man,

quàm liberare patriam periculis; esse
than to-deliver (his) country from-dangers; (that those) are

beatos, quibus ea res fuerit honori a suis civibus,
happy, to-whom this thing brought honour from their fellow-citizens,

nec tamen eos miseros, qui vicerint suos
nor however (that) those are-miserable, who have-surpassed their

cives beneficio;
fellow-citizens in-good-deeds (and who have not been rewarded therefor);

sed tamen ex omnibus præmiis virtutis, si
but however from-among all the rewards of-virtue, if (any)

ratio habenda esset præmiorum amplissimum
regard was-to-be-had (to) rewards (that) the-most-ample

præmium esse gloriam; esse
(and honourable) reward was glory; (that) it-was

hanc unam quæ consolaretur brevitatem vitæ,
this-glory alone that might-console (us for) the shortness of-life,

memoriâ posteritatis, quæ efficeret, ut absentes
by-the-recollection of-posterity, which effects, that absent

adessemus, mortui viveremus; denique
we-may-be-present, (that) dead we-may-be-alive; in-fine (that)

esse hanc, gradibus cujus homines etiam viderentur
it-is this, by-the-steps of-which men even seem

ascendere in cœlum. "De me," inquit, "Romanus
to ascend to heaven. "Of me," says-he, "the Roman

populus omnes gentes semper loquentur,
people (and) all nations 'will continually 'speak,

nulla vetustas unquam obmutescet.
no remote-age 'will ever 'be-silent (concerning me).

Quin hoc tempore ipso, quum omnes faces
But-even at-this time itself, when all the firebrands

invidiæ meæ subjiciantur, a meis
of-envy (and hatred) (of) me are-thrown-at (me), by my

inimicis, tamen celebramur in omni cœtu
enemies, yet-however we [I am] are celebrated in every company

hominum, agendis gratiis, et habendis gratulationibus.
of-men, by-returning thanks, and having congratulations

et omni sermone. Omitto
(among themselves), and by-every-kind (of) discourse. I-omit

festos   dies   Etruriæ,   et   actos   et   institutos,
the festival days   of-Etruria,   both   celebrated and   instituted

haec   est   centesima   lux
(on account of the death of Clodius);   this   is   the hundredth light

et,   opinor,   altera,   ab   interitu P. Clodii;
[day] and, (as) I-believe,   the second,   since   the death of-P. Clodius;

qua   fines   Romani   populi   sunt,   ea   non
as-far-as the boundaries of-the Roman   people   extend,   so-far   not

solùm   fama   de   illo,   sed   etiam   lætitia
only   the report of   this death,   but   also   the joy (thereat)

jam   peragravit.   Quamobrem,"   inquit,   " ubi
'has already 'extended.   Wherefore,"   says he,   " where

hoc   corpus   sit,   non laboro,   quoniam
this   body   (of mine) may-be,   'I-am not 'concerned,   because

gloria   mei nominis,   et jam versatur,   et   semper
the glory of-my   name,   both now   is,   and 'will always

habitabit   in   omnibus   terris."
'dwell   in   all   countries."

36.   Hæc,   Milo,   tu   sæpe   cum me,
These-things, O Milo,   you have often (conversed of) with   me,

his   absentibus;   sed,   iisdem
those (here now present) being-absent;   but,   these-same (persons)

audientibus, ego   hæc   cum te:
listening,   I (will converse of) these (following things) with you:

possum non   satis quidem laudare te,   quum   es
'I-can   not sufficiently indeed 'praise you,   when you-are

isto   animo;   sed   quò   ista virtus est magis
of-this   mind;   but in-as-much-as this   virtue   is   more

divina,   eò   majore   dolore   divellor   a te.
divine,   'by so-much 'the greater   grief   I-am-separated from you.

Nec   verò,   si   eriperis   mihi,   est
Nor   indeed,   if 'you (are made to) 'depart (from) me,   is

tamen illa querela   ad consolandum,   ut possim
in-fine that complaint (left) for   consoling   (me),   that I-may

irasci   his,   a quibus   accipero   tantum
become-angry with-those from whom I-shall-have-received   so-great

vulnus.   Enim non   mei   inimici   eripient   te
a wound.   For   not   my   enemies   will-snatch   you (from)

mihi, sed amicissimi, non aliquando
me, but my-greatest-friends, not (those who) at-any-time (may)

meriti male de me, sed semper
have deserved ill of me, but (those, who have) always (deserved)

optime. Judices, inuretis nullum tantum
the best. 'You-will O judges, 'inflict no such-great

dolorem mihi unquam, (etsi quis potest
grief (on) me at-any-time, (although what (grief) can

esse tantus) sed ne quidem hunc ipsum
be so-great) (as this), but not indeed this same, (so)

ut obliviscar quanti semper feceritis
that I-may-forget of-how-much 'you-have always 'made

me. Si quæ oblivio
me. [How much you have always esteemed me.] If which forgetfulness

cepit vos, aut si offendistis
(of this esteem) has-possessed you, or if you-have-been-offended

aliquid in me, cur non id
at-any-thing in me, why 'is not (the punishment for) it

luitur meo capite potius, quàm Milonis? Enim
'inflicted on-my head rather, than (that) of-Milo? For

vixero præclare, si quid accideret mihi
I-shall have lived perfectly-well, if any-thing should-happen to-me

prius, quàm videro hoc tantum
(if I should die) before, that I-shall-have-seen this so-much

mali. Nunc una consolatio
of-evil. [Such great evil befall him.] Now one consolation

sustentat me, quòd tibi T. Anni, defuit a
sustains me, that to-you O T. Annius, there-was-wanting by

me nullum officium amoris, nullum studii,
me [on my part] no duty of-love, none of-zeal,

nullum pietatis. Ego pro te appetivi
none of-attachment. I 'have for you 'sought

inimicitias potentium, ego sæpe objeci meum
the enmities of-the-powerful, I 'have often 'opposed my

corpus et vitam armis tuorum inimicorum, ego
body and life to-the-arms of-your enemies, I

abjeci me supplicem plurimis pro te, contuli
have-thrown myself (as) a suppliant to-many for you, I-have

bona,   meas fortunas ac   meorum
brought (my) property,   my   fortunes   and (those) of-my

liberorum in communionem tuorum temporum;
children   in   participation   of-your   times; [to share

denique hoc ipso die, si qua   vis
your misfortune;] in-fine   on this   same   day,   if   any violence

est parata,   si   futura   qua   dimicatio
is   prepared (against you), if   there-is-to-be   any   contest

capitis,   deposco.   Quid restat jam? quid
of·life,   I-demand (to share it).   What remains now?   what

habeo quod faciam pro tuis meritis in me, nisi
have-I   that   I-can-do   for   your   services   to   me, unless

ut quæcunque   erit   tua   ducam   eam
that   whatever   may-be   your (fortune) I-may-consider   that

fortunam meam?   Non abnuo,   non recuso,
fortune   mine?   'I-do not   ²reject, 'I-do not   ²refuse (this),

que obsero vos, judices, ut   aut augeatis vestra
and   I-entreat   you, O judges, that 'you either   ²add-to   your

beneficia,   quæ   contulistis   in me,   salute
benefits,   which   you-have-conferred   on   me,   by-the-safety

hujus, aut   videatis   occasura esse
of-this-man,   or   you-may consider (that these benefits)   will-fall

in   exitio   ejusdem.
(and be obliterated) in the destruction of-this-same-man.

37. Milo   non   movetur his lacrimis.   Est
Milo   ⁴is not   ³moved by-these   tears.   He-is-in

quodam incredibili robore animi;   putat
[he has] a certain   incredible   strength of-mind; he-considers (that)

exsilium esse ibi, ubi   non sit locus virtuti;
banishment is   there, where 'there-may not ²be   a place for-virtue;

mortem esse finem naturæ, non pœnam.   Sed
(that) death   is   the end of-nature, not a punishment.   But

hic est eâ   mente, qua natus est; quid
he   is in that (noble state of) mind, in which he-was-born;   what

vos,   judices?   quo   animo   tandem
do you,   O judges (think)?   in-what   mind 'will-you   in-fine

eritis?   Retinebitis memoriam Milonis,   ejicietis
be?   Will-you-retain   the memory   of Milo,   (and)   banish

ipsum? et erit ullus dignior locus in terris
himself? and will-there-be any more-worthy place on the earth

qui excipiat hanc virtutem, quàm hic, qui
which might-receive this virtue, than this, which

procreavit? Vos, vos, fortissimi viri appello,
produced (it)? You, you, O-most-brave men ¹I (now) ¹address,

qui effudistis multum sanguinem pro republica;
who have-shed much blood for the republic

appello vos in periculo viri, et in
I-address you in (the time of) danger of-a-man, and in (that)

invicti civis, vos centuriones que milites;
of-an-invincible citizen, you O centurions and (you) O soldiers,

vobis non modò inspectantibus, sed etiam armatis,
you not only looking-on, but also armed,

et præsidentibus huic judicio, hæc tanta virtus
and protecting this court, ¹shall this so-great virtue

expelletur, exterminabitur, projicietur ex hac urbe?
¹be-expelled, be-banished, be-thrown-out from this city?

O me miserum, O me infelicem! Tu potuisti revocare
O me miserable, O me unhappy! You could recall

me, Milo, in patriam per hos, ego non
me, O Milo, to my-country through these (men), ¹shall I not

potero retinere te in patriâ per eosdem?
¹be-able to retain you in (your) country through the same (persons)?

Quid respondebo meis liberis, qui putant te alterum
What shall-I-reply to-my children, who consider you a second

parentem? Quid tibi frater Quinte, qui
parent? What (shall I say) to-you O brother Quintus, who

nunc abes, consorti cum me illorum temporum?
¹are now ¹absent, a companion with me (in) these times

ne me potuisse non tueri salutem
(of my trouble)? (that) I-could not have-preserved the safety

Milonis per eosdem, per quos ille servasset
of-Milo through the same-persons, by whom he had-preserved

nostram? At in quâ causâ potuisse non?
our (safety)? But in what cause could-I not (do this)?

quæ est grata gentibus. A
(in a cause) which is agreeable to (all) nations (and people). By

quibus potuisse not? ab iis, qui acquierunt maxime
whom   could-I not? by those, who 'have-obtained the greatest

morte P. Clodii; quo deprecante? me.
'repose by-the-death of P. Clodius; who   entreating?   I.

Quodnam tantum scelus ego concepi, aut quod
What   such-great wickedness have I 'meditated, or   what

tantum facinus admissi in me,
such   atrocious-crime have-I-admitted in me, [have I committed

judices, quum indagavi, patefeci, protuli illa
O judges, when I-traced, laid-open, and brought-to (light) those

indicia communis exitii, exstinxi?
signs   of-common destruction, (and) I-destroyed (the conspiracy of

Omnes dolores redundant
Catiline which they indicated)?   All   my afflictions   overflow

ex illo fonte in me que meos.
(and spring) from that fountain on me and   my (friends)

Quid voluistis me esse reducem?
Why have-you-wished (that) I (should) be a restored person (to my

an ut, me inspectante, ii expellerentur
country)? whether that, I   looking on,   those might-be-expelled

per quos essem restitutus? Nolite,
(from their country) by whom I-was restored (to it)? Do-not

obscero vos, pati reditum esse acerbiorem mihi
I-entreat you, suffer (my) return to-be more-harsh to-me

quàm fuerit ille discessus ipse. Nam
than was that departure (and banishment) itself. For

qui possum putare me restitutum esse
how can-I think (that) I have-been-restored (to my country)

si distrahar ab iis, per quos restitutus sum?
if I-am separated from those, by whom I-have-been-restored (to it)?

38. Utiam immortales dei fecissent
Would   the immortal   gods   had-caused

(dixerim tuâ pace,
(may-I-have-said-this in your peace, [with your permission and without

patria; enim metuo, ne dicam
offence] O (my) country; for I-fear, lest I-may-say (something)

scelerate in te, quod dicam pie pro Milone)
wickedly as-respects you, which I-may-say piously for   Milo)

utinam   P. Clodius non modò viveret, sed etiam
would (that) P. Clodius not only might-live, but also

esset prætor, consul, dictator potius, quam viderem
'might-be prætor, consul, dictator rather, than I-should-see

hoc spectaculum. O immortales dii! fortem! et
this spectacle. O immortal gods! O brave man! and

virum   conservandum a vobis, judices! "minime,
a man (who) ought-to-be-preserved by you, O judges! "not-all,

minime," inquit.   "Immo vero   ille luerit
not-all," says-he [Milo]. "Rather indeed 'may he 'suffer (his)

debitas pœnas; nos subeamus, si ita est necesse,
merited punishments; we will undergo, if so it-is necessary,

                non debitas." Hiccine vir natus
(punishments) not merited." Is-it-that this man born for (his)

patriæ   usquam morietur, nisi in   patriâ, aut,
country 'should ever die, unless in (his) country, or,

si forte, pro   patriâ; vos retinebitis monumenta
if by-chance, for (his) country; you will-retain the monuments

animi,   patiemini nullum sepulcrum
of his mind (and courage), (but) you-suffer no sepulchre

        corporis esse in Italiam? Quisquam expellet
(for his) body to-be in Italy? 'Will any-one 'expel

hunc suâ sententiâ ex hac urbe, quem expulsum
this-man by-his vote from this city, whom banished

a vobis omnes urbes vocabunt ad   se? O illam
by you all the cities will-invite to themselves? O that

beatam terram, quæ exceperit hunc virum; hanc
happy country, which shall-have-received this man; O this

ingratam   si   ejecerit,   miseram si
ungrateful (country) if it-should-cast-him-forth, O miserable if

amiserit!   Sed   sit   finis. Neque enim
it-should lose (him)! But let-there-be an end. Nor indeed

possum jam loqui præ lacrimis, et hic   vetat
can-I now speak for tears, and he [Milo] forbids (that)

se defendi lacrimis. Oro que obtestor vos, judices,
he be-defended by-tears. I-pray and entreat you, O judges,

ut in ferendis   sententiis, quod sentietis, id
that in giving (your) votes, that-which you-may-think, that

audeatis.   Credite   mihi,   is   maxime
dare-to-do.   Believe   me, (that) he [Pompey] 'will   greatly

probabit   vestram   virtutem, justitiam   fidem,   qui,
'approve   your   virtue,   justice   and good-faith, who,

in legendis judicibus, delegit quemque optimum,   et
in selecting   judges,   selected   each-one   the best,   and

sapientissimum, et   fortissimum.
most-wise,   and most-brave (and fearless).

THE END

ab   eo   octaginta millibus passuum, in Oceanum.
from that (than) eighty   thousands   of paces, into   the Ocean.

Autem Rhenus oritur ex Lepontiis, qui incolunt
But   the Rhine arises out of the Lepontii, who   inhabit

Alpes : et fertur citatus longo spatio per   fines
the Alps : and is borne rapid in a long distance through the territories

Nantuatium, Helvetiorum, Sequanorum, Medio-
of the Nantuates,   Helvetii,   Sequani,   Medio-

matricorum, Tribocorum, que Trevirorum ; et ubi
matrici,   Tribocci,   and of the Treviri ; and when

appropinquat Oceano,   diffluit in plures partes ;
it approaches to the Ocean, it flows dividedly into more (several) parts :

multis que ingentibus insulis effectis ; magna pars
many   and   great   islands being formed ; great   part

quarum incolitur à feris que barbaris nationibus ;
of which is inhabited by wild and barbarous   nations ;

(ex quibus   sunt   qui   existimantur vivere
(out of which (there) are (some) who are thought   to live

piscibus atque ovis avium), que influit in
(on) fishes   and   the eggs of birds), and   it flows in into

Oceanum multis capitibus.
the Ocean by many   heads.

11. Quum Cæsar   abesset   ab
When   Cæsar might be distant (was distant) from

hoste non amplius duodecim millibus passuum,
the enemy not more (than) twelve   thousands   of paces,

legati   revertuntur ad eum, ut constitutum erat :
the ambassadors return   to him, as it had been appointed :

qui   congressi in itinere, orabant magnoperè,
who   having met (him) on the march, did pray   greatly

ne progrederetur longiùs. Quum   impetrâssent
he would not advance farther. When they might have (had) obtained

non id, petebant, "utì   præmitteret   ad
not   that, they did request, "that he would send before   to

eos equites, qui antecessissent   agmen,   que
those horsemen, who might have (had) preceded the troop (army), and

prohiberet eos pugnâ : que utì faceret potestatem
would prohibit them from battle : and that he would make   power

Sample Page, Cæsar Interlinear Translation
(Reduced in Size)